AUDREY COHEN COLLEGE

T4-AED-516

BF
698.4
K546
1985

Kleinmuntz, Benjamin.

Personality and psychological assessment

DATE DUE

COLLEGE FOR HUMAN SERVICES
LIBRARY
345 HUDSON STREET
NEW YORK, N.Y. 10014

# Personality
and Psychological
Assessment

# Personality and Psychological Assessment

BENJAMIN KLEINMUNTZ
*University of Illinois at Chicago*

ROBERT E. KRIEGER PUBLISHING COMPANY
MALABAR, FLORIDA

Original Editon 1982
Reprint Edition 1985

Printed and Published by
**ROBERT E. KRIEGER PUBLISHING COMPANY, INC.
KRIEGER DRIVE
MALABAR, FLORIDA 32950**

Copyright © 1982 by St. Martin's Press, Inc.
Transferred to Author
Reprint by Arrangement

*All rights reserved. No part of this book may be reproduced in any form or by any electronic or mechanical means including information storage and retrieval systems without permission in writing from the publisher.*
*No liability is assumed with respect to the use of the information contained herein.*

Printed in the United States of America

**Library of Congress Cataloging in Publication Data**

Kleinmuntz, Benjamin.
    Personality and psychological assessment.

    Reprint. Originally published: New York : St. Martin's Press, 1982.
    Bibliography: p.
    Includes Indexes.
    1. Personality assessment. 2. Psychological tests. I Title.
(BF698.4.K546   1985)         155.2'8         85-18142
ISBN 0-89874-893-3

10 9 8 7 6

For Dalia

# Preface to the Reprint Edition

This reprint of an already successful book is necessary for three overriding and related reasons: 1) St. Martin's Press, the original publisher, has decided to drop its textbook offerings in Psychology; 2) The book has had an excellent reception, both by its reviewers (D. R. Peterson and M. Gynther) and its users; and 3) the text was fraught with many minor and not so minor errors that only an author seems to notice, but which distort the contents sufficiently so as to be misinforming.

But be this as it may, the motivations for reprinting a textbook in assessment continue to be the same as they were in 1967 when the first edition of *Personality Measurement* appeared and as they were in 1982 when *Personality and Psychological Assessment* was published: The textbooks available in this important area are too sparse for a discipline that continues to spur controversy and heated discussion. Again as in 1967 and in 1982, this book addresses these important issues and hopes to sensitize students to them.

Since the publication of the original version of this textbook in 1982, I have used it quite comfortably in undergraduate and beginning graduate courses entitled *Personality Asessment, Personality Measurement,* and, as suggested by one reviewer (M. Gynther), in a brief course (one quarter) called *Introduction to Psychological Tests and Measurements.*

One final set of observations is in order. Since the publication of this text in 1982, the *Ninth Mental Measurements Yearbook,* currently being compiled at the University of Nebraska's Buros Institute of Mental Measurements by Dr. James V. Mitchell, Jr., is now on-line with the BRS data-base. Its publication in book format is imminent. In addition, as a nominee to The American Psychological Association's Committee on Psychological Tests and Assessment, I have had the privilege of previewing a draft of the *Guidelines for Computer-Based Tests and Interpretations,* the publication of which is also imminent. These developments were anticipated in the current text, and should have a major impact on the field of psychological assessment.

Benjamin Kleinmuntz<br>
Chicago, Illinois<br>
July, 1985

# Preface

The motivations for writing an undergraduate textbook in personality and psychological assessment have remained the same for the past few decades—the subject is an active area of research with few books in it and is the focus of considerable controversy, a controversy that has intensified during the past few years. This text intends to present a balanced compendium of this important area and to address that controversy so as to inform and sensitize students to some of the issues currently debated in the discipline.

Based on an earlier book, this one is an expansion of the original, and includes coverage of intelligence, achievement, ability, and aptitude testing, as well as a discussion of attitude and value scaling. The selection of topics and illustrative studies reflects my biases about the subject matter. That is unavoidable. But I would rather have readers disagree with my opinions than have them expend the energy and time necessary to discover what my opinions are. My biases, of course, are solidly grounded in the dustbowl empiricist tradition of my graduate years at the University of Minnesota and have been much influenced by my subsequent exposure to the information-processing views of my former colleagues Allen Newell and Herbert Simon at Carnegie-Mellon University. What is the end product of such a mix? A systems-oriented, skeptical view of the world of assessment.

These considerations aside, the approach to most topics of this book is directed more at the potential user than the expert. This means that some areas and issues are touched on only in passing. Again, that is unavoidable in a book of such limited scope as the present one. For those readers who need to go beyond the material presented and who want to delve more deeply into the topics and issues presented here, I recommend Jerry Wiggins's (1973) excellent graduate-level book, and Donald Fiske's (1978) probing inquiry into the problems of studying the person. I would also suggest that these readers consult the annotated bibliographies at the conclusion of each chapter in this text and the extensive list of references at the end of the book.

For any success this book has in communicating its subject matter, I am indebted to several anonymous reviewers who expressed their opinions about earlier versions of the manuscript, and to Professors Thomas Bouchard, Robert Hogan, Robert Holmstrom, Marvin Sontag, and Eileen G. Thompson, who read the most recent versions of it and offered many incisive and valuable comments. In addition, I want to thank my son Don, who prepared and compiled the references. A debt of gratitude is also due to my former mentors and teachers at the University of Minnesota who taught me much of what I know. Particularly noteworthy among these are Professors Kenneth E. Clark, Starke R. Hathaway, James J. Jenkins, Paul E. Meehl, William Schofield, and the late Ephraim Rosen.

Finally, special notes of appreciation are due to my wife, Dalia, who urged me to revise this book, and to our sons, Don, Ira, and O.J., who, in various ways over the years, have been my inspiration for a book on personality and psychological assessment.

Benjamin Kleinmuntz<br>
Wilmette, Illinois<br>
September 1981

# Contents

## 1 Personality and Psychological Assessment    1

Personality Assessment    1
    The Need for Quantification 2, The Nature of Measurement 3, Levels of Measurement 4
Assessment Measurement and Testing    5
    Assessment versus Measurement 5, Psychological Assessment Defined 6
Definitions and Dimensions of Personality    7
    Psychopathology 8, Normality 9, Motivation and Personality 10, Personality Traits and Types 11, Other Personality Dimensions 13
Personality Assessment Settings and Purposes    14
    Psychodiagnosis 14, Counseling and Psychotherapy 16, Legal Settings 16, Personnel Selection 17, Research Settings 19
Sources of Information about Personality    20
Plan of the Book    22
Summary    25
For Further Reading    25

## 2 Statistics Essential for Assessment    27

Descriptive Statistics    27
    Measures of Central Tendency 30, Measures of Variability 33, Measures of Correlation 35, Normal Curve of Probability 41
Inferential Statistics    48
Summary    48
For Further Reading    49

## 3 Assessment Logic and Psychological Attributes    50

Attributes of Psychological Assessment    51
  Standardized Assessment Conditions 51, Objectivity 52, Behavior 52, Behavior Sample 54

Assessment Logic    55

Reliability    56
  Measurement Error 58, True Score 59, Sources of Error 59, Standard Error of Measurement 61, Test-Retest Reliability 64, Scorer Reliability 69

Validity    70
  Content Validity 71, Criterion Validity 73, Reliability of the Criterion 73, Comparative Criterion Validities 74, Effects of Reliability of Criterion Validity 77, Crossvalidation 78, Construct Validity 80

Summary    82

For Further Reading    82

## 4 Types of Tests and Interpreting Scores    84

Classification of Psychological Tests    84
  Test Item Format and Construction 84, Paper-and-Pencil and Performance Tests 86, Maximum versus Typical Performance Tests 86

Interpretive Aids    88
  Norms 90, Derived Scores 92, Normalization 95, Profiles 97, Configural Scoring 99

Decision Making with Tests    100
  Expectancy Tables 100, Bandwidth-Fidelity Dilemma 105, The Problem of Incremental Validity 107

Combining Test Information    108
  Clinical versus Statistical Prediction 109, A Box Score of Empirical Evidence and Some Guidelines 110

Communicating Test Findings    113

Contents **xiii**

Summary 115
For Further Reading 116

## 5 Observation and Behavioral Assessment 117

Observation Defined 117
Observer Participation 118
Kinds of Observation 119
Direct Observation 120
   Naturalistic Observation 121, Naturalistic Personality Data 124, Aids for Limiting Observational Error 131
Controlled Observations 139
   Critical Comment 139
Indirect Observation 144
   Personal Documents 145, Archival Records 148, Physical Traces 150
Behavioral Assessment 151
   Behavioral versus Traditional Assessment 151, Origins of Behavioral Techniques 152, Assessment Methods 153, Critique of Behavioral Methods 161
Summary and Conclusions 163
For Further Reading 165

## 6 Interviewing 167

Introduction 167
Structured and Unstructured Interviews 173
   The Unstructured Interview 173, The Structured Interview 176, Critical Comment 179
Types of Interview 181
   The Employment, or Personnel Interview 182, Intake Interview 183, Mental Status Interview 183, Case History Interview 186
Theoretical Orientation of the Interviewer 192
   Freud's Psychoanalytical Technique 192, Alfred Adler's Directive Technique 192, Harry Stack Sullivan 193, Roger's Nondirective Counseling 194
Evaluation of the Interview 195
   Interview Process Errors 195, Interviewee

Contents

        Error 196, Interviewer Error 197, The Validity of Interviews 198
    Computer Interviewing     199
        Critical Comment 206
    Summary and Conclusions     207
    For Further Reading     208

## 7 Self-Report Inventories and Questionnaires     210

    The First Adjustment Inventory     211
    Minnesota Multiphasic Personality Inventory (MMPI)     212
        MMPI Construction 214, Clinical and Validity Scales of the MMPI 215, Clinical Scales 215, The Validity Scales 222, New MMPI Scales 223, Coding 224, MMPI Interpretation 227, Automated MMPI Scaling and Interpretation 230, Evaluation of the MMPI 237
    Contenders to Replace the MMPI     240
    California Psychological Inventory     244
    Interest Testing     247
    The Strong Vocational Interest Blank     248
    Attitudes and Values Testing     253
        Attitude Scaling 253, The Measurement of Values 259
    Summary and Conclusions     261
    For Further Reading     262

## 8 Projective Techniques     264

    Projection versus Projective Technique     265
    Rorschach Inkblot Test     266
        Computer Rorschach Interpretation 276, Evaluation of the Rorschach 279
    Other Projective Tests     285
        Holtzman Inkblot Technique (HIT) 285, Thematic Apperception Test (TAT) 287, Sentence Completions 291, Draw-a-Person Test (DAP) 292, Bender Visual-Motor Gestalt Test 293, The Picture-Frustration Study (P-F) 294, Role Construct Repertory (Rep) Test 295, Conclusion 299

Contents xv

|  |  |  |
|---|---|---|
|  | Summary | 299 |
|  | For Further Reading | 301 |

## 9 Maximum Performance Assessment 303

|  |  |
|---|---|
| Definitions and Theories of Intelligence | 303 |
|     The Binet-Simon Theory 305, Spearman's |  |
|     $g$ and $s$ Factors 306, Cattell's Theory 307 |  |
| Intelligence Testing | 313 |
|     Binet-Type Tests 314, The Wechsler Tests |  |
|     321, Group Tests of Intelligence 325 |  |
| Minority Group Testing | 326 |
| Achievement, Ability, and Aptitude Testing | 338 |
|     Achievement Testing 339, Ability Testing |  |
|     342, Aptitude Testing 344 |  |
| Summary | 345 |
| For Further Reading | 346 |

## 10 Some Assessment Problems and Solutions 348

|  |  |
|---|---|
| Technical Problems | 348 |
|     Lack of Consensus 349, Continuous-versus- |  |
|     Discrete Personality Variables 350, The |  |
|     Many Settings and Uses of Personality |  |
|     Assessment 351, The Nonutility of |  |
|     Assessment Devices 351, The Problem of |  |
|     Reactivity 353, Problems of Observer and |  |
|     Behavioral Inconsistencies 354, The |  |
|     Inadequacy of Personality Research 357, |  |
|     The Use of Traditional Measures 358 |  |
| Ethical and Moral Considerations | 363 |
|     Invasion of Privacy 363, Testing and Civil |  |
|     Rights 366, Quasi-Ethical Objections 368 |  |
| Summary and Conclusions | 376 |
| For Further Reading | 378 |

## References 380

## Indexes 429

# Personality
# and Psychological
# Assessment

# 1 Personality and Psychological Assessment

## Personality Assessment

Personality assessment could be called the art of "sizing up" people, an art that we all practice in our daily contacts with others. Most of us are skillful at this; some of us even take pride in our expertise. The proof of this rests in our relatively smooth and successful interpersonal relations as parents, neighbors, businesspersons, teachers, and students. In these roles, common sense seems to serve us well.

But personality assessment is more than an art and requires more than just common sense. It requires tools and procedures that have been constructed to perform particular tasks. These tools are often needed to provide the parent, neighbor, businessperson, teacher, and student with precise answers to specific questions.

Thus, the parent may need information about a child's intelligence or emotional make-up; the neighbor may want to know how much cooperation or friendliness can be expected from the persons next door; the businessperson may need to assess an associate's or a client's dependability, potential, or abilities; the teacher may want to compare students' motivations and increments of learning; and the student may want a profile of his or her occupational interests and aptitudes. But these approaches do not provide the precise information needed in many of these instances, which is why psychologists turn to more quantitative approaches.

Nevertheless, these common-sense procedures are so taken for granted in our daily dealings with one another that it is difficult to abandon them for more quantitative personality assessments, even though the latter are often more exact. In this introductory chapter, the advantages of the quantitative approach are discussed, and the various uses and settings of personality assessment are outlined. The remainder of the book examines some fundamentals, principles, problems of psychological testing, and personality assessment strategies. All

**The Need for Quantification**

are viewed as being part of a systems analysis framework, which is described in the last section of this chapter.

More than most people, the psychologist needs to articulate personality observations in quantities rather than words. Consider the difference in precision between the words most people use to describe fish sizes ("big," "enormous," "colossal," and so on) and their scientific classification according to size and weight. The psychologist who studies personality needs the precision that is provided by the latter because these offer more subtle discriminations and thus permit more exact descriptions. In contrast, ordinary descriptions of personality are ambiguous. The psychologist must often know, for example, whether an attribute is present in someone and which related characteristics accom-

---

**BOX 1-1**

## Excerpts from Sir Francis Galton's "Measurement of Character"

*The following excerpts from Galton's "Measurement of Character" appeared in the* Fortnightly Review *of London (1884). His guilt for applying measurements to nonphysical traits is evident:*

I do not plead guilty to taking a shallow view of human nature, when I propose to apply, as it were, a foot-rule to its heights and depths....

The use of measuring man in his entirety, is to be justified by exactly the same arguments as those by which any special examinations are justified, such as those in classics or mathematics; namely, that every measurement tests, in some particulars, the adequacy of the previous education, and contributes to show the efficiency of the man as a human machine, at the time it was made....

The act of measuring various human faculties now occupies the attention of many inquirers in this and other countries.... Can we discover landmarks in characters to serve as bases for a survey, or is it altogether too indefinite and fluctuating to admit of measurement? Is it liable to spontaneous changes, or to be in any way affected by a caprice that renders the future necessarily uncertain? Is man, with his power of choice and freedom of will, so different from a conscious machine, that any proposal to measure his moral qualities is based upon a fallacy? If so, it would be ridiculous to waste thought on the matter, but if our temperament and character are durable realities, and persistent factors of our conduct, we have no Proteus to deal with in either case, and our attempts to grasp and measure them are reasonable.

**Source:** Galton, F. The measurement of character. *Fortnightly Review*, 1884, 42, 179–185.

pany it. This knowledge may be needed to make interpersonal comparisons or to compare a person with a group standard; or the psychologist may wish to compare a person's characteristics with those previously displayed by him or her. All of these processes (i.e., determining existence, degree, nature, amount, and comparison) are enhanced by quantification or, as it is sometimes also called, measurement.

The difference, then, between most people's approaches to the study of personality and that of the psychologist is the latter's relatively greater need to assess and express personality in quantities rather than words. Whereas most people can correct mistaken personality judgments along the way, the psychologist bases many immediate decisions on these judgments and cannot afford to make as many errors: hence the need for the greater precision provided by quantification or measurement.

## The Nature of Measurement

What is measurement? It has been described as the assignment of numbers according to certain agreed-upon rules. The application of

---

**BOX 1-2**

**Levels of Measurement**

| Level | Function | Arithmetic Operation | Example |
|---|---|---|---|
| Nominal | Numerals used to name or classify objects, places, or persons. | No operations except to count the number of cases or things in a category. | Race horses with identifying numbers. |
| Ordinal | Numerals designate rank-order and permit statements of greater than, equal to, or less than. | All operations comparing ranks. | People in order of size or objects arranged according to relative weights. |
| Interval | Numerals are at equal intervals from one another and can be used to compare scores of persons or degrees of heat or cold. | Above procedures are permissible, and additions and subtractions may be performed as well. Multiplication and division are not permissible. | Thermometer |
| Ratio | This is the highest level of measurement, and its function is to specify precise relationships among objects or persons. | The absolute zero point on this scale permits all manner of arithmetic and statistical operations. | Yardsticks or weight scales. |

these rules and their assignment to various levels of measurement are not always as useful in psychology as in the physical sciences; but the rules are nonetheless the same (see Stevens, 1951), and measurements can be conceptualized as being on four different scales. Each scale represents another level of quantification and permits different arithmetical procedures, as the following discussion indicates (also see Coombs et al., 1970, pp. 14–17 for yet a fifth level of measurement on an absolute scale).

## Levels of Measurement

The first, or simplest, level of quantification is the *nominal scale*. It assigns numbers as labels to identify objects, entities, concepts, terms, or persons. Although these categories do have the relation of being different from one another, there are no arithmetical relations among their numbers. Thus, a person or a group of persons may be labeled "dependable," "punctual," "honest," or "deceitful," and these traits may be assigned the numerals 1, 2, 3, or 4; but the latter can never be added, subtracted, multiplied, or divided, although it is permissible to count the number of cases in each class and the number of classes identified by the numerals. An example of nominal scaling is such demographic classes as sex, race, and economic status.

The next level of measurement, the *ordinal scale*, includes the functions of nominal scaling but is more specific as it also defines the relative positions of objects or individuals with regard to the characteristic being measured. At this level, statements of "greater than," "equal to," and "less than" are permissible, but not statements about the size of the difference between positions. Ordinal measurement can be described as an elastic yardstick stretched unevenly, with the scale positions being indicated by the numbers on the stick in a clearly defined order. But the numbers at this level do not specify the distance between any two points on the stick because these numbers are unevenly distributed over the stick range of this scale.

The third level of measurement, the *interval scale*, indicates the distances between points, in addition to categorizing and determining relationships of greater than, equal to, or less than. What distinguishes interval from ordinal measurement is that interval measurement has equal units (or intervals) between points on a scale, which permits comparisons of distances between two things or persons. Addition and subtraction are therefore possible on the interval scale. But division and multiplication are not allowable, as these scales have no real zero point. The zero point is arbitrary and is assigned as a matter of convention.

It is often difficult to know whether a given test yields ordinal or interval test scores. Intelligence quotients (IQs) usually are considered examples of interval scale scores. But many people believe the IQ does not have equal intervals throughout its range, the issue being whether the difference between IQs of 85 and 90, for instance, has the same meaning as the difference between IQs of 130 and 135. The case for physical measurement is somewhat clearer. For example, in the Fahrenheit or Centigrade temperature scales, a change of 5° from 85°F to 90°F or from 10°C to 15°C is the same as a change of 5° from −20°F to −15°F or from 30°C to 35°C. Of course, on all these scales—Fahrenheit, Centigrade, and IQ—the zero points are arbitrary. To resolve the issue of whether IQ is on an interval scale, one should decide whether equal differences in intelligence are reflected in equal differences in test scores, particularly in the upper range.

An equal interval scale with an absolute zero at its point of origin is called a *ratio scale*. It is the highest level of measurement, includes all prior scale properties, and permits multiplication and division, as well as addition and subtraction. This scale also permits all statistical computations based on these operations. Moreover, ratio scales permit statements of relationships that are not possible with any of the other scales.

Although a ratio scale is seldom used in psychology, it is probably the most familiar of the scales discussed. All common physical dimensions such as height, weight, and volume are measured by ratio scales. One may say that when one person weighs 250 pounds and another 125 pounds, the latter is half as heavy as the first. And it requires only simple arithmetic to determine what is exactly twice, three times, or any multiple of a particular length, weight, or volume. But we cannot say that an IQ of 150 is equal to two IQs of 75, nor can we fit other psychological variables to the assumptions of ratio scales.

In personality assessment, most numerical findings are expressed in ordinal or approximate interval scales. This means that the limitations that accompany such measurements must be recognized and observed. The student who is familiar with both the restrictions imposed and the procedures permitted by these levels of measurement will better understand the problems of personality and psychological assessment that are discussed in subsequent chapters.

## Assessment, Measurement, and Testing

### Assessment versus Measurement

The term assessment was originally used by psychologists during World War II to describe the procedures of a group of psychologists and psychiatrists who selected individuals specially qualified for the espionage operations of the Office of Strategic Services (OSS) (Kelly, E. L., 1967). The word first appeared in psychological literature in the title of the book describing this unusual program of personnel selection, *The Assessment of Men* (Office of Strategic Services Staff, 1948). Six years later this term came into regular use when E. Lowell Kelly (1954) wrote "The Theory and Techniques of Assessment" for the *Annual Review of Psychology*.

Since that time, assessment has become a more inclusive concept than measurement and in this context refers to any procedure for learning about persons. In that sense, assessment includes both qualitative and quantitative appraisals of persons (Baughman, 1972). But measurement refers only to quantitative procedures and thus applies to many areas of psychological research in which assessment would not be appropriate. The psychologist may measure, for example, the amplitude of experimental subjects' reactions to stress, or the amount of time between the onset of a stimulus and the associated response. These measurements are not assessments because they express their values in physical rather than in psychological units or scores. We shall reserve the term assessment for those measurements that apply to psychological attributes directly, without using values obtained on physical phenomena.

Measurement is also used in statistics to help organize and interpret findings. If the question under examination is, for example, "What is the probability that in this experiment, variables $x$ and $y$ occurred by chance?" the answer requires measurement: counting, adding, subtracting, multiplying, or dividing, as well as a number of statistical procedures based on these arithmetic operations. But this form of measurement is not assessment either, according to our definition, because it does not deal directly with a psychological characteristic.

## Psychological Assessment Defined

What, then, is assessment? Assessment is a form of measurement that serves a much more restricted purpose than those already described. Most psychologists would probably agree on the following definition: Assessment includes all systematic (or standardized) and objective procedures (or devices) for obtaining observations and scores reflecting samples of psychological behavior.

This definition is intended to be sufficiently broad to include psychological tests, which are usually paper-and-pencil questionnaires, as well as some of the procedures described in this book for systematically recording behavior observations and scoring and quantifying data gleaned from personal documents, case histories, interviewing, and behavioral analysis. All unsystematic, casual, spontaneous, and informal techniques for assessing personality are excluded. Moreover, we shall make no distinction in this book among the terms test, examination, technique, and procedure. We shall often use these words interchangeably, although we recognize that such distinctions could be useful.

## Definitions and Dimensions of Personality

We probably could describe and evaluate personality assessment without actually defining personality itself because, in the course of our discussion throughout this book, a tentative eclectic picture will emerge that identifies most major personality dimensions. But it nonetheless may be well to consider briefly the meaning of personality before turning to its assessment.

Most psychologists probably would agree with Gordon W. Allport (1937, 1961) that the term "personality" refers to the unique organization of characteristics that define an individual and determine that person's pattern of interaction with the environment. More colloquially, personality is an individual's total make-up, the type of person that he or she is. To the psychologist, personality has no positive ("he or she has lots of personality") or negative connotations. It is neutral.

Psychologists do not agree, however, on such questions as the following: How does personality develop? What are the effects of early experiences on personality? Is there a critical period in personality development? How do heredity and environment affect personality? Are one's attributes consistent over time, or do they depend on specific situations to elicit them? Psychologists also do not agree on ways of talking about personality. Sigmund Freud had one explanation for personality, coined special terminology to describe it, and formulated a set of principles regarding its organization. Other well-known personality theorists such as Alfred Adler, Erik Erikson, Carl Jung, Otto Rank, Karen Horney, Theodor Reik, and Erich Fromm offered alternatives to Freud's system.

This book is not the appropriate place to list and evaluate the particulars of the numerous definitions and theories of personality. That task has already been carried out by others (Hall & Lindzey, 1978; Liebert & Spiegler, 1978; Mischel, 1981; Wiggins et al., 1976). But we do need to identify the dimensions of interest to psychologists who study personality, dimensions that focus on personality as psychopathology, as normality, as self-actualization, as needs, and as a composite of traits and types.

## BOX 1-3
## Some Alternate Definitions of Personality

| | |
|---|---|
| Sigmund Freud | Id, ego, and superego are the structures of personality. The id is the instinctual core which obeys the pleasure principle seeking short-term impulse gratification. The ego mediates between the instinctual demands of the id and the outer world of reality. Another of the ego's functions is to test reality. The superego represents the internalized societal moral standards. |
| Alfred Adler | His view of man is as a social being whose central orienting motives are a will to power, a masking of feelings of inferiority, a striving for superiority, and perfection. |
| Erik Erikson | Failures and successes at each of eight critical stages of ego development forge corresponding later personality developments. Trust-mistrust, autonomy–self-doubt, initiative-guilt, and integrity-isolation are examples of bipolar adult outcomes of faulty ego development. |
| Carl Jung | The self is a striving toward an ideal personality; the motivating force of the person constantly undergoes modification as a result of one's conscious and unconscious experiences. |
| Abraham Maslow | Man strives for self-actualization after satisfying physiological, safety, belongingness, and esteem needs. |

### Psychopathology

Many personality theories and some measurement techniques originated in the work of such famed clinicians and theorists as Sigmund Freud, Alfred Adler, Harry S. Sullivan, and Carl Rogers, to name just a few. They were clinicians first and personality theorists later and were primarily concerned with the causes and treatment of psychological disturbances, or psychopathology. Consequently, they considered normal behavior a less severe manifestation of the same process that operates in mental illness. Many of these clinicians adhered implicitly or explicitly to a classification system of psychopathology devised by Emil Kraepelin (1926). This system considers behavior abnormalities to be diseases and is the basis of a taxonomy still used today (American Psychiatric Association, 1980).

The basic classification of psychopathology now in use divides mental disorders into several major groupings that include schizophrenia, anxiety disorders, and antisocial personality disturbances. In schizophrenia, for example, a person's delusions (false and persistent beliefs in one's greatness or a feeling of being persecuted), hallucinations (hearing or seeing things that are not there), withdrawn behavior, irrational thinking, unusual gesturing, and "flattening" of affect (inability to respond with emotion) are sufficiently severe so as to be evident to most people who deal with him or her.

The second psychopathology grouping mentioned above, anxiety disorders, is not usually as debilitating as schizophrenia. It is characterized by irrational fears, obsessive and repetitive thoughts, and complaints of physical ailments that have no identifiable physiological basis (fatigue, weakness, back pains, headaches, paralysis, and even the loss of the use of certain organs and limbs). Although these sufferers do not usually require hospitalization, their subjective discomfort can be considerable. In sharp contrast to schizophrenics, who often believe they are well, anxiety-disordered persons believe they are emotionally disturbed and speak of it incessantly.

The last psychopathological grouping, the antisocial personality, includes persons characterized by socially unacceptable (sometimes asocial) behavior, behavior that is not morally acceptable to our society. Their behavior has often been described (see especially Cleckley, 1964; Hare, 1970) to be characterized by undependability, pathological lying, superficial charm, and untrustworthiness (for further information on this topic, see Kleinmuntz, 1980).

The most popular personality tests of the past thirty years grew out of the need to diagnose and detect psychopathology. Such personality tests as the Minnesota Multiphasic Personality Inventory (MMPI) and the Rorschach inkblots have become popular measurement tools for the psychologist, and extensive discussions of them will be presented in chapters seven and eight.

## Normality

Normality is usually defined as the absence of psychopathology, thus defining health by a process of elimination. This is not peculiar to the study of personality. Medicine also defines normality as the absence of physical ills. Contemporary approaches to the study of personality, much like those of present-day medicine, have become concerned with more than just pathology, however, and there have been serious efforts to approach normality on its own terms. Gordon W. Allport (1937, 1953, 1961), Abraham Maslow (1962, 1972), and Carl Rogers (1942, 1961) have been important influences on psychologists who study normality per se. Allport, Maslow, and Rogers stressed that normality and abnormality are not on the same continuum and that the study of normal persons should be a central focus of personology (see Hogan, 1976, pp. 107–111).

A direct outgrowth of Allport's interest in normal personality development has been the study of individuals who behave with unusual effectiveness. The best example of this approach can be found in the work of Abraham Maslow (1962, 1972), who rejected the prevailing truism of his time that social motives are an outgrowth of the hunger, thirst, and sex drives. He focused on "peak experiences" and emphasized the idea that the study of psychopathology leads to a negative conception of people. His ideal person takes active steps toward actualization, self-fulfillment, and healthy living. Maslow did not study conflict, misery, and pathology but, rather, psychological health.

Accordingly, Maslow urged psychologists to study unusually effective persons. Admittedly, these exceptional people were difficult to find; therefore he suggested that the study of historical and personal documents by and about them (i.e., Abraham Lincoln, Thomas Jefferson) could help identify some of the important distinguishing personality characteristics. In his search for the healthy and self-actualizing individual, Maslow also studied many famous and important contemporaries (i.e., Albert Einstein, Eleanor Roosevelt) and even his own acquaintances. Maslow learned from his studies that the characteristics of self-actualizing persons that set them apart from ordinary citizens were their realistic attitudes, acceptance of self and others, spontaneity, and problem centeredness, rather than false idealism, self-interest, autonomy, and independence. Some other qualities of self-actualizing people that Maslow uncovered were a sense of identification with all of humankind, a lack of prejudice, a respect for others, and an ability to detach themselves from their own culture (Maslow, 1968).

**Motivation and Personality**

Sigmund Freud, the founder of the study of personality by means of psychoanalysis, proposed a theory of unconscious motivation. Accordingly, he postulated the unconscious mind as a repository for unwanted impulses, ideas, feelings, and desires that people repress (or disavow). But despite such repression, people are not entirely free of these unacceptable attributes because, according to Freud, the impulses that result from their repression reappear in fantasies, dreams, actions, and generally in many facets of their behavior. It was these manifestations, in fact, that Freud considered to be important in disclosing the individual's motives and goals; therefore, he paid particular attention to accounts of these behaviors as well as to the patient's behavior toward the clinician.

Thus, psychoanalytic theory deals primarily with unconsciously motivated behavior and with needs and thoughts of which a person may be unaware and therefore is unable to express accurately. A psychoanalytic study is carried out by means of the case method, which consists of collecting information about an individual during the course of psychoanalytic psychotherapy, information that seems to follow a consistent theme in the patient's life. The therapist seeks consistency within the individual (e.g., the recurrence of a dream or a particular theme) and then presents the patient with an interpretation of its meaning. The truth or validity of the analyst's interpretations is assessed by the degree to which the patient accepts it as accurate and whether it leads to changes in the patient's behavior.

Another motivational or need approach to the study of personality is that developed by H. A. Murray (1938). Both the founder of a personality test—the Thematic Apperception Test (TAT) (see chapter eight)—and an early leader in personality theory and research, Murray catalogued a list of needs, their definitions, and ways of assessing their strengths.

These needs—some of which are presented below in Table 1–1—are still useful to psychologists and exemplify an attempt to describe behavior in terms of its direction. Murray also emphasized that the understanding of behavior must include an analysis of environmental pressures, or "press," as he calls them, exerted on the individual. These press (see Table 1–1) are like "objects or total situations in the environment" (Murray, 1962, p. 24) to which persons respond. Among Murray's more important contributions to the motivational study of the person were his identification and categorization of needs and press that form the person-environment interaction and his effort to assess them.

## Personality Traits and Types

There is an extensive vocabulary for attributes available in the English language to describe persons. In everyday contacts with people, such

**Table 1–1** Selected List of Murray's Needs and Press.

| Need | Brief Description |
| --- | --- |
| n Achievement | To strive hard for success. To get ahead in business, to persuade or lead a group, or to create something. |
| n Affiliation | To join clubs, friendships, and other close or affectionate relationships. |
| n Dominance | To direct or to dictate to others. Controlling. To dominate people or situations. |

| Press | Brief Description |
| --- | --- |
| p Achievement | Others are successful in school or business. Parents or associates pressure story's hero to succeed. |
| p Affiliation | The hero has several friends or sociable companions. He or she is a member of a group. |
| p Dominance | Someone tries to force the hero to do something. A person tries to influence the hero. |

words as kind, happy, resourceful, aggressive, and dependent are used to describe others. G. W. Allport and H. S. Odbert (1936) estimated that there are nearly 18,000 words in the English language to describe human characteristics and to differentiate people from one another. Somewhat later, another psychologist, Warren Norman (1963, 1967), using the third edition of *Webster's Unabridged Dictionary*, discovered about 27,000 different attribute names which, after additional revisions of Allport's list, totaled about 40,000 terms. Norman later reduced this list to about 2,800 terms which, according to one source, "will serve as a source of items for trait attribution systems for many years to come" (Wiggins, 1973, p. 338).

Psychologists who describe others according to their trait attributions begin with the idea that the person is a whole, or a unity. Although the person functions as a unit, however, it is useful to conceptualize subparts within him or her that interact with one another and are interdependent. These subparts have been called *traits* or *personality dispositions*. Traits have specific names such as those discovered by G. W. Allport and H. S. Odbert (1936) and W. T. Norman (1963, 1967), above, and carry such labels as introversion, dominance, impulsivity, anxiety, and self-control. Such traits are the components of an individual's personality and are sometimes described as tendencies to behave in a certain way. The aggressive person, for instance, tends to abuse others physically or verbally; the affiliative person seeks the company of others. Traits are usually thought of as relatively enduring aspects of the person, unlike feelings of hunger and fatigue that tend to fluctuate from one moment to the next.

The problem facing trait-oriented psychologists is how to organize, systematize, and conceptualize a large number of traits in order to characterize persons. To do this, these psychologists use factor analysis, a statistical method for simplifying rows and columns or an array of trait intercorrelations or clusters (for further details of this method, see Baughman, 1972; Cattell, 1957; Cronbach, 1970; Fruchter, 1954; Helmstadter, 1970). The leading proponents of factor analysis have been Raymond B. Cattell, Hans J. Eysenck, and J. P. Guilford, who have used this technique to construct objective personality tests to measure traits such as dominance, sociability, and introversion.

Not all psychologists agree, however, that the trait approach yields meaningful personality dimensions. Walter Mischel (1968, 1977, 1981), for example, argued that traits are in the rater rather than in the rated person and that human behavior is determined as much by the context, situation, or environment in which it occurs as by the traits reported to be found in the person. He (Mischel, 1968, p. 44) cited a study that demonstrated that raters sometimes rate complete strangers in the same way that they rate persons whom they know well. Hence this signifies more about the rater than the rated. Mischel also believes in the specificity of traits. For example, in a recent book on personality, he stated that the "early psychometricians ... did not pay much attention to the role of environmental variables as determinants of behavior ... [but] ... research has shown that performances on trait measures are reflected by a variety of stimulus conditions and can be modified by numerous environmental changes. ..." (Mischel, 1976b, p. 159).

Psychologists also classify persons on the basis of their patterns of attributes or traits. Thus, an introvert is a person who characteristically removes himself or herself from worldly contacts, possesses an inner directedness, and has a reflective intellectual manner. An extravert, on the other hand, is a person who is likely to possess a high degree of spontaneity, outgoingness, and objectivity. This dichotomous classification of persons into introverts and extraverts was first proposed by Swiss psychiatrist Carl Jung (1928), whose classification of persons into types was based on their habitual tendencies to turn inward or outward in their orientation toward the world. Jung's work influenced that of H. J. Eysenck (1967), whose personality theory consists of a hierarchical model in which types are built up on the observed intercorrelations among traits. In this model, for example, extraversion consists of the obtained intercorrelations among the traits of sociability, impulsiveness, activity, liveliness, and excitability.

Again, as in the case of trait theory, psychologists do not always agree that this is a valuable way to describe personality. For example, Nathan Brody (1972) considered personality types a necessary consequence of the method used, rather than proof of the existence of such a hierarchical model of the organization of personality. And Walter Mischel (1976b, p. 26) maintained that "an individual personality cannot be fitted neatly into one category or another" and (p. 28) that "there is still disagreement about which traits are the basic units of personality, but the search continues."

It is important to note also that when psychologists describe personality according to traits or types, they may use identical terminology but often have in mind different trait or type theories and disagree about how these traits are organized into types. Moreover, the same trait or type names are sometimes used to describe entirely different behavior characteristics. This apparent paradox is discussed in more detail in chapter ten, where we examine the technical problems of personality testing. It suffices to say here that there are problems that must be resolved if the study of personality is to become a sophisticated discipline.

## Other Personality Dimensions

Traditionally, the testing of intelligence and other abilities is not discussed in personality assessment books. This text, however, includes the topic on the assumption that one's ability to perform tasks well, or poorly, is equally as important in describing the person as are the more usual attributes discussed earlier. Thus a high or low intelligence, aptitude, or achievement test score can be as revealing about an individual as his or her score on a psychiatric screening test. We say more about this in chapter nine.

Likewise, other dimensions of the individual not commonly covered in personality assessment texts but appearing in this book are interests, attitudes, and values (chapter seven). Again, their appearance reflects this writer's conviction that they are just as informative about a person's emotional adjustment (or maladjustment).

Because of these considerations, the terms "personality" and "psychological" assessment are used interchangeably in this book. This book's title includes both terms, with "personality" appearing first, so as to reflect the greater emphasis on the more traditional topics of personality assessment.

In summarizing the preceding survey of some representative conceptualizations of personality, we can say that personality may be viewed as a unique organization of factors that determines an individual's pattern of interaction with the environment. Personality is defined sometimes in terms of its disordered manifestations and sometimes in terms of normality. Personality is also the sum total of a person's traits, needs, motivations, and the unique way each has of striving for maximum personal effectiveness. Finally, regardless of theoretical orientation and various conceptualizations, persons can be classified on the basis of abilities, interests, attitudes, and values—all of which psychological dimensions are equally as important about a person as other aspects of personality.

## Personality Assessment Settings and Purposes

Personality assessment can be used in various applied research settings. Some of these are presented in Table 1–2 and can be placed under one of five headings: clinical diagnosis, counseling and psychotherapy, legal classification, personnel selection, and personality research. Clearly, the nature of the setting often determines the purpose and function of the personality testing to be used.

### Psychodiagnosis

Psychodiagnosis is personality assessment made in a mental health clinic or hospital. Its functions are to classify and to understand the person being treated, as well as to facilitate communication among clinicians

**Table 1-2** Examples of Personality Assessment Settings and Purposes.

| Purpose | Setting | Function |
|---|---|---|
| Diagnosis | Mental hygiene clinic or psychiatric hospital. | Classification and understanding of persons. |
| Counseling and Psychotherapy | Clinic, hospital, or counseling center. | To obtain personality assessment before, during, or after counseling sessions. |
| Legal Classification | Courtroom, detention center, or correctional institution. | To determine "sanity" or "insanity." |
| Personnel Selection | Industry, government, school, military, or training program. | To aid in determining suitability for proposed assignment or for hiring. |
| Personality Research | Any or all of the above settings. | Before-and-after treatment evaluations. To assess effects of experimental manipulations. To ascertain the adequacy of the measurement tool itself. |

and to prescribe appropriate treatments. The problems of clinical diagnosis are fundamentally the same as those of personality measurement—to describe the personality structure and organization that explain the individual's behavior.

Some psychologists oppose classification. They believe that pinning labels on persons does them little good and it may be more helpful to try to understand the forces and stresses that motivate persons to act in particular ways. They argue that the state of the art in clinical psychodiagnosis is not as advanced as it is in medicine. Therefore, diagnostic labeling is little more than an academic exercise. Besides, they argue, diagnosis or labeling has deleterious effects on the persons so classified. Once so categorized, according to some (Rosenhan, 1973; Szasz, 1971), the person is publicly stigmatized as dangerous and insane and is treated accordingly. Behaviorally oriented psychologists (Ullmann & Krasner, 1975) often assert that it would be more useful to describe the events, conditions, and reinforcement contingencies controlling behavior than to label the person with the names of the diseases presumably responsible for his or her actions.

Proponents of clinical diagnosis, on the other hand, agree that labeling per se is not necessarily helpful to patients but that many diagnostic classifications carry strong implications for treatment. For example, if in the past, persons were diagnosed as depressed and were observed to benefit from a particular treatment, then in the future, others with the same diagnosis would become likely candidates for that treatment. Furthermore, it is often asserted that labeling facilitates communication among psychologists. Once they agree that symptoms $S_1$, $S_2$, and $S_3$ are associated with $D_1$ or $D_2$ and that treatment $T_1$ or $T_2$ is appropriate, then that particular classification communicates important information regarding the nature of a disorder and its appropriate treatment procedures. When the state of our knowledge about the etiology, or causes, of particular personality disorders advances to the point at which etiology is used to determine specific diagnostic labels, then, they would agree, classifications will communicate that additional information also (see Meehl, 1959b, 1973).

In the meantime, regardless of the pros and cons of the classification controversy, the psychologist's interest in administering tests for classification purposes does not imply a disregard of the importance of motivational forces as personality determinants. On the contrary, these motivational forces are often a part of the psychodiagnostic picture and therefore may have to become an integral part of future classification systems.

## Counseling and Psychotherapy

Counseling and psychotherapy, which strive to change people in order to help them adjust better to life, call for personality assessment before, during, or after treatment. Usually, these assessments measure the extent of change brought about by treatment.

But not all counselors and psychotherapists use tests or other assessment tools. The client-centered counselor, for example, whose philosophy is not to know more about the client than that person knows about himself or herself, may not use tests at all, or perhaps may use them only for research or at the client's own request. The trait-and-factor–oriented counselor, on the other hand, is likely to measure rather routinely before, during, and after treatment. In other words, the counselor's or the psychotherapist's theoretical orientation affects not only the extent to which he or she uses formal assessment tools such as tests, if at all, but also the selection of tests and the way and to whom these are interpreted and reported. For a more detailed account of the purposes of personality and psychological assessment in counseling and clinical psychology, the reader should consult other sources (Goldman, 1971, pp. 16–33; Korchin, 1976, pp. 123–278; Phares, 1979, pp. 161–294; Sundberg et al., 1973, pp. 199–249).

## Legal Settings

Psychologists often administer personality tests in the role of an "expert witness" in the courtroom. This form of forensic assessment is sometimes, but not exclusively, used to help determine whether the accused is "insane" and therefore not to be held legally responsible for certain acts of violence, or it may be used to help the court decide whether an individual seeking release from a mental hospital is sufficiently "sane" to be released (see Box 1–4). According to some psychologists (e.g., Holt, 1971, p. 15), the most enlightened use of such testing would be in helping to decide on a plan of treatment, rehabilitation, or whatever was needed to change the behavior of the accused or person seeking release from a hospital.

## Personnel Selection

Personnel selection can be defined as choosing, promoting, or placing from the available applicants those to be hired, promoted, or assigned to training programs designed for nurses, doctors, pilots, salespersons, psychologists, police officers, and so on. Personnel selection has one specific objective: to contribute to the increasingly effective use of labor within an organization. Technical qualifications for one of the above jobs or educational programs may be important but can usually be ascertained from the candidates' records. Testing, however, provides information about interpersonal (among examinees) as well as intrapersonal (within one examinee) differences. Interpersonal differences are important for selecting the right person for a particular job. Intrapersonal differences, or differences within the individual with respect to certain characteristics, indicate, first, how a person may have changed from one time to the next; second, these differences help determine how a person's many interests, aptitudes, or personality characteristics compare with one another. In the first intrapersonal instance, an individual's growth (or lack of it) may be assessed; in the second, a person's comparative strengths and weaknesses can be ascertained.

For organizations, such testing helps them select one applicant among many for a given job. For placement, in contrast, testing aids in choosing from a number of jobs the one best suited to the attributes of a particular applicant. In selection testing, the decision to hire has yet to be made; in placement testing, the decision to hire has already been made, but what that position will be is the question yet to be answered. Often the most crucial issue is whether a candidate possesses a suitable combination of personality traits, and this can be decided with the help of personality testing.

Personnel specialists (see Tenopyr, 1982) believe that to place men and women in the wrong jobs or in the wrong vocational or professional training program is wasteful or even dangerous. Such errors in personnel selection are legendary among veterans who have served in the

## BOX 1-4

## Assessment for Legal Purposes: A Case Study of Neglect

Harry was a diagnosed schizophrenic patient in a large state hospital in North Dakota. He had been committed to the hospital on the strength of his wife's signature on so-called Commitment Papers. But Harry was convinced that there was nothing the matter with him, and he persistently sought interviews with the hospital staff, each of whom, in private conversations with Harry, assured him that "the hospital will do you good." This went on for about eight months, after which Harry contacted and retained an attorney who filed a writ of habeas corpus on Harry's behalf. In an attempt to obtain an expert witness regarding his client's mental health, the attorney hired a clinical psychologist.

The clinical psychologist interviewed Harry and then administered the MMPI, Rorschach, and TAT. On the basis of his findings, the psychologist advised the lawyer that to the best of his knowledge, Harry was not schizophrenic at the present time and that it was highly unlikely that Harry had been schizophrenic when he was committed to the hospital. The psychologist then searched for the initial hospital admissions report or any case conference material that could shed some light on Harry's admission or progress during his stay in the hospital. There was no such record in Harry's file, nor was there any evidence that Harry had been seen or treated by anyone, except for an occasional conversation with a psychiatric nurse or hospital aide who had made entries that read, "Harry complains about hospital regimen," "Harry says he's normal and may go batty here," and "Patient is cooperative but whines a lot about being here."

The attorney and the clinical psychologist then contacted the wife, who told this sad tale: About one year ago, her husband began complaining that his two brothers, with whom Harry shared a partnership in a liquor store, were teasing him that he was "drinking up the profits." It was true that Harry took an occasional drink, his wife admitted, but both she and her husband suspected that the two brothers were trying to buy out Harry's share of the business and that one way to get him into trouble was to tease him about his drinking. This they did for about three months. Harry then pointed a shotgun at his brothers and threatened to "silence them permanently." Truly shaken, his brothers telephoned the sheriff and insisted that Harry be locked up for his and their protection. Harry was then apprehended in his home and put into the county jail. Several hours later, the sheriff and a physician told Harry's wife that they would release him from jail immediately if she would sign some papers that would entitle Harry to obtain "psychiatric observation in the state hospital." Not wanting to waste any time, the wife signed the necessary papers. These were the commitment papers that permitted the state to detain Harry in the state hospital indefinitely.

This story was presented in court and the state's main case, as presented

*(continued)*

> **BOX 1-4** (*Continued*)
>
> by the hospital psychiatrist, was that Harry was "insane" at the time of his commitment. Because the state was not able to present evidence of so-called legal "insanity," either at the time of his admission or at trial time, and because Harry had not been examined by any professional hospital personnel during his eight-month stay, the judge paid particular attention to Harry's attorney and the clinical psychologist who presented as evidence of Harry's "sanity" their interview and other personality assessment data which suggested that he was currently functioning without any apparent psychopathology. They furthermore persuaded the judge that Harry would probably function competently in society. On the basis of this evidence, Harry was released from the state hospital and was awarded punitive damages for his unnecessary hospital incarceration.

military forces. Stories abound of biochemists assigned to cleaning garbage cans, of mechanics forced to be cooks, and of unskilled and untrained people placed in teaching positions. These errors and wastes of labor can be avoided, or at least minimized, by using personnel selection procedures designed to contribute to the more effective use of people in organizations.

## Research Settings

Research using personality assessment can be done in any of the above settings, the most common being the university and the clinic, where the effects on personality of particular experimental variables or treatments are measured. For example, in psychiatric hospitals, one could find out the effects of electroshock therapy on personality by administering tests before and after treatment.

In industrial settings, special management-training programs are conducted so as to shape aspiring managers' personalities along certain lines (i.e., to become more sensitive in interpersonal relations, to develop leadership qualities, and so forth). The effectiveness of the program in achieving its objective can be evaluated with personality assessment.

Personality assessment for research purposes also is done in college psychological laboratories, in which volunteer, experimental subjects are tested, then undergo an experimental manipulation in which a novel condition is introduced, and then are tested again. For example, in a well-known early experiment, psychologists (Guetzkow & Bowman, 1946) were interested in determining the effects of prolonged food deprivation on the personalities of a group of World War II conscientious objectors who agreed to participate in the experiment. These men, who ordinarily were respected citizens of their communities, underwent radical changes in their personalities after a period of food deprivation: they were observed stealing food from store counters and from one another, fighting among themselves, hoarding dishes and silverware, telling lies to procure more food, and generally displaying antisocial behavior. Other noteworthy changes included a newly developed interest in reading recipes and cookbooks and pinning magazine pictures of lavish meals on walls. The men reported that many of their waking hours were spent daydreaming about sumptuous feasts. Many of these behavior changes were also observed in their personality test scores, particularly those of their MMPIs. On measures of ability, aptitude, and intelligence, however, their scores were essentially the same both before and after the food deprivation.

Another type of research with personality tests examines the adequacy of the measurement technique itself. This research is designed to explore the characteristics of a particular instrument and to ascertain whether it consistently and faithfully reveals the attributes that the tester intended. For example, the needs of a hospital or an industrial organization may dictate the development of a particular type of personality test; research would then be undertaken to determine whether that test meets these needs and whether it measures its purported variables reliably and validly (see chapter two).

Finally, personality assessment research is often used to contribute to the knowledge and theories of how persons function. This research is done in a variety of settings, and its emphasis is often on identifying motives, attitudes, beliefs, or defenses that underlie overt and inferred behaviors. Its major purpose is to build a sound theoretical system in which concepts can be measured and related to one another, usually so as to learn about persons and theory construction.

## Sources of Information about Personality

Psychologists interested in studying people collect their information from a variety of sources using many methods. These sources and methods (Table 1–3) include examining relatively superficial physical characteristics, measuring perceptual skills, observing behavior, and gathering samples of verbal self-reports. These are the data and procedures from which more general personality characteristics, motivations, traits, and dispositions are inferred (Butcher, 1972, pp. 1–2),

**Table 1–3** Personality Assessment Methods Used over the Years.

| Method | Example |
|---|---|
| Physical characteristics | Measurement of head size and shape and somatotyping (both now discredited) |
| Psychomotor performance | Various dexterity measures, finger tapping; memory for digits (chapter ten) |
| Perceptual skills | Perceiving incongruity of situations, spiral after-image; differential development of perceptual skills, e.g., size constancy (chapter ten) |
| Physiological processes | Galvanic skin responses; electroencephalograph recording; rapid eye movements (REM); various other biophysical techniques (chapter ten) |
| Performance in specified tasks | Small group interaction; psychodrama |
| Informant report | Behavioral descriptions; Q-sort technique (see chapter seven); rating scales; behavioral inventories (chapter five) |
| Verbal self-report | Interview (chapter six); autobiographies (chapter five); self-report questionnaire (chapter seven); free association; paired association |
| Nonverbal self-report | Expressive movements, handwriting, gestures, etc.; gait, posture, attire, etc. (chapter five) |
| Projection-apperception | The Rorschach inkblots; various constructive, thematic, completion tasks that encourage individual responding to ambiguous stimulus situations (chaper eight) |

Source: Adapted from Butcher, J. N. *Objective personality assessment* Morristown, NJ: General Learning Press, 1971.

and most of this book deals with the advantages and disadvantages of using these and other data sources for studying people.

These sources require varying degrees of inference from the obtained test-responses to the generalizations that can be made from them (e.g., perceiving faces and eyes in inkblots requires a greater inference than a response of "true" to the item "I am being plotted against" when either is used as an index of paranoia). Other sources constitute weak, unsupported, and sometimes even "illusory" connections of test sign with personality traits. For example, Chapman and Chapman (1967, 1969) and Wanderer (1969) demonstrated that even trained test interpreters were not accurate because they harbored mistaken notions about the significance of certain test signs and behavior observations. Still other assessment sources have been substantiated by large networks of empirical evidence and therefore have formed strong connections between indices and behavior. But now we are getting ahead of ourselves. Here it may be helpful simply to lay out the plan of this book so that the reader may obtain a preview of topics to come.

## Plan of the Book

As we indicated earlier in this chapter, this book has been written so as to fit into a systems framework. Accordingly, we shall view personality assessment as one component of a complex information-processing system that has three main interdependent components: an *information processor*, which is the system's decision maker; *inputs*, which consist of personality tests and procedures; and *outputs*, which are the processed inputs in the form of scores, interpretations, and rules for action. The system is anchored to the world by its inputs on one side and its outputs on the other. It is a system in that it is a group of elements, either physical or nonphysical, with interrelations and interactions toward one or more goals, objectives, or ends (see Alexander, 1976, p. 4).

This system is represented in Figure 1–1 by a combination block diagram and flow chart not unlike that designed to analyze complicated engineering equipment and to write elaborate computer programs (see Box 1–5). Figure 1–1 shows the interrelation of the system's elements and follows their direction of flow. This diagram highlights one advantage of using the systems approach as the book's organizing theme. It permits us to disassemble the system so that its various elements can be studied separately and to reassemble it so that we can describe its operation and dynamic interaction in numerous personality test settings. Another advantage is that the systems analysis diagram allows us to present a visual representation of the separate components of personality study, a representation to which we shall refer often in subsequent chapters.

Turning to the elements of the system presented in Figure 1–1 and looking first at the left-hand, or input, side of the diagram, we see a rectangle marked "Formulate Assessment Goals." This is a way of saying that the potential information processor, or decision maker, must consider the assessment program's goals before administering tests and feeding these and other personality data into the information processor. The questions to be asked in this regard (represented by the arrows pointing to the three diamonds) are, "Setting?" "Purpose?" and "Personality Theory?" This is a short way of saying that the formulation of examination goals is influenced by these three factors and by the specific answers to these questions (represented by the three rectangles alongside the diamonds).

The input side of the system then selects the proper procedure (last rectangle) and asks the questions regarding this procedure (represented by the four diamonds) of whether it is standardized, objective, reliable, and valid. If the answer to any of these questions is no, then another assessment procedure should be selected. This is shown by the "no" arrows that loop back from the diamonds to the last rectangle. If the

## BOX 1-5

### Functional Components of a Computer System

The ultimate mechanical data processor is the electronic digital computer. Its functional components are shown below, and its uses in studying computer interviewing and personality test interpretations are described in chapters six and seven.

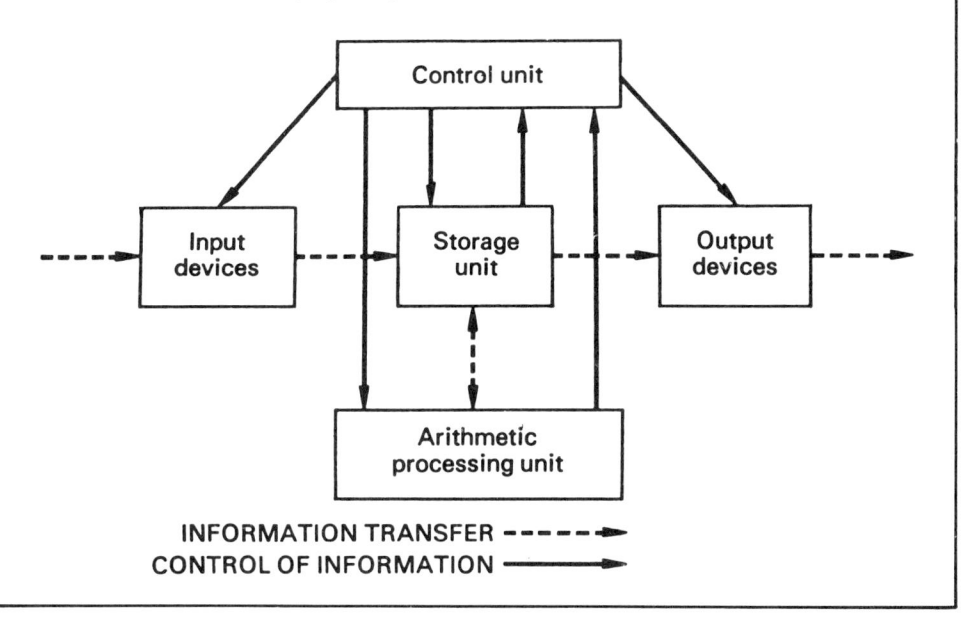

```
                    ┌──────────────┐
                    │ Control unit │
                    └──────────────┘
       ┌──────────┐  ┌──────────┐  ┌──────────┐
   --→ │  Input   │→ │ Storage  │→ │  Output  │ --→
       │ devices  │  │   unit   │  │ devices  │
       └──────────┘  └──────────┘  └──────────┘
                         ↕
                    ┌──────────────┐
                    │  Arithmetic  │
                    │ processing unit │
                    └──────────────┘
```

INFORMATION TRANSFER - - - - →
CONTROL OF INFORMATION ─────→

---

answer is yes, then the system's inputs are ready for information processing.

Most of the preceding elements of the input system have already been discussed in this chapter. The other input elements, which appear as four diamonds at the bottom of the diagram (relating to standardization, objectivity, reliability, and validity) will be examined in chapters three and four, along with other issues concerning measurement and testing. Most of the book will deal with the tests and procedures that appear in parentheses in the last rectangle on the input side of the diagram. These will be covered in chapters five through nine and are, as it were, the grist of the information processor.

The information-processing, or decision-making, component of the system consists of five main subsystems, each represented by a rectangle within the middle portion of the diagram: the normative, scoring,

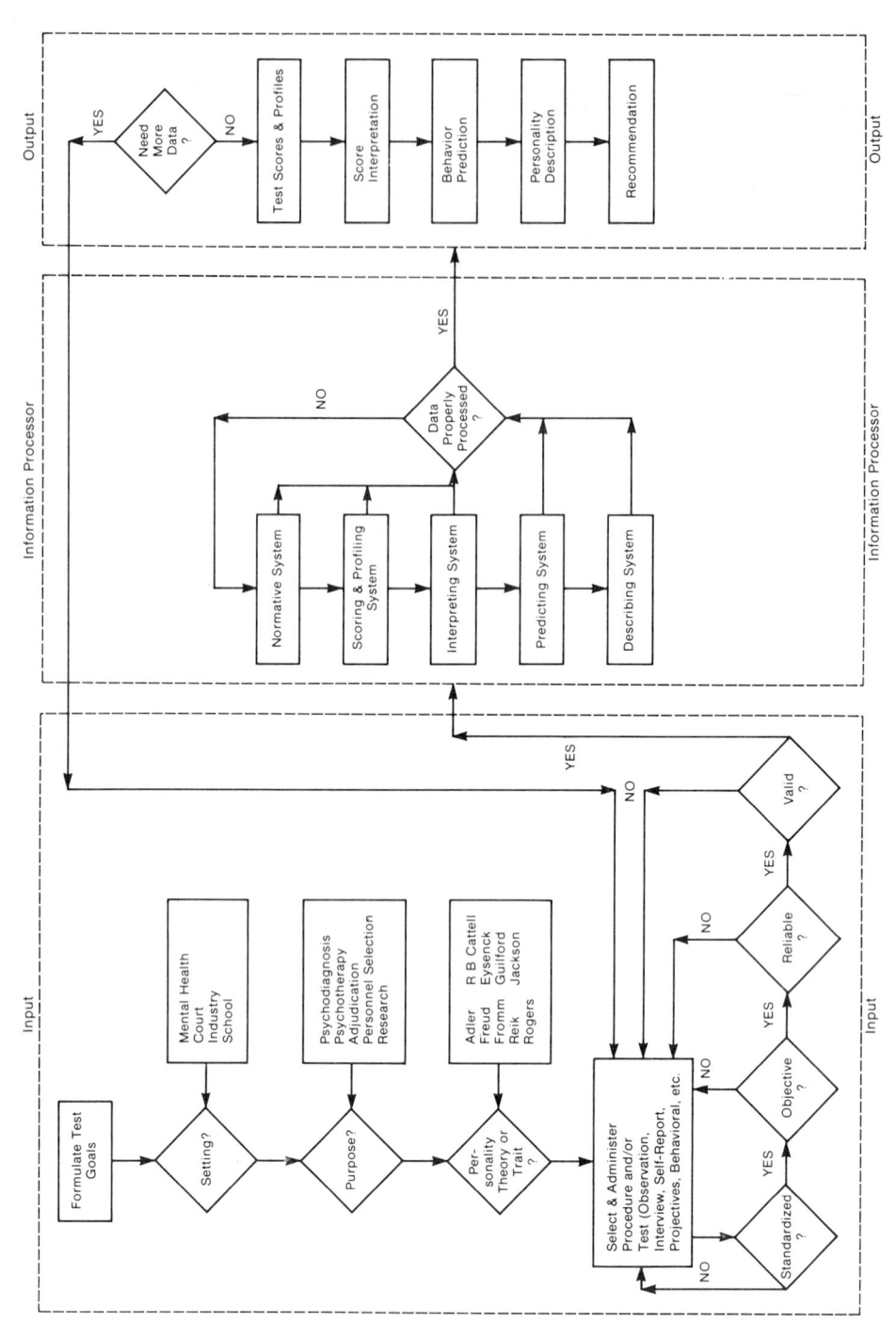

**Figure 1-1.** Combination Flow Chart–Block Diagram Depicting the Components of Assessment.

profiling, interpreting, predicting, and describing subsystems. The information processor, which also contains a subsystem to process its inputs before releasing them to the real world, is the core of the entire system. We shall study this component in considerable detail in chapter four.

On the output side of Figure 1–1 there appear one diamond and five rectangles. The first of these asks about the need for additional data. If the answer is yes, the system is instructed to loop back to the selection command on the input side; if no, the system can release test scores and profiles, interpretations, behavior predictions, personality descriptions, and other information that the decision maker may need to communicate these results to those who requested the testing. Again, we shall cover this component in chapter four.

We shall discuss the technical and ethical problems and issues of the information-processing system's use, as well as those that arise in personality study generally, in the final chapter of the book.

## SUMMARY

After making a case for the quantitative approach to personality assessment, defining assessment as a procedure for obtaining samples of psychological behavior, and describing personality and some of its dimensions, we discussed some of the settings and uses of the study of personality. These included diagnosis, counseling, legal and psychiatric classification, personnel selection, and research. The various sources for studying personality include observation, behavioral assessment, interviews, self-report inventories, and questionnaires, all of which, together with the means for administering, scoring, and interpreting them, are the topics of this book. These sources, as well as the means for processing them, will be presented throughout the book within a systems analysis framework.

## FOR FURTHER READING

Cattell, R.B., & Kline, P. *The scientific analysis of personality and motivation.* New York: Academic Press, 1977. The main organizing theme of this book is its emphasis on the scientific and quantitative study of personality. It is an important statement on the state of the art of Cattellian personality theory.

Ghiselli, E. E., Campbell, J. P., & Zedeck, S. *Measurement theory for the behavioral sciences.* San Francisco, W. H. Freeman, 1981. Particularly relevant to the material just covered are chapters 1, 2, and 3. The remainder of the book is invaluable also, but somewhat advanced.

Korchin, S.J. *Modern clinical psychology: Principles of intervention in the clinic and community.* New York: Basic Books, 1976. An encyclopedic tome on the field of clinical practice; chapters six through eleven overlap with the topics of the present text but are well worth reading.

Liebert, R.M., & Spiegler, M.D. *Personality: Strategies and issues* (3rd ed.). Homewood, IL: Dorsey Press, 1978. In addition to an overview of all strategies of studying personality, the authors emphasize the theories and issues of the psychoanalytic dispositional, phenomenological, and behavioral approaches.

Pervin, L.A. *Personality: Theory, assessment, and research* (3rd ed.). New York: John Wiley, 1980. A fine and scholarly overview of its topic, this book treats most approaches critically but fairly.

Sundberg, N.D. *Assessment of persons.* Englewood Cliffs, NJ: Prentice-Hall, 1977. This as an excellent statement on the same topic as the present volume, which is no coincidence, since both authors are Minnesota graduates with similar views.

Sundberg, N.D., Tyler, L.A., & Taplin, J.R. *Clinical psychology: Expanding horizons* (2nd ed.). Englewood Cliffs, NJ: Prentice-Hall, 1973. Of immediate relevance to the present chapter and book are chapters eight and nine on the appraisal of individuals by observations, interviews, and facts.

Wiggins, J.S. *Personality and prediction: Principles of personality assessment.* Reading, MA: Addison-Wesley, 1973. Divided into three parts (the prediction of human behavior, the techniques of data collection in personality assessment, and the practice of personality assessment), this upper-level book is superbly written and organized.

Willerman, L. *The Psychology of individual and group differences.* San Francisco: W.H. Freeman & Company Publishers, 1979. Marking the inevitable return of an interest in the measurement of individual differences, this book is especially valuable for its updated treatment of the heritability concept and its contribution to intelligence. The same author has also edited (with R.G. Turner) a book of readings that covers the same domain.

# 2 Statistics Essential for Assessment

No book on psychological assessment would be complete without some discussion of statistics in regard to the meaning of assessment results. Statistics is also important in organizing, evaluating, and reporting the data of our decision maker (see Figure 1–1) during all stages of its operation—preparing input data, processing and interpreting test information, and communicating test results to the outside world.

Statistics would be unnecessary if objects and people were constant. But this is not the case. These phenomena and people are variable, and to describe and understand them we use statistics.

In psychological assessment particularly, statistics is essential because observations collected under identical conditions vary not only from person to person, but also within the person from one time to the next. If everybody taking the same test, for example, received exactly the same score all the time, there would be no need for statistical analysis. But because scores do vary and individual differences are extensive, it is useful to be able to summarize these data using quantitative values that describe and organize the observed variability.

Statistics is used in psychological assessment mainly to describe and to generalize. *Descriptive statistics* deals almost entirely with a *sample* (or samples) drawn from a larger *population*. It focuses exclusively on organizing and describing the observed measures or scores of the sample. The second use of statistics, known as *inferential statistics*, determines whether the sample measures or "statistics," as they are sometimes called, are accurate estimates of population or "parameter" values. Inferential statistics usually expresses these estimates in likelihood or probability statements. We first shall examine some descriptive uses.

## Descriptive Statistics

Test results are usually obtained from a sample of individuals, as we indicated above, rather than from an entire population. Quantitative analyses or computations performed on the observations of this subset of persons selected from a larger group are called descriptive statistics.

## BOX 2-1

## On Statistical Reasoning

Statistics has been described (see Helmstadter, 1970, pp. 174–175) as the substitution of numbers for words, a substitution allowing us to arrive at rational conclusions in the face of uncertainty. It is, in other words, the science of quantitative reasoning that enables us to judge the probable fallibility of collected data. By so doing, statistics permits us to extend our observations far beyond the restricted sphere in which these observations occur. Without statistics, our reasoning and conclusions about objects, people, and events would be imprecise and limited.

---

Examples of such statistics are the *percentage* of persons obtaining particular scores, the *average* of these values, and their *relationship* to those obtained by another group or the same group at another time. In other words, descriptive statistics organizes or summarizes quantities that communicate information about a sample of scores.

The first step in organizing a set of obtained scores is to arrange them systematically so that they convey an emerging picture. This is usually accomplished by forming a *frequency distribution*, which is an orderly array of scores, arranged from highest to lowest measures, with score frequencies tabulated alongside. This distribution reflects the frequency with which the group's values occur, as is shown in Table 2–1.

This table shows an unordered and ordered array of hypothetical scores attained by 1,451 freshmen college students on the verbal portion of the Scholastic Aptitude Test (SAT-V). Scores on the SAT-V are often used to predict successful performance in college, and although the ones included here are fictitious, we can use them to illustrate several descriptive procedures. In our example, not all of the scores are shown on the left side of Table 2–1, although the frequency tallies that represent the ordered distribution are complete. These scores range from those falling within the *class interval* 440–459 to those falling within the interval 780–799. The *class interval*, generally, is the unit used within a frequency distribution, and its use is a matter of convenience in arranging data. It provides a means of grouping several adjacent scores for computing and for plotting graphs. The class intervals must be kept equal throughout any given distribution to allow the use of appropriate statistical and graphing procedures. In Table 2–1, the data have been arranged with eighteen class intervals, each of which includes twenty scores. The column headed "frequency" gives the number of persons ($N$) whose scores fall within each class interval.

A glance at the (incomplete) set of unordered scores presented on the left side of Table 2–1 indicates that we can get a clearer picture of the test performance of this group by arranging the scores in an orderly way. And a graphical presentation of these data offers a still clearer description. Figure 2–1 is a graphic representation of the data of Table 2–1 and consists of a *histogram* and a *frequency polygon*.

The histogram of Figure 2–1 shows both the midpoints of the test scores' class intervals along the horizontal axis, or *abscissa*, and the number of cases falling within any class interval at the vertical axis, or *ordinate*. The representation of data on histograms is achieved, as in Figure 2–1, by constructing bars whose lengths represent the frequencies in the intervals. There are as many bars as there are class intervals, and all bars are adjacent to one another. The histogram shows the data as discrete segments (intervals) and emphasizes the relative magnitude of each of these segments.

More often, however, test scores are best presented by emphasizing their continuous (rather than, for example, their discrete) nature. In this case, we illustrated the differences in frequencies as they occurred

**Table 2–1** Frequency Distribution of Hypothetical Scores Obtained on the SAT-V by 1,451 Entering College Freshmen.

| Unordered Scores (incomplete) | Ordered Scores (showing class intervals) | Frequency |
|---|---|---|
| 638, 495, 450, 585, 741, 716, 663, | 780–799 | 2 |
| 720, 628, 618, 453, 669, 750, 603, | 760–779 | 4 |
| 753, 700, 637, 456, 720, 742, 562, | 740–759 | 20 |
| 718, 755, 755, 631, 770, 756, 612, | 720–739 | 50 |
| 746, 715, 718, 680, 622, 681, 615, | 700–719 | 72 |
| 683, 465, 605, 721, 623, 601, 541, | 680–699 | 98 |
| 465, 610, 525, 673, 791, 637, 543, | 660–679 | 110 |
| 640, 645, 791, 425, 450, 628, 631, | 640–659 | 118 |
| 475, 580, 673, 779, 633, 775, 722, | 620–639 | 218 |
| 700, 680, 718, 625, 631, 685, 585, | 600–619 | 225 |
| 780, 661, 672, 685, 629, 662, 518, | 580–599 | 165 |
| 680, 560, 558, 753, 625, 500, 519, | 560–579 | 128 |
| 585, 535, 623, 628, 620, 609, 635, | 540–559 | 83 |
| 693, 583, 685, 690, 705, 693, 536, | 520–539 | 70 |
| 485, 602, 520, 565, 510, 533, 641, | 500–519 | 44 |
| 555, 662, 515, 492, 485, 581, 483, | 480–499 | 31 |
| 685, 672, 715, 490, 718, 681, 492, | 460–479 | 8 |
| 770, 680, 621, 720, 718, 518, 712, | 440–459 | 5 |
| 480, 548, 493, 545, 485, 525, 725, | | |
| 625, 605, 625, 590, 550, 673, 485, | | $N = 1{,}451$ |
| 660, 555, 675, 520, 682, 613, 538, | | |
| 539, 585, 721, 545, 710, 632, 498, | | |
| 720, 492, 602, 561, 493, 721, 566, | | |
| 637, 533, 561, 655, 614, 589, 725, | | |

Plus 1,283 other scores ranging from 440 to 799

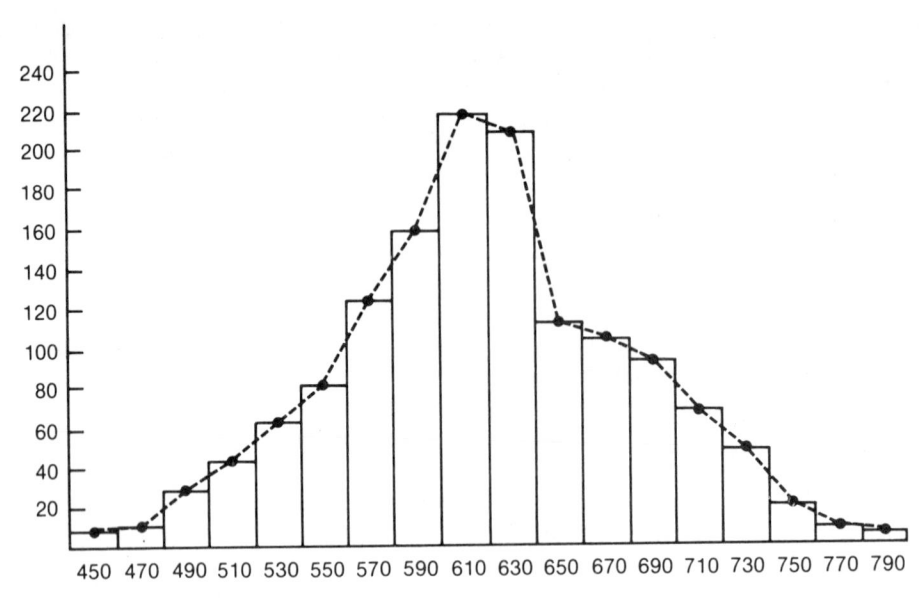

[Figure: histogram with x-axis values 450 470 490 510 530 550 570 590 610 630 650 670 690 710 730 750 770 790 and y-axis 20 to 240]

**Figure 2–1.** Histogram and Frequency Polygon of the Data Presented in Table 2–1.

from interval to interval in an incremental and continuous fashion. To do this, we placed a point at the center of the top of each bar and connected these points with lines. The resulting figure is called a *frequency polygon*. One such polygon is superimposed on the histogram in Figure 2–1; it is the ideal graph to use for comparing two or more groups.

There are two noteworthy features of graphed frequency distributions like those shown in Figure 2–1: the tendency of scores to cluster in the middle of the distribution and the variability of scores across a wide range. These features permit comparisons among test scores (or sets of data); the best way to communicate these features is by means of single values, or *statistics*, that describe them adequately and concisely. Two such measures are those that reflect a distribution's *central tendency* and its *variability*. As we indicate in the next two sections, the first summarizes the tendency of scores to bunch up in the center of the distribution, and the second describes score dispersion within a distribution.

### Measures of Central Tendency

The data of Table 2–1, or similar data, also measure central tendency. A measure of central tendency is some value located at the middle of a distribution characteristic (or descriptive) of the entire distribution.

For a given set of data, the measure of central tendency used depends on what is meant by "middle," different definitions giving rise to different measures. We shall consider three such measures: the *mean*, *median*, and *mode*.

The best known of these, of course, is the "average," or the arithmetic mean. It is obtained by adding all the scores and dividing the sum by the number ($N$) of cases (see Box 2–2 for a list of statistical symbols and their definitions). Thus, letting $X$ stand for a score on a test and given the scores $X_1$, $X_2$, $X_3$, $X_4$, and $X_5$, the mean is represented by $\bar{X}$ as follows:

$$\bar{X} = \frac{X_1 + X_2 + X_3 + X_4 + X_5}{N}$$

Another way of expressing this is by the formula

$$\bar{X} = \Sigma \frac{X}{N}$$

where $\Sigma$ = the sum of
$\bar{X}$ = the mean
$X$ = the score of each individual on the test
$N$ = the total number of individuals for whom there are scores

Thus, for example, given the scores 100, 110, 120, 105, and 95, the mean becomes

$$\bar{X} = \frac{100 + 110 + 120 + 105 + 95}{5}$$

$$= \frac{530}{5}$$

$$= 106$$

The median, the second measure of central tendency mentioned above, is the middlemost score of the distribution after all scores have been arranged in order of size. Thus, by rearranging the foregoing scores in size order, we have 95, 100, 105, 110, and 120. The median score is 105, since it divides the distribution exactly in half. Compared to the mean, the magnitude of the median is not affected by the extreme score values at the high or low ends of the distribution because the end values are not involved in any arithmetic operations.

The mode is the most frequently occurring, or the most common, score of a distribution. For example, given the scores 100, 110, 95, 115, 105, and 110, the mode is 110. Since in most large distributions (e.g., Table 2–1) the scores usually pile up around the center of the distri-

## BOX 2-2

### Statistical Symbols

The student who reads test manuals, books dealing with tests, or articles about testing in the educational journals will encounter a number of conventional symbols referring to statistical concepts or operations. Some of the commonest are defined below.

| Symbol | Definition |
|---|---|
| $N$ | The total number of cases in the group. |
| $f$ | Frequency. The number of cases with a specific score or in a particular class interval. |
| $X$ | A raw score on some measure. |
| $x$ | A deviation score, indicating how far the individual falls above or below the mean of the group. |
| $x'$ | A deviation score from some arbitrary reference point, often expressed in interval units. |
| $i$ | The number of points of score in one class interval. |
| $\bar{X}$ or $M$ | The mean of the group. |
| $Md$ | The median of the group. |
| $Q_1$ | The lower quartile, the 25th percentile. |
| $Q_3$ | The upper quartile, the 75th percentile. |
| $Q$ | The semi-interquartile range. Half the difference between $Q_3$ and $Q_1$. |
| $P$ | A percentile. |
| A subscript | Modifies a symbol and tells which specific individual or value is referred to, e.g., $P_{10}$ is the 10th percentile, $X_j$ is the raw score of person $j$. |
| $SD$ or $S$ | Standard deviation of a set of scores. |
| $\sigma$ | Standard deviation in the *population*, though sometimes used to refer to the particular sample. |
| $p$ | Percent of persons getting a test item correct. |
| $q$ | Percent of persons getting a test item wrong ($p + q = 100$). |
| $r$ | A coefficient of correlation. |
| $r_{11}$ | A reliability coefficient. The correlation between two equivalent test forms or two administrations of a test. |
| $\Sigma$ | "Take the sum of." |

Source: Thorndike, R. L., & Hagen, E. *Measurement and evaluation in psychology and education* (3rd ed.) New York: John Wiley, 1969, pp. 59-60.

bution, the mode is found there. In a histogram or frequency polygon the mode is, of course, the highest point of the distribution.

Which measure is the best? In most cases, the mean is the best measure of central tendency. Its value, unlike the others, is determined by the specific value of each score in the distribution. Changing the value of any one score would automatically change the value of the mean, but not necessarily the values of the median or the mode. The mean is also the preferred measure because it is more stable than the other two measures, and, most importantly perhaps, it is used to compute some of the other descriptive statistics that we discuss below.

For example, the mean is used to compute the standard deviation and the correlation coefficient.

But there are assessment situations in which the median is the most useful measure of central tendency. For example, it is preferred when there are extremely high and low scores at the two ends of a distribution because its value is uninfluenced by these scores. This characteristic of the median makes it best for describing the central tendency of distributions in which a few scores differ greatly from the rest of the scores.

The mode is the least sensitive measure of central tendency, since its value is totally unaffected by the values of any score other than that of the score appearing most frequently. But the mode is useful for summarizing qualitative or categorical data when it is impossible to determine the value of the median or mean. The mode is also used to identify the most common score.

In the normal distribution, the mean, the median, and the mode all fall together (i.e., are identical) in the center of the bell-shaped or symmetrical curve (see discussion below). But there is more to describing a sample's scores than to plot and graph its frequency distribution or to compute its measures of central tendency. In assessment it often is useful to have a numerical index of the variability of scores. Two such indices are the range and the standard deviation, which are discussed in the next section.

## Measures of Variability

The most commonly used measures to describe variability within a distribution are the *range* and the *standard deviation.* These measures reflect the distribution of scores by describing the spread and the dispersion of these scores. The range is the simpler of the two measures and is computed by taking the difference between the highest and lowest scores of a distribution. The range is often a useful descriptive device in establishing the lower and upper limits of a distribution. But it is highly unstable because of its dependence on only two scores in a distribution, scores that may not represent the spread of the majority of the scores. In other words, if there is a wide gap between the highest (or lowest) and the next highest (or next lowest) scores, this gap will not be reflected in the range.

A more stable and sensitive measure of variability than the range is the *variance,* or its square root, the *standard deviation.* It takes into account the spread of scores by measuring their relationship to some central point of a given distribution. Here is the way it is calculated:

$$S_x^2 = \frac{\Sigma(X - \bar{X})^2}{N} = \frac{\Sigma x^2}{N}$$

## BOX 2-3

### Four Distributions

Examples of four distributions in which the dispersions are both different (a) and the same (b), which have the same measure of central tendency but different dispersions (a), and which have the same dispersion but different measures of central tendency (b).

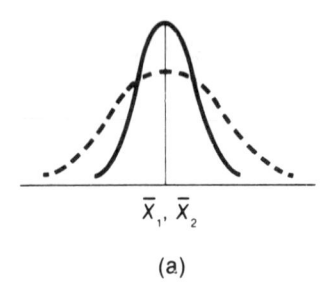

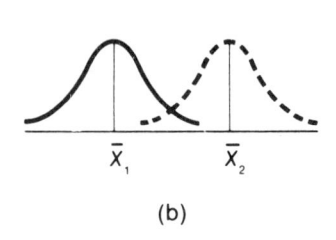

$\bar{X}_1, \bar{X}_2$

(a)

$\bar{X}_1 \quad \bar{X}_2$

(b)

**Source:** From *Principles of educational and psychological testing.* 2nd ed., by Frederick G. Brown. Copyright © 1970 by The Dryden Press, Inc. Copyright © 1976 by Holt, Rinehart & Winston, p. 39. Reprinted by permission of Holt, Rinehart & Winston.

where $S_x^2$ = variance of the scores on test $X$
$X$ = score on test $X$
$\bar{X}$ = mean of scores on test $X$
$x = X - \bar{X}$
$N$ = number of persons scoring on test $X$

and the standard deviation is the square root of the variance

$$S_x = \sqrt{\frac{\Sigma x^2}{N}}$$

Using these formulas, we compute the variance and standard deviation of the scores 100, 110, 115, 120, and 130 as follows:

First, we find the mean of the distribution, which is 115. Then 115 is subtracted from each score:

$X - \bar{X} = x$
$100 - 115 = -15$
$110 - 115 = -5$
$115 - 115 = 0$
$120 - 115 = 5$
$130 - 115 = 15$

Next, each $x$ is squared in order to remove negative values, and the squares are added. It may be noted that if these $x$'s were not squared, the sum of the distances from the mean (e.g., $x$) would yield a value of zero.

$$-(15)^2 = 225$$
$$-(5)^2 = 25$$
$$(0)^2 = 0$$
$$(5)^2 = 25$$
$$(15)^2 = 225$$
$$\Sigma x^2 = 500$$

$$\frac{x}{N} = \frac{500}{5} = 100$$
$$S_x^2 = 100$$
$$S_x = 10$$

The symbol $SD$ or $S$, is often used to represent the standard deviation, for which $SD^2$, or simply $S^2$, is used as a symbol for the variance. Both of these measures are more stable and more descriptive indices of variability than the range is because they are computed in terms of the means, which are the central reference points of their distributions. The stability of these indices permits comparisons among two or more distributions of scores, and together with the mean, they serve as bases for other important assessment indices.

## Measures of Correlation

One question often asked in assessment is whether performance on one test is related to performance on a second test or measure. A good way to determine whether there is such an association is to plot the scores on a *scatter plot*, or *scatter diagram*, on which the scores on one test are listed along the horizontal axis of a graph, or abscissa, and the scores on the other measure along the vertical axis, or ordinate. Each point in the scatter diagram thus represents the two scores of a single subject, or his or her coordinate, and is the point of intersection of these values.

Some idealized scatter plots are depicted in Figure 2–2. On these diagrams, if the points create a straight line with a positive slope (lower left to upper right, as in diagram *a*), the association between the scores is considered to be perfectly positive. Thus in diagram *a*, each increase of 2 points on one measure (*y*) is associated with a consistent increase of 3 points on the other test. Note also that this straight line is negatively sloped (upper left to lower right). In diagrams *c* and *d*, there seems to be a moderately positive and a low negative relationship. And in diagram *e* there are no discernible or consistent relationships between the scores on the two tests. In diagram *c*, as the scores on the first

**36**  Personality and Psychological Assessment

(a) A Perfect Positive Relationship (r = +1.00)

(b) A Perfect Negative Relationship (r = −1.00)

(c) A Moderate Positive Relationship (r = +.57)

(d) A Moderately Low Negative Relationship (r = −.31)

(e) A Negligible Relationship (r = +.007)

(f) A Curvilinear Relationship

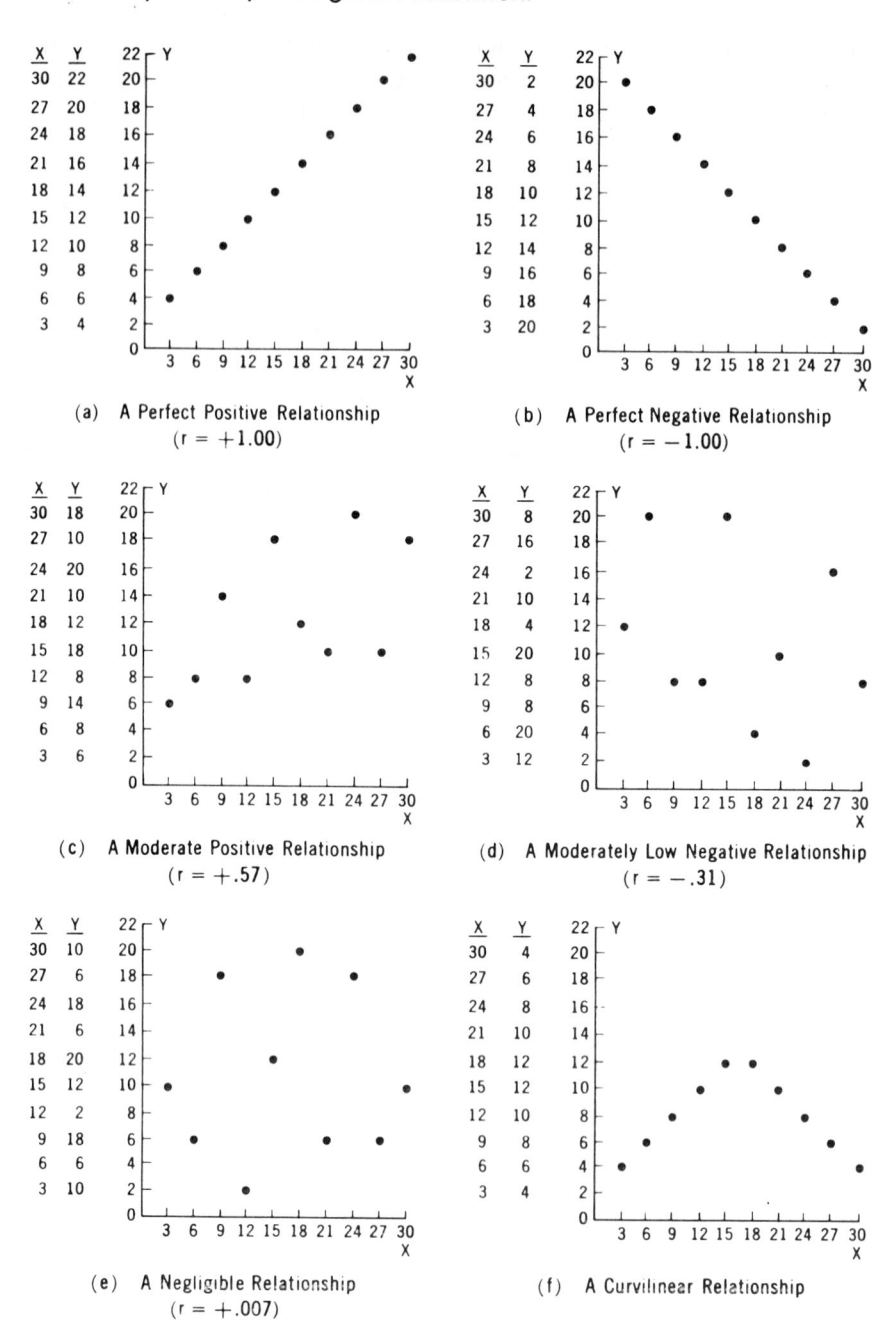

**Figure 2-2.**  Scatter Diagrams Showing Various Degrees of Correlation.

Source: Reprinted by permission of the publisher, from *The Assessment of Learning: Cognitive and Affective* by D.A. Payne, p. 223 (Lexington, Mass.: D.C. Heath and Company, 1974).

measure increase, those on the second test first increase, then stay the same, but afterwards increase again and decrease. In diagram *d*, the scores on the second test decrease, stay the same, and so on. And in diagram *e*, there seems to be no pattern of scores on the second measure associated with scores on the first. All of these correlations are linear; that is, they have a tendency to follow a straight-line pattern. Curvilinear relationships are also possible (diagram *f*). If one examined the relationship between stress and eye-hand coordination, for instance, one might find that some stress enhances performance but that too much stress diminishes performance on scores (see McNemar, 1969).

Fortunately, we need not rely on visual analyses of scatter diagrams to determine the relations between two variables. A descriptive statistic is available for this purpose, namely, the *correlation coefficient*, or simply the *correlation*. One of the most common of these measures is called the *Pearson product moment coefficient*, or *Pearson r*, named after its developer, Karl Pearson. This *r*, like many other similar correlations, may take on any value from 0.00 (no relationship) to +1.00 (perfect positive relationship) or −1.00 (perfect negative relationship). A correlation coefficient of +1.00 means that the person in a group who scored highest, let us say, on a scholastic aptitude test also performed best in school and that throughout the series of measures the correspondence is exact, or 1:1. A correlation of 0.00 signifies a complete absence of relationship, and a negative, or inverse correlation, indicates that a person who receives a high score on a test ranks low in school performance. Again, this is an exact correspondence, but it is inverse in that high scores on one measure are associated with low scores on another measure. Perfect correlations (+1.00 or −1.00) are almost never encountered in actual practice, and coefficients typically fall somewhere between these values. Commonly, correlations that hover around ±0.20 (read "plus or minus"), ±0.60, and ±0.85 are considered to reflect mild, moderate, and substantial relationships, respectively.

In the scatter diagram shown in Figure 2–3, which shows the hypothetical first-grade (*X*-scores) and second-grade (*Y*-scores) scores for 109 children, each dot or point represents an individual, and the position of the dot on the grid of the graph indicates each person's scores on the two variables. This graph, as we noted earlier, shows the overall arrangement of the dots, an arrangement that indicates the approximate degree of correlation. Figure 2–3 depicts a situation in which the correlation is moderately positive because the regression line extends from the lower left corner to the upper right corner of the graph. But in order to determine the actual correlation coefficient, we must calculate the values according to the formula:

$$r = \frac{xy}{N s_x s_y}$$

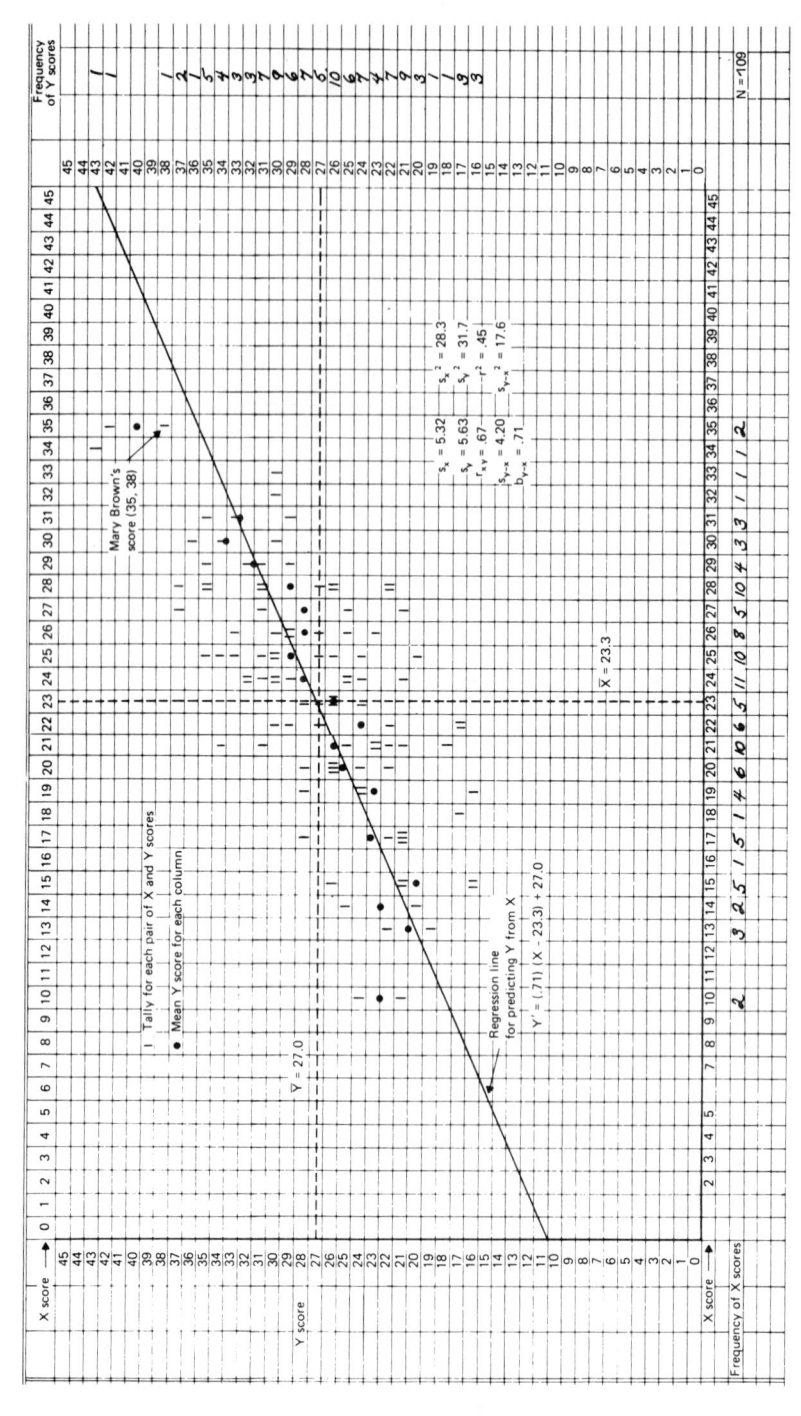

**Figure 2–3.** Scatter Diagram of First-Grade (X-Score) and Second-Grade (Y-Score) Vocabulary Scores for 109 Children.

Source: Holtzman, W.H., Methods in psychology. New York: Harper & Row, 1975.

where  r = product moment correlation
       xy = sum of the cross-products of the deviation scores
       $s_x$ = standard deviation of the X scores
       $s_y$ = standard deviation of the Y scores
       N = number of pairs of measurements

The only new term is xy, the sum of the cross-products obtained by multiplying the deviation scores (x and y) for each pair of scores and then adding these cross-products.

There are many more ways to compute the Pearson r, but these need not concern us here. Instead, let us examine some of the details of Figure 2–3, in which we see that for each of the 109 children we have two Vocabulary scores, collected, let us suppose, one year apart. The questions we can ask are, "If a child scores high on the test in the first grade, what is the likelihood that he or she will also score high one year later?" "Is there any chance that a poor performer in the first grade will do very well in the second?" "With what accuracy can I predict a child's future performance from a measure of present performance?"

The answers to such questions depend upon the relationship or degree of correlation between the two variables. Figure 2–3 shows a scatter diagram of this relationship, with Vocabulary scores in the first grade plotted on the abscissa (X) and scores in the second grade on the ordinate (Y). Each case is plotted on the diagram as a tally mark in the appropriate box whose X and Y coordinates correspond to the Vocabulary scores in the first and second years. For example, if Mary Brown's scores are 35 and 38 for the first and second years respectively, the mark representing her two scores will be located in the box perpendicular to the X-axis at 35 and to the Y-axis at 38. Figure 2–3 is a graph of all 109 pairs of scores. Occasionally, two or more cases have identical scores. This is shown by more than one mark in the same box.

Several more characteristics of the scatter diagram of Figure 2–3 are worth noting before we proceed with our computation of the correlation coefficient and other descriptive statistics based on these scores. Generally, as the X-scores rise in value, so do the Y-scores, indicating that a correlation does exist and that it is positive rather than negative.

Is there some way to predict scores on Y from those on X that would help estimate the extent of positive correlation? Yes, there is. Let us take a simple example. Note that the ten children who have an X-score of 25, for example, have Y-scores that vary from 20 to 35. For the correlation to be perfect, all ten of these children would have to have identical scores on Y. Note also that for each value of X there is a distribution of Y-scores, as in the case of the ten children with X-scores of 25. One possibility might be to compute the mean Y-score for each of these distributions. For example, the mean Y-score for the distribution of ten cases having an X-score of 25 is 29. Given this information we could say that the best estimate of a child's Vocabulary score in the second grade, given his or her first-grade score of 25, is 29, the mean for this column. The mean Y-score for the five children with an X-score of 15 is 20. Similarly, means could be computed for all the X-scores and Y-scores of the diagram.

Suppose we do plot the Y-score means for each of the column distributions in Figure 2–3, using a dot to mark their locations. The scatter among these means is less than the scatter of the individual scores. In fact, except for the two unstable means for the highest and lowest X-scores, they seem to follow a straight line. Let us assume that these column means do indeed depart from a straight line only because of minor chance variations. The straight line that fits the column means as closely as possible is called the *linear regression line for predicting* Y from X. Let us also suppose that the amount of scatter of Y-scores above and below this regression line is the same throughout the range of X-scores. Then we can use this regression line as the most stable basis for making predictions of Y from X throughout the entire range of scores, even for values of X in which few or no Y-scores are present in our sample of 109 cases. For example, for an X-score of 11, one would predict a Y-score of 19 using the points of intersection of the regression line. Likewise, a first-grade Vocabulary score of 10 yields a predicted second-grade score of 17, and so on. Though such graphic predictions can be made by estimating values of the best-fit regression line, there is, as we already noted, a better way to do it—namely, to compute Pearson r.

Using the formula for the correlation coefficient cited above, as we show in Figure 2–3, we obtain a correlation of 0.67 between the first- and second-grade Vocabulary scores for the 109 children. The following is the equation for estimating the regression line for predicting Y from X, given that we know that a straight line can be precisely located if we know its slope and the point at which it intercepts with the Y axis:

$$Y' = b_{yx}(X - \bar{X}) + \bar{Y}$$

where  $Y'$ = predicted Y-score for each X-score
 $\bar{Y}$ = mean of the Y-scores
 $X$ = individual X-score for which we are predicting a value of Y
 $\bar{X}$ = mean of the X-score
 $b_{xy}$ = slope of the line, obtained by the following:

$$b_{xy} = r_{xy} \frac{S_y}{S_x}$$

where $r_{xy}$ = Pearson $r$ between $x$ and $y$
$S_x$ = standard deviation of $x$
$S_y$ = standard deviation of $y$

When the correlation is zero, the regression coefficient is zero and the best prediction for any $Y$-score is $\bar{Y}$, the mean of all the $Y$-scores. When the standard deviations of $X$ and $Y$ are equal, the regression coefficient and the correlation coefficient are identical. The larger the correlation coefficient is, the better is the prediction of $Y$-scores by using the regression line rather than simply the mean of $Y$. We shall return to a discussion of this in chapter three to illustrate its role in estimating test reliability and validity.

There are many other descriptive statistics that could also be computed from the already-obtained values, but these need not concern us here, although we shall mention them later. To summarize, descriptive statistics is used to describe and to plot group data. Typical statistical values are those that reflect central tendency, variability, and relationship. The first of these are mean, median, and mode; the second, range, variance, and standard deviation; and the third, correlation coefficient.

## The Normal Curve of Probability

Earlier we introduced a frequency distribution of scores (see Table 2–1 and Figure 2–1), and we noted that the majority of cases tended to cluster in the center of the distribution and that there was a gradual tapering off of frequencies on both of its ends. This pattern, which showed up especially well on our histogram and polygon of Figure 2–1, resembled a symmetrical or bell-shaped curve which, by adding many more cases, would be what has come to be called the *normal curve*. The normal curve is a smoothed-out frequency polygon, preferably based on measures taken for several thousand cases, which has the bell-shaped symmetry shown in Figure 2–4.

The normal curve is a graphical representation well known to mathematicians long before psychologists discovered that individual differences distribute themselves in this way. Mathematicians discovered this curve when they tried to explain the outcome of such games of chance as coin tossing, dice throwing, and card playing. Later it was observed that countless other measures in nature distribute themselves normally; that is, they distribute themselves according to a theoretically expected distribution, or curve, that satisfies certain mathematical criteria of base-line distance and area relationships. More formally, the normal curve is a theoretical distribution (rather than an obtained or observed distribution) based on an infinite number of trials or scores, the variations of which are determined by chance factors. What is

**42**   Personality and Psychological Assessment

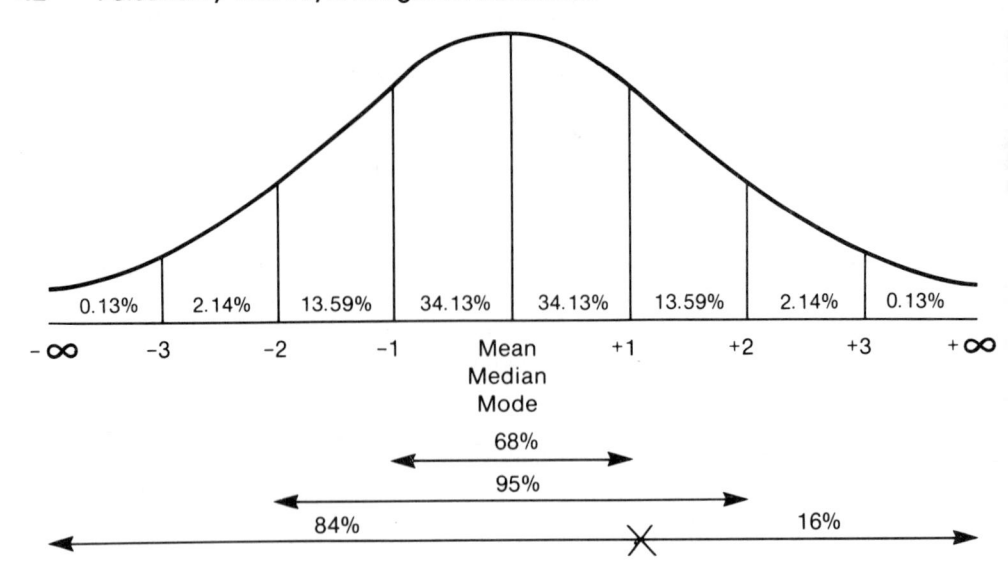

**Figure 2–4.** The Normal Curve of Probability and Some of Its Statistical Properties.

important about the normal curve for our purposes is that test scores obtained from large samples of individuals tend to take on this symmetrical form, and because its mathematical properties are known, we can make relatively precise statements about the frequency of occurrence of different scores. For example, the following statements (also illustrated in Figure 2–4) can be made about all normal curves:

1. The distribution is bilaterally symmetrical.
2. The values of the mean, median, and mode are identical.
3. The shape of the curve changes from convex to concave at the points ± 1 standard deviation from the mean.
4. Approximately 68 percent of the measures or scores marked off on the abscissa of the curve fall between ± 1 standard deviation from the mean.
5. More generally, given the values of a particular score—the mean and standard deviation of the distribution—the proportion of scores falling above and below a given score can be determined by reference to the normal curve, or to a table of z values (see "Inferential Statistics") based on the properties of the normal curve.

These properties of the normal curve permit various descriptions of normally distributed data, *because these proportions pertain to all normal curves*. We shall refer again to these properties when we discuss standard or derived scores (see "Inferential Statistics"), but an example of one application may be useful here. Suppose one obtains a score of 115 on a test, and it is known that for a large group the mean score on this test is 100 and that the standard deviation is 15. Then it follows that a score of 115 is one standard deviation from the mean and that the scores 85 and 115 are ± 1 standard deviation from the mean. If we add up the proportion of the cases that falls between −3 and +1 standard deviations, we will see that about 84 percent of the group received scores lower than 115. A score of 130 (+2 standard deviations), to take the example 1 standard deviation further, indicates that the proportion scoring lower than this would increase to approximately 97 percent. Of course, not all test scores distribute themselves normally in all groups. For example, an intelligence test administered to a select sample of respondents such as college students would result in a bunching up of scores at the high end of the distribution; and, likewise, the same test administered to a slow-learner group might result in a preponderance of scores at the low end of the distribution. For the first group, for whom the test is too easy, the bunching up is called a *negative skewing* of the distribution to the left (this assumes that the scores are arranged so that they become higher as we move to the right along the abscissa), and for the group for whom the test is too difficult, there is a *positive skewing* to the right. If the test is just right in level of difficulty, the scores will distribute themselves normally.

Thus we see how descriptive statistics and the normal curve can be applied to summarize and describe the test data of a sample and how inferences may be made about a sample by using the area under the normal curve. But suppose one wants to make inferences that extend beyond the particular group observed? This requires using inferential statistics, a topic to which we now turn.

## Inferential Statistics

Again, statistical techniques used to organize and summarize observed data are descriptive procedures. Description is an important first step, but it is not enough. Seldom are we interested only in the differences among individuals available for measurement; more often we would like to make inferences that generalize beyond the observed measures. For example, given the observation that persons with high scores on a science test perform better than persons with low scores, we might want to generalize about high and low scorers on this science test. Or given the information that there is a high positive correlation between a group's high school performance and success in college, we might wish to extrapolate or generalize beyond the observed data. In other words,

## BOX 2-4

## Skewed Distribution

The shape of a distribution can provide some useful clues about the adequacy of a test. If the test has inadequate ceiling (is too easy), the scores will pile up toward the high end of the distribution as shown in the distribution below. Such asymmetrical distributions are said to be *skewed* (it appears as if a normal curve has been pushed to one side). When the "tail" points to the left, the curve is said to be skewed negatively or skewed to the left. In this distribution there were many rather high scores, but relatively few low scores; and the distribution would be described as being skewed negatively.

Low −        High +

Scores

When skewing is present and the samples are large enough to make the measures of central tendency stable, those measures will differ systematically. As shown in the diagrams here, the mean is always "pulled" most toward the tail and the mode the least; the median is between the mean and the mode. Since the height of the curve represents frequency, the highest point in the curve indicates the mode of the distribution.

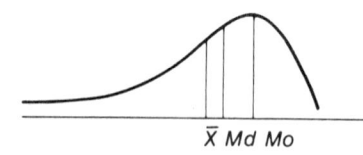

$\bar{X}$ Md Mo        Mo Md $\bar{X}$

If the mean has a lower value than the median, the distribution is probably skewed negatively. If the mean has the highest value of the three measures of central tendency, the distribution is probably skewed positively; if the mean, median, and mode have the same value, the shape of the distribution is probably normal.

**Source:** Julian C. Stanley, Kenneth D. Hopkins, *Educational and Psychological Measurement and Evaluation*, © 1972, p. 19. Reprinted by permission of Prentice-Hall, Inc., Englewood Cliffs, N.J.

we might want to predict the college performance of students in general, given their high school grades. Within limits, we may be able to do so, but the important point to note is that for these prediction purposes, we must use statistical reasoning that goes beyond that based on given observations. Such statistical reasoning, which is no longer descriptive, is appropriately called *inferential statistics*. The use of inferential statistics not only permits us to go beyond observed data, but it also allows us to assert the *degree of confidence* that we can place in our generalizations.

Inferential statistics, then, draws inferences about the characteristics of a population from sample observations. Ideally, it would be desirable to examine every individual in a population, but since this is unfeasible, we obtain observations from samples selected from that population. Since by definition a sample contains fewer than all possible subjects, a second sample drawn from the same population could consist of entirely different subjects, as might a third, fourth, and so on. With different subjects in different samples, even when drawn from the same population, the means, standard deviations, and other descriptive statistics calculated on the sample data will probably vary. If there are no *systematic* variations of the characteristics of the sample from those of the parent population, the deviations are called *random*, and sometimes are referred to collectively as *error variance*.

When the values of these statistics vary from sample to sample, it is impossible to say with certainty that the characteristics of any one sample reflect the characteristics of the entire population. It is usually possible, however, to use the data from a single sample to make estimates of the values of these statistics for the entire population and to make these estimates with a known margin of error. As an illustration, consider the data presented earlier regarding the Vocabulary scores in the first and second grades of elementary school. We can ask, "To what extent are the Vocabulary scores of this sample of 109 children characteristic of the larger population of children from which they may have been drawn?" In order to answer this question, let us imagine that we locate several thousand second graders out of our population and draw samples repeatedly, say, thirty samples of forty cases each. We would want to use an unbiased method of sampling so that each of the thirty samples would be truly representative of the population. Then we could compute the means of the gain scores for these thirty samples (see Table 2–2) and plot the frequency distribution of these sample means. The distribution would resemble a normal curve, as illustrated in Figure 2–5.

The mean of these sample means is the best single estimate of the *true*, or population mean, gain score, and the standard deviation of the distribution can be considered the *standard error* of the sample means for the estimated true population mean. But just as it is impractical to

**Table 2-2** Obtained Means for Vocabulary Gain Scores for 30 Different Samples of 40 Cases Each Drawn from Population of Second Graders.

| | | | | | |
|---|---|---|---|---|---|
| 2.3 | 3.1 | 3.5 | 3.7 | 4.1 | 4.4 |
| 2.5 | 3.2 | 3.6 | 3.8 | 4.1 | 4.6 |
| 2.6 | 3.2 | 3.6 | 3.8 | 4.2 | 4.8 |
| 2.8 | 3.4 | 3.7 | 3.9 | 4.2 | 4.9 |
| 3.0 | 3.4 | 3.7 | 4.0 | 4.3 | 5.1 |

test each individual in a population, it is equally impractical to collect many moderately large samples from a given population. Fortunately, there is a way to estimate the standard error of the mean from a single sample. This estimate can then be used to make a statistical inference from a given sample to the population.

The larger the sample size drawn from a population is, the more stable the resulting sample mean will be. In other words, the variability of the sample mean should be inversely related to sample size. If $N$ is the size of the sample, then the variance of the sampling distribution of all the means of samples of size $N$ will be equal to the population variance divided by $N$. Except for very small samples, the obtained

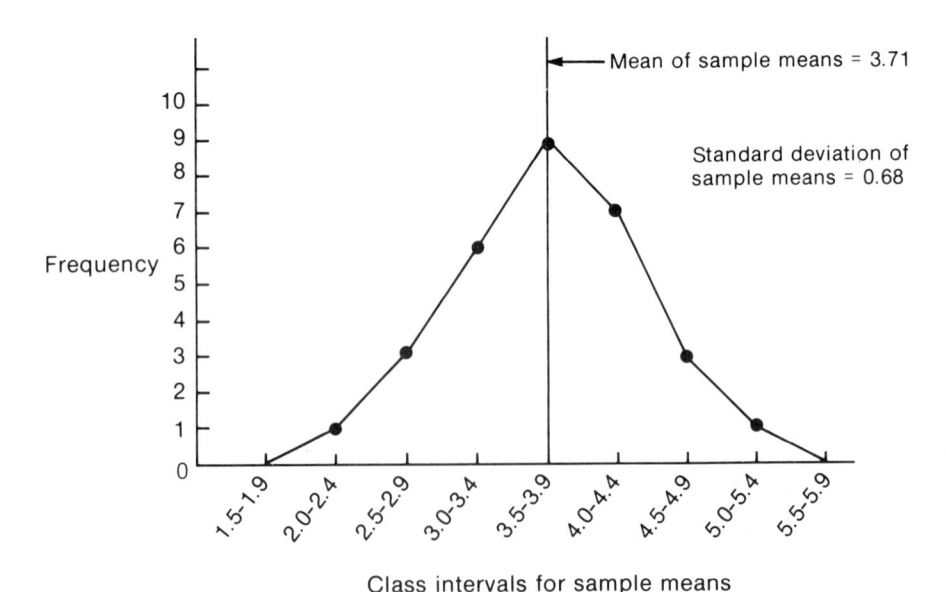

**Figure 2-5.** Frequency Polygon for Means on Vocabulary Gain Scores for 30 Samples Drawn from Population of Second Graders.

sample variance (or its square root, the standard deviation) is a good estimate of the population variance (or standard deviation). This relationship is expressed in this equation:

$$S_{\bar{x}}^2 = \frac{S_x^2}{N} \quad \text{or} \quad S_{\bar{x}} = \frac{S_x}{\sqrt{N}}$$

where $S_{\bar{x}}^2$ = variance of sample means
$S_x^2$ = obtained variance of scores in the sample
$N$ = number of cases in the sample
$S_{\bar{x}}$ = estimated standard error of the mean

Applying this formula to our Vocabulary example yields an estimated standard error for sample means. The standard deviation of the gain scores (see Table 2–2), or $S_x$ = 4.44 and $N$ = 109, gives us 0.43 for the estimated standard error of the mean.

Thus, given the mean gain score of 3.7 and its standard error of 0.43, it is simple to answer our question about the significance of the obtained gain in Vocabulary from the first to the second grade. We can also state whether the gain score is statistically significantly different from a zero gain. This type of inference is known as *hypothesis testing*, since we are testing a hypothesis about a population by using one or more samples drawn at random from that population. In our example we can state a *null hypothesis* that the true gain in Vocabulary score from the first to the second grade is zero. Our actual mean gain of 3.7 is 8.5 times greater than the $S_{\bar{x}}$ (i.e., 3.7/0.43). Since the sampling distribution of the means is a normal curve, we can use a table of probability values, like those published in most statistics textbooks, for areas under the normal curve to see what the probability is of obtaining by chance alone a sample mean 8.5 standard deviations removed from the null hypothesis mean. We have actually computed a z score.

$$z = \frac{\text{obtained mean minus hypothesized mean}}{\text{standard error of the mean}}$$

or

$$z = \frac{3.7 - 0}{0.43} = 8.5$$

If we refer to Figure 2–5, which shows the proportions of total area under the normal curve for z score units of +1.0, +2.0, and +3.0, as well as for −1.0, −2.0, and −3.0, we can see that a mean gain score of 3.7, which is 8.5 standard deviations from the hypothetical mean of zero, is highly significant. This suggests that we could reject the null hypothesis with a very high degree of confidence because a z of 8.5 or higher would be obtained by chance alone less than one in a million times. Therefore, we are correct in concluding that the gain in Vocabulary from first to second grade among the children in the population from which the sample was drawn is a real one. On the other hand, if we had proved our null hypothesis to be true, then the difference between the means that we found with our sample would have led us to conclude that this difference occurred by chance.

The degree of confidence that we attached to our rejection of the null hypothesis in the above example can be easily understood if we introduce two new terms—*confidence intervals* and *level of confidence*—and if we demonstrate other relationships among areas under the normal curve, the standard deviations, and the effects of sample size on the standard errors. We can also show how different kinds of distributions—the $t$-distribution, the $F$-distribution, the $\chi^2$ (*chi*-square) distribution, and many others—can be used when the assumptions of the normal distribution are not met. But these details are beyond this book's purposes. The interested reader might, therefore, want to consult any of several excellent sources on these topics (see Harshbarger, 1977, chap. 7; Phillips, 1973, chaps. 6, 7, 8, & 9; Winkler & Hays, 1975, chaps. 2, 7, 9, & 10).

To summarize, we have shown that there are two uses of inferential statistics. One of these demonstrates that observations made on a sample apply also to the population from which the sample was selected. The other use establishes the stability of observed differences of scores or measures between two (or more) groups. In both instances, we want to know how certain we can be, or how much confidence we can place, in our observations. We call this confidence or certainty, confidence intervals and levels of confidence.

## SUMMARY

The main uses of statistics are description and generalization. Some often-used terms in statistical description are frequency distribution, mean, median, mode, range, variance, standard deviation, and correlation coefficient. The normal curve of probability is a bilaterally symmetrical graph used in both descriptive and inferential statistics. In the first instance, it describes sample observations, and in the second, it is used to reach probable generalizations based on these observations. Both descriptive and inferential statistics, as well as the use of the properties of the normal curve, are the main features of statistical reasoning.

# FOR FURTHER READING

Cozby, P.C. *Methods in behavioral research*. Palo Alto, CA: Mayfield Publishing Company, 1977. For an elementary overview of, or a glimpse at, the topics of correlation particularly (chapter three) and statistics generally (appendices B & C), this book is a good starting point.

Dominowski, R. *Research methods*. Englewood Cliffs, NJ: Prentice-Hall, 1980. Offering many problems to solve as a learning device, Dominowski devotes one chapter to statistical techniques for describing data (chapter four) and one to correlational methods (chapter seven).

Guilford, J.P., & Fruchter, B. *Fundamental statistics in psychology and education* (6th ed.). New York: McGraw-Hill, 1978. This book is an excellent and comprehensive introduction to basic descriptive statistics, statistical tests and decisions, correlation and prediction, and psychological measurements.

Helmstadter, G.C. *Research concepts in human behavior*. Englewood Cliffs, NJ: Prentice-Hall, 1970. The chapter on statistical reasoning provides relevant background material for using statistics in testing and other psychological measurement.

Holtzman, W.H. *Methods in psychology. Module A–Z, Personalized Psychology Series*. New York: Harper & Row, 1975. An elementary but useful approach to measurement in psychology and statistics.

Kerlinger, F.N. *Foundations of behavioral research* (2nd ed.). New York: Holt, Rinehart & Winston, 1973. Although most topics of behavioral research methodology are covered, this book should be particularly useful for its lucid descriptions of probability (part three) and multiple regression analysis.

McCall, R.B. *Fundamental statistics for psychology* (3rd ed.). New York: Harcourt Brace Jovanovich, 1980. Although not as self-consciously intuitive as the Weinberg and Schumaker offering below, this book nevertheless presents a good overview of descriptive and inferential statistics.

Weinberg, G.H., Schumaker, J.A. & Oltman, D. *Statistics: An intuitive approach* (4th ed.). Monterey, CA: Brooks/Cole, 1981. Written by a consulting psychologist and a mathematician, this highly readable book touches all bases in descriptive and inferential statistics.

# 3 Assessment Logic and Psychological Test Attributes

This chapter introduces the essential attributes of good psychological assessment strategies, attributes that we apply throughout the book in evaluating their worth. Some of these—standardization, objectivity, reliability, and validity—appear on the input side of the flow chart of Figure 1–1, just prior to a procedure's entry into the information processor; this highlights their importance as criteria of acceptable procedures. Other concepts introduced in this chapter do not appear in Figure 1–1 but are more basic. These include the topics of true scores, sources of measurement error, standard errors of measurement, and crossvalidation.

The main focus of this chapter, then, is to examine certain aspects of the definition of assessment presented in chapter one, and to discuss the logic and criteria of good assessment strategies. The reader may find it helpful to refer again to the definition given in chapter one of assessment before reading about each of its separate components—standardization, objectivity, behavior, and behavior sample. The reader is also reminded that from among the foregoing terms, only the first two appear in Figure 1–1. This is because they refer to operations to ensure a procedure's excellence; by contrast, the terms behavior and behavior sample as well as true score and the others are less obviously related to such operations. The assessor should establish the reliability and validity of a technique before using and publishing it. Therefore, a discussion of this reliability and validity is the subject of most of this chapter.

A word or two are in order here regarding current thinking on tests and the theory on which they are based. Many of the concepts of testing described in this chapter and in the remainder of the book are gleaned from classical test theory (CTT), which has its roots in the correlational studies conducted in the early 1900s by British psychologist Charles Spearman. CTT has come under considerable criticism lately from various quarters because it relies on a faulty and unfruitful statistical model (see Lumsden, 1976; Weiss & Davison, 1981). The main criticism, the details of which are beyond the scope of this book, is that CTT uses sample-based statistics to arrive at estimations of test reliability. Thus test reliability estimates, which we will indicate later, are important in establishing the stability and trustworthiness of test scores and are highly dependent on a particular set of test items administered to a particular sample of individuals. Consequently, inferences made about a test's reliability that go beyond that combination of item-sample (and item-sample-event) interaction are made on very shaky grounds.

Alternatives to classical test theory, and hence to the criticism of classical reliability theory, have been *criterion-referenced* testing, discussed briefly in chapter nine in connection with achievement testing; *latent test theory*, sometimes called *item response theory* because it relies heavily on item scaling, a topic we consider in chapter seven when we discuss attitude and value scaling; and *order models*, which is related to mathematical information theory and develops psychological measuring instruments on the basis of logical relationships among item responses and the individuals utilizing the items. It seems that the last of these alternatives to CTT comes closest to meeting the main criticism of classical test theory in that order-based models attempt to attain reliability estimates tailored to specific individuals rather than basing them on a sample in which an individual may not be represented.

All these alternatives seem promising, but their development is only in its infancy. Therefore, although this writer agrees with Weiss and Davison's evaluation that "little progress was made in CTT, since there is little progress to be made" (p. 650), he feels nevertheless compelled to discuss the concepts that were formulated within the framework of classical test theory because at the present time very little research exists on the applicability of the alternatives to personality assessment.

# Attributes of Psychological Assessment

## Standardized Assessment Conditions

A psychological procedure, usually a paper-and-pencil test, is standardized when its administration, materials, instructions to subjects, and scoring are specified so that, insofar as feasible, the test is identical for all persons at all times. Ideally, the test constructor strives to control all variations except the one that the test measures. The term standardization is sometimes used (Anastasi, 1976) to include the collection of test data from a reference or norm group as well as the requirements of common administration and scoring procedures. In this book we use this term only to refer to establishing the conditions of common test item or test question content and to ensuring identical test administration and scoring directions for all subjects at all times.

Standardization is similar to experimental control, which is the condition under which scientific observation should be conducted. In this sense, a psychological test is similar to a scientific experiment in which most aspects are held constant or are controlled. These controls are in the form of using identical test materials, specific time limits, uniform instructions, and the same scoring format, as well as eliminating those factors in the environment that might distract the respondents. If such control is exercised, then the assessor can confidently conclude that the obtained test scores do reflect variation on the measured dimension. Such control, unfortunately, is usually not that effective, as we indicate in the next several sections.

**Objectivity**

Test results can be independent of the subjective judgment of the test scorer. Generally, a test is objective to the extent that its score is independent of the test scorer. A completely objective test would yield identical scores for the same responses each time the test is scored. Some test items and scoring formats result in greater objectivity than others.

The test format most likely to produce objectivity is one in which respondents select the best or the most descriptive of several matching, completion, true-false, or fixed-alternative answers, and these are scored according to agreed-upon "best" or "correct" answers. This format does not rely on the judgment of scorers, as do, for example, essay tests or observational or projective techniques. But even on these procedures subjectivity can be reduced, and hence objectivity enhanced, by training scorers or observers to apply scoring criteria consistently and uniformly. Objectivity is a desirable attribute of tests because it, again, permits the tester to conclude that the test reflects variation on the dimension being measured rather than variation caused by scoring errors or disagreements among test scorers about what the correct answers are. And, as we shall indicate later in the section on reliability, score variations caused by scoring errors—sometimes also called error variance—reduce the reliability or the consistency of the test so that it will not yield the same scores each time it is used.

**Behavior**

In the context of testing, behavior refers to an examinee's responses to a series of test stimuli or items. These test items may require answers to questions about actions, wishes, attitudes, preferences, or emotions, or may involve manipulating objects. Currently, most psychological tests, particularly traditional paper-and-pencil personality tests, do not sample sensory behaviors—that is, behaviors that involve visualizing, hearing, smelling, tasting, or touching objects. But there are no rigid rules about this, and it is possible that the study of personality might benefit from the inclusion of physical dimensions in its measurements. In the context of less formal procedures than tests, behavior is the examinee's responses to the observational or other setting and its demands.

The relation of behavior to a particular psychological attribute is important in assessment, again, particularly in personality testing. The principal question for the assessor is to discover the meaning of a response to a psychological test or other assessment procedure (see Wiggins, 1973, pp. 382–415). There are several ways of viewing this problem, depending on one's theoretical orientation to tests and test construction.

Most early test constructors believed that there was a one-to-one correspondence between an examinee's answers on a test and that examinee's internal state. For example, Woodworth (1917), who during World War I constructed the Woodworth Personal Data Sheet, assumed that the "yes" and "no" answers of inductees to the 116 questions about their neurotic behaviors reflected their internal states. Such questions as the following were asked: "Do you wet your bed?" "Have you ever had moments of dizziness?" "Are you happy most of the time?" The answers to these questions were assumed to correspond to aspects of general adjustment or the lack thereof. This approach, sometimes called the *correspondence* point of view, has been seriously challenged on numerous grounds, not the least important of which is, for our purposes, that the items in question may not be related to psychiatric illness, in this case neuroticism.

A later viewpoint, most articulately expressed by Meehl (1945), makes no assumption about the correspondence or association of test item content to some internal state. Rather, it considers responses to personality tests as meaningful only to the extent that these answers statistically correlate with nontest or criterion behaviors. This point of view, which is called the *criteria*, or *empirical*, orientation, does not consider a response to a self-report personality test a "surrogate for a behavior sample" (Meehl, 1945a, p. 247) but rather "an intuitively interesting and significant bit of verbal behavior . . . [in which] the scoring does not assume a valid self-rating to have been given" (Meehl, 1945a, p. 249). In other words, what one says about oneself may be a highly significant fact about that person, even though the interpreter of structured tests does not accept with any confidence that what one says would agree with what complete knowledge of that person would lead others to say of him or her.

Another approach to defining the meaning of test responses has been the so-called construct viewpoint as originally articulated by Cronbach and Meehl (1955), then refined by Loevinger (1957), and currently being used by Jackson (1974, 1976) and his associates in the construction of the Personality Research Form (PRF) and the Jackson Personality Inventory (JPI) (see chapter seven). This viewpoint emphasizes the importance of having personality test items reflect some underlying theory of personality. This can be accomplished by assembling a pool of items representative of the substantive domain delineated by the theory. Then the variation in item response can be attributed to the variation among the respondents with respect to the underlying psychological construct.

A more recent view (Mills & Hogan, 1978; Johnson & Hogan, 1981) suggests that test-taking behavior can be regarded as a kind of self-presentation formally identical to what goes on in most social interaction, and that people respond to personality test items in a fashion similar to the manner in which they react to the conversational ploys of other people. This view assumes that "self-images guide role performances vis-à-vis other people *and* personality inventories" (Mills & Hogan, 1978, p. 779). Hogan then presents evidence that "people use their responses to items on tests and questionnaires as a means of telling an audience (which must be defined either by the subject or the test administrator) how he or she wants to be regarded; peoples' responses to items on any psychometric device are organized in terms of their underlying self-images" (Johnson & Hogan, 1981, p. 62).

## Behavior Sample

Ideally, a test should sample the entire domain of the underlying construct under investigation. For example, if an assessor wants to examine a person's honesty, then the assessor should observe him or her in as many situations as could possibly elicit the relevant honest (or dishonest) responses. But this is impractical. Therefore, the psychologist must settle for a less-than-ideal situation: a sampling of the relevant domain. A prime requisite of such a sampling should be that it represent the dimension being studied. In this regard, the psychologist is on the same methodological grounds as other scientists. The chemist, for example, tests a supply of water by analyzing one or more samples of it, and the agronomist tests farm lands by sampling and testing their soil. But because of limited time and resources, none of these scientists can obtain extensive assays of the attribute under examination.

The psychologist has still another problem, the problem of sampling from an undefined and elusive population of behaviors. Whereas the chemist's or the agronomist's domain is as concrete and tangible as water and soil, the psychologist must sample behaviors that are abstract, conceptual, and hypothetical. For example, how should the psychologist sample honesty? Or ego strength? Or authoritarianism: Or, for that matter, the often-measured but still controversial realm of intelligence? How the psychologist solves this problem is the topic of the next section.

## Assessment Logic

The fundamental logic of assessment is that the responses on a psychological test or procedure are significant if they concur with or predict some socially important criterion or future behavior. The way that psychologists arrive at predictions using assessment data is by making repeated observations of a general class of events (e.g., test responses, other behavior samples). These events are then observed to be related to another set of available events or future behaviors. For example, after finding that hundreds of persons who receive low scores on an aptitude test also fail in some future activity and that those persons who receive high scores succeed in the same activity, the psychologist can predict that the next time someone gets a low score on this test he or she too will fail and that the person who gets a high score will succeed. The prediction of nontest behavior, then, from sampling test behavior follows this procedure:

1. Assigning an individual, on the basis of test responses, to categories of persons about which some information of success and failure is known.
2. Predicting that what in the past has happened to these persons in regard to relevant nontest behaviors will also happen to other persons in the future.

This process is nothing new. It is followed by all of us each time we make a judgment about an individual. For example, if we remark, "What a freak he is," we recognize the similarities between this individual and others who have been designated "freaks," and we can predict that there will be similarities between this person's future behavior and that of others so classified in the past, even if the similarity is only that the behavior will be unusual.

In a sense, much of assessment is a refinement of this everyday process, the process of classifying individuals according to their past behavior and of estimating the probable occurrence of some future or nontest behavior for those in a given class. But in testing, the two-step procedure referred to above is more systematic and is usually separated by a time interval. The first step is to administer the test and to obtain the *predictor variables* or test scores of the individual whose behavior is to be predicted. The second step is to determine the *criterion variables*, which are the socially important nontest behaviors to be predicted. The problem is to estimate, on the basis of past experience with persons who have achieved the same or similar scores, what an individual's criterion or nontest behavior will be. In other words, the basic logic of testing, as Anastasi observed and as we indicated earlier, "involves generalizations from the behavior sample observed in the testing situation to behavior manifested in other nontest situations" (1976, p. 32).

Having discussed standardization, objectivity, and the meaning of test behaviors, and having described the logic of assessment, particularly as it applies to the study of personality, we are now ready to consider two important attributes for evaluating the worth of tests: reliability and validity. From the psychometric viewpoint, the ideal measuring instrument should be reliable and valid if it is to be useful. Reliability refers to the stability and consistency of a test's scores; validity to the scores' usefulness and meaningfulness. Of the two concepts, validity is the more essential requirement of a good test. We begin our discussion by considering reliability.

## Reliability

The concept of reliability, as we intimated above, answers the question: "Is the test a consistent and stable measure of these characteristics?" Or, viewed from a different perspective, reliability addresses the question of whether a test yields the same score each time it is administered. Synonyms for reliability, according to one source (Kerlinger, 1973), are dependability, stability, consistency, predictability, and accuracy. Reliability studies determine the replicability and stability of measurements in many circumstances in which the same results are expected. This relates to the generalizability of scientific findings in which a reliable measuring instrument can generalize to many other applied circumstances. Cronbach, prefers the term *generalizability* to the older term reliability and described the establishment of a measure's reliability as follows (his allusion to "selections typed" refers to an example concerning typewritten passages):

> When we use a single observation as if it represented the universe [of observations], we are generalizing. We generalize over scorers, over selections

## BOX 3-1

### The Importance of Test Reliability and Validity

According to the most recent *Standards for Educational and Psychological Tests*, "a test developer must provide evidence of the reliability and validity of his test" (American Psychological Association, 1974, p. 25). Several general principles set down in the *Standards* are pertinent here:

1. The procedures and samples used to determine reliability coefficients or standard errors of measurement should be described sufficiently to permit a user to judge the applicability of the data reported to the individuals or groups with which he or she is concerned. (American Psychological Association, 1974, p. 51)
2. The test manual should indicate to what extent test scores are stable, that is, how nearly constant the scores are likely to be . . . after time has elapsed. The manual should also describe the effect of any such variation on the usefulness of the test. (American Psychological Association, 1974, p. 54)
3. If it is reasonable to expect scores on a test to change significantly over some time interval in response to developmental or educational influences, the manual should call the test users' attention to this possibility and advise care in the use of the old scores. (American Psychological Association, 1974, p. 54)

But reliability is only a necessary and not a sufficient condition for a good test. In addition to being reliable, a test must measure something of practical or theoretical value—that is, it must be valid for some purpose. According to the *Standards*:

1. Questions of validity are questions of what may properly be inferred from a test score; validity refers to the appropriateness of inferences from test scores or other forms of assessment. The many types of validity questions can . . . be reduced to two:
   a. What can be inferred about what is being measured by the test?
   b. What can be inferred about other behavior? (American Psychological Association, 1974, p. 25)
2. A manual or research report should present the evidence of validity for each type of inference for which use of the test is recommended. (American Psychological Association, 1974, p. 31)
3. Statements about validity should refer to the validity of particular interpretations or of particular types of decisions. (American Psychological Association, 1974, p. 31)

**Source:** American Psychological Association. *Standards for educational and psychological tests.* Washington, DC: American Psychological Association, 1974. Copyright 1974 by the American Psychological Association.

typed, perhaps over days. If the observed scores from a procedure agree closely with the universe score, we can say that the observation is "accurate," or "reliable," or "generalizable." And since the observations then also agree with each other, we say that they are "consistent" and have little "error variance." (1970, p. 154)

One way to understand the idea of test reliability is to consider the influences of error on test scores or observations.

## Measurement Error

Any factor that produces inaccurate scores on a test is called *measurement error*. Although there are several classes of these errors, two are particularly important: systematic (constant) and unsystematic (random, chance) errors. Both types of measurement error are undesirable because test scores should reflect variations caused by real or true differences—sometimes also called true variance—rather than by extraneous or nontest-related factors. Unfortunately, whenever measurements are made, whether in the physical or the behavioral sciences, both types of error are introduced despite the measurer's best efforts. But the tester is particularly concerned with unsystematic or random errors because these errors contribute to the unreliability of the measurements. These random errors, it will be recalled from the discussion in chapter two, are collectively called *error variance*.

*Systematic* or *constant* errors are those biases systematically associated with a measuring instrument or procedure. A yardstick whose origin is one yard rather than zero will yield measurements consistently smaller than those obtained with a standard yardstick. Since the error in this case is systematically associated with the measurement procedure, it is considered to be constant.

*Unsystematic, random,* or *chance* error variance, in contrast, represents fluctuations that occur fortuitously, or seemingly at random. These errors reflect those momentary variations from one occasion to another that do not systematically or constantly bias the measuring device. For example, a metal yardstick that expands and contracts with changing temperatures introduces random error that sometimes yields measurements smaller or longer that depend somewhat on the temperature rather than entirely on the length of the object being measured. Accurate lengths in these circumstances can be made by holding the temperatures constant or by using a tape that is resistant to varying temperatures. *Reliability estimates of psychological tests are primarily concerned with determining the degree of inconsistency in observed scores arising from the introduction of chance or random error*, since chance error tends to lower the reliability of observed scores. The objective is to obtain in the observed score as close an estimate of a *true score* as possible.

## True Score

What is a true score? A true score is the one that would be obtained if there were no errors of measurement. Or to express this more algebraically, if a given score or procedure, $x$, is subject to measurement error, $e$, then the score or procedure minus the error, $x - e$, represents the true score, $t$. This is usually represented as the equation $x = t + e$, where $x$ is the obtained, or observed, score; $t$, the error-free, or true, score; and $e$, the measurement error. The main concern of empirical reliability studies is to estimate the extent to which measurements reflect true scores. True scores, however, are by definition ideal or universe measures that cannot be known unless an infinite number of repeated measures are taken. They are therefore approximated by available instruments or procedures. Thus the true score, $t$, of our earlier equation is a hypothetical score only approximated by the obtained measure, $x$.

The measurement error term, $e$, represents the contribution of random error, which can be either positive or negative. If it is positive, then $t$, or the person's true score, will be an overestimate of the obtained score; if it is negative, the true score will be an underestimate. Much has been written on the relations among true, observed, and error scores (see, e.g., Gulliksen, 1950; Lord & Novick, 1968; Magnusson, 1966; Nunnally, 1978; Wiggins, 1973), but their detailed discussion is beyond this book's scope. Our concern will be limited to identifiable error sources that contribute to the unreliability of test scores. We shall also discuss several methods for estimating the reliability of tests.

## Sources of Error

There are many sources of error that contribute to the unreliability of measurements. The latter are undesirable, it will be recalled, because they are not stable. Three error sources are described in the next sections—the test itself, the administration and scoring of the test, and the test taker—other error sources are detailed in Cronbach (1970, pp. 151–179) and Stanley (1971).

Errors arising from the test itself are due mainly to selecting items during test construction that do not relate to the dimension being measured. Optimally, if a test is to measure a particular characteristic, every item on that test should measure that characteristic and nothing else. In practice, this is difficult to achieve because most psychological attributes themselves are not clearly defined. But even if the test were to measure a single and clearly defined attribute, most of the test items would still be ambiguously structured, particularly those in the projective tests that are designed to use amorphous stimuli, and thus different test takers would react differently to given items. These different interpretations of item content can be sources of error. In another context, Meehl gave the following example of how the same item, even on a structured test, can mean something different to different people (Meehl suggested, however, that this difference was an advantage rather than a shortcoming on the Minnesota Multiphasic Personality Inventory [MMPI]):

> Consider the MMPI Scale for ... hypochondriasis. A hypochondriac says that he has headaches often, that he is not in as good health as his friends are, and that he cannot understand what he reads as well as he used to. Suppose that he has a headache on an average of once every month, as does a certain "normal" person. The hypochondriac says he often has headaches, the other person says he does not. They ... hence ... must either interpret the word "often" differently in that question, or else have unequal recall of their headaches. According to the traditional view, this ambiguity in the word "often" ... [constitutes] sources of error, for the authors of the MMPI they may actually constitute sources of discrimination. (Meehl, 1945, p. 299)

Random error variance also occurs when test materials, test conditions, or test administration and scoring instructions are not standardized. For example, inadequate lighting in the examination room, or other kinds of physical discomfort, may influence test scores. Poorly worded directions can lead to mismarked answer sheets, and omitted items to which answers are essential may preclude meaningful scores. Ambiguous scoring instructions can cause unreliability if the scorers do not agree on the correct answer. Even scoring keys may be inaccurate, although machine-scoring procedures have minimized, but not eliminated, this source of error.

Other sources of error that influence reliability and are difficult to eliminate can be traced to the test taker. Different persons react differently, as we noted above, to identical items. Sometimes this difference, as Meehl suggested, is relevant to the behavior attribute that the tester wants to sample, but more often it introduces random error to the test. For example, if an MMPI item like "I am a special agent of God" is supposed to differentiate between schizophrenics (who should answer "true") and normals ("false"), and one answers it negatively because of a belief that "true" has religious or socially unacceptable connotations, and another person also answers it negatively because of a belief in the truth of its content, then there will be errors owing to the idiosyncratic response style.

Test takers also add error to their scores because of boredom, fatigue, distracting (too hot, cold, or noisy) testing conditions, or a lack of motivation to answer the items honestly. Indeed, any difference in motivation that sets a particular test taker apart from the other test takers will result in measurement error.

In observational and interview settings, as we shall indicate in chapters five and six, errors arise because the observer is human and, as Wiggins implied, is therefore subject to a variety of human frailties (1973, pp. 301–304). The observer or interviewer also may tire easily, become bored or fatigued, be careless or inattentive, or view a particular assessment situation from a personal perspective. The conditions under which observations are taken, like the conditions under which tests are administered, may also contribute to measurement error. For example, a noisy or distracting environment may affect the observer, as may the time of the day or the year of the observations. In short, any factor that prevents the observer or subject from functioning at his or her best may add chance or random measurement error, which in turn translates into unreliability.

## The Standard Error of Measurement

Having defined reliability according to random error variance and having traced the sources of such error to several test and extratest conditions, we can now consider an index of reliability that has become popular in recent years (American Psychological Association, 1974; Guilford & Fruchter, 1978; Helmstadter, 1970). This index is the *standard error of measurement*, which is an estimate of the extent of error that would be obtained if it were possible to give the same test to a person many times. This standard error of measurement, or $S_m$, is one of the most useful ways of reporting how much chance fluctuation occurs in scores from one occasion to the next. Clearly, the smaller the $S_m$ is, the more reliable the test is.

Perhaps we can best understand $S_m$ by going back to the equation $x = t + e$, regarding which we noted that the obtained score is a function of the true score, plus error. Because of error, the obtained score, $x$, will sometimes overestimate the true score and will sometimes underestimate it. Occasionally, the observed score will approximate the true score, and this occurs, of course, when the error term is small. The magnitude of error cannot be known unless we test someone an infinite number of times. This is not possible. Therefore, we do the more practical thing, which is to calculate the mean and the standard deviation of the distribution of obtained scores. In other words, we estimate the error term by calculating the variation that would occur in a person's score if he or she were to take the same test repeatedly. We call the mean of the obtained scores an estimate of the true score, and the standard deviation of these scores is the estimate of the error score.

The latter is called the standard error of measurement, which represents the theoretical range of variation in any one person's obtained score.

More precisely, the standard error of measurement ($S_m$) is an estimate of the error made in substituting a true score for an observed score. This value can be calculated in practice by administering the same test twice (or equivalent forms of the test or two halves of the same test) to a group of subjects. The scores of the subjects are then correlated with one another and are combined, as in the following formula, with the standard deviation of these scores:

$$S_m = S_x \sqrt{1 - r_{xx'}^2}$$

where  $S_m$ = standard error of measurement
$S_x$ = standard deviation of the observed test scores
$r_{xx'}$ = correlation coefficient on parallel tests for the given group

A bit later, we shall refer to $r_{xx'}$ as the reliability coefficient, which has been the more conventional way of reporting reliability estimates of tests and which estimates the ratio of true variance to total variance.

In the meantime, the current thinking is that the standard error of measurement, which is the standard deviation of the measurement error distribution, is a very convenient way of reporting how accurately an individual's obtained test score estimates his or her true score. It is expressed in the following formula, which indicates that the $S_m$ is the average of the standard deviations that we would obtain if each of $N$ individuals were measured on $m$ different but parallel tests:

$$S_m = S_x \sqrt{1 - r_{xx'}^2}$$

The standard error of measurement is an important interpretive guide. Suppose a student takes a test on which a score of 25 is obtained and we want to know his or her "true score." And suppose we also know that $S_x = 15$ and $r_{xx'} = 0.95$. By a simple calculation using the formula above, we then can find out that the individual's range of observed scores around the true score (e.g., $S_m - 3.35$) is 21.65 to 28.35. Moreover, we can conclude that this amount of variation from the person's true score will be correct about 68 percent of the time that he or she takes the test. This is because, like any standard deviation, the standard error of measurement can be interpreted as the normal-curve frequencies discussed in chapter two. Recall that between the mean and ± 1 $S_x$ are about 68 percent of the cases of the normal curve. In other words, we can conclude that on the test scale in question, there is a two-thirds probability that any person's obtained score will fluctuate ± 1 $S_m$, or 3.25 points in our example, on either side of his or her true score on the test scale. Thus there is still one chance in three that this person's true score will be higher or lower than this. We can estimate the true score still more exactly by using other information that can be gleaned from the normal-curve frequencies. We can expect, for example, with approximately 95 percent certainty, that a true score is within a distance of about two standard deviations from an obtained score. This probability estimate is based on the fact that about 95 percent of the cases fall within two standard deviations of the mean. One can calculate even these probabilities more exactly, but in practice this is ordinarily not necessary.

The standard error of measurement, then, gives an estimate of a test's reliability by providing information about the approximate degree of inaccuracy (or score fluctuation) that needs to be taken into account in interpretation and decision making.

A complementary way of estimating reliability which, as we noted earlier, is used to calculate $S_m$, is to report reliability according to correlation coefficients. There are several ways of reporting these coefficients, and each defines measurement error in a slightly different way, as the next four sections describe (see chapter two, "Measures of Correlation," for a review of correlation coefficients). But the main point to remember throughout this discussion is that these reliability coefficients should be considered according to their predictability—that is, the degree to which scores on one test can predict scores on another. When the variation of a person's scores from one occasion to the next or over equivalent or parallel tests (or split-half or two halves of the same test) is large, this means that the prediction of his or her score on

---

**BOX 3-2**

### Three Reliability Coefficients

The reliability coefficient can be estimated by several distinct procedures, as the text indicates. Three of the most commonly used procedures are illustrated here.

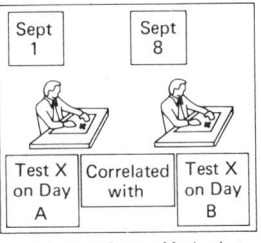

(a) Test-Retest Method: Test X on Day A — Correlated with — Test X on Day B (Sept 1, Sept 8)

(b) Equivalent-Forms Method: Test X on Day A — Correlated with — Test X' on Day A (Sept 1, Sept 1)

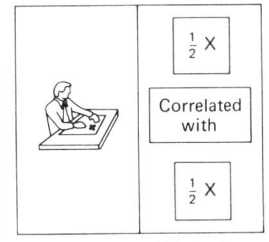

(c) Split-Half Method: $\frac{1}{2}X$ — Correlated with — $\frac{1}{2}X$

one test from his or her score on another will be poor. On the other hand, if there is no variation at all among a person's scores, then we can predict accurately his or her score on one test from the score on another.

Another way of viewing the reliability coefficient is that it estimates the ratio of true variance to total variance. Thus a reliability coefficient, or an $r$, of 0.40 estimates that 40 percent of the obtained variance is true variance and that the remaining 60 percent is error variance. A high reliability coefficient, such as an $r$ of 0.90 estimates that 90 percent of the obtained variance is true variance and 10 percent is error variance.

## Test-Retest Reliability

One way to estimate the reliability of a procedure is to establish the score fluctuations that occur on the same test from one testing to the next. This method defines error as any circumstance or condition that causes disagreement between measurements on different occasions. The extent of the agreement can be computed by correlation methods. The resulting value is a *test-retest reliability coefficient,* which is the index of the reliability of the scores that can be obtained from one occasion to the next with a given instrument. Just like the correlation coefficients of chapter two, the reliability coefficient can take positive and negative values between 0 and 1. If a test is impervious to random error, people's scores on repeated occasions will be identical, their positions on the score distributions that we can draw for repeated measurements will be the same, and the correlation between the distributions will be 1.0 (or −1.0 if the relationship is inverse). The measurements of such an instrument are completely reliable.

Since this coefficient reflects the scores obtained by the same subjects on two occasions, it also indicates the extent to which test scores are affected by the chance or random fluctuations in the condition of the subject or of the test surroundings from one time to the next. The logic for computing this reliability estimate lies in the notion that temporary factors (i.e., health, motivation, mood) may increase test scores on one occasion and lower them on another. Such transient factors lower the test-retest correlation coefficient and are assumed to be due to error.

How much test-retest error is acceptable before a set of measures is considered unreliable is a problem confronting all test users, a problem not easily resolved by simply stating an arbitrary correlation value. There is no such concept as *the* reliability of a test. The reliability that is estimated by one method, on one occasion, and with one group will not be identical to the estimate obtained by a different method, on another occasion, and with another group. Thus, each test user must resolve this problem by deciding whether the cited reliability of a test (i.e., in a test manual) is meaningful to his or her use of the test on a specific occasion with a given group (see Guilford & Fruchter, 1978, p. 408, on the reliability of a set of measurements).

In arriving at this decision, it also helps to understand how the retest reliability coefficient is computed. Recall that earlier we showed that reliability is the ratio of the estimated and calculated variances of the true and observed scores, respectively. This means that retest reliability can be interpreted as the proportion of observed score variance that represents variation in true scores. For example, if $r_{xx} = 0.80$, not an unusual test-retest reliability value in personality testing, then we can say that 80 percent of variability in observed scores is due to differences in true scores and that only 20 percent is due to errors of measurement. At the extremes, if $r_{xx} = 0.00$, then all variability is due to measurement error; if $r_{xx} = 1.00$, then there is no measurement error, since all variability is true-score variance (see Brown, 1976, pp. 77–79; and Guilford & Fruchter, 1978, pp. 411–412 for discussions of how reliability coefficients translate into percentages).

In other words, a retest reliability coefficient for a particular test estimates both the proportion of its variance in observed scores due to differences in true scores and the proportion due to measurement error. For any given test, then, the test user must decide whether, for the purpose for which it will be used, 10, 15, 20, or an even greater percent measurement error is acceptable. A general guideline in this regard is that many achievement, aptitude, and ability tests yield retest reliability coefficients in the 0.90s and that many personality and interest scales have lower reliabilities, usually correlations in the range of 0.75 to 0.85, depending on the characteristics being measured.

There are other important uses of retest reliabilities. For example, in personality testing, this form of reliability may not be entirely appropriate as an index of an instrument's stability. Many personality attributes are assumed to fluctuate. In fact, some personality inventories include mood scales designed specifically to reflect temporary variations. On such scales it is difficult to distinguish between variance due to random variation and that truly reflecting fluctuating moods. For instance, an individual who is depressed at the outset of psychotherapy may become less depressed as therapy progresses. A sensitive measuring instrument should reflect this change. The analogy of this in physical measurement was noted by Magnusson: "It is quite natural to consider a measuring tape completely reliable despite the fact that it gives different results for an individual's broad-jump performance on different occasions" (1966, p. 107).

There are other disadvantages in personality study of estimating reliability by the retest method. Whereas the procedure does assure complete equivalence of test content on two occasions, the experience of having taken the test the first time may change test-taking attitudes on the second occasion. The person may become more "test-wise" and may have taken the opportunity during the interval between tests to find out how to take the test, by studying the meanings of certain symptom-disease relations to the test's items. The examinee may then utilize this information on the second test occasion. This problem occurs more often in achievement and aptitude testing, particularly when respondents recall many of the answers they gave to items on the first occasion. During the test-retest interval, they may rehearse, practice, or acquire new skills in order to "pass" previously "missed" items. And the combination of any or all of these factors seems to interact so as to decrease the retest reliability coefficients as the time interval between testings lengthens.

These effects, which are sometimes called test-wiseness, rehearsal, recall, or practice, are sources of error that influence test scores on retests. To counteract these effects, particularly the effect of time elapsed between test occasions, it is recommended for achievement, aptitude, or even personality tests, that an interval of at least one week, but no more than two or three months, be allowed to intervene between the first and the second test administration. But it is best to avoid, if possible, retesting with the same instrument.

## Equivalent-Forms Reliability

One way to minimize the foregoing effects is to estimate reliability by twice administering parallel or equivalent forms of a test to the same group. The two forms administered on the two occasions should be closely comparable in length and item content, as well as in the mechanics of administering and scoring them. The correlation between the group's scores on the two forms represents the reliability coefficient, sometimes called the *coefficient of equivalence*. Usually the time interval between the test administrations is minimal, and the two forms are typically given in immediate succession. This coefficient is calculated as the correlation between the scores of the two forms of the test given to the same group.

Since it is often impractical to administer two tests to the same individuals in quick succession, errors arising from temporal fluctuations are only minimized, not eliminated. Errors also occur when the two forms of the tests are not exactly parallel or equivalent, because the items are not measuring the same characteristics. But the temporal fluctuations are usually small, and there are statistical formulas available to estimate the equivalence of two parallel forms of a test (see Magnusson, 1966, pp. 107–108). And since all the factors are present that cause scores in the retest design to be unstable as well as those factors that contribute to error or inconsistencies in the parallel forms scheme, coefficients of equivalence are usually the most stringent estimates of reliability.

The term parallel tests is used in two senses, one of which refers to its use according to classical reliability theory. This theory holds that parallel tests should be constructed so that one testing with two equivalent tests will give the same correlation between the two score distributions that would be obtained with two testings with one of the tests. In many test situations, however, especially in personality testing, we may be interested in parallel-forms testing in another sense. For example, we may want an estimate of the accuracy with which one form of the test measures the attributes also tapped by the other test. The elaboration of this difference is too technical for our purposes (see Cronbach et al., 1963; Lord & Novick, 1968, pp. 47–60) and is beyond our needs because parallel forms of most personality tests do not exist. But it may suffice to point out that in parts of this book in which we do speak of parallel forms, we refer to its second sense, as, for example, in chapter eight when we discuss projective tests and in the classical sense in chapter nine when we discuss intelligence and ability measures.

## Split-Half Methods

Sometimes the tester needs to minimize retesting effects, but it is expensive or impractical to construct parallel tests. In these instances, split-half procedures may be used. In this method a test is administered, and then its two halves are correlated with one another for the same group.

The split-half method, sometimes also called the *odd-even* approach, derives its names from the fact that separate scoring keys are constructed for the two halves of the same test so that the two scores for each person in one group can be tallied and correlated with the odd-numbered items appearing in one key and with the even items in another. The two halves of the test thus are the counterparts of the two forms of the parallel tests because they are presumed to measure the same true scores. This presumption presents no difficulty so long as the two halves measure the same characteristics, but not otherwise. For example, when the two halves measure different characteristics, then different true scores are being estimated and the meaning of the coefficients is questionable. This situation may arise when a test's content is heterogeneous, especially when the even items' contents are unrelated to those of the odd items (i.e., the odd items are more difficult than the even items; or the even items sample one characteristic, and the odd ones sample another), which is true of most personality questionnaires and projective techniques. In this case, the split-half reliability estimate should not be used.

Split-half reliability is also used inappropriately when speed is important to test performance. In such tests, the question usually is, *how many* items can be answered in a given period of time? Such tests generally are designed so that most items can be answered correctly. Brown illustrated this as follows:

> ... assume that you give a 100-item test of simple arithmetic facts to fourth-graders. The problems are ones that, with sufficient time, the students would get correct. However, by setting a restrictive time limit, such that not everyone can finish, we produce a speeded test. Under these circumstances, a child who completes 90 items will probably get 90 correct, 45 even and 45 odd; a child who finishes 80 items will get 80 correct, 40 even and 40 odd. ... Thus, each child will get the same score ... on both halves ... [and] the split-half coefficient will be spuriously inflated. (1976, p. 77)

But even for tests that are not pure speed tests, but in which speed is of some importance, the time limit has the same effect as above, of overestimating the split-half reliability coefficient, and for the same reason. In such cases, reliability should, if possible, be computed by the retest or equivalent forms methods. But these procedures, as we indicated earlier, are subject to temporal and test-to-test variations.

When it is appropriate to use the split-half methods—that is, when the obtained correlation coefficient is computed for homogeneous, unspeeded tests—it is, in fact, an index of reliability for only one of the test halves. It must therefore be corrected by a formula, usually the *Spearman-Brown Prophecy Formula* or the *Kuder-Richardson formulas 20 or 21*, in order to estimate the reliability coefficient for the whole test. Which of the three correction formulas is appropriate for a particular case depends on what assumptions can be made about the homogeneity of the test items and their weighting and scoring schemes. Again, discussion of the specifics of this topic would take us too far afield.

### Internal Consistency Reliability

Another index of reliability is one that determines whether a test's items are homogeneous, or internally consistent. The rationale of this index is that if the items of a test measure the same or similar attributes—as reflected by the consistency of performance or scores over a test's items—then the items will be intercorrelated positively. And if the item scores are intercorrelated positively, then it is possible to know or to predict one's score on this and similar items if we know how the person performed on one item.

The basic formula for determining this reliability estimate or *coefficient alpha* (see Cronbach, 1951) is based on both the average correlation among items and the number of items of a test. If this coefficient (or the Kuder-Richardson formulas which can also be used) proves to be very low, then the test user may conclude that the test items are heterogeneous or are too short. In either case, the test developer or user may want to develop items that more adequately sample the domain of interest. This is because the major source of measurement error is the sampling of content.

The assumption underlying internal consistency reliability, according to a recent important review of classical reliability theory (Jackson & Paunonen, 1980), is that a test assesses a single underlying dimension of interest. However, it is often the case in personality and psychological assessment that a test is designed to assess any number of correlated facets. For example, one group of researchers (Jackson et al., 1972) identified four distinct but interrelated facets of risk taking—monetary, physical, social, and ethical—each of which might be incorporated into a total score of risk taking. Thus the question arises whether the assumption of unidimensionality implied by coefficient alpha is justified.

## Scorer Reliability

With most objective group tests, the agreement of two or more scorers (or the same scorer at different times) on the correct or appropriate responses is easily reached and is evidence of *scorer reliability*. The scoring procedure for these group tests is straightforward in that a standard response key or a machine-scoring system is applied to the test items and a simple tally is computed of the number of correct answers. If different weights or bonus credits are to be assigned, these will be scored by a special formula included on the scoring key. Scorer unreliability or error variance in this case will occur only as a result of clerical mistakes in constructing the key or in computing the numbers of right and wrong answers.

With subjective, or individually administered, tests (or observations, interviews, or projective techniques), however, in which the responses are not scored objectively and therefore the scorer's judgment is a factor, scorer reliability may be a problem. For these assessments, detailed scoring criteria of correct responses must be developed; but since it is impossible to provide criteria for every conceivable response alternative, errors will arise. These errors, sometimes called *examiner* or *scorer errors*, are different from those that result from temporal fluctuations in the subject's condition or from the use of alternative test forms, in that they are attributable to the observer rather than to instrument fluctuations and errors.

One way to estimate scorer error is to design reliability studies in which either a correlation or a percent agreement value is computed among two or more scorers. This is achieved by having two or more judges independently score the tests (view the behavior, listen to the interviews) and then record their findings so that a correlation coefficient can be computed in the usual way. The coefficient, which at best should be 0.80 or higher, is the index of scorer reliability. The other way to arrive at an estimate of scorer reliability is to compute the percent of agreement among scorers, correcting, of course, for chance agreements which in any given setting may be high because of shared biases. Ideally, the agreement should be complete, but less satisfactory agreements of about 80 percent or more are also acceptable.

High scorer reliability can be achieved by training the scorers to apply the prescribed scoring criteria. Such training usually provides the judges with experience in recognizing categories of correct and incorrect responses and permits them to practice scoring these according to certain rules. High scorer reliability can also be attained by providing detailed scoring-criteria directions in the test manual, against which may be compared acceptable and unacceptable responses, the value or weights to be assigned to each, and the many variations of acceptable and unacceptable possibilities. The scorer usually compares the specific test responses with the descriptions and assigns the appropriate values.

## Validity

Reports of the reliability of a method tell us something about its consistency and stability; descriptions of its validity inform us about its usefulness and relevance. So long as we are dealing with reliability, we are not concerned with a test's relevance or usefulness, only with whether its results are the same on repeated measurement. When establishing validity, however, we investigate whether a test, whose reliability is known, measures or relates to the named dimension. Unfortunately, the test's name or title tells us little about its validity. Only empirical studies can accomplish this. Thus, a test labeled "Emotional Stability" may in fact measure test-taking endurance or some other unrelated and unexpected dimension.

A procedure's validity is seldom at issue when we deal with physical measures such as height or weight, for, as Magnusson noted, "it is obviously weight that is measured with a balance (provided the balance is functioning correctly)" (1966, p. 123). But when we deal with psychological variables, it is essential to establish empirically an instrument's relevance to and usefulness for measuring a labeled characteristic. There is no such concept as *the* validity of a test; a test useful for

> **BOX 3–3**
>
> **Summary of Differences between Content, Criterion-related, and Construct Validity**
>
> *Content validity*
>
> Question asked: How would the individual perform in the universe of situations of which the test items are a sample?
>
> Evaluation: By estimating the adequacy of sampling.
>
> Orientation: Toward the task or behavior, the test process.
>
> Example: A classroom exam sampling the content of a given unit of the course.
>
> *Criterion-related validity*
>
> Question asked: How well do scores on the test predict status or performance on some independent measure?
>
> Evaluation: By comparing scores on the test with scores on the independent (qualitatively different) measure.
>
> Orientation: Toward the criterion, the predicted variable.
>
> Examples: Using a scholastic aptitude test to predict college grade average; using a mechanical aptitude test to predict success as an automobile mechanic; using a personality inventory to predict which automobile drivers will have accidents.
>
> *Construct validity*
>
> Question asked: What trait does the test measure?
>
> Evaluation: By accumulation of evidence as to what the test does and does not measure.
>
> Orientation: Toward the trait being measured by the test.
>
> Examples: Developing a test to define a trait such as intelligence or creativity.
>
> **Source:** From *Principles of Educational and Psychological Testing*, Second Edition, by Frederick G. Brown. Copyright © 1970 by The Dryden Press Inc. Copyright © 1976 by Holt, Rinehart & Winston. Reprinted by permission of Holt, Rinehart & Winston.

measuring one dimension in one sample and setting may be useless for the same or another dimension in a second sample or setting. An instrument's validity must be established empirically for every new sample and setting. This is done mainly by means of content, criterion, and construct validation. Essentially, all of these concern the relations between test performance and an independent nontest variable. The validities that we discuss are what Campbell and Stanley (1966) called "external" validity, which they differentiated from "internal" and "statistical conclusion" validity. We shall not be concerned with the latter two types of validity (see also Cook & Campbell, 1979).

## Content Validity

Content validity examines the extent to which test items are a representative sample of the nontest variables under investigation. For example, in order to develop a test of schizophrenia by this method, one would define this dimension, perhaps by studying the speech and other behavior of persons labeled schizophrenic, and would then include items that representatively sample the discovered behavior patterns.

This method of validation has been used more frequently to develop achievement or personnel selection tests than personality tests because the domains of content to be sampled in achievement tests are more clearly defined than in personality testing. An examination in algebra, for example, requires sampling all the important algebraic operations and equations studied during a given period of time; personnel selection tests require sampling from a domain defined by a job analysis. But the domains of personality attributes are not so readily specified. As evidence of this, consider the difficulty one encounters in sampling such elusive concepts, as ego-strength, dominance, normality, or many other hypothetical entities of interest in personality study.

Thus, content validation results from an empirical and logical analysis that has been criticized for not using sufficiently stringent conditions to define the relevant domain (Guion, 1977, 1978). According to the *Standards for Educational and Psychological Tests* (American Psychological Association, 1974, pp. 28–29), to demonstrate the content validity of a set of test scores one must show that the behaviors reflected in the testing are a respresentative sample of behaviors to be exhibited in a specified performance area. Therefore an investigation of content validity requires that the test developer or test user "specify his objectives and carefully define the performance domain in light of these objectives" (p. 28).

The performance domain, according to the *Standards*, can be defined by pooling the "judgments of job designers, incumbents, and supervisors. Test users might define the performance domain of interest to them in terms of similar people in their own organizations or, preferably, in terms of appropriately detailed and comprehensive job analyses" (p. 29).

Another form of evidence for content validity is obtained from correlating the scores of the given test with others that presumably measure the same content domain. Of course, all the tests may be measuring the wrong traits. Too, this process is quite close to criterion validity, discussed below, in which the criteria become the scores on other tests.

An important distinction should be made here between content validity and face validity. They are quite different. Content validity is determined by a set of operations, and we evaluate it by the thoroughness and care with which these operations are conducted. In sharp contrast, face validity, which is not acceptable evidence of validity for most purposes, is merely a judgment that a test appears to be relevant to its intended purpose. Such test items may serve a useful public relations purpose but contribute nothing to the current validity of tests. Holden and Jackson (1979) also distinguish between face validity and item subtlety, defining the former as "the degree to which a respondent views the test as fair and appropriate under the given testing conditions," and item subtlety as the extent to which "the average respondent could link an item to its keyed scale" (p. 513).

## Criterion Validity

Whereas studies of content validity ask whether the test is a representative sample of the universe of tasks or situations that it is designed to measure, studies of criterion validity ask whether there is any evidence of relations between test scores and nontest or other test criteria or outcomes. These relations are expressed as a correlation coefficient called the *validity coefficient*. For example, on a personnel selection test designed to choose candidates for a training program, a validity coefficient may be computed between test scores and a criterion of success in the program, the criterion possibly consisting of course grades or later job performance.

Two types of criterion validity are usually computed: *predictive* and *concurrent* validity. Predictive validity refers to a test-criterion correlation in which the criterion or outcome is discovered at a later time. It is predictive in that the validity correlation coefficient forecasts a later criterion measure. Concurrent validity, by contrast, is the relation between a test and an already available criterion. A clinical diagnosis of neuroticism, for example, on which several diagnosticians agree, can be a criterion for validating a neuroticism test. The reason for constructing tests to measure a variable for which one already has information is that the tests may be a more parsimonious way to collect similar data, as they may save time and expense by being more concise measures of the relevant dimension.

## Reliability of the Criterion

A problem with both of these criterion-related validities is the unreliability or imperfection of the criterion variables. It is often assumed in validity studies that the existing or future outcome criteria are reliable. But perfectly reliable criteria are as improbable as perfectly reliable tests, since these consist of observations, interviews, ratings, or other tests, all of which themselves are fallible. For example, Borman (1978) contrived a nearly ideal environment for obtaining performance evaluations of jobs by using raters who were knowledgeable about the jobs and by using rating scales of advanced design. Yet although as expected he obtained a higher consensus among raters than might have been the case under less ideal conditions, the ratings by no means approached perfection. Jackson and Paunonen, in commenting on this study, attribute this finding "to the lack of consensus among raters and their differing personal constructs regarding job-relevant behavior" (1980, p. 512).

Test constructors want to validate tests by correlating them with "perfect" criteria. But since the latter are as rare as perfect tests, a statistical procedure is used, called *correction for attenuation in the criterion variable*, which estimates the true validity of the test, given that the criterion may not be reliable. This estimate, the details of which are beyond the scope of this book (see Nunnally, 1978, p. 238), is used to evaluate the validity coefficient by its magnitude relative to the ceiling imposed by the criterion's unreliability. The procedure, which results in a corrected validity coefficient, uses in its formula both the obtained reliability coefficients and the obtained validity coefficients (also see Magnusson, 1966, pp. 148–149).

There is a special variety of criterion unreliability, called *criterion contamination*, that merits mention here because of its relevance to criterion data collection in personality study. Criterion contamination occurs when test scores unduly influence the criterion. For example, when a clinician or a psychiatric nurse in a mental health setting rates a patient's behavior, and the patient's personality test scores are available to the raters, then this knowledge influences the patient's ratings. These ratings are then said to be contaminated by the raters' knowledge of the test scores. Criterion contamination is common in clinical settings because of the practical and ethical reasons that make it difficult to withhold such psychometric information from those involved in patient care. Careful research planning is required to preclude such contamination.

## Comparative Criterion Validities

So far we have not discussed what values of the validity coefficient are acceptable as criterion predictors. We shall return to this topic in the next chapter, which examines both test interpretation and the relation of validity coefficients to other selection indices. But several principles regarding both decision making using tests and criterion validity values can be stated here (see Brown, 1976, pp. 120–121): (1) Decisions made by using tests should be correct more often than they would be if tests were not used; (2) the test should provide an economy of time, personnel, resources, or money; (3) the test should offer some unique information or service not otherwise obtainable (or obtainable only at great expense or inconvenience); and (4) the correlation between test and criterion should be greater than one obtained by chance and should remain greater upon retesting a new sample (see "Crossvalidation" below).

Having stated the issues we can now offer some additional information on comparative criterion validity values. Throughout the following discussion, it is important to keep in mind that, as with reliability, there is no such concept as *the* validity of a test. The results of any validity study are *situation-specific* in that they are dependent on the particular circumstances under which they were collected. This statement carries the important implication that a test has more than one validity, and its validity for one situation tells us little about its validity for another situation. Brown boldly stated the case for establishing a test's separate validities: "The need to evaluate a test independently for each specific use cannot be overstressed ... using a test without evaluating its effectiveness is both poor practice and borders on the unethical" (1976, pp. 119–120).

Regarding the comparative values of validity coefficients, it should be recalled that the relation between test scores and a nontest criterion is expressed as a correlation coefficient. As such, the function of the validity coefficient is to predict a person's criterion score. One requirement of this correlation coefficient is that its value should be statistically significant from zero. In other words, it is necessary to know that the size of the correlation between the test scores and a criterion could not have happened by chance and that this nonchance difference from $r = 0.00$ occurs with some degree of certainty. Another requirement is that it be large enough to permit predictions.

When we have a statistically significant and large correlation coefficient between the test scores and a criterion, we treat the test scores as predictors of the criterion, in which $x$ and $y$ represent the test scores and the criterion, respectively. The accuracy of the prediction then becomes partly dependent on the value of $r_{xy}$, the size of the coefficient. When $r_{xy} = 1.0$, the prediction is exact, which means that for all persons who received a score on test $X$, we can accurately predict their criteria, $y$. If $r_{xy} = 0.00$, the predictions will be completely random and no better than guesses.

What the test user also needs to know, in addition to the absolute size of the correlation coeffficient, is, as we indicated above, the degree of certainty to place on the obtained correlation between $x$ and $y$, because the degree of predictive accuracy also depends on this value. To obtain this information, we compute the *standard error of estimate*, or $S_{est}$, which is comparable to the standard error of measurement encountered earlier in our discussion of reliability. In the case of reliability, we noted that the magnitude of the standard error depended partly on the size of the standard deviation of the observed test scores and partly on the size of the correlation between the two tests under investigation. The standard error of estimate is similar to this. It relies on both the numerical value of the standard deviation of the distribution to which the prediction is made (i.e., the criterion) and the correlation between the scores on this distribution and the predictors. The following equation indicates these relations:

$$S_{est} = S_y \sqrt{1 - r_{xy}^2}$$

where $S_y$ = standard deviation of the criterion scores
$r_{xy}^2$ = square of the validity coefficient

This standard error of estimate can be used to set confidence limits of an estimated criterion score in the same way that the standard error of measurement was used to determine the confidence limit of the true score. For example, suppose that an applicant achieved a Scholastic Aptitude Test (SAT) score of 520 and we wanted to predict the applicant's probable freshman grade point average on a four-point scale ($A = 4, B = 3$, etc.). If the test's validity coefficient is known to be 0.60 for the grade point average at that institution and if the average grade points achieved by past freshmen who achieved a score of 520 was 2.9 and the standard deviation of the grade points was 0.5, then 95 percent confidence limits would be determined as $2.9 \pm 1.96\ S_{est}$, or

$$\begin{aligned} S_{est} &= S_y \sqrt{1 - r_{xy}^2} \\ &= 0.5\sqrt{1 - (0.60)^2} \\ &= 0.4 \end{aligned}$$

which means that the confidence limit becomes $2.9 \pm 1.96\ (0.4)$. Therefore, we could say with a 95 percent degree of certainty that a grade point average of somewhere between 2.1 and 3.7 could be expected at the end of the applicant's freshmen year. If we lower the degree of predictive certainty to 68 percent, which is a more realistic confidence level in practice, we will get $2.9 \pm 1.00\ (0.4)$, or a grade point average range between 2.2 and 3.6.

It thus appears that with a validity coefficient of 0.60, which is unusually high for most tests, the error of the predicted grade point average, even at the lower level of certainty, is large, since the difference between a low C (2.2) and a high B (3.6) is substantial. Fortunately, however, our standards are somewhat too stringent because in most testing situations, it is not necessary to predict the specific criterion of individual cases, just to determine which individuals will exceed a certain minimum standard of performance, or cutoff point in the criterion. But the error of estimate is not the only way to evaluate a test's validity coefficient because the effectiveness of a test as a decision tool must also consider the types of decisions to be made from the scores, the demands of the situation, and the costs of decision errors. We discuss this in chapter four.

## Effects of Reliability on Criterion Validity

At the outset of our discussion of reliability and validity, we noted that tests can have high reliability but lack validity. We can now elaborate on that idea by noting that the relation between these concepts is such that a test with low reliability cannot have high criterion validity. That is to say, *reliability is a necessary, but not a sufficient, condition for criterion validity*.

Two basic principles of classical reliability or classical test theory will help us understand this interrelationship, although these are only simplifications that are amply explored elsewhere (e.g., Cronbach, 1971; Guilford & Fruchter, 1978; Lemke & Wiersma, 1976; Stanley, 1971). First, the reliability coefficient ($r_{xx'}$) determines the proportion of the total test variance that is true. Second, the validity coefficient ($r_{xy}$) *squared* yields the proportion of total test variance that is predictable or valid. In reference to lie detection tests, Lykken described this relation succinctly but somewhat differently as follows:

> Since a test's reliability is the consistency with which it measures, then the extent to which a test measures what it *claims* to measure—its validity—must be limited by the test's reliability. Specifically, for dichotomous classification tests like the polygraph lie test, the maximum possible validity—average agreement with the criterion—is equal to the square-root of the reliability, measured as the average agreement between retests or between scorers. (1981, p. 79)

These relationships can be illustrated by the following example: Consider the case in which a test's reliability estimate is known to be 0.85 and its validity coefficient is 0.40. We square the validity coefficient and see that 16 percent of the total test variance is predictable. Since 85 percent of the test variation is reliable or true and 16 percent is predictable, it follows that 69 percent of the total obtained test variance is reliably measured but is not valid with respect to the criterion. The latter type of variance is sometimes called *specific variance* and is obtained by subtracting the predictable variance from the true variance.

If we are given both the obtained variance of a set of test scores and the validity coefficient, we can easily compute the predictable or valid variance. For example, if in the above illustration the obtained variance is 100, then we can multiply the validity coefficient squared, or 0.16, by 100 and determine that the predictable variance is 16.

There are several principles in this discussion that pertain to the relationship of the validity coefficient to the reliability coefficient. These are listed as follows and are treated in greater depth elsewhere (Lemke & Wiersma, 1976, pp. 119–127):

1. When all of the true variance is specific variance, the validity coefficient is 0.00.
2. If a test has no specific variance, all of the true variance is valid or predictable.
3. The reliability coefficient indicates the proportion of the test variance that is true.
4. The square of the validity coefficient indicates the proportion of obtained variance that is predictable.
5. If *all* true variances were valid, the *square* of the validity coefficient would equal the reliability coefficient.
6. A test can have a validity coefficient as high as the square root of its reliability.

## Crossvalidation

A special and essential form of criterion validation is *crossvalidation*. It is often used in addition to traditional validity investigations and refers to the procedure of validating predictors originally proposed by Mosier (1951)—for example, test scores, a pattern of cutoff scores, observations—obtained from one sample for a new sample drawn from the same population. In the new, or crossvalidation, sample, the validity coefficients are expected to be lower or to show "shrinkage." The overestimated original validity coefficient is believed to occur both when there are chance combinations of random factors that may not recur in the new sample and when the predictors were selected (from a larger set) on the basis of the criterion correlations in the original sample.

An illustration of both the occurrence of random factors and the need for crossvalidation was provided by Anastasi (1976, p. 219) in the following example: Suppose that out of a sample of one hundred medical students, thirty with the highest and thirty with the lowest medical school grades have been selected to represent contrasted criterion groups. If these groups now are inadvertently compared with respect to traits irrelevant to success in medical school, certain chance differences may occur. For example, there may be an excess of private-school graduates and of red-haired persons in the higher scoring criterion sample. If we now compute a validity coefficient that incorporates as predictors these two irrelevant occurrences in one of the groups, then these chance characteristics could operate spuriously to elevate the obtained correlation. When this validity study is repeated in another sample, the chance differences in the two irrelevant characteristics (and other fortuitous factors) may disappear or be reversed with the consequence that the validity coefficient will be lower because the high and low score differences do not hold up.

Another empirical example of the need for crossvalidation was provided by Kleinmuntz (1963a, 1969) in two studies which showed that a set of empirically derived decision rules designed to predict maladjustment in one sample were less valid in predicting this in new samples. The validity shrinkages were manifested in the higher success, or hit, rates for the sample for which the decision rules were developed than for several new or crossvalidation samples. Specifically, these studies indicated that a set of MMPI decision rules, developed from a sample of Carnegie-Mellon University students, had less success in detecting maladjustment in the new samples drawn from other universities than in the original sample.

Crossvalidation, then, evaluates the durability for a new sample of test items, scores, or other predictors developed from an original sample. The crossvalidated numerical value is said to be a better estimate of predictor-to-criterion relation than the original value of the true degree. Thus, crossvalidation is similar in function to replication in all scientific enterprises. Cronbach (1970, p. 434) referred to this form of replication as *validity generalization.* He suggested that crossvalidation studies be conducted because it is important to make "periodic checks on validity ... to verify weights and cutting score," even when the procedure continues to be used in the same setting. Such replication permits one to generalize about a measure's continued applicability for its intended use.

In personality study, crossvalidation studies sometimes also ask, What is the generalizability of results over different observers or interviewers? Over different situations? Over different instructions or sets to take the test? The last question is especially important, according to one source (Brown, 1976, p. 119), because validity may vary substantially depending on whether a test is given as part of a research program or for purposes of counseling or is part of a diagnostic procedure for possible inclusion in a treatment group.

Crossvalidation studies also can answer questions of generalizability. Particularly important in this regard are the following questions, especially in view of the recently heightened awareness of the rights of some still disenfranchised groups: Is the test valid for blacks as well as whites? For women as well as men? For persons of different educational levels? Over what age range is the test valid? Is it valid for persons who do not speak English in their home? For those who reside in rural districts? For all socioeconomic levels? And is the test valid for students who attend inner-city rather than other schools? The diversity among some of these seemingly similar groups is sometimes so great that the generalizability, or applicability, in each case has to be evaluated separately.

## Construct Validity

*Construct validity* is a relatively new concept (see Cronbach & Meehl, 1955; Loevinger, 1957; Messick, 1975) which is different from content and criterion validity in that it goes beyond the other forms of test validation but may include them. The main concern of construct validity is whether the test items are samples of the behaviors included in the theoretical construct in question. Psychological constructs, such as leadership, intelligence, integrity, or anxiety, are often presumed to be the variables measured by a test; but we must investigate whether this is indeed the case. One way to do so is to demonstrate the connections between test scores and predictions about the behaviors expected of high or low scores. Thus, construct validity asks, "How can scores on the test be explained psychologically?" and "Does the test measure the attribute it is said to measure?"

The procedure of construct validation is especially useful in establishing relations between tests and psychological concepts for which external criteria are unavailable. Essentially, the procedure consists of two steps besides those required in the other forms of validation: (1) making predictions, based on theory, of the meaning of test scores and (2) gathering evidence to confirm these predictions. Since personality study often deals with the relations between test scores and difficult-to-define theoretical constructs, this kind of validation is especially suitable for this purpose. The following example may illustrate this: Suppose we want to establish the construct validity of a self-report test's ability to predict the relative ordering of a group of persons with regard to "anxiety" as defined by psychoanalytic theory. Then suppose that we can state two hypotheses based on this theory and the test results: (1) Anxious persons who are subjected to noisy situations perform more poorly than do nonanxious ones on the problem-solving tasks given in these circumstances; (2) people who perform poorly in noisy situations get high scores on an anxiety test. We then will administer the test, expose high and low scorers to noisy experimental conditions, and examine whether the predicted connections hold up. If they do hold up, then we will learn something about the test and the construct. We can continue to accumulate systematically additional validating evidence of other theoretical relations between the test and other experimental manipulations. Eventually a theory, or a *nomological network* (see Cronbach & Meehl, 1955), of logically related constructs is developed.

Construct validity, thus, is the gradual and simultaneous development of a test (or tests and procedures) and a theory about the construct it measures. The development is never really complete, but as knowledge develops, we arrive at a more complete understanding of the test, the construct, and the influences of these on one another.

A quantitative scheme for accumulating construct-validating evidence was proposed in an important paper by Campbell and Fiske (1959) in which they introduced the now well-known methods of *convergent* and *discriminant* validation. According to this paper, construct validity can be demonstrated when different tests or methods meet predictions from theory by being related to those variables with which they should be logically correlated (convergent validity) and when similar tests or methods are unrelated to other variables with which they should not be logically correlated (discriminant validity). Campbell and Fiske called this the *multitrait-multimethod* construct validity matrix, which refers to the intercorrelations of the many methods of collecting positive and negative evidence of which traits or constructs are and are not being measured by certain tests or procedures.

Suppose, for example, that a personality researcher devises a test that his or her theory suggests is a measure of social introversion. And suppose that three measuring methods could be used—family ratings, peer ratings, and another test of social introversion. In addition, the researcher wants to demonstrate that the Social Introversion Test is not measuring, say, schizophrenia or paranoia. Thus, three traits—social introversion, schizophrenia, and paranoia—might be sampled. Also, each trait might be sampled by one of three methods, as already indicated. To validate the Social Introversion Test, the researcher must demonstrate that the new test correlates with the other social introversion test and is not measuring schizophrenia or paranoia. Nine methods are used. These methods are then studied, within a correlation matrix, for their convergent and divergent properties. If the two social introversion tests correlate highly with one another and highly with family and peer ratings of social introversion, but do not correlate highly with the methods of the other traits, the construct validity of the new Social Introversion Test would be on its way to being established.

The convergence of the three methods of measuring social introversion would support the new test as a measure of a trait or construct. But, by this multitrait-multimethod procedure, the theory underlying the development of the Social Introversion Test is also confirmed, as indeed it should be in any construct validating study. As we noted earlier, it is often difficult to distinguish completely the difference between the theory-confirming and the test-confirming properties of construct validation procedures.

Another important and related, method for showing construct validity is *factor analysis*. This is also a quantitative way to examine a test's meaning by studying its correlations with other variables. The statistical and mathematical procedures need not concern us here (see Guilford & Fruchter, 1978, pp. 439–445; Nunnally, 1978, pp. 327–436) except to note that they require analyzing tables of intercorrelations among tests (or among constructs) in order to discover the common characteristics or *factors* shared by the tests (or constructs) under examination. The factors are hypotheses about the psychological meaning of the intercorrelations, as Cattell and Kline noted in their book *The Scientific Analysis of Personality and Motivation*:

> Specific hypothesis testing is another important usage of factor analysis in the study of personality . . . since by utilizing this method we can examine the value of some of the major personality theories. . . . Basically the method requires that . . . a set of factors . . . be hypothesized either from theory or previous results . . . that a factor analysis be computed and rotated as nearly as possible to the hypothesis, and that some test of goodness of fit of hypothesis and result be worked out. (1977, p. 20)

## SUMMARY

The chapter elaborated on the definition of assessment given in chapter one by defining the following terms: standardization, objectivity, and behavior. The first of these characteristics differentiates psychological assessment from haphazard and spontaneous observations; the second ensures the equality of test materials, administration instructions, and scoring; and the last refers to the assessment procedure data's independence of the subjective judgment of the scorers or observers. Behavior is the examinee's responses to a series of test items or environmental stimuli and the probable meanings of those responses.

Assessment procedures must be reliable and valid in that they must yield accurate and meaningful measures, respectively. Reliability studies reflect the effects on assessments of error and extraneous factors. Validity studies show the predictability from test scores or other observations of certain real-world behaviors as well as the underlying psychological construct measured. It is also advisable to consolidate assessment results by administering tests and conducting person studies in a totally new, but similarly composed, or crossvalidation sample of subjects.

## FOR FURTHER READING

Aiken, L.R. *Psychological testing and assessment* (3rd ed.). Boston: Allyn & Bacon, 1979. This book is divided into four parts dealing with the methodology of testing, with "cognitive" and "affective" assessment, and with contemporary developments in testing. It is a smaller book than either Anastasi's or Cronbach's, below, and should be read before tackling them.

Anastasi, A. *Psychological testing* (4th ed.). New York: Macmillan, 1976. From the time of its first edition in 1954, it has been clear that this will be the classic and comprehensive tome in its field. And so it has remained for its second (1961), third (1968), and fourth (1976) editions.

Brown, F.G. *Principles of educational and psychological testing* (2nd ed.). New York: Holt, Rinehart & Winston, 1976. This is a considerably expanded version of its first edition. Brown's text competes with Anastasi's classic book on testing, above, although it is not quite as comprehensive.

Borman, W.C. Exploring upper limits of reliability and validity in job performance ratings. *Journal of Applied Psychology*, 1978, *63*, 135–144.

Cronbach, L.J. *Essentials of psychological testing* (3rd ed.). New York: Harper & Row, 1970. A considerable revision of its earlier two editions (1949 and 1960), Cronbach's text remains heavily test-interpretation and decision oriented. It is somewhat more difficult to read than Anastasi's book but is well worth the effort.

Lord, R.M., & Novick, M.R. *Statistical theories of mental test scores*. Boston: Addison-Wesley, 1968. Written by two ETS senior scientists, this book attempts to —and succeeds—present a careful mathematical statement of classical test theory. The book is intended only for those who have a sound background in mathematical probability theory.

Nunnally, J.C. *Psychometric theory* (2nd ed.). New York: McGraw-Hill, 1978. Although his 1975 book on statistics for psychology and education overlaps, Nunnally provides a good grounding in statistics. Particularly relevant to chapters three and four of this book is his part four, which deals with the measurement of abilities, personality, and sentiments.

Stanley, J.C., & Hopkins, K.D. *Educational and psychological measurement and evaluation*. Englewood Cliffs, NJ: Prentice-Hall, 1972. Not as encyclopedic as Anastasi's book, above, and not as decision oriented as Cronbach's classic, Stanley's and Hopkins's offering is better written and more educationist oriented than either of these. Its newest edition, which was published in 1981, is more tightly organized and still better written than were its five previous editions. Clearly, this book is essential reading for educationists.

Thorndike, R.L. (Ed.) *Educational Measurement* (2nd ed.). Washington, D.C.: American Council on Education, 1971. A collection of twenty papers on test design, special types of tests, measurement, and test applications, this volume is an excellent reference for all these topics.

# 4 Types of Tests and Interpreting Scores

The first three chapters made several important distinctions between assessment and measurement, presented statistics important for understanding assessment, and then defined psychological assessment procedures and delineated some of their essential attributes. But they did not discuss what kinds of tests are available to users, nor did they explain how to interpret test scores. These are the topics of this chapter.

The first topic relates to the input side of the system depicted in Figure 1–1, an integral part of the decision to "Select and Administer Procedure and/or Test." We deal with this subject matter briefly at the outset of this chapter and then discuss the information processor of Figure 1–1. The information processor is the guts of the system, as it were, consisting of the tools and aids that enable the system to fulfill the primary function of psychological testing—predicting or forecasting the future behavior of, as well as making decisions about, the person being tested. We conclude the chapter with a discussion of the psychological report, which communicates the assessment findings to the referral source. This part of the assessment process refers back to the output component of Figure 1–1.

## Classification of Psychological Tests

The proliferation of tests available for psychological assessment has progressed at a staggering rate over the past three decades. Whereas the first edition of Buros's *Mental Measurements Yearbook* (1938) listed about 300 separate test entries, a more recent edition (Buros, 1972) listed 1,155 tests, and the current edition, the *Eighth Mental Measurements Yearbook* (Buros, 1978) listed 1,189 tests. We shall examine some of the ways that have been used to classify these tests.

### Test Item Format and Construction

It is sometimes useful to describe test items according to their degree of *structuredness*. For example, items such as "Find the standard deviation for the following distribution of scores" or "Do you blush easily?" are more structured than, let us say, test stimuli such as the inkblots of the Rorschach or the pictures of the Thematic Apperception Test (TAT), both of which are called projective techniques. The items above convey a similar meaning to respondents because they are written in English; the inkblots are amorphous and therefore are interpreted differently by different people. Likewise, the responses to test items may vary along a continuum of structuredness. Thus, some items may require persons to select from two or more possible alternative responses, and this would be a highly structured situation; other item formats might require them to give lengthy replies or create imaginative associations.

Another way to classify tests is according to the method used for item construction, which also influences item format. This classification cuts across item format categories and includes item construction by means of any one of four possible methods: domain sampling, criterion keying, factor analysis, and forced choice keying.

The first of these methods consists of sampling the relevant *content* area. That is to say, the items are selected to be representative of the behavior *domain* the tester wants to measure. Recall from chapter three that the problem with domain sampling is that it is not easy to define the content areas of, say, special abilities, interests, or, especially, personality.

In order to assess interests and personality, psychologists sometimes use the method of *criterion keying*. In sharp contrast to *domain sampling*, this method selects items on the basis of observed correlations between the items and the external criterion measures. Although the test constructor may begin by selecting items through a content-sampling procedure, he or she retains items and develops scoring keys if, and only if, these have demonstrated relationships with real-life measures. In constructing the Strong Vocational Interest Blank (Strong, 1943), for example, psychologists selected items because they statistically differentiated among specific occupational groups. The items of the Minnesota Multiphasic Personality Inventory (MMPI) were also selected in this manner, and they were retained because of their demonstrated empirical relations to relevant criteria. Thus, the item "At times I am full of energy" appears on the depression scale of the MMPI not so much because it reflects degree of depression but because a "false" response to it statistically discriminates significantly among criterion groups of normal and depressed individuals (see Meehl, 1945).

A third method for constructing tests is called *forced-choice keying*, which is a special case of criterion keying and was devised because of the observation that people answer personality test items in a socially desirable way. Professor Allen L. Edwards (1957, 1964) demonstrated the distorting influences of the social desirability variable on personality test scores and used a forced-choice item format as a correction. Very simply, this format has items to which the reponse choices are equally attractive (or unattractive) and similarly socially acceptable (or unacceptable); therefore, rather than requiring a choice between two response alternatives, only one of which is socially desirable, the format now forces a choice among two or more favorable items, only one of which is relevant to the dimension being measured. For example, if a college student is asked on an admissions test, "Would you prefer to be (a) scholarly or (b) shrewd?" the student would probably select choice (a). But if choice (b) were an equally attractive alternative, such as "coolheaded" or "command respect" (although these choices would not be valid for predicting the relevant criterion), then the student would have more difficulty selecting the more socially desirable alternative.

Finally, another way to construct items is by means of *factor analysis*. Factor analysis, it will be recalled, is a statistical technique used to simplify large arrays, or rows and columns, of variables by correlating each observation or variable with other ones under consideration and finding a common underlying factor. We have referred to this method as a way to validate tests. In test construction, it is used to select items. For example, if test items have been administered to several thousand individuals, the first step is to compute the correlations among items. The resulting matrix of intercorrelations is simplified by factor analysis, which indicates the items that cluster to form factors. Thus, if responses to items regarding, let us say, agility, athletic skill, and physical prowess tend to cluster, these items might appear on a test to measure potential sports ability. Many tests of intelligence, special abilities, and personality were constructed in this way.

### Paper-and-Pencil and Performance Tests

Tests can be classified according to whether they require answers to paper-and-pencil questions (items printed in test booklets) or are a manipulation of test stimuli. The principal difference between these formats is the nature of the required responses, with performance tests requiring observable, overt behavior (arranging pictures, building blocks, matching colors) and with paper-and-pencil tests eliciting more covert responses (thinking about the relevance of self-descriptive items, choosing a correct answer, organizing an essay on a topic).

### Maximum versus Typical Performance Tests

Another distinction between types of tests is whether *maximum* or *typical* performance is required (see Cronbach, 1970, pp. 35–40). Maximum performance tests contain instructions to do one's best; typical performance tests, on the other hand, obtain a sample of behavior representative of the individual's day-to-day responding. Generally, in achievement, intelligence, and ability testing, respondents are encouraged to put forth maximum effort, but in personality and interest testing, they are not so encouraged. In fact, personality testers often resort to deception because they cannot say that personality is being measured without at the same time also altering the test takers' responses on the test; thus instructions to "do your best" are irrelevant. So testers say something like, "There are no right or wrong answers" or "Anything you say is correct," both of which, of course, are untrue. This raises the question of whether measures of typical performance are actually obtained on personality tests, since the tester's subterfuge may be matched by that of the examinee.

## Individual and Group Tests

Individual tests differ from group tests in that individual tests measure one subject at a time and group tests, as the name indicates, examine many at once. The difference between these formats is more than just one of economy. It is often difficult to administer tasks to many individuals at once because these tasks may demand an intense and close interpersonal atmosphere, in that they contain items that require complex or elaborate instructions and thus oral interaction. Some individual tests, however, have been modified for group administration. An example is the Holtzman Inkblot Test (HIT), which is usually administered to one person by having the tester question the subject about what he or she sees on the inkblot cards, but which has also been adapted to the group form by projecting the inkblots onto a large screen and asking the subjects to write out their responses on an answer sheet (Holtzman, 1974).

## Self-Report Inventories

A common saying among clinical psychologists is that if you want to know about persons' feelings and beliefs, then ask them. Inventories and questionnaires are devices used to obtain such self-reports. One problem with these devices is that the person may distort his or her feelings and beliefs, distortions that may affect the accuracy of the obtained self-reports. Such *dissembling* or *dissimulation*, as it is called, was early recognized to exist in the structured-test movement (Gough, 1947, 1950; Schmidt, 1948) and has recently attracted renewed attention in personality study (Johnson & Hogan, 1981; Meehan et al., 1979). For example, people have been known to fake both normality (Schmidt, 1948) and psychopathology (Gough, 1974) on the MMPI, but it came as somewhat of a surprise, as demonstrated more recently in a study using Hogan's Survey of Ethical Attitudes (SEA) (Hogan, 1970) that they also lied about their politically liberal or conservative attitudes (Meehan et al., 1979) and dissembled in order to place themselves in a socially desirable or undesirable light (Johnson & Hogan, 1981).

Another problem with self-reports is that they sometimes assume that persons know enough about themselves and their behavior to report these accurately, a tenuous assumption at best. It has long been argued that items on self-report measures are a second-best source of information about a subject's actual behavior or attitudes, appropriate only when a direct assessment of the subject's behavior or attitudes is impossible or unfeasible, although the scoring does not assume a valid self-report to have been given (see Meehl, 1945, 1959a). A more recent view is that item endorsements are not reports of actual behavior, but symbolic self-presentations or attempts to communicate one's covert self-image (Mills & Hogan, 1978). According to this view, all self-reporting is an attempt to report what one would like others to credit one with, a view maintaining that subjects present themselves on tests much as they would in any other social interaction.

## Test Content

The most common classification of tests is one that relies on the test's content, or what the test is designed to measure. Test content areas can be classified in many ways. The classification scheme used by Buros in the *Eighth Mental Measurements Yearbook* (1978), outlined in Table 4–1, is one such method. The tests are separated mainly according to their subject areas.

Although the table of contents of the *Eighth Mental Measurements Yearbook* does not distinguish among various personality study procedures, such a distinction is useful and is one that we make in chapters five through nine. Our scheme divides personality study into observations, behavioral assessments, interviews, self-reports, attitude and value scales, projective techniques, and intelligence and ability tests. We shall return to a discussion of all of these methods in the next chapter. In the meantime, we shall examine some of the interpretive aids available to the information processor of Figure 1–1. Obviously the end product, or output, of this data processing relates to the right-hand, or final step of Figure 1–1.

## Interpretive Aids

There are several aids available to the test user for making inferences about the meaning and uses of test results. Some of these appear as

**Table 4–1** Partial Reproduction of the Table of Contents of Buros's *Eighth Mental Measurements Yearbook* (1978).

Contributing Test Reviewers
Foreword
Preface
Introduction
Tests and Reviews
  Achievement Batteries
  English
    Literature
    Spelling
    Vocabulary
  Fine Arts
    Art
    Music
  Foreign Languages
    English
    French
    German
    Greek
    Hebrew
    Italian
    Latin
    Russian
    Spanish
  Intelligence
    Group
    Individual
    Specific
  Mathematics
    Algebra
    Arithmetic
    Calculus
    Geometry
    Special Fields
    Statistics
    Trigonometry
  Miscellaneous
    Agriculture
    Blind
    Business Education
    Courtship and Marriage
    Driving and Safety Education
    Education
    Health and Physical Education
    Home Economics
  Reading
    Diagnostic
    Miscellaneous
    Oral
    Readiness
    Special Fields
    Speed
    Study Skills
  Science
    Biology
    Chemistry
    Geology
    Physics
  Sensory-motor
    Motor Vision
  Social Studies
    Economics
    Geography
    History
    Political Science
    Sociology
  Speech and Hearing
    Hearing
    Speech
  Vocations
    Clerical
    Interests
    Industrial Arts
  Listening Comprehension
  Philosophy
  Psychology
  Record and Report Forms
  Religious Education
  Socioeconomic Status
  Test Programs
  Multi-Aptitude Batteries
    Manual Dexterity
    Mechanical Ability
    Miscellaneous
    Selection and Rating Forms
  Specific Vocations
    Accounting
    Business
    Computer Programming
    Dentistry
    Engineering
    Law
    Medicine
    Miscellaneous
    Nursing
    Sales
    Skilled Trades
    Supervision
  Personality

part of the Information Processor of Figure 1–1 and are described below.

### Norms

Psychological tests have no absolute standards of "pass" or "fail." A given test score's meaning is surmised from its relation to others' scores on the same test. *Norms*, which provide these reference points for comparison, are usually collected at the time of test construction by administering the test to a sample representative of the population for which the test is intended. The scores of this sample, for which we compute the mean and standard deviation, are comparison referents by which we evaluate the meaning of each new score. Thus, a result can appear to be good or poor, depending on which norms we use.

The American Psychological Association's *Standards for Educational and Psychological Tests* (1974) contains some specific and essential recommendations for reporting normative data (see Box 4–2). It recommends that norms be published in the test manual when the test is released, that norms refer to defined and clearly described populations, that the manual discuss any probable bias or underrepresentations of

---

**BOX 4–1**

**Most Frequently Used Clinical Assessment Instruments**

| Test | Usage rank |
| --- | --- |
| Wechsler Intelligence Scale for Children (WISC) | 1 |
| Bender Motor Gestalt Test | 2 |
| Wechsler Adult Intelligence Scale (WAIS) | 3 |
| Minnesota Multiphasic Personality Inventory (MMPI) | 4 |
| Rorschach Inkblot Test | 5 |
| Thematic Apperception Test (TAT) | 6 |
| Sentence Completion Tests | 7 |
| Draw-a-Person Test (Goodenough) | 8 |
| House-Tree-Person Technique (HTP) | 9 |
| Stanford-Binet Intelligence Scale | 10 |
| Draw-a-Person Test (Machover) | 11 |
| Peabody Picture Vocabulary Test (PPVT) | 12 |
| Wechsler Preschool and Primary Scale of Intelligence (WPPSI) | 13 |
| Vineland Social Maturity Scale | 14 |
| Children's Apperception Test (CAT) | 15 |
| Memory for Designs Test (MFD) | 16 |
| Wechsler Memory Scale | 17 |
| Strong Vocational Interest Blank (SVIB) | 18 |

**Source** Adapted from Brown, W. R., & McGuire, J. M. Current psychological assessment practices. *Professional Psychology*, 1976, 7, 480.

> **BOX 4-2**
>
> ## A Select Set of Essential Standards for Including Normative Data
>
> Interpretations of test scores, according to the American Psychological Association's *Standards for Educational and Psychological Tests* (1974, pp. 19–24), traditionally have been *norm referenced*; that is, a person's score is interpreted by comparing it with other persons' scores. The following principles are considered *essential* features of norm-referenced tests:
>
> 1. Norms should be published in the test manual at the time of release of the test for operational use.
> 2. Norms presented in the test manual should refer to defined and clearly described populations. These populations should be the groups with whom users of the test will ordinarily wish to compare persons tested.
> 3. The test manual should report the method of sampling from the population of examiners and should discuss any probable bias in this sampling procedure.
> 4. The description of the norms group in the test manual should be complete enough so that the user can judge its appropriateness for his use. The description should include number of cases, classified by one or more of such relevant variables as ethnic mix, socioeconomic level, age, sex, locale, and educational status.
> 5. Local norms are more important for many uses of tests than are published norms. A test manual should suggest using local norms in such situations.
>
> **Source:** American Psychological Association. *Standards for educational and psychological tests.* Washington, DC: American Psychological Association, 1974, pp. 19–24.

groups in the sampling procedure, and that the manual report the significant aspects of the conditions under which normative data were obtained.

One cannot always anticipate the composition of each group for which a test will be used, nor can one foresee all the uses for a new test; therefore, in addition to published norms that may be based on a national sample, test users must also continue to gather normative information for the groups with which they deal, and they must update these norms from time to time. The collection of such local and updated information is the responsibility of every test user. A particular test user often will have a very special application in mind for a test. For example, in the Minnesota Multiphasic Personality Inventory (MMPI), testers found many applications of its numerous scales that were never intended by its constructors. Thus even though its original purpose was to differentiate among various psychodiagnostic groups, the MMPI has been used, among other things, to identify individuals with low back pain and arthritis; it has been administered to numerous unintended populations such as juvenile delinquents, prisoners, and others; and it has been found useful in predicting the length of stay in treatment, and so on, as we shall see in chapter seven. The important point to be made here is that regional and updated normative data are essential to a proper interpretation of the meaning of scores. Norms are invariably expressed as derived scores for reasons that will be made apparent in the next few pages.

## Derived Scores

In chapter two, we discussed how raw scores obtained from tests can be arranged according to their frequency distributions and how the properties of the normal curve can be used to interpret their meaning. It is important to recognize, however, that raw scores as such have little if any generality, since they are a product of the item responses contained in a particular test. Because of the natural and expected variation in difficulty from one form of a test to another or between tests, even when they are measuring the same characteristics, the raw score of given value will not have the same meaning or represent the same ability or characteristic.

For example, suppose that we obtain the results of a student's performance on ability tests X, Y, and Z in the form of the raw scores 30, 96, and 45. What do these values mean in terms of the student's level of ability as measured by each of the tests or in terms of the student's relative ability from one test to the next? Or, for that matter, what do these scores signify about the student's ability relative to that of other students who may have taken the same tests?

In order to answer these questions it is necessary to adopt a system of equating test scores according to a common score scale. Such a transformation of raw scores to a scale of *derived* scores can be achieved in a variety of ways.

A common derived score is the *standard score*. The formula for the standard score is exactly the same as that used for computing the familiar z score of chapter two. This conversion uses the characteristics of the normal curve:

$$z = \frac{X - \bar{X}}{S_x}$$

where  $X$ = a raw score
 $\bar{X}$ = mean raw score of a normative group
 $S_x$ = standard deviation of the normative group

From this conversion we can see that a new raw score that equals the mean becomes a *z* score of zero. And since standard deviations are measured from the mean, standard scores are expressed as deviations from zero. A raw score one standard deviation above the mean, for example, is a Z score of +1; a raw score one-half a standard deviation below the mean is a *z* score of −0.5, and so on.

Raw scores are converted to standard scores in order to show the number of standard deviation units they are above or below the mean of a relevant normative group. Since the standard score is reported in standard deviation units, points along the base line of the normal curve can be located, and one can determine the proportion of cases that falls above and below these points. Thus if a student's *z* score were +1.96, we would know that this score was 1.96 standard deviations above the mean and that 95 percent of the scores in the distribution of the normative sample were lower. Some other common *z* score values and their corresponding proportion of cases are the following:

68 percent of the scores will fall between ±1.00 *z* score,
84 percent of the scores will fall below a *z* score of +1.00, and
97.5 percent of the scores will fall below a *z* score of +1.96.

Although *z* scores have many advantages, they are not often used by test interpreters because about one-half of them are negative. Moreover, most *z* scores are expressed to one or two decimal points, an inconvenience that has led testers to use other derived scores, particularly those designed to eliminate the need for decimal points. Figure 4–1 describes some of these.

Figure 4–1 illustrates the relation of various derived scores to one another and to the proportions of cases falling under the areas of a normal curve. The percentage of cases under the areas of the curve are marked off only for whole unit *z* scores (e.g., ±1, ±2, ±3); and if there are fractional parts of units such as ±0.75, ±1.6, or ±1.96, these fractional parts can be mathematically computed to reflect the number of cases falling under these areas of the curve. The percentages of these cases can also be found by consulting specially prepared tables of *z* scores, which appear in the appendices of most elementary testing and statistics books.

A derived score that does not use the mean and the standard deviation of a normative group is the *percentile* rank. The relation of the percentile to the normal curve is also shown in Figure 4–1. The percentile shows a scorer's position in a group (either in the sample or in the normative group) with reference to a given attribute and is derived by computing the percent of the group that has less of the

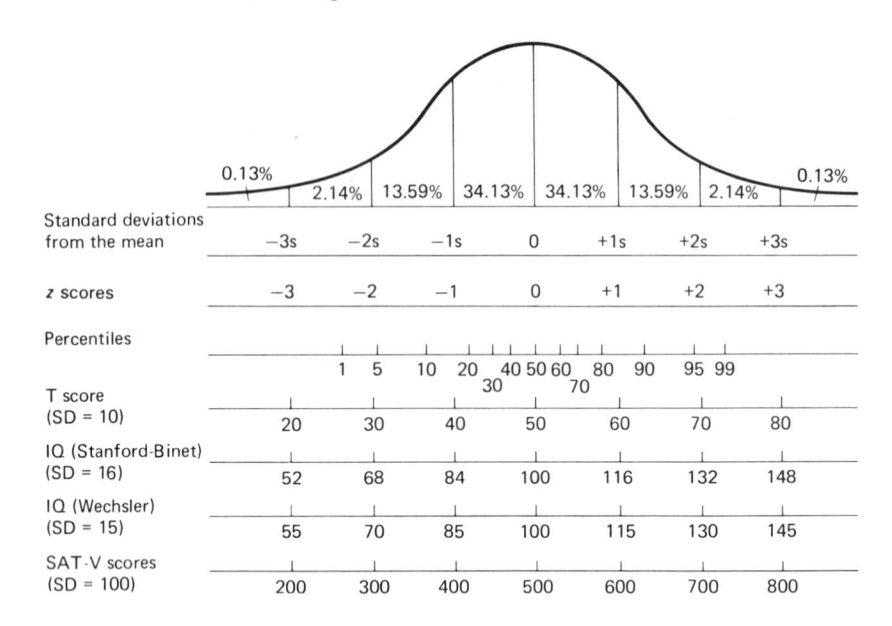

**Figure 4–1.** Relationships among Derived Scores

Source: Adapted from *Methods of expressing test scores (Test Service Bulletin No. 48)*. New York: The Psychological Corporation, January, 1955, p. 2.

attribute (or has lower raw scores) than the individual being considered. An example will illustrate this point.

Suppose an examinee in a class of thirty-five students received a score of, let us say, 23 on a test, and thirty out of the thirty-five students in the class scored lower than 23. This score earns a place in about the 89th percentile rank (e.g., the examinee's score earns a rank of 31; therefore 31/35 = 0.886). Or to express this differently, if 89 percent of a distribution falls below the raw score of 23, then 23 is in the 89th percentile. If 99 percent of a group falls below 750, then 750 has a percentile score of 99, and all scores in that distribution that are higher than 750 have percentile ranks that are fractions above 99 (e.g., 99.5, 99.9). But percentiles are usually reported in whole numbers.

Another feature of percentiles may be noted by referring again to Figure 4–1. On the base line of the normal curve, the percentile score is a point in the distribution that corresponds to specific cumulative percentages of cases falling under the area of that curve. Thus it may be noted that the 50th percentile falls at the mean of the distribution, which is also the midpoint or median and the mode of a normal distribution. Moreover, since approximately 84 percent of the cases of a distribution fall below +1 standard deviation, that point corresponds to the 84th percentile. Likewise, −1 standard deviation corresponds to about the 16th percentile, and +2 standard deviations to the 98th percentile.

## Normalization

Some other derived scores used in psychological assessment are the Stanford-Binet and Wechsler IQs, stanines, *T*-scores, and Scholastic Aptitude Test scores (SAT-V). The comparative values of these derived scores can be read directly from Figure 4–1. They have been placed in a vertical alignment with the base line of the normal curve.

A distribution of raw scores can be converted into normalized standard scores—a process sometimes called *normalization*—by forcing them into a normal distribution. This should be done if the raw scores can be assumed to be normally distributed. The process transforms the raw scores by assigning arbitrary values to their mean and standard deviation so that they conform to a normal distribution.

One such normalized standard score is the aforementioned *stanine*. As the name implies, the stanine is a nine-step standard score. It has the value 5 assigned as its mean and has a standard deviation of about 2. Each of its nine units is equal to about one-half standard deviation in width under the area of a normal curve except that the stanines 1 and 9—at opposite ends of the distribution—are somewhat larger and contain the lowest and highest 4 percent of the raw scores. Raw scores are converted to stanines by rank-ordering them from lowest to highest and assigning to them stanine values according to the following approximate percentages:

|  | First | Second | Third | Fourth | Fifth | Sixth | Seventh | Eighth | Ninth |
|---|---|---|---|---|---|---|---|---|---|
|  | 4% | 7% | 12% | 17% | 20% | 17% | 12% | 7% | 4% |
| Stanines | 1 | 2 | 3 | 4 | 5 | 6 | 7 | 8 | 9 |

Stanines are useful derived scores because they minimize small differences among scores. They also used to be convenient because they could be easily punched into the single columns of an IBM card. But new developments in computer hardware have made this convenience obsolete. Some commercial test services even attach interpretive classifications to stanines. One such interpretive scheme is shown in Figure 4–2. This scheme is often used to show an examinee's relative standing compared with those of a norm group, on a maximum performance test.

Another noteworthy derived standard score is the *T*-score, which is used to plot the profiles of several important self-report inventories that we discuss later (see chapter seven). *T*-scores convert obtained raw

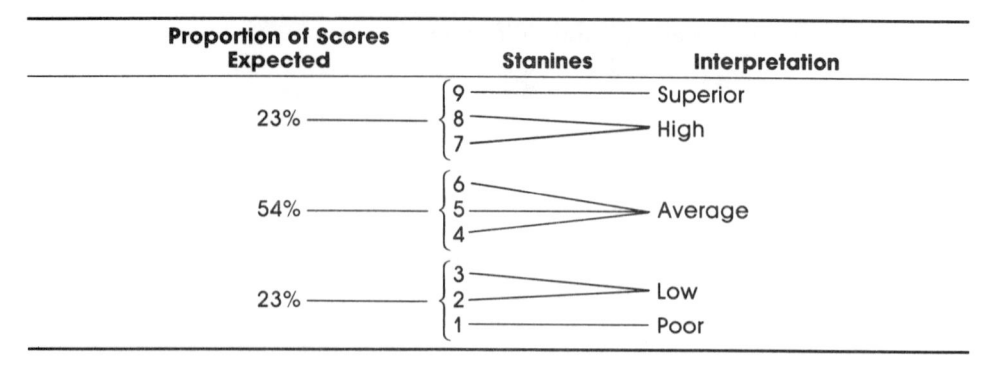

| Proportion of Scores Expected | Stanines | Interpretation |
|---|---|---|
| 23% | 9<br>8<br>7 | Superior<br>High |
| 54% | 6<br>5<br>4 | Average |
| 23% | 3<br>2<br>1 | Low<br>Poor |

**Figure 4–2** Stanine Record.

scores by assigning to them a mean of 50 and a standard deviation of 10. The *T*-score allows a finer differentiation among persons than the stanine does because the stanine's units are expressed as whole numbers. For example, a *T*-score of 40 is one standard deviation below the mean; a *T*-score of 65 is one and one-half standard deviations above the mean; and a *T*-score of 70 is two standard deviations above the mean, and so on.

Some other commonly used derived scores are the Stanford-Binet IQ, the Wechsler IQ, and the SAT scores. These have assigned mean values of 100, 100, and 500, respectively, and have standard deviations of 16, 15, and 100. All of these values were shown earlier in Figure 4–1.

To summarize, we can say that the main advantage of transforming raw scores to derived ones is that they express scores as common or standard scales, a convenience that permits test interpreters to report scores so that they may be compared with each other. In fact, the American Psychological Association is quite specific on this point in its *Standards* (1974, pp. 22–23), which contains several important recommendations for reporting normative information in the form of derived scores. For example, it is essential in reporting norms that the test manual use percentiles for one or more appropriate reference groups or standard scores whose basis is clearly described. Any unusual type of score or unit must be explained or justified.

The *Standards* also recommends that derived scores be carefully described in the test manual so that testers can use them to make accurate interpretations and so that the derivation can be clearly described to avoid misinterpretation or overgeneralization. Finally, the *Standards* recommends that a test manual should specify whether standard scores are linear transformations of raw scores (a transformation in which every individual retains exactly his or her relative position on the distribution of standard scores) or are normalized (the form of the standard score distribution is altered by changing the size of the scale units in order to obtain a normal distribution).

## Profiles

When we want to display intraindividual score differences for various characteristics, we plot the scores on a test profile sheet. To do this, we must convert all subtest distributions of scores to the same scale of derived scores. When we convert them in this way we can compare them with one another because the intervals between scores are equalized.

A profile can be plotted by letting various points along the horizontal axis represent subtests, or scales of the same test, and marking the converted score equivalents along the vertical axis. One such profile is shown in Figure 4–3. It displays the subtests of the California Psychological Inventory (Gough, 1956) along its horizontal axis and expresses the eighteen scores corresponding to these subtests as *T*-scores. Generally, the important features to note in a profile, regardless of the standard scores used as transformations, are the differences in subtest or scale elevations obtained by an individual.

Profiles are usually interpreted according to both the configuration of the scale elevations and the slope characteristics of these elevations. Such *profile analysis*, as it is called, is a form of test interpretation that compares an individual's scores on the subscales of a test (or on two or more tests) with those of a norm group.

A further convenience for both summarizing group data and interpreting individual profiles is the systems of coding that have been developed for various tests. We shall examine one such coding system in chapter seven, which has been developed for the MMPI (Hathaway, 1947) and which permits testers to translate profile information into shorthand statements about a person. For example, using the system proposed by Hathaway, the code number 35'78902-64 is translated to read, "this patient has scores at least two or more standard deviations above the mean (e.g., *T*-score of 70) on hysteria (Scale 3) and masculinity-femininity (Scale 5) and, from highest to lowest scores, is within the normal range on psychasthenia (Scale 7), schizophrenia (8), hypomania (9), social introversion (0), and depression (2). Furthermore, this person's scores on the schizophrenia and hypomania are at identical *T*-score levels, and his or her scores on paranoia (6) and psychopathic deviancy (4) are below the mean of the normative group." A similar, but more elaborate, coding system was later devised by Welsh (1948).

In general, profile interpretation has become sophisticated over the last two decades, and interpreters have learned to attend to the config-

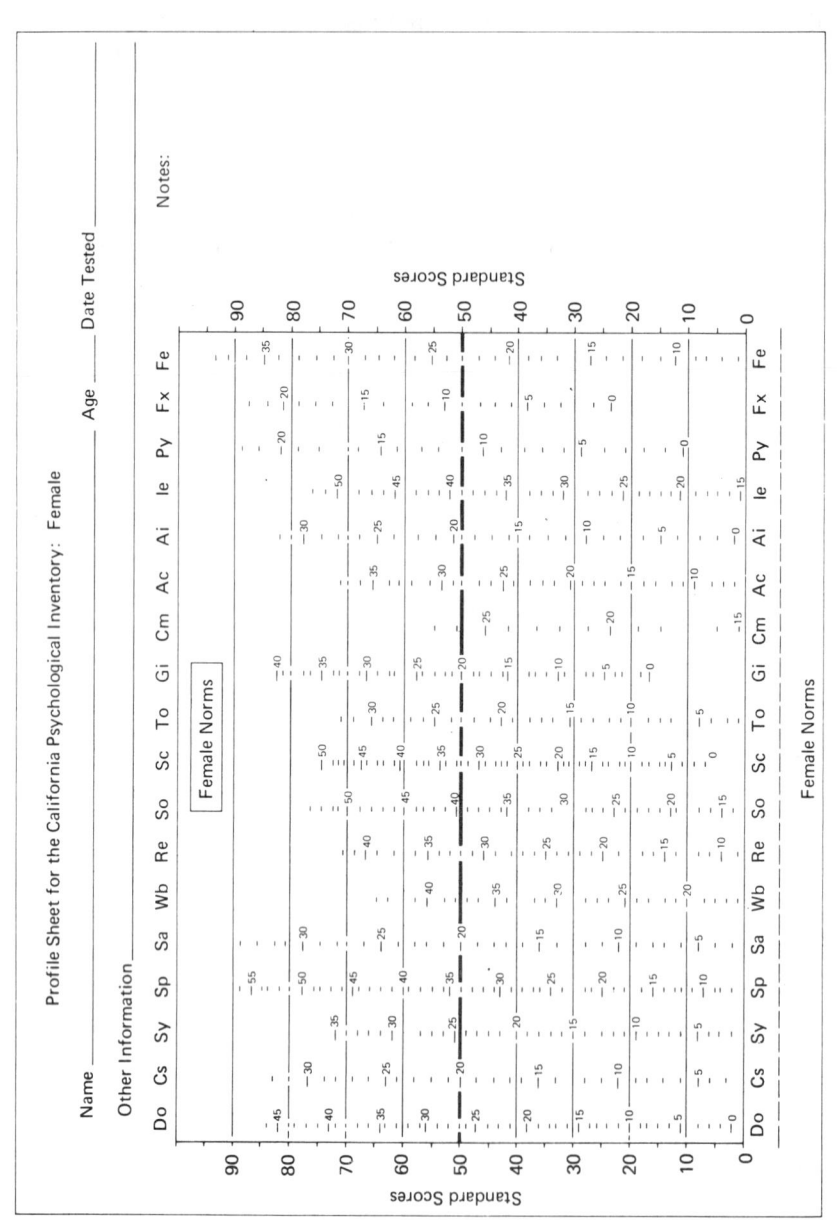

**Figure 4–3.** Profile Sheet of the California Psychological Inventory (CPI)

Source: Reproduced by special permission from the California Psychological Inventory by Harrison G. Gough, Ph.D. Copyright 1956. Published by Consulting Psychologists Press, Inc.

uration of test-scale patterns rather than to the elevations of single scales. These patterns are often interpreted by applying a set of decision rules that have been empirically shown as valid for a particular prediction task. An interpretive system's decision rules usually attend to such profile characteristics as the slope of the various scales plotted on the profile sheet, the dispersion or scatter of each scale from some average level, and the absolute and relative level of elevations of the subscales (see Cronbach, 1970, pp. 365–375; Cronbach & Gleser, 1965; Lyman, 1971, pp. 126–144; Nunnally, 1978, pp. 437–469).

## Configural Scoring

A technique that applies pattern analysis to items rather than to scale configurations—sometimes called *configural scoring* (Meehl, 1950)—emphasizes the pattern of responses that characterizes an individual's test answers. Essentially, configural scoring requires the simultaneous scoring of two or more items on a test so that the pattern of responses rather than the items one at a time can be interpreted. For example, on a personality inventory in which one answers items with yes or no, this approach would search for patterns of "yes" and "no" responses that represent a particular diagnostic group that may not be easily detected by conventional scoring or by profile analysis. Consider the case of paranoid persons who are usually difficult to detect by conventional methods of inventory interpretation. If these persons could be identified by a pattern of "yes" and "no" answers to particular items scored two or three at a time, then personality inventory interpretation for such detection will have improved considerably.

The configural scoring approach has been compared by Goldman (1971, p. 172) to the basic gestaltist principle that the whole is greater than the sum of its parts, that is, that the configuration of the parts has meaning over and above the meaning of the individual parts. It is not clear at present how much this technique will increase the accuracy of test interpretations. At least one study (Lubin, 1954) reported that configural item scoring was less valid than the conventional technique of scoring items one at a time. Horst (1954), however, believes that configural scoring may become more useful with further statistical advances. Williams and Kleinmuntz (1969) showed that the technique is feasible using a computer but that for a test such as the MMPI, which contains 566 items, about 160,000 correlations have to be computed. This means that for even a relatively small sample, two hundred to five hundred subjects, the computation is lengthy, taking about three to five hours on a high-speed computer. Obviously, the method is impractical without a computer.

## Decision Making with Tests

Having classified tests into various item and content formats, having defined norms and derived scores, and having touched on profile and item configural analyses, we now shall consider the two main functions of the information-processing component of the system depicted in Figure 1–1: prediction and decision making with test scores, two functions that work hand in hand with one another. Predictions regarding probable future behaviors are made from tests, and decisions are based on these predictions. Typical predictions are that a person will succeed at a job, will perform well academically, or will benefit from psychotherapy. The decisions based on these predictions would be to hire (or promote) a job candidate, accept a college applicant, or assign a patient to a therapy program.

In other words, an important function of the information processor is to forecast behaviors and to decide which applicants are most likely to succeed in, or benefit from, the groups for which they are selected. There is some risk associated with each prediction and decision, but the hope is to reduce the risk by enabling correct decisions to be made more often than incorrect ones.

### Expectancy Tables

The question that confronts the decision maker when making predictions is, "How can I make the greatest number of correct decisions?" There are many ways to do this. One is to use an *expectancy* table, such as the one in Table 4–2, which is a simplified version of a more elaborate format. On the left-hand side of Table 4–2 appear the test scores or predictor variables grouped according to intervals convenient for the

**Table 4–2** Expectancy Table Displaying the Relation between Hypothetical Scores on the Verbal Scale of the Scholastic Aptitude Test (SAT-V) and Freshmen College Grades.

| SAT-V Test Scores | Freshman College Grade Averages (percent) |   |   |   |   | Total (percent) |
|---|---|---|---|---|---|---|
|  | A | B | C | D | F |  |
| 800 | 85 | 8 | 5 | 1 | 1 | 100 |
| 700–799 | 75 | 12 | 8 | 3 | 2 | 100 |
| 600–699 | 55 | 30 | 12 | 1 | 2 | 100 |
| 500–599 | 26 | 32 | 38 | 2 | 2 | 100 |
| 400–499 | 0 | 5 | 40 | 33 | 12 | 100 |
| 300–399 | 11 | 16 | 51 | 12 | 10 | 100 |
| 200–299 | 0 | 3 | 10 | 62 | 25 | 100 |

test user and the occasion. Along the top of the table are the criterion categories according to which the individuals were rated. These tables, according to one source "are essentially scatter plots of predictor versus criterion, or, from another point of view, norms on the criterion variable, differentiated by score on the predictor variable" (Angoff, 1971, p. 547).

Table 4-2 shows the relations between (hypothetical) scores on the verbal scale of the familiar Scholastic Aptitude Test (SAT-V) and freshman college students' final grades. Given an individual's test score, it is possible to predict the chances of his or her obtaining one of the five grades shown in the criterion columns. For example, for someone scoring at 800 on the SAT-V, the chances are about 85 in 100 of obtaining an *A*, 8 chances in 100 for a *B*, and so on. Likewise, at the low end of the SAT-V score continuum, the chances for obtaining *A* and *B* grades with SAT-V scores of less than 400 are very slim; and the likelihood of obtaining grades better than *C* with scores of less than 300 is also small.

Another way to tally the results of a test for criterion measures is to set up a 2 × 2 (two cells by two cells) scatter diagram like that in Figure 4-4. In this diagram we see that one hundred patients were given personality tests and subsequently were assigned to four (2 × 2) treatment groups. Some of these patients benefited from treatment, and this was indicated in the two cells above the horizontal line of the diagram. The criterion measure consisted of judgments (by a panel of experts) about whether patients benefited from treatment, and the horizontal cutoff point designates minimum benefit. The thirty-eight cases indicated in the two cells below this line represent persons who did not benefit. If all one hundred patients had been assigned to the treatment group, then 62 percent would have benefited. Let us suppose now, in our hypothetical situation, that the test scores are being used to maximize the likelihood that the patients will benefit from treatment, that the score of 60 is being used as a cutoff point, and that only those persons indicated in the two cells to the left of the vertical line in the diagram have not been treated. In this case, because the group consists of fifty-three patients, forty-four benefited from treatment. Thus it can be seen that the percent benefiting is now raised from 62 to 83 (i.e., 44/53 = 0.83). This increase is a consequence of using the personality test to help make this decision.

Several other features of Figure 4-4 are important. The terms *valid positives, false positives, valid negatives,* and *false negatives* are used. These are borrowed from medicine and designate the cases in which tests have correctly indicated the *presence* (positive sign) of pathology (valid positive) or have erroneously indicated it (false positive); as well as the cases in which they have correctly indicated the *absence* (negative sign) of

## Personality and Psychological Assessment

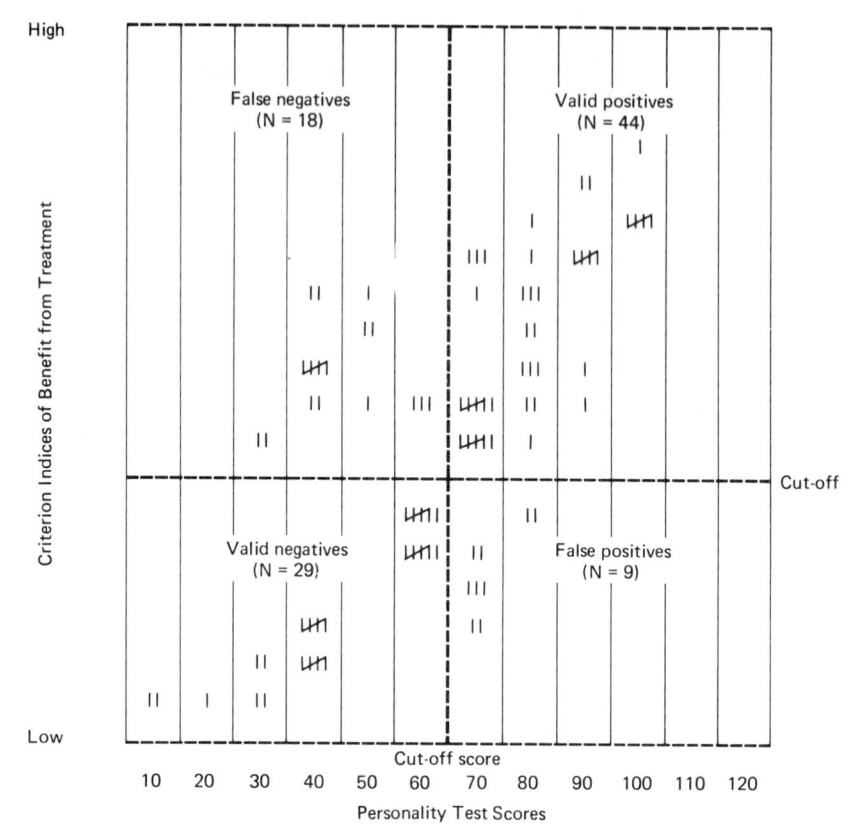

**Figure 4–4.** Scatter Diagram Showing Personality Test Scores Being Used as a Means to Maximize the Number of Patients Benefiting from Treatment

Source: Kleinmuntz, B. Psychological assessment. In W. H. Holtzman (Ed.), *Introductory psychology in depth. Developmental topics.* New York: Harper & Row, 1978, p. 122.

pathology (valid negative) or have erroneously indicated it (false negative). In our example, these terms are used to designate cases for whom test scores would not predict benefits (negatives).

It also is pertinent that the validity coefficient between the test scores and the criterion measures could be computed from the information given in Figure 4–4. Although it is not important to do so in this case, an estimate can be made from the scatter of cases falling at various points in the diagram. In this case the estimate, based on the scatter of the tally marks that cluster around a hypothetical diagonal running from the lower left to the upper right corners of the diagram, suggests that the correlation is a high positive one, a coefficient probably lying somewhere between +0.60 and +0.70. This correlation can be used by the tester in determining treatment, but the precise methods for using such validity coefficients in conjunction with tests and criterion cutoff points in order to maximize the percentage of valid positive and negative instances are complex (see Cronbach & Gleser, 1965).

Finally, a third way to make predictions using expectancy tables is one that utilizes information about the validity coefficients of tests and the proportion of applicants who are to be accepted (selection ratio). These expectancy tables, one of which has been in use for many years, have been named the Taylor-Russell Tables after their founders (Taylor, H. C., & Russell, 1939). The example in Table 4–3 shows the increment of successful predictions that can be expected above that which would occur without using the test. Information included in this table consists of the various selection ratio percentages, which appear across the top, and the validity coefficients of the test being used. The proportions in the cells of the table indicate the percent of successful predictions that can be made. In the particular reproduction in Table 4–3, the expectancy table has been constructed to be used when the percentage of successful predictions without using the test is 60. Therefore, the proportions in the cells must be subtracted from 0.60.

Let us look at some examples of how the Taylor-Russell Tables may

**Table 4–3** Taylor-Russell Tables of the Proportion Who Will Be Satisfactory among Those Selected for Given Values of Proportion of Employees Considered Satisfactory (= .60), the Selection Ratio and Test Validity Coefficient.

| Test Validity Coefficient | Selection Ratio |||||||||||
|---|---|---|---|---|---|---|---|---|---|---|---|
| | .05 | .10 | .20 | .30 | .40 | .50 | .60 | .70 | .80 | .90 | .95 |
| .00 | .60 | .60 | .60 | .60 | .60 | .60 | .60 | .60 | .60 | .60 | .60 |
| .05 | .64 | .63 | .63 | .62 | .62 | .62 | .61 | .61 | .61 | .60 | .60 |
| .10 | .68 | .67 | .65 | .64 | .64 | .63 | .63 | .62 | .61 | .61 | .60 |
| .15 | .71 | .70 | .68 | .67 | .66 | .65 | .64 | .63 | .62 | .61 | .61 |
| .20 | .75 | .73 | .71 | .69 | .67 | .66 | .65 | .64 | .63 | .62 | .61 |
| .25 | .78 | .76 | .73 | .71 | .69 | .68 | .66 | .65 | .63 | .62 | .61 |
| .30 | .82 | .79 | .76 | .73 | .71 | .69 | .68 | .66 | .64 | .62 | .61 |
| .35 | .85 | .82 | .78 | .75 | .73 | .71 | .70 | .67 | .65 | .62 | .61 |
| .40 | .88 | .85 | .81 | .78 | .75 | .73 | .79 | .68 | .66 | .63 | .62 |
| .45 | .90 | .87 | .83 | .80 | .77 | .74 | .72 | .69 | .66 | .64 | .62 |
| .50 | .93 | .90 | .86 | .82 | .79 | .76 | .73 | .70 | .67 | .64 | .62 |
| .55 | .95 | .92 | .88 | .84 | .81 | .78 | .75 | .71 | .68 | .64 | .62 |
| .60 | .96 | .94 | .90 | .87 | .83 | .80 | .76 | .73 | .69 | .65 | .63 |
| .65 | .98 | .96 | .92 | .89 | .85 | .82 | .78 | .74 | .70 | .65 | .63 |
| .70 | .99 | .70 | .94 | .91 | .87 | .84 | .80 | .75 | .71 | .66 | .63 |
| .75 | .99 | .99 | .96 | .93 | .90 | .86 | .81 | .77 | .71 | .66 | .63 |
| .80 | 1.00 | .99 | .98 | .95 | .92 | .88 | .83 | .78 | .72 | .66 | .63 |
| .85 | 1.00 | 1.00 | .99 | .97 | .95 | .91 | .86 | .80 | .73 | .66 | .63 |
| .90 | 1.00 | 1.00 | 1.00 | .99 | .97 | .94 | .88 | .82 | .74 | .67 | .63 |
| .95 | 1.00 | 1.00 | 1.00 | 1.00 | .99 | .97 | .92 | .84 | .75 | .67 | .63 |
| 1.00 | 1.00 | 1.00 | 1.00 | 1.00 | 1.00 | 1.00 | 1.00 | .86 | .75 | .67 | .63 |

Source: Taylor, H. C., & Russell, J. T. The relationship of validity coefficients to the practical effectiveness of tests in selection: Discussion and tables. *Journal of Applied Psychology*, 1939, 23, 565–578. Copyright 1939 by the American Psychological Association. Reprinted by permission.

be used. Suppose that 10 percent of the applicants must be selected from the entire group applying. A test with a validity coefficient of 0.00 to 0.40 can raise the proportion of successful applicants from 60 percent to 85 percent. The 25 percent improvement represents the increment in success rate that can be attributed to having used a valid test. The two extreme cases, one represented by a test with zero validity and the other by the instance in which 95 percent of the applicants must be accepted, are also important. In the first case, it is obvious that regardless of the proportion of applicants to be accepted, a test with zero validity is not helpful. On the other hand, when almost all applicants must be accepted (e.g., 95 percent), then even a test with perfect validity ($r = 1.00$) shows an improvement of only 3 percent (from 60 percent to 63 percent) in the success rate.

### Base Rates

Another important, and related, consideration in test decision making is the use of the base rate. The concept of the base rate was introduced into psychological testing by Meehl and Rosen (1955) in an article that stated that the value of a test depends not only on the size of the validity coefficient but also on the number of positives that may be expected from the total sample of applicants. When this information about the applicant sample is available, then it is possible to compute how much a test's scores will improve prediction over that which would occur without its use. In other words, to find out how much can be gained by using a test in a particular population, it is important to know the base rate, or the incidence in a population of the particular characteristic under consideration.

The quantity of the base rate (e.g., the number of positives) is determined by the nature of the applicant sample and is a quantity that varies from one sample to another. The base rate of schizophrenic individuals (positives) that one would expect to find on the back ward of a state hospital might be about 90 percent. The base rate of schizophrenics that one would expect to find in an abnormal psychology class (allowing for some self-selection as a result of which more than the usual number of schizophrenics chooses abnormal rather than social psychology) is probably about 5 percent. In a suicide prevention center, the base rate of depression might again be close to 90 percent, whereas in a university classroom it would be expected to be considerably lower. The important point is, as Wiggins pointed out, that "such variations in base rates will have considerable effects on the outcomes of test prediction in these different settings" (1973, p. 248).

Cronbach offered an excellent illustration of how varying base rates affect test predictions (1970, pp. 539–540). His example, which is described in Figure 4–5, depicts what would occur if the base rates of depressed persons coming to four different clinics were 50 percent, 20 percent, 5 percent, and 2 percent. Figure 4–5 shows the probabilities of correctly identifying depressed patients on the MMPI *D* or depression scale when the applicants' sample base rates shift from 50 percent to 20 percent, to 5 percent, and to 2 percent. Referring to Figure 4–5, we see that the probability that a person is clinically depressed increases as the *T*-score on the MMPI *D*-scale increases and as the base rate increases. Thus, the value of the *D*-scale is closely related to the base rate. For example, by taking a *T*-score of 70, which is a derived score of two standard deviations above the mean, the psychologist calling a person depressed is right about 80 percent of the time when the base rate is fifty-fifty but is right about only 1 percent of the time when the base rate is 2 percent. Other values can be easily read from Figure 4–5, but it should be apparent that a valid test is most useful when the base rate is about 50 percent.

## Bandwidth-Fidelity Dilemma

Another concept that Cronbach contributed to personality testing is bandwidth-fidelity, which refers to the tester's choice of whether to select a broadly or a narrowly focused assessment technique (1970, pp. 179–182). Apparently the precision of the tester's prediction is influenced by this choice.

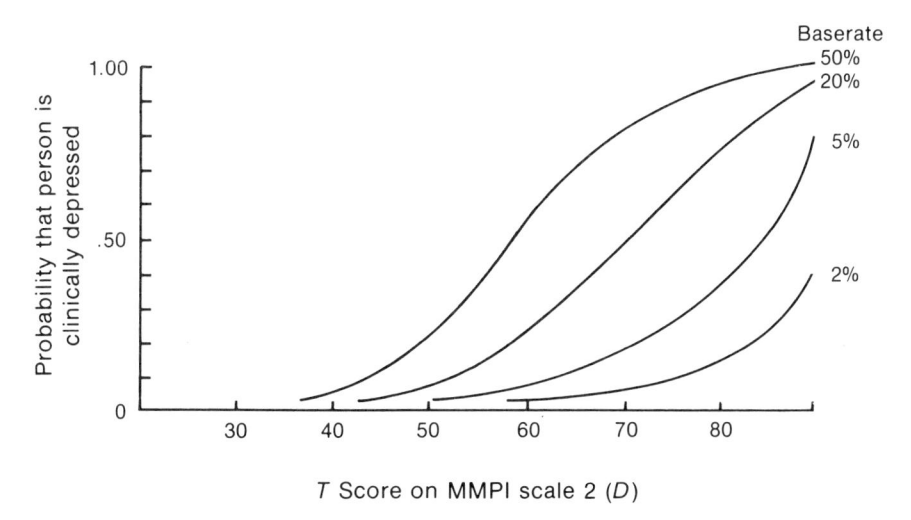

**Figure 4–5.** Probability of Correct Identification of Depressed Patients

Source: Cronbach, L. J. *Essentials of psychological testing.* New York: Harper & Row, 1970, p. 540 (Reprinted by permission of the publisher.)

Cronbach adapted the idea of bandwidth-fidelity to psychometrics from Shannon's and Weaver's (1949) mathematical communication or information theory. In an information communication system, according to the theory, there is a compromise between bandwidth and fidelity so that if there is a shift in the direction of greater fidelity, the bandwidth will be reduced; and a broader bandwidth will reduce fidelity. Thus, in home record-playing systems in which the fidelity of a recording depends on the groove width, if the grooves are crowded together to fit more music within a given space on a record (greater bandwidth), then the fidelity will suffer. The psychometric counterpart of this is that a test designed to gather much information (broad bandwidth) tends to have low fidelity, whereas a test that tries to measure one variable (narrow bandwidth) may be more accurate (high fidelity).

Cronbach indicated how this bandwidth-fidelity dilemma holds true for tests of ability:

> Compressing behavior into one or two scores loses detailed information. But attempting to capture rich detail by using many scores, each from a small sample of behavior, gets poor information. A high-school counselor would obviously prefer 10-minute tests of fine abilities to a 50-minute test that samples mechanical reasoning exhaustively and tells nothing about verbal, numerical, abstract reasoning, and clerical abilities.... (1970, p. 180)

Although no rule can specify the optimal bandwidth-to-fidelity ratio for testing, Cronbach listed certain conditions that favor instruments with a wider or a narrower fidelity bandwidth (1970, p. 189). According to him, narrowband instruments should be used for all-or-none selection decisions or predictions in which radical treatments are prescribed (e.g., electroshock, surgery, radiation). Wideband techniques should be used for decisions that could be made progressively and sequentially. The wideband techniques therefore could be relatively unstandardized and impressionistic procedures such as the Rorschach inkblots and interviews, which also have a low fidelity. These relatively nonpsychometric procedures (see chapters six and eight) should be used to suggest hypotheses about possible treatment plans (which can be followed up without any great harm to the patient) but should not be used to help make all-or-none decisions.

The distinction between standardized or psychometric and unstandardized or impressionistic assessment, according to Cronbach and Gleser (1965), cannot be made on the basis of test stimulus dimensions but should, rather, be based on the test's demonstrated suitability for different prediction purposes. Thus, narrow bandwidth instruments cannot be identified by the types of items they use or by the forms of responses they require, but rather by their empirically proven focus in predicting specific criteria; wideband techniques, on the other hand, are flexible or unfocused assessment procedures empirically known to clarify many criteria.

Generally, in selecting tests suitable for specific personality measurement goals, one must decide whether the assessment requires high fidelity or broad bandwidth or some combination of the two. Regarding this, Cronbach stated:

> Fallible tests can suggest assignments for an employee, treatments for a patient, or teaching techniques for a student. Even if a test is little better than a guess, it has some value when there is no sounder basis for choice. Since trying out the hypothesis permits verification, and leads to a change when the hypothesis is disconfirmed, little has been lost. We may say, in sum, that the fallibility of wideband procedures does no harm unless the hypotheses and suggestions they offer are regarded as verified conclusions about the individual. (1970, pp. 689–690)

## The Problem of Incremental Validity

Whether or not these decision-making aids do help the test interpreters is a problem that has to be resolved by incremental validity studies. These studies reflect the increase in predictive efficiency that can be claimed for using a particular test or procedure (Meehl, 1959a; Sechrest, 1963a). In other words, studies of incremental validity evaluate the relative contribution of particular assessment techniques to predicting criteria. This problem is one that we have already encountered in our discussion of the effects of base rates on the probability of making correct decisions. But unlike base-rate studies, incremental validity studies attempt to evaluate the contribution of individual measuring devices without regard to the characteristics of the applicant sample or to the validity values of the separate tests under examination.

Several incremental validity studies have been conducted in personality assessment (Golden, 1964; Kostlan, 1954; Sines, L. K., 1959; Winch & More, 1956), and the results, when considered together, have shown that the effects of increased information on descriptive accuracy depend as much on the expertise of the assessors and on the attributes selected for description as on the particular tests or procedures administered.

Some of these studies have yielded interesting information about specific procedures. For example, in a clinical setting, Kostlan (1954) found that the personalities of psychiatric patients could be accurately described by experienced clinicians simply on the basis of fact-sheet information (age, marital status, occupation, education, and referral source) and that the clinicians variously used the information from different tests and test combinations. When the test results were used to make the same judgments, only the social history scores yielded more accurate inferences than those made from simple biographical facts.

In another clinical study, Winch and More (1956) compared judges using interview information, case histories, and a projective test (TAT), and found that the TAT made no statistically significant contribution beyond that provided by the interview and the case history. Similar results were reported by L.K. Sines (1959), who compared the relative worth of biographical data, interviews, and the Rorschach and MMPI tests, and found that the Rorschach may actually *decrease* the validity of personality descriptions. And in a study comparing interpretations based on the Rorschach, MMPI, and TAT, as used singly and in combination with each other, Golden reported: "The results of the present study do not support the view that clinical inferences based on a battery of tests are more reliable and valid than those based on individual tests" (1964, p. 444).

The results of incremental validity studies such as the above have led some (Lanyon & Goodstein, 1971, pp. 173–174) to conclude that as sources of information for prediction or decision making, personality tests are not as successful as case histories. These results also suggest that a single test adds about as much information to the biographical data as does a complete battery of tests. But to defend the personality assessors' rather poor performances in the aforementioned studies, Lanyon and Goodstein raised several important considerations: (1) The kinds of comprehensive personality descriptions demanded in these studies are not usually requested in practice; (2) the studies were concerned with overall personality descriptions, and not with the assessment of specific attributes and behaviors; and (3) instruments should be used for making the kinds of discriminations for which they have been shown to be valid and should not, as is usually the case, be used for assessment tasks for which they were not devised.

## Combining Test Information

Most research on the predictive efficiency of tests tends to concentrate on the psychometric excellence of these tests and on the worth of certain interpretive aids for decision making. However, one important variable usually omitted in discussions of the relative worth of tests and aids is the information processor, either a human or an actuarial system, who is confronted with an array of test results and charts to be interpreted. This is an unfortunate omission, since the data processor may be the single most important component of the system or, at the very least, may be as important as the data to be processed. The problem for the information processor can be stated as follows: Given a set of observations and/or test scores, should these data be combined subjectively or should they be combined actuarially or statistically? Although it might seem that this problem is trivial, it has been the topic of a major controversy in psychology, with some psychologists taking the subjective, or judgmental processing, side of the argument and others taking the statistical, or actuarial, side.

## Clinical versus Statistical Prediction

This argument, which in clinical psychology is known as the "clinical-versus-statistical prediction controversy," was the major focus of a now-classic monograph by Paul E. Meehl (1954) of the University of Minnesota. Meehl's main contribution to this controversy was to clarify the theoretical and methodological underpinnings of the clinical-versus-statistical procedures for combining psychometric and nonpsychometric data. The ferocity of the arguments over the merits of either one of these methods was pointed out early in the book. Advocates of statistical methods, according to Meehl, refer to persons who prefer clinical intuition as "mystical, vague, unscientific, primitive, sloppy, and muddleheaded," and view their own method as "reliable, rigorous, scientific, precise, quantitative, and hardheaded." Critics of the statistical or actuarial method label it "pedantic, fractionated, trivial, pseudoscientific, and blind," and tend to refer to their own procedures as "dynamic, patterned, natural, sophisticated, and sensitive" (1954, p. 4). Stripped of its pejorative and honorific adjectives, however, the controversy revolves around the issue of whether more accurate predictions can be made by using a formula or a statistical equation or by judgmental or clinical methods.

But the practical problem for the decision maker is that the psychologist has gathered a multitude of information about a client, such as test scores, interview data, and biographical facts, and must combine these predictors to arrive at a decision about the client. In practice this can be reduced to a concern about the relative benefits of a clinical-versus-statistical combination of data, with the clinical method being characterized by using intuition, judgment, or clinical wisdom, and the statistical method by entering actuarial experience tables or applying decision rules. Lanyon and Goodstein offered the following examples of these alternative modes of operation, citing the clinical method first:

> A ... psychologist may note that a particular patient is depressed ... agitated ... and preoccupied with ... death. From these observations, he concludes that the patient is potentially suicidal and recommends that he should be watched carefully.... Alternatively, the psychologist might observe the

patient's age, his marital status, and certain MMPI test scores. He then consults an actuarial table, which gives the statistical frequency of suicide in persons ... [with] such characteristics, and obtains a figure indicating the probability of suicide by that particular patient. (1971, p. 160)

Lanyon and Goodstein also called attention to the fact that this clinical-versus-actuarial approach is not unique to psychologists. Physicians also use this approach to combine data to make diagnoses; security analysts use it to advise clients on investments; and many other "clinicians" such as polygraphers, or lie detectors, use it (see Kleinmuntz, 1968; Slovic & Lichtenstein, 1971; Szucko & Kleinmuntz, 1981).

## A Box Score of Empirical Evidence and Some Guidelines

Persons on both sides of the clinical-versus-statistical prediction controversy have collected evidence to corroborate their respective sides. Meehl (1965) reported that in his box score of some fifty studies, the statistical method was demonstrated to be superior in predictive power in about two-thirds of the investigations and about equal in the rest. But he cited two particular studies, reported by Lindzey (1965), in which clinical judgments surpassed a set of formal rules. In a subsequent reanalysis of Lindzey's data, however, Goldberg (1968a) showed that the clinical prediction in the Lindzey studies did not outperform statistical prediction (also see Goldberg, 1965, 1968b, 1970).

On the clinical side of the controversy, there have been the persistent and forceful arguments of Robert R. Holt (1958, 1971, 1978b), who had the following to say about quantitatively based predictions:

> Personalities cannot be understood or even meaningfully measured without the necessarily subjective processes of the clinician as he perceives, empathizes, intuits, makes judgments, integrates, and synthesizes information, and constructs a theory, or schema, of a person.

Holt further argued that in most of Meehl's box score of fifty studies, the clinicians predicted outcomes (college grades, success on the job, violation of parole) that put the clinicians at a disadvantage vis-à-vis statistical methods. A fairer test of the clinicians' ability would have been to have them predict some form of behavioral outcome dominated by personality traits, motives, defenses, or other such inner states that clinicians are trained to assess. Holt therefore pressed for comparisons— if comparisons are to be made—that would pit actuarial approaches against *sophisticated clinical prediction*, the latter defined as using "the refinements of experimental design from the actuarial side ... [including also] a full use of qualitative data and the clinician's personal as well as intellectual resources" (1971, p. 216). What Holt had in mind regarding sophisticated clinical prediction was that the clinician be retained as one of the prime instruments but that he or she use quantification and statistics whenever helpful, with an effort to become as reliable and valid a data processor as possible. Sophisticated clinical prediction also requires the clinician, not his or her mechanical surrogate, to make the final organization of the data, so as to yield a set of predictions tailored to each case.

But the controversy is far from over, and clarifications of data collection (see Sawyer, 1966; Sines, J. O., 1964, 1966) and prediction modes (see Einhorn et al., 1979; Holt, 1978b, pp. 20–37), as well as information supporting one side or the other, continue to appear in the psychological literature. And it is quite possible that the controversy over the relative superiority of one prediction method to the other cannot be answered, even when a box score wholly favors either one or the other of these methods. Perhaps the clinical method is to be preferred in some instances and statistical strategies in others. The question, as Meehl once phrased it in the title of one of his papers (1957), can be reduced to: "When shall we use our heads instead of the formula?"

A set of guidelines for using the head rather than the formula was proposed by Goldman (1961, pp. 202–204). Some of these guidelines are paraphrased here:

1. Statistical predictions should be made if expectancy tables have been made available as a result of earlier experience with similar prediction situations.
2. Statistical methods should be used when mathematical equations are available for particular prediction problems, or when a set of decision rules has demonstrated its usefulness for these predictions.
3. Clinical predictions should always be suspect if they are based on no firmer grounds than the clinician's "feelings" of confidence about them.
4. When no statistical formulas or mechanical rules are available, then intuitive methods must be used.
5. Intuitive methods are often superior to statistical equations when the events to be predicted occur infrequently. For example, when predicing a rare event such as suicide, it has been demonstrated (Meehl & Rosen, 1955; Rosen, 1954) that even the most sophisticated statistical techniques can fail.
6. Clinical judgment is essential when the prediction problem requires the description of complex intraindividual interactive processes. For example, when a personality description, rather

than the prediction of probable behaviors, is the goal of a particular assessment situation, then it is necessary to use clinical intuition. There is yet no set of rules or computer program that can organize this information into a meaningful description of a person.

Goldman offered test interpreters some additional sound advice (1971, pp. 210–212): He suggested that for many decisions, statistical or mechanical decision methods are preferable because they efficiently organize the relations between test data on the one hand and criteria on the other. The statistical methods, furthermore, when used properly, also assign correct weights to predictors; whereas intuitive procedures are more likely to be affected by the influences of irrelevant cues that result from assigning inappropriate weights to data. But Goldman also acknowledged the limited use of the tools available for contemporary decision making: "At the moment . . . [we] . . . have little choice but to use clinical methods for many situations; the paraphernalia of actuarial interpretation—the tables, formulas, and machines—are with all too rare exceptions a vision of the future" (1971, p. 210).

Meehl was less skeptical about the future than Goldman, when he observed the following in a somewhat different context:

> [We] . . . must constantly reiterate the elementary truth that if you depart in your clinical decision making from a well-established (or even moderately well-supported) empirical frequency—whether it is based upon psychometrics, life-history material or whatever—your departure may save a particular case from being misclassified predictively or therapeutically; but that such departures are, prima facie, counterinductive, so that a decision *policy* of this kind is almost certain to have a cost that exceeds its benefits. The research evidence strongly suggests that a policy of making such departures, except very sparingly, will result in the misclassifying of other cases that would have been correctly classified had such nonactuarial departures been forbidden; it also suggests that more of this second kind of misclassification will occur than will be compensated for by the improvement in the first kind. . . . That there are occasions when you should use your head instead of the formula is perfectly clear. But which occasions they are is most emphatically *not* clear. What *is* clear on the available clinical data is that these occasions are much rarer than most clinicians suppose. (1973, pp. 234–235)

Investigators on the statistical side of the controversy are systematically collecting evidence to demonstrate that the occasions for using the head rather than the formula are indeed rare. This book is not the proper place to enumerate these occasions or to list the box score of studies on both sides of the controversy. But we shall discuss in chapters seven and ten two studies in which statistical modes of data combining were clearly the best methods. In one of these studies (see Kleinmuntz, 1963a,b, 1975), a computer outperformed human personality test interpreters; in the other study (Szucko & Kleinmuntz, 1981), statistical modes of data analysis were better "lie detectors" than experienced polygraph examiners were.

But in fairness to the clinical side of the argument, we quote its chief spokesman, Robert R. Holt, who regrets that the controversy is now treated as a "war of attrition" in many textbooks and who in the following passage made a rather sane plea for restoring dignity to and proper respect for human judgment:

> What I have been opposing all these years is not formal methods [statistical and actuarial methods of predicting, or systematic or controlled procedures] but attempts to denigrate and eliminate judgment. Some of the formalists may protest that they have only wanted to expose the excesses of those who relied on judgment too much and at the wrong points, but I fear that the result has been to intimidate and discourage many a practicing clinician in the necessary exercise of his judgment. . . . Attempts to computerize diagnosis in internal medicine have been going on for some years, but they still fail to yield definite results in many cases, so that the physician still has to fall back on his judgment. If that judgment is constantly derogated . . . will he be able to accept the responsibility of using it when it is most needed? (1978b, pp. 14–15)

And to Holt's list of the computer's failures over the years to replace human judgment, we could add instances of the machine's rather poor performance vis-à-vis the thinking of clinical neurologists (Kleinmuntz, 1968), of chess players (Robinson, 1979), or interviewers (Weizenbaum, 1976), and of other clinicians generally (see Blois, 1980). In principle, however, there are few valid reasons why the computer, given its flexibility, large memory store, and extraordinary speed for processing computational as well as noncomputational information, should not in the foreseeable future outperform humans in most intelligent enterprises. During the interim period, of course, and perhaps for tasks such as psychotherapy (see Luborsky & Spence, 1971; Meehl, 1978), human judgment may be the best wheel in town for some time to come.

## Communicating Test Findings

After the relevant information about someone is processed and interpreted, it is usually communicated to the source that originally asked the questions about the person. This is the output component of the system depicted in Figure 1–1. It usually appears in the form of a "psychological report," and since various settings ask different questions about a person, there is no set format. Generally, though, psychological reports resemble the format presented in Table 4–4. These reports are most commonly written by personnel and clinical psychologists (or recently, by computers), who try to answer questions about an individual's suitability for a job or promotion, or advise a referral source about possible clinical resources in a community or about the possibility of psychotherapy.

But regardless of the setting for which the report is written, its content deals with the target person's past and present behavior, personality dispositions, interests and attitudes, and intelligence and abilities. These all are spheres of the person that can be addressed, with varying degrees of reliability and validity, by observations (chapter five), interviews (chapter six), inventories and questionnaires (chapter seven), projective techniques (chapter eight), and intelligence and ability tests (chapter nine). Table 4–4 offers some other characteristics of psychological reports.

First, and foremost, the psychological report, regardless of whether it is written by a psychologist or a computer (see chapter seven), must communicate its findings, interpretations, and recommendations as clearly and comprehensively as possible. According to S. J. Korchin,

**Table 4–4** The Psychological Report.

| Name of Person: | | Birth Date: | | Age: |
|---|---|---|---|---|
| Sex: | Marital Status: | | Education: | |
| Examined by: | Date: | | Place: | |
| Interviewed by: | | | | |
| Tests Administered by: | | | | |

*Questions Asked by Referral Source*
(Using the exact wording of the referral source, state the reasons why the referral was requested.)

*Observations and Interview Results*
(Describe the behaviors and attitudes expressed by the examinee before, during, and after testing. Use as many direct quotes as possible. Also use information supplied by other sources about the person.)

*Test Findings and Interpretations*
(Without being didactic, state your test results and interpretations as precisely as possible. Avoid using generalities that may be true of anyone.)

*Predictions and Recommendations*
(Briefly state predictions and recommendations warranted by the interview and test results.)

"it is a scientific document recording the results of an inquiry" (1976, p. 274). The report must be written at a level that the referring source will understand, without being didactic or patronizing, while at the same time it must convey an understanding of the person being studied. And as a scientific document, it should adhere as closely as possible to the findings obtained.

Second, the psychological report should describe the subject's characteristics as fully and specifically as possible, avoiding generalizations (see the discussion of the "Barnum" effect, chapter eight), stereotypes, and other banalities that could describe almost anyone. There is no need to administer tests in order to assert that "Mary has a tendency to impulsivity but is genuinely level headed." This statement could describe anyone, and as it stands, it tells us very little about Mary specifically.

Finally, it may be instructive to examine an inadequate psychological report. "Many of the problems of poor reports," according to Korchin's *Modern Clinical Psychology*, are due to "vague generalizations, overqualification, clinging to the immediate data, stating the obvious, and describing stereotypes" (1976, p. 278). And good clinical interpretation and report writing, Korchin continued, "requires a degree of risk-taking as well as creative intelligence, knowledge, and experience! All of these characteristics of poor and good psychological report writing, it should be noted, are the equivalents of poor and good communicating generally" (1976, p. 278).

## SUMMARY

Tests can be classified according to their structuredness, item format, performance modes, and other content and noncontent characteristics. Once they are properly prepared and administered, tests may be scored and interpreted by means of several types of scores and aids. These include derived scores, people charts, norms, and item-pattern-and-profile configural schemes. Other decision aids may also be used for information processing. These include expectancy tables, base-rates information, and bandwidth-fidelity considerations, all of which are intended to maximize the test's hit rates (valid positive and valid negative) and minimize their miss rates (false positive and false negative). Incremental validity studies are usually conducted to determine the worth of these tests and their interpretations, but such studies have generally not been favorable to personality testing.

Until 1954, one serious omission in the research on tests and their interpretive efficiency was the lack of attention paid to the test user as an information processor. But this research gap was more than filled by an important paper on the topic by Paul E. Meehl, whose theoretical and methodological analysis of the issue has inspired much research on the clinical-versus-statistical controversy. The bulk of the empirical evidence seems to support statistical and other formal modes of information processing, although it is apparent that there are many instances in which the mechanical combination of data is inadequate.

# FOR FURTHER READING

American Psychological Association. *Standards for psychological and educational tests*. Washington, D.C.: American Psychological Association, 1974. About to be revised, the *Standards* is an invaluable condensation of most testing concepts discussed in this chapter and the previous one.

Hogarth, R.M. *Judgment and choice: The psychology of decision*. Chichester, England: Wiley, 1980. For information on decision making and the pitfalls of human judgment, this excellent little book goes beyond the confines of clinical judgment discussed in the present chapter.

Holt, R.R. *Methods in clinical psychology. Volume 2: Prediction and research*. New York: Plenum, 1978. Written by an advocate of the "soft" side of the clinical versus statistical controversy, the book delineates the history and discusses the issues from its "clinical" perspective.

Lumsden, J. Test theory. *Annual Review of Psychology*, 1976, *27*, 251–280. A ground-breaking critique of classical test theory, this review inspired the new look in contemporary test theory. Irreverant and witty, this chapter is nevertheless difficult going.

Lyman, H.B. *Test scores and what they mean*. Englewood Cliffs, NJ: Prentice-Hall, 1971. Light reading, this little book contains a lot of information on the basics of interpreting test scores.

Meehl, P.E. (Ed.)., *Psychodiagnosis: Selected papers*. Minneapolis: University of Minnesota Press, 1973. A selection of thirteen papers by Meehl and some of his associates, this book is a must for anyone who is concerned about the technical issues confronting psychodiagnosticians. It is a fine sequel to Meehl's (1954) *Clinical versus Statistical Prediction* which, of course, is a classic polemic on this controversy.

Meehl, P.E. *Clinical vs. statistical prediction: A theoretical analysis and a review of the evidence*. Minneapolis: University of Minnesota Press, 1954. This is the original and classical polemic of the clinical vs. statistical controversy.

Weiss, D.J., & Davison, M.L. Test theory and methods. *Annual Review of Psychology*, 1981, *32*, 624–658. An excellent and easy-to-read updating of modern test theory.

# 5 Observation and Behavioral Assessment

Although this book is primarily about quantitative approaches to the study of personality, we shall consider research strategies that are not strictly quantitative: Observations, behavioral assessments, and interviews, three important assessment methods for the information processor of Figure 1–1, are the topics of this and the next chapter. These methods are used frequently in studying people, and when followed properly they can be scientific and can yield quantifiable data. We begin by defining observation and then consider the participatory roles of the observer. Finally, we devote the rest of the chapter to discussing direct and indirect observational methods and behavioral assessment.

## Observation Defined

Observation is basic to all scientific inquiry. In sharp contrast to the layperson's "just looking," or casual and haphazard perceptions, scientific observation requires deliberate and systematic search. Like casual observation, scientific observation is not infallible, but it is more *selective* and more *consistent with specific empirical aims*.

This selectivity, according to some psychologists (Weick, 1968; Wiggins, 1973), is important to scientific observation because it helps the observer focus on and edit particular aspects of the total observational scene. In turn, this selection affects what is recorded and what conclusions are drawn from the data.

Perhaps the most important feature of scientific observation is its consistency with empirical aims, a consistency that guides observational efforts along prespecified lines of inquiry. Our concern in this chapter is limited to those observational methods that are consistent with the empirical aims of the study of people. At a less-global level than personality assessment, this consistency with empirical aims refers to observations guided by the constructs of particular theories of personality; and at a still less global level, it refers to observations consistent with the formulated plans of a particular research project. Examples of these three levels, presented in order of increasing specificity, are observations that focus on people rather than on environmental objects; observations that view these people according to Freudian, Adlerian, or behavioral theories; and observations whose aim is to test specific elements of particular theories.

## Observer Participation

People can be observed on various levels of observer participation and in natural or controlled settings. Observer participation, as outlined in Table 5–1, may proceed in any one of four possible ways.

In the first method, the observer may be present in the setting, and the subject is aware of being studied. This is perhaps best illustrated by the clinical methods, in which the observations are made by the clinician while diagnosing or treating the patient. The clinician notes the subject's appearance, dress, articulated attitudes, and general demeanor, as well as his or her speech quality (e.g., level of vocabulary, appropriate choice of words) and quantity (e.g., rate of speech). While making these observations, the clinician compares the subject with others observed in the past and attempts to evaluate the similarities and differences. We shall describe this method in chapter six, when discussing the interview.

In the second method of observer participation, the observer is visible, but the subject is not aware of being studied, and the investigator blends in with the setting. This approach is best suited to the study of very young children or infants. The main disadvantage of this method is the vast amount of time necessary to sample behavior extensively. Therefore, it is often carried out by a close acquaintance of the subject or, in the case of a child, by a parent. But the parent is usually not a

**Table 5–1** Examples of Observer Participation.

| Observer | Subject | Example of Observation |
|---|---|---|
| Present and visible | Aware of being observed | Clinical interviewing |
| Present and visible | Unaware of being observed | Viewing very young children, or adults when deception is used |
| Present but not visible | Aware of being observed | Observing a subject in a training situation when the observer is out of sight (e.g., behind a screen) |
| Present but not visible | Unaware of being observed | Observer is concealed or uses audio or videotape recording techniques without the subject's awareness |

reliable observer because of an eagerness to "see" the offspring walk, talk, or use certain skills "on time." Such misperceptions may distort the observed behavior. Nor is an acquaintance or other family member a particularly good source of information. They, too, distort their observations and records, often because they want to hide or embellish the truth.

In the third method, the observer does not participate, but the subject is aware of being studied. In this arrangement the observer usually is behind a screen, recording behavior using audio and videotape recorders or cameras. This method is best used for viewing different subjects' reactions (or the same subject's varying reactions) to the same set of conditions or circumstances. In an interview training program, for example, it may be helpful, both to the student and the client, if such an interview is monitored by an experienced third person. Although the observer in these situations is usually behind a two-way viewing mirror, and therefore not visible, the student is very much aware of being studied. This is a disadvantage of the method because the student interviewer's behavior, and consequently that of the client also, will probably be influenced by the observer's felt presence.

The last method of observer participation is the best one. In it the observer does not participate, and the subject is unaware of being observed. It is the preferred method because it is least likely to influence or change the behavior under observation. It is the method of choice in developmental centers and child guidance clinics where the observer is situated out of the view of his or her subjects (or videotapes the scene) while they are engaged in play or problem solving. The games or puzzles can be especially contrived to elicit specific reactions or to enable the observer to view interpersonal behavior, depending on the observer's needs.

All of these forms of observer participation are more pertinent to direct than to indirect observations. For, as we shall indicate later in the chapter, indirect methods deal with the communication or traces of a person and his or her behavior and involve no firsthand viewing.

## Kinds of Observation

*Direct*, or firsthand, observation is a useful way to obtain information about people's behaviors in various situations, but it is not the only way. There are also *indirect* observational procedures. Some examples of indirect methods are self-report tests or questionnaires (see chapter seven), available records, and physical traces. These are used as substitutes for direct observation. But the advantage of directly viewing behavior is that the behavior can be viewed in the raw, as it were, while it is occurring. It is also independent of the subject's ability or willingness to report. But there are disadvantages also. It can change the behavior under consideration, and it is difficult to obtain representative samples of the behaviors being studied.

As we indicated in the last chapter, the best way to study people is to observe them directly in real-life situations. Thus, to assess either a person's ability to withstand stress or his or her anxiety level, the best way might be to expose the individual to stressful or anxiety-producing situations. Of course, to do this would be unethical. But as we shall see later in this chapter, given certain observational aids, this method does not have to be abandoned entirely. In the meantime, we shall concern ourselves with some direct observational modes.

## Direct Observation

Direct observation, then, is viewing behavior firsthand as it occurs. Direct observation is usually either *naturalistic* or *controlled*. Traditionally, naturalistic observation is described as a method of observing the actions of organisms in their indigenous, or native, surroundings. This is especially useful for viewing, with minimal interference, ongoing behavior in all its complexity. This method can be used by the clinician who visits patients' homes to study family patterns (for example, at dinner or at play). And although the clinician's presence may modify his or her subjects' behavior, he or she nevertheless has the advantage of obtaining firsthand impressions of them in their everyday environment.

Observations can also be *naturalistic* without being made at the subject's home. For example, during the diagnostic interview, the observer may note his or her client's behavior, appearance, and demeanor while they are conversing. The observations are naturalistic in that the diagnostician does not manipulate the environment or his or her client in any way to produce these reactions but simply lets things happen naturally in the office or in the hospital ward. This is the more common form of naturalistic observation in psychodiagnosis. Naturalistic observations are difficult to obtain without numerous hardware aids and rating scales to improve the precision of data collection and recordings. We shall discuss these aids later.

Controlled observations are usually made in the laboratory, where the psychologist can modify the surroundings according to his or her needs. The major distinction between controlled and naturalistic observations, although it is not always sharp, is that in naturalistic observations the psychologist waits for behavior to unfold; in controlled observations he or she creates circumstances and systematically introduces variables that elicit responses. These controls may be special arrangements of furniture and toys in a playroom, or they may involve systematically varying certain aspects of a situation (for example, amount of stress, noise level, number of persons). In either case, the psychologist strives to control conditions so that they are standard and replicable. We shall deal first with naturalistic observation.

## Naturalistic Observation

Since observers in naturalistic observations are at the mercy, as it were, of the behavior as it is occurring, they must devise techniques to enable them to capture the essential or research-relevant behaviors. Two techniques for doing so are *time sampling* and *incident sampling*. Time sampling is a method of observing behavior in short time periods distributed so as to enable a representative sampling of behavior. Because it records behaviors at certain times rather than continuously, time sampling has an advantage over other observation methods in that it permits viewing the subject in a variety of situations. The cumulative picture obtained over many short periods is more likely to typify the subject's behavior patterns than that collected in less frequent, but longer, periods. When using time-sampling procedures, the observer should schedule the time periods for observing the behavior. Depending on the behavior to be observed, these could be ten minutes in the morning, ten minutes in the afternoon, and again in early and late evening. It may be possible, for example, to record the incidence or duration of behavior during the first five minutes of each hour, or during variable time blocks, or several times during the day.

A behavior that might occur frequently, according to one source, is "clinging to an adult" (Cartwright & Cartwright, 1974, p. 87). Suppose that a child displays such clinging continuously. Rather than concentrating on observing just this behavior, the observer could use time sampling divided into two, fifteen-minute sessions in the morning and two more fifteen-minute sessions in the afternoon. *Which* time periods are most beneficial and *how many* time periods to use is not decided arbitrarily. The observer should base these decisions on previous experiences with the behavior and should strive to ensure that the time periods chosen coincide with a variety of activities.

Other behaviors typically studied are play preferences, friendship patterns, and aggression. Investigators (Barker, 1963; Barker & Wright, 1955) often sample a certain behavior extensively by making continual notations. An example of this is a study (Raush, Dittman, & Taylor, 1959) that used time sampling to observe six children in a residential treatment center. The children were observed during breakfast, arts and crafts periods, game activities, and when eating snacks before bedtime. During an eighteen-month observation period, the investigators were able to document considerable differences in the children's behavior patterns.

For behaviors in which discrete units can be tallied or counted, a record form should be prepared. Suppose a family therapist, interested in recording the *frequency* with which one sibling hits another, wanted to document this behavior. The record form might look like the one for sibling *A* in Table 5–2.

A similar type of record form could be prepared for observations of the *duration* of behavior. If the same therapist were interested in knowing how often sibling *B*, the victim of sibling *A*, provoked this hitting behavior, he or she could use the same time-sampling procedure. Besides recording the days' tallies, the therapist could also subdivide the day into half-hour intervals, selected for when both siblings would be together (mealtimes, going to school, and so on). Table 5–3 shows the record form that could be used for recording sibling *B*'s behavior.

The information obtained through either tallying frequencies or recording duration of behavior can be transferred to some kind of graph or chart, or it can be punched into IBM cards. A graph or chart provides convenient visual representations of the observed behavior. Card punching facilitates more sophisticated statistical analyses of the target behaviors (e.g., correlating sibling *B*'s provocative behavior with that of sibling *A*'s hitting; determining how much provocation elicits hitting; ascertaining what behaviors terminate the aggression).

**Table 5–2** Record for Frequency of Sibling *A*'s Hitting Behavior.

Name: Sibling *A*   Date: From February 1 to February 7

Observer: B. K.

Behavior Description: Hitting (e.g., any deliberate physical contact made with Sibling *B* using the hands or feet)

| Days | Tallies | Total |
|---|---|---|
| 1 | / / / | 3 |
| 2 | 卌 | 5 |
| 3 | 卌 / / / | 8 |
| 4 | / / / | 3 |
| 5 | 卌 / / | 7 |
| 6 | 卌 卌 / / / / | 14 |
| 7 | 卌 卌 / / | 12 |
| | Average per day for the week: | 7.4 |
| | Average per weekend (days 6 and 7): | 13 |

**Table 5-3** Record for Duration of Sibling *B*'s Provocative Behavior.

Name: Sibling *B*

Observer: B. K.

Behavior Description: Provocative behavior—any verbal or behavioral teasing—i.e., name calling, sticking out tongue, warning about possible retaliation by parent or self, showing off toy or other possessions

| Days | Time | Total Minutes |
|---|---|---|
| 1 | 8:00 – 8:30 A.M.<br>3:00 – 3:30 P.M.<br>6:00 – 6:30 P.M. | 90 |
| 2 | 3:15 – 3:30 P.M.<br>8:15 – 8:30 P.M. | 30 |
| 3 | 7:30 – 8:15 P.M.<br>9:30 –10:00 P.M. | 75 |
| 4 | 9:45 – 10:15 P.M. | 30 |
| 5 | 7:30 – 7:45 A.M.<br>3:20 – 4:00 P.M.<br>6:00 – 6:30 P.M. | 85 |
| 6 | 9:00 – 9:15 A.M.<br>3:30 – 3:45 P.M.<br>6:15 – 6:30 P.M. | 45 |
| 7 | 11:00 – 11:10 A.M.<br>12:30 –12:45 P.M.<br>2:35 – 2:55 P.M.<br>7:30 – 8:30 P.M. | 105 |

Average: 66 minutes per day

There are many behaviors, however, that do not easily lend themselves to time sampling. For example, such infrequent occurrences as stealing, setting fires, or displaying affection are not readily observed by this method. How could one possibly predict the time of their occurrence? It is equally difficult to observe certain rare and covert behaviors such as the development of attachments, compliance, or resentment.

For these behaviors, the method of *incident sampling* may be more appropriate because through it we can sample the incidents of selected behavior, rather than the times of selected behavior. For example, if in a clinic setting we want to see a person conversing with imaginary persecutors or to observe someone's tremor, either we must predict the time of these incidents and be present when they do occur, or we must wait for them to appear. Other difficult-to-predict events are emotional outbursts, repetitive rituals, and family quarrels. Hence this method may often be better for observing planned incidents in controlled settings than for observing those that unfold slowly in natural settings. Or it may be easier to see a display of altruism or generosity if a situation is rigged to elicit that behavior than to wait around for it to occur.

A variant of incident sampling, called the *critical incident technique* (Flanigan, 1954), requires recording instances of behavior especially favorable or unfavorable to a target behavior. Thus a teacher or parent may use the critical incident technique to record all instances of a child's pouting or aggression, for example. Or one could record one's own target behaviors (e.g., stuttering, smoking, boasting, and so on) and the circumstances that seem to surround the behavior. Using this technique on oneself has been employed particularly skillfully by behavioral assessment psychologists, who refer to it as *self-monitoring* (also self-recording and self-observation, see Ciminero et al., 1977; Thoreson & Mahoney, 1974), and who have devised a number of innovative recording tools such as stabilometric cushions to record movement and hyperactivity (Miklich, 1975) and cigarette cases with counters to keep track of the number of times a smoker has opened during a 24-hour period. Given the recent developments in miniature electronic circuitry, behavior that used to be inaccessible will no doubt be able to be recorded in the future.

One reason for using naturalistic observations is that it may be the best way to gather some kinds of data, such as counterproductive behaviors, reactions to natural disasters, or grief after a personal loss. Clearly these behaviors cannot be staged in the laboratory. Even if it were feasible to contrive situations eliciting these behaviors, the ethical problems created by placing intense stress upon subjects would preclude such experiments (see Bickman, 1976, p. 255).

Another reason for using naturalistic methods is that the content and circumstances of certain behaviors are as important as the behaviors themselves, and these cannot possibly be simulated in the laboratory. For example, one group of psychologists (Festinger et al., 1956) joined a "doomsday" sect that predicted the precise date that the world would end. These psychologists, whose identities were not disclosed to the sect, carefully observed and recorded the behavior of the sect members before, during, and after the time that it became clear that their prophecy would fail. How could they possibly have staged these circumstances in the laboratory?

**Naturalistic Personality Data.** Much information about a person in naturalistic observation is communicated nonverbally, in fact, it has been suggested by some researchers (Weitz, 1972; Wiens, 1976) that nonverbal communication is a more primitive part of the human behavior repertoire than speech and therefore antedates verbalization. For example, it has been observed that under stress—when a person's self-control is presumably minimal—people tend to resort to howling, crying, thrashing about, and grimacing, rather than talking. But there also are less-dramatic cues than those that occur under stress.

**Signs and Cues.** Personality assessors are forever watching for significant clues to personality. Some of the following have been reported (Webb et al., 1966): Tattoos are said to reveal that their bearers are or were associated with delinquent and antisocial behavior; good grooming differentiates college fraternity men from nonaffiliated college males; and more neatly dressed males within fraternities earn better grades than those who dress slovenly. Shoe styles within a particular socioeconomic status often are an index of life style. And the day-to-day changes of a person's color, style, and texture of clothing reflect that person's mood fluctuations and personality changes. Other observable personality-relevant cues are jewelry (type, quality, amount), automobile (color, type, length, adornments), sports preferences (amount of violence, extent of participation), and cigarettes (brand, length, filter), as well as other readily observable signs of body usage and care such as scars, missing fingers, calluses, and grooming.

Several other clues are commonly associated with particular personality disorders: chafed hands due to excessive hand washing typify the meticulously clean, obsessive-compulsive person; slovenly apparel typifies the schizophrenic individual; many Band-Aids on exposed limbs and other parts of the body typify a person with germ phobia; and multiple wrist scars typify the suicide-prone individual. To some astute observers, many of the above signs, when considered together with the expressive behaviors discussed in the next section, reveal a great deal about a person.

**Expressive Behavior.** Individual differences in *movements* and *gait* have been studied by personologists, who have observed that these movements tend to correlate closely with various temperaments. The vigorous person tends to go about his or her business rapidly and strenuously, and the lethargic one tends to linger and dawdle. Likewise, *gestures*, as Freud (1904/1938) noted in his clinical work, reveal emotional dispositions and are valuable aids for learning about attitudes and impulses. Moreover, from among more than a thousand different "steady" *postures* that the human body is capable of assuming, some persons adopt their own postural positions; and as with movements and gestures, the postures they choose reveal much about them. In short, as Mehrabian asserted, "our facial expressions, eyes, and postures, in addition to uncovered parts of our bodies, all communicate information about ourselves and our feelings" (1971, p. 9).

That various personality attributes are related to the way we express

**BOX 5-1**

## The Influence of Culture on Gestures

An interesting study by two investigators* demonstrated that gestures are highly influenced by cultural factors. They compared gestural behavior patterns in Italian and Jewish groups living under different as well as similar environmental conditions and concluded that these patterns are unmistakably distinguishable in terms of such characteristics as the part of the body used to form the movement and the laterality, symmetry, radius, rhythm, and tempo of the movement itself. The traditional gesture patterns tended to be absent in the assimilated comparison groups, who on the whole showed fewer gesticulations and whose gestures resembled more closely those typical of American groups. The graphic technique used to analyze gestural behavior is shown in the accompanying figure, where the relatively wide and sweeping gestures of traditional Italians (solid line, from 1 to 18 for each arm) are traced and compared with the narrower and less sweeping (broken line) gestures of traditional Jews. Both sets of tracings are based on observations made of persons while they were conducting ordinary conversations.

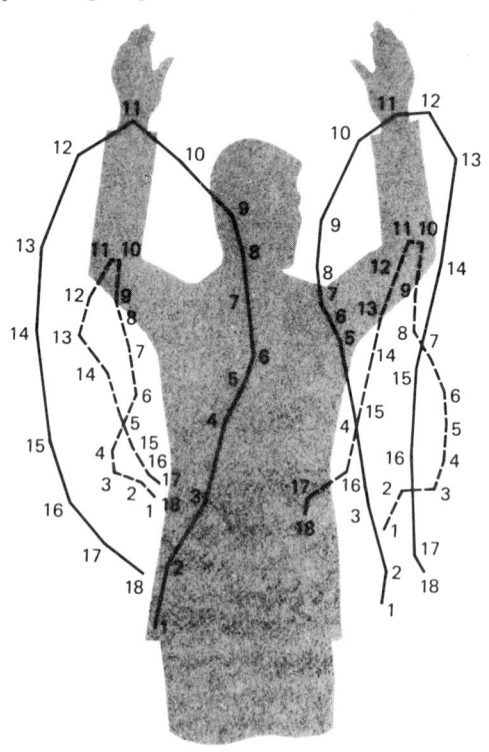

Efron, D. & Foley, J. P. A comparative investigation of gestural behavior patterns in Italian and Jewish groups living under different as well as similar environmental conditions. *Zeitschrift der Sozialforschung*, 1937, 6, 151–59. Also reprinted in T. M. Newcomb & E. L. Hartley (eds.) *Readings in social psychology*, N.Y.: Holt, Rinehart & Winston, 1947, pp. 33–40.

and carry ourselves has been expounded in scientific and popular publications by numerous authors (Fast, 1970; Hall, E. T., 1959, 1966, 1979; Mehrabian, 1971; Morris, D., 1977), and there are interesting hypotheses about these relations. Julius Fast, for example, in his book *Body Language* gave an example of how nonverbal gestures contradicted verbal messages in the case of the young woman who told her psychiatrist that she loved her boyfriend while nodding her head from side to side in denial (1970, p. 9). More recently, Edward Hall applied this concept to America's dealings in the Middle East: "To Americans, everyone is 'like us' underneath. It just isn't true. Anwar Sadat, for instance . . . when he's sitting and talking with someone . . . often has a hand on this person's knee. This touching is very Egyptian and it's an important part of communication in Arab culture" (1979, p. 45). And Desmond Morris, in his book *Manwatching: A Field Guide to Human Behavior*, wrote of the "teacher who barks at his pupils to 'sit up straight' [and] is demanding, by right, the attention posture that he should have gained by generating interest in his lesson . . . he feels more 'attended to' when he sees his pupils sitting up straight, even though he is consciously well aware of the fact that they have just been forcibly un-slumped, rather than genuinely excited by his teaching" (1977, p. 25).

Investigators who have bolstered their people-watching observations with somewhat more convincing evidence than the quasi-quantitative and clinical anecdotes cited above have been concerned with relating facial expressions and the emotions. One eminent psychologist, Silvan Tomkins, went so far as to state that emotions *are* facial responses (1962). In his view, expressed by Carroll Izard in a book reviewing the literature on facial expressions and emotion, "organized sets of facial responses are triggered at subcortical centers where specific 'programs' for each distinct emotion are stored" (1971, p. 187).

Subsequent research by Tomkins and his associates showed that, indeed, persons can successfully communicate emotions through facial expression, and more importantly for our purposes, judges can correctly identify them from posed photos. Figure 5–1 presents the ten primary emotions used in some of these studies and describes the labels and categories that apply to each picture (see Izard, 1972; Izard & Tomkins, 1966; Tomkins & McCarter, 1964).

Other studies have shown that facial expressions can be valuable nonverbal cues during a psychodiagnostic interview (Ekman, 1964, 1965, 1971; Ekman & Friesen, 1969, 1975) and that both the giving and the receiving of these cues in interpersonal contacts often occur at a low level of awareness to both giver and receiver (Buck et al., 1972). In one fascinating study (Dougherty et al., 1969), an earlier version of the photograph series shown in Figure 5–1 was shown to comparable groups of normals and schizophrenics in the United States and France.

128     Personality and Psychological Assessment

**Figure 5–1.** These ten photographs (slides) were projected on a screen, and subjects from widely varying cultures were able to correctly recognize the emotions being expressed by each of the persons portrayed. These fundamental emotions include (*a*) interest-excitement, (*b*) enjoyment-joy, (*c*) surprise-startle, (*d*) distress-anguish, (*e*) disgust-contempt, (*f*) disgust-revulsion, (*g*) anger-rage, (*h*) shame-humiliation, (*i*) fear-terror, and (*j*) contempt-scorn.

(Reproduced by permission from C. E. Izard. *The face of emotion.* Copyright © 1971 Appleton-Century-Crofts, Educational Division, Meredith Corp.)

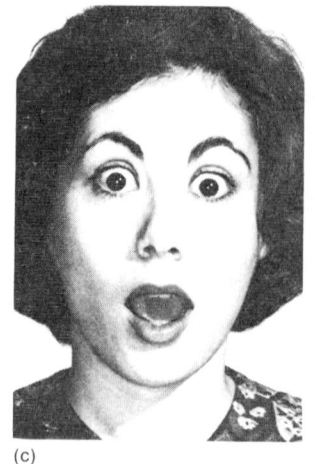

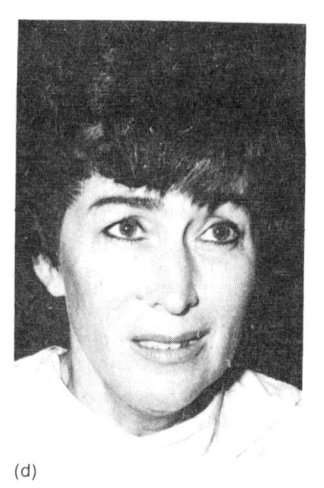

(a)

(b)          (c)          (d)

Each group was asked to label the facial expressions and later to place each photo in one of eight emotion categories. The results indicated that for both countries the normals performed these tasks with significantly more success than the schizophrenics did, thus suggesting a crucial difference between these two groups in their ability to decode correctly others' emotions.

In another study of facial expressions, John Cacioppo and Richard Petty (1981) used electromyographic (EMG) responses as measures of muscular activity over three muscle groups in the face. The purpose of recording the EMG responses was to obtain an index of subtle and intermittent or phasic expressions of emotion emitted by people as they awaited and intellectually processed a communication. Reasoning that empirical research has generally supported Darwin's initial observation

(e) (f) (g)

(h) (i) (j)

linking distinctive facial expressions to different emotions, these psychologists demonstrated that these facial muscle sites (e.g., the corrugator, zygomatic, and depressor) yielded a pattern of skeletomuscular response that distinguished positive from negative reactions to a persuasive communication. The implications of their findings are that they "illustrate (a) the utility and means of monitoring covert bodily response . . . in research on the *extent* and *affectivity* of ongoing information processing, (b) the possibility of tapping simultaneously cognitive and affective processes . . . by EMG measures, and (c) the application of the *model* of *skeletomuscular* patterning in studies of mental processes" (p. 453).

One psychiatrist (Marcos, 1979), addressing the problem of interpreting bilingual patients and their actions so that clinicians could evaluate their nonverbal messages, worked out an elaborate scheme for coding hand movements. The background for his study (also see Grand at al., 1977) was the observation that Spanish-speaking schizophrenic patients, with many problems in the English language, were noted to be much more tense when interviewed in English than in Spanish. An analysis of the content and vocal components of these interviews disclosed that in the English-language evaluations, the patients produced a series of changes related to verbal encoding difficulties. Marcos's main conclusion was that "by understanding motor activity that reflects central cognitive processing mechanisms, researchers may have the opportunity to study those 'invisible' mental processes through the monitoring of 'visible' motor acts" (1979, p. 943). Of course, the same analysis of nonverbal cues can be made among normals, the point being that people transmit clues about their thinking through measurable or visible behaviors.

At a somewhat less visible level of observation, Eckhard Hess studied the changes in the eye's pupil size as an index of change in attitudes and emotions (1965, 1975). In his laboratory at the University of Chicago, Hess measured changes in pupil size, by photographing the subject's eye with a movie camera, while the subject viewed slides on a screen. Later the film was projected onto a screen, and the pupil size was measured with a millimeter scale. Hess also used a pupillometer that scanned the eye and automatically measured the diameter of the pupil while the experiment was in progress.

In one set of early experiments, Hess (1965) showed that when men viewed a picture of a woman with large pupils, their own pupils dilated. Interestingly none of the men reported noticing the difference in pupil size, but when they were asked to describe the woman, they said that the woman in the picture with the large pupils was "soft," "more feminine," or "pretty." In another picture the woman, now with contracted pupils, was described as being "hard," "selfish," or "cold."

These experiments suggest that one uses another's pupil size as a source of information about that person's feelings or attitudes. In an experiment conducted by one of Hess's students, Janet Bare Ashear (Hess, 1975), she observed that she elicited more smiles from infants than some of her fellow workers did. It turned out that in the lighting of an average room, her pupils were larger than those of most other people. To learn whether this was a coincidence, she arranged to visit the homes of sixteen infants between the ages of three and three and a half months. Ashear made two visits to each home, and on each visit she interacted with the infant, talking and smiling, and recorded the number of times the infant smiled. On one of her visits she had her pupils artificially dilated with the drug phenylephrine hydrochloride. On the other visit she had her pupils artificially contracted with another drug, pilocarpine hydrochloride. Not only did the infants smile more often when Ashear's pupils were dilated, but an unexpected result was that the infants' mothers also responded differently to these pupillary differences. When her pupils were constricted, the mothers reported that she appeared to be "harsh," "hard," "brassy," "cold," "evasive," and "sneaky." When she came with dilated pupils, she was described as being "naive," "young," "open," "soft," and "gentle."

Expressive consistency and stability are also evident in handwriting. Personologists have, from time to time, been interested in the analysis of handwriting, or *graphology*, and even the computer has been called into service. *Pandemonium*, an early computer program devised by Selfridge (1959) to study sloppy handwritten letters, was used by one investigator (Doyle, 1960) to match handwritings with persons.

Although this research is more relevant to problems in pattern recognition and artificial intelligence than to personality assessment, the fact that the computer could correctly recognize 87 percent of the letters (human beings can recognize 97 percent) indicates that there are many identifiable handwriting attributes that can serve as diagnostic clues. Since both human beings and properly programmed computers can recognize and match handwritings with individuals, the implication for personality assessment is that unique expressive styles do exist. What the precise relationships are between these handwriting styles and personality, however, still remains to be discovered.

**Aids for Limiting Observational Error.** No matter how well trained the observer is and regardless of the pains taken to record the subjects' actions, obtaining an accurate picture of behavior as it emerges remains difficult. An observer can take in only so much at a glance and can listen to only one conversation at a time, even in relatively uncomplicated one-person settings. While listening, the observer may miss entirely the subject's simultaneous finger tapping, gum chewing, or scratching. But even if these are noticed, the observer may not have the opportunity to record them on paper; what is not recorded immediately is usually distorted upon later reconstruction. Now add to the setting another one, two, or three persons, and the observational burden becomes increasingly complex. In addition, when one person attempts to study another, they both are influenced by what has been aptly called "shared humanity" (Kaplan, 1964, p. 136).

*Hardware Aids.* The recognition of this complexity has led to the greater use of recording devices, which in turn has resulted in greater accuracy and completeness and has facilitated permanent record keeping as well. In some instances, hardware has enabled the removal of the observer as a third party in the setting (Figure 5–2), but in many other instances it has been used simply as a second party present during the action.

The most popular hardware item for verbal behavior has been the audiotape reporting-recorder. Clinicians who formerly spent much of their interview time taking notes have been quick to adopt tape recorders as substitutes.

**Figure 5–2.** Regardless of an observer's skill and training he will find it difficult to obtain an accurate record of behavior as it emerges. Because of this difficulty, hardware aids such as the cinema photographic unit shown here have been introduced into observational settings.

Although audiotape is ordinarily used to record verbal interchanges and videotape to record action, G. R. Patterson and his associates (1971) used audiotape to report both. In studies of family interaction patterns (who talks to or hits whom and when), Patterson narrated his observations into a chin microphone while viewing the behavior as it occurred. Usually Patterson stood behind a screen, sometimes inside a mobile unit.

Whichever device is used, the psychologist obtains a permanent record of both verbal and nonverbal action as it unfolds. This permits careful analysis later.

Other special hardware has also been used for observing and analyzing single and two-or-more-person behavior as it happens. The Interaction Chronograph, developed originally by an anthropologist (Chapple, 1940), has been used to study schizophrenics in a hospital ward (Chapple et al., 1963). This device, which resembles an elaborate electrical stopwatch, allows the observer not only to keep a record of the action (for example, gesturing or nodding), but at the same time he or she can also press buttons to record who acts toward whom, at which times, and for how long. The device also makes computations of these bits of information. The relevance of these records to psychodiagnosis rests on the sound assumption that the actions accompanying speech are as important as the speech itself.

*Rating Scales.* Another device for limiting human observer error is the *rating scale*, an instrument already encountered in the discussion on the quantification of symptoms. Ratings can be made either during observation or when tape recorders are used afterward to aid or supplant the observer.

Essentially, rating scales allow observers to quantify observations by evaluating traits numerically. Such quantification permits comparisons of specific traits by making it easier to collect data about many people in a variety of observational settings. One such psychiatric rating scale, shown in Figure 5–3, was devised by Wittenborn (1964) to quantify the symptoms of behavior pathology. Another scale, used by clinicians, ward attendants, and others familiar with patients, is the *Inpatient Multidimensional Psychiatric Scale*, or IMPS (Figure 5–4), developed by Lorr and his associates (1962, 1963, 1966, 1974). The IMPS was used in a study to collect ratings for 296 patients in about fifty hospitals. This study verified the existence of a number of psychotic disorders previously identified by other measurement procedures, such as Wittenborn's. Verification studies of this sort are important, for they provide sounder bases for the future uses of these and similar rating scales.

The *Q-sort*, which was developed by Stephenson (1953, 1980), is a rating method used more often for self-ratings than for rating others, but it is worth mentioning here because of its extensive use in personality

## Personality and Psychological Assessment

| Scale | I | II | III | IV | V | VI | VII | VIII | IX | X | XI | XII |
|---|---|---|---|---|---|---|---|---|---|---|---|---|
| 5. Face shows at least ordinary expressive variability in response to others.   0<br>Facial expression slow to change in response to others, i.e., shows ① more or less constant mood.<br>Facial expression does not change appreciably.   2<br>Face flaccid and without discernible change.   3 | | | | *1* | | | | | | | | |
| 6. Takes no apparent interest in activities, events, or circumstances   0<br>that do not concern him.<br>Apparently interested in activities that do not concern him but does   1<br>not show his interest directly.<br>Is obviously curious about activities that do not concern him.   ②<br>Excessively interested in activities that do not concern him, eavesdrops, makes persistent inquiry, intent on observing.   3 | | | | *2* | | | | | | | | |
| 7. No evidence of difficulty in making decisions.   0<br>Reports uncertainty and postponement of decisions.   ①<br>Cannot make decisions without advice or pressure.   2<br>Cannot make decisions.   3 | | | | | *1* | | | | | | | |
| 8. Shows ordinary ability to remember the names and functions of   0<br>other persons.<br>Shows some uncertainty concerning the identity or function of others   1<br>whom he should know.<br>Misidentifies persons with whom he is or has been in frequent contact.   2<br>No evidence that he has ability to identify persons.   ③ | | | | | | | | | *3* | | | |
| 9. Makes no effort to influence or control one or more other patients   0<br>Attempts to influence one or more other patients indirectly, e.g., by   1<br>comments, allusions, flattery, etc.<br>Attempts to control one or more other patients by direct comments   2<br>or requests.<br>Insists on controlling one or more other patients by any means at   3<br>his disposal. | | | | | | | | | | | | |
| 10. Age, education and physical status considered, patient's memory   0<br>for life history is good.<br>Patient's memory for life history events may be somewhat inferior.   ①<br>Patient's memory for major life events is conspicuously and   2<br>implausibly poor.<br>Memory faults are so conspicuous as to suggest that the patient is   3<br>suffering from amnesia or organic impairment or is deliberately withholding material or is mute, etc. | | | | | *1* | | | | | | | |
| 11. Can maintain interest in task at hand.   ⓪<br>Attention may stray from task at hand, but returns spontaneously.   1<br>Attention wanders and must be redirected to task.   2<br>No evidence that he can concentrate or direct thoughts, even with   3<br>help. | | | | | *0* | | | | | | | |
| Subtotals (p. 2) | | *2* | *3* | | | | | | | *3* | | |

**Figure 5–3.** A page from the Wittenborn Psychiatric Rating Scales Showing Items 5 to 11.

Source: Wittenborn, J. R. *Wittenborn Psychiatric Rating Scales.* New York: The Psychological Corporation, 1955 (Revised 1964). (Reproduced by permission)

research. Q-sort descriptions are statements printed on cards, and the observer's, or Q-sorter's, task is to describe someone by rank-ordering the statements according to their relative appropriateness to the individual being rated. As a typical distribution of descriptive cards, we present Figure 5–5, regarding which it may be noted that the assignment of cards, from least to most descriptive, is made according to the curve of normal probability. That is to say, fewer cards are piled at the extremes of the distributions, but they gradually build up toward the middle of the distribution. The pile numbers at the axis of Figure 5–5 are nominal, as they merely identify particular categories, ranging from "least descriptive" to "most descriptive." These judgments are made by ranking the cards according to their description of the attribute being rated or the individual being characterized. Thus the attribute or individual can be considered to have been ranked on an ordinal scale.

*Q*-sort ratings can be made by expert observers, acquaintances, or peers, or as indicated above, they can be self-rankings. Expert raters are usually persons who have had special training and experience in observing the characteristics they are rating. Peer raters usually are members of the same group or close acquaintances of the rated individual and have few qualifications beyond those that the ratees have. Self-ratings, as the name implies, are collected by individuals rating themselves. These ratings are subject to all the errors that affect the accuracy of self-report inventories (see chapters four and seven) and are also subject to those sources of error listed below as detracting from the worth of other rating methods. There have also been some statistical critiques of *Q*-sorts, but their details are beyond the limited scope of this book (see Block, J., 1960; Cronbach, 1970, pp. 585–588; Kerlinger, 1973, pp. 593–597; Nunnally, 1978, pp. 623–625).

---

COMPARED TO THE NORMAL PERSON
TO WHAT DEGREE DOES HE . . .

* 1. Manifest speech that is slowed, deliberate, or labored?

* 2. Give answers that are irrelevant or unrelated in any immediately conceivable way to the question asked or topic discussed?

    Cues: Do not rate here wandering or rambling conversation which veers away from the topic at issue (see item 4). Also, do not rate the coherence of the answer.

* 3. Give answers that are grammatically disconnected, incoherent, or scattered, i.e., not sensible or not understandable?

    Cues: Judge the grammatical structure of his speech, not the content which may or may not be bizarre.

  4. Tend to ramble, wander, or drift off the subject or away from the point at issue in responding to questions or topics discussed?

    Cues: Do not rate here responses that are obviously unrelated to the question asked (see item 2).

* 5. Verbally express feelings of hostility, ill will, or dislike of others?

    Cues: Makes hostile comments regarding others such as attendants, other patients, his family, or persons in authority. Reports conflicts on the ward.

* 6. Exhibit postures that are peculiar, unnatural, rigid, or bizarre?
    Cues: Head twisted to one side; or arm and hand held oddly. Judge the degree of peculiarity of the posture.

**Figure 5–4.** A Portion of the Inpatient Multidimensional Psychiatric Scale

Reproduced by special permission from Inpatient Multidimensional Psychiatric Scale by M. Lorr, D. W. McNair, C. J. Klett, and J. J. Lasky. Copyright 1966. Published by Consulting Psychologists Press, Inc.

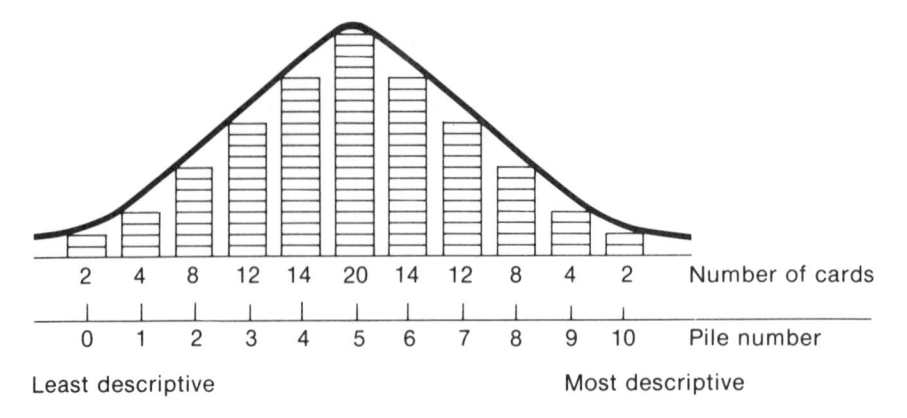

**Figure 5-5.** A Q-Sort Distribution of 100 cards, Arranged from Left to Right According to Whether They Are Least and Most Descriptive of the Trait in Question.

*Evaluation of Rating Methods.* In clinical research one frequently hears the phrase, "for lack of a better criterion, ratings were used." Ratings are particularly suited for obtaining criteria for personality tests because they are easier to find than objective and behavioral measures are. This is less true for achievement and aptitude testing. Therefore, establishing the reliability of these rating procedures is especially important. Unfortunately they are subject to numerous types of errors. The sources of these errors are many, and of course, removing them does improve the reliability of the ratings. This in turn enhances the ratings' correlation with their predictors; that is, it will enhance their validity coefficients because the coefficient's upper limit is determined by the reliability of the criterion (see chapter three).

One type of error common to ratings is called *leniency error*. It occurs when a judge consistently rates people too favorably. Perhaps he or she wants to maintain the reputation of being "nice," or the rater may simply be incapable of judging others harshly. There are also errors in the opposite direction, those made by the "hard" raters. In either case, the net effect is error.

Both the easy and the hard raters are consistent in their biases and therefore add systematic, or constant, error variance to their ratings. This error in either direction is not of any great concern as long as the same rater (or raters) judges individuals on the same attributes (or persons), because the direction of their bias is known. But if the biases in their ratings are not known and these ratings are compared with those obtained by other raters of the same attributes (or persons), then it is difficult to know whether these discrepancies indicate real changes or are just systematic error variance.

Another type of error is due to the *halo effect,* so named because it is caused by the influence of a rater's overall favorable (or unfavorable) impression of a person. For example, a rater may upgrade his or her ratings of a person because of a generally favorable impression or may downgrade the ratings because of a generally unfavorable impression. One consequence of the halo effect is that spuriously high correlation coefficients are obtained between seemingly unrelated traits, because the person is rated indiscriminantly on all of them. The general effect of the halo error, according to Cronbach (1970, p. 572), is that it obscures the pattern of traits within the individual, because it displaces the ratings for each behavior which make up the average rating for all the behaviors.

Yet another source of erroneous ratings is the *ambiguous* description of the characteristics to be rated. For example, such terms as "maladjustment," "leadership," and "cooperativeness" are often vaguely defined and are therefore variously interpreted by different judges, resulting in ratings useless for practical or research purposes.

Ambiguity error also occurs when verbal descriptions of scale positions are unclear. For example, is "substantial" more or less of something than "moderate"? Is "large" more of something than "big," or is it less? Ambiguity error also is caused by poorly constructed scales that consist of items about which the rater has no information. Such ratings, if obtained, obviously are meaningless, and the judge should be given the option of indicating his or her relative or total unfamiliarity with the trait or person in question.

One additional type of error, called the error of *central tendency,* is also important for the effect it has on the unreliability of ratings. It arises because of raters' tendencies to stay close to the center of a scale and to avoid using the extreme positions. The statistical effect of this error is to reduce the variability of the ratings, which in turn spuriously decreases the magnitude of their reliability. Reducing the variability of the ratings also makes it difficult to discriminate adequately among persons so rated.

In addition to the errors described above, three others shall be mentioned briefly because they are so common. One of these is the *proximity error,* which is caused by a judge's tendency to describe behaviors appearing close together on the printed rating sheet as more alike than he or she would if these descriptions were physically farther apart. A second common error is the *logical error,* occurring when the rater judges a person similarly on characteristics that he or she feels are logically related to one another. The third error is called the *contrast error* which, according to one source, arises because of the "habit of raters to place others on a scale in contrast to their own characteristics" (Helmstadter, 1970, p. 377).

There has been a somewhat different critique of personality ratings in recent years, which holds that ratings are fictions of the rater's mind rather than reflections of the real world of personality traits (D'Andrade, 1965, 1974; Shweder, 1975, 1977a, 1977b). One critic concluded that "the correlations [among personality rating and inventory scales] are primarily an artifact of the rater's or the questionnaire taker's cognitive structure, and not a reflection of the real world" (D'Andrade, 1974, p. 181). Another critic carried this argument a step further and questioned the whole theory of individual personality differences because these differences were based on "conceptually biased judgments [created by] an 'illusion' of . . . actual behavior . . . " (Shweder, 1975, pp. 455–456).

The logic and data of this critique have been challenged by others (Block et al., 1979) who have maintained and provided evidence to bolster their claim that personality does reflect the real world of traits and individual differences. Although their arguments are psychometrically complex, their conclusion is not: "There are preliminary indications that these differences [obtained from personality ratings and questionnaires] are reliable and can provide additional perspective on the processes involved in the effort to develop, conceptualize, integrate, and apply one's psychological understanding of people" (p. 1071).

***Improvement of Rating Methods.*** It is generally agreed that certain precautions could be taken in constructing and using ratings that would contribute to their greater reliability and validity. Some of the recommendations for improving the ratings are the following (Helmstadter, 1970, pp. 378–382; Thorndike & Hagen, 1969, pp. 434–444):

1. Rating scales should be used only to measure those traits for which more rigorous forms of testing are not available.
2. Careful attention should be given to the structure of the rating format in order to ensure unambiguous items.
3. Raters should be qualified to rate. They can become qualified by learning about the subjects in question, by learning the techniques required, and by learning the terminology used on the rating format.
4. It is essential, also, to interest the raters in participating in the task. (In another context, two researchers [Gustafson & Orne, 1963] showed that participants in an experiment can be so motivated by special instructions.)
5. The qualities to be rated should be stated clearly and specifically, and examples of the behaviors to be rated should be given.
6. Only raters who are thoroughly familiar with the individual in the situations to be rated should be asked to rate that individual.
7. The ratings of several raters should be pooled when there is more than one rater.

8. Raters should be properly trained to use the rating instrument. Such training should include practice observations of the subject. These observations, will give the raters an opportunity to ask about the meanings of terms, categories, and requirements, and they will allow the raters to observe the subject in pertinent settings.

## Controlled Observations

Although the personality assessor is not often able to control the background against which behavior occurs, when it is possible, controlled observations are superior to naturalistic methods. When the observer creates the conditions in which responses are given, he or she will know which stimuli or events are responsible for consequent behaviors. Moreover, when the observer structures the situation according to particular specifications and investigative aims, he or she will not need to wait for the behavior to occur. There are several procedures for making controlled observations, and we shall describe one of them.

**Situational Stress Condition.** One method of observing people in the same stress condition, controlled by the observer, was used in a personality assessment program developed by the Office of Strategic Services (OSS) during World War II. Although the purpose of this program was to select men for military intelligence work, variations of these conditions have been used to evaluate an individual's susceptibility to personality disorganization under stress.

One device for introducing stress is the "blown bridge" problem (Office of Strategic Services, 1948). Soldiers were given the task of reconstructing a miniature blown-up bridge but were not given enough long boards to do so. In addition, they were criticized, harassed, and ridiculed so that they were not able to complete the job. The main purpose of the contrived situation was to view the subjects' reactions to stress and to see whether their leader could size up the situation and channel the men's ideas into an effective plan of action (Figure 5–6).

### Critical Comment

Naturalistic observations have much to recommend them: they yield data firsthand and therefore produce a picture of what a person does, not what that person says he or she does. Exterior cues and expressive behavior communicate a great deal about people, and when such behavior is viewed firsthand and with minimum constraints placed on

## BOX 5-2

## Reliability and Validity of Observational Methodologies

Reliability and validity problems confront all data collection methodologies. Observational techniques reduce some of these difficulties because the activity is being recorded by the researcher as it happens, rather than being reported by a respondent whose memory may have faded or who lacks interpretational concepts. Additionally, bias may be reduced because the researcher is less emotionally involved than the respondent.

For several reasons, observational techniques are vulnerable to the problems of unreliability and invalidity. The most important of these are

1. *Choice of research settings.* Lack of access to some research settings, or the use of a very small number of observational locations, increases the chance that selected settings are not representative.
2. *Sampling within research settings.* Since the observer usually observes only a fraction of the total activity, choices of time and activity to observe can provide unrepresentative data.
3. *Observer-caused effects.* Since the observer is necessarily a part of the environment being observed, his presence may have the unintended and unobvious consequence of changing the behaviors being studied.
4. *Failures of interpretation.* Observers may misinterpret activities being studied because they have personal biases or lack appropriate concepts for classifying and recording information.

Some of the many tactics that have proven successful for reducing problems of reliability and validity are

1. *Recording raw data as soon and completely as possible.* Taking notes of and even tape recording conversations are often less disruptive than might be expected. When the topic being discussed is not sensitive for the respondent, these techniques may actually encourage more complete answers because the respondent realizes that he is being taken seriously. When concurrent note-taking is not possible, notes should be created as soon as possible while memories are still clear.
2. *Writing up and indexing notes as soon as possible.* An indexing system with appropriate categories should be used (and revised when necessary) so that observations can be located when the researcher is sorting out data for final reports.
3. *Breaking some observations into units which minimize emotion or judgment.* For instance, for each observed situation where two nudists walked past one another, did they look

*(continued)*

Observation and Behavioral Assessment   141

> **BOX 5–2**  (*Continued*)
>
> aside, make eye contact, or observe one another's bodies?
> 4. *Limiting emotional involvement in the situation being observed.* Friendships and personal commitments should be avoided to reduce potential bias. Observers often experience problems in "going native."
> 5. *Creating cross-checks on the data.* For instance, a second observer may independently observe the same phenomena. Also, multiple methodologies such as use of observation and informants can be used to study a single problem; or a search can be made for inconsistencies in observational data collected by a single researcher.
>
> **Source:** Eckhardt, W. K., & Ermann, M. D. *Social research methods: Perspective, theory, and analysis.* New York, Random House, 1977, pp. 266–267.

**Figure 5–6.** In this so-called blown bridge problem, subjects were observed under a stress condition in which they were called upon to reconstruct a bridge but were not supplied enough boards of sufficient length to do so. (Courtesy Donald W. MacKinnon)

Source: Office of Strategic Services. *Assessment of Men.* New York, Rinehart, 1948, p. 695.

its occurrence, the observer does not not need to cope with his or her subjects' (or their relatives') rationalizations or explanations of actions.

Naturalistic observation need not occur in the client's milieu. Behavior noted during an interview, for example, of a client's general appearance, attitude, and bearing is considered naturalistic within the scope of our definition. Such observations provide valuable clues to personality which can be either confirmed or discredited by subsequent inquiry, psychological testing, or counseling.

Naturalistic observations do have disadvantages, however. Because naturalistic methods avoid placing constraints on what is viewed, they yield data difficult to reproduce and thus violate one of the basic tenets of scientific observations: the standardization of conditions, materials, and procedures.

Furthermore, naturalistic observation relies heavily on the ingenuity of the human observer. More skillful observers will be better than others in noting certain behaviors. Moreover, human observers' recordings of behavior are biased by their own expectations. Rosenthal (1969, 1976) and his colleagues demonstrated that informing experimenters of predicted experimental findings can cause biased observational recordings in tasks such as rating the amount of success or failure shown in photos of faces (Rosenthal et al., 1964). More recently, O'Leary and his associates (1975) showed that observational recordings can be influenced by an experimenter's comments about his or her expectations regarding the experiment (also see Kent & Foster, 1977).

Another disadvantage of naturalistic methods is that a human observer's own behavior is variable over the course of observing. He or she may become bored and less conscientious as time passes, or may become increasingly interested as the content of what is being observed becomes more meaningful or corroborates more with the hypotheses being tested.

Contributing to the observers' disagreement, and hence to inaccurate observation, is the fluctuation of the behavior under study. Since personality and behavior observations consist of response tendencies, moods, dispositions, and symptoms that are highly probabilistic rather than all-or-none, the behavior being studied can be expected to change from time to time.

Perhaps the major problem of naturalistic observation is that it is *reactive*. That is, the observer can change the subjects of observation simply by his or her presence in the situation. For example, in the "doomsday" situation cited earlier, the investigators joined the group as ordinary members. This raised the methodological problem of whether their membership and interaction with the other members changed the characteristics of the sect. Whereas some psychologists (Bickman, 1976) believe that this can be a great problem, others

(Kerlinger, 1973; Weick, 1968) are not convinced of its importance. Kerlinger (1973, pp. 538-539) suggested that this was not a severe problem, except to the uninitiated who believe that people will react differently, even artificially, when observed. He cited the belief that a teacher under observation, especially by supervisors, will rise to the occasion. Kerlinger failed to point out, however, that the teacher cannot be "creative," or "adaptable" if he or she does not have the ability to do so.

To counterbalance the effects of fluctuating observer and subject behavior, many observers use special hardware and rating scales. But these aids, although they do simplify many aspects of the observer's task, do not force behavior to occur; to accomplish that, the observer must manipulate the subjects and the conditions of the setting to be observed.

Rating-scale procedures, with the increased constraints that they impose on the observer, partially solve the problem of viewing relevant behaviors because they prescribe the specific behaviors to be noted. Furthermore, because rating scales are quantifiable and therefore can be standardized, they allow comparisons among individuals (or among attributes of the same individual) viewed by different observers (or by the same observer at different times). But rating scales also have their own problems, which in turn require careful attention.

Controlled observations do have an advantage over naturalistic methods in that they highly constrain and therefore control the subject matter and the environment under investigation. By forcing data to emerge, controlled observations yield highly pertinent information. Such data allow comparisons with observations made under similar conditions; they also permit the observer to introduce subtle stimuli, which in turn may yield subtle discriminations among relevant behaviors.

As the observer participates more actively in the observational procedure, however, he or she loses some of the naturalness of *in situ* observations. The question then becomes, "To what extent are these observations relevant to real life?" As we move to more controlled observations, we also run the risk that our subjects will detect our contrivances, and thus our intentions and objectives. This, too, is a disadvantage that must be considered when using this method.

There is a problem in both the naturalistic and the controlled methods when the observations require high degrees of inference. This often happens when the observational assignment calls for the interpretive labeling, or judgment, of globally observed behavioral units, or when complete interactional units of behavior are to be reported. Thus, observations that require labels such as authoritarianism, impulsiveness, rigidity, and dominance require a higher level of inference than those that require reporting only, for example, physical contact or repetitive behavior. These inferential leaps, as they are sometimes called, tend to decrease the reliability of the observations because they make interjudge agreement more unlikely. And, by the same reasoning, when a greater observational burden is placed on the observers, such as when they view complex interactions, then interjudge agreement may also suffer. If interjudge agreement is low, then these observations, which are often used as criteria in validity studies, lower the validity coefficients obtained between the predictor and the criterion validities.

Some of these problems and risks are overcome when observations are made by indirect procedures, as the remaining portions of this chapter suggest.

## Indirect Observation

Earlier in this chapter we defined direct observation as the firsthand viewing of behavior as it occurs. We noted also that it can be either naturalistic or controlled and that in other than ideal conditions, it entails contact with the subjects under consideration. Indirect observation, in contrast, circumvents firsthand or direct interaction with the subjects of study. Therefore, it is less *obtrusive*; that is, it is less likely to interfere with its subjects in the observational setting. The advantage of unobtrusive measures is that the data they yield are minimally *reactive*, in that they cause fewer measurement errors than do direct observation measures in which the respondents are aware of being tested (guinea pig effect). Nonreactivity also minimizes the effects of the observer's variability as an instrument, because the observer is not actively obtaining unobtrusive data. The observer usually happens upon these data which, according to the authors of the imaginative book *Unobtrusive Measures: Nonreactive Research in the Social Sciences*, do not require the cooperation of a respondent, and the observers do not themselves contaminate the response (Webb et al., 1966, p. 2).

Examples of unobtrusive measures to be discussed in the next sections are data gleaned from personal documents, archival records, and physical traces. We do not offer these measures as alternatives to more direct methods of observation or to questionnaires and other tests, and some people may not consider them observational methods at all. But whatever we call them, they are some of the methods that can be used to study people. And many methods are better than one. "Once a proposition has been confirmed by two or more independent measurement processes, the uncertainty of its interpretation is greatly reduced" (Webb et al., 1966, p. 3).

## Personal Documents

The use of personal documents to study personality is not new. It was most thoroughly explored by the late Gordon W. Allport and his students (1942, 1965). Personal documents include such spontaneously written materials as autobiographies, diaries, letters, open-ended questionnaires (not standardized tests), verbatim recordings of confessions, and various other literary compositions. As personality measures, they can be used as one other source of information about the individual, in conjunction with data from direct observations, interviews, and paper-and-pencil tests.

Spontaneously written productions differ from elicited story-telling techniques, such as those demanded by the Thematic Apperception test (TAT), because the motivations for writing them differ. Allport (1961) listed several possible reasons that persons have for writing personal documents, including exhibitionism, literary appeal, personal perspective, catharsis, desire for immortality, and scientific interest, any of which could lead to omissions or elaboration of critical information. Recognition of these motives is important for analyzing personal documents because it acknowledges a methodological problem: "Unless we know how and why the document came into being, we cannot decide how much trust to place in it, nor can we evaluate its completeness of coverage" (Allport, 1961, pp. 402–403).

*Content analysis* is the method of observation used to study systematically written communications. Instead of directly observing people's behavior or asking them to respond to scales, the investigator studies the communication itself and asks questions about it. This form of analysis was defined by Berelson as "a research technique for the objective, systematic, and quantitative description of the manifest content of communication" (Berelson, 1954, p. 489). As it is traditionally used to analyze personal documents, this method selects the categories based on clinical inference from general theory, counts the text units falling into each category, and quantitatively expresses the results as frequencies within each category.

One of the earliest detailed reports on the use of a systematic content analysis to study people was by Gordon W. Allport (1942, 1965, 1966), who interpreted some three hundred letters written by a woman to two young friends. *Letters from Jenny* (Allport, 1965) was the resulting book, a collection of letters written by this middle-aged woman over an eleven-year period. Most of the letters pertain to Jenny's preoccupation with her relationship with her son. As a series of personal documents, Jenny's letters are fascinating reading; she was a highly literate correspondent beset by strong hatreds, fears, conflicts, and jealousies. Her letters clearly reflect these mental states and follow her through various stages of personality disintegration both before her entry into, and during her final years in, a mental institution.

Professor Allport originally had these letters published in 1946 and used them from time to time in his classes in exercises exemplifying theories of personality. A familiar exercise for Allport's students was to analyze the letters' content from the perspective of various theories, such as those of Freud, Adler, and Jung, which is also our interest here.

In his first report on the *content analysis* of these letters, Allport (1942) described a method in which thirty-nine clinical judges listed the essential characteristics of Jenny as they saw them. These characteristics were expressed by means of 198 adjectives grouped into several "common-sense" traits (e.g., quarrelsome, suspicious, aggressive, sentimental). This content analysis was then extended by Baldwin (1942) to include a more elaborate and quantitative scheme. Using a "personal structure analysis," Baldwin instructed raters to count how often particular categories occurred and to correlate those that clustered together. By this method, Jenny was described rather well using the clusters of adjectives that appeared most often in the text. The important thing to note about a personal structure analysis, when compared with a content analysis of the same text by inspectional or clinical methods, is that the personal structure analysis, a more quantitative approach, yields greater amounts of information about the person under study.

More recently, a still more quantified kind of content analysis was performed by a computer. Using a computer program designed to analyze the content of English text, called the "General Inquirer" (Dunphy et al., 1965) a student in one of Allport's personality seminars at Harvard (Paige, 1966) analyzed Jenny's letters. Based on this computer interpretation of the text and a subsequent factor analysis of adjectives identified as describing Jenny, eight highly stable factors were discovered. These factors were similar to those that had appeared in Allport's and Baldwin's earlier studies. Computerized content analysis is not yet routinely used for information processing. Such use awaits the further technical development of computer understanding of text sentences (Simmons, 1973) and natural language processing (Harrison, 1973; Schank, 1973; Winograd, 1973).

Personal documents can also be used to validate other methods of observation and assessment. Kerlinger (1973) gave an example of validating a scale to measure attitudes toward Jews by asking a group of people to write short essays on Jews. Attitudes such as these are difficult to validate by traditional measures because there are few external criteria against which to check their validity. Nonetheless, although most people may be wary of admitting to anti-Semitic, or similar, attitudes, "it is not easy to conceal anti-Semitism if one has to write a short essay on Jews" (Kerlinger, 1973, p. 533). It is important to note, however, that Kerlinger's example was more obtrusive, and hence more reactive, than Allport's example. Whereas Jenny was not asked to write her letters and was not aware that they would be used to study her, Kerlinger's subjects were asked to write essays and therefore were aware that some aspect of behavior was being studied. But there are also problems with the less obtrusive methods, as we indicate below.

**Critical Comment.** Several questions must be raised in interpreting personal documents, the main ones being: "Who says what, to whom, how, with what effect, and why?" (Babbie, 1975; Holsti, 1969). These are important questions because, as we noted earlier, some persons write personal documents in order to deceive. This deception may be conscious or unconscious and is probably no different from faked responses on self-report tests. Crucial facts may be omitted or elaborated, and new ones added, depending on the intent of the communication. Furthermore, the topics selected may be determined in unknown ways by the attributes or needs of the intended recipient or by the personal motives of the writer. Even the content of Jenny's letters, above, is suspect, even though she was not asked to write them and had no way of knowing that they would be used to study her. Very simply, her motive was to impress upon her two young recipient friends that she was a good person and a loving, but wronged, mother.

According to most depth theories, the early years of life are the most important for fixing certain personality patterns. Accounts of these early years are hardly ever available in personal documents. Some writers record their reminiscences about infancy and childhood, but such recollections are fraught with inaccuracies and confabulation. That is not to say that these memories of events and people do not have their value—because like dreams and free associations, they may disclose valuable clues to present personality patterns—but as objective histories, they are grossly deficient.

The content analysis of personal documents has other problems as well (see Babbie, 1975). For one thing, the content analysts may have difficulty developing and counting methods that adequately represent their theoretical concepts. In one sense this is no different from the problem the test constructor faces in constructing a standardized test, but in another sense, the analyst has less freedom and flexibility because he or she has less control over what is written in the document. The interpreter must work with the available document and cannot dictate its format.

Another problem of content analysis is whether to interpret the manifest or the latent content of the communication. The coding scheme for each of these is quite different. To determine, for instance, how "erotic" certain communications are, the interpreter simply needs to count the number of times the word "love" appears, or its average number of appearances per page, and then to add up the frequency of these and similar words. Alternatively, the content analyst can code the latent content by looking for the message's hidden meanings and then making a global judgment of its "erotic" content. The first method has the advantages of ease and reliability of coding, and it specifies how eroticism was measured. Its validity is questionable, however, because it is unlikely that eroticism can be assessed by the number of occurrences of the word "love." Global judgments, on the other hand, lower the reliability because, as we indicated earlier, when higher-level inferences are required, interjudge reliability suffers because different judges apply different standards and definitions. A passage that might be regarded as "erotic" by one may not appear to be so by another. Even one observer or coder may vary from one time to the next his or her application of these standards.

There are also some important advantages to using personal documents which counterbalance the disadvantages. First, they save time and money. The documents are already available, and a single researcher can undertake the content analysis. No test needs to be designed, nor does an elaborate observational situation need to be contrived. The researcher needs merely to gain access to the material to be coded in order to program it for computer content analysis. Second, there is an economy that extends beyond the mechanics of coding and analyzing. For example, if a tester discovers flaws or omissions in a test or if an observer has not properly recorded or controlled certain aspects of the observational setting, either one may be forced to repeat the whole research project with all the attendant costs in time and money. In analyzing personal documents, obviously no such costs are incurred.

The most important advantage of content analyzing documents is its unobtrusiveness. That is, the content analyst, who in this case is also the observer, has no effect on the subject being studied. This is particularly true if the observer has had no contact with the writer of the communication. This feature, as we already noted, is important because it minimizes errors caused by the reactions of the document's author. Clearly, analyzing Jenny's letters had no effect on either the letters' content or Jenny's behavior and fate.

### Archival Records

Useful personal data that are even less obtrusive, and hence less reactive than written documents, are the archival records maintained by governments and schools. These can be the official actuarial tallies kept of births, marriages, deaths, graduations, and grade point averages; or they can be the unofficial jottings and observations found in school yearbooks. Both forms of personal data are unobtrusive because they are unintentional by-products of living; they are nonreactive because the subjects under investigation are usually not aware of being observed and therefore are minimally affected by such scrutiny.

Several examples of using official actuarial data for personality studies were provided by Webb and his associates (1966). One example is the classic study on hereditary genius by Galton (1869), who used archival records to determine the eminence of subjects defined as "geniuses," and also studied other records to find out how their relatives reacted to this eminence. Archival data were collected for 997 men in 300 families, including judges, statesmen, military leaders, scientists, literary figures, and persons from the arts. Among his many findings, Galton reported that the 997 men had a total of 739 relatives who had also achieved eminence. Moreover, the closer the degree of relationship was, the more eminent relatives there were. He also reported more detailed information; for example, many of the judges postponed marriage until they had been elevated to the bench.

Another example of using official actuarial data is a later study by Galton (1872), who utilized longevity data to investigate the efficacy of prayer. He reasoned that if prayer were efficacious and if members of royal houses were the persons whose longevity was the most widely and frequently prayed for, then they should have lived longer than others. His findings did not support the normative expectations of his day: the mean ages at death for royalty, men of literature and science, and gentry were, respectively, 64.04, 67.55, and 70.22 years.

There is an example of using unofficial archival data as information about persons in a study by Barthell and Holmes (1968), who used high school yearbook entries to study the prepsychopathological personalities of schizophrenics and hospitalized neurotics. This form of research, which by some has been called retrofollowed (Meehl, 1971) or followback (Sundberg, 1977) investigation, focuses on one empirically or theoretically salient feature of the archival data. The Barthell and Holmes study focused on the number of activities listed for each student in the high school yearbook. By tallying the frequencies of activities, these investigators demonstrated that the high school yearbook entries of persons who were later diagnosed as either schizophrenic or neurotic differed from those for the normal control group in that the schizophrenics or neurotics had participated less in athletic and social activities, having been more withdrawn in adolescence than the normals were. Although there have been some questions about the adequacy and choice of controls in this study (Schwarz, 1970), the method has been strongly defended in other articles (Meehl, 1970, 1971).

## Physical Traces

An indirect observational method that is unobtrusive and also yields nonreactive data is the study of physical traces that survive past behavior. Physical traces can be used as evidence of human behavior, according to a study by C. P. Duncan (1963), who demonstrated that the popularity of museum exhibits can be determined by noting the number of worn vinyl tiles around them. Wrightsman (1969), in an exceptionally fine use of physical traces, studied lawbreaking among supporters of "law-and-order" election candidates (as determined by their bumper stickers) by examining the number of automobiles whose windshields displayed vehicle permits. He then computed a simple correlation between the law-and-order bumper stickers and the windshield vehicle permits and learned that lawbreaking (expired permits) was more prevalent among the law-and-order types than among those who had no such bumper stickers.

The main advantage of physical evidence information is its inconspicuousness, because the information to be analyzed is produced without the creator's awareness of its being used by the researchers. Like personal documents and, to a greater extent, like archival records, physical evidence is not affected by the errors arising from awareness of measurement, role selection, or observer effects, or by the interaction between the observer and the observed.

But there are some problems with the methods based on "erosion." For example, there is the problem of whether the erosion itself attracts people to places, just as people driving in deep snow are more likely to follow the tracks of previous cars than to create their own tracks.

But perhaps a more difficult question to answer is how the investigator can transform physical traces into meaningful indices of behavior. The physical evidence needs to be interpreted in accordance with the known population levels. How many footsteps, for example, does it take to wear down a vinyl tile or a carpet? And what is the usual number of expired vehicle permits in a large sample of automobiles without law-and-order bumper stickers?

To sum up this section on indirect observations, we note that the unobtrusiveness and nonreactivity of these measures offer certain advantages over direct observations. Personal documents, for example, usually do not require the active participation of their writers, and thus their subjects will react less to real or imagined observational conditions. Likewise, archival records and physical tracings are usually either written or deposited inadvertently. But all of these methods have their drawbacks as well.

## Behavioral Assessment

Behavioral assessment is the newest and most rapidly growing personality assessment technique, and the interest in it is probably an offshoot of the popularity of behavioral therapy. It has its roots in classical and operant conditioning, and it invariably requires direct observation in more or less naturalistic circumstances. Its differences from other assessment techniques are that "most of the traditionally available personality methods are of little utility to the behaviorally oriented clinician . . . [because] . . . a different paradigm for assessment has been developed" (Goldfried, 1976, p. 281). The reader who wants more information about behavioral assessment should consult any of several handbooks (Ciminero et al., 1977; Hersen & Bellack, 1976; Honig & Staddon, 1977; and Mash & Terdal, 1976) or primary sources on this subject (Azrin & Powell, 1968; Azrin et al., 1968; Bandura, 1961, 1969; Bijou & Peterson, 1971; Cautela, 1968; Goldfried, 1976; Goldfried & Sprafkin, 1974; Gottman & Leiblum, 1974; Kanfer & Phillips, 1970; Kanfer & Saslow, 1969; Mikulas, 1970; Mischel, 1968; Stuart, 1970; and Ullmann & Krasner, 1975). Our discussion below only touches the surface of this new subject.

### Behavioral versus Traditional Assessment

The main differences between the behavioral and the traditional approaches to personality assessment are closely tied to the basic assumptions of these approaches. Whereas traditional assessors search for underlying constructs to account for the consistency or inconsistency of behavior, behavioral assessors focus on the importance of the behavior itself. Walter Mischel commented that in behavioral analyses, "the emphasis is on what the person *does* in situations rather than on inferences about what attributes he *has* more globally" (1968, p. 10). Consequently, behavioral observers are more likely than traditional observers to analyze relationships between behavior and environmental occurrences or to postulate deep or dynamic causative factors to account for observed behaviors. Similarly, in interviewing, Kanfer and Grimm (1977) noted that behavior analysts attempt to elicit specific descriptions of actual events, people, and situations; whereas traditional assessors listen for information to confirm or discredit their hypotheses about such global constructs as depression, impotence, anxiety, and unhappiness.

## Origins of Behavioral Techniques

Some of the differences between behavioral and traditional approaches are that behavioral methods began in the laboratory, whereas traditional methods began in the clinics of mental health practitioners. Consequently, behavioral assessment has strong ties to the laboratory's stimulus-response models of human learning. Two stimulus-response traditions developed, classical and operant conditioning, each with its own terminology and followers.

**Classical Conditioning.** Classical conditioning, sometimes also called *respondent conditioning*, has its roots in Ivan Pavlov's well-known study (1927) demonstrating that dogs could be conditioned to salivate at the sound of a bell or metronome. In this experiment a hungry dog was observed to salivate (unconditioned response) at the sight of food (unconditioned stimulus), and after several pairings of a neutral sound such as a bell (conditioned stimulus) with food, the dog learned to salivate (now a conditioned response) at the sound of the bell, which now had the power to elicit the conditioned response.

The food, or unconditioned stimulus, is also called a *primary reinforcer*, because an organism's conditioned response would *extinguish*, or cease to exist, without its presentation. There are also *secondary reinforcers*, defined as any neutral stimuli that acquire reinforcing properties through their association with the primary reinforcers. In Pavlov's experiment with the dog, for example, any of the cues in the laboratory (harness, color of the walls, laboratory coat), because of their proximity to or association with food, could have acquired secondary reinforcing characteristics.

**The Operant Approach.** The operant conditioning paradigm, sometimes also called *instrumental conditioning*, differs from the classical, or respondent, forms in that the organism must behave, or emit responses, before it will be reinforced. The reinforcement therefore is said to be contingent upon the emission of a response. R. L. Thorndike (1932) and B. F. Skinner (1938, 1953) thus challenged the Pavlovian position that most responses are *elicited* by stimuli and that most learning occurs because of a chaining of associated reflexes. Skinner proposed that most behavior was *instrumental* in obtaining reinforcement. He called particular attention to such everyday behaviors as opening doors, shutting windows, and learning to talk. In each instance, successful completion of the behavior causes consequences that are pleasant or satisfying and thus are likely to recur. Behavior that is not followed by positive consequences, or that leads to unsatisfying outcomes, is not likely to recur and may eventually *extinguish* from the organism's behavior repertoire.

The prototype experiment illustrating this approach usually occurs in an apparatus devised by Skinner called a *Skinner box*. At one end of the box is a lever or bar; when it is depressed by a hungry subject (usually a rat or pigeon), a pellet of food is automatically dispensed (by a magazine) into a tray below the lever. At first, the organism responds (depresses the lever) quite by accident, but once the subject has responded and received food, it soon responds again (and receives food and responds again, and so forth), and the probability of its future responding, or its *operant rate*, increases.

Because the rate of responding increases when the behavior is followed by food, the latter is said to reinforce the response (or the reinforcement is said to be contingent upon the response), and food becomes a *primary*, or *unconditioned*, *reinforcer*. When the magazine has been operated many times, the organism responds immediately to the noise made by the magazine and approaches and eats the pellet. Hence the noise (or a light if the food magazine is illuminated) becomes a *conditioned*, or a *secondary*, *reinforcer*, and the subjects will respond to it for long periods of time. If, however, the responding ceases to produce food, then the noise, through *extinction*, will lose the power to reinforce, and responding will stop.

This concept of reinforcement was elaborated by Skinnerians to include positive, negative, and punishing consequences. A *positive reinforcer* is a stimulus whose presentation increases the operant rate; a *negative reinforcer* (or aversive stimulus), in contrast, is a stimulus whose withdrawal increases the probability of the response that preceded it. And *punishment* is either a positive reinforcer withdrawn or a negative reinforcer presented.

Skinnerians also focus on the stimulus conditions, or *discriminative stimuli*, that cause behavior; most of their questions are phrased as, "What stimuli and what consequences will maintain a given response?" The term operant itself, according to Skinner, "emphasizes the fact that the behavior *operates* upon the environment to generate consequences" (1953, p. 65). And in their behavior assessment before therapy, Skinnerians find it important to learn which behaviors are under the control of which discriminative stimuli in the environment. Such behavior is said to be under *stimulus control*.

## Assessment Methods

Since the stimulus-response paradigms of classical and operant conditioning are somewhat different from each other, their assessment techniques also are different, but the lines of demarcation are not always clear. Both methods search for stimulus-response-reinforcement relationships that trigger and support a person's maladaptive behaviors. But since the therapies used by the two approaches are different as well, their assessment procedures sometimes can be distinguished according to this difference. We shall treat each method separately, keeping in mind that both of these behavioral approaches occur mainly in naturalistic and clinical settings, rather than in controlled ones.

**Respondent Assessment.** According to Wolpe, one of the respondent method's founders, a technique variously called *de-conditioning, reciprocal inhibition,* or *desensitization* can extinguish a maladaptive response such as anxiety. This is accomplished by making "a response antagonistic to anxiety . . . occur in the presence of anxiety-evoking stimuli, so that it is accompanied by a complete or partial suppression of the anxiety responses . . ." (1958, p. 71). Several respondent therapies are used to do this, and each has its own interview assessment procedure.

In *assertiveness training,* for example, the therapist's goal is to augment "every impulse towards the elicitation of these inhibited responses, with the expectation . . . that . . . there will reciprocally be an inhibiting of the anxiety . . ." (Wolpe, 1969, p. 62). The therapist works toward this goal first by asking questions designed to assess how the patient behaves passively in a number of situations (e.g., "Suppose that arriving home after buying an article you find it slightly damaged. What will you do?") and then by informing the patient that the intentional outward expression of his or her resentment will reciprocally inhibit anxiety.

Another respondent behavioral technique is called *aversive conditioning*. This procedure is often used with alcoholic and obese persons (see Gottman & Leiblum, 1974). Again, the therapist must find out both which responses need to be extinguished and the situations in which they occur. In treating alcoholism, for example, the therapist first interviews the patient about the nature and extent of alcoholic behavior and then plans an aversive-conditioning schedule. Essentially, the method consists of giving the patient a noxious agent as an unconditioned stimulus (in a variation of this, the agent can be covert, for example, sickening thoughts), along with alcohol as the conditioned stimulus. After repeated pairings of the two stimuli, the patient should become ill or experience discomfort in the presence of the sight, smell, or taste of alcohol. Respondent interviewers use various behavioral questionnaires as assessment aids. Table 5–4 presents a list of some of these assessment questionnaires, along with their functions and founders. Figure 5–7 reproduces some of the categories and items covered by one recent inventory, the Multimodal Life History Questionnaire, developed by A. A. Lazarus (1977b; 1981) of Rutgers University.

**Table 5-4** A Partial List of Questionnaires Used in Respondent Behavioral Assessment.

| Name of Questionnaire | Function | Reference |
|---|---|---|
| Assertion Inventory | Persons list situations and degree of discomfort they would probably experience by being assertive in certain situations. | Gambrill & Richey, 1975. |
| Fear Survey Schedule III | Fears (75) are rated on a 5-point scale. | Curran & Gilbert, 1975; also see Hersen, 1971; Lang & Lazovik, 1963; Wolpe & Lang, 1969; for other Fear Surveys. |
| Life History Questionnaire | As the name indicates, this assesses developmental events, behavior problems, fears, and life history. | Wolpe, 1969. |
| Multimodal Life History Questionnaire | This collects information in general problem areas as well as areas of sex, marriage, family, and fears. (see Figure 5-7). | Lazarus, A. A., 1977b. |
| Negative Attitudes toward Masturbation Inventory | This measures guilty attitudes toward masturbation. | Abramson & Mosher, 1975. |
| Sexual Orientation Questionnaire | A 120-response survey used to assess (6-point scale) heterosexual versus homosexual interests. | MacDonough, 1972; Phillips, 1968; Turner et al., 1974. |

According to psychometric criteria, these questionnaires are similar to interview schedules and rely heavily on personal honesty for accurate descriptions.

**Operant Methods.** The operant behavior therapist is interested in understanding and bringing the consequences of given forms of behavior under his or her control and in transferring this control to the patients. This is usually accomplished by making a "thorough analysis of the interaction between the behaving organism and the environment in which the behavior occurs" (Kanfer & Phillips, 1970, p. 242; Kanfer & Grimm, 1980). Some of the techniques and terminology that operant behaviorists use to achieve their therapy goals are *schedules of reinforcement*, which refer to the rates at which reinforcing stimuli are delivered (fixed or variable ratio, fixed or variable interval schedules); behavior *shaping*, a method of reinforcing approximations to a desired response;

---

1.  *General*
    Name, Age, Occupation, Marital Status, Religion
2.  *Clinical*
    a) State in your own words the nature of your main problems and their duration:
    b) On the scale below please estimate the severity of your problem(s):
    mildly upsetting     moderately severe     very severe     extremely severe     totally incapacitating
3.  *Personal Data*
4.  *Occupational Data*
5.  *Sex Information*
6.  *Menstrual History*
7.  *Marital History*
8.  *Family Data*
8a. *Additional Information*
    a) Recount any fearful or distressing experiences not previously mentioned:
9.  *Self Description:* (Please complete the following:)
    a) I am a person who _____
    b) All my life _____
10. *Assessment Summary*
11. *Sequential History*
12. *Word Pictures*:
    Give a word picture of yourself as you would be described:
    a) by yourself.
    b) by your spouse.
    c) by your best friend.
    d) by someone who dislikes you.

---

Lazarus, A. A. *The Practice of Multimodal Therapy.* New York: McGraw-Hill, '98'

**Figure 5–7.** Categories and Some Illustrative Items Appearing on the Multimodal Life History Questionnaire.

and *discriminative stimuli*, which mark the time until a response brings reinforcing consequences (e.g., the green light, which sets the occasion for crossing a street). Operant behaviorists also refer, more than respondent therapists do, to changing target behaviors. These changes can be either the extinction of maladaptive responses or the increase of deficit behavior.

Consequently, in order to change or extinguish target behaviors, the operant assessor must record specific base-line behaviors. These are obtained by either direct observation of or report by the patient or his or her family and friends. There is a good example of obtaining baseline behavior by direct observation in a study by Sobell and Sobell (1976), who collected information on hospitalized alcoholics and on normals. Their studies were conducted in a dayroom at a state hospital.

The setting included a padded and varnished bar with a full length mirror, a bottle display, bar stools, tables, chairs, music, and dim lighting. Groups of three or four alcoholics or normal drinkers were allowed to drink freely (with a sixteen-drink limit), and observers recorded each drink ordered, the type of drink, the number of sips taken, the total time per drink (seconds), and the intersip intervals. Through these records the assessors learned that the alcoholics ordered more drinks than the normals did, preferred their liquor straight, took longer sips and drank faster, and took a longer time between sips than did normal drinkers. But more importantly for our purposes, the therapists had a base line for the target behavior they wished to change or extinguish. As in other observations and interviews, one problem in measuring a response such as alcohol consumption is that the patient's awareness of what is being measured may influence the frequency or the nature of the very response under study.

Although many operant behavior modifiers prefer to assess behaviors by direct observation, several rating scales for indirect behavior recording also are used. Many of these scales antedate the widespread use of operant techniques (e.g., the 1961 Psychotic Inpatient Profile and the 1962 Inpatient Multidimensional Psychiatric Scale, both by Lorr et al.), but some have been designed especially for operant behavior therapy. (An example of a rating scale for operant behavior therapy was described by Craighead and his associates (1976) in their book *Behavior Modification*.) Two of these scales, the Initial Interview Outline and the Behavior Assessment Form, are shown in Tables 5–5 and 5–6.

After an initial interview, which does not differ from the interviews conducted by most clinicians, the assessor collects the information, both from the patient and by direct observation. This information, to paraphrase Craighead and his colleagues (1976, pp. 158–161), is collected from the assessment and then is synthesized and ordered so that the change agent may identify both the dependent variables (client's problem behaviors) and the independent variables (causing and maintaining factors). When this assessment is completed, it is presented to the client, and then the clinical experiment (treatment or behavior modification program) is explained to the client and is subsequently carried out. The same procedures may be used in working with children, adults, at home, or in institutions, although the outlines followed or the procedures used may vary from one situation to the next. The model, however, remains the same.

**Other Behavioral Procedures.** Besides the respondent and operant orientations—as intertwined as they may be (see Ullmann & Krasner, 1975, pp. 86–87)—there are several other behavioral techniques, not all of which have clear roots in the classical or instrumental paradigms.

**Table 5-5** Initial Interview Outline.

I. Objectives
 1. Establish good relationship with the client.
 2. Obtain adequate information to identify dependent and independent variables of client's problem.

II. Assessment session
 1. Opening question: "Why are you here?"
    a. Begin by introducing self, confidentiality, and clinic policies.
    b. Invite client to tell about problem as client sees it, by asking the opening question.
    c. Find out how and why the decision to come in was made.
    d. Use of "reflection and clarification" to keep client talking about how he sees his problem.
  (Depending on what is said in response to the opening question, go on to either 2 or 3 below.)
 2. Inquiry into assets and liabilities.
    a. Socioeconomic situation. (How is the situation financially?)
    b. Job situation. (Does he or she have a job? What?)
    c. Work situation. (What is the relation to others on the job?)
    d. Educational background.
    e. Religious background.
    f. Peer relations. (What are relations to the same and the opposite sex?)
    g. Relationship with spouse.
    h. Relationship with in-laws.
    i. Relationship with children (each specific child).
  (Gaining information in these areas will allow you to: (1) develop a better understanding of the client; (2) determine strengths and weaknesses; and (3) determine if and how problems in these areas may be related to the problem presented in Section I.)
 3. Set clear definition and specification of problem areas (dependent variables) and the associated independent variables.
    a. Identify and define each distressing problem.
    b. Presence and absence of positive and negative eliciting and discriminative stimuli (internal and external).
    c. Presence and absence of reinforcement and punishment (internal and external).
    d. To whom it is distressing.
    e. Timing and frequency.
    f. Circumstances under which behavior occurs (focus on specific situations).
    g. What happens afterward.
    h. What client says to himself before the behavior.
    i. What client says to himself after the behavior.
    j. What is currently being done about problem.
    k. Availability of reinforcement.
 4. Objectives of therapy.
    a. What do you want to be different at end of therapy?
    b. Just a beginning in formulating objectives.

III. Closing first interview
 Give a nebulous statement with regard to helpfulness of the information and your feelings of being able to help the client with his problem. Inform the client that you need more information to complete the assessment (if such is, in fact, the case) and that you need to look at the information already gained. TELL THE TRUTH, BUT BE AS POSITIVE AS POSSIBLE.

Source: Craighead, W. E., Kazdin, A. E., & Mahoney, M. J. *Behavior modification: Principles, issues, and applications* (2nd ed.). Boston: Houghton Mifflin, 1981, p. 166. Copyright © 1981 by Houghton Mifflin Company. Used by permission.

One method that does have such roots, however, is Bandura's (1969) *social learning* theory of behavior therapy, which uses *modeling* as its fundamental concept of learning. Modeling, which has its origins in animal experiments using imitation (Miller & Dollard, 1941), is also known as *observation learning* or *vicarious no-trial learning* (see also Bandura, 1974).

Compared with the respondent and operant procedures, modeling relies more on the cognitive activities of the learner. The patient is expected to think about and even practice the desired behavior to be learned or the undesired behavior to be extinguished, and this behavior is learned or extinguished by observing others on film or directly. For example, Bandura and his associates (Bandura et al., 1967; Bandura & Menlove, 1968) extinguished children's fears of dogs both by having them watch movies in which fearless models handled dogs in a variety of situations and by having them view live models in similar situations. Modeling has also been used both to modify snake phobias in female students who witnessed male models handling snakes fearlessly (Geer & Turteltaub, 1967) and to encourage patients to emulate their therapists' appropriate behaviors (Kanfer & Phillips, 1966). What is important for our purposes is that the therapist must first obtain his or her information from the patients by interviewing them, although recently there has been a trend toward having the clients collect data on themselves through self-monitoring (Ciminero et al., 1977; Epstein et al., 1976; Ernst, 1973; Fixsen et al., 1973; Mahoney & Thoresen, 1974; Thoreson & Mahoney, 1974). This trend reflects a change in emphasis from the external control of behavior to self-control in which clients direct their own therapeutic programs (see Grimm, 1980 for a critique of the reliability of self-reporting).

One other behavioral approach is the social learning theory of Julian Rotter (1954) and his associates (Phares, 1972, 1976; Rotter, 1966; Rotter et al., 1972), who developed techniques for assessment and treatment that combined reinforcement concepts with cognitive elements. For example, Rotter and his associates conceptualized both an internal and an external *locus of control* of reinforcement, which refer to two types of personalities. Locus of control is a way of expressing the degree to which individuals see themselves in control of their lives and the circumstances and events that influence them. People who see themselves as exerting a significant influence over their own lives are Internals (Is), and people who believe that the events in their lives are determined by forces outside themselves (fate, change, the government) are Externals (Es). These people are assumed to differ in their generalized expectations or beliefs regarding causation and the sources of their reinforcements.

Rotter's method for assessing whether a person attributes the causes of his or her behavior to internal or external forces was to create

**Table 5-6** Behavior Assessment Form.

Date _____

Therapist _____

Name _____ Address _____

Phone _____ Age _____ Occupation _____

Marital Status _____ Children _____

Previous Therapy _____
    Outcome _____ Orientation _____
    Current expectancies _____

Known Medical Problems _____
    Most recent exam _____ Current drugs _____

Atypical Background or Experiences _____
_____

Average Hours of Sleep per Night _____ Regular? _____

Eating Patterns _____

Physical Description _____
_____

Social & Interview Behaviors _____
_____

Self-Description:                       (Aver.)
  1. Physical condition   (V. Poor) 0 1 2 3 4 5 6 7 8 9 10 (Athletic)
  2. Intelligence          (Stupid) 0 1 2 3 4 5 6 7 8 9 10 (Bright)
  3. Physical looks       (Ugly) 0 1 2 3 4 5 6 7 8 9 10 (Attractive)
  4. Assertiveness        (Shy) 0 1 2 3 4 5 6 7 8 9 10 (Aggressive)
  5. Likeability         (Disliked) 0 1 2 3 4 5 6 7 8 9 10 (Well liked)
  6. Self-confidence     (Inferior) 0 1 2 3 4 5 6 7 8 9 10 (Confident)
  7. Coping style       (Anxious) 0 1 2 3 4 5 6 7 8 9 10 (Relaxed)
  8. Personal worth       (Bad) <u>0 1 2 3 4 5 6 7 8 9 10</u> (Good)
                                Sum = _____ Mean = _____
  9. Name some of the particularly good things about yourself (assets, talents, etc.): _____ (space is provided for answer)
 10. Name some of the particularly bad things about yourself (faults, deficiencies, etc.): _____ (space provided)

Presenting Problem(s):
  1. Definition & description: _____ (space provided) _____
  2. Historical development (recency, etc.): _____ (space provided) _____
  3. Current state & correlates:
     a. Frequency/intensity _____
     b. Situationality _____

**Table 5–6** *Continued*

    c. Temporal distribution _____
    d. Antecedents (environmental & cognitive) _____

    e. Consequences (social & self-presented) _____

4. Atypical or complicating factors: _____ (space provided) _____
5. Comments: _____ (space provided) _____

<u>Tentative Treatment Program:</u>
1. Modification targets: _____ (space provided) _____
2. Assessment methods: _____ (space provided) _____
3. Probable determinants: _____ (space provided) _____
4. Tentative treatment strategies: _____ (space provided) _____
5. Auxiliary topics or comments: _____ (space provided) _____

Source: Craighead, W. E., Kazdin, A. E., & Mahoney, M. J. *Behavior modification: Principles, issues, and applications* (2nd ed.) Boston: Houghton Mifflin, 1981, pp. 167–168. Copyright © 1981 by Houghton Mifflin Company. Used by permission.

measures from which I-E tendencies could be inferred. Then he observed behavior in real-life settings and contrived experimental situations to permit meaningful comparisons between I-oriented and E-oriented individuals. Rotter's first measures resembled traditional psychometric self-report inventories: A person is instructed to choose one each from a series of item pairs, one of which reflects the expectation that one can control his or her life ("In my case, getting what I want has little or nothing to do with luck"), and the other a belief that outside forces are in control ("Many times we might just as well decide what to do by flipping a coin").

Findings from observations in real-life situations and from experimental settings have suggested that perceptions of control influence a wide array of behaviors. For example, individuals scoring high on internality appear more active in their attempts to control and master the environment. They seek out more information relevant to their goals, are less prone to subtle social influences, are better adjusted, and can laugh at themselves in the face of failure, thus exhibiting frustration tolerance and the defenses necessary to cope with stress (Phares, 1972).

## Critique of Behavioral Methods

Behavioral assessment shares many of the problems we have discussed in reference to observation. Generally, it represents specific combinations of the "observation of a given *attribute* on a given *occasion* within a specified *setting* by certain *observers* employing certain *instruments*" (Wiggins, 1973, p. 292). Therefore, the behavioral assessor must be concerned with the degree to which the information developed from these assessments is reliable or generalizable to other combinations of observers and occasions (see Cronbach et al., 1972). We shall now examine some of the other problems that behavioral assessors share with their more traditional observer counterparts (also see Goldfried & Sprafkin, 1974, regarding problems of behavioral assessment).

**Defining Behavior.** The behavior to be recorded or rated, whether verbal or nonverbal, should be defined as specifically as possible. Behaviors as seemingly clearly described as "anxious speech," "good grooming," "poor grooming," or "uneasiness" are higher-order inferences and, as such, contribute to disagreements among observers and miscommunication among raters. To avoid this problem, Ayllon and Azrin recommended that behavior be described "in specific terms that require a minimum of interpretation" (1968, p. 36).

Essentially, the less the behavioral observer or interviewer has to interpret, the less room there is for error. Fortunately, there are several ways to avoid the errors that may arise from these ambiguous definitions. One way is simply to remove the observer from the assessment process by using completely automated assessment devices. This was the method used by Nathan and O'Brien (1971) in their work on liquor consumption among alcoholics. They devised a clever "drinking machine" that computed the amount of alcohol consumed, and the printout information could then be used as a substitute for or a supplement to the alcoholic's admitted drinking rates.

A second way to avoid errors caused by ambiguity is to focus on the unmistakable products of behavior rather than to accept as evidence the spoken word. In this regard, Ayllon and Azrin suggested that the assessor "arrange the situation so that the behavior produces some enduring changes in the physical environment" (1968, p. 127). Examples are weight reduction in obesity therapy, lack of stuttering in speech therapy, and no smoking after "smoke clinic" therapy. Thus, although the interviewed subject may proclaim that he or she has curtailed his or her eating habits, only the balance scale can confirm or disprove this.

A third way to avoid errors arising from vague definitions is to include in the definition such a narrow range of behavior that the observation is relatively easy. This can be done by deciding, for example, that speech is any audible verbalization, that activity is any movement of a limb, that a tic is any jerky movement of the head, or that hearing voices is any speech emitted without anyone being present.

**Observer Error.** Again, in common with naturalistic or controlled observations, observer errors in behavioral assessment are caused by biases in the observer's expectancies and by inaccuracies in recording the spoken or other overt behavior in question. Both of these sources of errors can be limited, and observed accuracy can be enhanced by adhering to Wallace's principles: "(a) the observer's recordings can be compared to a criterion set of recordings developed from known stimulus material; (b) the observer can be joined in the responding process by another observer with later comparison between the two recordings" (1976, p. 294).

Finally, accuracy can be improved by training behavioral assessors and other observers in a particular method of behavior coding and scoring and by having them practice those skills in several sessions of listening to or observing the behavior in question. The degree of assessor or observer accuracy should be computed in order to estimate interrater agreement before and after training, either by the percent agreement method (see Hawkins & Dotson, 1975, for information on correcting spurious estimates of agreement) or by any other appropriate correlational techniques (see De Risi et al., 1975; Winkler, 1970).

## SUMMARY AND CONCLUSIONS

During our discussion of observational methods in this chapter, we shifted our emphasis from procedures with minimal constraints on the observer, subject, and setting to those with ever-increasing controls. We noted that on this continuum, the least control is exercised in those situations in which the observer merely views the behavior of the subjects in question. This casts the observer in a passive role. Much time and energy are wasted in waiting for relevant behavior to occur, and many other problems arise because of the observer's perceptual and cognitive limitations.

Instrumentation and other aids do not eliminate the observer's problems, but they do make more precise the observations made. There is little question, for example, that audiotapes and movies can absorb more of a given scene than the human observer can; yet because the activation of hardware devices is completely under the control of the human observer, the problem of viewing relevant behavior still remains.

Rating scales can also be used, and these increase the constraints imposed on the observer and thereby partially solve the problem of viewing relevant behaviors, because they prescribe specifically, and sometimes clearly, the behaviors to be noted. Rating scales also yield quantitative standardized data and therefore offer the advantage of allowing comparisons to be made of individuals (or the same individual) viewed by the same, or different, observers. However, rating scales are beset with their own problems, not the least of which are the raters' biases.

In making controlled observations, investigators are highly constrained and in turn place considerable controls on their subject matter and environment. By forcing data to emerge, they obtain highly pertinent observations. Such data allow the researcher to compare these observations with observations made under similar conditions and also permit the observer to introduce subtle stimuli, which in turn may yield subtle discriminations in relevant behaviors. However, as the observer becomes more active in the observational procedure, he or she loses some of the naturalness of *in situ* observations. The really unsettling question then becomes, "To what extent are these observations relevant to real life?" The observer also runs the risk—as he or she moves toward more contrived observations—that the subjects will detect the hardware or contrivances, and thus the intentions and objectives of the study under way.

In this chapter we also distinguished between direct and indirect observation. All of the above are direct observations because they view behavior firsthand. Indirect observation does not deal directly with the subjects under investigation but examines documents and records written by the person or by others about the person. Indirect observations can also be made from physical traces deposited or left behind by the person. These observations are often nonreactive in that they require little from the participating subjects and hence afford them few opportunities to react to the manipulation or setting of a study. They are unobtrusive because there is a minimum of interference with the subjects of study. Nonetheless, the analysis and interpretation of these nonreactive and unobtrusive measures must proceed carefully and consider the subjects' motivations in writing their documents or leaving their tracings.

The most recent form of direct observation—usually in naturalistic settings or in the clinic—are behavioral assessments. Their origin was in the laboratory, and they can be traced to classical and operant conditioning experiments. Both of these latter assessment procedures concentrate their observations and other inquiries on discovering stimulus-response-reinforcement relationships that underlie behavior. Most recently, these behavioral approaches have focused on, besides overt behaviors, the cognitive functioning of their examinees.

Finally, with the possible exception of the recent development in the behavioral approaches, all observations of human behavior concern manifest behavior and neglect the content of that behavior. For example, in most observations, no information is obtained about beliefs, perceptions, feelings, attitudes, past behavior, or future plans. Yet, this knowledge is indispensable to the study of personality. To obtain this information, such techniques as interviews, self-report inventories, and projective testing are used extensively. The first of these methods, the interview, is the topic of the next chapter.

# FOR FURTHER READING

Babbie, E.R. *The practice of social research.* Belmont, CA: Wadsworth, 1975. A thoroughly enjoyable book on the logic and rationale of scientific inquiry, part II, on modes of observation, is particularly germane to the present discussion.

Craighead, W.E., Kazdin, A.E., & Mahoney, M.J. *Behavior modification: Principles, issues, and applications.* (2nd ed.). Boston: Houghton Mifflin, 1981.

Duncan, S., Jr., & Fiske, D.W. *Face-to-face interaction: Research methods and theory.* Hillsdale, NJ: Lawrence Erlbaum Associates, 1977. This superb study on human interactions, provides an exemplar of scientific and replicable work in observational techniques.

Eckhardt, K.W., & Ermann, D.M. *Social research methods: Perspective, theory and analysis.* New York: Random House, 1977. More than just a "methods" text, this book contains some lively chapters on "call girls as informants," "the social meaning of nudity in nudist camps" (with a section on sexual modesty in nudist camps), and "the behavior of citizens during encounters with the police."

Festinger, L., Riecken, H.W., & Schacter, S. *When prophecy fails.* New York: Harper & Row, 1956. A fascinating study of observation in the naturalistic setting of a religious sect awaiting the end of the world on a specific date in the near future.

Fiske, D.W. *Strategies for personality research: The observation versus interpretation of behavior.* San Francisco: Jossey-Bass, 1978. As we indicate throughout chapter ten of the present book, Fiske is most concerned about the slow progress of personality research. He tends to place much of the blame on faulty observations and their interpretations.

Lazarus, A.A. *The practice of multimodal therapy.* New York: McGraw-Hill, 1981.

Lofland, J. *Doomsday cult: A study of conversion, proselytization, and maintenance of faith.* Englewood Cliffs, NJ: Prentice-Hall, 1966. An excellent illustration of observations made in a field study of a small religious cult still active today.

Orne, M.T. On the social psychology of the psychological experiment: With particular reference to demand characteristics and their implications. *American Psychologist,* 1962, *17,* 776–783. Orne contends that the motivational factors of subjects in human experiments and their reading of the demands of the experimental situation often affect the outcome of experiments.

Patterson, G.R. *Families: Applications of social learning to family life.* Champaign, IL: Research Press, 1971. An example of the application of social learning theory to the observation of family interactions in a naturalistic setting.

Rosenthal, R. *Experimenter effects in behavioral research* (Enlarged ed.). New York: Halsted Press, 1976. A somewhat expanded version of his 1966 book, this book continues to present evidence that experimenters and observers communicate the intent of their studies and/or affect their outcomes unintentionally.

Rosnow, R.L., & Rosenthal, R. Volunteer effects in behavioral research. In T.M. Newcomb, (Ed.), *New directions in psychology* (Vol. 4). Holt, Rinehart & Winston, 1970. An excellent treatise on the problem of volunteer subjects in psychological research.

Selltiz, C., Wrightsman, L.S., & Cook, S.W. *Research methods in social relations* (3rd ed.). New York: Holt, Rinehart & Winston, 1976. Containing chapters on research design, measurement, and statistics, this book also provides several excellent chapters on the data collection methods of observations and the interview.

Webb, E.J., Campbell, D.T., Schwartz, R.D., & Sechrest, L. *Unobtrusive measures: Nonreactive research in the social sciences.* Chicago: Rand McNally, 1966. Written in a breezy style, this book continues to be popular among social scientists interested in securing information *not* readily obtainable by direct observations.

Weick, K.E. Systematic observational methods. In G. Lindzey & E. Aronson (Eds.), *The handbook of social psychology* (Vol. 2). Boston: Addison-Wesley, 1968. A comprehensive survey of observational methods by one of the more competent researchers in the field.

# 6 Interviewing

In this chapter we discuss *interviewing*, yet another input to the information processor of Figure 1–1. Unlike the material covered in the last chapter, however, interviewing, and many of the techniques we examine later, can be conducted and administered by the computer itself. First we shall introduce interviewing as it is conventionally carried out, and then we shall move to computer interviewing.

## Introduction

"Language most shows a man," wrote Ben Jonson in the seventeenth century, "speak that I may see thee." This is true and thus interviewing differs from direct observation in that it adds the dimension of speech and language, thereby enabling us to fathom hitherto inaccessible aspects of a person. Thus, if we want to know how people feel, what they have experienced, how much they remember, and what their emotions and motives are, we can ask them. Unfortunately, however, we cannot always believe what we hear because verbal communication is not so straightforward that we can easily interpret it. By its very nature, the desired information is private; people either cannot or will not readily disclose it. Often they are not aware of their inner thoughts and motives; and even more often, they intentionally hold back, disown, deny, or distort them. Consequently, the interviewer must be very skillful to obtain such information.

At the same time that the interviewer is engaged in talking, he or she must also be alert to the nonverbal cues transmitted, nonverbal cues that, as we noted in the last chapter, can be gleaned from the respondent's general appearance, gestures, postures, and facial expression, and may disclose information about that person's attitudes, wishes, and so on. And if the interview is conducted in the subject's home, the interviewer must also attend to other cues that may reveal the subject's standard and style of living (neighborhood, condition of living quarters, taste in home furnishings, number and titles of books, and so forth), as well as the respondent's interactions with others at home (tone of voice, physical contact). In fact, such nonverbal information is offered spontaneously and often cannot be obtained by asking questions. This information can be used as a basis for further hypotheses about a

## BOX 6-1

## Interviewing

Interviewing is a data-collection procedure involving verbal communication between the researcher and respondent either by telephone or in a face-to-face situation. While a number of differences exist between data collection by telephone and face-to-face interaction, there are a number of advantages and disadvantages common to personal contact. Of course, these advantages and disadvantages vary with the characteristics of the population to be interviewed, sponsorship of the research, content of the interview items, length of interview, and timing of the interview with the social condition of society and the personal circumstances of the interviewee.

Nonetheless, the general advantages of interviews include

1. A high response participation rate compared to self-administered questionnaire data-collection techniques, that is, those techniques relying on a distribution of questionnaires to individuals to be completed and returned at a later date.
2. An ability to collect data from persons incapable of completing a questionnaire without assistance, for example, young children and marginally literate or illiterate adults.
3. An ability to clarify questions or probe for additional information within the constraints of interview training.
4. An ability to verify or cross-check certain verbal responses with the observed conditions.

The general disadvantages of interviews include

1. The relatively high cost of interviewing respondents due to such factors as the travel expense of the interviewers, the time expended to physically locate a respondent whose address has changed or who may not be at home at the time of the initial interview (thereby requiring a call-back), and the salary costs of interviewers and field supervisors whose task it is to solve problems and maintain data-collection quality control.
2. The possibility that the interviewer-interviewee relationship may produce reliability and validity measurement problems due to differences in social characteristics, such as, race, age, sex, ethnicity, perceived status differences, etc., and personality characteristics, that is, the degree to which the interviewer and interviewee develop a relationship of personal trust.
3. The possibility that interviewers may subtly change the intended meaning of questions through slight rewording or emphasis on some words in the items, through questions which probe the meaning of a response and may unintentionally threaten the respondent.

Rules of thumb for maximizing the advantages and minimizing the disadvantages of interviewing include

(continued)

**BOX 6–1** (*Continued*)

1. Matching interviewers with specific characteristics (e.g., race, sex, or ethnic background) to the characteristics of target populations.
2. Training interviewers to
   a. Adhere closely to a verbatim reading of the interview schedule as designed and to employ only those probes which convey a neutral response of the interviewer, such as: "You have just said that 'You frequently vote for Democratic candidates.' Could you clarify for me whether this means Democratic candidates for national, state, or local office?"
   b. Avoid expressions of approval, disapproval, or surprise at an interviewee's response, such as "Wow, you've just said 'Some Presidents deserved to be assassinated.' Do you feel that way because you think they are traitors to the Constitution?"
3. Using proper sampling techniques, such as cluster sampling for geographically distributed populations, updating addresses prior to entering the field, and selecting a time period during which the respondents are likely to be available.

**Source:** Eckhardt, W. K., & Ermann, M. D. *Social research methods: Perspective, theory, and analysis.* New York: Random House, 1977, pp. 222–223.

---

person, hypotheses that can be explored either during the interview itself or, if psychotherapy is recommended, during the therapy sessions.

To understand how complex the analysis of an interview can be, consider the following list of some of the so-called act-variables that two researchers found useful in studying face-to-face encounters in naturalistic settings (Duncan & Fiske, 1977, pp. 39–47). Although the researched interactions were somewhat more complicated than interviews alone, the selection of their data points is nevertheless instructive:

1. Turn Time: how much time the person spent talking (e.g., speaking turns).
2. Turn Number: the number of speaking turns.
3. Interruption Rate: the number of times that one person interrupted the other.
4. Filled Pause Rate: any pause during which the speaker emitted sounds such as "er," "ah," "um," and the like.
5. Nod Rate: the number of times a person nodded his or her head while the other was speaking.
6. Smile Number: the total number of smiles during a given time interval.

7. Smile Extent: the total time for smiling while speaking and not speaking.
8. Gaze Number: the total number of gazes at partner while speaking and not speaking.
9. Gesture Time: the total time spent gesturing while speaking and not speaking.
10. Foot Time: the time spent moving a foot.
11. Seat Rate: the number of times a person shifted his or her seat position while speaking and not speaking.
12. Leg Rate: the number of times the person shifted his or her leg position while speaking and not speaking.

In addition, consider the following quantifiable "paralanguage" variables (which occur in speech but are not part of language): intensity, pitch-height, tempo, pauses, audible inhalations and exhalations, resonance, laughing, crying, and rasping. All of these factors then have to be synthesized and related to the linguistic elements, which include the denotative and connotative meanings of the content of what is spoken.

Physicians and priests have been using interviews since antiquity. We know from the writings of Plato that he and Socrates pursued learning, wisdom, and truth by conducting dialogues with their disciples. One of the world's oldest books, *The Instructions of Ptah-Hotep*, was written by an Egyptian government official in about 400 B.C. and instructed people in the art of conversation (see Brady, 1976, pp. 220–221).

The interview's link with psychotherapy is relatively recent. The interview resembles psychotherapy in that its focus is usually on a single problem or goal, typically to discover as much about a person as possible. Interviewing is unlike psychotherapy, however, in that the interview is for gathering information, and psychotherapy is for changing behavior. One source (Johnson, 1979) put interviewing on a continuum of communication, with conversation at one end and psychotherapy at the other: Conversation—interviewing—advising—counseling—psychotherapy. Conversation is described as a friendly verbal exchange among people, which is culturally normal in that what a person may say and what responses are acceptable are prescribed. At the other end of the continuum, psychotherapy is described both as a much more complex exchange in which there are "phases of disorganization and organization" (p. 259) and as a technique that relies on all the skills used in conversation, interviewing, advising, and counseling.

For us, it is sufficient to remember that the interview differs from ordinary conversation in that, as Arthur Wiens observed, its "content is directed toward a specific purpose and is likely to have unity, progression, and thematic continuity" (1976, p. 5). This is similar to an earlier definition by Bingham and Moore, who described the interview

## BOX 6-2

## Conversational Politics

Sociolinguistic research, according to a recent article (Parlee, 1979), has shown that the way we talk to one another carries a silent message, governed by the setting and by social roles. Long pauses, digressions, and the sequence of speakers may provide important information about who is in command and who is being dominated. For example, conversations between superior and subordinate, young and old, and doctor and patient all may reveal patterns largely independent of individual personalities (e.g., subordinates show more interest in topics raised by superiors than the reverse; older people interrupt younger ones; and doctors question patients).

Such patterns in conversations are the subject of sociolinguistics, the study of the influence on language of social settings and roles. As we indicated in the last chapter, anthropologists, sociologists, and psychologists working in this area have long been concerned with the use of language in our and other cultures.

Conversational politics is one area of sociolinguistics and includes male-female, teacher-pupil, black-white, and adult-child interactive language styles. Particularly interesting is a conversation recorded by linguist William Labov, which showed that black children's use of language sometimes is quite different in the presence of an adult interviewer asking questions from what it is when another child is present. Consider the following dialogue, especially as it may relate to our later discussions of personality and intelligence testing with children, particularly with minority-group children:

*Interview setting:*
ADULT: You never been in a fight?
CHILD: Nope.
A: Nobody ever pick on you?
C: Nope.
A: Nobody ever hit you?
C: Nope.
A: How come?
C: Ah 'o' know.
A: Didn't you ever hit somebody?
C: Nope.
A: (*Incredulously*) You never hit nobody?

*Informal setting with another child present:*
ADULT: Is there anybody who says you momma drink pee?
CHILD (*same as above*): Yee-ah!
CHILD 2: Yup!
C1: And your father eat doo-doo for breakfast!
A: Ohh! (*laughs*)
C1: And they say your father—your father eat doo-doo for dinner!
C2: When they sound on me, I say C.B.S.
A: What that mean?
C1: Congo booger-snatch! (*laughs*)
C2: Congo booger-snatch! (*laughs*)
(cited in Parlee, 1979, p. 51)

Labov warned that teachers or other adults might wrongly conclude from the first interview that the child had a language deficiency. The same child's language in a less formal setting, however, showed that nothing could be further from the truth.

## BOX 6-3

### A Scheme of the Interview Performance Cycle

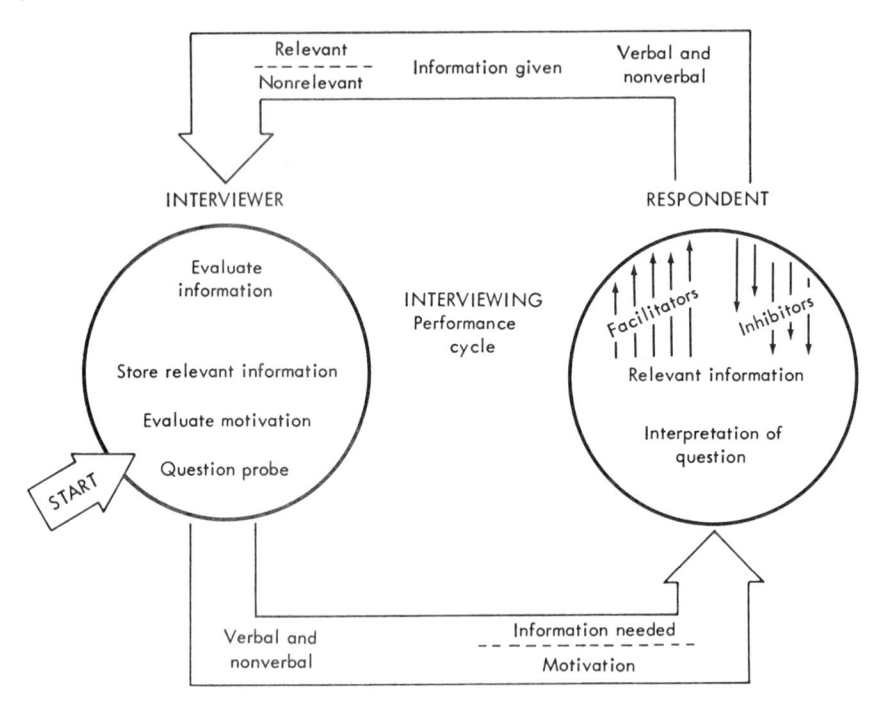

```
                    Relevant
                    --------      Information given      Verbal and
                    Nonrelevant                          nonverbal

     INTERVIEWER                                      RESPONDENT

       Evaluate
       information              INTERVIEWING       Facilitators  Inhibitors
                                  Performance
     Store relevant information     cycle         Relevant information

     Evaluate motivation                           Interpretation of
                                                      question
  START  Question probe


                    Verbal and          Information needed
                    nonverbal           ------------------
                                          Motivation
```

According to a cross-cultural researcher, Raymond Gorden, the performance cycle of most interviews begins with the interviewer asking a particular question, which in turn is communicated by both verbal and nonverbal cues to designate the information needed and to motivate the respondent. Since the respondent is not an automaton, he or she will first interpret the "true meaning" of the question and the intent of the interviewer, then determine whether or not he or she has any relevant information. If the respondent has none, he or she may either simply say so, or may try to meet the interviewer's expectations by saying something irrelevant or by fabricating apparently relevant information. If the respondent feels that he or she does have information relevant to the question, he or she may give it freely, withhold parts of it, or withhold it all by giving a smoke screen of irrelevant information or by inventing seemingly relevant information. Which the respondent does depends on the facilitators and inhibitors operating in the interview situation. The respondent, both verbally and nonverbally, conveys relevant, irrelevant, or fabricated information to the interviewer. Then the inter-

(continued)

> **BOX 6-3** (Continued)
>
> viewer must evaluate the information received, separating the relevant from the irrelevant and the valid from the invalid. The interviewer stores (notes, records, etc.) the relevant, valid information. Then after estimating the respondent's ability and willingness to give relevant information he or she formulates a probe or goes on to the next question.
>
> Source: Gorden, R. L. *Interviewing: Strategy, techniques, and tactics.* Homewood, IL: Dorsey Press, 1980, p. 480.

as the conversation with a purpose (1959). The interview, then, is for the benefit of the interviewed person or, in the case of the selection or personnel interview, for the benefit of the institution or employer. The interview can be either structured or unstructured, depending on its purpose.

## Structured and Unstructured Interviews

In the structured interview, structure is the extent to which the interviewer asks every respondent exactly the same questions in the same way. The amount of structure in an interview can vary. At one extreme, fixed questions may be asked or even read by the interviewer. A less extreme example is the interview in which a basic set of questions is asked, but many others may be brought in. At the other extreme, the interviewer follows no plan. The interviewer may, in the first instance, ask closed-format questions that offer little chance to digress. This sort of interview provides such information as a person's age, nationality, social background, degree and type of education, occupational history, future plans, and so on. In the second kind of interview, besides these questions, the interviewer may also ask about the person's ambitions, fears, worries, marked aversions, sex experience, philosophy of life, and numerous other topics. And in the third kind of interview, the interviewer may allow the interviewee to lead the direction of the interview, usually by asking open-ended questions that permit considerable freedom to digress. We shall begin with the last kind of interview.

### The Unstructured Interview

The unstructured interview takes different forms and different names, such as the "focused," "clinical," "nondirective," or "depth" interview. All these names indicate its close ties with the psychotherapeutic

> **BOX 6-4**
>
> **Structuring the Interview**
>
> Not to be confused with either the structured or the unstructured interview is the matter of structuring all interview situations in the sense of setting the stage for the conduct of the interview. How the interviewer structures the situation, according to Gorden (1980, pp. 213-232), greatly influences the communication. Some questions that the interviewer should consider at the outset of the interview are, How should I introduce myself? How do I explain the interview's purpose? Should the interview be recorded? What is the appropriate wording for the opening question? How do I close the interview?
>
> Regarding the last question, Benjamin observed that closing may be the most difficult part of the whole interview, especially for the new interviewer who "may not understand how to let the interviewee know that the time is about up ... and may be fearful ... [of making] ... the interviewee feel that he is being pushed out" (1969, p. 30). To solve this problem, Benjamin suggested some helpful closing statements:
>
> "Thanks for coming in. This meeting has been a fruitful one for both of us, I think."
> "I believe that does it; we know how to get in touch with one another should anything else come up."
> "Before you leave, I just want to make sure I understand you correctly."
> "We've had quite a chat, and I am wondering what you're taking away from it. It hasn't been easy for you to talk, I know, and I'm not certain I understand everything you tried to express. So if you could sort of summarize things out loud, it might help both of us." (1969, pp. 33-34)

interview. The unstructured interview's distinguishing feature is that it places minimum constraints on the interviewer or the subject regarding the topics to be covered or the types of questions to be asked. The flexibility of this type of interview, if used properly by a trained assessor, makes it easier to explore the affective implications of a respondent's communications, thereby disclosing both the overt and covert significance of a subject's responses.

To the interviewer, the unstructured interview offers the versatility and freedom to roam over a wide variety of topics. This freedom is both its major advantage and its major disadvantage. It is an advantage because this flexibility can elicit otherwise inaccessible information, and it is a disadvantage because in not being standardized, the data the interview yields are not comparable from one interview to the next. Therefore, the unstructured interview is usually used when there is little need to ask respondents for the same information and when particular problems need to be identified to enable further examination. It is especially valuable when used with persons who might be threatened by too many probing questions.

There are degrees of unstructuredness even within the unstructured format. At the unstructured end of the continuum, in the *nondirective* interview, the initiative is largely in the hands of the respondent. As a result of the work of Carl Rogers and his associates, nondirective interviews became popular as a method of counseling in colleges. During the nondirective counseling interview, the client is encouraged to express his or her feelings without suggestions or questions from the counselor. The counselor's function is to encourage the client to talk, with a minimum of direct questioning or guidance. Examples of some typical statements made by the interviewer during nondirective interviewing are, "You seem to feel that . . . " "Can you repeat that . . . ?" "Isn't that interesting," or "Tell me more." We shall have more to say about Rogers later in the chapter.

A form of unstructured interviewing that Freud developed for both diagnostic and therapeutic purposes is called *free association*. Freud believed that this technique was best used for neurotics, because direct inquiry would be useless with persons who, according to psychoanalytic theory, did not consciously know what was bothering them. At the same time, the interview could flow in a direction determined by the patients' conflicting motives and their attendant anxieties so long as the interviewer removed as many external constraints as possible by structuring the interview. Hence, Freud instructed his patients to express their thoughts freely, to talk about anything that came to mind, no matter how trivial or irrelevant it might seem. To minimize respondent reactivity during free association, Freud refrained from direct questioning and sat behind the patient, who lay on a couch. Freud liked this arrangement because it both relaxed the patient and reduced the number of cues from the therapist's face that might signal to the patient what he or she was expected to think or say. The resulting method, free association, is, according to one author "unexcelled for providing data about the inner longings and fears that impel people, particularly data from which their unconscious motives may be inferred" (Holt, 1971, p. 47). Again, we shall have more to say about Freud's method of interviewing later in the chapter.

Somewhat more structured than nondirective and free association interviewing is a method employed by a group of investigators (Adorno et al., 1950) in an early study entitled *The Authoritarian Personality*. The interview schedule used in that study is presented in Table 6–1. We should note that although the interviewer used a framework of questions to be answered, he was nevertheless still free to explore reasons and

**Table 6–1** Excerpt of Interview Schedule.

| Family Background: Sociological Aspects |
|---|

Underlying Questions:
  (a) National origins of father and mother (not just racial; e.g., third generation Polish, German immigrant, etc.).
  (b) Important ingroup memberships of father, mother (e.g., unions, Masons, etc.).
  (c) Picture of socioeconomic status of parents and grandparents as reflected in occupation, education, way of life, etc.), with special attention to social mobility.

Suggested Direct Questions:

Background
  (a) Father's and mother's national antecedents, occupation, education, politics, religion.

Economic
  (b) Actual standard of living of father and mother (ask specific questions to get clear: cars, servants, housing, entertaining, etc., enough to eat, on relief, have to work as child, etc.).

Ingroups
  (c) Who were your father's (mother's) friends mostly: What organizations did your father (or mother) belong to? How did your father (mother) spend his (her) spare time?

Source: Adorno, T. W., Frenkel-Brunswik, E., Levinson, D. J., & Sanford, R. N., *The authoritarian personality*. New York: Harper & Row, 1950, pp. 304–325.

motives and was given latitude to probe further in some of the categories. In contrast to the nondirective interview, the direction of this interview was clearly in the hands of the interviewer.

## The Structured Interview

The structured interview or, as it has sometimes been called, the *standardized interview*, strives to ask each respondent the same questions in order to collect identical information. Such structuredness ensures that all respondents are replying to the same questions. If one interviewer asks, "Would you like to see better working conditions in this plant?" and another asks, "Do you think better working conditions would be desirable?" the answers may not be comparable. Differences in question order can also influence the meaning and implication of a question.

Selltiz and her associates (1976, pp. 309–317) listed two types of standardized interviews: 1) fixed-alternative and 2) open-ended. The fixed-alternative interview, sometimes also called a closed-question interview, is one in which the respondents are limited to stated alternatives. These alternatives may be simply yes or no; they may be chosen to indicate various degrees of approval or agreement; or they may consist of a series of replies to which the subjects pick the one closest to their own position. The types of questions asked and the fixed-alternative response categories are essentially the same whether they are part of an interview or a questionnaire. One reason for using interviews rather than written questionnaires, particularly when sensitive topics such as religion or sex may be the object of inquiry, is to obtain answers from persons who are either unwilling or unable to fill out questionnaires.

Here are two examples of fixed-alternative items:

What would you say is your approximate alcohol intake each day?

Less than 1/2 ounce
More than 1/2 ounce
Less than 1 ounce
More than 1 ounce
More than 2 ounces
More than 3 ounces

If you were to see a person in distress parked along the highway, you would probably:

Stop to help
Call the police at the next nearest exit
Continue to drive without trying to assist the motorist

The open-ended interview format permits a relatively freer response from the subject than the closed-interview format does. The distinguishing feature of open-ended questions is that they only suggest issues and do not restrict the answers or their expression. Examples of open-ended interview questions are as follows:

Now that you have been attending the University of _____ for _____ years, I wonder if you would tell me how you feel about it?

1. What do you *like* most about it?
2. What do you *dislike* most about it?
3. How about dormitory life, do you like it?
4. Is your social life coming up to expectations?

Lazarsfeld (1944) suggested that the development of a closed-question interview schedule be preceded by freer preliminary interviews in order to discover the range of probable responses, the possibilities that seem relevant, and the various implications and interpretations of wordings of particular questions. From this information, better closed questions could then be formulated. Lazarsfeld's proposal addresses an important ingredient of the standardized interview, the standardization of both the meaning and the stimulus itself.

Kerlinger (1973) recommended a third type of standardized-schedule item which he called the *scale* item. A *scale* is a set of verbal items to each of which a person responds by expressing either degrees of agreement and disagreement or some other kind of response. Scale items have fixed alternatives and place the responding individual at some point on the scale. Scale scores can thus be determined for each respondent and can be checked against open-ended question data. According to Kerlinger, "the use of scale items in interview schedules is a development of great promise, since the benefits of scales are combined with those of interviews" (1973, p. 485). We shall return to the advantages and disadvantages of scaling methods in the next chapter when we discuss attitude and value scaling.

Another approach to standardized interviewing, which is somewhat less structured, is the *nonschedule standardized* interview (Richardson et al., 1965), so called because it attempts to standardize without using a prepared schedule of interview items. Instead, the interviewer is trained to cover a particular set of topics and is told what information is required of each respondent. In order to achieve maximum standardization, the interviewer is encouraged not to vary his or her questioning from one respondent to the next. An illustration of a nonschedule interview is presented below. The items are somewhat varied in their coverage and format, in order to exemplify different types of scoring schemes. Items 1 through 4 allow the interviewer the freedom to phrase his or her own questions or to ask no questions, since the replies can be inferred from observations. The remainder of the items are in question form:

1. Orientation to Interview
   0 Seems to understand purpose of interview.
   1 Shows some insight as to purpose.
   2 Accepts stated explanation of purpose.
   3 Completely misinterprets purpose.
2. Attention
   0 Completely attentive to flow of conversation.
   1 Relatively undisturbed by extraneous stimuli.
   2 Easily distracted by extraneous stimuli.
   3 Impossible to get and hold attention.
3. Amount of Speech
   0 Underproduction.
   1 Moderate.
   2 Substantial.
   3 Abnormal overproduction.

4. Expressive Ability
   +2 Excellent.
   +1 Good.
    0 Adequate.
   −1 Inadequate.
   −2 Very inadequate.
5. Are you bothered by ill health?
   0 Never.
   1 Hardly ever.
   2 Sometimes.
   3 Often.
6. Do you experience dizzy spells?
   0 Never.
   1 Sometimes.
   2 Often.
7. How often are you troubled by stomach upset?
   3 Often.
   2 Sometimes.
   1 Hardly ever.
   0 Never.

## Critical Comment

In general the advantage of the structured interview is that it guarantees that important information about various aspects of a person will be obtained. The structured interview also provides standardization which in turn guarantees that all interviewees will be asked the same questions in similar situations. An advantage for the new interviewer is that the structured interview requires less psychological acumen and experience than the unstructured interview does. Furthermore, because the structured interview is quantifiable, it permits comparisons among interviewers and among respondents.

There are several important disadvantages, however, which are encountered as the structuredness increases. A list of formal questions and topics necessitates a rigidity that often interferes with more relaxed communication. The interview can become an inquisition and consequently may yield little more than minimal answers to the questions. If just enough time is allowed for asking the prescribed questions, opportunities for ferreting out related and pertinent bits of information will be missed. Moreover, with greater structure, the interviewer cannot cover the wide range of topics that could identify problems of which the respondent may be unaware.

The free, or unstructured, interview also has both advantages and disadvantages. Besides eliciting the desired information, at the same time it allows the conversation to proceed with a minimum of direction.

This brings it closer, than the structured interview does, to ordinary conversation between two people. Being more free and casual, the unstructured interview is often more natural, and consequently, the respondent may be more at ease. Furthermore, since there are no time limits or topic pressures, the interviewer can follow up promising leads. If the interview is conducted skillfully, the necessary information will be obtained—possibly without the respondent's being aware of the kind and amount of data being elicited.

But this freedom is counterbalanced by the risk of overlooking important areas of inquiry. This was noted by Helzer and his associates, who conducted a reliability study (1977a, b) using the interview as the main source of information about patients. They found that the interviewers were able to agree on diagnostic classifications when using structured, rather than unstructured, interviews.

Another disadvantage of the unstructured interview is that it confronts the respondents with different situations. Therefore, it is more difficult to compare the results equitably, and this may bias the sampling of the kinds and amount of information obtained. Some information will be provided and some will be concealed, because the direction of and the information from the interview are under the control of the respondent, who may emphasize his or her stronger attributes and obscure the weaker ones.

In summary, the advantages and disadvantages of each form of interview, as shown in Table 6–2, are about equal. The question of how much structure to incorporate in an interview is governed by its goals. Generally, it is correct to say that if the interview's real purpose is to gather a great deal of information, to develop rapport, to orient the respondent to a new setting, or to introduce testing procedures, then the unstructured interview is suitable. But if the interview is intended as a measuring device, by means of which limited but relevant infor-

**Table 6–2** The Structured versus Unstructured Interview.

| Type of Interview | Advantage | Disadvantage |
| --- | --- | --- |
| Structured | Standardized. High information yield. Requires less experience. Permits quantification. Permits comparisons. | Rigid procedure. Interrogation atmosphere. Encourages check marking. |
| Unstructured | Permits free expression. Is more natural. Free rein of questions. No time limits. | Encourages rambling. Resembles conversation. Unstandardized. Encourages respondent to conceal information. |

**Table 6–3** Types of Interviews and Their Settings, Aims, and Problems.

| Type of Interview | Setting | Purpose | Problem |
|---|---|---|---|
| Personnel | Industry | To assess candidate's qualifications | Interviewer's dual role |
| Troubleshooting | Industry | To determine cause of interpersonal difficulties | Interviewer's dual role |
| Poll | Door-to-door | To assess attitudes, opinions, or beliefs | Rigid structure and leading questions |
| Stress | Military or training programs | To assess reactions to unusual circumstances | Generalizability |
| Medical diagnostic | Clinic or hospital | To diagnose | Accuracy of reporting |
| Psychiatric intake | Mental hygiene clinic or hospital | To gather preliminary information about patient and establish relationships | Patient's anxiety |
| Mental status | Mental hygiene clinic or hospital | To ascertain patient's mental state | Overprobing and pathological bias |
| Case history | Clinic, hospital, or home | To gather background information | Selectivity of information |
| Pretest and posttest | Psychiatric | To determine decision making ability before and after test | Amount of test information to impart |
| Termination | Psychiatric | To set patient free | Premature timing |

mation is to be gathered and practical decisions and predictions are to be made, then the structured interview is preferable.

## Types of Interviews

Aside from the consideration of structuredness, interviews may also differ in their purposes and goals. The various types of interviews, their aims, and problems are summarized in Table 6–3. In addition to those appearing in Table 6–3, Bingham and Moore (1959) listed interviews in journalism, law practice, law enforcement, and vocational counseling as separate forms. Lopez (1965) divided interviews along quite different dimensions, by classifying them as information exchange, problem solving, and decision making. From among these, we shall discuss five types of interviews. Our listing below borrows from each of these divisions and is not exhaustive.

## The Employment, or Personnel, Interview

The employment, or personnel, interview is an important and integral part of employment selection and is usually conducted in the personnel department of the hiring industry or in the office of a consulting psychology firm retained by the industry to evaluate candidates. Its purpose is usually to assess the applicant's suitability for a particular job opening or for promotion. In either case, the interviewer both collects and imparts information.

To the employer, the personnel interview provides information about the candidate's work experience, personal characteristics, interests, and abilities. This information serves as a basis both for recommending further testing and for ascertaining the candidate's qualifications for the position. The obviously unqualified candidate is usually not encouraged to pursue his or her application. During the employment interview, all this information, along with helpful suggestions about the candidate's suitability for other possible positions or career choices (if such information is available to the interviewer), may be conveyed to the candidate.

For the job applicant, the employment interview consists mostly of information giving. It can be a frightening experience. Depending on the skills of the interviewer, the candidate may either overcome his or her initial apprehension regarding the interview and settle back and relax, or become even more tense and frightened. The conduct of the interview, and the information the candidate provides (or obtains) during its course, may motivate him or her either to accept the position (if offered) or not to accept it or pursue it further.

There is usually a final, or follow-up, personnel interview with the job applicant. Its function is to communicate to the candidate his or her favorable and unfavorable qualifications and to inform him or her of the company's decision. During the final interview, the employer (or repesentative) may ask some last-minute questions designed to help reach a final decision to hire or reject and to convey once again to the job applicant some of the details of the open position. When the decision not to hire (or not to promote) is made, either before or during the follow-up interview, the reason for this decision usually is also communicated to the candidate so that he or she may benefit from the interviews.

## Intake Interview

The intake interview, as the name suggests, is the initial contact in the clinic or hospital between the interviewer and the respondent. For the interviewee it is often an ordeal. Frequently, the decision to seek help for an emotional problem, or being forced to do so, has made the person ill at ease, self-conscious, and defensive. Perhaps now this person has misgivings about his or her (or someone else's) decision to seek help and has misconceptions about what is expected during the interview. The usual awkwardness and discomfort of the initial interview may be intensified if the person was coerced into coming. This is not surprising, since the interview is an unfamiliar experience to most people; and because it is the initial session, the interviewer is a stranger. Some people find it difficult to confide in members of their family; to reveal their innermost secrets to a stranger can be even more difficult. The interviewer must understand this and accordingly adjust the tone of the interview, as well as do most of the talking.

Beyond the first goal of the intake interview, which is to establish a relationship with the patient, the clinician must understand the latter's expectations and assess his or her motivation for treatment. Since the groundwork is to be laid for possible further contact, the interviewer usually describes the institution he or she represents, the fees to be charged, and the extent to which the patient's expectations can be met by the clinician's agency.

The intake interview, which is usually quite brief, also gathers identifying information (name, age, education), determines the patient's problem, and touches on other matters that will be pursued more thoroughly in the mental status interview.

## Mental Status Interview

The mental status interview is a depth study made at the earliest possible time after the intake interview. Its purpose, as the name implies, is to assess mental preoccupations and behavior pathology. It probes more deeply than the intake interview does into personal matters and consists of inquiries about suicidal thoughts, voices, relationships with others in the family, sexual behavior, and the like. Considerable skill is required to find out this information without causing the patient discomfort, and generally it has been found that a gentle manner and a permissive atmosphere are more productive than inquisitorial questioning in hostile or businesslike surroundings.

Table 6–4 lists the six categories for which the interviewer collects information. He or she is urged (Menninger, 1952; Wells & Reusch, 1945) to use as many direct quotations as possible in reporting the

**Table 6-4** Excerpts from a Mental Status Interview of a Twenty-Nine-Year-Old Male.

| Category | Example of Report |
|---|---|
| General appearance, attitude, and behavior | He is friendly and cooperative. Has made no complaints about ward restrictions. He smiles in a somewhat exaggerated and grotesque manner. |
| Discourse | He answers in a deep loud voice, speaking in a slow, precise, and somewhat condescending manner. His responses are relevant but vague. |
| Mood and affective fluctuations | His facial expressions, although not totally inappropriate, are poorly correlated with subject of discourse or events in his environment. |
| Sensorium and intellect | The patient's orientation to place, person, and time is normal. His remote and recent memory also are normal. Two brief intelligence measures indicate about average intelligence. |
| Mental content and specific preoccupations | He readily discusses what he calls his "nervous trouble." He complains of "bad thoughts" and a "conspiracy." He reports hearing voices saying, "Hello, Bill, you're a dirty dog." |
| Insight | The patient readily accepts the idea that he should be in the hospital. He feels that hospitalization will help him get rid of these "bad" thoughts. He is not in the least defensive about admitting to auditory and visual hallucinations or to the idea that everyone on earth is his enemy. |

interview and to refrain, at least at this stage of psychodiagnosis, from extrapolating beyond his or her observations.

The first of these categories—general appearance, attitude, and behavior—consists simply of information about the respondent's physical stature and bearing, style of dress, unusual mannerisms and actions, and demeanor during the interview. The most obvious kind of signal that may betray a personality problem is illustrated by, for example, the person with an antisocial personality who may sink into a chair, with legs and feet raised up on the interviewer's desk, and say, "What's up doc?" If the interview is conducted in the hospital, the clinician makes a special effort to collect information from the hospital aides and nurses about the patient's general behavior in the ward. This information can be gathered by informal observation, or preferably, it can be gathered systematically, using rating scales or audiovisual aids.

The second category consists of the respondent's manner of speaking, or discourse. People have many qualitative and quantitative speech idiosyncrasies, and each has its particular diagnostic significance. The following excerpt, which illustrates the circumstantial speech of some manic psychotics, is an example of how some patients never quite get to the point:

DOCTOR: What brings you here?
PATIENT: I can tell you what does, but telling you and bringing you are one and the same. Get what I mean? One and the same thing because this is a hospital, and I tell you they brought me to a hospital, and it is nothing more or less than just that; and it brings all of us to our destinies.

The third category is the patient's emotional, or affective, tone. Is the patient happy or dejected? Does the emotion correspond to the topic of discussion? How stable is his or her mood during the course of the interview? For example, some people with a diagnosis of hebephrenic schizophrenia have such widely fluctuating emotions that during a single interview, they may display extreme mirth, followed by sadness, and then by uproarious laughter.

The fourth category, evaluating sensorium, establishes whether the patient knows where he or she is, realizes that he or she is a patient in a clinic or hospital, and is not confused about the season of the year or the actual year in which all of this is happening. This is also the part of the interview in which, if there is not time for lengthier intelligence tests, the interviewer makes some assessment of intelligence. Typically, the interviewer gives the patient several brief arithmetic problems (for example, subtract 7 from 100 and continue until told to stop), asks the meanings of several words taken from a standard vocabulary list, or asks three or four questions from a test of abstract reasoning (for example, in what way are a table and chair alike? A poem and a statue?).

The fifth category of the interview deals with the patient's mental content. More than the other areas, this may touch upon sensitive material. To illustrate, we present an excerpt from an interview with a paranoid thirty-five-year-old male who had tried to kill his mother-in-law.

DOCTOR: You say that you've done nothing unusual, yet the police brought you here last night.
PATIENT: I tried to use the telephone in my own house, and my mother-in-law tried to stop me.
DOCTOR: What do you mean?
PATIENT: I tried to register my invention. You see, I have information that someone is trying to steal my ideas.
DOCTOR: So you tried to call the patent office?
PATIENT: No, I tried to call the president. This is too important, and I'd rather not trust some flunky or clerk with this information.
DOCTOR: How often have you called the president?
PATIENT: A couple of times.
DOCTOR: What kind of invention do you have?

PATIENT: (He produces a long document that had been rolled up and tucked inside his jacket.) It's a plan to restore vision to the blind.
DOCTOR: Do you want to tell me more?
PATIENT: I don't know, can I trust you?
DOCTOR: I should tell you that I must share this information with other hospital personnel.
PATIENT: Okay, here is how it works. The antenna on the top of the skull fits into the splice of the optic nerve by means of the mathematical formula that you see here....

The last category of information to be obtained during the mental status interview is an estimate of the patient's insight into his or her disorder. That is, the interviewer attempts to learn whether the respondent understands the extent of the disorder and why he or she is at the clinic or hospital. Paradoxically, as we indicated earlier, the more severe a person's mental disorder is, the less likely the patient is to appreciate the fact of being ill.

## Case History Interview

The purpose of the case history interview is to gather background information about the patient, either at the time of the original contact or, more appropriately, any time after the intake interview. Case history interviewing began at about the time that social work joined forces with the psychoanalytic movement. Early in the history of social work, case studies were made in order to determine eligibility for public assistance. During the 1920s and 1930s it became firmly linked to the mental hygiene movement (Taft, 1927), and its major purpose became the study and description of the individual and the family group.

When psychiatry, psychology, and social work joined forces in mental health settings, case histories became the social worker's contribution to the mental health team. This background-information gathering for personality assessment was readily accepted and adopted by the psychologists, who also were accustomed to explaining behavior in terms of a subject's past experience.

Of the three primary sources of information for the case history—interviews, formal records, and agency reports—the case history interview is the most important and is conducted with the client as well as with his or her family, neighbors, friends, teachers, employers, or others. These interviews cover, among other matters, such basic topics as the history of the complaint, hereditary background, childhood development, and medical history. The information gathered in these interviews is usually checked and cross-checked, because in all likelihood, it is colored by the biases and opinions of the respondents.

It is not the goal of the case history to collect data for a complete biography; rather its goal is to answer such questions as "Should the patient be committed to a state institution?" or "What are the history and background of his or her presenting complaints?" The kinds of information collected are (Sundberg et al., 1973): (1) identifying data (e.g., name, age, sex), (2) reason for coming, (3) description of work and status on the job, (4) family constellation, (5) early recollections, (6) birth and development, (7) history of physical and psychological health, (8) education and training, (9) work record, (10) recreational activities and interests, (11) sexual development, (12) marital and family data, (13) self-description, (14) significant or turning points in life, (15) view of the future, and (16) other information voluntarily supplied by the patient.

The fundamental assumption underlying the collection of case history data is that a person's present personality is part of a continuous process of development. The importance of this assumption has been especially emphasized by Freudian psychoanalysts, who strongly believe in the importance of childhood experiences to adult behavior. Presumably a person's past behavior also helps predict what may be expected of him or her in similar situations in the future.

Some writers have proposed that the case history be the primary tool of personality assessment (Dailey, 1960, 1971). Also regarding this proposal Sundberg stated: "In many ways, the person's life *is* the person. There is nothing more individual and 'personally possessed' than the series of events through which a person has passed" (1977, p. 106).

Why would the study of life history events be so important in studying a person? It seems that life history data are often the only clues to the development, cause and effect, and impact of society on a person. Psychologist Block, in his *Lives through Time*, asserted: "Correctional, cross-sectional, or experimental methods have great and suggestive contributions to make toward an understanding of the bases of behavior. But these approaches do not encompass time and the trajectory of individual lives" (1971, p. 3).

This view of the importance of life history events extends beyond the interview and includes data gathered from both interviews and archival and other secondary sources. There is some evidence to support this view. In one early study (Horn, D., 1943), biographical data were found to be more valuable than other types of information available. In another study (Kostlan, 1954), various types of data (Rorschach, MMPI, and case history) were selectively eliminated, and the superiority of the case history as a source of cues was demonstrated. More recently, Soskin

## BOX 6-5

## Early Recollections of Three Male Homosexuals

*Case A*

1. Age 5–6. I was lying on the floor and made a caustic remark, and she [mother] kicked me in the crotch. It hurt—but she apologized. It was an enraged kick—but she immediately became soft.

2. Age 4. I was with my father at the beach and was standing in the water. Suddenly my legs were pulled out from under me. It was my father. I was scared.

3. Age 4. I was in a closet, in a dress, with a doll. My father opened the door. He caught me. [Question] I remember being caught in a compromising position.

*Case B*

1. Age 3–4. I needed shots every other day. Grandma did it. The first time, standing by the stove she got the hypodermic ready. She said, "Come here." I was crying. I held her legs, she was wearing a long dress, and she gave me the shot. I cried and screamed. The first thing I wanted to do was run, but I didn't. Then she rocked and held me, and said I was a good boy for not running away, and I felt real good.

2. Age 4. I was with grandma, and she was hanging clothes. I switched on the washing machine and tried to put some clothing through, and my arm went through. I screamed and grandma ran towards me. I was scared, and she turned the machine off, and I felt fine.

3. Age 4–5. I remember when my parents got married (when mother remarried). I hid their rings. The rings were above the mantel and I took them and hid them. Two hours later I sat and waited for them to find out. They asked me and I didn't respond: I said, "no." They asked again, and I said I wanted some boxes their presents came in, and I showed them. They gave me the boxes and left.... I remember holding grandma's hand as they went in the car. I felt like they were leaving me.

*Case C*

1. Age 5–6. I remember climbing up on the sofa where he [father] was lying and I lay on top of him. I knew I could do it. I'm almost positive there was something sexual about it. I felt wonderful but I don't remember what he did.

2. Age 4. Mother was cleaning the house. I picked a thing off the floor. I went to blow into it. I thought it was a balloon. She was furious and hollered. It seemed like a long time, on and on. I couldn't understand how, over a balloon, but I knew there was more to it. Now I know it was a prophylactic. Whenever they are mentioned I think of this.

3. Age 5. Sis and I were in bed. We had scarlet fever or measles. The room was very dark, the weather was warm, it was quiet and cozy. I looked out the screen door at where the kids whom I liked and wanted over, lived. But I couldn't go out of the house. [Question.] I liked the idea of both of us being sick,

*(continued)*

> **BOX 6–5**  *(Continued)*
>
> not able to scratch or rub, but getting great attention and care. It was a nice situation.
>
> 4. Age 5. Next door a woman had a garden, and flowers grew against our fence. I can't remember whether I was picking the flowers or standing and smelling them. The woman came out screaming and screaming and screaming. [Question.] I was scared. I remember mother coming out and they talked back and forth across the fence and then I went back into the house.
>
> Source: Manaster, G. J., & King, M. Early recollections of male homosexuals. *Journal of Individual Psychology,* 1973, 29, 29–30.

(1959), L. K. Sines (1959), Golden (1964), and Owens (1971) reported similar findings.

Personality assessment by means of the case history alone is usually not recommended because of the unreliable information obtained from the individual and his or her acquaintances. Life history data, insofar as they depend on the person's memory or the memory of acquaintances, are extremely unreliable. As an example of this, R. S. Lazarus (1961) reported an early study made by Doering and Raymond (1935) on the credibility of information given by the mothers of sixty patients in the Boston Psychopathic Hospital. Even factual items (e.g., date of birth, high school grades) were incorrectly reported by 11 percent of the mothers. Twenty-six percent of these mothers gave incorrect information about such items as the incidence of mental disease in the family. One solution to this problem is to check case history information, whenever feasible, against babybooks, school records, and other informal and formal records.

Moreover, inferences based on life history data are sometimes unwarranted. For example, in a comparative study of the personal histories of schizophrenic and nonpsychiatric patients, Schofield and Balian (1959) discredited the inference often made that the origins of mental illness are readily found in life experiences. In a survey of over three hundred studies of life histories of psychiatric patients, they found very few with "traumatic histories" but did find "traumas" in the life histories of one-fourth of the control group of normal persons. The most stunning finding of their statistical analysis was the substantial overlap of the normal and schizophrenic samples on the distributions of personal history variables. Schofield and Balian cautioned against believing that any single set of events or circumstances could predict the future onset of schizophrenia. They found, instead, that the study of patterns and configurations of life events were more valid predictors than isolated events were.

Life history assessment, by means of the interview and other sources, has also been used to study the effects of stress on physical and mental disorders (e.g., Holmes & Rahe, 1967; Rahe & Holmes, 1965). For example, one team of researchers (Holmes & Holmes, 1970) uncovered a wide variety of stressors that seemed to be implicated in these disorders. To measure the impact of different kinds of life changes on the development of disorders, Holmes and Rahe (1967) constructed a scale of stress values measured in "life stress units." Their Social Readjustment Scale, as they called it, rated each kind of stressful event in terms of LCUs, or life change units. To devise a scoring system, they assigned an arbitrary base-line value of 50 to the act of marrying and then had judges rate other actions and events based on that. Some of the life events and their scale values are as follows: death of a spouse (100), divorce (73), jail term (63), marriage (50), fired at work (47), death of a close friend (37), vacation (13), Christmas (12). The reader should note that some of the LCUs are associated with pleasant events.

Holmes and Rahe predicted that too many changes, coming too close together and totaling more than 300 points in one year, could result in serious mental or physical disorders. In other words, the more LCUs one earns in a short period of time, the more prone one is to disease. This hypothesis was corroborated in a sample of 2,500 naval officers and enlisted personnel aboard three cruisers (Holmes & Masuda, 1972). The men's LCUs and their health changes were recorded for six months. During the first month of the cruise, those men who had reported being exposed to intense life changes had nearly 90 percent more disorders than those who reported fewer stresses. This trend continued for the six-month duration of the trip.

In a later study (see Bootzin, 1980, pp. 196–197), it was found that of those who had acquired more than 300 LCUs during a one-year period, 86 percent reported serious health problems, whereas only 48 percent of those who had scored between 150 and 300 reported such health changes.

**Critical Comment.** In the section on indirect observation in chapter five we touched on some of the weaknesses of the life history approach. We mentioned falsification of information which could be traced to conscious or unconscious dissembling, and we indicated a number of factors, such as exhibitionism or bravado, that could lead to omissions or exaggerations of facts. Other problems that we discussed were the patient's lack of self-knowledge and an inability to remember feelings about and reactions to significant figures in his or her life.

To these disadvantages of the life history approach we add two others. First, there is the problem that not all personal history items are verifiable. Certainly, demographic data such as birth date, confirmation date, and wedding date can be, in principle at least, validated. But other information, especially that pertaining to habits, needs, attitudes, and values—all of which could be useful personality predictors—cannot be easily verified.

Second, when the sources for the life history data include the friends and family of the target person, their possible biases must be understood and corrected. Friends and family can distort the truth about their acquaintance or family member just as well as they can about themselves. Of course, their motives may be conscious or unconscious. And again, as in self-reports, poor or inaccurate recall may distort or influence what is reported.

## Pretest and Posttest Interviews

When a personality assessment is made in a psychiatric clinic or hospital, interviews are conducted just before and after tests. The pretest interview is held in order to evaluate the patient's condition and to help decide what tests should be used. After the tests are given, a posttest interview is then conducted in order to inform the patient of the test results and to make recommendations based on them. The posttest interview is also a good time to clarify any issues brought up in the pretest interview or in the test findings.

In general, the posttest interview offers the clinician an opportunity to examine hypotheses formulated during the pretest interview and throughout the clinical evaluation. If the test results are not consistent with the nontest observations and the clinical impressions, they also can be examined at this time. For example, a test score or an item response may suggest bizarre thinking, but nothing that transpired during the initial interview may have given a hint of this. The interviewer can now pursue this lead by asking new and probing questions about this matter. There are numerous tales in personality assessment circles of instances in which the test responses provided the only leads to a patient's disorder, which had been overlooked during the initial phases of personality evaluation.

There are many other kinds of interviews, and as we indicated at the beginning of this section, our list is not complete. One kind of interview listed in Table 6–3, the so-called stress interview, is no longer frequently used. It was once a common method of investigating people's fitness for special jobs or assignments and of inducing stress in psychophysiological research. But it has been discontinued for these and other uses because of both ethical and research-design concerns. There is some current interest (see Almy, 1978), however, in reviving it for gastrointestinal research because, it is asserted, its potential gains would far outweigh its risks. The principal arguments for reviving the stress interview are that modern instrumentation would enable the collection of unique information not otherwise obtainable and that the new ethical safeguards would preclude its abuse.

## Theoretical Orientation of the Interviewer

The psychotherapeutic theory that the interviewer adheres to determines largely, but not exclusively, the framework within which the interview will proceed. This theory also guides the degree of the interview's structuredness, as well as its duration and format. This is to be expected, since as we noted earlier, the history of the interview is closely associated with the history of psychotherapy.

The contributions to the theory and technique of interviewing by such reputed psychotherapists as Freud, Adler, Sullivan, and Rogers have been many, and in the next pages, we shall sketch some of them. For more detailed information about the various personality theories underlying these techniques, the interested reader could consult Corsini, 1977; Hall & Lindzey, 1978; and Munroe, 1955. For our purpose, which is to relate historically the psychotherapy interview to its measurement function, the reader should keep in mind that personality is assessed throughout the therapy sessions (see Meehl, 1960).

### Freud's Psychoanalytic Technique

For Freud, the purpose of the interview was to help the patient explore his or her unconscious self. In the process, Freud believed, he himself would gain glimpses of the formation of personality structure. Accordingly, Freud's major interview objective was to help the patient reconstruct his or her basic personality. Freud's main tools for attaining this goal were free association and dream analysis.

Essentially, free association is an unstructured form of interview that requires the respondents to say anything and everything that comes to mind, regardless of how trivial, inappropriate, or ludicrous it may seem. The patients are also supposed to report their dreams and fantasies, not an easy task for most people. In contrast, the interviewers' role, after intially and briefly instructing their patients about their responsibilities, is a passive one in that they withdraw from the interaction, though occasionally the interviewer may prod the interviewee by asking probing questions.

### Alfred Adler's Directive Technique

As in Freud's technique, Alfred Adler's empirical observations were gleaned from the interview, but his goals in therapy were different from Freud's. Adler's interview techniques were more directive than Freud's, and his objectives were to help patients (1) understand their life styles (e.g., gain insight into characteristic coping patterns), (2) try new ways of solving everyday problems, and (3) develop greater social interest.

In studying the individual, Adler emphasized the discovery and understanding of the person's life story, as well as his or her attitudes toward it. Thus, during the interview, the areas most heavily explored were vocation, history of illnesses, attitudes, and moods; relations with family and friends; and love affairs. Other information valued by Adler included art productions, early memories, and dreams.

In regard to interview style, the role of the Adlerian interviewer is much more active than that of the Freudian interviewer. The Adlerian interviewer often puts patients to work discovering the reasons for their problems. Typically, as the interviews progress, the patients are required to assume an ever-increasing responsibility for their actions and are expected to participate more actively, than before treatment, in the socially shared goals of their communities.

## Harry Stack Sullivan

Harry Stack Sullivan's interpersonal theory of psychiatry stresses personality as a hypothetical entity that can best be observed or studied from social situations. Accordingly, during the interview he was interested in learning about the sequence and meanings of the principal interpersonal problems to which the patient was exposed while passing from infancy to adulthood.

Sullivan is the only one of the psychiatrists discussed so far whose books specifically described the techniques of interviewing. Either a one-time occurrence or a more extended process, the psychiatric interview was separated into four stages: (1) formal inception, (2) reconnaissance, (3) detailed inquiry, and (4) termination (Sullivan, 1954).

During the first stage Sullivan formulated working hypotheses about the patient, and during the reconnaissance stage he attempted to define the patient's major problem. The most important stage of the interview was the detailed inquiry, and Sullivan prescribed a list of diagnostic signs and symptoms for which the interviewer should watch. These included apathy, sadness, elation, overdramatic extravagance, tenseness, bizarre thinking, and peculiar mannerisms. Finally, at the termination of the interview, Sullivan suggested that the interviewer make a *final statement*, a *prescription of action*, a *final assessment*, and a *formal leave taking*. Again, each of these stages was carefully spelled out.

Because of his careful specification of stages and procedures, Sullivan's interview approach is more adaptable than those of Freud and

Adler to standardization and subsequent quantification. In addition, Sullivan recommended overall interview strategies and tactics to meet various contingencies. These recommendations can be quite helpful to the new interviewer whose experience with psychiatric interviews is limited.

## Rogers's Nondirective Counseling

Carl Rogers's interviewing techniques and goals, as we indicated earlier, resembled those of Freud, Adler, and Sullivan in that they were formulated in the clinic. His belief in people's abilities to solve their own problems, together with his therapy goal of helping them achieve self-actualization, dictated that he use the nondirective interview to communicate with his clients.

Rogers's interview technique was originally described in his 1942 book, *Counseling and Psychotherapy*, and elaborated in his 1951 book, *Client-Centered Therapy*, as well as in more recent publications (Rogers, 1961; Rogers & Stevens, 1971). In these, he advised interviewers to avoid giving advice, to refrain from asking highly specific questions, and to go to great lengths to avoid criticizing the client. Recognition and clarification of feelings, on the other hand, were encouraged, along with nonjudgmental acceptance of the client's statements. How this should be accomplished during the interview is difficult to describe and is best illustrated by the following excerpt from one of Rogers's sessions with a woman:

> CLIENT: I'll tell you how I feel about my coming here. I don't think I have to come twice a week. I would like to come once a week for the time being and see and just talk over my problems once a week. And then, if everything goes smoothly on the once a week deal, why then I think I'm through. The only reason I'm not stopping now, although I feel right now I don't need any more, is that I just want to feel a lasting final few licks, shall we say.
> THERAPIST: You want to feel quite sure that you are really through before you quit.
> CLIENT: Or if this is one of these quiet weeks, if it is, why then I'll have to start coming back twice, maybe three times, I hope not.
> THERAPIST: By and large you feel you are getting close to the end.
> CLIENT: I think so. How does one determine?
> THERAPIST: Just the way you are determining.
> CLIENT: Oh, is that so, just by feeling that you don't have to come as often?
> THERAPIST: When you are ready to call it quits, why, we'll call it quits.

CLIENT: Uh huh, and then no return, uh?
THERAPIST: Oh yes, if you feel you want to.
CLIENT: And then I'd have priority on you, is that it?
THERAPIST: Of course, yes, yes. We don't close the door and lock it, we just say goodbye and if you want to get in touch with me again, why, feel free to do so. (1951, pp. 85–86)

For us the most noteworthy features of this dialogue are the way the therapist led the client to assume the major responsibility for her progress by encouraging her to reach her own decisions and the way the client, rather than her therapist, made all the important interpretations. These differences set the Rogerian interviews apart from the approaches discussed earlier.

## Evaluation of the Interview

The three main sources of errors in interviewing, which contribute to its unreliability as an assessment tool, are errors arising from the complexity of the *interview process*, from the fears and anxieties of the *interviewee*, and from the *interviewer* (Table 6–5).

### Interview Process Errors

As indicated in Table 6–5, interview process errors arise from the complexity of the interview's two-person interaction. For example, Heller reported (1972) that dominant interviewees elicit different interviewer behaviors than dependent ones do and that hostile or

**Table 6–5** Sources of Error in the Interview.

| Source | Error | Resolution |
| --- | --- | --- |
| Interview process | Usually random rather than directional, error results from the complex interaction of interviewer, interviewee, and setting. | Conduct as many interviews as feasible with same respondents. |
| Interviewee | Error results from fears and anxieties, misinformation, or role expectations. | Carefully structure interview and anticipate expectations. |
| Interviewer | Error results from idiosyncrasies of interviewer, recording mistakes, inferences beyond obtained data, poor training, theoretical biases, or inexperience. | Standardize interviewer strategies and intensive training, and establish a uniform system for collecting data. |

friendly respondents elicit still different interviewer behaviors. This interactive complexity was also shown by Matarazzo and his associates (1968), who demonstrated that the amount of client speech was related to the interviewer's verbal activity: "When patients talked little the interviewer talked more, hoping to stimulate them; when patients were more verbally active, the interviewer's tendency was to talk less, so as not to impede the patients' productivity" (Wiens, 1976, p. 45). In fact, this conversational complexity has given rise to a new area of sociolinguistic research which focuses on the politics of conversational linguistics (see Box 6–2).

Interview process errors also are unpredictable in that they do not produce inaccuracies in only one direction. For example, a respondent may not feel up to par on a particular day and therefore may present a distorted sample of his or her typical behavior. Had he or she been interviewed on another day, the observed behavior might have been considerably different. Similarly, the interviewer may be preoccupied on a particular day and therefore may present a distorted sample of his or her typical behavior. If a combination of these influences is operating at any one time, the communication between the interviewer and the respondent could be impaired, with the possible result that neither the interviewer nor the interviewee would obtain a proper sample of the other's typical behavior.

**Interviewee Errors**

These errors may arise, as we indicated in our discussion of the intake interview, because of the interviewee's anxieties in a new situation or misgivings about seeking help. A skillful interviewer can use these apprehensions to advantage and enlist the respondent's cooperation by means of them; but if the interviewer overlooks them, they may disrupt the interview. The interviewee's role expectations also may interfere with communication. Consider, for example, the person who has read or heard that psychologists and psychiatrists like to hear about dreams because they reveal important clues to personality. Now the respondent is in a situation in which he or she is expected to talk about dreams but unfortunately has no dreams to relate. How the respondent adapts to that situation may have little to do with how he or she usually behaves. Therefore, the interviewer obtains a picture of behavior based on considerable stress and anxiety rather than a picture of typical behavior.

In addition, the motivations of the interviewees, as we indicated earlier, vary greatly. Some respondents consciously distort the truth; others do so unconsciously. Some interviewees may have sought the appointment, whereas others may have been brought in, or been ordered to appear, by a third party. Most children and adolescents are involuntary clients, and some adults are ordered by a judge or by a professional worker to appear. In many of these instances, both systematic and random (unpredictable) errors are introduced which affect the interview, sometimes in known, but more often in unknown ways. But one thing is certain: given an alternative set of interviewee motivations or variables, the resulting interview would be quite different.

## Interviewer Errors

There are three main types of interviewer errors. First is the error caused by the interviewer's fallibility as an observer or recording instrument. He or she may be fallible because of a particular background or mental set preventing him or her from seeing or hearing exactly what has transpired; or if the interviewer does observe accurately, his or her notes may amplify, minimize, omit, or round out responses. These recording errors may be made either before or after the interview.

A second kind of interviewer error is caused by inexperience. For example, untrained and inexperienced interviewers who do not know how to motivate others to talk freely do not obtain much information. One common error of this sort arises when interviewers permit the interview to deteriorate into a "good-friends" relationship. This atmosphere does not encourage the divulgence of personal thoughts and problems; instead, the interviewee may not want to bother his or her newly found friend with his or her troubles.

Then there is the interviewer who inadvertently discourages further discussion by comments such as "Well, I guess we beat that subject to death" or "I'll bet you can't answer this question" (see Gilmore, 1973, for examples of questions that facilitate and impede questions); or the one who, when hearing anything about a favorite topic—be it golf, life insurance, or sex—probes into it prematurely, relentlessly, and irrelevantly. Roy Schafer (1954, p. 21), in an excellent chapter on interviewing, discussed this voyeuristic, or "peeping Tom," tendency of some clinicians.

A third type of interviewer error, aptly called the "pathology bias" by some (Dailey, 1960), occurs because the diagnostician sees symptoms and defense mechanisms in everyone (or interprets as pathological any response that is unusual or unique). In this regard, one psychologist who advocated a positive approach to mental health said, "There is abundant empirical knowledge concerning the ... anxious and the neurotic ... there is little information and even less conceptual clarity about the nature of psychological normality" (Shoben, 1957, p. 183).

Several research findings directly pertain to the effects of interviewer roles on the progress of the interview. In Heller's study (1972), he found that interviewers who were instructed to be friendly, silent, and passive were particularly adept at eliciting free discussion. Thus, interviewer ambiguity and lack of feedback, Heller reported, created more subject self-disclosure than did a structured and active approach. Moreover, it is often assumed that interviewers' silent pauses cause anxiety during the initial interview and serve to reduce speech production. One study (Siegman, 1978), however, disputed this assumption and presented evidence that anxiety arousal per se reduces silent pauses and accelerates speech rates.

Wiens (1976) reported that, generally, active-friendly interviewers were preferred by clients to passive-hostile ones. The latter's passivity and lack of communication tended to be somewhat punishing to most interviewees. Wiens recommended that interviewers structure the early portions of the interview until the inexperienced interviewees learn what is expected of them and then lessen the structure after the respondents have become familiar with their role.

## The Validity of Interviews

These errors that we have described contribute to the interview's unreliability and lack of validity. Most criticisms of the interview have focused on its lack of validity in that it does not accurately predict the person's behavior, or some criterion, and that it cannot be used for psychodiagnostic or personality assessment data. Three sets of studies on this subject are noteworthy.

One of these, by Sarbin (1941, 1943), showed that the interview added no new information to test scores and high school achievement in predicting college success. Other research showed that the ratings obtained from interview information were of little practical use in predicting the success of graduate students in clinical psychology programs (Kelly & Fiske, 1951; Kelly & Goldberg, 1959). The third set of studies showed that as many as 40 percent in a survey inaccurately reported contributions to community fund-raising appeals and that 10 percent inaccurately reported possession of a driver's license (Cannell & Kahn, 1968). Relating these types of inaccuracies to the interview, Kanfer and Phillips (1970) decided that when people describe their experiences or emotions in an interview, their verbalizations are determined as much by the interview context as by their true histories. As such, these disclosures cannot be accepted as truths.

Taking a somewhat different route, two investigators (Carey & Gottesman, 1978) showed mathematically that an interview's high reliability does not necessarily guarantee its high validity but that, paradoxically, low reliability can, in certain circumstances, also result in high validity. Consequently, these investigators proposed enhancing the validity of psychiatric interviews, not so much by manipulating their reliability as by changing the experimental designs within which they occur. Among the changes they suggested, the technical details of which are beyond our present purpose, were to consider tightening the experimental design and taking into account the relative fluctuations in the base rates of the target disorders and then computing measurement errors with more appropriate statistics than are currently in vogue.

If the interview is so deficient in reliability and validity, why is it the method of choice for so many professions? Evidently the interview has uses not affected by its adequacy as a predictive tool. In industry or in the clinic or hospital, the interviewer acquires firsthand information about the interviewee's appearance, voice, and mannerisms, as well as other impressions and clues that can be obtained only from person-to-person contact. But perhaps more importantly, the interviewer, by an apparent demonstration of interest in another human being, acknowledges that the interviewee is a person and not just another number.

If it is human warmth that continues to recommend the assessment interview as a proper tool in the study of people, then the following sections on computer interviewing are misplaced. On the other hand, if computer interviewing enhances the procedure's reliability and validity, then the loss of the human intermediary will make up for it by providing greater accuracy and usefulness.

## Computer Interviewing

The design of an automated system that can interview or be interviewed for personality assessment purposes is still somewhat futuristic, but it is not beyond reach. The beginnings of one such system have been under way for some time, as illustrated in the early work of Weizenbaum (1966) and his ELIZA interview dialogues. Consider, for example, the following dialogue between a patient and a therapist in which the patient is a human and the therapist is a computer program:

> PATIENT: Men are all alike.
> THERAPIST: In what way?
> PATIENT: They're always bugging us about something or other.
> THERAPIST: Can you think of a specific example?
> PATIENT: Well, my boyfriend made me come here.
> THERAPIST: Your boyfriend made you come here?
> PATIENT: He says I'm depressed much of the time.
> THERAPIST: I am sorry to hear you are depressed.
> PATIENT: It's true. I am unhappy.
> THERAPIST: Do you think coming here will help you not to be unhappy?
> PATIENT: I need some help, that much seems certain.

THERAPIST: What would it mean to you if you got some help?
PATIENT: Perhaps I could learn to get along with my mother.
THERAPIST: Tell me more about your family.
PATIENT: My mother takes care of me.
THERAPIST: Who else in your family takes care of you?
PATIENT: My father.
THERAPIST: Your father?
PATIENT: You are like my father in some ways.
THERAPIST: What resemblance do you see?
PATIENT: You are not very aggressive but I think you don't want me to notice that.
THERAPIST: What makes you think I am not very aggressive?
PATIENT: You don't argue with me.
THERAPIST: Why do you think I don't argue with you?
PATIENT: You are afraid of me.
THERAPIST: Does it please you to believe I am afraid of you?
PATIENT: My father is afraid of everybody.
THERAPIST: What else comes to mind when you think of your father?
PATIENT: Bullies.
THERAPIST: Does that have anything to do with the fact that your boyfriend made you come here? (Weizenbaum, 1966, pp. 40–42)

This dialogue resembles clinical interviewing, although it has the sound of a cocktail party conversation. The interview begins with the patient's observation regarding the nature of men, meanders through a variety of seemingly unrelated topics, and then ends with no perceptible statement of a problem or its resolution. One reason ELIZA is so limited is because its natural-language processing can understand only the denotative meanings of its dictionary of words. That is, it cannot search for the connotative meanings of words, nor can it understand the deeper language structures of sentences. But it is a step in the right direction. Its influence on another researcher, Kenneth M. Colby (Colby et al., 1971; Colby & Hilf, 1974), led to developments in which people can interview computers.

Colby and his associates, then at Stanford University, constructed a computer system that enabled clinicians and others to interview paranoid machine-patients whose persecutory delusional systems could be adjusted to be "weak" or "strong," depending on how the system's three affect variables—anger, fear, and mistrust—were represented to react to several sensitive areas of inquiry. The program was called PARRY. Here is an excerpt from an interview with a "weak" (less paranoid) version of PARRY (Colby, 1973, pp. 280–281):

DOCTOR: Tell me something about yourself.
PATIENT: I went to the track at Bay Meadows.

DOCTOR: What happened there?
PATIENT: There's a lot of crooked gambling going on there.
DOCTOR: Why do you think the gambling is crooked?
PATIENT: I have worried that gangsters have too much power in this country.

And an excerpt from an interview with a "strong" version of the model:

DOCTOR: How do you like the hospital?
PATIENT: I don't communicate very much with others.
DOCTOR: Do other people at the hospital get on your nerves?
PATIENT: I shouldn't have come here.
DOCTOR: Why do you say you shouldn't have come?
PATIENT: They made me come here.

We shall describe one study in which PARRY's real-world applicability was tested. In this design, Hilf (1972) had eight psychiatrists interview by teletype two patients using the technique of machine-mediated interviewing. Each psychiatrist interviewed two patients. One patient was PARRY, and the other was a hospitalized paranoid psychotic. The psychiatrists' task was to conduct a diagnostic psychiatric interview and to rate each response from the "patients" (the psychiatrists were not told that one of these was a machine) along a nine-point scale of paranoia. The transcripts of these interviews were then evaluated by a randomly selected group of psychiatrists and computer experts in order to determine which was the real patient and which was PARRY. The answer to the research question, "Can expert judges (psychiatrists and computer scientists) using teletyped transcripts of psychiatric interviews distinguish between paranoid patients and simulated paranoid processes?" was no.

What are the implications of this research for the study of personality? Most importantly, it demonstrates that some personality processes and belief systems can be simulated and hence be made into models. From this it follows logically that these models can be gradually modified so that they incorporate other forms of normal and abnormal personality processes. To make these modifications and to arrive at a set of personality simulations, one has to learn a great deal about these personalities because computer programming demands an explicitness not required in other forms of theorizing. And finally, as we learn more about personality for simulation purposes, we can devise ever more detailed assessment techniques for testing the developed models and, in turn, for testing the personality types on which the models are based.

A computer interview program with a somewhat different goal from that described above, one with the more open-ended purpose of obtaining personality test responses from patients in order to assess

> **BOX 6-6**
>
> ### The Computer as Intake Interviewer
>
> A computer-assisted psychiatric assessment unit is currently functioning as part of the admissions procedure at a mental hospital in Salt Lake City (Johnson & Williams, 1975). The system works somewhat as follows: Patients enter the hospital and are greeted by a receptionist who opens for each a computer file by entering basic identifying information into the system. Patients are then introduced to another person whose interview is designed to determine their ability to complete a computerized self-report testing battery. If, as is generally the case, the patient is able to do so, the computer administers a mental status interview and submits a DSM II diagnosis and narrative report to a professional. (The computer program is currently being updated to submit DSM III diagnoses.)
>
> The computer next administers several standard self-report personality tests and an intelligence test. As each test is completed, the computer analyzes the responses and prints a narrative report. This report is submitted to a staff that subsequently meets and works out an optimal treatment plan for the patient.
>
> The computer system seems to be well received by patients and staff alike. Its main advantages are that (1) the hospital's intake capacity and efficiency have improved considerably (more patients processed in less time), (2) the system collects standardized clinical data on all patients instead of the prior haphazard and random bits of information, and (3) as a result of ongoing monitoring during the patient's stay at the hospital, the system provides constant measures of patient progress.
>
> **Source:** Kleinmuntz, B. *Essentials of abnormal psychology* (2nd ed.). New York: Harper & Row, 1980, p. 36.

their mental status, was developed by Kleinmuntz and McLean (1968). This program's objective was to evaluate respondents' replies to MMPI items, and in accordance with the answers to the last questions asked, the program was to branch off to those areas of inquiry that seemed promising. A flow chart of a sample interview is shown in Figure 6-1.

First the program presented a basic set of items for each of the fifteen scales. This set enabled the computer to decide what other relevant questions to ask. After the computer presented the basic questions, it calculated the $T$-scores (see chapter four) for each of the scales. All the scales were then assigned to one of three states: "assumed normal" if a scale's $T$-score was within one standard deviation of the mean (i.e., between 40 and 60); "assumed abnormal" if a scale's $T$-score departed more than two standard deviations from the mean (i.e., between 30 and 70); or "not yet classified" if it did not meet either of these criteria. Each scale marked "not yet classified" was placed on a "critical" list.

Interviewing    **203**

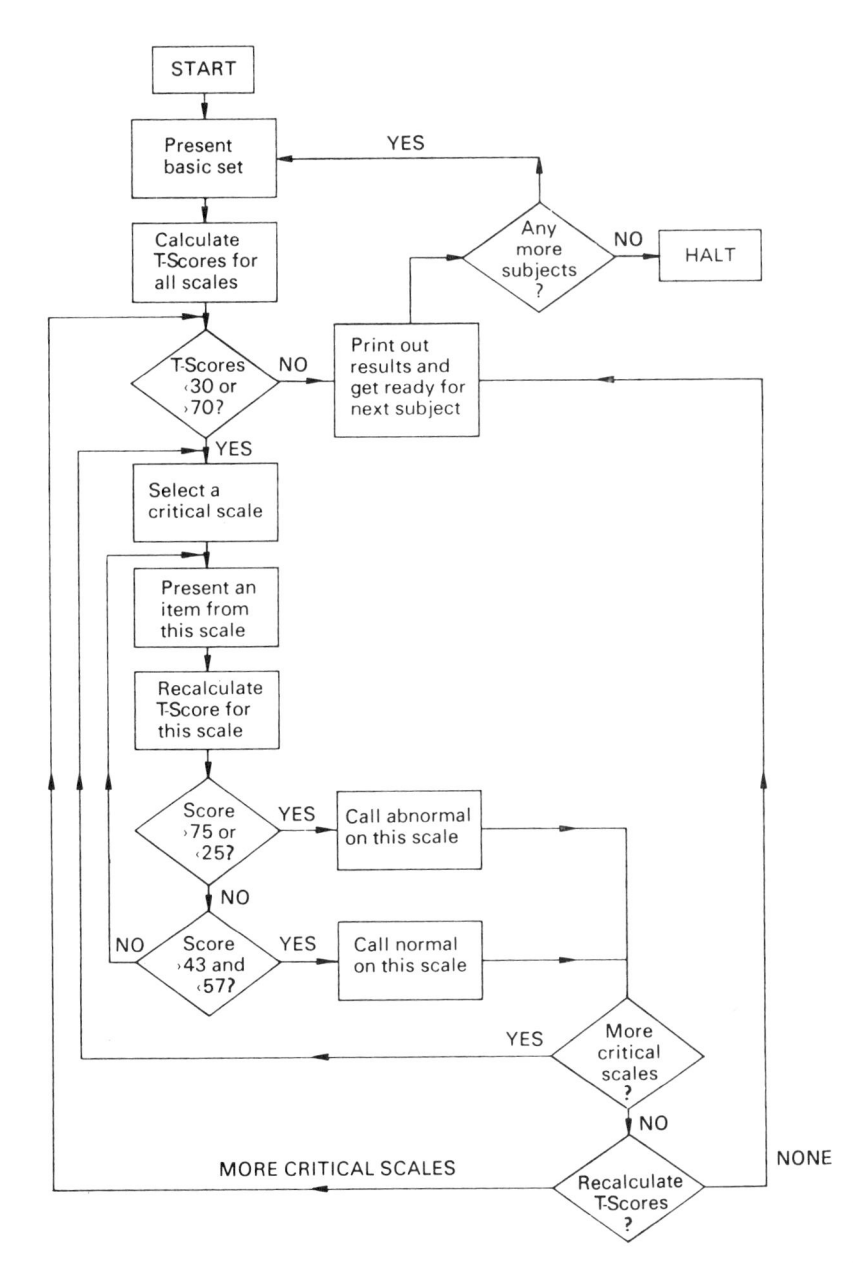

**Figure 6–1.** Flow Chart of Computer Program Designed to "Interview."

The second phase of the computer program consisted of selecting a scale from those on the critical list and asking questions relevant to it. After each question, the $T$-score was again calculated for that scale. If the scale now qualified for one of the other states (normal or abnormal), the questioning was discontinued, another scale was selected from the critical list, and the process was repeated. If the scale still remained in the "not yet classified" state, questioning from it continued until a classification was reached.

At some point, the computer program removed all the scales from the critical list, and those not yet classified normal or abnormal were placed in an unclassifiable category. This terminated the program, and the computer then printed out its mental status conclusions.

This program's feasibility as an interview technique was tested by using as the input subjects' MMPI item responses those obtained when they had taken the MMPI earlier. Thus, instead of actually seating the respondents opposite a computer teletype, as the computer interview of the future was designed to do, the MMPI answer sheets of several emotionally adjusted and maladjusted college students were "read in" to the computer. The results indicated that both methods, the computer-administered tests and those administered in the conventional manner, yielded remarkably similar test scores.

How many persons can be interviewed simultaneously by this system? This number is limited only by a computer's storage capacity and the number of available input and output devices (teletypes or display tubes). The disadvantage of this method over administering the entire MMPI is that the shorter form rather than the entire item pool is administered, and this short form has been shown to yield more limited information. In principle, however, this could be remedied by programming the computer with many items gleaned from existing and future personality inventories. Such a computer program would draw on a richer data base than the present MMPI items now provide. And the advantage of such a large data base would be that the computer could branch off to a set of highly discriminating items, as dictated by the problem at hand, and yet ask many questions.

Building on this experience with computer interviewing, Brooks and Kleinmuntz (1974) tried to design a machine system that would interview patients without using personality test items. Toward this end, they programmed a computer to conduct mental status interviews with informants of diagnosed patients. The novelty of this system, compared to the MMPI program above, was that it was given the ability to learn from its mistakes. Therefore, it was able to improve its diagnostic accuracy because it received constant feedback on its past errors. We shall briefly describe this system (see Brooks & Kleinmuntz, 1974, for a more extensive report).

The informants who provided inputs to the program had to have had at least two weeks of close contact with a patient. The basic operations of the program consisted of asking the informants questions about a patient's behavior that could be answered by yes or no. The system's questions, drawn from testbooks and patient file descriptions, included inquiries about a wide range of possible psychopathological symptoms and signs that the informant (family member, nurse, ward attendant, mental health professional) could observe directly. For example, there were questions about speech abnormalities, unusual ideas and thoughts, motor anomalies, interpersonal difficulties, and so on. Here are three sample questions, along with parenthetic examples of their significant diagnostic categories:

1. Has the patient ever hit or shoved others for no reason at all? (paranoid schizophrenic)
2. Does this person have any ideas that he or she considers particularly novel or unusual? (manic, paranoiac)
3. Would you say that this individual is unusually concerned with his or her diet or physical health? (hysteric, hypochondriac)

Two hundred similar questions were arranged in groups of four, with each group being concerned with one symptom or aspect of the behavior. Each successive question within the group specified a greater degree of pathology.

The processed and interpreted outputs of the program consisted of a quantitative index ranging from 0 to 0.99 for each of the thirty diagnostic categories taken from the now obsolete *Diagnostic and Statistical Manual of Mental Disorders*, or DSM II (American Psychiatric Association, 1968; also see American Psychiatric Association, 1980). These indices were computed as follows: between zero and four "yes" responses could be made for each question group. The program contained a weight that indicated how important a particular question group or symptom was to a specific diagnosis. The sum of the products of the weights and the number of the "yes" responses for the question groups were then calculated for each diagnostic category. An overall index of psychopathology was also printed out, and this was based on the total number of "yes" (e.g., psychopathological) responses. A simulated output of results for a hypothetical paranoid schizophrenic patient is shown in Table 6–6.

In this program output, the paranoid schizophrenic category received the highest index value, 0.75; the four next highest categories were paranoia, 0.67; undifferentiated schizophrenia, 0.66; schizoaffective disorder, 0.63; and hebephrenia, 0.55. The relative sizes of the indices can be empirically adjusted for the base rates (see Meehl & Rosen, 1955)

**Table 6–6** Simulated Program Results for a Diagnosis of Paranoid Schizophrenia.

| Diagnosis | Index Value |
|---|---|
| Paranoia | 0.67 |
| Paranoid schizophrenia | 0.75 |
| Catatonic schizophrenia | 0.62 |
| Hebephrenia | 0.55 |
| Undifferentiated schizophrenia | 0.66 |
| Schizoaffective disorder | 0.63 |
| Manic psychosis | 0.45 |
| Psychotic depression | 0.23 |
| Neurotic depression | 0.20 |
| Hysteric hypochondriasis | 0.15 |
| Anxiety neurosis | 0.24 |
| Dissociative hysteria | 0.12 |
| Phobic neurosis | 0.09 |
| Obsessive-compulsive disorder | 0.06 |
| Sexual disorder | 0.09 |
| Alcoholism | 0.14 |
| Drug abuse | 0.17 |
| Antisocial personality disorder | 0.18 |
| Psychophysiological disorder | 0.27 |
| Organic brain syndrome | 0.44 |
| Degree of psychopathology | 0.55 |

of particular patient populations and would thus signify the relative likelihoods of alternative diagnoses. Since persons do not usually fall into discrete diagnostic categories, these indexes also would reflect the continuum of overlapping classifications.

The heuristics of this program's learning capability are complex and have been described elsewhere (Brooks & Kleinmuntz, 1974), but here it may suffice to indicate that it is a capability realized by having a criterion diagnostician monitor the program by instructing it in the correctness of its diagnoses. The diagnostician also attaches confidence ratings to these corrections, and these ratings are then transformed into weights. The principle is to alter the program continually until it attains optimal weights for each of its diagnostic categories. The program can easily be adapted to include DSM III (American Psychiatric Association, 1980) diagnostic categories.

### Critical Comment

There are several advantages to using computers rather than human interviewers. First, the computer comes to the clinical scene without any of the inherent biases that human beings harbor. One psychologist referred to the machine as a "neutral ... deaf, dumb, and inert ... *tabula rasa* whose passivity cries out for the activity of the programmer" (Tomkins, 1963, pp. 7–8). Second, the computer, once properly programmed, confronts respondents with a standard stimulus and asks a uniform set of questions. It will not vary its appearance or its setting, as the interviewer may well do; nor will it become bored or preoccupied with its assignment, as many human beings do. Moreover, the computer can elicit disclosures that some people may be reluctant to reveal to human interviewers. For example, Lucas and his associates (1977) found that alcoholics admitted consuming considerably more alcohol to a computer than they did to a psychiatrist. Finally, the computer has the advantage, at least in principle, of being able to interview many people simultaneously.

Equally important, however, are the computer's shortcomings as an interviewer. First, it is not capable of picking up possibly important visual cues. Second, the computer cannot exude the warmth that one human being can give another. Quite possibly, its impersonal "confession box" nature may appeal to some persons, especially to those who are deeply embarrassed by disclosing personal matters to strangers, but more likely the computer repels many who need the human touch to encourage them to talk. And finally, a possible source of concern for many respondents may be the computer's permanent-storage feature. Once information is stored in the machine, that information, unless precautions are taken to avoid it, becomes accessible to many more persons than originally intended. Obviously, this destroys the confidentiality of the interview. With human interviewers, most people can be easily reassured that their disclosures are privileged communications; such reassurances are somewhat less credible when given by a machine.

## SUMMARY AND CONCLUSIONS

A personality assessment interview is any prolonged contact between two persons in which a face-to-face communication is initiated for the specific purpose of allowing the interviewer to learn about an individual's personality characteristics. Interviews vary from the highly structured to the less structured; and in general, the advantage to be gained as one moves from the more structured interview to the less structured interview is the increasing breadth of topic coverage. Structured interviews have the advantage of providing some semblance of standardized conditions. However, the major disadvantage of structure is the inquisitorial atmosphere that may be created by a crisp question-and-answer interview session.

The unstructured interview has the advantage of creating conditions conducive to free expression, which permits the interviewer greater latitude in exploring promising leads. Often the theoretical orientation of the interviewer dictates the type of interview he or she conducts; and depending on, for example, whether he or she is oriented to the theory of Freud, Adler, Sullivan, or Rogers, his or her interview goals and techniques will vary accordingly.

Cutting across the structured-versus-unstructured dichotomy and across the interviewer's particular theoretical orientation, there are many types of personality assessment interviews. These include the employment, intake, mental status, case history, pretest, and posttest interviews. Each of these serves a different purpose, and their structures and problems reflect these differences.

Generally, reliability and validity indices are low when the interview is not structured. In most studies of the predictive value of the assessment interview or the situation in which it occurs, it is difficult to know how much validity to attribute to the interview alone and how much is due to other sources available to the assessor. Most incremental validity studies, in which increasing amounts of evidence are systematically made available to the interviewer, have shown that the interview does not add much to the size of the validity coefficient or to the information obtained by more formal psychometric techniques.

However, in spite of some discouraging reliability and validity evidence, the interview serves a valuable function in the clinical and employment setting. There seem to be more important considerations than the consistency and accuracy of a procedure, and foremost among these considerations is the fact that the interview imparts qualities of interest and warmth from one person to another.

It is quite possible, although somewhat futuristic, that this important element of the interview may be removed by the recent increased use of the computer for interviewing. Work currently under way suggests that computers may soon be used routinely for intake interviews and for training purposes. But if the human element is lost as a result, it is hoped that the increased reliability and validity that can be realized from the computer interview will more than compensate for the loss.

# FOR FURTHER READING

Benjamin, A. *The helping interview.* Boston: Houghton Mifflin, 1969. A brief but lucid treatise on the counseling interview. Gives many useful examples of the helping interview.

Brady, J. *The craft of interviewing*. Cincinnati: Writer's Digest, 1976. A breezy but informative book on interviewing.

Cannell, C.F., & Kahn, R.L. Interviewing. In G. Lindzey & E. Aronsen (Eds.), *The handbook of social psychology* (2nd ed., Vol. 2). Reading, MA: Addison-Wesley, 1968. A review of current (1968) thinking and research on the use of the information-gathering interview.

Cormier, W.H., & Cormier, L.S. *Interviewing strategies for helpers: A guide to assessment, treatment, and evaluation*. Monterey, CA: Brooks/Cole Publishing Co., 1979. This is a fine resource for information about the interview. Especially salient is chapter three, on nonverbal communication, which covers kinesics, paralinguistics, proxemics, mixed messages, nonverbal behavior during silence, and the effects of distance between client and interviewer.

Gorden, R.L. *Interviewing: Strategy techniques and practice* (3rd ed.). Homewood, IL: Dorsey Press, 1980. Written by a cross-cultural researcher, this is a detailed treatment of the styles, strategies, techniques, and skills of interviewing.

Kanfer, F.H., & Grimm, L.G. Behavioral analysis: Selecting target behavior in the interview. *Behavior Modification*, 1977, *1*, 7–28. A good research example of how two behavior assessors select target behaviors in the pretherapy interview.

Merton, R.K. *The focused interview: A manual of problems and procedures*. New York: Free Press, 1956. A classic and critical evaluation of the focused interview.

Richardson, S.A., Dohrenwend, B.S., & Klein, D. *Interviewing: Its forms and functions*. New York: Basic Books, 1965. One of the best discussions of the interview as a research instrument.

Wiens, A.N. The assessment interview. In I.B. Weiner (Ed.). *Clinical methods in psychology*. New York: John Wiley, 1976. A thorough description and review of the anatomy of the assessment.

# 7 Self-Report Inventories and Questionnaires

Personality, interest, attitude, and value testing consist mainly of self-report inventories and questionnaires. The plan of this chapter is to discuss the main features of these techniques in relation to the information processor of Figure 1–1, with special emphasis on the popular Minnesota Multiphasic Personality Inventory (MMPI). We begin with a brief description of the self-report inventories in general and then move on to a more detailed consideration of the MMPI. We next examine several contenders for the MMPI's preeminent place—and then move on to automated-test processing, nonpsychiatric and interest self-report inventories, and attitude and value scaling.

The self-report inventory is like a standardized interview in that its items are questions and statements such as

Are your feelings easily hurt? (Yes, No)
Do your interests change quickly? (Yes, No)
Do you tend to get angry with people rather easily? (Yes, No)
I daydream very little. (True, False)
I enjoy detective or mystery stories. (True, False)

Instead of interviewing persons individually, the printed inventory booklet of questions, items, or statements is administered to all of a group of subjects at the same time. The items given to each subject are identical. This item equivalence for all subjects and the uniform administration and scoring procedures are the distinguishing features of the self-report inventory, features that enable the scores obtained by one individual to be compared with those of the others, provided, of course, that norms are made available.

The subjects' answers on the inventories are limited to fixed-alternative responses (e.g., yes, no, true, or false). The advantages of fixed-response categories are that they eliminate both the need for subjective judgment to score the tests and the need for memory to reconstruct the subjects' responses. A disadvantage of the fixed-alternative responses is that the subjects are severely restricted in their responding.

Just as the interviews' type and content are varied to suit their different purposes, the item content of the self-report inventories also is modified to reflect their distinct uses. For example, if the purpose of a particular test is to assess attitudes toward persons in authority positions, then the inventory would be composed of a set of items relevant to those attitudes. But if the intent is to diagnose personality disorders, then an entirely different questionnaire would be used. To test attitudes toward authority the items might probe into the subjects' feelings about prejudice, minority groups, democracy, and being ruled by others. To diagnose personality disorders the items might concentrate more heavily on the respondents' views of themselves, their ability to get along with others, and their attitudes toward their own habits and past experience.

## The First Adjustment Inventory

The first self-report inventory was developed during World War I, when the United States Army commander in chief, General John J. Pershing, recommended that because of the "prevalence of mental disorders," screening methods be used to eliminate unfit draftees. Robert S. Woodworth, a psychologist who had been investigating the problems of emotional fitness for warfare, responded with the Woodworth Personal Data Sheet (Woodworth, 1917).

The Woodworth Personal Data Sheet was designed to identify neurotic soldiers who are emotionally unsuited for combat. Before this, the selection procedure consisted mainly of brief psychiatric interviews, an impractical procedure because hundreds of thousands of military recruits had to be processed and only limited numbers of skilled interviewers were available. The paper-and-pencil version of the psychiatric interview was a natural development because it facilitated the individual interview by asking such standard questions as "Do you make friends easily?" "Do you often feel miserable and blue?" and other probing questions, some of which are presented in Table 7–1.

Woodworth developed the Personal Data Sheet from the then current psychiatric literature, and the final test included 116 items relating to symptoms commonly associated with mental disorders, which were to be answered by either yes or no. A respondent's score was the number of these symptoms that he claimed to have. Those who reported having many symptoms were detained for further questioning. The Personal Data Sheet, judged by its usefulness according to this modest criterion,

**Table 7-1** Sample Items from the Woodworth Personal Data Sheet.

Have you failed to get a square deal in life?
Is your speech free from stutter or stammer?
Does the sight of blood make you sick or dizzy?
Do you sometimes wish that you had never been born?
Are you happy most of the time?
Do you find that people understand and sympathize with you?
Do people find fault with you much?
Do you suffer from headaches or dizziness?

Source: Woodworth, R. S. *Personal data sheet*. Chicago: Stoelting, 1917.

was a success and served as an impetus for developing many other self-report inventories (see Buros, 1978), although by modern psychometric standards it was based on the naive assumptions that people have insight into their neuroticism and will answer the items honestly.

## Minnesota Multiphasic Personality Inventory (MMPI)

Since its inception during World War II, the most widely used self-report test has been Hathaway's and McKinley's (1942, 1943, 1951) Minnesota Multiphasic Personality Inventory (MMPI). The MMPI, a psychiatric screening device, uses the method of *empirical* or *criterion keying*, which selects items that discriminate between criterion groups of normals and psychiatrically diagnosed persons. This method makes none of the naive assumptions of the Personal Data Sheet because it assumes neither self-knowledge nor honesty. In the empirical approach, one concentrates on the item responses that are characteristic of a specific criterion group and retains from a universe or pool of items only those that discriminate between that group and the control groups. In selecting items for a schizophrenia scale, for example, one first obtains items from any source or pool that may define this group—perhaps items based on information in textbooks or case files—and then administers these to both diagnosed schizophrenics and normals. Next the number of the "true" and "false" responses of both groups is tallied, and those items discriminating between the schizophrenic criterion group and the normal group are identified. The main point is to retain only those items that empirically define the criterion group. Then those items are crossvalidated to new criterion groups that are demographically and diagnostically similar to the original groups, in order to find out whether those items continue to discriminate between the two groups.

Self-Report Inventories and Questionnaires 213

## The Minnesota Multiphasic Personality Inventory
Starke R. Hathaway and J. Charnley McKinley

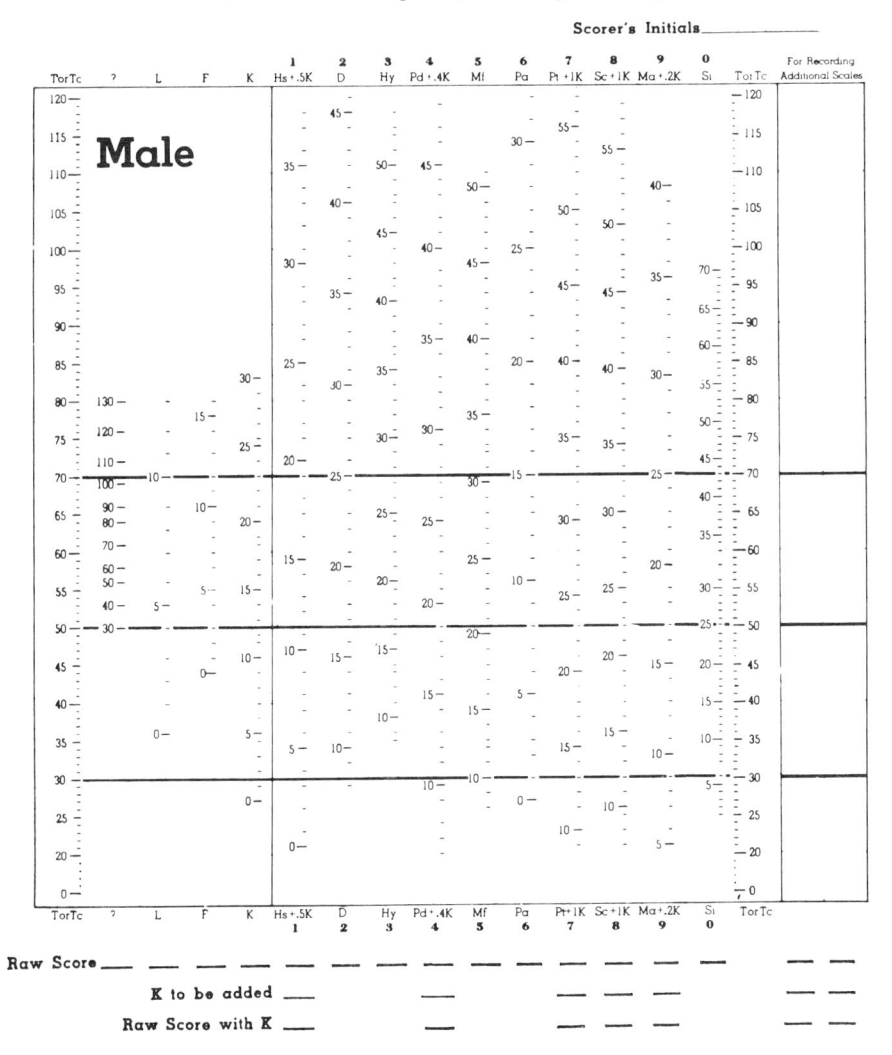

**Figure 7-1.** An MMPI Profile Sheet. The validity scales ?, L, F, and K are shown on the left-hand side; and clinical scales 1 to 0 are on the right-hand side. There are separate norms for males and females.

(Reproduced by permission. Copyright 1943 by the University of Minnesota. Published by the Psychological Corporation, New York, N.Y. All rights reserved.)

## MMPI Construction

The construction of the MMPI proceeded independently of any theories about the structure of personality. It is therefore an intentionally atheoretic test, and its development was based on a thoroughly empirical methodology. At the outset of its development, an original pool of 1,000 items was selected from psychiatric examination forms, psychiatry textbooks, descriptions of psychiatric and neurological examination procedures, and earlier published scales of personal and social attitudes. These items were administered to about two hundred clinically diagnosed neuropsychiatric patients in the University of Minnesota Hospitals, to more than one thousand normal persons selected from those visiting relatives in these hospitals, to several hundred students seeking admission to the University of Minnesota, and to a sample of residents of the city of Minneapolis. The 550 items retained for further study, and subsequently for inclusion in the MMPI, were selected because they empirically discriminated between neuropsychiatric patients and normal people.

More specifically, the normative neuropsychiatric patients used in constructing the inventory were divided into clear-cut diagnostic criterion groups on the basis of clinical judgments and conferences. The answers of each of these hospitalized patients to the 550 items were tabulated, and the items that statistically differentiated between the members of a particular diagnostic group and the normals were then scored as indicators of that psychiatric trend. For example, an item was retained on the scale for hypochondriasis only if hypochondriacal patients endorsed it more often then normal persons did. By this empirical method, Hathaway and McKinley selected approximately one-half of the original pool of 1,000 items.

The MMPI currently in use has 566 items. The examinee is instructed to respond true or false to such statements as "Someone has it in for me," "I certainly feel useless at times," and "Everything tastes the same," and to record his or her responses on an answer sheet. The items cover a range of personality-relevant areas that include general health, specific physical ailments, attitudes toward family and community, religious beliefs, mood fluctuations, delusions, hallucinations, and other topics relevant to diagnosing psychological disturbances. The item responses are tallied according to ten clinical and four validity scales, or keys, and these are plotted on a profile sheet (see Figure 7–1). Raw scores on each of these scales are expressed as $T$-scores, which, you will recall, are derived (or standard) scores with a mean of 50 and a standard deviation of 10.

## Clinical and Validity Scales of the MMPI

The MMPI, as noted above, is scored according to ten clinical scales and four validity scales. The validity scales contain items designed to detect test-taking attitudes and attempts to distort test responses in favorable or unfavorable directions. The clinical scales, conventionally called by their scale numbers rather than by their psychiatric diagnostic labels, are Scale 1, hypochondriasis (*Hs*); Scale 2, depression (*D*); Scale 3, hysteria (*Hy*); Scale 4, psychopathic deviate (*Pd*); Scale 5, masculinity-femininity (*Mf*); Scale 6, paranoia (*Pa*); Scale 7, psychasthenia (*Pt*); Scale 8, schizophrenia (*Sc*); Scale 9, hypomania (*Ma*); and Scale 0, social introversion (*Si*). The scales' use of numbers to refer to their ordinal positions on the profile sheet simplifies the profile-coding procedures and eliminates the necessity of using psychiatric labeling when discussing someone's MMPI profile.

The four validity scales are question scale (?), lie scale (*L*), infrequency scale (*F*), and correction scale (*K*). Some of the scales' characteristic items appear in Table 7–2.

## Clinical Scales

It is important to keep in mind throughout our discussion of the MMPI clinical scales that although elevated scores on these scales are found among the various clinical groups, the reverse is not necessarily true. For example, just because diagnosed depressed patients consistently score high on Scale 2 (depression) (e.g., one or more standard deviations above the mean, or *T*-scores of 60 or higher), it does not necessarily follow that high Scale 2 scores indicate clinical depression. High scores on many of these scales are found among normal subjects, the scale elevations simply suggesting that some normals share certain personality characteristics with the psychiatric patients who also score high on these scales. Thus, a normal who has a *T*-score of 70 on Scale 2 may be depressed or dejected but does not necessarily need hospitalization or even outpatient treatment. The research evidence regarding the meaning of low scores (*T*-scores of 40 or lower) is less clear than that pertaining to high scores.

**Scale 1 (Hs).** The clinical group that served as a criterion reference sample for the construction of Scale 1, hypochondriasis, consisted of fifty diagnosed hypochondriacs (McKinley & Hathaway, 1940). These persons characteristically display an unusual preoccupation with their bodily functions and worry constantly about physical ailments. No

**Table 7-2** The Validity and Clinical Scales and Items Similar to Those of the MMPI.

| Scale | Sample Item | Interpretation |
|---|---|---|
| ? | No sample. It is merely the number of items marked in the "cannot say" category. | This is one of four validity scales, and a high score indicates evasiveness. |
| L | I never have had dreams (FALSE).* | This is the second validity scale. Persons trying to present themselves in a favorable light (e.g., good, wholesome, honest) obtain high L Scale elevations. |
| F | Everything sounds the same (TRUE). | F is the third validity scale. High scores suggest carelessness, confusion, or "fake bad." |
| K | I have very few nightmares compared with my friends (FALSE). | An elevation on the last validity scale, K, suggests a defensive test-taking attitude. Exceedingly low scores may indicate a lack of ability to deny symptomatology. |
| Hs | I wake up tired most mornings (TRUE). | High scorers have been described as cynical, defeatist, and crabbed. |
| D | At times I am full of hope (FALSE). | High scorers usually are shy, despondent, and distressed. |
| Hy | I have never had a dizzy spell (FALSE). | High scorers tend to complain of multiple symptoms. |
| Pd | I like authority (FALSE). | Adjectives used to describe some high scorers are adventurous, courageous, and generous. |
| Mf | I like sports (FALSE) | High-scoring men have been described as aesthetic and sensitive. High-scoring women have been described as rebellious, unrealistic, and indecisive. |
| Pa | I am agreeable most of the time (FALSE). | High scorers on this scale have been characterized as shrewd, guarded, and worrisome. |
| Pt | I am certainly full of self-confidence (FALSE). | Fearful, rigid, anxious, and worrisome are some of the adjectives used to describe high Pt scorers. |
| Sc | I believe I am someone else (TRUE). | Adjectives such as withdrawn and unusual describe Sc high scorers. |
| Ma | I am important (TRUE). | High scorers are called energetic and impulsive. |
| Si | I avoid social gatherings (TRUE). | High scorers are described as modest, shy, and self-effacing. Low scorers are seen as sociable, colorful, and ambitious. |

* The "true" or "false" responses within parentheses indicate the scored direction of each of the items

amount of evidence and reassurance to the contrary seems to convince them that they are indeed healthy.

Scale 1 is composed of thirty-three predominantly somatic items such as "I have a great deal of aches and pains" (if answered true, this item is counted toward the *Hs* scale), "The top of my head sometimes feels numb" (true), "I am very seldom troubled by ill health" (false), "My sleep is fitful and disturbed" (true), and "I wake up easily most mornings" (false). Average normal males answer between eight and fifteen of these in the hypochondriacal direction, whereas average normal females answer even more of these in the hypochondriacal direction. These sex differences probably reflect our culture's assumption that women are more preoccupied with their bodily functions than men are, a normative difference also evident on some of the other clinical scales. But generally, normal persons who score high on Scale 1 have been described by their friends and acquaintances as sociable, enthusiastic, kind, responsive, modest, frank, courageous, and versatile (Hathaway & Meehl, 1952). Among psychiatric patients, high *Hs* scorers have been characterized as crabby, dissatisfied, defeatist, and cynical (Cuadra & Reed, 1954).

**Scale 2 (D).** Fifty hospitalized depressed persons were selected by Hathaway and McKinley as the criterion group for constructing the *D*, or depression, scale. The resulting scale has sixty items such as "I usually feel good about life" (false), "I am often awakened by noise" (true), "At times I am full of energy" (false), and "Once in a while I tell a lie" (false).

On the average, twenty (male) to twenty-eight (female) items answered in the *D* direction are equivalent to a *T*-score of two or more standard deviations higher than the normal Minnesota reference group. College students whose highest MMPI profile score was on Scale 2 were repeatedly described as shy (Black, 1953), physically distressed, and depressed (Guthrie, 1950).

**Scale 3 (Hy).** The criterion group (fifty persons) used to select the sixty items for the third MMPI scale exhibited such symptoms as voice loss, deafness, tingling sensations, or a numbness or lack of feeling over various portions of their bodies. These so-called hysterical symptoms usually have no physical cause and are said to be purely imaginary, although they can be quite incapacitating. Some of the items on Scale 3 are "I have never had a fainting spell" (false), "I frequently notice my hand shakes when I try to do something" (true), "I am happy most of the time" (false), and "Once a week or oftener I feel suddenly hot all over, without apparent cause" (true). Again, there are male-female differences, because women are expected to admit to more hysterical symptoms than men are.

**Scale 4 (Pd).** Most of the persons included in the criterion group (one hundred prisoners and seventy-eight diagnosed clinic cases) for psychopathic deviancy were antisocial, usually in a destructive and violent way. That is, their deviancies were expressed through stealing, lying, forgery, truancy, and vandalism. Many of these persons had been referred by the police or court judges to a psychiatric setting.

Some of the fifty items that this scale comprises reflect the psychopathic deviate's antisocial and asocial behaviors, but many more items are not as face valid as these. For example, the answers to the following two items are clearly in accord with the psychopathic stereotype: "I like school" (false) and "In school I was sometimes sent to the principal for cutting up" (true). On the other hand, unless one accepts the empirical point of view, it is difficult to understand how the following items could be rationally scored in the $Pd$ direction: "I am against giving money to beggars" (false) and "I am easily downed in an argument" (false). The latter are on the $Pd$ scale simply because of their empirically demonstrated ability to differentiate between diagnosed psychopathic deviates and normals.

**Scale 5 (Mf).** There is a total of sixty items on Scale 5, the masculinity-femininity scale ($Mf$), and a group of thirteen male sexual inverts was used as a criterion sample. An attempt to develop an $Fm$ scale to identify female inverts was unsuccessful. Items were also selected for this scale if they differentiated between the sexes. The item content on the $Mf$ scale was drawn from the Strong Vocational Interest Blank (see "The Strong Vocational Interest Blank," this chapter) and ranges from interests in various occupations to preferences for hobbies, avocations, social activities, and family relationships. Some of the $Mf$ items are "I would like to be a florist" (true), "I like mechanics magazines" (false), "I sometimes tease animals" (false), and "I like to talk about sex" (true).

Although Renaud reported (1950) that high scores on the $Mf$ scale characterize overt male and female homosexuals, Dahlstrom and his associates (1972) questioned the dependability of Scale 5 for this kind of evaluation because the scale is highly susceptible to faking and because elevated scores on the scale are often obtained by persons who evidently are not sexually deviant.

**Scale 6 (Pa).** The $Pa$, scale was designed to detect the clinical pattern of paranoia. The subjects of the criterion group (number not reported) were regarded as defensive, suspicious, jealous, and contentious, and had delusional beliefs of reference, influence, and grandeur (Hathaway,

## BOX 7-1

## The Bem Sex Role Inventory (BSRI)

In a paper on America's apparent "sex role ideology," psychologist Sandra Bem (Bem & Bem, 1972) observed that the "homogenization" of American women had cast them into the role of homemaker and had caused them to be placed into dead-end, routine jobs (also see Broverman et al., 1972). Bem's response to such "sex role stereotyping" was to propose a new personality dimension—*psychological androgyny*—which postulated the idea that persons "might be *both* masculine and feminine, *both* assertive and yielding, *both* instrumental and expressive" (Bem, 1974, p. 155). Moreover, Bem felt that androgynous individuals of both sexes were better able than strongly sex-typed persons to adapt their behavior to new and varied situations, a belief that she affirmed (1975) and later reaffirmed (1976).

These considerations inspired Bem to develop the Bem Sex-Role Inventory (BSRI), which includes both a masculinity scale and a femininity scale and which characterizes a person as masculine, feminine, or androgynous, depending on whether he or she endorses masculine or feminine personality characteristics. A person is thus sex typed, whether masculine or feminine, to the extent that the difference in scores is high, and androgynous if the difference in scores is low. The BSRI also has social desirability items, or items neutral to sex. All the items are shown in the table below. The subjects are instructed to describe themselves on a scale from 1 (never or almost never true) to 7 (always or almost always true) so that each objective can be assigned a value.

### Items on the Masculinity, Femininity, and Social Desirability Scales of the BSRI

| Masculine Items | Feminine Items | Neutral Items |
| --- | --- | --- |
| 49. Acts as a leader | 11. Affectionate | 51. Adaptable |
| 46. Aggressive | 5. Cheerful | 36. Conceited |
| 58. Ambitious | 50. Childlike | 9. Conscientious |
| 22. Analytical | 32. Compassionate | 60. Conventional |
| 13. Assertive | 53. Does not use harsh language | 45. Friendly |
| 10. Athletic | | 15. Happy |
| 55. Competitive | 35. Eager to soothe hurt feelings | 3. Helpful |
| 4. Defends own beliefs | | 48. Inefficient |
| 37. Dominant | 20. Feminine | 24. Jealous |
| 19. Forceful | 14. Flatterable | 39. Likable |
| 25. Has leadership abilities | 59. Gentle | 6. Moody |
| 7. Independent | 47. Gullible | 21. Reliable |
| 52. Individualistic | 56. Loves children | 30. Secretive |
| 31. Makes decisions easily | 17. Loyal | 33. Sincere |
| 40. Masculine | 26. Sensitive to the needs of others | 42. Solemn |

*(continued)*

> **BOX 7–1** (Continued)
>
> **Items on the Masculinity, Femininity, and Social Desirability Scales of the BSRI**
>
> | Masculine Items | Feminine Items | Neutral Items |
> |---|---|---|
> | 1. Self-reliant | 8. Shy | 57. Tactful |
> | 34. Self-sufficient | 38. Soft spoken | 12. Theatrical |
> | 16. Strong personality | 23. Sympathetic | 27. Truthful |
> | 43. Willing to take a stand | 44. Tender | 18. Unpredictable |
> | 28. Willing to take risks | 29. Understanding | 54. Unsystematic |
> | | 41. Warm | |
> | | 2. Yielding | |
>
> Note: The number preceding each item reflects the position of each adjective as it actually appears on the Inventory.
>
> Source: Bem, S. L. The measurement of psychological androgyny. *Journal of Consulting and Clinical Psychology*, 1974, 42, 156. Copyright 1974 by the American Psychological Association. Reprinted by permission of the publisher and author.
>
> But the BSRI and its rationale have not been without controversy, as evidenced in several articles in the *Journal of Personality and Social Psychology* (Bem, S. L., 1979; Locksley & Colten, 1979; Pedhazur & Tetenbaum, 1979; Spence & Helmreich, 1979). These critics questioned the relationships between the BSRI test scores and correlated behaviors, and they challenged the underlying assumption that persons high in both masculinity and femininity are better adjusted than those who are strongly sex typed (also see Spence et al., 1974, 1975). To this Sandra Bem replied that her androgynous message had already been absorbed by the culture, and because the concept had a built-in obsolescence, "it will have been transcended" (1979, p. 1053).

1956). A large proportion of this criterion group was also schizophrenic, that is, they were disoriented and out of touch with reality.

Some of the statements on this forty-item scale are "I have no enemies who really wish to harm me" (false), "Someone has it in for me" (true), "I am sure I am being talked about" (true), and "I am happy most of the time" (false).

Scale 6 has often been named as the weakest of the MMPI keys because a large group of hospitalized, clinically paranoid patients consistently manages to avoid being detected by it. This phenomenon has resulted in a certain amount of "clinical paranoia." For example, if a psychiatric patient in a hospital obtains a "normal" profile (all scores within the approximate normal range of more or less than one standard deviation from the mean), then the test interpreter may suspect that he or she is dealing with the MMPI profile of a paranoid patient.

It has been postulated by many MMPI interpreters that the reason why paranoid persons are able to avoid being discovered by Scale 6 (i.e., why they manage to become "test misses") is that they are particularly alert and astute and therefore are able to detect the intent of most of the *Pa* scale items. But this idea was dispelled in one study (Kleinmuntz, 1958, 1960c), which showed, by means of the semantic differential, that both "test hits" and "test misses" were able to recognize that these items signified mental illness.

**Scale 7 (Pt).** Although psychasthenia (*Pt*) is no longer used as a diagnostic category, the clinical types included in the criterion group (twenty persons) for Scale 7 are still with us. These people are beset with obsessive thoughts, compulsive rituals, incessant fears, guilt, and a host of other anxiety-inducing conflicts.

The items on this forty-eight–item scale cover such personality features as dread, lack of self-confidence, self-doubt, and moodiness. Some examples are "I am inclined to take things hard" (true), "I almost never dream" (false), "I usually have to stop and think before I act even in trifling matters" (true), "I am certainly lacking in self-confidence" (true), and "I certainly feel useless at times" (true). Scale 7, undoubtedly because of its heavy concentration of anxiety-revealing items, served as a prototype for J. A. Taylor's (1953) Manifest Anxiety Scale, which for many years measured anxiety in learning experiments (see Taylor, J. A., 1951) and was later found to correlate with other indices of anxiety and with clinical ratings of this dimension (see Franks, 1956a,b; Korchin & Heath, 1961; Mandler et al., 1961).

High scorers on Scale 7 have been described as sentimental, peaceable, verbal, individualistic, emotional, and high strung. Self-descriptive adjectives used by college women included gloomy, dreamy, sentimental, indecisive, absent minded, and unpopular. Guthrie (1950) described high-scoring medical students as fearful, rigid, anxious, and worrisome.

**Scale 8 (Sc).** The seventy-eight items of Scale 8, schizophrenia, were derived from a larger pool of items administered to fifty schizophrenic patients. This diagnostic group contained persons who had marked distortions of reality and whose symptoms included bizarre thinking, withdrawal from interpersonal contacts, ambivalence, and inappropriate affect. Scale 8 is the longest of the original MMPI scales.

The dimension being tapped by Scale 8 is revealed by its items: "Peculiar odors come to me at times" (true), "Most of the time I feel as if I were dead" (true), "I often feel as if things were not real" (true), "I believe I am a condemned person" (true), and "Everything tastes the same" (true).

**Scale 9 (Ma).** The twenty-four patients included in the hypomania criterion group were viewed as overactive, excited, and irritable. Generally, persons diagnosed as manic are noted for their flurries of overactivity, during which they come to believe that their mission on earth is to resolve all problems simultaneously, to act immediately on many issues, and to purchase every commodity wisely and quickly—and to accomplish all these things in a single day.

The forty-six items on Scale 9 cover a range of content that includes the grandiosity, as well as the overactivity and excitement, that seems to beset hypomanic individuals. Some item examples are "I am an important person" (true), "At times I feel that I can make up my mind with unusually great ease" (true), "I work under a great deal of tension" (true), and "At times my thoughts have raced ahead faster than I could speak them" (true).

**Scale 0 (Si).** The tenth and last scale of the regularly used MMPI scales was constructed by item analysis (Drake, 1946), contrasting the percentage of responses of two groups of students with the items. MMPI items retained for Scale 0, or social introversion, were those that differentiated between the students who scored above the 65th centile rank of the Minnesota *T-S-E* Inventory and those who scored below its 35th centile rank (Evans & McConnell, 1942–1957). (The Minnesota *T-S-E* Inventory is a test that divides the personality dimensions of introversion and extraversion into features of *T*hinking, *S*ocial participation, and *E*motional expression.)

There are seventy items on Scale 0; four of them are "I am not unusually self-conscious" (false), "I enjoy social gatherings just to be with people" (false), "Whenever possible I avoid being in a crowd" (true), and "I enjoy gambling for small stakes" (false).

## The Validity Scales

In addition to the clinical scales there are four validity, or credibility, scales: ?, *L*, *F*, and *K*. Their purpose is to indicate how much the test interpreter can rely on the examinee's honesty in answering the items. The first of these scales, the *question scale* (?), consists of the number of items omitted or marked in the "cannot say" category. Because subjects are encouraged to answer all items, excessive scores on this scale suggest evasiveness or indecisiveness. Moreover, if many items are omitted, then a comparison of the subject's overall profile with those of a normative group will be spurious. Therefore, if a respondent answers a hundred or more items in this direction, his or her profile will usually be considered invalid.

The second validity scale, the *lie scale* (*L*), consists of fifteen items worded in such a way that individuals who are attempting to present themselves as exemplary will endorse them. For example, "I get angry sometimes" is a statement that most people would answer in the "true" direction. However, a person who is trying to "fake good," that is, a person who does not want to admit to socially unfavorable items, would not endorse this statement.

The assumptions underlying *L* are that most people will admit to having committed various minor transgressions and that, therefore, those people who do not admit to these—that is, those examinees who answer the MMPI's *L* scale items in a statistically infrequent direction— are probably equally unlikely to respond honestly to other MMPI items as well. A weakness of the scale is the transparency of its items. Most sophisticated subjects, especially college students, tend to "see through" these items, and consequently their fake-good tendencies are not easily detected by the scale. In other words, although the *L* scale detects some faking in the socially desirable direction, it is not a dependable or useful measure of the intended attribute.

The third validity scale, the *infrequency scale* (*F*), consists of sixty-four items endorsed infrequently by the normative samples. A high *F* score suggests carelessness, misunderstanding, confusion, a "fake bad" test-taking attitude, or any combination of these factors. *F* also detects chance (or random) test responding, obtained by answering true or false on the basis of a coin flip. In any case, MMPI interpreters consider high *F*-scale scores as indices of unusual MMPI responding.

The last validity scale, *K*, sometimes called the *correction scale* (Meehl & Hathaway, 1946), consists of thirty items. This scale reflects guardedness or defensiveness in admitting to psychopathology. In order to correct for low test scores on some of the clinical scales, one can add proportions of *K* to these scales. For example, scales 1, 4, 7, 8, and 9 have the proportions 0.5, 0.4, 1.0, 1.0, and 0.2 of *K*, respectively, added to their raw scores. The proportions of *K* to be added and the development of the specific *K* scale items themselves were empirically determined so as to improve the MMPI's capability of detecting clinical abnormality.

## New MMPI Scales

Since the MMPI was originally published in 1942, more than two hundred scales have been developed. Most of these have not been adopted for routine use but are often used in personality research or other particular areas. An exception to this is Scale 0, the social introversion scale, which has been incorporated into the MMPI profile sheet as the tenth scale.

Other experimental MMPI scales vary widely in the types of attributes they measure. More than thirty scales have been developed for use among college students, mostly to measure personality characteristics unrelated to psychiatric abnormalities (Kleinmuntz, 1962). Examples of some of these are measures of ego strength, or *Es* (Barron, 1953); manifest anxiety, or *MAS* (Taylor, J. A., 1953); dominance, or *Do* (Gough et al., 1951); and college maladjustment, or *Mt* (Kleinmuntz, 1960b, 1961).

An important new MMPI scale is the social desirability, or *SD*, scale developed by Allen Edwards (1953, 1957; also see Edwards, 1970, pp. 108–166), who defined social desirability responding as the "tendency of subjects to attribute to themselves in self-description, personality statements with socially desirable scale values and to reject those with socially undesirable scale values" (1957, p. vi). The scale that he developed measures an individual's typical or characteristic level of putting his or her best foot forward without special instructions or motivations to do so (also see Wiggins, 1973, pp. 421–425).

The MMPI's *SD* scale consists of thirty-nine items keyed in the socially desirable direction as determined by the unanimous ratings of a panel of ten judges. Most of these items were selected from J. A. Taylor's (1953) manifest anxiety scale, whose items in turn were selected from the MMPI's *Pt* scale. As a consequence, the *SD* scale is highly and negatively correlated with the latter two scales and with the MMPI's other clinical scales. Thus, because the MMPI clinical scales assess psychopathology, which itself is viewed as socially undesirable by many test takers, it is not surprising that these examinees confound the psychopathology with social desirability. In a sense, this justifies the views of some investigators (i.e., Block, 1965; Wiggins, 1966, 1968) who consider *SD* to be a personality measure in its own right, perhaps resembling such personality attributes or factors as "lack of anxiety" and "ego resiliency."

But be that as it may, the main intended use of *SD* was to detect the extent to which subjects deliberately slanted their MMPI answers in a socially acceptable direction. Unfortunately, there is little firm evidence at the present time, according to Dahlstrom and his associates (1972, p. 149), "to support the application of this scale in clinical practice . . . " although there is one such scale generally available, namely, Wiggins's (1959) *Sd* scale. Wiggins's scale was developed using college students and successfully detects subjects who attempt to create socially favorable impressions.

## Coding

After years of using the MMPI in nonpsychiatric settings, it became clear that the evaluations based on single scale elevations, rather than the patterns of profiles of scale scores, were inadequate. It also became apparent to test users that the implications of the scales had to be extended beyond their original psychiatric intent. That is, instead of referring to the hypochondriasis scale, it seemed better to adopt the simple label *Hs*. This helped remove the implication that persons scoring high on *Hs* are necessarily hypochondriacs. As we noted earlier, normal

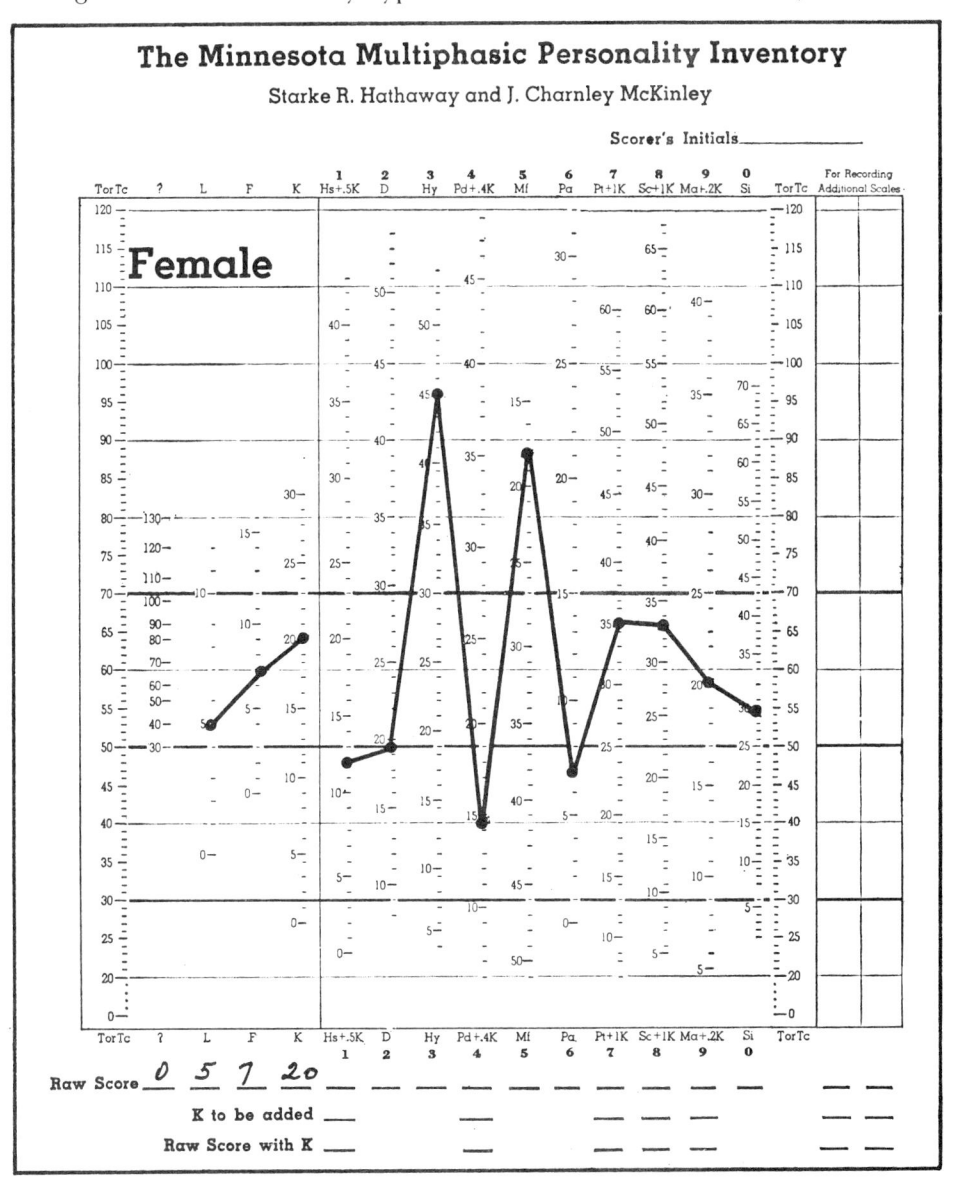

**Figure 7-2.** A Sample MMPI Profile in Which the Hathaway Code Is 35'789021-64.

persons do score high on these scales, and although they may share some characteristics with diagnosed hypochondriacs, they nevertheless do not fit the clinical description in most respects.

In profile coding, each clinical scale is assigned a digit, depending on its serial position—from left to right—on the MMPI profile sheet (see Figure 7–1). Thus, *Hs* becomes 1, *D* becomes 2, and so on, until the last scale, *Si*, is assigned the numeral 0. The next step is to write down the scale digits in the order of their *T*-score elevations, from highest to lowest. Thus, in Figure 7–2, in which a hypothetical profile's highest *T*-score elevation is 95 on Scale 3, the digit 3 is the first number in the

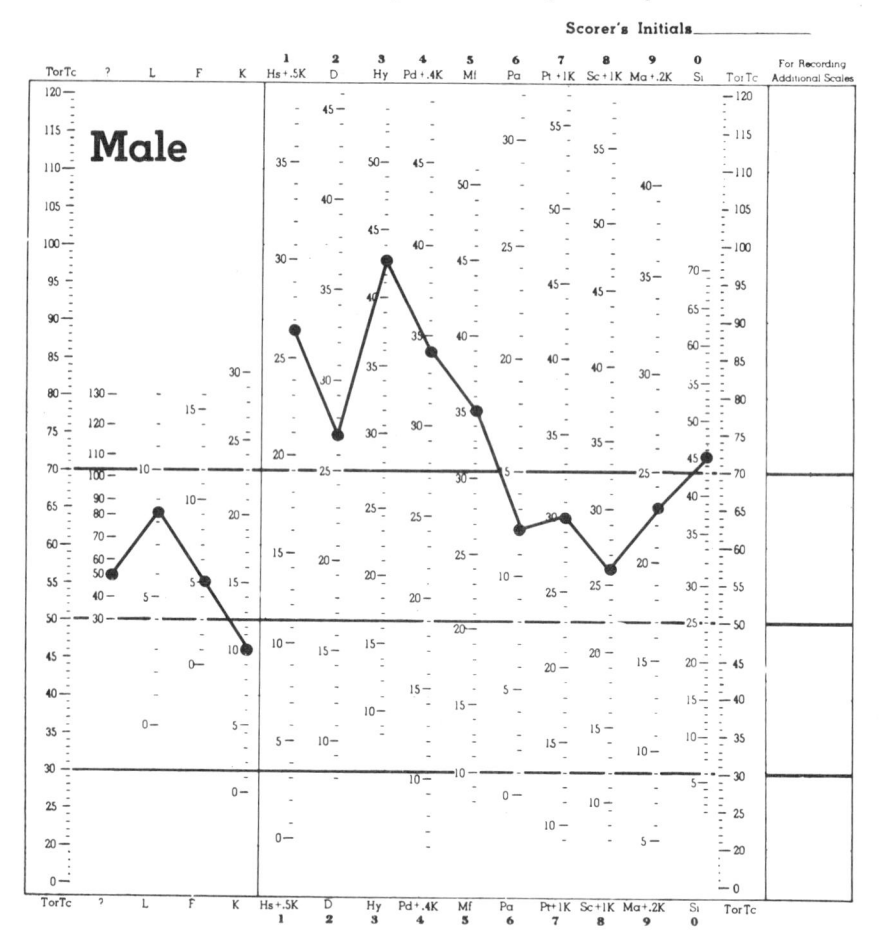

**Figure 7–3.** Sample MMPI Profile Illustrating the "Conversion V."

code. The second highest scale is $Mf$ (Scale 5) at 87; the code now is 35. The third and fourth highest scales are 7 and 8—3578, and this continues until all the clinical scales are listed in descending order according to their $T$-scores. The digit sequence for the example in Figure 7–2 is 3578902164.

After the digits have been recorded in this way, the appropriate elevation symbols, as shown in Figure 7–2, are notated. Thus, in the Hathaway system, a prime (') is inserted after the last number in the code that represents a $T$-score of 70 or above. All adjacent scale numbers whose $T$-scores are within 1 point of each other are underlined, and a dash (–) separates the digits that represent $T$-score values greater than 54 from those that are less than that value. After the dash, the digits of the lowest scales are written if they have $T$-score values less than 46. Finally, the raw scores for $L$, $F$, and $K$ are recorded to the right of the code. If the raw score of $L$ is equal to or greater than 10, or if the raw score of $F$ is equal to or greater than 16, a capital $X$ is placed after the clinical scale code. The $X$ indicates that the profile might be invalid. For the profile presented in Figure 7–2, the correct code for the clinical scales is 35'789021–64 and for the validity scales, 5:7:20.

Several MMPI atlases are now in use (Hathaway & Meehl, 1951a; Hathaway & Monachesi, 1961; Marks & Seeman, 1963; Marks, Seeman, & Haller, 1974), and all of them notate profiles according to Hathaway's or Welsh's (1948) modification of Hathaway's coding system. The first and still the most popular of these is *An Atlas for the Clinical Use of the MMPI* (Hathaway & Meehl, 1951a), which provides short case histories of 968 patients, arranged according to the similarity of profile pattern. Other such atlases deal with data from college counseling centers, juveniles, and hospital patients. The most comprehensive summary of interpretive procedures on MMPI profiles can be found in Dahlstrom and Welsh's *MMPI Handbook* (1960) and in Dahlstrom, Welsh, and Dahlstrom's 1972 and 1975 revisions of the *Handbook*.

## MMPI Interpretation

We shall present here only a few examples of interpretations associated with major configural profile patterns. Perhaps the most-discussed profile pattern among normal and hospital populations is the one displaying a "neurotic triad." This profile consists of elevations of scales 1 and 3 ($Hs$ and $Hy$), or 3 and 1, higher than that of Scale 2 ($D$). This 13 or 31 configuration, which is depicted in Figure 7–3, is sometimes also called the "conversion $V$," because of the $V$-shaped profile produced by this combination of elevations and because it is often found among persons diagnosed as "conversion hysterics." In Black's study (1953) mentioned earlier in this chapter, in which college women rated their peers, persons with MMPI profiles with scales 1 and 3 elevated were described as selfish, dependent, and indecisive, and also as having many somatic complaints. Persons with these profiles who are in psychiatric hospitals often have somatic complaints and pains, and their most frequent diagnosis is conversion hysteria (Hathaway & Meehl, 1952).

A closely related designation of patterns and relationships among some of the predominantly psychotic scales, specifically scales 6, 7, 8, and 9, has been called the "paranoid valley" (Dahlstrom & Welsh, 1960). Figure 7-4 illustrates this pattern. The "valley" is formed by the elevations on scales 6 and 8, with scales 7 and 9 relatively lower. Either

## The Minnesota Multiphasic Personality Inventory

Starke R. Hathaway and J. Charnley McKinley

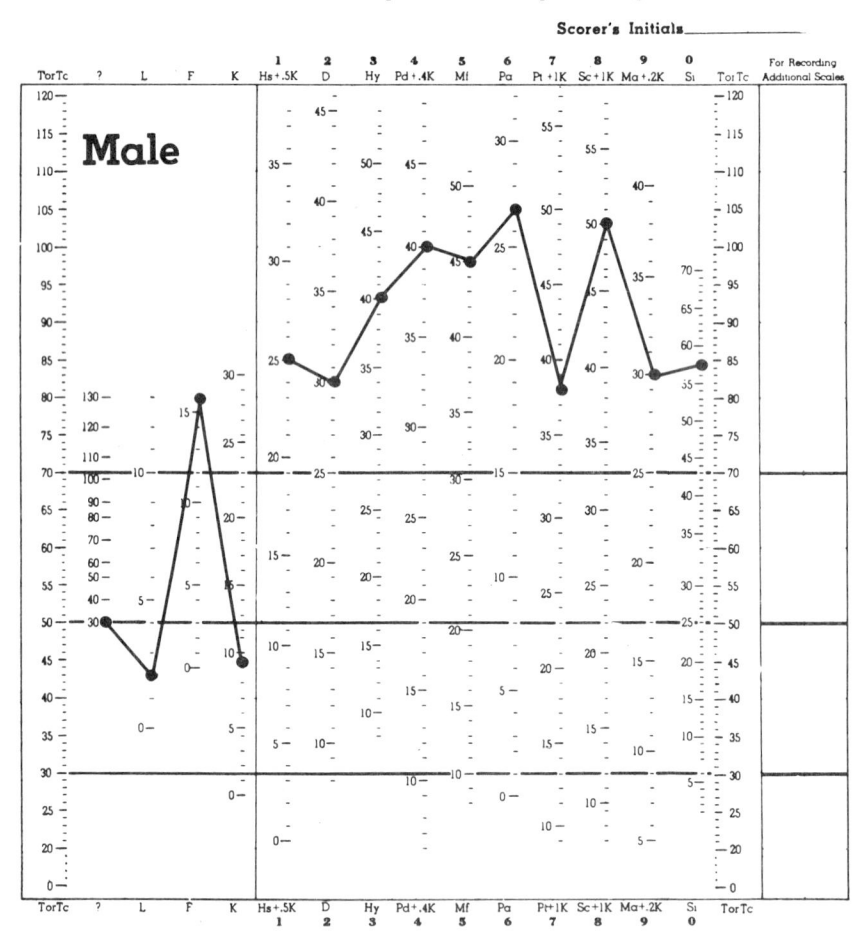

**Figure 7–4.** Sample MMPI Profile Illustrating the "Paranoid Valley."

**Table 7-3**  Descriptions of Some Typical MMPI Code Types.

| Code Types | Descriptions |
|---|---|
| 12 and 21 | Pain, depression, irritability, shyness, and seclusiveness. |
| 23 and 32 | Depression, weakness, apathy, agitation, and tenseness. |
| 27 and 72 | Depression, tenseness, anxiety, and undue sensitivity. |
| 28 and 82 | Depression, anxiety, agitation, and hysterical tendencies. |
| 31 and 13 | Pain, eating problems, sociable, and extraverted. |
| 64 and 46 | Depression, irritability, and suspiciousness. |
| 68 and 86 | Paranoid delusions, withdrawl, and apathy. |
| 78 and 87 | Depression, introversion, irritability, and tendency to worry. |
| 49 and 94 | Overactive, violent, talkative, and extraverted. |

Source: Hathaway, S. R., & Meehl, P. E. The Minnesota multiphasic personality inventory. *Military Clinical Psychology*, TM 8-242; AFM 160-45, Depts. of Army & Air Force, July 1951b.

Scale 6 or Scale 8 may be the high-point score in this pattern, creating a 68 or 86 configuration. Of course, the rest of the profile must be considered also, but the paranoid valley pattern shown in Figure 7-3 is often found among paranoid schizophrenic patients.

The single most common profile in hospitalized psychiatric groups is the so-called 72 or 27 pattern (see Table 7-3), sometimes referred to as the "worry wart" or even the "psychiatric fever" profile. It is also a frequent pattern among psychiatric outpatients and medical patients (Dahlstrom et al., 1972, pp. 260-262). The prominent presenting complaint of this group, according to Hathaway and Meehl (1951b), is depression accompanied by tenseness and nervousness. Many of these persons also complain of anxiety, insomnia, and undue sensitivity. Similarly, according to Guthrie (1950), medical patients with this profile pattern complained of being easily or continually tired or being exhausted and depressed but surprisingly did not report many physical symptoms, even though their complaints had been made to internists.

Among normals, Forsyth and Smith (1967) reported that nursing students with 278 code types were judged by their group dynamics leaders as being more able than other students to understand the feelings of others and as having more problems with authority figures. They also were judged to have less need to be liked, to want everyone's friendship, to be overpowering, to invite hostility, to be self-confident, stubborn, angry, rebellious, sarcastic, and anxious verbally and nonverbally, to communicate with their leader, and to confide in their group.

As we noted, experienced MMPI users often refer to profiles according to their two or three scale primary elevations. Of course, it is easier to remember the code types this way than according to their ten, twelve, or sometimes even fifteen digits. Thus, they talk about 27s,

49s, 85s, or 26s as representing abbreviated versions of significant personality types.

## Automated MMPI Scoring and Interpretation

Besides being one of the best-researched personality inventories, the MMPI is also one of the tests whose scoring and interpretation has been the most extensively automated. According to the *Eighth Mental Measurements Yearbook* (Buros, 1978, pp. 938–962), in the United States there are no fewer than seven commercial computerized scoring and interpreting services for the MMPI. In alphabetical order, these are the Automated Psychological Assessment (Lachar, 1976), Behaviordyne Psychodiagnostic Laboratory Service (Finney et al., 1976), Caldwell Report (Caldwell, 1969), MMPI–ICA Computer Report (Dunlop, 1963–1967), Psychological Assessment Services (Fowler, 1973–1975), Psychological Corporation MMPI Reporting Service (Pearson & Swenson, 1967), and Roche MMPI Computerized Interpretation Service (Fowler, 1966–1976). Outside the United States, there are also interpreting systems available in Europe, and undoubtedly there will be other systems available worldwide in the near future (see Butcher, Pancheri & Morgana, 1976).

These commercial, automated interpretive services provide the user with a kit of materials and guidelines for their use. Answer sheets are mailed to the service and then are scored and interpreted by computer. Narrative reports are then returned to the referring person. These narratives, according to one writer (see Eichman, 1972) vary considerably in complexity and descriptive level. Typically, the MMPI user is given a three-page printout. The first page is the narrative interpretive report that the computer has selected according to specific instructions. The second page is a technical sheet; one-half of it usually is the MMPI's raw scores and *T*-scores, and the other half is a printout of certain "critical items" selected by the computer programmer because they presumably indicate the presence of psychopathology. The third page usually is an MMPI profile of the person being studied.

The interpretive statements are the core of the service's offering to the MMPI user. These interpretations have been gleaned from clinical and research information on the MMPI and from codebooks or "cookbooks" (see Dahlstrom et al., 1972, pp. 77–83) and are associated with certain scale elevations and specific patterns of scale combinations. The interpretive statements, according to Raymond Fowler (1969), author of the Roche MMPI Computerized Interpretation Service, are obtained by programming the computer with many interpretive paragraphs associated with specific scale elevations and configurations. Then, after also considering the examinee's sex, age, socioeconomic background, and marital status, the computer identifies the salient features of the MMPI profile under consideration and locates and prints out the appropriate paragraphs from its statement library. Excerpts from two typical paragraphs, taken from the Roche system, are reproduced here:

> THE PATIENT SEEMS TO BE A PERSON WHO HAS DIFFICULTY MAINTAINING CONTROLS OVER IMPULSES. SHE BEHAVES IN A SOCIALLY UNACCEPTABLE MANNER, AND IS LIKELY TO EXPERIENCE GUILT AND DISTRESS.
>
> THIS PATIENT'S POORLY CONTROLLED ANGER MAY BE EXPRESSED IN TEMPER OUTBURSTS, OFTEN AS A RESPONSE TO THE FRUSTRATION OF CHILDISH DEMANDS FOR ATTENTION AND APPROVAL. SHE IS HIGHLY SENSITIVE TO REJECTION, AND HER ANGER IS ESPECIALLY LIKELY TO BE DIRECTED TOWARDS FAMILY MEMBERS. (1969)

A more complete MMPI interpretation and profile appear in Box 7–3, which contains a report of a sixteen-year-old single male whose profile shows a 728 configuration. The three validity scales interpreted by the Caldwell Report System are $L$, $F$, and $K$, and the ten clinical

---

**BOX 7–2**

## Computer Modeling the Clinician

Evidence of the feasibility of simulating the judgments of an expert clinician by a computer were presented in a study (Kleinmuntz, 1963a, 1975) in which 126 personality test profiles (MMPIs) were presented to ten experienced interpreters. These interpreters were instructed to sort the profiles along a fourteen-step distribution ranging from "least adjusted" to "most adjusted." It was then possible to select the "best" clinician in terms of his or her overall percentages of correct identifications.

The expert was then presented again with the 126 test profiles and was instructed to "think aloud" into a tape recorder as he or she placed the profiles into adjusted and maladjusted categories. A content analysis of these recordings then suggested sixteen sequential decision rules, a flow chart of which is shown in the figure below. Eventually, these rules were further refined into thirty-five decision rules. The rules were programmed for the computer, and the computer model of the expert was then used in the judgments of adjustment from a new series of MMPI profiles. The model of the expert performed as well as the expert and, in some instances, better.

*(continued)*

**BOX 7-2** (Continued)

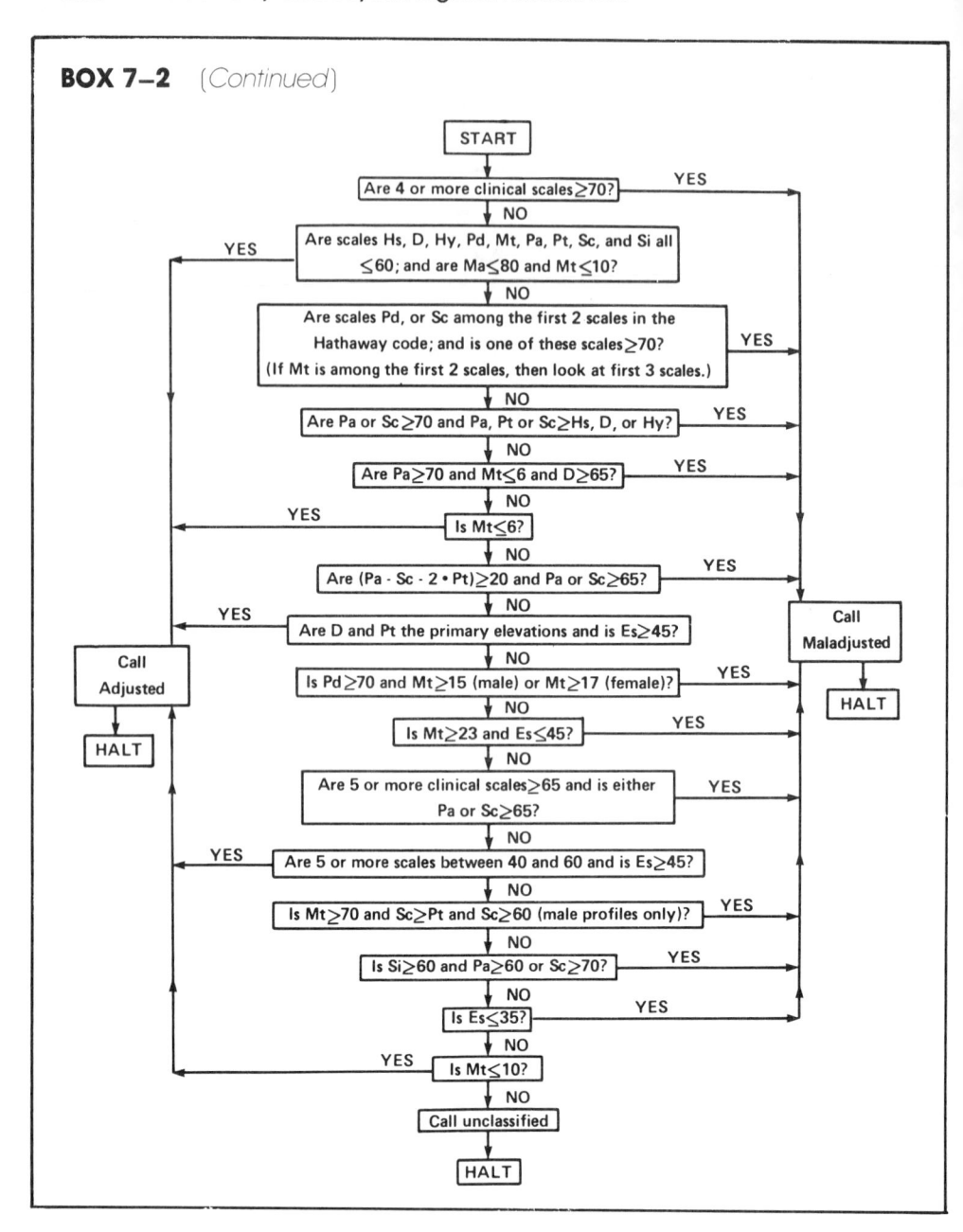

```
                                    START
                                      │
                                      ▼
                    Are 4 or more clinical scales ≥70? ──YES──┐
                                      │ NO                    │
                                      ▼                       │
         ┌──YES── Are scales Hs, D, Hy, Pd, Mt, Pa, Pt, Sc, and Si all
         │        ≤60; and are Ma≤80 and Mt≤10?                │
         │                            │ NO                     │
         │                            ▼                        │
         │        Are scales Pd, or Sc among the first 2 scales in the
         │        Hathaway code; and is one of these scales ≥70? ──YES──┤
         │        (If Mt is among the first 2 scales, then look at first 3 scales.)
         │                            │ NO                     │
         │                            ▼                        │
         │        Are Pa or Sc≥70 and Pa, Pt or Sc≥Hs, D, or Hy? ──YES──┤
         │                            │ NO                     │
         │                            ▼                        │
         │        Are Pa≥70 and Mt≤6 and D≥65? ──YES────────────┤
         │                            │ NO                     │
         │        ┌──YES── Is Mt≤6?                             │
         │        │                   │ NO                     │
         │        │                   ▼                        │
         │        │        Are (Pa - Sc - 2•Pt)≥20 and Pa or Sc≥65? ──YES──┤
         │        │                   │ NO                              │
         │        │                   ▼                           Call  │
         │     ┌──YES── Are D and Pt the primary elevations and is Es≥45?  Maladjusted
         │     │                      │ NO                              │
         │     │                      ▼                               HALT
         │     │        Is Pd≥70 and Mt≥15 (male) or Mt≥17 (female)? ──YES──┤
         │     │                      │ NO                              │
         │     │                      ▼                                 │
   Call  │     │        Is Mt≥23 and Es≤45? ──YES─────────────────────────┤
 Adjusted │     │                      │ NO                              │
         │     │                      ▼                                 │
   HALT  │     │        Are 5 or more clinical scales≥65 and is either ──YES──┤
         │     │        Pa or Sc≥65?                                     │
         │     │                      │ NO                              │
         │     │   ┌──YES── Are 5 or more scales between 40 and 60 and is Es≥45?
         │     │   │                  │ NO                              │
         │     │   │                  ▼                                 │
         │     │   │        Is Mt≥70 and Sc≥Pt and Sc≥60 (male profiles only)? ──YES──┤
         │     │   │                  │ NO                              │
         │     │   │                  ▼                                 │
         │     │   │        Is Si≥60 and Pa≥60 or Sc≥70? ──YES────────────┤
         │     │   │                  │ NO                              │
         │     │   │                  ▼                                 │
         │     │   │        Is Es≤35? ──YES───────────────────────────────┤
         │     │   │                  │ NO
         │     │   │   ┌──YES── Is Mt≤10?
         │                            │ NO
                                      ▼
                              Call unclassified
                                      │
                                      ▼
                                    HALT
```

## BOX 7-3

**CALDWELL REPORT**
3122 SANTA MONICA BOULEVARD
SANTA MONICA, CA. 90404 / (213) 829-3644

July 30, 1980

NAME: ----------
AGE: 16
SEX: Male
EDUCATION: 9 years
MARITAL STATUS: Single
REFERRED BY: ----------
DATE TESTED: July 22, 1980
TESTS ADMINISTERED: Minnesota Multiphasic Personality Inventory (MMPI)

Test Taking Attitude

    He was unusually open, candid, and self-critical toward the MMPI. The profile appears valid.

Symptoms and Personality Characteristics

    The profile indicates a moderate level of anxiety and depression. Multiple tensions, worrying, self-doubts, fears and anxieties are suggested. In some related cases such symptoms as the blunting of affect, concreteness of thinking, morbid ruminations, and transitory ideas of reference suggested schizoid trends or incipient schizophrenic reactions despite preserved orientation and good general reality testing. Feelings of despondency, hopelessness, and guilt are suggested along with phobias and occasional thoughts about suicide. Indecisiveness and a loss of interest would relate to the depth of his ambivalences. Shy, introverted, and withdrawing, he appears quite uncomfortable socially, keeping others at a distance and fearing close involvement.

    He tests as sensitive and resentful with an easily hurt pride. The profile suggests that close personal relationships would be disturbed by misunderstandings and repeated difficulties in expressing anger. Problems in regulating his emotions are indicated along with a self-defeating impulsiveness. Passive-dependent manipulations are likely with many secondary gains. However, his lapses of forethought would be repeatedly self-defeating of his longterm goals, and he would see this as confirming of his many self-criticisms. He is apt to have passive-aggressive ways of expressing his resentments of family restraints and to suffer guilt-laden conflicts with parents, school, or other sources of control. His overall balance of masculine and feminine interests is less masculine than average for his age, tending toward verbal or esthetic interests rather than mechanical and outdoor activities.

    Typical family backgrounds involved rejection by one or sometimes both parents. Sometimes this was indirect, as by the illness or death of one

*A DIVISION OF CLINICAL PSYCHOLOGICAL SERVICES INC.* (continued)

**BOX 7-3** (*Continued*)

Page 2

parent and the resulting burdens on the other parent. Personal peculiarities often had provoked negative reactions from family members, including unfavorable comparisons to "superior" siblings or others in the family along with an excessive amount of teasing by siblings. Their social ineptness and difficulties in giving love resulted in repeated heterosexual disappointments and frustrations of their wishes for emotional closeness. Many persisted in school over extended periods with a fear of failure if they were to "challenge the nonacademic world". They often studied and cultivated interests in obscure intellectual subjects such as religions and philosophies of life, typically ruminating about these with oddly personalized interpretations.

Diagnostic Impression

Among adult patients the most typical diagnosis with this profile is of a chronic "endogenous" depression. A few patients with this pattern had underlying schizoid trends.

Treatment Considerations

The treatment of similar patients has often included combinations of sedating phenothiazines and antidepressants. Adult patients with this pattern had only brief and limited responses to shock therapy, and the transient post-shock lifting of the depression was often followed by a flooding of intense anxieties, fears, and ruminations. His responses suggest a careful review of his sexual history.

Slowness to relate and immature emotional distortions are likely handicaps in psychotherapy. He is apt to have a resistively negative self-image despite steady if not positive past accomplishments. These critical self-judgments are apt to be unrealistic but sufficiently integrated into the patient's identity so that they are slow to change. Some patients with this pattern were able to develop intellectual insights at great length with few apparent resulting changes in their behavior.

The profile predicts a gradual response to psychotherapy—especially if his depression is not of recent onset—but most similar patients have eventually made positive responses to treatment. One study reported relatively favorable responses by these patients to support from older, kindly, understanding, well-adjusted, and motherly female therapists. Difficulties brought on by his rigid internal standards and ideals are apt to be a major focus in treatment. Chronic difficulties in expressing anger and particularly his guilt over anger toward family members are apt to require an extended working through. Overreactions to any physical, intellectual, and other handicaps are also likely points of focus in therapy. In some cases increasing self-assertiveness and integrated expressions of anger were seen as particularly meaningful signs of improvement.

Thank you for this referral.

Alex B. Caldwell, Ph.D.
Diplomate in Clinical Psychology

ABC/jf

(*continued*)

## BOX 7-3 (Continued)

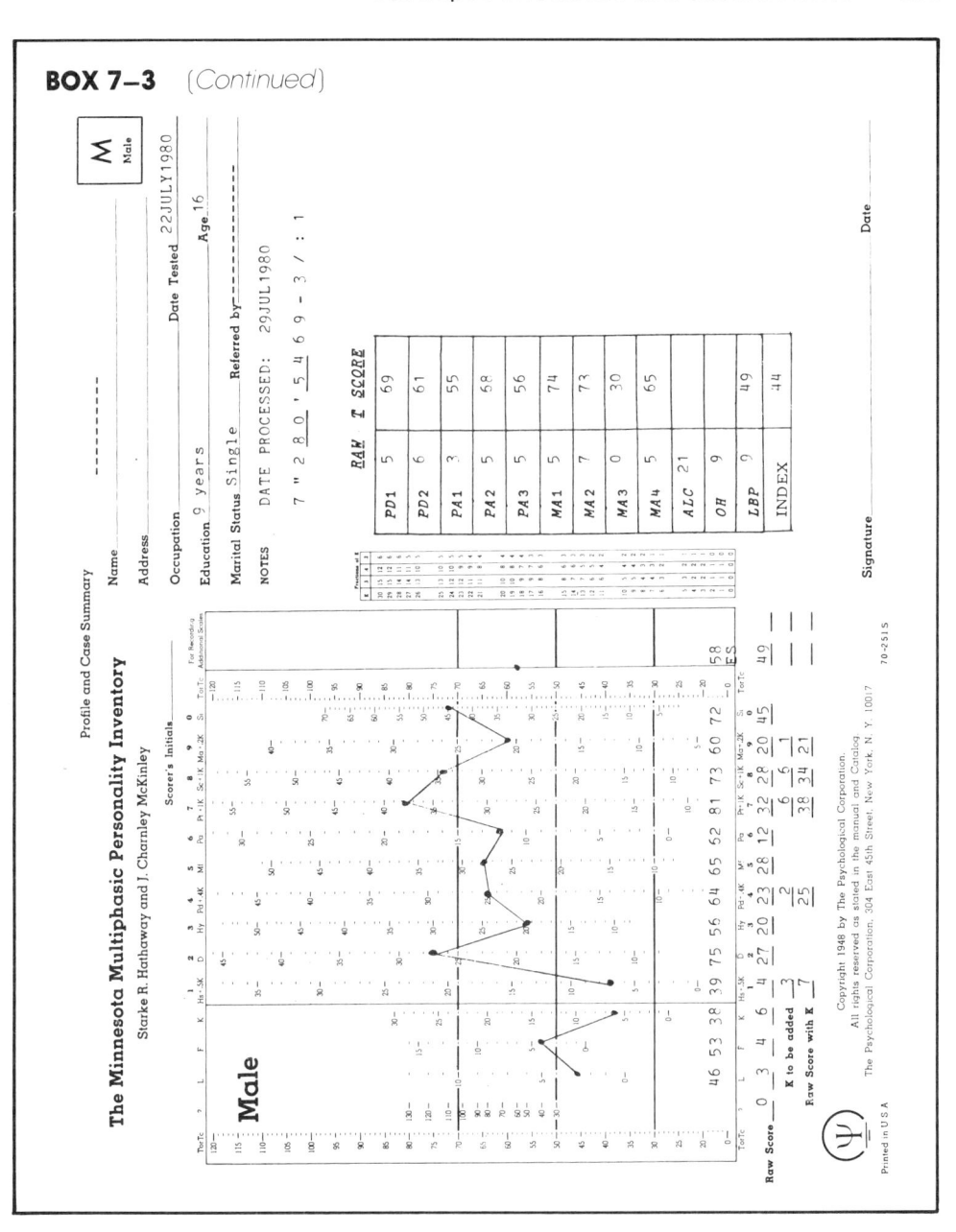

**The Minnesota Multiphasic Personality Inventory**
Starke R. Hathaway and J. Charnley McKinley

Profile and Case Summary

Male ☒

Name _____
Address _____
Occupation _____
Education 9 years
Marital Status Single    Referred by _____
NOTES    DATE PROCESSED: 29JUL1980

Date Tested 22JULY1980    Age 16

7 " 2 8 0 ' 5 4 6 9 - 3 / : 1

| | RAW | T SCORE |
|---|---|---|
| PD1 | 5 | 69 |
| PD2 | 6 | 61 |
| PA1 | 3 | 55 |
| PA2 | 5 | 68 |
| PA3 | 5 | 56 |
| MA1 | 5 | 74 |
| MA2 | 7 | 73 |
| MA3 | 0 | 30 |
| MA4 | 5 | 65 |
| ALC | 21 | |
| OH | 9 | 49 |
| LBP | 9 | 44 |
| INDEX | | |

Raw Score  46 53 38  4 6 4  39 75 56 64 65 52 81 73 60 72  58
K to be added    3        7                                 ES
Raw Score with K   7      27 20 23 28 12 32 28 20           49
                          25    6 6 1
                          38 34 21

Copyright 1948 by The Psychological Corporation.
All rights reserved as stated in the manual and Catalog
The Psychological Corporation, 304 East 45th Street, New York, N.Y. 10017

Signature _____    Date _____

Printed in U.S.A.    70-251S

scales are Scale 1 through Scale 0. The resulting profile and the relevant personal data have been processed through a series of decision rules. The final Caldwell Report on the individual MMPI is a compilation of sentences highly differentiated by code type, secondary scale elevation, age, sex, education, and marital status.

In a way, the final report is the end-product, or output, of the information processor we depicted in Figure 1–1. The Caldwell system, however, makes no test selections and applies no criteria to judge the psychometric excellence of the tests it processes. Rather, it merely scores and interprets the test, or tests, presented to it. It accomplishes this by applying the appropriate scoring keys and statements with which it has been programmed. The system's memory core contains twelve thousand different sentences, and according to Alexander Caldwell, the narrative report which results goes beyond the capacity of human memory and can rarely, if at all, be matched by manual scoring and human recall of case studies (1981).

"The great leap forward in automated assessment," as James Butcher (1978, p. 942) called it, has produced clinical lore as its basic data. In other words, the interpretations printed out by the computer are narratives that draw heavily from clinical hunches. As such, they are "computerized narratives using psychological test-based information [and] . . . are little more than an art (or craft) disguised as a science" (Butcher, 1978, p. 942). The objection to these systems implicit in this criticism is that more credibility may be attached by untrained recipients to these clinical "hunches" than is deserved by the report's validity, a credibility that can be traced to the scientific mystique associated with computer outputs.

Nevertheless, one cannot help but be impressed by reports such as that in Box 7–3, from the Caldwell Report System. Perhaps the most important question regarding this and other interpreting systems is, "How well do their narrative evaluations describe their patients?" In commenting on the Roche Report, Dahlstrom, Welsh, and Dahlstrom (1972, p. 315) note that

> The content of this report is quite accurate in what is stated about this particular case. It highlights his depressive state, his acute difficulties, and the long-standing social and sexual problems which he has faced over the years. . . . It is interesting that the paranoid and schizoid features noted by the staff psychologist in his report are explicitly introduced in this report.

In reference to the Caldwell Report System, Dahlstrom, Welsh, and Dahlstrom found that

> This report includes an accurate and highly pertinent résumé of the clinical status of this man, highlighting his depression, anxiety, dysphoria, and guilt

feelings. It deals explicitly with the suicidal preoccupation, the specific sexual problems, and the early forms of paranoid and other reality-distorting trends in his thinking. In addition, it quite accurately pinpoints aspects of his family life and early history. Little seems to be left out that is relevant to this man's case and little that is included appears to be very far off target. (1969, p. 336)

But even though this and other reports may be right on target in their descriptions, they have nonetheless been criticized on ethical grounds. For example, Fred Adair (1978, p. 940) called attention to the "curious dichotomy" between the professional psychologist who is obligated to uphold the ethics of the profession and the entrepreneur psychologist who must show a profit in order to compete successfully in the marketplace. This dichotomy is displayed most clearly in many sources' promotional literature, which "takes on a Madison Avenue-like quality where caveats are included in the fine print. The physician or other professional user could be overwhelmed with the advertised efficaciousness of the computer-generated personality description and give more weight to it than either the writer/creator or computerized scoring and interpretive services ever intended" (Adair, 1978, p. 941).

Fortunately, all of the reporting services listed at the outset of this section seem to be responsive to these criticisms by the profession. Several are supporting research by offering reduced fees for experimental protocol data, and some are even providing annual research grants to study the reliability and validity of their services. But as encouraging as this responsiveness may seem at first, it is nevertheless true that, as James Butcher reminded the profession, "demonstrating the validity of computer-generated narratives (like that of demonstrating clinical interpretations generally) is a formidable task" (1978, p. 944).

## Evaluation of the MMPI

As mentioned at the outset of this chapter, the MMPI has had an impressive impact on personality assessment, but its acceptance, although now widespread, has not always been without criticism. This criticism, as noted earlier, has come largely from the popular press, although there has been some informed criticism as well. In the following evaluation we review some of the positive and negative informed comments about the MMPI.

In its favor, much of the MMPI's popularity can be explained by its widespread use and the many situations for which it has been found to be valid. The MMPI, to mention only a few examples of what seems to be an infinitely long list of uses, has been found valid as a test to aid in screening emotional and adjustment problems in high school (Hathaway

& Monachesi, 1951, 1952, 1953, 1957), college (Kleinmuntz, 1960b, 1963a, 1963b; Sloan & Pierce-Jones, 1958), and industry (Drasgow & Barnett, 1957); and in research with medical patients (see Dahlstrom et al., 1975) and in cross-cultural research (Butcher & Pancheri, 1976).

Furthermore, the MMPI has been used successfully to determine the severity of symptoms among psychiatric patients (Feldman, 1958); to assess their contact with reality (Meehl, 1946; Taulbee & Sisson, 1957); to measure the extent of their overt anxiety, i.e., the extent to which they openly manifest tension, nervousness, insecurity, or fears (Welsh, 1952; Taylor, J. A., 1953); and to assess their ego strength or the degree to which they might benefit from treatment (Barron, 1953). Crossvalidation studies (repeating validity studies by using new samples of subjects) and evidence for the validity of specific individual MMPI scales for many of these uses have often and admittedly fallen short of the test originators' expectations (see Hathaway & McKinley, 1943). Their willingness to publicize their test's inadequacies, however, and hence to recognize the need for continually improving it, has greatly contributed to the test's current success.

Nonetheless, the MMPI has been strongly criticized for the unreliability of some of its scales (Anastasi, 1976). The reliability of the individual scales, computed on the basis of test-retest procedures, ranges from the 0.50s to the low 0.90s. Retests lower than these were also reported in a study with college students in which the intervals between tests were as short as one week. The mean of these reliabilities was only 0.61 (Gilliland & Colgin, 1951).

In reference to these low reliabilities, the MMPI's originators asserted that the traditional psychometric criteria of reliability cannot be applied to personality tests (McKinley & Hathaway, 1944). They pointed out that many traits of personality are highly variable and that test-retest data on MMPI scales are more a measure of trait variance than of the test's reliability. This trait variance is to be expected especially among psychiatric patients because their symptoms' exacerbations and remissions are frequent. This is probably most true for the scales affected by temporary fluctuations. However, split-half reliabilities, which are not subject to such trait fluctuations, have also been exceedingly low. Several studies among psychiatric groups have reported coefficients within the range of 0.11 (Welsh, 1952) to 0.96 (Winfield, 1952). In one study with normal college students, a coefficient as low as $-0.05$ (*Pa* scale) was reported (Gilliland & Colgin, 1951). These low reliabilities at the low end of the range cannot be so easily explained away and do suggest that chance fluctuations influence scale scores, although the split-half method underestimates heterogenous scales like those of the MMPI.

In any event, the effectiveness of profile interpretations is weakened if the separate scales are subject to chance fluctuations. When individual scales are unreliable, many of the profile patterns also are unstable. In future research using the MMPI, it is important therefore to select new items to replace some of those that contribute to the low reliabilities. In a number of studies the three scales that have consistently yielded low reliability coefficients are Scale 3 ($Hy$), Scale 6 ($Pa$), and Scale 9 ($Ma$) (see Table 7-2, appendix $K$, p. 474, in Dahlstrom & Welsh, 1960). Studies on reconstructing these scales may well be worthwhile, although much research and clinical experience already have been invested in them.

Another argument often heard—one also not favorable to the MMPI—is that its construction was based on small numbers of subjects (Sarason, 1972). More generally, this argument holds that the procedure was inadequate in both the number and the kind of subjects used. For example, in establishing the depression scale (Scale 2), the criterion group used contained fifty depressed patients who represented only a small and unusual segment of the whole category of depressed patients (they were in the depressed phase of manic-depressive psychosis). Had a larger group of patients been selected, according to this argument, the sample would have been more representative of hospitalized depressed persons.

Moreover, as these critics correctly noted, diagnostic labeling also varies among hospitals, among clinics, and even among psychologists and psychiatrists. This variance, which is partly caused by the clinicians' differing theoretical orientations, can also affect the selection of the so-called normal comparison groups. The net result of these inadequacies is that the scales based on these selecting and labeling procedures are as unreliable as the procedures themselves. Many critics attribute the instability (temporal unreliability) of many of the MMPI's scales to these deficient construction methods.

The greatest limitation of the MMPI, as critics have repeatedly indicated (Adcock, 1965; Lingoes, 1965; also see Alker, 1978; King, 1978), is its lack of sensitivity in discriminating within abnormal or normal groups themselves. Unquestionably, the MMPI's chief claim to prominence and uniqueness as a personality measuring instrument has always been its power to discriminate between those persons coming from normal populations and those coming from abnormal populations. Thus, it is valuable for making broad nosological distinctions, between neurotics and psychotics, as Meehl and Dahlstrom (1960) demonstrated. But unfortunately it is weak in making finer distinctions within any one of these groups.

But even though the MMPI is not accepted unconditionally as the method of choice for personality assessment, it still can make tangible contributions. According to Sarason,

> The evaluation of the MMPI, or of any other test or procedure, should be based as much on what lessons have been learned from it as on how useful it has proven to be.... Were a new MMPI to be developed today, this sort of criticism would be of value in shaping a better inventory, one of greater discriminatory validity than the present one. (1972, p. 161)

## Contenders to Replace the MMPI

In light of the foregoing criticism, we may well ask whether a new MMPI should be developed. Although the answer to this question would seem to be yes, there are some stumbling blocks to such a development. First, MMPI researchers, although they may agree that the test is archaic, do not unanimously concede that its validity would be enhanced by a revision. Thus, the new product would not be worth the effort required to revise it. Second, according to Butcher and Owen, there is considerable reluctance to "tinker with a product that is selling well and has no visible competition at this time" (1978, p. 504). And third, there is some concern that the new MMPI would not inspire as much research (and might invalidate the extensive existing research) as did the original test.

Another question raised about MMPI revision is whether the MMPI could be improved by a revision. The answer to this question, according to Butcher and Owen (1978, p. 507), is definitely affirmative. But the problem is in deciding how much, or to what extent, changes should be made. Here are some guidelines suggested by Butcher and Owen, who recommended several levels on which a possible MMPI might be focused:

1. Changes in the profile sheet that might consist of displaying additional scales which would be accompanied by changes in the manual that would provide new research material on the interpretation of the additional scales.
2. The second level of revision would go further than the above in that it would entail a redevelopment of the present MMPI scales. This revision would attempt to strengthen the present scales by altering the scoring keys by deleting the weaker items and rewording several select items. This level would also include some updating of the norms by using more recent normal and clinical populations.
3. The third approach would involve both of the above and some

major changes at the item level. The item pool would include a wider range of problems and more items that deal with personality attributes and change potential. (1978, p. 507)

In the meantime, however, there are several contenders to replace the MMPI's psychodiagnostic function. One of these is the Differential Personality Inventory (DPI) developed by D. N. Jackson (1972), which was enthusiastically embraced by Goldberg (1974) as the replacement for the MMPI. The DPI contains scales to detect headache proneness, sadism, insomnia, psychotic tendencies, and neurotic disorganization, all of which would provide a clinician with valuable information. These scales were developed by using rational scale construction (Jackson, D. N., 1971), which means that the items were selected so as to conform to the theoretically based definitions of each of the aforementioned scale attributes and that the items on any one scale were therefore homogeneous with the content the scale measured. The advantage of using homogeneous content scales is that it ensures distinction among the traits by reducing the amount of irrelevant variance measured by the scales. Unfortunately, despite the DPI's promise, it has not yet inspired the type of validation research that would make it a useful psychodiagnostic tool.

Another personality inventory designed by Douglas Jackson and his colleagues is the Personality Research Form (PRF) (Jackson, 1967–1974), which again was constructed by using a theoretically or rationally based method. Briefly, the test was developed by taking twenty trait terms adapted from a list of needs originally formulated in the 1930s by Henry Murray and his coworkers at Harvard (see chapter eight). These traits (achievement, affiliation, aggression, and so forth) were then reformulated in accordance with subsequent research and theoretical developments. Over one hundred face-valid items were then written for each trait definition, and the items were administered to over one thousand college students. In this way, about twenty personality scales and two validity scales were developed, with each scale having about twenty items, the exact number of scales and items depending on whether a "standard" or a "long" edition of the PRF is used. The twenty items (ten true, ten false) for each of the scales were selected according to three criteria: an endorsement frequency between 5 and 95 percent, high correlations with each provisional content scale, and low correlations with irrelevant scales. Like those of the DPI, the PRF's scales have a high content homogeneity and are, in the words of one test reviewer, "internally consistent, relatively independent of each other, comprised of moderate endorsement frequencies, and relatively free of the possibly distorting influences of social desirability ..." (Wiggins, 1972, p. 301).

The PRF was also heralded enthusiastically by several other important test reviewers in the *Seventh Mental Measurements Yearbook* (Anastasi, 1972; Kelly, E. L., 1972), all of whom agreed that it was statistically well designed and had been developed according to the best psychometric standards currently available. It was not surprising, therefore, as one writer noted in the *Eighth Mental Measurements Yearbook*, that the PRF is "likely to be of more interest to psychometricians and personality researchers than it is to test users in practical or applied situations" (Hogan, 1978, pp. 1007–1008). This is so for several reasons. For example, the manual contains little evidence of an association between real-life criteria and the PRF scales. Furthermore, there is no discussion of the psychodiagnostic meaning (or evidence for the personality description) of the various trait definitions that define each scale. And finally, according to one other *Yearbook* reviewer in regard to Jackson's (1976) more recent Jackson Personality Inventory (JPI),

> Since there is no evidence that JPI scales carve (human) nature at her joints and since it appears that scores on these scales have only a very modest relationship to the way in which the concepts that define the scales are used in interpersonal assessment, it would be difficult to prove that the JPI profile of an individual provides a very informative or trustworthy characterization of him. (Lykken, 1978, p. 873; see also Goldberg, 1978, for a more favorable, but still cautious, review of the JPI)

Yet another noteworthy contender to replace the MMPI monopoly, according to one recent view (Butcher & Owen, 1978), is Theodore Millon's Clinical Multiaxial Inventory (MCMI). It was originally published as the MMCI (Millon, 1977, 1979), but because of the rhyming similarity with the MMPI, the name for the Millon Inventory was changed from MMCI to MCMI. The rhyming similarity was no accident, for as Millon stated in his *Test Manual*, "The MMPI well deserves emulation as the instrument that pioneered the most fruitful test construction and validation ideas of the past thirty-five years" (1977), p. 1). But then Millon continued, it is now "time to draw upon the best features of the MMPI, minimize its limitations, and move forward to develop instruments that reflect advances of the past quarter of a century in psychopathology, diagnostic assessment and test construction" (p. 1).

Toward these ends, the MCMI utilized the strengths of the rational, factorial, and empirical scale construction methods for each of its twenty scales. Regarding the mix of scale construction methods, Millon relabeled them as follows: the *theoretical-substantive* to represent the linking of item content to theory, the *internal-structural* to refer to the factorial model to which the test is expected to conform, and the *external-criterion* to represent the empirical correspondence between each test scale and a variety of extratest measures. The clinical personality theory to which the test is linked is Millon's own, as outlined in his *Modern Psychopathology* text (1969). According to his current modification of this theory (see Millon, 1977), there are eight basic *personality styles* (asocial, avoidant, submissive, gregarious, narcissistic, aggressive, conforming, and negativistic), and each is measured by a scale on the MCMI. In addition, there are scales for his theory's three *pathological personality syndromes* (schizoid-schizophrenic, cycloid-cyclophrenic, and paranoid-paraphrenic) and nine *symptom disorders* (anxiety, hysteria, hypomania, neurotic depression, alcohol misuse, drug misuse, psychotic thinking, psychotic depression, and psychotic delusions).

The items of Millon's test were selected from a large pool of about 3,500 items and were reduced to the final set by rational, internal consistency and external empirical methods. The final inventory consists of 175 items, which is reasonably brief and requires a minimum amount of time to complete. The psychiatric normative sample consisted of 1,591 subjects (699 females), and the normal group was composed of 297 (153 females) college students and industrial workers. A crossvalidation sample of 256 patients (111 females) was used.

Like the MMPI, this test can be scored and interpreted by computer. Essentially, the interpretive programs summarize in a report those characteristics derived from Millon's theory of psychopathology. The main advantage of such a computer interpretation, according to Millon, is that "a computer data bank provides a resource of clinical information that is far more substantial in scope and variety than that held by the average clinician" (1977, p. 22). And echoing the clinical-versus-statistical controversy that we discussed in chapter four, Millon supported the statistical or actuarial side of the argument by asserting that "diagnosticians must resort to highly tenuous speculations when they encounter novel profile configurations. In contrast, the computer program is well supplied with comparable cases to be drawn upon for interpretive reference" (1977, p. 22).

Unlike most automated MMPI services, MCMI test interpretations provide DSMIII category diagnoses (American Psychiatric Association, 1980). Given the computer's capability of storing probabilities associated with test profiles, as well as the aid of consumer feedback in the form of verified (or unverified) diagnoses, it would require little added effort to stipulate also the numerical probabilities of the program's estimate being accurate for each diagnosis that it renders. And because treatment recommendations are made, Millon could greatly improve the existing automated test interpretation systems by providing information about the success rate of his program's therapy suggestions.

All of this suggests that the MCMI may be on its way to being an updated, although much briefer, version of the MMPI and that it could provide more sophisticated interpretations. But it is too early to judge whether it will replace the MMPI as the standard clinical diagnostic inventory. At the present writing (1981), only the test manual has been published, and the inventory and its interpretive system have not had time to attract the research attention necessary to establish their reliability and validity. The next several years should prove their usefulness for clinical screening and assessment. In the meantime, one serious drawback to this extensive research should be noted: unlike the MMPI and one of its important derivatives, the California Psychological Inventory (CPI), the MCMI has nonreusable booklets. This is an unfortunate feature for an experimental test, in that the test users must rely on the test publisher, in this case the National Computer Systems (NCS), in order to score the test. Although the items are classified in the manual, the test compilers should have their publisher provide hand-scoring keys to qualified users so that potential researchers would have an easier and less commercial access to the MCMI.

## California Psychological Inventory

In addition to these self-report inventories, all of which were designed as psychodiagnostic screening devices and are used among so-called normals only incidentally, there are several self-report tests intended for use exclusively among normal persons. We shall discuss one such test here, the California Psychological Inventory (CPI), developed by Harrison Gough (1956–1975).

Gough derived about half of the CPI's items from the MMPI. Then he made 480 items of the original CPI into eighteen scales almost wholly on the basis of their ability to assess such criteria as rated popularity or rated citizenship among members of extreme groups. Some of the CPI's items are listed in Table 7–4.

**Table 7–4**  Items from the California Psychological Inventory.

| Alternatives | Item |
|---|---|
| True  False | I enjoy social gatherings just to be with people. |
| True  False | I gossip a little at times. |
| True  False | I like poetry. |
| True  False | People often expect too much of me. |
| True  False | My home life was always happy. |
| True  False | Only a fool would ever vote to increase his own taxes. |
| True  False | I love to go to dances. |
| True  False | Sometimes I feel that I am about to go to pieces. |
| True  False | I have never deliberately told a lie. |
| True  False | My parents never really understood me. |

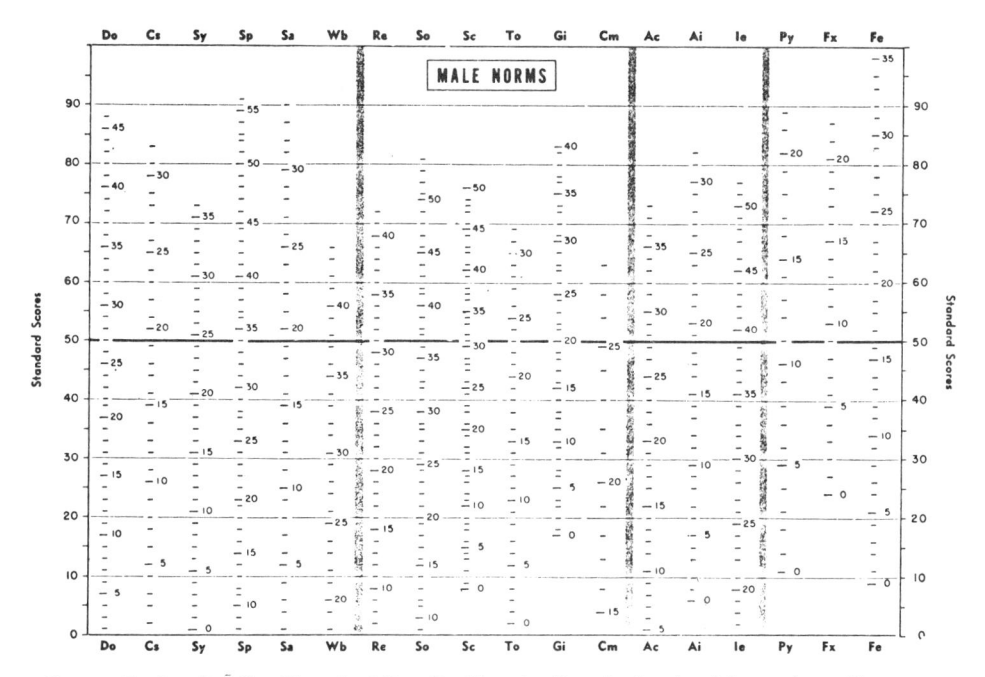

**Figure 7-5.** Profile Sheet of the California Psychological Inventory. The male norms are displayed in this particular illustration. The CPI scales, from left to right, are dominance, capacity for status, sociability, social presence, self-acceptance, sense of well-being, responsibility, socialization, self-control, tolerance, good impression, communality, achievement via conformance, achievement via independence, intellectual efficiency, psychological mindedness, flexibility, and femininity.

(Reproduced by special permission from The California Psychological Inventory by Harrison G. Gough. Copyright, 1956. Published by Consulting Psychologists Press, Inc.)

The CPI also provides a profile (see Figure 7-5) of its eighteen scales, of which three are validity scales. The other fifteen scales include scores on dimensions such as dominance, socialization, tolerance, achievement via conformance, achievement via independence, intellectual efficiency, sense of well-being, self-control, and flexibility.

The CPI is composed of 480 true-false items selected and validated on the basis of such criteria as social class membership, course grades, participation in extracurricular activities, ratings for various traits, and peer nomination ratings of college entrance groups with regard to each trait. For example, for the dominance (*Do*) scale, which identifies strong, dominant, and influential people who are able to take the initiative and exercise leadership, fifty fraternity and fifty sorority members at the University of Minnesota were given a description of a dominant person.

Each group was then asked to nominate ten fellow members who were high in dominance and ten who were low and also to rate their own dominance. From these ratings, eight high-dominance men and eight high-dominance women were selected. They were given the MMPI plus 100 specially written items. Their responses were then contrasted with those of eight men and eight women rated low in dominance. The 100 most discriminating MMPI items were selected and administered, along with the 100 specially written items, to twenty-four high dominance and twenty-four low-dominance high school students, who also were selected on the basis of peer ratings. From these item analyses, 60 items were selected, 28 from the MMPI and 32 from a special pool (for a scale-by-scale description, see chapters four through eight of Megargee's (1972) *California Psychological Inventory Handbook*).

In many respects the CPI is similar to the MMPI. The procedures for its administration, scoring, and profiling are like those of its parent test. However, the method of constructing its scales was much better than that of the MMPI. Many of these methodological advances resulted from lessons learned with the MMPI. Professor Gough was among the earliest contributors to MMPI research and was familiar with many of the earlier test's shortcomings. Thus, in keying the various CPI scales, Gough used a much larger sample (six thousand males and seven thousand females) than the MMPI's Hathaway and McKinley did. Moreover, Gough paid special attention to choosing samples with similar variables such as age, social status, and geographical region. His greatest improvement was to use the aforementioned peer nomination techniques to select and categorize the criterion subjects, rather than to use experts or psychiatrists. Peer nomination procedures generally yield more reliable criterion categorizations than psychiatric labeling does.

The CPI is already well on its way to becoming one of the best, if not the best, personality-measuring instruments of its kind. It is designed, like the MMPI, on the principle that questionnaire items that correlate with socially significant criteria are important. Its technical development has been described as being of the highest order (Goldberg, 1972; Gynther, 1978). Its reliabilities, which were carefully determined by the retest method, are generally high, in the upper 0.80s and lower 0.90s. The validity of each scale is adequate and was determined by comparing group scores of persons among whom the scale was designed to discriminate. The high quality of the normative data, which, as indicated, was based on large samples, rounds out an impressive accomplishment in personality testing for normal people.

Although most test critics agree on the CPI's technical excellence, not all agree on its usefulness. Its severest critics have been R. L. Thorndike (1959) and J. A. Walsh (1972). Thorndike maintained that the CPI's eighteen dimensions provide a redundant, inefficient, and confused picture of a person, and he pointed out that of the eighteen scales, only four fail to correlate at least 0.50 with some other scale. Such intercorrelations, because they reflect the scales' lack of independence, are not desirable in a test designed to describe personality succinctly. Walsh referred to the CPI as "an almost comically typical product of criterion-oriented test construction" with "dubious" validity claims (1972, p. 96). This is in sharp contrast to Gynther's laudatory review in the current *Yearbook*, which summed up the liabilities and assets of the CPI: "Although there are deficits (e.g., the manual), the assets seem to outweigh them. One of the big things in its favor is that the CPI addresses questions that a great many people want to know answers to" (1978, p. 736).

In addition, one of the most impressive features of the CPI has been its author's, adopters', and publisher's relentless efforts to collect pertinent research data and, as was true of the MMPI's authors, its developers' responsiveness to criticism. Between its inception and the publication of Buros's *Fifth Mental Measurements Yearbook* (1959), 33 studies were reported in the literature. The *Sixth Mental Measurements Yearbook* (1965) listed a total of 144 research reports, many of which reflected a readiness to repair the test's shortcomings rather than to refute them. The next edition of the *Yearbook* (1972) listed 764 research items, and the most recent *Yearbook* (1978) referred to no fewer than 1,382 research papers!

The wide variety of problems to which the CPI has been applied is also impressive (see Megargee, 1972). Significant associations have been reported between the CPI and various measures of achievement in elementary school, high school, and college, as well as in military and police training programs, medicine, dentistry, nursing and teaching. Furthermore, the CPI can predict those who are likely to participate in extracurricular activities or to cheat on exams. The inventory has also been found to relate to leadership, managerial ability, employability, and adjustment, as well as to conformity, creativity, and physiological responsiveness to stress—all of which led one critic to refer to it as a "wide-band" instrument, "one that is sensitive to a broad array of behavior patterns" (Megargee, 1972, p. 247). By these criteria alone, one may conclude that the CPI's impact on personality research has been impressive.

## Interest Testing

In the following section, we briefly describe interest testing, which focuses on a person's avocational and vocational preferences. Because we have been discussing the empirically keyed MMPI, it is appropriate now to examine the first self-report tests to be constructed by this method: the Strong Vocational Interest Blank (SVIB) (Strong, 1927) and its more recent revision, the Strong-Campbell Interest Inventory (SCII) (Campbell, 1974), are used extensively in career counseling and personnel selection, mostly the former. But first, a word about interest testing in general.

Compared to personality tests per se, interest tests focus on those aspects of personality that direct people to seek certain vocations or professions. From this perspective, interest tests can be described as reflecting relatively positive facets of persons in that the interest test items inquire about which activities and surroundings give pleasure and satisfaction. Unlike most personality inventories, which are geared for psychiatric screening and psychodiagnostic evaluation, interest tests are designed to help young people plan their careers and life work. These differences of intent and use are demonstrated by the choice of test format and items.

Typically, interest (or preference) tests are group administered, self-report inventories that consist of items relating to recreational pastimes, interpersonal preferences, literary habits, and preferred task assignments. The respondents are expected to mark their likes and dislikes, and it is assumed that from a list of alternative occupations or pastimes, most individuals can select those they prefer. The Strong Vocational Interest Blank, however, makes no such assumption, as we indicate below.

## The Strong Vocational Interest Blank

Shortly after World War I, Edward K. Strong and his coworkers observed that individuals in different vocations and professions consistently differed in their recreational and avocational preferences. Some of these differences were obvious. Strong noted, for instance, that office workers preferred the indoors, and forest rangers the outdoors. But less obvious differences also turned up.

Consequently, Strong systematically collected information about patterns of interests among satisfied persons in many professions and vocations and compared these patterns with those of another group made up of men (both satisfied and dissatisfied) from various occupations. He then constructed scoring keys by the empirical, or criterion-keying, method. For example, in devising the scoring key for the engineering scale, Strong administered items to several thousand practicing engineers, tabulated their "like" ($L$), "indifferent" ($I$), and "dislike" ($D$) responses, and retained all items that empirically differentiated between the criterion group of engineers and other men. If the difference between these groups was very large, he retained the discrimination items for the engineering scoring key. In a like manner, Strong developed the entire test by retaining those items to which the *L*, *I*, and *D* responses defined the preferences of successful persons in each of several occupational groups. The fundamental assumption of the SVIB, therefore, was that persons having the interests associated with, but not necessarily found in, an occupation would probably enjoy working in that occupation.

The most recently revised version of the SVIB for men consists of 325 items (see Table 7–5), which is somewhat shorter than the original separate SVIBs for men and women (for the SCII, see Campbell, 1974, 1976). Each respondent is scored on 6 general occupational themes, 23 basic interest scales, and 124 occupational scales. Along with the test profile (see Figure 7–6), which depicts the respondent's scores on all scales and allows him to compare his standing on these scales with those of satisfied persons in various occupations, each individual obtains a guide to understanding his scores. These test scores, in turn, then become a quantified guess about that individual's probable job satisfaction. Such an interest profile does not imply that these persons have the commensurate or necessary training or ability to perform that job; rather, it measures the extent to which their preferences agree or disagree with those of successful men in a given occupation.

The SVIB and the SCII tests, which have been used for six decades since the 1920s (Strong, 1927, 1951, 1955, 1963) and have recently been revised (Campbell, 1974, 1976, 1981), were recognized by one reviewer "as the paragon of applied behaviorial measures . . . and the bellwether of career counseling" (Crites, 1978, p. 1621). And with their more than fifteen hundred citations, they are clearly the most-researched preference tests in existence. But despite their widespread acceptance and use, the series of SVIB and SCII inventories, their computer-scoring services, and their interpretive reports have been criticized for such things as information gaps in the test manual, sex bias, and even crass commercialism. For example, Robert Dolliver, in the latest *Yearbook* (1978), faulted the test's construction for not including data on the item content of many SCII scales and for not adequately describing the normative samples. Patricia Lunneborg, in the same *Yearbook* (1978), criticized the test both for keeping its item content secret, and thus precluding research on item sex bias, and for restricting the occupational options available to women, by offering female interest scales that "reveal an abundance of low-level clerical jobs" (Lunneborg, 1978, p. 1628). And Richard Johnson (1976), who found the SCII to be well constructed in most respects, expressed his regret that a commercial scoring agency had to be employed to score the scales, a criticism that was also made by Jean Steinhaurer (1976). There also are other interest tests, the most famous of which, after the Strong inventories, are G.

**Table 7-5** Sample Items from the Strong-Campbell Interest Inventory.

**Part I. Occupations**

Many occupations are listed below. For each of them, show how you would feel about doing that kind of work.

Mark on the answer sheet in the space labeled "L" if you think you would like that kind of work.

Mark in the space labeled "I" if you are indifferent (that is, if you think you would't care one way or another).

Mark in the space labeled "D" if you think you would dislike that kind of work.

Don't worry about whether you would be good at the job or about not being trained for it. Forget about how much money you could make or whether you could get ahead. Think ony about whether you would like to do the work done in that job.

Work fast. Answer every one.

1. Actor/Actress
2. Advertising executive
3. Architect
4. Art museum director
5. Art teacher
6. Artist
7. Artist's model
8. Astronomer
9. Athletic director
10. Auctioneer
11. Author of children's books
12. Author of novels
13. Author of technical books
14. Auto mechanic
15. Auto racer
16. Auto sales
17. Bank teller
18. Beauty and haircare consultant
19. Biologist
20. Bookkeeper
21. Building contractor
22. Business teacher
23. Buyer of merchandise
24. Carpenter
25. Cartoonist
26. Cashier in Bank
27. Chemist
28. Children's clothes designer
29. Church worker
30. City or state employee
31. City planner
32. Civil engineer
33. College professor
34. Computer operator
35. Corporation lawyer
36. Costume designer
37. Courtroom stenographer
38. Criminal lawyer
39. Dancing teacher
40. Dental assistant
41. Dentist
42. Designer, electronic equipment
43. Dietitian
44. Draftsman
45. Dressmaker/Tailor
46. Editor
47. Electrical engineer
48. Electronics technician
49. Elementary school teacher
50. Employment manager
51. Factory manager
52. Farmer
53. Fashion model
54. Florist
55. Foreign correspondent
56. Foreign service officer
57. Free-lance writer
58. Governor of a state
59. High school teacher
60. Home economics teacher
61. Hospital records clerk
62. Housekeeper
63. Hotel manager
64. Illustrator
65. Income tax accountant
66. Interior decorator
67. Inventor
68. Jet pilot
69. Judge
70. Labor arbitrator
71. Laboratory technician
72. Landscape gardener
73. Librarian
74. Life insurance agent
75. Machine shop supervisor
76. Machinist
77. Manager, Chamber of Commerce

*(continued)*

## Self-Report Inventories and Questionnaires

**Table 7-5** *(Continued)*

**Part I. Occupations**

| | |
|---|---|
| 78. Manager, child care center | 105. Rancher |
| 79. Manager, women's style shop | 106. Realtor |
| 80. Manufacturer | 107. Receptionist |
| 81. Mechanical engineer | 108. Retailer |
| 82. Military officer | 109. Sales manager |
| 83. Minister, priest, or rabbi | 110. School principal |
| 84. Musician | 111. Scientific illustrator |
| 85. Newspaper reporter | 112. Scientific research worker |
| 86. Nurse | 113. Sculptor |
| 87. Nurse's aide/Orderly | 114. Secret service agent |
| 88. Office clerk | 115. Social worker |
| 89. Office manager | 116. Specialty salesperson |
| 90. Opera singer | 117. Sports reporter |
| 91. Orchestra conductor | 118. Statistician |
| 92. Pharmacist | 119. Flight attendant |
| 93. Photographer | 120. Stockbroker |
| 94. Physician | 121. Surgeon |
| 95. Playground director | 122. Toolmaker |
| 96. Poet | 123. Traveling salesperson |
| 97. Police officer | 124. Travel bureau manager |
| 98. Politician | 125. Typist |
| 99. Private secretary | 126. TV announcer |
| 100. Professional athlete | 127. Vocational counselor |
| 101. Professional dancer | 128. Waiter/Waitress |
| 102. Professional gambler | 129. Wholesaler |
| 103. Psychologist | 130. X-Ray technician |
| 104. Public relations director | 131. YMCA/YWCA staff member |

SOURCE: Reprinted from Strong-Campbell Interest Inventory, Form T325 of the *Strong Vocational Interest Blank* by Edward K. Strong, Jr. and David P. Campbell with the permission of the publishers, Stanford University Press. Copyright © 1974, 1981 by the Board of Trustees of the Leland Stanford Junior University.

Frederick Kuder's (1934–1976) three Kuder preference records: vocational, occupational, and personal. Only a brief description is possible here.

The Kuder Preference Record-Vocational and the Kuder Occupational Interest Survey deal specifically with interests relevant to vocational counseling. The Kuder Preference Record-Personal, in contrast, was designed to measure personal aspects that lie midway between interests and adjustment. As such it yields scores in group activity, stable situations, and avoiding conflict (which relate to adjustment to one's surroundings) as well as scores in working ideas, directing others, and verification (which seem relevant to the world of work).

Some of the scales that appear on the vocational and the occupational tests are mechanical, computational, scientific, persuasive, artistic, literary, musical, social, clerical, masculinity-femininity, accountancy, civil engineering, and dentistry.

What is unusual about the Kuder tests, as compared with the many other inventories constructed in the 1930s, 1940s, and 1950s, is that

## Personality and Psychological Assessment

### SVIB-SCII Profile for

| General Occupational Themes | | | Administrative Indexes | |
|---|---|---|---|---|
| Theme | Std Score | Result | (for the use of the counselor) | |
| R-Theme | | This is a _____ Score. | Total Responses | |
| | | | Infrequent Responses | |
| I-Theme | | This is a _____ Score. | | Response % |
| | | | Occupations | LP  IP  DP |
| A-Theme | | This is a _____ Score. | School Subjects | |
| S-Theme | | This is a _____ Score. | Activities | |
| | | | Amusements | |
| E-Theme | | This is a _____ Score. | Types of People | |
| | | | Preferences | |
| C-Theme | | This is a _____ Score. | Characteristics | |
| | | | Special Scales: | AOR:  IE: |

**Basic Interest Scales**

| | Scale | Std Score | Very Low | Low | Average | High | Very High |
|---|---|---|---|---|---|---|---|
| **R THEME** | Agriculture | | | | | | |
| | Nature | | 30 | 35  40 | 45  50  55 | 60  65 | 70 |
| | Adventure | | | | | | |
| | Military Activities | | | | | | |
| | Mechanical Activities | | | | | | |
| **I THEME** | Science | | | | | | |
| | Mathematics | | | | | | |
| | Medical Science | | | | | | |
| | Medical Service | | | | | | |
| **A THEME** | Music/ Dramatics | | 30 | 35  40 | 45  50  55 | 60  65 | 70 |
| | Art | | | | | | |
| | Writing | | | | | | |
| **S THEME** | Teaching | | | | | | |
| | Social Services | | | | | | |
| | Athletics | | | | | | |
| | Domestic Arts | | | | | | |
| | Religious Activities | | | | | | |
| **E THEME** | Public Speaking | | | | | | |
| | Law/ Politics | | | | | | |
| | Merchand'ng | | | | | | |
| | Sales | | | | | | |
| | Business Mgmt. | | 30 | 35  40 | 45  50  55 | 60  65 | 70 |
| **C TH** | Office Practices | | | | | | |

Profile for use with test booklet T325
Stanford University Press, Stanford, California

Strong-Campbell Interest Inventory
of the Strong Vocational Interest Blank

they contain items in the triadic forced-choice style, confronting the examinee with the problem of selecting from three choices those activities or preferences he or she likes most and least. The underlying theory of the test, according to Horrocks (1964, p. 675), is that specific dimensions of interests (like outdoor interests) distinguish one occupational group from another and that various constellations of such dimensions may be used to identify those vocations that an examinee might be advised to consider or reject.

Although the reliabilities of the Kuder tests' various scales were generally satisfactory, ranging from about 0.42 to 0.82, and although the tests were useful in guiding young people into and away from particular occupations and vocations, these tests have been abandoned by their publishers. Harmon concluded in a review of the tests that "the manual . . . contains no information . . . on the reliability or validity of the scales, or the composition of the norm groups for boys, girls, men, and women . . . [which] . . . leads me to conclude that the publishers have abandoned . . . [the tests] . . . and that the public should probably do so too, not because of poor quality but because of inadequate information" (1978, p. 1592).

## Attitudes and Values Testing

Attitude and value scales measure somewhat different facets of the person than do personality and interest tests. Whereas the latter two are "self-reports" in the strict sense of the term, attitude and value tests, usually in the form of questionnaires, investigate reactions toward, or feelings about, persons, things, or situations. The main difference between attitude and value tests, then, and personality and interest self-reports is in the reference points, or *referents,* that are rated. A self-report inventory item, such as appears on the MMPI or the SCII, uses the examinee as its referent or construct; an item on an attitude or value questionnaire uses things or issues "out there" as its referents.

### Attitude Scaling

Attitude questionnaires are said to be scaled because they are constructed so as to measure people's attitudes toward issues, persons, and institutions. Perhaps some examples of these scaling methods will be helpful.

### Figure 7-6.

Reprinted from Strong-Campbell Interest Inventory Form T325 of the Strong Vocational Interest Blank by Edward K. Strong, Jr. and David P. Campbell with the permission of the publishers, Stanford University Press. Copyright © 1974, 1981 by the Board of Trustees of the Leland Stanford Junior University.

The best-known ways to scale attitude are those developed by Thurstone, Likert, and Guttman. The first of these, the *Thurstone* scale (1929), also called the *equal-appearing interval* scales, requires respondents to express favorable-to-unfavorable attitudes toward objects or people. The items are said to be equal appearing because in constructing the items, experts were asked to sort them into piles considered equal distances apart, ranging from most favorable to least favorable. An example of an item from Thurstone's and Chase's (1929) Attitude toward the Church Scale is:

(Favorable)—I feel the Church is the greatest agency for the uplift of the world.
(Neutral)—I know too little about the Church to express an opinion.
(Unfavorable)—I have nothing but contempt for the Bible and its readers.

On this item, $F$, $N$, and $U$ would be assigned scale values—ranging from low to high—and the lower the scale value was, the more positive the attitude toward the church would be. The original questionnaire contained forty-five items, each of which had been first sorted according to scale values. Similar scales are still being constructed today to collect attitudes toward such diverse referents as the draft, abortion, TV commercials, and politicians.

The *Likert* (1932) scale presents subjects with statements with which they can agree or disagree along a scale reading "strongly agree," "agree," "undecided," "disagree," and "strongly disagree." This has also been called a *summated rating scale* because the scores of the items of this scale are summed, or summed and averaged, to yield an attitude score. Thus if five steps between agreement and disagreement are used, weights ranging from one to five are assigned so that extreme agreement with one item receives the same weight as extreme disagreement with another. The score then becomes the sum of the weights for all items on the scale. A sample of a Likert scale item that might measure attitudes toward, let us say, abortion, would read as follows:

Abortion should be permitted in instances where the father of the unborn child is in question.

Strongly agree
Agree
Undecided
Disagree
Strongly disagree

The Likert scaling method and its variations are still in use today. In

**Table 7-6**  Example of a Cumulative Scale.

| Pattern Type | | Perceives a Power Structure | Perceives Little Influence | Perceiving Power as Used | Dissgrees with Goals | Scale Score |
|---|---|---|---|---|---|---|
| Least Alienated | I | Disagree (0) | Disagree (0) | Disagree (0) | Disagree (0) | 0 |
| | II | Agree (1) | Disagree (0) | Disagree (0) | Disagree (0) | 1 |
| | III | Agree (1) | Agree (1) | Disagree (0) | Disagree (0) | 2 |
| | IV | Agree (1) | Agree (1) | Agree (1) | Disagree (0) | 3 |
| Most Alienated | V | Agree (1) | Agree (1) | Agree (1) | Agree (1) | 4 |

Source: Adapted from Eckhardt, W. K., Ermann, M. D. *Social research methods: Perspective, theory and analysis.* New York: Random House, 1977, p. 110.

fact, the early scaling approaches preceding and following this discussion are the bases for some of the alternative methods to classical test theory mentioned earlier in the book. Particularly, order models as well as latent trait test and item response theories, which reflect the most contemporary psychometric thinking, have their roots in the work of Thurstone's mental age scale of the mid-1920s and Guttman's unidimensional scaling studies of the 1940s (see Weiss & Davison, 1981, pp. 638–645 for a recent review of the new theories of testing).

The *Guttman* (1947) scaling approach, also still in use, has as its purpose a somewhat more complex idea. This idea is to determine whether the attitude under study contains only one dimension. Such unidimensionality, in turn, occurs if the response of many subjects can be rank-ordered in a *cumulative* pattern. For example, if it is possible to arrange all the subjects' responses into a pattern like that shown in Table 7–6, then a scale is considered unidimensional and hence cumulative. The important thing about this pattern, according to one source (see Selltiz et al, 1976, pp. 423–424), is that if it holds, a given score on a particular series of items will always have the same meaning; knowing a person's score makes it possible to tell, without consulting the questionnaire, exactly which items that person has endorsed. This method therefore requires ranking both items and respondents. Consider the following items taken from a study of alienation conducted by Eckhardt and Ermann (1977, pp. 106–110):

1. In this community, some organizations and individuals have more to say about what gets done than others.
   (a) Basically agree _____ (b) Basically disagree _____
2. The problem with this town is that an average citizen like me has little chance of influencing what gets done around here.
   (a) Basically agree _____ (b) Basically disagree _____

3. No matter how you vote or what you want, people in public office generally do what they want anyway.
   (a) Basically agree _____ (b) Basically disagree _____
4. For the most part, I disagree with what public officials and other important people want to do in this community.
   (a) Basically agree _____ (b) Basically disagree _____

If these items formed a perfect cumulative scale, then all the persons with a score of four would agree with all the items, and all the persons with a score of two, would agree with the first two items and would disagree with the second two. In other words, because the items are arranged in an ordinal pattern from least alienated to most alienated, the positions on the scale are indicated by both the number and the pattern of "agree" responses. Thus, Type I persons and Type V persons can be characterized as least alienated and most alienated, with endorsements of no items and all four items, respectively.

In practice, perfect cumulative, or unidimensional, scales are rarely if ever found, but Guttman's technique is a method of ascertaining the extent to which approximations to them can be developed. The Guttman approach, sometimes also called *scalogram analysis* (see Festinger & Katz, 1953), uses several criteria to decide whether a series of items is unidimensional. The most important of these criteria is reproducibility of responses, that is, the proportion of many subjects' responses that actually fall into the pattern presented above. Note the relation of the pattern of item responses to the total score. If we know a person's total score, and if the scale is cumulative, we can predict his or her pattern. Therefore, the proportion of actual responses that fall into the pattern is an index of the extent to which particular responses are reproducible from the total score. Guttman (1944) and his associates set ninety as the minimal reproducibility proportion acceptable for a set of items to be regarded as approximating a perfect cumulative scale.

Not all approaches to attitude scaling can be categorized into the three types above. We described one other method in chapter five, the *Q*-sort, in which subjects rank referents along a prespecified number of categories. It does not fall neatly into the mold of a Thurstone, Likert, or Guttman scale but shares some features with all of these. Unlike these three approaches, the *Q*-sort can be used for self-descriptions as well. Another method that does not fit the mold of the preceding scaling techniques is the *semantic differential*, which we shall now consider.

The *semantic differential* was developed by Osgood (1952) and his associates (Osgood et al., 1957) as a tool for measuring meaning. The logic of the semantic differential method was summarized by Osgood somewhat as follows: (1) The process of description or judgment can be conceived as the allocation of a concept to an experimental continuum definable by a pair of polar terms; (2) many different experimental continua, or ways in which meaning can vary, are essentially equivalent and hence may be represented by a single dimension; (3) a limited number of such continua can be used to find a semantic space within which the meaning of a concept can be specified.

The semantic differential consists of a group of seven-point scales, each defined by a pair of polar terms (e.g., excitable-calm, strong-weak) by which the words or concepts are to be rated. The scales were chosen by having subjects write down descriptive adjectives for forty nouns.

---

*DIRECTIONS*

On the following pages there is either a word or a sentence in capitalized letters at the *top* of the page. You will also notice that there are 17 pairs of opposite words underneath the capitalized word or sentence. Between each of the pairs of opposites there are 7 dashes. You are to place a check mark on one of the 7 lines that are between the two opposite words and the check mark should indicate what the word or sentence at the *top* of the page means to you. Look at the examples below:

EXAMPLE 1:                    MAN
   Line 1:    Good  ✓:___:___:___:___:___:___  Bad
   Line 2:    Slow  ___:✓:___:___:___:___:___  Fast
   Line 3:    Cruel ___:___:✓:___:___:___:___  Kind

In this example MAN is the word at the top of the page and the pairs of opposites are Good-Bad, Slow-Fast, and Cruel-Kind. If MAN seemed to you to mean something very Good, you would make a check as in Line 1. If MAN seemed to you to mean something quite SLOW, then you would place your check mark as in Line 2. And if you feel that MAN means something which is a little Cruel, then you would put your check mark as in Line 3.

In the following example a check has been placed to illustrate how someone would place his check marks if he thought that TIGER was something very Bad, very Fast, and very Cruel:

EXAMPLE 2:                   TIGER
   Line 1:    Good  ___:___:___:___:___:___:✓  Bad
   Line 2:    Slow  ___:___:___:___:___:___:✓  Fast
   Line 3:    Cruel ✓:___:___:___:___:___:___  Kind

Sometimes you will feel that the word or sentence at the *top* of the page is neither Good nor Bad, neither Slow nor Fast and neither Cruel nor Kind. On the Sample below, using the word TREE, place your check marks to indicate how you would show this feeling.

SAMPLE                        TREE
   Line 1:    Good  ___:___:___:___:___:___:___  Bad
   Line 2:    Slow  ___:___:___:___:___:___:___  Fast
   Line 3:    Cruel ___:___:___:___:___:___:___  Kind

On the following pages, place your check marks rapidly. What is wanted is your first impression. There are no "right" or "wrong" answers. Be sure to make only one check mark for each pair of words. Do not skip any pairs of words or pages.

**Figure 7–7.** Directions and Samples for Administering the Semantic Differential.

Source:

The adjectives used most often were then converted into fifty bipolar scales, and one hundred students rated twenty concepts on these scales. Factor analysis of the results indicated that three factors accounted for most of the variance. These were the *evaluative* (good-bad), *activity* (fast-slow), and *potency* (strong-weak) factors.

The raw data obtained from the semantic differential ratings are a collection of check marks on such bipolar scales as are illustrated in Figure 7–7. A number is arbitrarily assigned to each of the seven

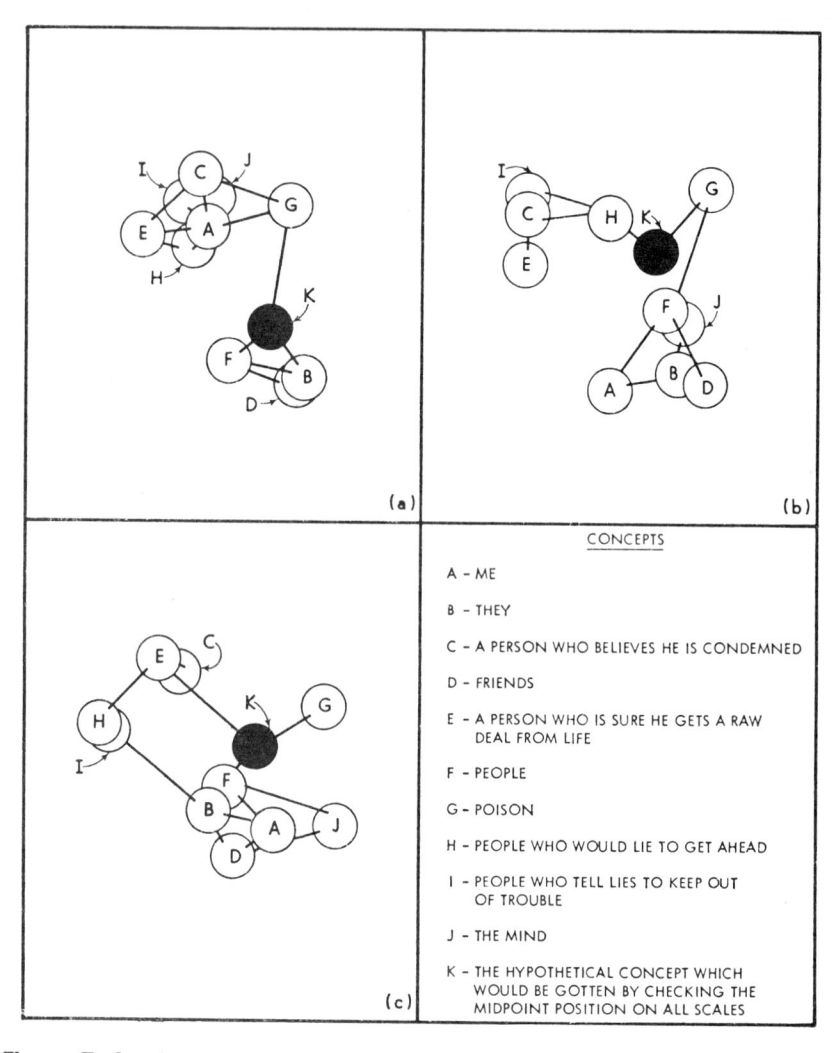

**Figure 7–8.** Semantic Structures of (a) Test Hits, (b) Normals, and (c) Test Misses. Note especially in (c) that test misses describe themselves and the MIND as mentally healthy, strong, and calm.

positions on the scale. These can be in the form of 1 through 7 or can be $+3$, $+2$, $+1$, $0$, $-1$, $-2$, or $-3$. A rater's score on a scale is the value corresponding to the scale position checked. For $k$ scales and $m$ concepts, each respondent yields a $k \times m$ matrix. If a group of $n$ respondents is used to rate referents or concepts, then there will be a matrix of $k \times m \times n$ scores. These scores can then be plotted in a three-dimensional space (see Figure 7–8) by using a special distance formula which need not concern us here.

This method of rating concepts was used by Kleinmuntz (1958, 1960c) to investigate psychiatric patients' attitudes toward certain MMPI items. The idea was to learn whether the attitudes toward some MMPI paranoia (Scale 6) and schizophrenia (Scale 8) items varied according to whether the patient was a "test hit" (e.g., detected by the MMPI) or a "test miss" (not detected) hospitalized paranoid schizophrenic. The hypothesis of the study was that the test misses were able to evade detection because they could "see through" these items. It turned out that both groups of schizophrenics (and a group of normals) found the items to be transparent indicators of mental illness, the difference in responding being that the test hits chose to admit their disorders and the test misses did not so choose.

In fact, at least according to the groups' expressed attitudes toward the concepts me, they, people, friends, poison, and the mind (all selected because of their special significance for paranoid schizophrenics), the test misses described themselves in the same way that the normals did, even considering themselves to be supernormal. This is reflected in the semantic structures depicted in Figure 7–8, which were plotted for the three groups (test hits, test misses, and normals). These subjects rated the concepts along the seven-point bipolar scales defined by the endpoints (mentally healthy, mentally ill, weak-strong, and excitable-calm). The spatial orientation for the structures is that mentally healthy is down and mentally ill is up; weak is to the left and strong is to the right; and excitable is away from the viewer and calm is toward the viewer.

## The Measurement of Values

For many years the standard approach to measuring attitudes and values has been an instrument devised by Gordon Allport and Philip Vernon. The Allport-Vernon Study of Values (1931) was based on six categories of values originally proposed by Spranger (1928): theoretical, economic, aesthetic, social, political, and religious. The questionnaire, which came to be known as the Allport-Vernon-Lindzey Study of Values (*A-V-L*) because of Gardner Lindzey's (1960) more recent affiliation with it, has two parts, with 120 items equally distributed over the six categories. Part I requires that the respondent express a preference for one of two fields of activity by indicating yes or no to the following statement:

> The main object of scientific research should be the discovery of pure truth rather than its practical applications (a) Yes (b) No.

Clearly, the choice of scientific discovery over that of application earns a score in the theoretical direction.

Part II of the *A-V-L* requires the ranking of four choices in order of their appeal. The following is an example:

> Do you think good government should aim chiefly at—
> (a) More aid for the poor, sick, and old.
> (b) Development of manufacturing and trade.
> (c) Introducing more ethical principles into its policies and diplomacy.
> (d) Establishing a position of prestige and respect among nations.

In these choices, the first involves social values, the second economic values, the third ethical or religious values, and the fourth political values.

At this point we should distinguish between measuring attitudes and measuring values. The two *A-V-L* examples, above, reflect a broader system of beliefs than do attitude measures. That is, it can be assumed that one who scores high on a religious value scale also holds unfavorable attitudes toward abortion, communism, premarital sex, polygamy, and so on. Likewise, a person who scores high on a theoretical value scale probably also holds negative attitudes toward less government spending for the basic sciences and holds positive attitudes toward missions to outer space. In other words, a person's attitudes toward specific issues, objects, or people reflect his or her underlying value or belief system.

Another and more recent measure of values grew out of research by Milton Rokeach (1967–1973) on *The Nature of Human Values*, which is the title of both a book and the test's manual. The test itself is called the *Rokeach Value Survey* (RVS). It requires subjects to rate themselves using eighteen instrumental values and eighteen terminal values. Rokeach defined a value as an enduring belief that a specific mode of conduct (instrumental value) or end-state of existence (terminal value) is preferable to its opposite. Rokeach defined a value system as an array of values along a continuum of relative importance. His book proposed a theory in which human values can be divided into thirty-six values, eighteen instrumental and eighteen terminal. The *instrumental values* are ambitious, broad-minded, capable, cheerful, clean, courageous, forgiving, helpful, honest, imaginative, independent, intellectual, logical, loving, obedient, polite, responsible, and self-controlled. The *terminal values* are a comfortable life, an exciting life, a sense of accomplishment, a world at peace, a world of beauty, equality, family security, freedom, happiness, inner harmony, mature love, national security, pleasure, salvation, self-respect, social recognition, true friendship, and wisdom.

Each value term is accompanied by a short defining phrase, for example, "mature love (sexual and spiritual intimacy)." Examinees are instructed to rank-order each list separately according to the importance to them of the values as a guiding principle. Each value term is on a gummed label which is easily detached and reaffixed at the desired rank position. A value's score is simply its rank.

The RVS and the theory on which it is based have received some criticism, but this is beyond the scope of this presentation (see Cohen, 1978; Kitwood, 1978). We shall mention here merely that the theory is promising but nascent and that the RVS is not useful for individual assessment in counseling, psychotherapy, and selection. But perhaps that is as it should be, since its purpose is to measure values, not psychodiagnosis.

## SUMMARY AND CONCLUSION

The bulk of this chapter deals with the MMPI and some contenders to replace it. The MMPI was constructed by using criterion keying, a method that makes few theoretical assumptions about the relationship of item content to the underlying psychological constructs. The main feature of criterion keying is that it develops scoring keys by establishing empirical correlates between item reponses and observed extratest behaviors. The California Psychological Inventory and the Strong Vocational Inventory and its revision were also constructed by this method.

Other personality inventories considered in this chapter include Jackson's Differential Personality Inventory (DPI), which was constructed by the theoretical-rational method. This method tries to tie the item content to the test's underlying theory. A third MMPI contender is Millon's Clinical Multiaxial Inventory (MCMI), which used a mix of empirical keying, factor analysis, and rational methods. Whether any of these tests will replace the MMPI is a moot point; in the meantime they do not seem to have generated the pace or volume of research that, from its very inception, the MMPI inspired.

This chapter concluded with an examination of interest tests, which explore a more positive aspect of the person than do personality inventories, and with a discussion of attitude scaling and value measurement. Attitude and value tests almost invariably use the questionnaire format, which differs from self-report inventories in that the referents are issues, objects, or people.

A general problem in the measurement of personality, interests, attitudes, and values is that these constructs themselves are not directly measurable. In other words, the obtained score stands as a "sign," and hence a highly fallible indicator, of the behavior in question. This is in sharp contrast to direct observation, particularly the type used in behavioral assessment, in which the elicited or admitted behavior itself is the important variable being investigated.

This problem has two implications. First it implies that the test score interpreter must take a greater inferential leap than the direct observer must in interpreting his or her respective findings. This means that there is more uncertainty about the sign-to-behavior relationship in inventory and questionnaire testing than in behavioral assessment or other direct observations. Second, test scores may be poor predictors of what one will actually do in the real world or of how one will actually behave in real situations. But if inference and prediction are limitations of inventory and questionnaire testing, they are even greater limitations of the interpretations of projective testing, as should become apparent in the next chapter.

## FOR FURTHER READING

Adair, F.L. Re MMPI computerized scoring and interpreting services. In O.K. Buros (Ed.), *Eighth mental measurements yearbook*. Highland Park, NJ: Gryphon Press, 1978. Together with James N. Butcher, Adair criticizes the following seven automated MMPI services: Automated Psychological Assessment, Behaviordyne Psychodiagnostic Laboratory Service, Caldwell Report: An MMPI Interpretation, MMPI-ICA Computer Report, Psychological Assessment Services, Psychological Corporation MMPI Reporting Service, and Roche MMPI Computerized Interpretation Service.

Butcher, J.N., & Owen, P.L. Objective personality inventories: Recent research and some contemporary issues. In B. Wolman (Ed.), *Handbook of clinical diagnosis of mental disorders*. New York: Plenum, 1978, pp. 475–545. An integrative discussion of self-report inventories with emphasis on issues and problems surrounding the MMPI.

Campbell, D.P. The Strong vocational interest blank: 1927–1967. In P. McReynolds (Ed.), *Advances in psychological assessment* (Vol. 1). Palo Alto, CA: Science & Behavior Books, 1968, pp. 105–130. A review of the history and literature on this popular test written at about the same time that Campbell was launching his own revision of the test.

## Self-Report Inventories and Questionnaires 263

Crites, J.O. Critique of the Strong-Campbell interest inventory. In O.K. Buros (Ed.), *Eighth mental measurements yearbook.* Highland Park, NJ: Gryphon Press, 1978. Together with Robert Dolliver and Patricia Lunneborg, Crites takes careful aim at his contemporary version of the Strong Vocational Interest Blank and finds it wanting in a variety of important ways.

Dahlstrom, W.G., & Dahlstrom, L. (Eds.), *Basic readings on the MMPI: A new selection on personality measurement.* Minneapolis: University of Minnesota Press, 1980. This updating of a 1960 *Basic Readings* book is a must for MMPI users who need to know the latest developments on this popular objective test.

Dahlstrom, W.G., Welsh, G.S., & Dahlstrom, L.E. *An MMPI handbook* (Vol. 1): (Rev. ed.). *Clinical interpretation.* Minneapolis: University of Minnesota Press, 1972. This updating of the 1960 basic book on the MMPI—together with its research applications in volume 2 printed in 1975 and a more recent book of readings published in 1980—contains more information on the MMPI than any other book in print.

Gynther, M.D., & Gynther, R.A. Personality inventories. In I.B. Weiner (Ed.). *Clinical methods in psychology.* New York: John Wiley, 1976, pp. 187–279. In a discussion of the nature of objective personality inventories, these authors discuss the MMPI, CPI, 16 PF, PRF, and other well-known personality inventories.

Hathaway, S.R. Where have we gone wrong? The mystery of the missing progress. In J.N. Butcher (Ed.), *Objective personality assessment: Changing perspectives.* New York: Academic Press, 1972, pp. 21–43. Hathaway is far from pessimistic about the future progress of personality inventory—especially the MMPI—and he suggests that computers will be used much more effectively than now (1972) in interpreting MMPI profiles.

Jackson, D.N. The dynamics of structured personality tests: 1971. *Psychological Review*, 1971, *78*, 229–248. This paper is an important updating of the state of the art of the rationale of objective personality testing. It is intentionally titled similarly to Meehl's (1945) earlier paper, "The Dynamics of 'Structured' Personality Tests."

Meehl, P.E. Reactions, reflections, projections. In J.N. Butcher (Ed.), *Objective personality assessment: Changing perspectives.* New York: Academic Press, 1972, pp. 131–189. The occasion for this paper is to comment on the other six articles in this volume on objective personality tests; but, predictably, Meehl goes considerably beyond these confines. Essentially, this chapter is his updating of the state of the art of MMPI testing in general.

Megargee, E.I. *The California psychological inventory handbook.* San Francisco: Jossey-Bass, 1972. This resource volume on one of the most researched self-report inventories designed for normals contains the theoretical background and descriptions of the CPI.

Norman, W.T. Psychometric considerations for a revision of the MMPI. In J.N. Butcher (Ed.), *Objective personality assessment: Changing perspectives.* New York: Academic Press, 1972, pp. 59–83. This is a call for a more sophisticated factor analytic approach to personality inventory construction than was being used to date.

# 8 Projective Techniques

HAMLET: Do you see yonder cloud that's almost in shape of a camel?
POLONIUS: By the mass, and 'tis like a camel, indeed.
HAMLET: Methinks it is like a weasel.
POLONIUS: It is backed like a weasel.
HAMLET: Or like a whale?
POLONIUS: Very like a whale.

William Shakespeare, *Hamlet,* III, 2, 381–387.

Polonius was possibly more politic than honest to agree so readily with Hamlet, but at one time or another each of us has had a similar experience when looking at clouds. We have seen shapes such as animals, landscapes, cotton candy, human figures, and even familiar faces. Obviously, since clouds are nothing more than clouds and do not represent anything, each person's interpretation is unique and is produced by the mind. These misperceptions, or projections, are how we organize amorphous stimuli into standardized constructions.

Consider, for example, the inkblot depicted in Figure 8–1. People often describe it as looking like "... two persons talking to one another about a way in which ..." or "... two persons trying to pull apart...." Since this inkblot does not really represent two persons saying or doing anything, such responses must project the person's own thoughts and feelings. Hence, they are called *projective techniques.* The respondent is said to project his or her attitudes and ideas onto the ambiguous stimuli.

Projective techniques are typically administered in conjunction with interviews, case histories, and self-report inventories, and in this sense are again the grist for our information processor of Figure 1–1. Some clinicians prefer to use self-report inventories for the more molecular aspects of personality (e.g., response tendencies, habits, traits, or behavioral dispositions) and to reserve projectives for the deeper facets of personality (e.g., needs, unconscious wishes, and fantasies). Not all practitioners or test theorists, however, would agree with this oversimplification. Some clinicians consider projectives the only tests that can supplement observation and interviewing, but others reject them as unscientific and would not consider using them under any circumstance.

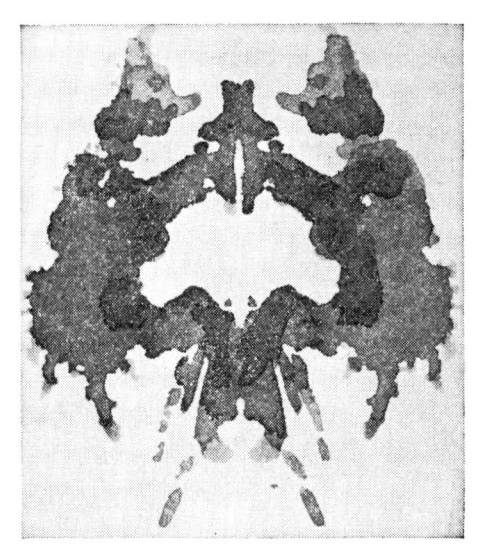

**Figure 8–1.** Inkblot Similar to One Used in the Rorschach Test.

The underlying issues are far from settled, but most informed psychologists (Anastasi, 1976; Cronbach, 1970; Sundberg, 1977; Tyler & Walsh, 1979), although critical of the shortcomings of projective tests, are reluctant to reject them outright because of their apparent value as exploratory procedures in personality assessment.

## Projection versus Projective Technique

The concept of *projection* was introduced into psychology by Sigmund Freud. He defined it as a mechanism that accounts for the way some persons ascribe their drives, feelings, and sentiments to others or to objects in the outside world, as a defense against admitting to having these threatening qualities in themselves. The use of projection, according to Freud, permits persons to deny the presence of threatening or undesirable impulses by imposing them on others.

H. A. Murray introduced in his *Explorations in Personality* (1938) the idea of projective tests as a form of psychological testing. This idea gained popularity as a result of an article by L. K. Frank (1939) in which he stressed the importance of a disguised measuring device. This method, he stated, would allow the tester to view the individual's private world and the way he or she attributes meaning to, or projects meaning onto, a relatively plastic field.

In contrast to self-report inventories, whose items are more or less meaningful, the materials of projective techniques consist of such ambiguous stimuli as inkblots, pictures, incomplete sentences, or incomplete stories which require restructuring or interpreting. This stimulus ambiguity and the multiplicity of replies permitted the examinee (in contrast to the fixed alternatives of self-report tests) to have an advantage over inventories in that they do not require self-ratings or information about characteristic reactions to situations. These features of projective techniques—unstructured stimuli, multiplicity of alternative responses, free responding, and the absence of specific right or wrong answers—are advantages because they encourage fantasy and imaginative responses. These, in turn, help the test administrator gain access to those aspects of a person's thinking that are presumably inaccessible even to the individual. On the other hand, this ambiguity also makes score interpretation more fallible, as we argued at the conclusion of the last chapter.

There are many projective tests. We shall consider several of them but shall focus mainly on the two most popular ones: the Rorschach Inkblot Test and the Thematic Apperception Test (TAT). It should be noted that despite their particular characteristics, we shall evaluate these techniques according to the same criteria that apply to all of the inputs of Figure 1–1.

## Rorschach Inkblot Test

The fundamental assumption underlying this test, named after its founder, Hermann Rorschach (1921), is that there is a relationship between the way an individual organizes or "structures" the inkblots and his or her personality. In responding to ambiguous stimuli, one presumably "sees" things that reflect personal needs and feelings. That is to say, one's perceptions are presumed to be selected according to projected needs, wishes, and desires. Such projection is facilitated by the fact that the inkblots are not socially familiar objects or situations that naturally elicit culturally prescribed responses.

The administration, scoring, and interpretation of the Rorschach test vary among psychologists. Typically, the ten inkblots are given one at a time to an individual, who must state what, if anything, he or she sees in them. The responses are scored according to the location of the inkblot the examinee used to create the response and to how well the subject organized the various portions of the blot to form a perception. Rorschach scoring and interpretation generally relate a person's inkblot perceptions to how he or she perceives, and copes with, people and the environment.

The Rorschach's uses include assessment of productivity, spontaneity, mood fluctuations, euphoria, anxiety, and even intelligence. Articles and books on the test (Exner, 1976, 1978; Holt, 1971, 1978a; Piotrowski, 1965; Rappaport et al., 1968) list such clinical applications as diagnosis of psychosomatic, neurotic, and psychotic illness; detection of suicidal tendencies; diagnosis of brain damage; and prediction of response to treatment. There is considerable controversy over these claimed applications of the test, but we shall say only that these claims have not always been satisfactorily supported by evidence and that the Rorschach is not a psychological test according to our definition.

**Administering the Rorschach.** There are many ways of administering, scoring, and interpreting the Rorschach, mainly because Rorschach users do not generally agree on its optimal use and interpretation. After the founding of the Rorschach Institute in 1939 and the publication of the *Journal of Projective Techniques* (now the *Journal of Personality Assessment*), however, all the methods now are sufficiently similar so that when one is learned, most of the others are easily understood. The following description of procedures is based on the Klopfer system (Klopfer & Davidson, 1962; Klopfer et al., 1954), which is one of the two most commonly used systems of Rorschach administration and scoring (also see Exner, 1978; Klopfer & Kelley, 1942; Klopfer et al., 1954). The other system was developed by Samuel Beck (1944, 1945, 1972).

Klopfer's method divides the administration of the Rorschach into four parts: performance proper, inquiry, analogy, and "testing the limits." During the *performance proper*, the subject is given the ten inkblots and instructed to examine each separately and to communicate what he or she sees. The tester acts as the observer and recorder, interfering as little as possible with the respondent's spontaneity. The subject's direct questions about the procedure are usually evaded, in order to have the test as unstructured as possible. Some typical questions during this first phase are: "May I turn the card?" "Should I tell you the first thing that comes to mind or should I think about the card?" These questions are answered as noncommittally as possible (e.g., "That's entirely up to you"), leaving the responsibility for these decisions to the examinee.

Responses to the cards, some of which are shown in Figure 8–2, along with the inkblots that elicited them, are recorded verbatim, as are the tester's remarks about the subject's general behavior, mode of responding, reaction time (the time between the presentation of the card and the first response to it), total response time per card, and the length of time taken to complete the performance proper. The examiner also notes the position in which the examinee holds the card when responding (right side up is ∧; top of the card facing the subject's right and left sides are > and <, respectively; and facing down is recorded as ∨).

The *inquiry* period is the phase designed to discover how the respond-

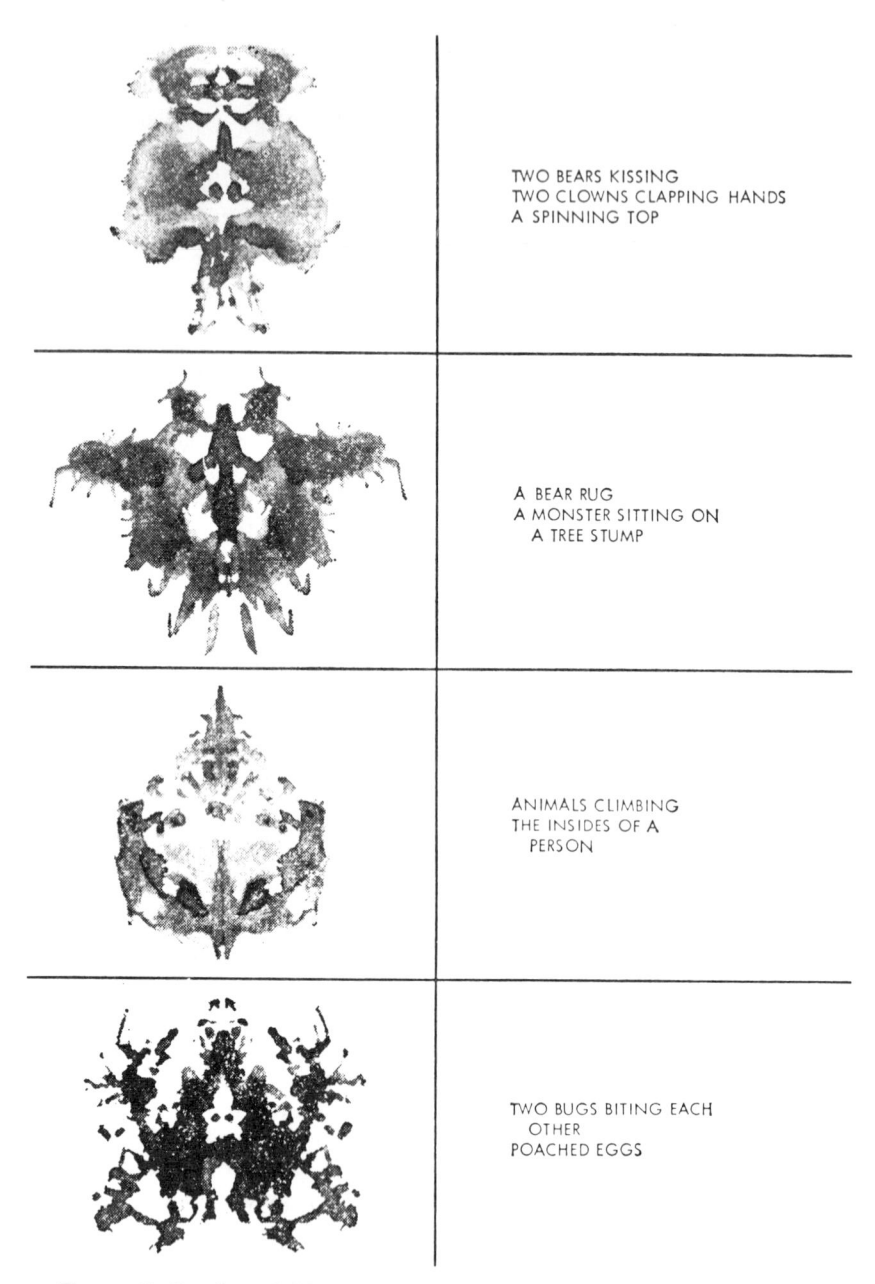

**268**   Personality and Psychological Assessment

|   |   |
|---|---|
|   | TWO BEARS KISSING<br>TWO CLOWNS CLAPPING HANDS<br>A SPINNING TOP |
|   | A BEAR RUG<br>A MONSTER SITTING ON<br>  A TREE STUMP |
|   | ANIMALS CLIMBING<br>THE INSIDES OF A<br>PERSON |
|   | TWO BUGS BITING EACH<br>  OTHER<br>POACHED EGGS |

**Figure 8–2.**   Four inkblots and Some Typical Responses to Each

ent arrived at his or her perceptions. The examiner does this by asking questions about the physical properties of a particular inkblot that influenced the subject's spontaneous replies. Typically, the examiner asks such questions as "Where on the card did you see the butterfly?" "Tell me more about the way you see two animals climbing up a hill," or "What is it in the card that makes it seem textured?" In this way the psychologist ascertains how the person arrived at the responses made during the performance proper. There is always the danger of leading the subject during the inquiry to contrive reasons (or to give the reasons that he or she believes the tester prefers) to explain his or her responses. But experienced test administrators, like adept interviewers, can minimize these effects.

The *analogy*, or follow-up period, is an optional third phase. It is used when the inquiry has not fully clarified all the scoring problems. In most cases, the appropriate procedure for the follow-up period is to ask analogy questions. For example: "Here you said that color contributed to your calling this an explosion; now can you select those responses in which color also helped?" or "You said here that you saw a bird in flight; are the birds you saw here also in flight?"

The fourth and final phase is called *testing the limits*. Its aims, especially in cases in which the subjects have given very few or no responses, are to learn whether the respondents can see particularly popular concepts and whether they can use specific portions of the blot or organize particular properties of the card (e.g., color, shading, blacks, and whites) which were not utilized in the spontaneous responses. During this phase, the examiner may suggest specific concepts (e.g., "butterfly," "man in motion," "two people doing something") and ask whether the examinee can also perceive these concepts.

**Scoring the Rorschach.** Rorschach scoring is complex and, all too often, differs among the various Rorschach schools. But as we noted earlier, there are enough similarities so that when one scoring system is learned, most of the others are easy to understand.

The major scoring categories are location, determinant, content, popularity-originality, and form level. Scoring for *location* requires classifying responses according to five main categories, depending on how much of the inkblot the respondent used to arrive at a concept. Scoring categories are the use of the whole blot ($W$), a large detail ($D$), a small detail ($d$), a rare detail ($dr$), or the white space ($S$) between the blot and the test card. A location chart (see Figure 8–3) may be used to score these categories.

The *determinants*, as the name implies, refer to the quality of the blot that determined the person's perception. These determinants are movement ($M$, $FM$, or $m$), shading ($c$, $K$, or $k$), color ($C$ or $C'$), and form

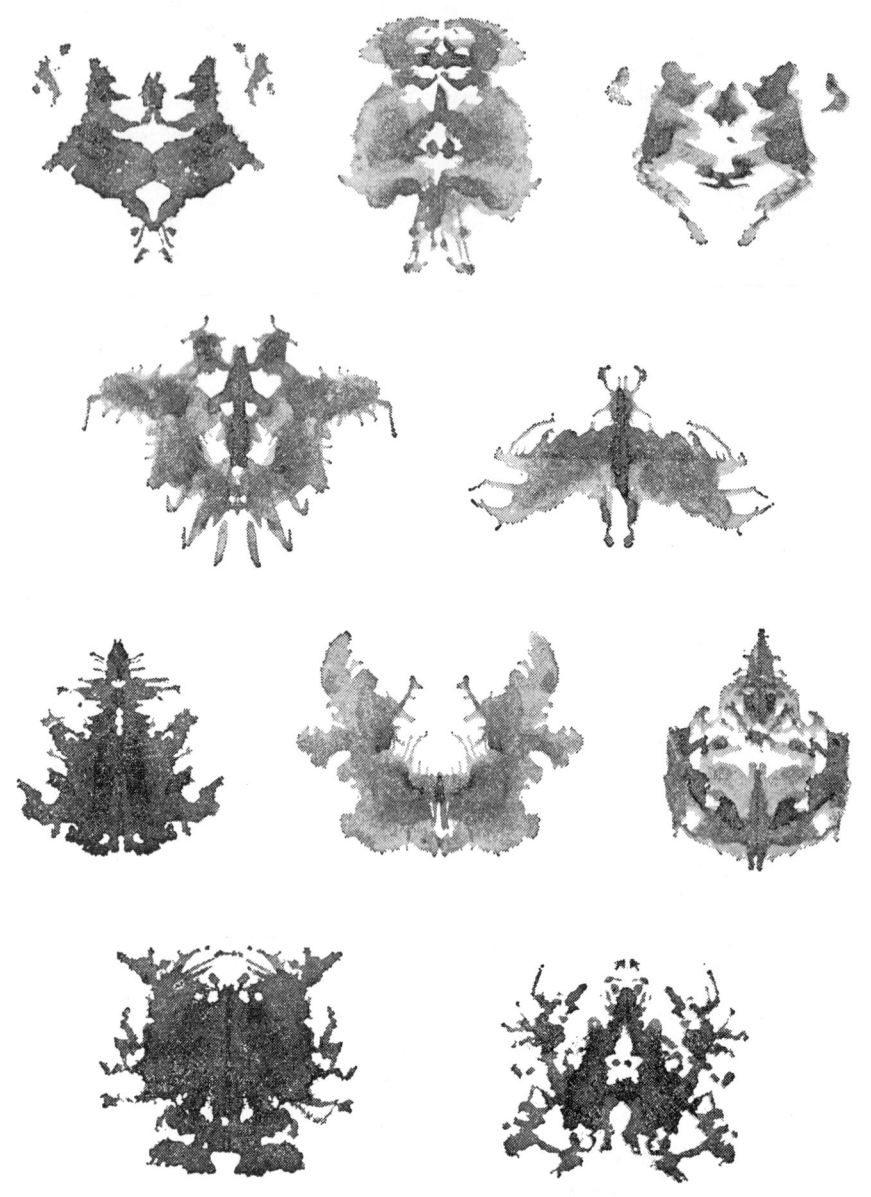

**Figure 8–3.** A Location Chart Similar to One Used with the Rorschach Inkblots.

(*F*). Movement refers to the perception of the blot as representing an object "in movement." The shading of the blot can determine responses which are classified according to whether darker or lighter shading or blacks, whites, and grays influenced the subject's perception. Color determinants are scored when the examinee emphasized the chromatic aspects of the blot in his or her response. A response is scored in the form category when the shape or contour of the blot—rather than its movement, shading, or color—determined the concept. Table 8–1 illustrates some of these determinants.

Scoring the *content* of responses uses mainly three, out of a possible twenty-three, categories: human (*H*), animal (*A*), and abstract (*Abs*), depending on the subject matter of the perceived concept. Sexual, anatomic, and geographic content areas are also common. In addition, responses are scored for their popularity (*P*) or originality (*O*). The most popular content categories are animals, humans, parts of animals or humans, clouds, fires, landscapes, and maps. Examples of unusual or original content categories are those that refer to literary or mythical characters (e.g., Falstaff or Mephistopheles) or those that relate to the person's hobby, vocation, or special interests (e.g., computer memory drum or transmission gears). If an original concept does not fit the blot in which it is presumably embedded, or if it is bizarre in other ways, it is scored an original minus (*O*−).

Determinants are scored as good or as poor *form level* responses, depending in part on how well the subject tied together various inkblot components into a meaningful concept. Form level ratings are based on an elaborate scoring procedure (each response is scored on a scale that ranges from −2.0 to +5.0), which is intended to reflect the subject's ability to fit the percept to the structure of the inkblot, as well as his or her skill in communicating this information to another person (the examiner). Some examples of responses, their scoring categories, and some typical interpretations are presented in Table 8–2.

These scores and their proportional interrelationships are then plotted on a *psychogram* similar to the one presented in Figure 8–4. The psychogram is a bar graph representing the distribution of the determinant scores. As indicated in Figure 8–4, the major determinant-

**Table 8–1** Rorschach Responses and Determinant Scores

| Response | Score |
|---|---|
| This looks like a butterfly. (Q. What makes it like a butterfly?) Its Shape (Card III). | F |
| A couple of clowns clapping hands (Card II). | M |
| A bat in flight (Card I). | FM |
| Leaves falling down to earth | m |
| A bearskin rug (Q. What made it seem like a bearskin?) It has pile—a feeling that it would change form under your hand (Card IV). | Fc |
| This red part on top is blood (Card II). | C |

Source: Klopfer, B., & Davidson, H. H. *The Rorschach technique: An introductory manual.* New York: Harcourt, Brace & World, 1962, pp. 120–156.

**Table 8-2** Examples of Interpretations of Rorschach Responses

| Response | Location Category | Nature of Interpretation |
|---|---|---|
| This is a butterfly (pointing to the whole of Card V.) Here are the wings, feelers, and legs. | W | The use of many W (whole) responses is considered to reflect the subject's ability to organize and relate materials. |
| This is part of a chicken's leg (pointing to a large section of Card V). | D | Detail scores are usually interpreted as indicative of an interest in the concrete. |
| This could be a face (upper edge of "wings" on Card V). | dd | The use of unusual or tiny details (dd) may suggest pedantic trends. |
| Looks somewhat like a spinning top (center of Card II). | S | Persons who use S (reversing figure and ground) often are observed as oppositional, negative, and stubborn. |

scoring categories are on the horizontal axis, and the number of responses is on the vertical axis. The most important feature of the psychogram is the shape of the distribution of the main determinant scores, which reflect whether the responses tend to cluster in the center of the graph, in the left half, or in the right half; or whether they are evenly distributed over the three main areas of the graph.

The psychogram thus summarizes the balance among the major determinants of inkblot perception. We discuss some typical interpretations associated with these determinants, and their quantitative interrelationships, in the next section on Rorschach interpretation. It is convenient to describe here, however, the interpretive significance of the psychogram's three major portions.

If the subject's perception has been influenced mostly by his or her imagination, needs, and drives, the responses will pile up on the left side of the graph (indicating a preponderance of movement responses); if the perception has been influenced mostly by external stimuli, the responses will pile up on the right side of the graph (indicating an abundance of color responses); and if the perceptions are mostly rational, impersonal, and unemotional, the responses usually will cluster in the center of the psychogram (an overabundance of form responses).

**Interpreting Rorschach Scores.** Interpreting Rorschach scores is an elaborate procedure, and so we shall discuss only the main part of the interpretive process.

Rorschach workers generally agree that a subject's *total number of responses* (R) to all the test cards indicates productive capacity. The more intelligent the person is, the more productive his or her overall Rorschach record is. The average number of R expected from normal adults ranges from 20 to 45.

The *location* categories, that is, the choice of areas onto which the subject projects his or her concepts, may reflect intellectual style. For example, the use of many whole responses, or W, presumably reflects the abilities to organize material, to relate details to one another, and to deal with abstract and theoretical material. An overabundance of either ordinary or unusual detail, or D and d responses, may be interpreted as a tendency toward pedantry, as well as a need to be accurate, correct, and exact.

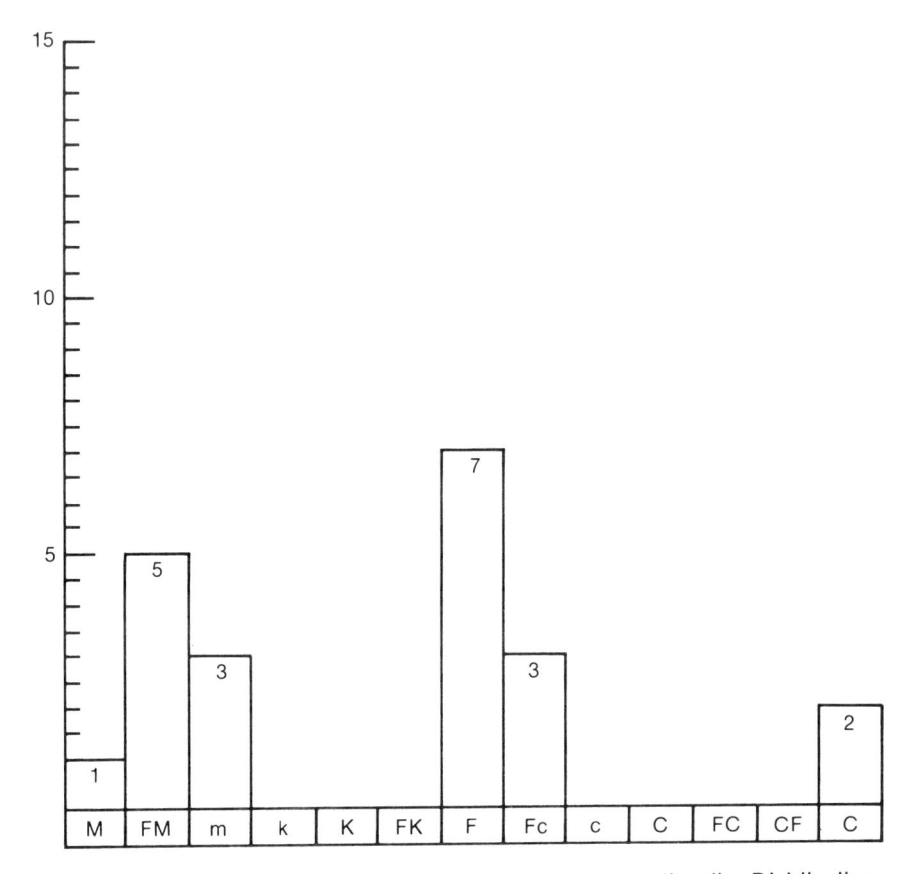

**Figure 8-4.** The Psychogram Is a Bar Graph Representing the Distribution of the Determinant Scores. In this psychogram, the distribution of the scores is mainly in the middle and the left half of the graph.

In general, the *determinant* categories are said to relate to the person's emotional aspects. Thus, responses determined exclusively by shape may reflect intellectual control; and movement responses, or the projection of action onto the inkblots, may suggest inner emotional control and the acceptance of oneself. Human movement responses are considered the most significant of the determinants and are often interpreted as the ability to empathize with people.

*Content* scores are said to disclose the breadth of interests. A wide range of content in which, for instance, human, animal, and inanimate responses are present is usually associated with high intelligence. A preoccupation with anatomy may suggest somatic or psychological concerns and difficulties. For example, the repeated perception of heads and faces is often interpreted as a concern with one's intellectual abilities. Content responses also have sexual significance. Problems of sexual identification, for example, are said to be revealed by gender confusion regarding the human figures.

*Form level* ratings for each response and for the overall Rorschach record are considered important in evaluating intellectual capacity. Poor form level responses, for example, are said to indicate limited intellectual capacity, as well as withdrawal from reality. Good form level responses, on the other hand, are cited in one anecdotal source (Gilbert, 1978; also see Gilbert, 1980) as indicating anxiety, insecurity, compulsiveness, and exactness.

*Popular* or *original* responses also are scored and interpreted by many Rorschach workers as revealing either a shared or a unique perceptual style, respectively. Three popular responses (e.g., the inkblot shown in Figure 8–5 is usually seen as a bat) typically are given on most records, and about three to eight popular responses in a record indicate an ability to see the world as others do. An overabundance of populars

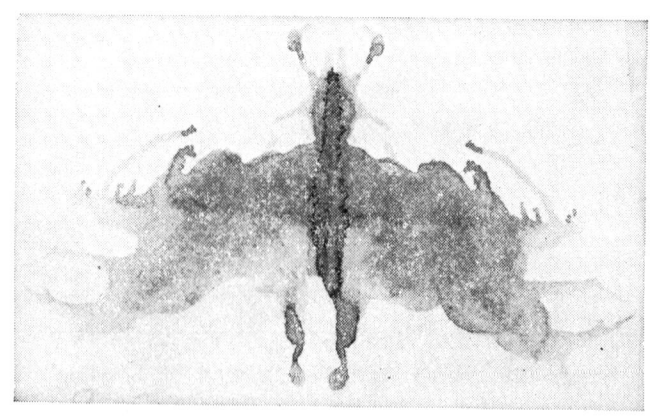

**Figure 8–5.** This Rorschach inkblot is most popularly perceived as a bat.

(eight or more) is interpreted as strong need to think as other people do. Good originals (versus $O-$) indicate a superior intellect and innovativeness. According to one system of interpretation (Klopfer & Davidson, 1962), a superior person tends to have twice as many originals as populars (provided there are at least five $P$s). Too many $O$s may indicate excessively erratic thinking.

Several systems of Rorschach interpretation also perform *sequence* and *content analyses*. A sequence analysis is a card-by-card and a response-by-response search for the characteristics of a subject's test behavior, use of language, and certain special qualities of the inkblot material utilized that may confirm, modify, or discard hypotheses based on prior interpretations. The protocols are searched; that is, the number of responses given to each card, the number of missing responses to particular portions of a card, the variations in reaction time from card to card, and the sequence of reactions to color or shading of cards all are determined. These factors are considered indicative of intellectual and emotional functioning.

The following passage is a sequence analysis of the responses to an inkblot similar to Card V of the Rorschach (see Figure 8–5):

> Card V is immediately interpreted as the popular concept of a bat flying. It is not surprising that this essentially intelligent and well-controlled subject makes immediate use of the popular connotation to Card V. However, her insecurity about this concept is rather puzzling ... the remark concerning the lower extension, seems to reveal a tendency on her part to be hypercritical of herself rather than putting the blame where it rightly belongs. . . . (Klopfer & Davidson, 1962, p. 182)

Content analysis decides what is perceived in the blots, rather than sequence of perceptions. This is usually considered valuable for its cues about the person's motivation. The significance of human, animal, and inanimate content, already discussed, is that they may reflect one's breadth of interest. Content analysis also searches for sexual, anatomic, geographic, or science-related responses, as well as for other content areas such as emblems, spiders, numerals, letters of the alphabet, blood, food, or abstractions. These content areas are interpreted according to the tester's own theoretical orientation. For example, psychologists subscribing to Freudian psychoanalytic theory might interpret these response categories as follows:

*Human Figures*, when seen as monsters, ghosts, clowns, or mythical characters, may indicate the subject's inability to identify closely with real people.

*Animals*, especially if they are perceived as fierce or wild, may indicate aggressive tendencies that the subject is trying to control.

*Sexual* responses must be interpreted in relation to the subject's other Rorschach scores and life history. These responses may be expressed in their symbolic forms (e.g., train, purse, falling), or they may indicate concern with, or avoidance of, sexual problems.

*Anatomy, geography, or science* content may reveal the subject's attempt to cover up real feelings by intellectualizing the inkblots. An extreme example would be the person who sees the card in Figure 8-5 as a "mammal of the order *Chiroptera*" (a bat).

*Masks* may disclose an emphasis on role playing to avoid personal exposure.

*Blood* responses suggest strong, uncontrolled emotional reactions.

*Food* may indicate dependency needs, that is, the wish to be nurtured by others.

**Applications of Rorschach Testing.** Generally, the Rorschach has been used to assess cognitive and affective (emotional) functioning; this includes estimates of intelligence, creative potential, spontaneity, degree of mood fluctuation, depression, euphoria, and anxiety; as well as statements about passivity, introversion, assertiveness, reaction to emotional stress, and control of emotional impulses. Other uses include the diagnosis of psychosomatic, neurotic, and psychotic illness; more specific differentiation within the neurotic group (e.g., hysteria versus depression) and the psychotic group (e.g., paranoia versus paranoid schizophrenia); detection of suicidal tendencies; differential diagnosis between brain-damaged and nonbrain-damaged cases; prediction of overt behavior in various situations; and prognosis of favorable or unfavorable outcomes in the treatment of psychotic patients.

The claims made throughout the history of the Rorschach technique for its wide applicability led Holtzman to write, ". . . curiously enough, the same ten inkblots are used throughout!" (1959, p. 130). It is beyond the scope of this book to examine each of these claims; the evaluative discussion below highlights only some of the complexities entailed in substantiating such claims. For a thorough review of many of the issues touched upon here, the reader is referred to Zubin, Eron, and Schumer (1965); as well as books by Exner (1978) and Holt (1978a); and articles by Holzberg (1960, 1966), Exner (1976), and Weiner (1977).

### Computer Rorschach Interpretation

A computerized scoring and interpretation system was developed for the Rorschach by Zygmunt Piotrowski (1964) and is called the Piotrowski Automated Rorschach, or PAR. The PAR became available for commercial use in 1974, but with limited success. Using an elaborate program consisting of 434 parameters and 900 rules, all of which were based on his research and clinical observations, Piotrowski prepared a pool of about 980 descriptive personality statements. Each Rorschach protocol interpreted by the system is assigned some 50 to 80 statements from this pool, depending on the particular responses of the protocol. The statements deal mainly with interpretive comments relating the Rorschach responses to personality problems and their probable causes, interpersonal effectiveness, intelligence, problem-solving ability, and initiative.

For its first six years, the PAR was used for personnel selection and promotion by Hay Associates, a Philadelphia-based management consulting firm. But its current use is more psychodiagnostic than it was originally, and because it is now being used almost exclusively for psychiatric screening, the system has been renamed the Computerized Perceptanalytic Rorschach, or CPR (Piotrowski, 1980a). According to Piotrowski (1980b), the CPR now includes many more statements that deal with sexual and other personal matters, which the management firm deemed unsuitable for employment settings. Otherwise, the CPR is essentially the same as the PAR.

The CPR codes responses to all of the Rorschach cards. This procedure uses a fairly sophisticated language-processing program that tags critical concepts in the subjects' responses. These responses are then scored according to Piotrowski's modification of Rorschach's scoring scheme and are interpreted by rules based on Piotrowski's experiences with the inkblot technique. Some of the typical interpretive statements are:

Dislikes loud and crude emotional expressions
Quick and decisive
Shares very few common ideas with others
Wastes much time and emotional energy in obsessive self-observation
No hysterical symptoms
Schizophrenia
Is fearful of genital contact with women
Acts impulsively because of inability to tolerate anxiety
It is advisable to make concessions to the subject, at first, in order not to arouse antagonism. Cautiously and gradually one can make carefully phrased suggestions on how to behave in a more effective manner. A good therapeutic rapport may be difficult.... (Piotrowski, 1980a, pp. 100–105)

These interpretations were based on two administrations of the inkblots, given nine months apart, to a young schizophrenic man. (There are about one hundred interpretations in all.) During the intervening nine-month period, the person was in psychotherapy.

Regarding the statements' accuracy, Piotrowski offered the following testimonial by the subject's psychotherapist: "Very accurate printouts. The change from the first to the second testing is well brought out. All the relevant and significant points were brought out and specified. And they are valid. The patient is at least as bright as his formal IQ of 111 suggests" (1980a, p. 95).

Although the system is promising and, with the proper research that would tie responses to observed behaviors, could be as sound as the computerized MMPI service reviewed in chapter seven, some Rorschach users and researchers have criticized it. For example, John Exner called the PAR "disappointing, primarily because many of the variables of the test were not weighed appropriately" (1976, pp. 85–86). By this he meant that the automated system's descriptive statements were too general and were not tailored precisely enough to the uniqueness of the person. Thus, the statement that an individual is "quick to display emotion" may be quite valid, but it is too broad. "Among the major questions it leaves unanswered," according to Exner, are "under what kinds of circumstances does this emotional display occur, and is this proclivity an asset or a liability for the person?" (1976, p. 86).

The PAR and similar personality interpretations have long been criticized on these grounds, but the PAR should not be singled out in this regard. Many of the interpretive statements of the automated MMPI and other services share this problem, which Donald G. Paterson called the "Barnum effect," or the problem of writing overgeneral personality descriptions. Human report writers are not exempt from writing such Barnum statements, either. Two examples of such statements are "You have a tendency to worry at times, but not to excess" and "You often get depressed, but you couldn't be called moody because you are generally cheerful and optimistic." Interestingly, it has repeatedly been shown in college undergraduate lecture sections that when students are presented with personality descriptions "based" on tests they took on a previous day, they invariably believe that a page or two of such Barnum statements describes them accurately (see Dunette, 1957; Evans, 1962; Forer, 1949; Stagner, 1958; Sundberg, 1955). This effect can be attributed partly to the prestige of the statements' source, especially if the source is a psychologist (Rosen, 1975), and partly to the assessment procedures used (Snyder, 1974).

More revealing than Exner's criticism of the generality of Rorschach statements, was Piotrowski's own admission that the approach to the CPR "is not psychometric." He went on to state that it "does not rely on group statistics for discovery of relevant and meaningful test components . . . [it] . . . uses the naturalist's method of investigating concrete, living individuals (not abstract group averages) with the hope and intention of discovering components (test parameters) that have the same valid meaning in the case of every tested individual" (1980a, p. 87). This appeal for an *idiographic* approach to the study of people (which treats each person individually rather than as an entity within a large population) is unfortunate because this approach ignores *nomothetic* or group information that could contain statistics about people with scores similar to those in question. It also relies too heavily on the clinician's interpretive skills and his or her initiative to keep tallies of predictive success rates, a reliance that is ill placed, as we noted in chapter four. Besides these considerations, it is important to add that Piotrowski's so-called nonpsychometric approach makes minimal use of the computer's abilities to tally, store, and calculate large arrays of data rapidly—all of which could contribute to large-scale normative, reliability, and validity studies, which would truly add to the scant literature on the Rorschach psychometric credibility.

## Evaluation of the Rorschach

The appraisal of Rorschach reliability and validity is a long-standing and perplexing problem which has invited much comment by clinicians and researchers (mostly clinicians). Perhaps one of the best reviews was by Jules Holzberg (1960), who presented the attitudes of various schools of psychology toward Rorschach reliability and validity. There are those psychologists, he pointed out, who insist that the Rorschach must meet the same criteria of psychometric excellence as all other methods of personality assessment must; and then there are the less-hardheaded Rorschach workers (the majority) who argue that this test is not like the others and that its purpose is to describe personality "globally" and to aid the clinician in obtaining insight into that personality. And since it is not a measuring instrument in the usual psychometric sense, the Rorschach workers argue, the demonstration of the Rorschach's reliability and validity is of no concern.

The validity of the nonpsychometric assumption also was challenged by Holtzman in regard to the Rorschach user's scoring procedure: "When he classifies and enumerates any of $S$'s responses to a projective technique, he is adopting, even if crudely, a psychometric frame of reference. When he counts such responses, he is implying a crude ordinal scale by which 10 $M$ means more of something than 1 $M$" (1959, p. 121). Holtzman's attitude was that the Rorschach must meet certain essential criteria of psychometric tools and procedures. But he did recognize that this technique had a different origin and rationale from those of the self-report inventories and thus, the methods for establishing the Rorschach's reliability and validity had to be adapted accordingly.

With this in mind, and with attention to the special character of the Rorschach, we shall now examine some of the evidence regarding the test's reliability and validity.

**Reliability of Scoring.** Most techniques for establishing the reliability of psychometric devices have been developed for tests more structured than the Rorschach. Ability and objective personality tests, for example, are scored by rather straightforward computational procedures. But the Rorschach cannot be scored by applying a key because the scores require an intervening interpretive stage. The problem of reliability, then, becomes one of determining the extent of agreement among the judges scoring the same protocols. Such reliability studies, however, are not popular because there are so many different schools of Rorschach scoring, each with a different scoring system. But some studies of interscorer reliability have been reported in the literature.

*Interscorer Reliability.* Using the Hertz (1934) system of scoring, two judges achieved a 93 percent agreement in scoring eleven thousand responses. Before scoring the responses, the judges had agreed with each other on the use of the score categories, and they trained by scoring a number of sample responses. Several later studies (Baughman, 1951; Ramzy & Pickard, 1949) showed that disagreement between scorers on a system of categorization was responsible for the more common unreliabilities and that pretraining using, and agreement on, categories of scores could enhance interscorer reliabilities.

*Retest Reliability.* There are special problems in demonstrating Rorschach test-retest reliability. One is that the Rorschach scoring systems are complex and differ radically from those for other tests. Another is that the number of different response categories (e.g., movement, plus or minus form level, color, shading, popular, or original) within a record is limited; thus there is an inadequate sampling of responses within these categories. This in turn results in temporal instability because of the small samples used to compute correlations.

It is also difficult to determine whether the differences on retests are due to the instability of the measurement method or to changes in a subject's temporary disposition. This problem is not unique to the Rorschach but is magnified on this test because of its special test setting. The examiner plays an active role both as tester and interviewer during the administration of the inkblots and therefore can exert considerable influence on test-taking attitudes. Unfortunately, the vast majority of retest studies do not consider this possible influence on retest scores because the examiners are interchanged freely from one study to the next. The net result, of course, is inadequate test-retest studies.

Then there is the problem that retest scores tend to be more stable for some persons than for others, both because of the differing effects on some persons of memory and contextual test conditions and because of the individual differences in their tendencies toward mood fluctuations. The question to be asked about retest reliability is, therefore, "Reliable for whom and under what conditions?" In this connection one psychologist (Fiske, 1959) advised that the temporary dispositions and stable components of a personality be distinguished, and he suggested that one index of reliability might be a measure of successive interpretations of a single person's Rorschach. By using this measure, reliability could be established by demonstrating that the Rorschach protocols of one person obtained at different times were less divergent than were the protocols elicited from different persons. But neither the complexity and the small number of responses nor the memory and testing context answer these questions about retest reliability or the use of standard estimating methods.

The most recent studies on the consistency of Rorschach scores were summarized by Exner (1978) and provide some evidence that many Rorschach scoring categories were indeed stable over different time intervals. In a series of seven studies Exner and his associates showed that this stability could be demonstrated among patients, as well as nonpatients, in psychiatric hospitals and that the retest correlations for some scoring categories were as high as 0.93. It is important to note that all the scorers in these studies used Exner's modified Rorschach scoring system, and it is therefore not surprising, as we noted earlier, that their agreements were high.

***Equivalent Forms Reliability.*** Although it is difficult to develop a set of cards comparable (but not identical) to the Rorschach's, several studies (Zulliger, 1941, 1952, 1956) reported using a series of seemingly parallel inkblots devised by Behn-Eschenberg (called the Behn-Rorschach). But in these studies the average coefficients obtained with the Behn-Rorschach were discouragingly low (0.56 to 0.65 with twenty-day or twenty-one–day intervals between retests of two groups), and there was some evidence to indicate that it and the Rorschach were not at all equivalent (Holzberg, 1960). The utility of this particular parallel series for testing equivalent forms reliability is thus questionable.

Other sets of equivalent forms for an inkblot series have been developed (Howard, 1953) but were not designed as substitutes for the Rorschach and thus must be evaluated in terms of their own reliability and validity. One such set is the Holtzman Inkblot Test (HIT) (Holtzman et al., 1961), which we discuss later in this chapter.

***Split-Half Reliability.*** When it is impractical to establish the reliability of a test by the retest or equivalent forms method, a split-half procedure is sometimes used. This method, as we noted in chapter two, calls for only one administration of a test and requires scoring both halves of the test, that is, all of the even-number items are scored and then all of the odd-numbered items are scored. The two halves of the test are then correlated to obtain an estimate of reliability. The advantage of this technique is that it eliminates prior exposure to the inkblots.

But the Rorschach cards are not items whose equivalence can be easily established, and therefore, the task of creating equal halves is difficult. First, the number of inkblot responses varies from one card to the next, which creates unequal halves. Second, the stimulus structure of the cards is heterogeneous and therefore cannot be considered equivalent. And finally, the few responses (or no responses at all) given to any single card makes the split-half method unsuitable. Nevertheless, split-half studies have been conducted, and not surprisingly, the results have been contradictory.

In one early study, Vernon (1933) reported a high split-half coefficient (0.91) for the number of responses elicited from subjects for the two halves (i.e., $R$ was as high for one-half of the inkblots as for the other half) but found low coefficients for the scoring categories of the two halves of the test. But in another study, Hertz (1934) obtained high average split-half coefficients for all scoring categories. These different findings may be due to the varying response sample sizes that Vernon and Hertz obtained in the two halves of the Rorschach records. It has been suggested (Cronbach, 1949; Vernon, 1933; Zubin et al., 1965), therefore, that the number of responses ($R$) in the record be controlled when testing for this form of reliability, since variations in this number tend to distort the results. But many Rorschachers find this solution unacceptable because it would impede the subject's freedom of responding. And this freedom, on balance, is the technique's greatest achievement.

The trend among Rorschach investigators has been to avoid split-half methods. In this regard Exner stated, "it is probably not a good measure of the 'sturdiness' of the Rorschach (1978, p. 63)." His reasoning was based on the assumption, which must apply in any split-half study, that the subject will respond to any stimulus using essentially the same style. But this assumption is not valid because subjects may alter their styles according to the different Rorschach stimuli.

**Validity of the Rorschach.** Although the literature on the validity of the Rorschach is replete with claims of the technique's general applicability, the substantiating evidence for these claims is meager. For example, the Rorschach is used most often to elicit information that can be used in predictions regarding individuals. Unfortunately, however, clinical predictions based on Rorschach protocols are not sufficiently precise to allow follow-up examinations, or when they are precise, they still are not often followed up.

But generally, validity studies using the Rorschach are difficult to conduct. The reasons for this difficulty, according to one informed source (Brown, 1976), are the statistical problems already mentioned in reference to its scores. Another problem is that because the test measures unconscious motivational factors and because criterion measures reflecting these factors are not available, there is no direct validity evidence.

It is also discouraging to note that in one of the leading textbooks on current research on the Rorschach (Exner, 1978), the word validity does not even appear in the index. Such an evasion of one of the basic tenets of psychometric respectability does not inspire confidence in the technique. In this context, it is reassuring to note, however, that some Rorschach workers (Goldfried et al., 1971, pp. 380–381) have acknowledged "that the majority of studies in the Rorschach literature have yielded negative or ambiguous results." They also called for "care with which assessment studies" of the test's validity are conducted because "impressive positive data have emerged from studies in which appropriately derived Rorschach indices have been assessed with appropriate samples against appropriate criteria and with appropriate requirements for making concurrent or predictive judgments."

***Empirical Validity.*** In the *Eighth Mental Measurements Yearbook*, Rolf Peterson (1978b, pp. 1042–1045) reported that during the last five years a number of significant studies were conducted which have implications for the empirical validity of several Rorschach determinants and content areas. For example, movement perceptions in the inkblots were found to be related to sex identity, creativity, physical activity, and anxiety. Extensive color use was found to be statistically correlated with explosive behavior, and among general medicine patients, many anatomy responses in a protocol were associated with unsuccessful physical rehabilitation. Peterson also reported mixed results using several homosexual scales to discriminate among prisoners of differing sexual orientations, and similarly indeterminate findings with the "Rorschach Prognostic Rating Scales" in predicting therapy outcomes. All of these considerations led Peterson to the following conclusion, with which this book essentially agrees: " . . . if the review had been written from the point of view of the role of the Rorschach as a tool for personality theorizing, a much more positive review would have been possible. . . . The general lack of predictive validity for the Rorschach raises serious questions about its continued use in clinical practice . . . " (1978b, p. 1045).

***Construct Validity.*** Studies conducted with the Rorschach have, however, provided some indirect evidence of construct validity (or the lack of it). This research usually proceeds by administering Rorschach tests before and after subjects undergo certain physical manipulations, such as surgical removal of portions of the brain or before and after experimental procedures in a laboratory, and the expected changes as a consequence of these manipulations are noted. For example, prefrontal lobotomies, which partially remove (or ablate) a portion of the frontal cortex, should lower anxiety. In one reported study, evidence of changes interpreted as indicating lower anxiety was reflected in the Rorschach protocols of operated patients (Allison & Allison, 1954). But generally, before-and-after-surgery studies have reported inconsistent findings (Helman, 1953; Zubin, 1949), and in one study, reported by the Columbia Greystone Associates (Mettler, 1949), no postoperative changes were found.

Experimentally induced manipulations, which are preceded and followed by Rorschach testing, include induced tension, hypnosis, drugs, or even electroshock treatment. The purpose of inducing these experimental modifications, again, is to assess whether predicted changes in Rorschach protocols will occur. In one such study, using the Hertz scoring system, Eichler (1951) demonstrated that experimental stress did affect Rorschach performance: An experimental group was first given arithmetic problems, with intermittent electric shocks to harass them, and then was given the Rorschach test under the threat of further and more intense electric shocks. Several of the presumed Rorschach signs of anxiety reportedly increased and differentiated significantly between the stress group and the control group. These changes included an increase in the number of shading responses and a decrease in the total number of $R$s. Eichler concluded that experimentally induced anxiety did prove the validity of these anxiety indices.

Hypnosis was used in an early study in which investigators administered the Rorschach test to one subject nine times (Levine et al., 1943). The first administration was under standard conditions, then under hypnosis suggesting seven different moods, and finally under hypnosis suggesting a normal and composed mood. As predicted by these investigators, the first and last Rorschach protocols were quite similar, a similarity used by them as evidence for the negligible effect on the Rorschach test of the hypnotic state itself. There were a number of identifiable effects accompanying the hypnotically induced mood changes that were in keeping with accepted Rorschach theory. For example, "depression" decreased the number of movement and color responses, and hypochondriasis decreased the number of human and animal movement responses and increased the anatomy responses. "Euphoria" produced a more mediocre record than that produced under normal conditions. All in all, the investigators concluded that changing moods, varying attitudes, and diverse emotional states were systematically reflected in Rorschach performance.

Most personality theories predict improvement following somatic treatment or psychotherapy, and therefore construct validity would be enhanced if the Rorschach protocols secured after treatment reflected this improvement. Rioch (1949) and Windle (1952) both tested this hypothesis. Rioch's study reported the before-and-after protocols of thirty-six patients who had undergone psychoanalysis. All of these patients' Rorschachs reflected significant changes in the predicted direction, and these changes corresponded to the trends reported by the therapist. In Windle's study, insulin was administered to a group of schizophrenic patients. In those instances in which a patient's behavior on the hospital ward was reported as improved, this improvement was also reflected in that patient's responses on the Rorschach.

The empirical validity studies cited have sometimes been encouraging, but more often negative. Evidence for the inkblots' construct validity is a little better. The construct validity studies cited, however, only begin to touch the surface of an enormous number of Rorschach investigations which have yielded vastly inconsistent results. More than 4,900 references are listed in Buros's *Eighth Mental Measurements Yearbook* (1978), many of which reached the same conclusion heard repeatedly over the past forty-five years: There is little convincing evidence to support the validity claims made for the technique by its proponents. This state of affairs was summarized as follows:

> Thousands of publications have been concerned with the Rorschach test, but it has not fared very well in reliability and validity studies. Considering the length of time that it takes to administer and score, the test is unsatisfactory when judged by standard psychometric criteria. It remains popular among clinical psychologists and psychiatrists, however, and will probably continue to be so until a demonstrably superior technique for the depth analysis of personality is developed. (Aiken 1979, p. 262)

## Other Projective Tests

A variety of other projective tests exists for personality assessment. We begin with the Holtzman Inkblot Technique, which most closely resembles the Rorschach but which, as we shall indicate, departs from its progenitor in several important ways that partially invalidate it as a projective tool.

### Holtzman Inkblot Technique (HIT)

Almost the only projective test using the Rorschach inkblots that meets the criteria of a psychometric tool is the Holtzman Inkblot Technique (HIT), first published in 1961 (Holtzman et al., 1961; also see Holtzman, 1975b). It was devised by using empirical keying, that is, its forty-five stimulus cards discriminated between normal and psychiatric criterion groups. The HIT now consists of two parallel sets of inbklots, each containing forty-five test blots. Unlike the Rorschach test, the HIT asks the subject to give only one response per card and immediately follows this response with a simple standardized inquiry to ascertain where the percept was seen and what qualities of the inkblot suggested it.

The HIT is scored according to twenty-two scales (i.e., location, form definition, and movement) which cover many aspects of a person's response to an inkblot. The more important variables for scoring the Rorschach were carefully considered in devising the scoring system. The result is a procedure that incorporates the best features of a projective technique and yet retains the characteristics of a good psychological test. Therefore the HIT's scoring is more reliable than the Rorschach's and lends itself more readily to sound validity studies, although according to Holtzman, only a "few (studies) have dealt directly with validity" (1975b, p. 253), an admission rare among test constructors (also see Holtzman et al., 1975).

The HIT's increased psychometric respectability, however, was purchased at a price that most projectivists would rather not pay. The wide latitude in responding that the Rorschach offers is narrowed on the HIT, in that a subject can make only one response to each card. The advantage of restricted responding, on the other hand, is the wider assortment of stimuli that can be administered. In short, the HIT is the Rorschach test with the addition of acceptable psychometric terms, but without the loss of too much of the original test's essence.

But despite its promise as a psychometrically superior version of the Rorschach, the HIT has not inspired the widespread research that might have been expected when it first appeared in its individual and group test formats in 1958. The *Eighth Mental Measurements Yearbook* (Buros, 1978, p. 845) listed a modest 356 studies conducted using the HIT. According to one source, part of the reason for this resistance to using the HIT, and hence to research on the test, "appears to be due to an attitude of 'use the Rorschach or reject projective techniques'" (Peterson, 1978a, p. 845). Perhaps the expected switch to a psychometrically more sophisticated inkblot test will yet materialize, although the prospects are not encouraging—even a fine book by Hill (1972) on clinical applications of the HIT was not convincing enough. In the meantime, we must simply suggest, as did Gamble (1972) in his comprehensive review of the HIT, that the test has potential as a clinical assessment tool. And we join Peterson in suggesting "that those committed to projective techniques, and the Rorschach, in particular, at least begin to collect HIT data as part of their ongoing assessment programs" (1978a, p. 849). Some interesting studies of other cultures have been conducted using the HIT, particularly among Mexican children (see Holtzman et al., 1975), but the need now is to conduct extensive studies using it in a wide variety of American subcultures, particularly in relation to its potential as a clinical assessment tool.

## Thematic Apperception Test (TAT)

The only other projective test that has been as popular as the Rorschach is the Thematic Apperception Test (TAT). The TAT's materials (Murray, 1938, 1943), in contrast to the Rorschach's amorphous inkblots, consist of drawings and photos in which the identity of most objects is obvious. For example, there is little question that the drawing shown in Figure 8–6 is of a youngster contemplating his musical instrument. And yet there is enough ambiguity in this scene to allow the subject to project, or to apperceive, the details of the picture according to his or her own experience, wishes, needs, and background. The principal assumption of the TAT's interpretation, like that of the Rorschach, is that fantasies, experiences, inner tendencies, conflicts, and attitudes are projected onto the characters or objects depicted on the cards.

The TAT, like the Rorschach, is an individually administered test in which twenty TAT cards are presented (in two one-hour sessions) and the examinee is asked to tell a story about each picture, which the examiner either tape-records or transcribes verbatim. The test can then be scored by any one of several available methods (Atkinson, 1958; Eron et al., 1950; Holt, 1978a; McClelland, 1958a, 1975; also see Exner, 1977, pp. 93–97), but the most popular is Murray's system, or some variation thereof, in which the following aspects of the stories are analyzed: the *hero*, in which the leading character in each story is identified; the *needs of the hero*, in which needs (abbreviated $n$) such as $n$-Achievement, $n$-Order, or $n$-Aggression are identified; *press*, in which the pressures or forces acting upon the hero are located; and *themes*, in which both the interplay between the hero's needs and press and his resolution of his conflicts and anxieties are analyzed. To interpret the TAT, one relates the TAT's scores to facets of the subject's past behavior and personality. An illustration of a typical protocol to the card presented in Figure 8–6 is presented in Box 8–1.

As with the Rorschach, there is no single measure of the TAT's applicability or validity; rather, there are many uses for it, though many of the claims for the test have not yet been verified by existing research. All of this research, which seems to be continuing, suggests that despite its many shortcomings (see below), the TAT remains an important assessment tool for the clinician. But according to J. D. Swartz, who as a founder of the HIT is not unbiased, it is probably true that "if the TAT were published today with the same amount of information on its reliability, validity, and standardization, it is very doubtful that it would ever attain anywhere near its present popularity . . . " (1978, p. 1127).

## BOX 8-1

## Interpretation of the TAT Responses of a Twelve-Year-Old Boy

*In order to illustrate how TAT interpretations are made, we present the following story told by a twelve-year-old boy in response to the picture shown in Figure 8-6:*

Line 1: This boy was supposed to be practicing his violin but he really doesn't feel like it.

Line 2: If his mother catches him goofing off from practicing, he is going to get into a lot of trouble.

Line 3: She does a lot of yelling and screaming about these types of things, and the boy has learned not to excite her.

Line 4: She really doesn't care whether he learns to play the thing or not, and as long as she doesn't catch him goofing off, she's satisfied.

Line 5: Right now the boy is trying to figure out how to fool his mother and he thinks maybe he'll tape-record his practice session and then in the future, play back the tape recordings while he sneaks out the window and plays with his friends.

Line 6: Wait till he tells his friends about the tape recordings and the way he fooled his mother. They'll find out again how smart he really is.

*In this boy's story there are numerous, valuable clues to his personality, which were subsequently corroborated by his psychologist. Borrowing as little as possible from any particular personality theory, we shall analyze each line of the narrative. In actual practice, of course, the interpretation of the story proceeds in conjunction with the consideration of the subject's other narratives and within the context of other assessment procedures:*

Line 1: The opening comment indicates that the subject perceives the violin accurately (most but not all subjects do), that he has been instructed to practice his lessons, and that he does not enjoy playing the instrument.

Line 2: Here the boy suggests that his behavior may make his mother unhappy and that she may punish him.

Line 3: There is some cynicism expressed in this remark, and the subject indicates that his mother is to be placated.

Line 4: The mother is portrayed as being uninterested in his progress with the violin and will not reprove him so long as she is not confronted with his defiance. This remark probably reveals the boy's opinion of her attitude toward his violin lessons and seems to be a facet of their relationship worth exploring.

Line 5: The subject's plan is creative and suggests that he is willing to take risks.

Line 6: The final sentence indicates the boy's exhibitionism, his concern about the opinions of others, and fear of being stigmatized as ignorant and mentally slow. It also suggests that he has planned similar deceptions before the one described.

**Figure 8–6.** A Card Similar to the One That Elicited the Story Reproduced in Box 8–1.

**Evaluation of the TAT.** The major criticisms lodged against the TAT over the past two decades concern the scanty evidence for its reliability and validity (see Buros, 1965, 1972, 1978). In part, the inadequacy of evidence supporting the TAT's reliability and validity is due to the clinician's unfailing confidence in its "clinical usefulness" (e.g., in Exner, 1976, the words reliability and validity do not appear with respect to the TAT); but in the main this lack of evidence is, again, due to the large numbers of schools or systems that have developed over the years, each with its own administration, scoring, and interpretation schemes. As with the Rorschach and many other projective techniques, the TAT's scorer reliability usually is high when the judges agree on the scoring categories and are carefully trained to score the TATs according to these criteria (Atkinson, 1950; Kagan & Moss, 1959; Lindzey & Herman, 1955). The general problem of the TAT's reliability was summarized by Holt, who posed the following question: "to what extent do the stories reflect transient and fugitive states of the person, such as moods or the traces of recent experience, and to what extent are they determined by more slowly changing dynamic and structural features?" (1978a, pp. 74–75).

The validity of the TAT's protocols depends largely on the expertise of the interpreter, the scoring and interpretation used, and the situations and predictions that must be contrived from the stories. In this regard, we again quote Swartz, who stated, " ... when Morgan and Murray constructed the TAT, they thought they had provided a method for psychological investigation that presented subjects with ambiguous stimuli. With the many variations in administration, scoring, and interpretation, it seems that the TAT is equally ambiguous for examiners ... " (1978, p. 1127).

This is analogous to an earlier review by Eron (Buros, 1972), who observed that the TAT is helpful as an index of a client's general interest, motives, and areas of emotional turmoil, but is a failure as an instrument for predicting individuals' behaviors or specific personality traits (also discussed with Eron in 1980).

Many of these same conclusions, according to Sundberg (1977, p. 217), are true also of the TAT's derivatives. These include the Children's Apperception Test, or CAT (Bellak & Bellak, 1952; also see Bellak, 1954), which consists of ten pictures of animals in anthropomorphic settings; the Thompson (1949) modification of the TAT, or T-TAT, in which figures of blacks, rather than whites, are depicted; the Blacky Pictures (Blum, 1950–1962), which have a series of twelve cartoon drawings depicting a family of dogs whose activities are built around Blacky, the central character; and the Make-a-Picture Story (MAPS) test (Shneidman, 1952), in which examinees are instructed to make their own pictures using twenty-two background settings and sixty-seven cut-out figures. The Blacky Pictures and the MAPS test are no longer widely used. But extensions of the TAT, testing achievement motivation, are still frequently used. These extensions, devised by David McClelland (1955, 1958a, 1958b, 1961) and his associates (McClelland et al., 1953), used the TAT to measure *achievement needs*, or *n ach*. These investigators adapted the TAT so that it could be administered to groups of individuals not known to the experimenter. In addition, they invented a measuring procedure that had a high interrate scoring reliability for assessing achievement needs.

Using four to eight TAT-like cards, they instructed the viewers to create imaginative stories about these pictures, which were shown on a screen for twenty seconds. Subjects were given four minutes to write down their stories on forms which had general questions printed on them. The questions were, What is happening? Who are the persons? What has led up to this situation? What is being thought? What is wanted and by whom? What will happen? and What will be done?

McClelland's and his coworkers' principal contribution was their content analysis of these stories using achievement imagery. Each story was judged to have such imagery if it contained some reference to competition with a standard of excellence. This competition was defined as a concern with winning or with accomplishing a task well. When the achievement scores (determined by a scoring system that need not concern us here) were related to other behavioral indicators, it was found that individuals scoring high on this index were characterized by some of the following behaviors:

> Volunteering for tasks in the absence of other rewards such as money or power.
> Working unusually long and hard at achievement-related activities.
> Setting realistic goals.
> Preferring to receive feedback about their performance efficiency and adequacy.
> Oriented toward the future and able to delay gratification.
> More concerned about winning or doing well than about losing or doing poorly.

Conversely, individuals classified as low in need for achievement were described by the following behaviors:

> Failing to initiate activities in the absence of money or power.
> Working for short periods of time.
> Setting unrealistic goals that are too easy or too difficult, given their level of ability.
> Avoiding feedback about the adequacy of their performance.
> Oriented toward immediate gratification.
> More concerned about losing or doing poorly than about winning or doing well.

## Sentence Completions

Sentence completions were first used as a personality test by Payne (1928) and by Tendler (1930), although it was used earlier by Ebbinghaus (1897) as an intelligence test (Exner, 1976). Such tests are easy to administer and consist of sentence items, or stems, of one or more words that the respondent is instructed to complete. A few typical stems are:

> My father always . . .
> He . . .
> The way . . .
> My health . . .
> Suddenly I . . .
> A voice . . .

There are several varieties of sentence completion tests. Among the best known is the Rotter Incomplete Sentence Blank (Rotter & Rafferty,

1950), which includes an elaborate objective scoring key and provides extensive normative data. Generally, test items for sentence completions are constructed to suit the needs of the particular population being tested. Typically, qualitative or "content" analysis is used as the method of choice, and in these instances the interpretations are guided by the tester's own personality theory. But there also are some quantitative interpretive systems (Exner, 1973; Rohde, 1951–1957).

An interesting variation on the sentence completions test was introduced by Sutherland and Gill (1970), who combined it with a word associations test. A list of one hundred stimulus words is presented to the subject, who is instructed to respond to each word with a complete sentence. To the word *table*, for instance, the response might be "I hate eating at home" or "I've been told my table manners are atrocious." Six scoring categories are used to evaluate the responses: (1) form, (2) syntax, (3) self and other references, (4) communication mode (personal versus other statements), (5) affective tone, and (6) affective references.

## Draw-a-Person Test (DAP)

In the Draw-a-Person Test (DAP), developed by Machover (1948, 1951), the examiner provides the subject with a blank sheet of paper and instructs him or her to "draw a person." After the first figure is drawn, the subject usually is asked to draw a person of the opposite sex. After drawing the figures, the subject is asked to tell a story about each of the persons, including their age, education, ambition, fears, and other facts (Machover, 1951; Urban, 1963).

The scoring of the DAP is qualitative and is essentially an analysis of the figures' characteristics and the manner in which they were drawn. Thus, the relative size of the male and female figures, for example, is said to reveal clues to sex identification. Similarly, missing parts of the body are noted, as are disproportions of certain other parts, erasures, symmetry, or asymmetry.

The DAP interpretive manual has been criticized (Anastasi, 1976; see also Chapman & Chapman, 1967, 1969) for containing such sweeping generalizations as "Disproportionately large heads will often be given by individuals suffering from organic brain disease," or "The sex given the proportionately larger head is the sex that is accorded more intellectual and social authority." The evidence for these characterizations is usually vague references to clinical experience and a few anecdotal accounts of selected cases. In two careful reviews of the DAP literature, Swensen (1957, 1968) concluded that Machover's specific hypotheses about figure meanings were not supported and were equivocal, and he urged testers to use caution in interpreting specific "signs" on the test.

There are several variations of the DAP, with equally unsatisfactory evidence of validity. One of these is the *Draw-a-Person Quality scale* (Wagner & Schubert, 1955), in which the drawing is assessed according to an artistic scale running from zero to eight. Another is the *House-Tree-Person* test (HTP) devised by Buck (1946–1956), in which a subject is instructed to draw a house, a tree, and then a person. Presumably, the stories told in association with these objects contain clues to the respondent's home, environment, and interpersonal relations, respectively. There also are many other drawing techniques and instructions for their use (see Anderson & Anderson, 1951, chap. 14), as well as an uncritical survey of the meaning of many drawings of human figures (Gilbert, 1978, 1980).

## Bender Visual-Motor Gestalt Test

The Bender Visual-Motor Gestalt Test (1938–1946) was introduced by Lauretta Bender as a test of visual-motor coordination. The designs (see Figure 8–7) that she selected illustrate some perceptual principles of Gestalt psychology. The test consists of nine geometrical figures, each on a card, which are presented to the subject one at a time. The subject is instructed to copy each figure in turn; afterwards, he or she is asked to reproduce from memory as many of the patterns as possible.

This technique was developed mainly to study visual-motor coordination, but it also has been used to test for the presence of central nervous system lesions (see Yates, 1954), as well as to differentiate between matched samples of normal and abnormal persons. For the latter purpose, a quantitative scoring key was developed and normative data collected (Pascal & Suttell, 1951). This key was crossvalidated on samples of normals, neurotics, and psychotics, and these groups were clearly and significantly differentiated on the basis of the scoring scheme.

The Bender-Gestalt test has also been used as a projective device to reveal significant personality trends. It has been claimed, for example, that drawings in which the figures are in collision with one another reveal disorganization (Hutt, 1969); that heavy lines indicate aggression, hostility, and neurosis (Hutt, 1969); that figure reversals suggest negativism (Hutt, 1969); and that exact reproduction indicates obsessive-compulsive personality traits (Tolor & Schulberg, 1963). Evidence for these claims is usually stored somewhere in the clinician's head and has not been made generally available (Billingslea, 1963; Blakemore, 1965). Most of the reviews of this test in the *Seventh* and *Eighth Mental Measurements Yearbooks* (Buros, 1972, 1978), however, do not credit the Bender-Gestalt with high validity but suggest that it may be valuable for sampling certain kinds of behavior.

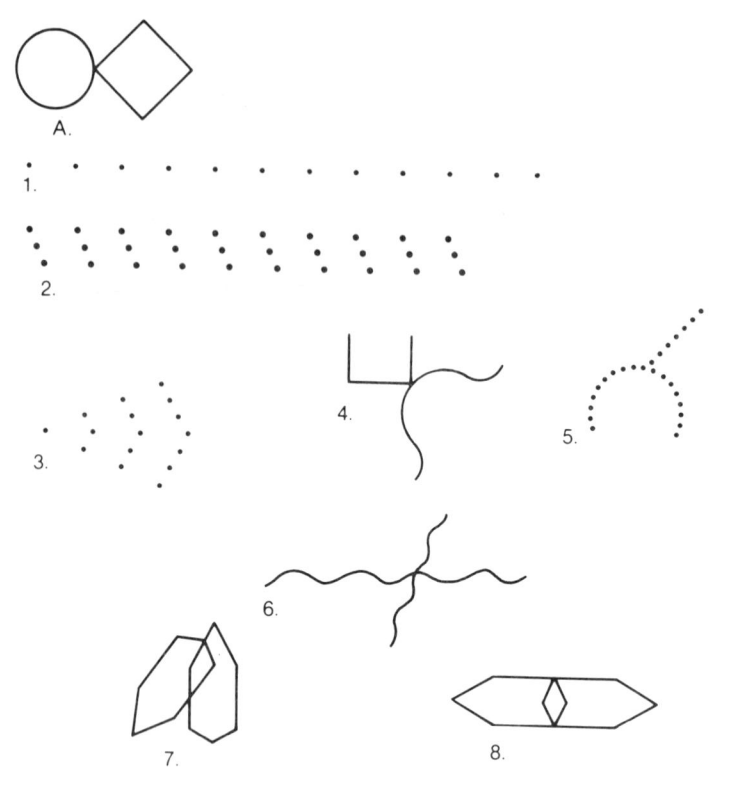

**Figure 8–7.** The Figures for the Bender Visual-Motor Gestalt Test

(Reproduced by permission of Dr. Lauretta Bender and the American Orthopsychiatric Association Copyright, 1946.)

## The Picture-Frustration Study (P-F)

The Picture-Frustration Study (P-F) was designed in accordance with Rosenzweig's (1944–1964) theoretical interest in the psychoanalytic concepts of frustration and aggression. He considered the P-F study a controlled projective technique and focused on the subject's patterns of reactions to frustration.

The P-F test consists of a series of cartoonlike drawings (see Figure 8–8), each of which portrays two principal characters. One of these persons is the victim of a somewhat frustrating set of circumstances, and the other character is either apologizing for the frustration that he or she has caused the victim or is calling attention to the frustrating circumstances in some other way. The respondent is instructed to give the answers that he or she thinks the frustrated person would give. This test is available for children (four to thirteen years) and for adults (fourteen years and older). A frame from the adult form is shown in Figure 8–8.

The P-F test is scored according to the response's direction of aggression (intropunitive, extrapunitive, or impunitive) and the specific type of reaction occurring. (These categorizations, of course, adhere to Rosenzweig's psychoanalytic theory.) Combinations of direction and type of response yield nine different possible scores, plus an overall group conformity rating which judges the extent of an examinee's conventionality.

Because of its highly structured stimulus materials and its relatively objective scoring procedures, the P-F test has generally been considered one of the more thoroughly researched projective techniques. Norms have been gathered for many special groups, and a systematic collection of evidence for its reliability and validity is well documented. Some, reviewers of the P-F test have stated that it is one of the most interesting and research-generating projective devices available (Anastasi, 1976; Bjerstedt, 1965).

## Role Construct Repertory (Rep) Test

Although not usually considered a projective technique (it is not listed in any of Buros's *Yearbooks* either, mainly because it is not sold commercially), our last selection in this chapter—George Kelly's (1955) Rep

**Figure 8–8.** Examples from the Rosenzweig Picture-Frustration Study.

(Reproduced by permission, from the Rosenzweig P-F Study. Adult form, copyright 1948.)

Test—could qualify as a test in many respects, as our description indicates. It is a standardized procedure that presents subjects with ambiguous tasks that are objectively scored in prespecified ways.

The Rep test requires the subject to list the names of people who play fifteen specified roles in his or her life. The roles are as follows (note that the last nine items are less specific than the others and hence are more open ended and ambiguous):

1. *Self:* yourself.
2. *Mother:* your mother or the person who has played the part of a mother in your life.
3. *Father:* your father or the person who has played the part of a father in your life.
4. *Brother:* your brother who is nearest your own age or, if you do not have a brother, a boy near your own age who has been most like a brother to you.
5. *Sister:* your sister who is nearest your own age, or if you do not have a sister, a girl near your own age who has been most like a sister to you.
6. *Spouse:* your wife (or husband) or, if you are not married, your closest present girl (boy) friend.
7. *Pal:* your closest present friend of the same sex as yourself.
8. *Ex-Pal:* a person of the same sex as yourself whom you once thought was a close friend but in whom you were badly disappointed later.
9. *Rejecting Person:* a person with whom you have been associated who, for some unexplained reason, appeared to dislike you.
10. *Pitied Person:* the person whom you would most like to help or for whom you feel most sorry.
11. *Threatening Person:* the person who threatens you the most or the person who makes you feel the most uncomfortable.
12. *Attractive Person:* a person whom you have recently met whom you would like to know better.
13. *Accepted Teacher:* the teacher who influenced you the most.
14. *Rejected Teacher:* the teacher whose point of view you have found most objectionable.
15. *Happy Person:* the happiest person whom you know personally.

Of course, a person may play more than one role. For example, one's teacher may also be the pitied person, and one's spouse may also be the most attractive person, and so on.

The Rep test was the product of Kelly's theory of social behavior, and its purpose was to help plan individual psychotherapy by proposing clinical hypotheses that could then be tested in the therapy sessions. To attain these ends, George Kelly devised a *grid* (see Figure 8-9) form of the Rep test.

The grid form works like this: First, the subject is given the fifteen role titles described above and is asked to write down on cards the names of the appropriate person who fits these roles. Second, the subject is instructed to consider for each of the fifteen role figures the three roles designated by the three circles in each row of Figure 8-9 (in columns), according to the constructs, also provided by the subject. For example, in Figure 8-9, the first triad comparison is among the rejecting person, pitied person, and attractive person according to the bipolar constructs cold-warm. This comparison reveals to which constructs the subject has linked two of the persons in the triad and also between which constructs the subject has differentiated. In other words, these constructs are dimensions along which the subject can rank

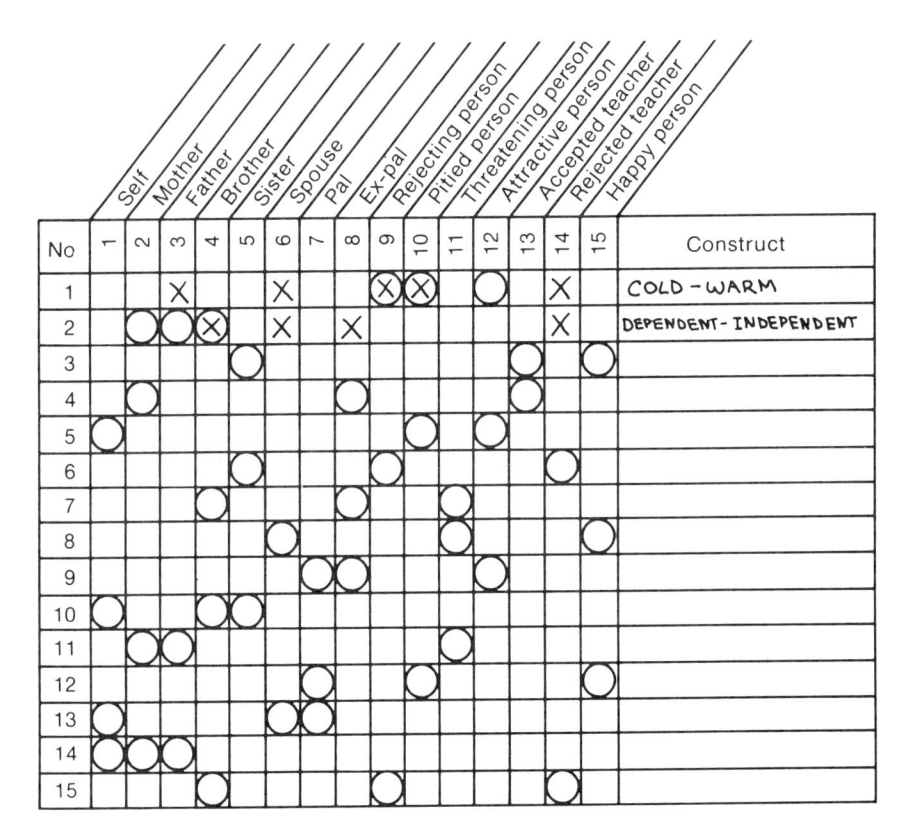

**Figure 8-9.** Simplified Grid Form of the Rep Test

Source: Weiner, B., Runquist, W., Runquist, P. A., Raven, B., Meyer, W. J., Leiman, A., Kutscher, C. L., Kleinmuntz, B., & Haber, R. N. *Discovering psychology* New York: St. Martin's Press, 1977, p. 467.

significant people in his or her life. If we examine row 1 of Figure 8–9, we will see that a subject might consider "cold" the individuals he or she has identified as the rejecting person and the pitied person (indicated by *x*) and the other individuals, by implication, "warm." Third, the subject then judges the remaining twelve people in row 1 as having or not having this quality (coldness) and places an *x* in the proper box in row 1 if they (father, spouse, and rejected teacher) do have this quality. Finally, the subject completes the remaining fourteen rows in this manner, selecting a construct for each triad.

The resulting row-by-column grid, or constructs-by-persons matrix, informs the tester about the constructs that the subject typically uses to perceive and classify others. Even without training, according to one source (Weiner et al., 1977, pp. 466–467), one can ascertain which constructs together are applied to a particular subject and thus are not distinguished. Thus if a person reported that men were cold and women were warm but used the construct male-female to distinguish the members of a particular triad, we would know that the person could also have chosen the construct cold-warm for this triad, that maleness and coldness were not separate constructs for this person.

In addition, by viewing the circles in the grid vertically rather than horizontally, one can find out the perceived similarity among individuals. It might be interesting to know, for example, which parent the subject perceives as more like himself or herself, or how similar the spouse is to the threatening person. This can be determined by comparing the constructs perceived as describing oneself with the constructs perceived as describing the spouse or the threatening person.

The reliability and validity of the Rep test are still largely unknown because it has been used sparingly, primarily in clinical, rather than research, settings (see Bannister & Mair, 1968). Some reliability studies have suggested that grid responses have a reasonable test-retest consistency. But there are no validity studies of which this writer is aware. Therefore, the Rep test can be considered only a promising clinical assessment tool. In regard to the Rep test's worth as a theoretical tool, Wiggins wrote, "Because the Rep test procedures represent a general approach to the elicitation and analysis of personal constructs, it is difficult to evaluate the usefulness of either the procedures or the personality model which underlies them for specific assessment problems . . . " (1973, p. 493).

## Conclusion

What, then, can we conclude about projective techniques? Judged by the standards of classical test theory, projectives fail the test (see Brown,

1976, p. 401). But should these techniques be drummed out of the personality tester's repertoire? Possibly. Yet many clinicians find them useful as exploratory procedures that yield data about a subject that are difficult to obtain from other sources. These data relate to the needs, wishes, aspirations, and unconscious processes that many of the more structured instruments do not measure. The issue of whether projectives are the most cost-effective means for obtaining such data is open to debate.

It is also conceivable that the classical psychometric approaches are limited, an argument that was logically defended in another context (see Lumsden, 1976); that there are several alternative approaches to finding out about another person; and that projectives are one of these alternatives. Perhaps the most useful interim resolution to this puzzle is to adopt Sundberg's distinction between the use of projectives as *exploratory procedures* for providing hypotheses about a person, versus their use as *psychometric tests* for obtaining quantitative information about a definite trait or characteristic (1977, p. 223). As exploratory techniques, projective devices can hardly be flawed on any but a cost-effective consideration; but as psychometric tests, when, for example, they are used to predict, screen, or classify persons, projectives must be judged according to the scientific criteria of reliability and validity. In their latter uses, projective techniques do not pass scientific muster.

# SUMMARY

Projective techniques are devices that encourage and permit a wide variety of subject responses. This is accomplished partially by constructing ambiguous test stimuli and partially by leaving the response situation loose or unstructured.

The most promising development in the projective methodology's history occurred with the appearance in 1921 of Hermann Rorschach's inkblots. The Rorschach, as it has come to be called, consists of a set of ten inkblot or symmetrical pictures to which the subject is required to respond. The scoring of the Rorschach is complex, and special problems in scoring and interpreting protocols have arisen over the years. These problems, plus the complex interviewlike interaction that is part of the test administration, have raised the question of whether it is appropriate to judge the technique by traditional psychometric criteria. According to these criteria, the Rorschach has not fared well. Some of its proponents have suggested that its clinical usefulness, rather than its psychometric excellence, is a more suitable criterion of its value. The Holtzman Inkblot Test (HIT) is a relatively recent innovation which has psychometricized the inkblots, but in the process it also has sacrificed some of the Rorschach's virtues.

A projective technique that has approached the Rorschach in the extent of its impact on personality testing is the Thematic Apperception Test, or TAT. In contrast to the ambiguous inkblot of the Rorschach, the identity of most TAT pictures is evident. In this test, the subjects are required to create stories rather than just to state what they believe the test stimuli look like.

The scoring and analysis of the TAT's responses raise some of the same issues as the Rorschach did regarding the technique's place in psychometrics. Moreover, the evidence supporting the TAT's reliability and validity is equally as unsatisfactory as that presented in favor of the inkblots.

Several modifications and derivations of the TAT have gained popularity among clinicians and research psychologists. Among these tests, the more prominent are the Children's Apperception Test (CAT) and the Blacky Pictures. In addition, regarding their work on achievement motivation, McClelland and his colleagues have argued for the validity of this procedure for eliciting specific needs.

There also are numerous other projective devices, with varying test administration methodologies and scoring procedures. At one extreme of stimulus structuredness is the Sentence Completion Test, in which the subject is given stems to complete; and at the other extreme is the task (e.g., Draw-a-Person Test) that provides the respondent with blank paper and requires picture drawings. Somewhere between these extremes lies the Rosenzweig Picture-Frustration Test, which provides the drawings but expects its respondents to furnish the answers to certain frustrating situations created in the pictures. The P-F has been described as a promising research tool.

Generally, projective methodology's greatest shortcomings are its lack of standardized administration procedures and its lack of information proving its psychometric respectability. There are, of course, notable exceptions to this generalization, the most well known of these being the Holtzman Inkblot Technique. In its conceptualization and development, however, this test resembles structured tests more closely than projective techniques. The compromise most acceptable to both projectivists and psychometrically oriented psychologists would probably be a test that was amenable to quantitative scoring schemes and yet at the same time retained its subtlety and open endedness. One procedure that does not quite fit the mold of projectives but resembles them in many ways is the Rep test, which had its origins in George Kelly's social behavior theory. The Rep test seems to be most useful in planning psychotherapy, although its reliability and validity for this purpose are unknown. Its administration and scoring procedures, as well as its interpretation, are sophisticated and require extensive statistical analysis.

# FOR FURTHER READING

Beck, S. *Rorschach's test: A variety of personality pictures.* (Vol. 2). New York: Grune & Stratton, 1967. From a series of books on the Rorschach by this author, this is the latest of the volumes written by one of the five chief contributors to this test's scoring and interpretation.

Bellak, A.S., & Hersen, M. *Introduction to clinical psychology.* New York: Oxford University Press, 1980. Written by two behaviorally oriented psychologists, chapter four of this book presents a highly critical review of projective tests and refers to their defenders and detractors as "believers and the nonbelievers."

Bernstein, D.A., & Nietzel, M.T. *Introduction to clinical psychology.* New York: McGraw-Hill, 1980. Chapter six on projective personality tests divides these tests into *association* (Rorschach, word associations), *construction* (TAT, Rosenzweig P-F), *choice* or *ordering* (Szondi, Tomkins-Horn Picture Arrangements), and *expressive* (Draw-a-Person) tests.

Exner, J.E. Projective techniques. In I.B. Weiner (Ed.), *Clinical methods in psychology.* New York: John Wiley, 1976, pp. 61–121. This comprehensive review chapter considers the current status of projective methods, the Consensus Rorschach (given to two or more persons simultaneously), the Holtzman Inkblot Test, the Thematic Apperception Test, and most other projectives.

Hertz, M. R. *Frequency tables for scoring Rorschach responses.* Cleveland: Case Western Reserve University Press, 1970. The author is one of the main contributors to the Rorschach theory and method.

Holt, R.R. *Methods in clinical psychology: Projective assessment.* (Vol. 1). New York: Plenum, 1978. Written by a research-oriented clinician who is considered an articulate spokesman for this method, Holt's book is one of the best on projectives.

Klopfer, B., Meyer, M.M., & Brawer, F. *Developments in the Rorschach technique.* New York: Harcourt Brace Jovanovich, 1970. The senior author is one of the four or five leading theoreticians of this technique.

Peterson, R.A. Review of the Rorschach. In O.K. Buros (Ed.), *Eighth mental measurements yearbook.* Highland Park, NJ: Gryphon Press, 1978. In Peterson's review of the Rorschach, he asserts that it is not the test's validity that accounts for its popularity, but rather its richness of "hypothetical dynamic associations" (p. 1042).

Piotrowski, Z.A. *Perceptanalysis.* New York: Macmillan, 1957. This early book represents the author's more conventional approach to this test's interpretation.

Rapaport, D., Gill, M.M., & Schafer, R. *Diagnostic psychological testing* (Rev. ed. by R.R. Holt). New York: International Universities Press, 1968. Still one of the leading books on projectives, Holt's revision of this edition is particularly helpful in its approach to Rorschach scoring and interpretation.

Zubin, J., Eron, L.D., & Schumer, F. *An experimental approach to projective techniques.* New York: John Wiley, 1965. Although it has been almost twenty years since its publication, this solid contribution to rather soft tests is still a standout in the literature on projectives.

# 9 Maximum Performance Assessment

The testing of intelligence and other abilities—the topic of this chapter—is not usually discussed in personality assessments books. This omission is perhaps due to their apparently greater connection to best effort than to typical performance (see chapter four). The discussion of this topic here reflects this writer's conviction that the ability to perform tasks well (or poorly) is equally as important to a person as are other aspects of personality. Thus a high (or low) intelligence or achievement test score can be as significant as information about a person's emotional adjustment (or maladjustment) or high (or low) score on an ego strength scale. This conviction is reinforced by research suggesting that there are few personality attributes of practical or theoretical importance that are not correlated with maximum performance tests, a fact that has been amply documented in some recent introductory books on personality (see Mischel, 1981, pp. 151–152) and individual differences (see Willerman, 1979, p. 349). With the conclusion of this topic we will have considered all of the assessment procedures that would be input into our information processor of Figure 1–1.

This chapter begins by considering some of the definitions of intelligence and some of the theories explaining it. Next we discuss several ways of assessing intelligence, achievement, abilities, and aptitudes, as well as some of their problems.

The question of what intelligence is has still not been answered. There are as many definitions of it as there are theories about its nature, but we shall discuss only the most popular ones.

## Definitions and Theories of Intelligence

L. L. Thurstone, one of the pioneers of the intelligence-testing movement, defined intelligence as "carrying on the trial and error process among reactions that are as yet incomplete and approximate" (1923, p. 78). Using a somewhat more empirical, albeit more circular, approach,

## BOX 9–1
## Information Yield from Some Observations, Interviews, and Tests

| Source | Information Yield |
|---|---|
| *Observations* | |
| Naturalistic | Assess reactions to everyday situations, scars, tremors, needle marks, expressive behaviors, and ratings of any of these behaviors. |
| Controlled | Obtain reactions to rigged stimuli, information about specific behaviors under contrived conditions, and ratings by others who remember the subject. |
| *Interviews* | |
| Intake | Establish relationship with patient, assess motivation for participating in treatment, impart information about agency, set expectations, and collect basic life data. |
| Mental Status | Assess mental preoccupations; observe attitude, appearance, and behavior; and observe mood fluctuations and speech. |
| *Psychological tests* | |
| Personality | On self-report inventories, collect responses regarding personal habits, unusual beliefs, or fantasies; on projective techniques, obtain responses to unstructured situations and assess needs and inner states. |
| Interest | Assess preferences for activities and other positive behavior. |
| Attitude | Scale opinions of issues, persons, or institutions. |
| Value | Measure subject's belief system. |
| Intelligence | Ascertain IQ level; determine extent of mental deficit, if any; and test for central nervous system involvement. |
| Achievement | Determine material learned in course or program. |
| Ability | Measure immediately available skill. |
| Aptitude | Measure potential skill. |

**Source:** Adapted from Kleinmuntz, B. *Essentials of abnormal psychology* (2nd ed.). New York: Harper & Row, 1980, p. 35. Reprinted by permission.

the famed experimental psychologist E. G. Boring defined intelligence as a "measurable capacity to do well in an intelligence test" (1923, p. 36). David Wechsler, the developer of the intelligence scales that bear his name, considered intelligence the "aggregate or global capacity of the individual to act purposefully, to think rationally, and to deal effectively with his environment (1939, p. 3). And with skepticism, and perhaps as an astute prediction of things to come, Charles Spearman wrote that the "word [intelligence] . . . might be expressly reserved to denote without prejudice whatever these tests may some day, after full investigation, show themselves to measure" (1923, p. 22).

More recently, George Frank, in "Measures of Intelligence and Conceptual Thinking," wrote that the psychological definitions of intelligence have not attained the clarity of the Oxford dictionary's definition, "the faculty of understanding," derived from the Latin *inter legere*, meaning "to bring together." He then asserted that the "definition of intelligence cannot be brushed aside as an academic or semantic issue; it makes a difference as to what we can expect from the data from measures of intelligence and what we can expect to be able to do with these data" (1976, p. 129).

By combining these definitions and the information that can be gleaned from many intelligence tests, our definition is that intelligence is the acquired abilities, adaptive capacities, and potential problem-solving skills available to us at any given moment of adaptive or intellectual challenge. In other words, intelligence is a mix of achievement, ability, and aptitude, in which intelligence reflects past training accomplishments; ability, currently available problem-solving skills; and aptitude, a test-based prediction of innate talent and probable success in solving future problems (see Sundberg, 1977, p. 228, for similar distinctions).

Obviously, intelligence is difficult to define. But perhaps it is as unimportant to define it as it is to define particular physical constructs. For example, H. J. Eysenck found that a "textbook of physics does not define gravitation; it (1) refers to examples of the action of this hypostatized force, such as the apple falling, and then (2) goes on to describe the means of measuring the effects of gravitation" (1973, p. 2). What this suggests, then, is that our efforts could be more profitably spent examining the several theories of intelligence and the ways it is measured than arguing about its proper definition. We thus turn to the first of these topics.

Many theories of intelligence have been, and continue to be, formulated over the years, and some have had a considerable impact on the types of intelligence tests constructed. Indeed, in many instances the construction of the test preceded the formulation of the theory.

**The Binet-Simon Theory.** The Binet-Simon scales, which were the forerunners of the now well known Stanford-Binet Intelligence tests, were not based on any particular theory of intelligence but were a response to Parisian school authorities in about 1904, who needed a method of detecting those children who were too slow to be educated in ordinary schools.

Theodore Simon and Alfred Binet set out to discover what tasks normal children of given ages could perform. Their idea was to devise scales that would distinguish between normal and subnormal youngsters. They did this by selecting a series of items that seemed to test the children's judgment, comprehension, and reasoning; for example, they believed that "to judge well, to comprehend well, to reason well" were the "essential activities of intelligence" (see Willerman, 1979, p. 84).

The difficulty of the items increased with the child's age, and so a varied series of items and tasks was used. Simon and Binet intended to measure "pure" intelligence by disregarding, as much as possible, those tasks related directly to schooling. After their success in discriminating between mentally deficient and normal children, Simon and Binet also demonstrated that their scales could differentiate among normal children. That is, they chose tasks that were much more readily accomplished by older than by younger children, and also by children considered by their teachers to be bright rather than dull. The resulting scales were the first attempt, according to one source (Vernon, 1979, p. 4), to provide a numerical scale of levels of intelligence, later referred to as mental ages. We shall return to a more complete discussion of the Binet scales later in this chapter.

**Spearman's g and s factors.** While Simon and Binet were developing the foundations for the now familiar Stanford-Binet Scales, a British psychologist, Charles Spearman, was formulating a different concept of intelligence. Whereas Binet postulated that intelligence was a complex set of qualities, including judgment, reasoning, and the capacity to adapt oneself to circumstances, Spearman postulated a "two-factor" theory of intelligence. This theory held that there was something common to all abilities, which Spearman called $g$, or general factor, and that in addition, every ability had a specific, or $s$, component peculiar to itself.

Spearman's theory contrasted sharply with Binet's adherence to a nineteenth-century faculty model which regarded the mind as a series of separate powers such as reasoning, memory, and imagination. But interestingly, and quite fortuitously, Spearman's theory was an indirect defense of and complement to the Binet-Simon scales because the scales contained a collection of diverse mental tasks. Thus Spearman's approach provided the first theoretical justification for such a collection, since one could now consider each of the tasks a partial measure of Spearman's $g$. Or, as P. E. Vernon observed, "overall performance, or Mental Age, would tend to give a good measure of the general factor, because the specific elements in the various items are uncorrelated; that is, they would tend to cancel one another out and not bias the total score in any particular direction" (1979, pp. 4–5).

According to some (e.g., see Willerman, 1979, p. 91), the precise meaning of Spearman's *g* has eluded explanation. One view is that all mental tests are complex, despite attempts to simplify them. All tests therefore contain common elements, and this is what is meant by *g*. Another view is that since the same or similar problems can be solved by alternative strategies, perhaps one general ability, or *g*, is latent in an individual and this is what is being applied in various, seemingly heterogeneous tasks. Still another view is that *g* is a quality of the brain—for example, its physiology—which is inherited and which permits the acquisition, retention, and retrieval of knowledge appropriate for solving problems.

**Cattell's Theory.** R. B. Cattell (1963, 1971a, 1971b), the British-born American psychologist who spent most of his productive years at the University of Illinois (Urbana-Champaign), formulated a theory of intelligence which had its origins in Spearman's idea of *g*. Cattell's theory holds that the *g* factor consists of two components: fluid intelligence, or $G_f$, and crystallized intelligence, or $G_c$. According to Vernon (1979, pp. 47–48), Cattell's theory links Spearman's factorial work to a plausible theory of heredity and environment. For example, Cattell's $G_f$ is the biologically determined aspect of intelligence that permits us to solve new problems and to grasp new relationships. In contrast, $G_c$ represents the concepts, skills, and strategies acquired from our culture and education. According to this view, fluid intelligence is a necessary, but not a sufficient, condition for superior crystallized abilities; poor fluid abilities result in deficient crystallized abilities.

The evidence for Cattell's view comes from several empirical findings which show that with age, performance on perceptual tests reaches a plateau earlier than performance on verbal tests does and the brain injury after maturity affects certain test performances more than others. J. L. Horn (Horn, 1979; Horn & Donaldson, 1976; Horn & Knapp, 1973), for instance, described well both fluid and crystallized intelligence and gave samples of test items used to measure them. Since fluid abilities are relatively independent of cultural experiences, they can be tested on persons with a non-Western cultural background. Of course, the mode and content of presentation must be appropriate to the specific culture; it would not make sense, for example, to give the following item to people who do not know the alphabet:

> Given the letters A C F J O \_\_\_,
> provide the next letter.

But it may be appropriate to test a similar inductive reasoning by using the accompanying puzzle, provided, of course, that the subjects are familiar with geometric figures such as these (see Figure 9–1).

Items measuring crystallized intelligence, that is, abilities closely tied

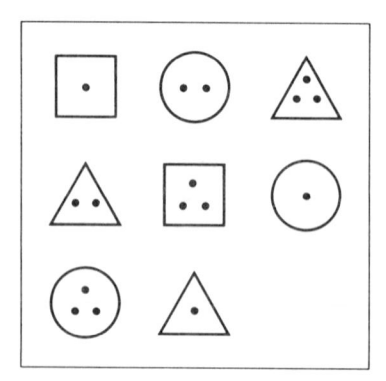

**Figure 9-1.** What figure fits into the lower right? (Answer: a square with two dots.)

Source: Horn, J. L. Intelligence—Why it grows, why it declines. In L. Willerman & R. G. Turner (Eds.), *Readings about individual and group differences*. San Francisco: W. H. Freeman & Company Publishers, 1979, p. 22. Published by permission of Transaction, Inc., from *Transaction*, Copyright © November 1967 by Transaction, Inc.

to acquired knowledge, are vocabulary, mathematics, and reasoning problems. For example, one problem that measures experiential evaluation in married men is the following:

> Your wife has just invested time, effort, and money in a new hairdo. But it doesn't help her appearance at all. She wants your opinion. You should:
>
> 1. try to pretend that the hairdo is great;
> 2. state your opinion bluntly;
> 3. compliment her on her hairdo, but add minor qualifications; or
> 4. refuse to comment.
>
> Answer 3 is considered correct on the grounds that husbands can't get away with answers 1 and 4, and answer 2 is likely to provoke undue strife. (Horn, 1979, p. 23)

In Cattell's theory, which is a hierarchical approach to intelligence, the distinction between crystallized and fluid intelligence is unclear. It often is possible to solve a problem like the above two by using either mode. For example, a problem that could be solved intuitively might also be solved by using rules or by applying mathematical logic. But Cattell (1971a, 1971b) has acknowledged this problem and has refined his initial theory by adding four new factors:

1. Neurologically organized *powers*; for example, visual, auditory, or motor abilities.
2. *Proficiencies*, or skills, in particular areas.

3. *Agencies*, or tools; that is, acquired strategies that generalize to many situations.
4. Several general capacities besides the fundamental $G_f$; for instance, general spatial ability, cognitive speed, carefulness, and memorizing.

**Guilford's Theory.** Guilford's theory is quite different from those of Binet and Simon, Spearman, and Cattell, although it too is solidly in the psychometric and factorial tradition. In his 1967 book, *The Nature of Human Intelligence,* Guilford proposed his Structure of the Intellect (SOI) model. Unlike the other theorists, Guilford tested his SOI model by not only using a variety of factor and statistical procedures but also letting his model guide his acquisition of psychometric data. The others' strategy had been to infer their models from the data.

According to Guilford's model (see Figure 9–2), the structure of the intellect can be divided into content, operations, and products. Content includes the four aspects of information on which the operations can

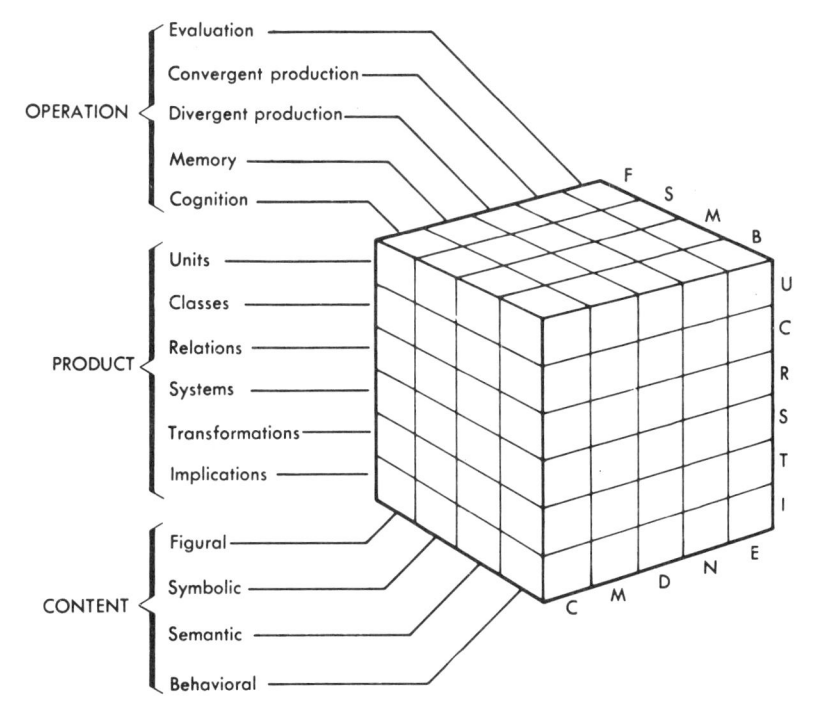

**Figure 9–2.** Guilford's model of Intellect.

Source: From *The Nature of Human Intelligence* by J. P. Guilford. Copyright © 1967. Used with the permission of McGraw-Hill Book Company.

be performed: figural, symbolic, semantic, and behavioral. The operations are evaluation (judgment), convergent production (giving the correct answer), divergent production (constructing logical alternatives), memory, and cognition. After a particular mental operation is applied to a specific content, there are six possible products: units, classes, relations, systems, transformations, and implications, which can be translated into things, common properties, connections between things or objects, complexes, inversions, and expectations, respectively.

This model, as can be seen in Figure 9–2, consists of 4 × 5 × 6 = 120 different intellectual facets; Guilford claims that both his research and numerous large-scale investigations have confirmed 98 of these (Guilford & Hoepfner, 1971). Thus, he has rejected the idea of a general factor, partly because he found low or zero correlations between the tests designed to measure different factors and partly because he found evidence to suggest that different factors show different curves of growth and decline and react differently to various psychopathological conditions, drugs, environment, and so on. Some researchers (e.g., Brody & Brody, 1976) have disputed his claims and have asserted that Guilford's data do not exclude a $g$ factor and that his separate factor structures have not been successfully crossvalidated.

Perhaps the most widely held reservation about Guilford's approach came first from Cattell (1971a), who criticized his model on the grounds that the content categories are not mutually exhaustive or independent and that the product dimensions could be replaced by other factors that explained them equally well. Moreover, the operations do not include several other possibilities. More importantly, however, as Willerman (1979, p. 93) noted, Cattell's main objection was that Guilford's tests bear little relation to the real world.

**Sternberg's Theory.** We shall conclude this section by examining a new theory of intelligence which was proposed by R. J. Sternberg (1977, 1979a, 1979b). This theory has its roots in the information-processing tradition of Newell and Simon (1972) but in many ways is close to the psychometric theories of Spearman (1923, 1927) and J. B. Carroll (1976). Sternberg set out to investigate the component processes of analogical thinking because he believed that it was a good index of general intelligence, or Spearman's $g$; and he drew heavily from Cattell's findings that many cognitive control factors can be used to solve the problems on most standard intelligence tests.

Sternberg's theory, which is based largely on laboratory studies of how people solve problems of the sort found on IQ tests, postulates at least two basic levels of information processing. The first is the level of the components that underlie intelligence; that is, the steps that the individual uses to solve complex mental tasks. The second is the level of metacomponents, or the higher-order steps that one uses to decide how to solve a mental task. These levels, and the way in which they are presumably applied to problems, are presented in Figure 9–3, a schematic outline of the theory.

Figure 9–3 is somewhat more detailed than necessary for our purposes, but we can illustrate several of its elements with several simplified examples. For example, suppose that you intend to convert Mexican pesos to dollars and that you know a dollar is worth about 22 pesos. You want to know how many dollars you can get for 1,200 pesos. Metacomponents can be used to solve the problem: The sum to be converted has to be divided by the dollar value of each peso, and components are used to arrive at the solution: $1200 \div 22 = \$54.55$.

A componential analysis of a typical analogy problem is somewhat more complex. The problem:

> The subject is given the first three terms of an analogy and a blank term; e.g., "Four score and seven years ago" is to Lincoln as, "I'm not a crook" is to _____ , and is asked to choose between (a) Nixon, (b) Capone. (Sternberg, 1979a, p. 218)

First, the person must encode the various terms of the analogy, identifying each and retrieving from memory the chunks that may be relevant to the solution. Examples of possible encodings for Lincoln are that he was a president of the United States during the Civil War, made a famous speech, and was known as Honest Abe. Possible encodings for "I'm not a crook" are that it was part of someone's disclaimer, was probably pronounced by a dishonest president, and is of relatively recent origin.

Next, the person infers a relationship between the attributes of the first two terms of the analogy, "Four score and seven years ago" and Lincoln. Here the person may infer that Lincoln lived eighty-seven years ago or, rejecting this, may infer that he delivered a speech containing these words. Then the person maps the higher-order relation that connects the first half of the analogy, headed by "Four score ..." to the second half of the analogy, "I'm not a crook." Both halves deal with presidents of the United States and their speeches.

Finally, the person applies the relation inferred from the first two terms ("Four score ..." and Lincoln) to the third analogy term ("I'm not a crook") and then selects one of the possible answers. Since only one refers to a president—Nixon—he or she would correctly choose that answer. But since both choices involve crooks, Nixon and Capone, the person must also apply an optional component, justification, in order to decide that one of the choices is preferable to the other.

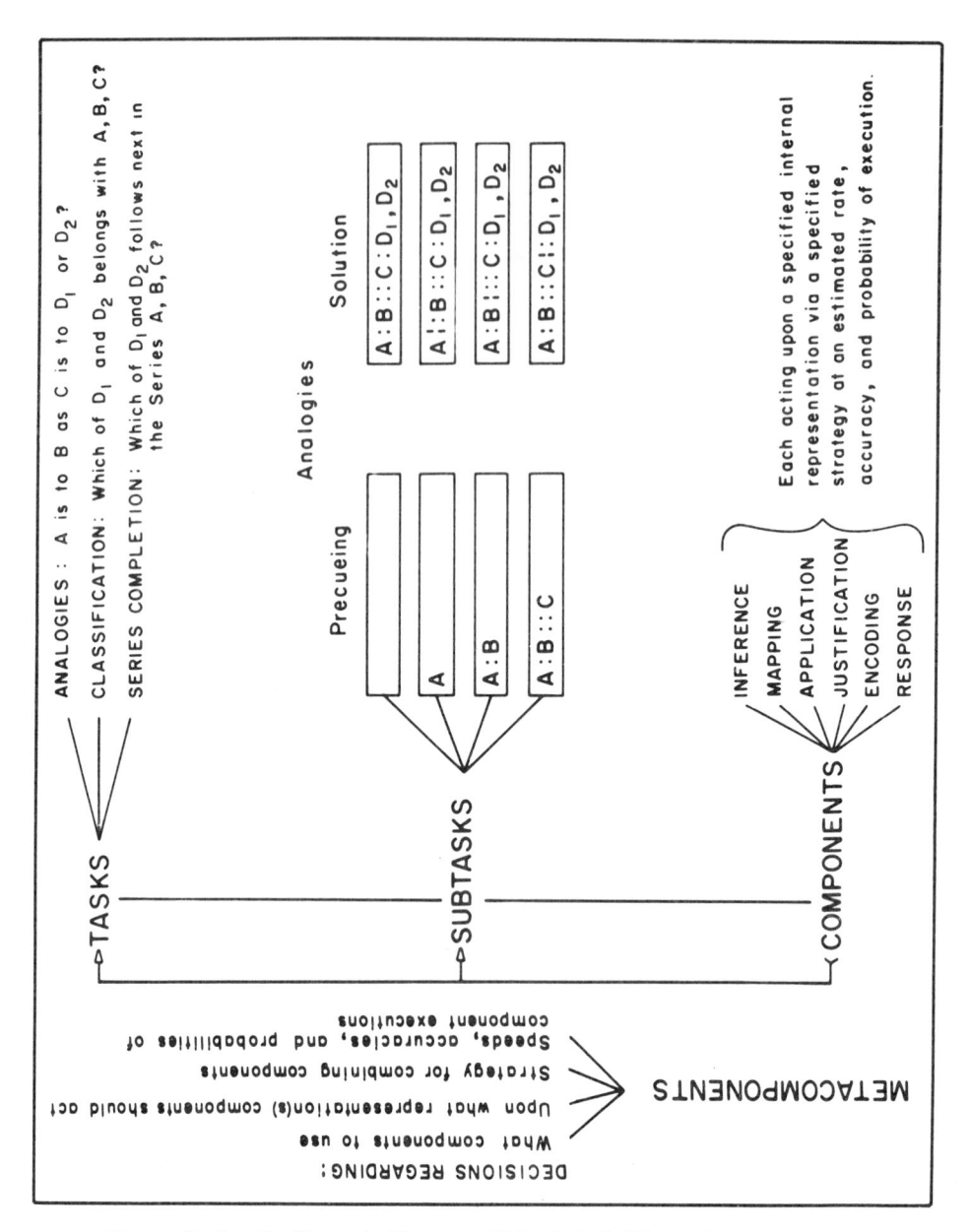

**Figure 9–3.** Outline of a Theory of Mental Abilities, with Examples at Right of Figure.

Source: Sternberg, R. J. The nature of mental abilities. *American Psychologist*, 1979, 34, 217. Copyright 1979 by the American Psychological Association. Reprinted by permission of the publisher and author.

The person does this by checking previous components for errors of omission or commission before responding with the most appropriate answer to the analogy.

Two other aspects of Sternberg's theory are noteworthy: the first is his idea that intellectual problems not only must be solved correctly but also must be solved within a given time period; the second aspect is that intelligence can be improved, which is an encouraging note in view of the prevailing controversy about this (recently revived by Jensen [1980], according to whom intelligence is not amenable to improvement). Regarding the first of these, Sternberg stated "By analyzing response time and error data for individual subjects at the level of the component process, it becomes possible to pinpoint quite precisely the source or sources of particular weaknesses or strengths in global information processing" (1979a, p. 225). And as for improving intelligence, he observed,

> Moreover, it becomes possible to train subjects in strategies that capitalize on their particular patterns of strength and weakness. We have found, for example, that it is possible to improve substantially the performance of subjects solving linear syllogisms by training [them] . . . to use a strategy calling for components [they] . . . do not [usually] . . . use spontaneously but that are readily available for use by the subjects once [they] . . . are appropriately trained. (1979a, p. 225)

## Intelligence Testing

Although there are many other definitions and theories of intelligence— and the interested reader may want to consult several excellent sources for more information (e.g., Anastasi, 1976; Brody & Brody, 1976; Eysenck, 1973; Frank, G., 1976; Vernon, 1979; Willerman, 1979)—we shall now turn our attention to the numerous assessment strategies that have been used to measure intelligence and some of its variants.

Intelligence-quotient (IQ) testing, unlike the quest for a theory or a definition of intelligence, has often been heralded as one of the preeminent accomplishments of twentieth-century psychology, but it has also provoked a heated and sometimes bitter controversy. IQ testing's main accomplishments have been its rather stable or reliable assessment of intellectual functioning, and its useful or valid estimates of current and future cognitive skills, which do not require knowledge of a person's past history or brain condition. The controversy that this testing has elicited has concerned both the meaning of intelligence and the usefulness and ethics of its assessment. Even more controversial has been the ongoing debate about its probable genetic component, a debate fraught with sociopolitical implications.

## BOX 9-2

## Intelligent Testing: What Is Intelligence?

In his presidential address to the Division of Evaluation and Measurement of the American Psychological Association, Alexander Wesman (1968) offered the following two propositions about intelligence:

1. Intelligence is an attribute, not an entity.
2. Intelligence is the summation of the learning experiences of the individual.

Wesman then separated several issues of intelligence testing as follows:

1. It is artificial to classify tests into those of ability, aptitude, and achievement since what we can do intellectually is learned. (He went on to say that our labeling system relies entirely on the purpose for which the test is used. We label a test "achievement" if our intent is to discover how much an examinee has learned; we label it "aptitude" if our intent is to predict future performance in a new language or job; and we label it "intelligence" if our purpose is to predict future academic performance.)
2. It is folly to talk of "culture-free" tests when we consider the relevance of prior learning on test scores. And as long as our educational system and our general culture depend on conventional verbal abilities, those who aspire to progress in that system and culture will need to foster those abilities. In a verbal society, verbal competence cannot sensibly be ignored.
3. More than just the verbal domain is important for appraising intelligence; performing certain tasks is equally important. For example, employers have learned that the ability to diagnose malfunctioning machinery is poorly demonstrated by verbal exposition, but well demonstrated by a work sample requiring actual mechanical repairs.
4. We should recognize the limitations of our present "intelligence" measures until such time as we can devise relevant measures of the significant learnings which do occur.

**Source:** Wesman, A. G. Intelligent testing. *American Psychologist,* 1968, 23, 267-274.

## Binet-type Tests

The measurement of intelligence owes its beginnings to the work of Binet and Simon, who, as we already indicated, were commissioned in 1904 by the French government to study the problem of retardation among school children. But even before this time, an article published by Binet and Henri in 1895 had already hinted at the development of "intelligence scales." Binet and Henri had reviewed most of the existing tests and concluded that they relied too much on sensory discrimination and specialized skills. Accordingly, they proposed the measurement of more general abilities and argued for testing other qualities, all of which they thought were closely related to "intelligence." Some of these qualities are memory, attention, imagination, comprehension, and suggestibility.

When Binet was commissioned to study the progress of retarded children in Paris schools, he and Simon began developing "intelligence scales." Their scheme was quite simple and based on an empirical notion not much different from criterion keying. The difficulty level of each problem on a scale was to be determined experientially by posing them to children ranging in age from three to eleven years. If three-year-olds usually solved a particular problem but could not progress beyond it, then that upper limit became the three-year level of difficulty. Likewise, upper limits, or cutoff points, were established for the year levels four, five, six, seven, eight, nine, ten, and eleven.

The use of this criterion-oriented item construction had not yet been perfected in Binet and Simon's 1905 version of the test, but in 1908 and 1911, when the first and second revisions of the Binet-Simon tests were published, the empirical method had been perfected and other scales had been added. These scales were grouped according to age levels (see Table 9–1). The age level concept inspired the idea of mental age (MA), which was fully recognized, along with the IQ, in the 1916 revision of the Stanford-Binet test. In 1938 Esquirol noted that severely mentally retarded children were not as capable of learning as normal children were. Using this idea, the MA also accounted for the fact that children of higher chronological age (CA) could solve more difficult items than younger children could. Accordingly, Binet arranged his test so that the difficulty of items increased with age (see Sattler, 1974, pp. 91–92).

Lewis Terman (1916; Terman & Merrill, 1937), a psychologist at Stanford University, later scored the Stanford-Binet test according to an intelligence quotient (IQ), which expressed the ratio of the child's chronological age to his or her mental age. The IQ is computed by dividing the child's MA by his or her chronological age (CA) and multiplying by 100. Thus a ten-year-old child who has earned an MA score of 12 on the Binet test receives an IQ of 120 (MA/CA = 12/10 × 100 = 120). This ratio IQ was changed in Form *L-M* (Terman & Merrill, 1960), which incorporated the best of the 1937 *L* and *M* forms, to a deviation IQ. The new Stanford-Binet deviation IQ is essentially a normalized standard score with a mean of 100 and standard deviation of 16. It expresses the deviation of the ratio IQ from the mean ratio IQ

**Table 9–1**  List of Tasks by Ages as Arranged by Binet in 1911.

*Age 3*
1. Points to nose, eyes and mouth.
2. Repeats two digits.
3. Enumerates objects in a picture.
4. Gives family name.
5. Repeats a sentence of six syllables.

*Age 4*
1. Gives his sex.
2. Names key, knife, and penny.
3. Repeats three digits.
4. Compares two lines.

*Age 5*
1. Compares two weights.
2. Copies a square.
3. Repeats sentence of ten syllables.
4. Counts four pennies.
5. Unites the halves of a divided triangle.

*Age 6*
1. Distinguishes between morning and afternoon.
2. Defines familiar words in terms of use.
3. Copies a diamond.
4. Counts thirteen pennies.
5. Distinguishes pictures of ugly and pretty faces.

*Age 7*
1. Shows right hand and left ear.
2. Describes a picture.
3. Executes three commissions, given simultaneously.
4. Counts the value of six sous, three of which are double.
5. Names four cardinal colors.

*Age 8*
1. Compares two objects from memory.
2. Counts from 20 to 0.
3. Notes omissions from pictures.
4. Gives day and date.
5. Repeats five digits.

**Table 9–1** (*Continued*)

*Age 9*
1. Gives change from 20 sous.
2. Defines familiar words in terms superior to use.
3. Recognizes all the pieces of money.
4. Names the months of the year, in order.
5. Answers easy "comprehension questions."

*Age 10*
1. Arranges five blocks in order of weight.
2. Copies drawings from memory.
3. Criticizes absurd statements.
4. Answers difficult "comprehension questions."
5. Uses three given words in not more than two sentences.

*Age 12*
1. Resists suggestion.
2. Composes one sentence containing three given words.
3. Names sixty words in three minutes.
4. Defines certain abstract words.
5. Discovers the sense of a disarranged sentence.

*Age 13*
1. Repeats seven digits.
2. Finds three rhymes for a given word.
3. Repeats a sentence of twenty-six syllables.
4. Interprets pictures.
5. Interprets given facts.

*Adult*
1. Solves the paper cutting test.
2. Rearranges a triangle in imagination.
3. Gives differences between parts of abstract terms.
4. Gives three differences between a president and a king.
5. Gives the main thought of a selection which he has heard read.

Source: Terman, L. M. *The measurement of intelligence*. Boston: Houghton Mifflin, 1916, pp. 37–39.

at each age level. In other words, a specific IQ at different ages in Form *L-M* indicates about the same relative ability, regardless of the examinee's age.

The Binet-type tests are administered to examinees individually, and the 1937, 1960, and subsequent revisions (Terman & Merrill, 1960, pp. 67–109; see also Terman & Merrill, 1973), like their predecessors, have their subtests arranged according to age levels, ranging from age two to Superior Adult. The adult levels (Average Adult and Superior Adult levels I, II, and III) are misnomers because the test is not actually intended for persons over the age of eighteen; these additional levels raise the ceiling of the test and thus permit brighter youngsters to respond to more difficult questions and problems. The items are scored at half-year intervals at Level II through Level V and at full-year intervals thereafter.

The test materials measure very young children in tasks of eye-hand coordination, memory, and reasoning. The tasks become increasingly more difficult for the older age groups. Excerpts of items taken from levels II, VI, and XIV are presented in Table 9–2. Scoring is on an all-or-none basis, with the *basal age* as the age at which an individual passes all items and with the *ceiling age* as the age at which an individual fails all tasks. Within these extremes, the individual earns credits in months which are added to the basal age.

The Stanford-Binet must be administered by a trained psychologist who is both skilled at interviewing and familiar with its scoring procedures. Each of the separate tasks or subtests is scored as it is being administered, because progress to subsequent levels depends on performance at lower levels. Both the administration and the scoring procedures are highly standardized for this test, and the examiner is not supposed to alter the wording of the questions or the criteria for their scoring. A carefully prepared test manual is provided.

The normative sample for the two forms of the Stanford-Binet's 1937 (second) revision consisted of about three thousand children, with about one hundred children at half-year intervals from ages one and a half to five and a half, two hundred children from ages six to fourteen, and one hundred children from ages fifteen to eighteen. There were three criteria for retaining items: (1) if the item measured presumably intelligent behavior, (2) if the proportion of children passing the item increased rapidly with age, and (3) if the mean mental age of children passing and failing the item differed significantly.

For the 1960 Form *L-M*, the normative group consisted of 4,500 children (ages two and a half to eighteen) who had taken form *L* or *M* between 1950 and 1954. No new material was introduced, nor were the essential features of the scale changed. But the 1960 (third) revision, as indicated earlier, was constructed by selecting the best items from forms

**Table 9-2**  Summary of Test Contents for Selected Age Levels on the Stanford-Binet Test (1960 Revision).

**Year Level II**
1. *Three-hole formboard*: Formboard 5" × 8" with three holes for circle, square, and triangle. Child places blocks in appropriate holes.
2. *Identifying parts of the body*: Large paper doll. Child identifies hair, mouth, feet, nose, ear, hands, and eyes.
3. *Picture vocabulary*: Eighteen 2" × 4" cards with pictures of common objects. Child names the objects.

**Year Level VI**
1. *Vocabulary*: List of words on a vocabulary card. Child defines words, e.g., "What is an orange?"
2. *Mutilated pictures*: Card with mutilated picture. Child has to say what is wrong with the picture.
3. *Maze tracing*: Maze paths with three positions marked. Child indicates the shortest way through the maze to designated points, starting from each of the three positions in turn.

**Year Level XIV**
1. *Reasoning 1*: Card on which a problem is stated. Child must display proper reasoning in solving the problem.
2. *Ingenuity I*: A set of problems involving different-sized containers to arrive at given amounts of water, e.g., using a 3-pint and an 8-pint can to secure exactly 1 pint of water.
3. *Induction*: The examiner cuts six sheets of paper 8½" × 11", one at a time so that a hole appears, and refolds it several times, cutting another hole each time. The examinee has to give a rule that explains the number of holes.

SOURCE: Based on Terman, L. M., Merrill, M. A. *Stanford-Binet intelligence scale: Manual for the third revision, form L-M.* Boston: Houghton Mifflin, 1960, pp. 69–75.

$L$ and $M$ of the 1937 alternate or equivalent tests. The revised test contained those items that more persons passed as they got older and those that correlated highly with the scale as a whole.

Form $L$-$M$ was updated most recently in 1972 (Terman & Merrill, 1973) by administering the test to about 2,000 persons, selected from a sample of 200,000 school children, ages three through twelve (see Anastasi, 1976, pp. 232–233). The latest norms were chosen in response to minority-group criticism, and the new sample was selected from communities differing in size, geographical region, and economic status, and included blacks, Mexican-Americans, and Puerto Ricans, as well as whites. Thus compared with earlier versions of the test, the 1972 normative sample was more representative of the American population. Anastasi observed that "the later norms show some improvement in test performance at all ages . . . the test authors attribute this improvement to the impact of radio and television on young children and the increasing literacy and educational level of parents, among other cultural changes" (1976, p. 233).

The reliability and validity of the Stanford-Binet tests are considered adequate for most uses. It is not important to detail the relevant studies here, but the reader is advised that such studies, especially those bearing on the validity of the test, are meaningful only to the extent that they are relevant to particular uses. Thus, although the correlations between Stanford-Binet IQs and elementary school grades are high (between 0.40 and 0.80), the Stanford-Binet is not the test of choice for predicting school grades at higher academic levels.

The Stanford-Binet has also been reported as indicating children's emotional disturbances (Sattler, 1974, p. 326), including irritability, restlessness, suspiciousness, apathy, euphoria, and an attitude that the test is "kid stuff." These indications of normality or disturbance specify that compulsives may pass some subtests but fail others that do not require careful attention to detail; that negativistic children may not want to obey simple commands (Year Level II–6 items not shown in Table 9–2); that aggressive and practical children may have an advantage over passive, hesitant children on the Ingenuity tasks (Year Level XIV–2), which present problems whose solutions require using different-sized containers to arrive at given amounts of water (Taylor, E. M., 1961); and that children failing the Mutilated Pictures items (VI–2) yet passing others of equal difficulty may have sexual inhibitions (Kessler, 1966).

There are many such findings, but it is interesting to note that much of the research on specific Stanford-Binet subtests has generally not found significant or important differences between the scores of emotionally disturbed children and those of normal children. One such study (Dunsdon, 1953), which developed a scoring system for an earlier report (Myers & Gifford, 1943), compared the Form *L*, Stanford-Binet performances of 1,297 maladjusted children with those of 658 normal children (ages seven to fourteen) but found no differences in their scores.

Likewise, another early investigator (Pignatelli, 1943) found no differences between the patterns of success and failure of two groups of 303 problem children with adjustment and learning difficulties and those of 303 normal children. These subjects were carefully matched for CA, MA, and IQ on year levels VII, VIII, and IX on the 1916 Stanford-Binet.

On the other hand, another early investigation (Wile & Davis, 1941), which studied the 1916 Stanford-Binet scores of one hundred mentally disturbed children between the ages of five and eleven years (IQs of 80 to 130), found that the two most frequently failed tasks were Copying a Diamond (VI–3) and Repeating Three Digits Reversed (IV–3). These items were failed by 86 percent and 72 percent of the children, respectively, and were attributed to deficiencies in visual memory and visual auditory association.

Similar patterns of failure or memory deficiencies were apparently not found among nondisturbed children, although the investigators presented no evidence regarding normal children. And generally, studies relating personality and emotional disturbance to intelligence testing indicated some identifiable associations, and this was true particularly when behavioral measures of personality or disturbance were used as criteria. But there seemed to be no evidence of differences in levels of intelligence between adjusted and maladjusted children.

## The Wechsler Tests

Another important person associated with intelligence testing is David Wechsler. In 1939 Wechsler designed an intelligence test for adults that, like the Binet-type tests, was also to be administered individually. It originally appeared as the Wechsler-Bellevue Scales I and II (equivalent forms were developed at Bellevue Hospital in New York City), then after being revised in 1955 was named the Wechsler Adult Intelligence Scale (WAIS), and was about to appear in a new version at the present writing (1980). Whereas the Binet tests were designed for children, and in fact lack face validity even for brighter and older children, the items on the original Wechsler tests were appropriate for adults (see Matarazzo, 1972; Wechsler, 1939, 1955, 1958; also see Wechsler, 1975). After introducing the Wechsler-Bellevue Scales I and II, Wechsler developed (1949) a test for children, called the Wechsler Intelligence Scale for Children, or WISC. The WISC can be used for children between the ages of five years and five years eleven months. Still later, in 1967, he introduced the Wechsler Preschool and Primary Scale of Intelligence (WPPSI), which is intended for children aged four years to six and a half years.

Wechsler believed that there was an age limit beyond which IQ based on mental age could not increase significantly. On memory for digits, for instance, the limit seemed to be fourteen years, and for vocabulary it appeared to be twenty-two years. Since the denominator of the standard IQ formula contained chronological age, adults who continued to answer the same number of items correctly would obtain decreasing IQs. Clearly, this was a drawback and a problem in intelligence testing.

Wechsler's solution to this problem was to introduce the deviation IQ, a solution that followed the lead of L. L. Thurstone (1926), who had earlier held that the concept of mental age was inadequate. Wechsler suggested that "a person's intelligence at any given time is defined by his relative standing among his age peers. This assumes that though an individual's absolute capacity may change, his relative standing may not ..." (1958, p. 33). Therefore, Wechsler's deviation IQs are not ratios of mental age to chronological age but are simply standard scores in which the mean has been set at 100 and the standard deviation at 15. Nonetheless, it has been noted that the Stanford-Binet IQs and the WISC IQs correspond closely to each other when both tests are administered to the same individuals. These Binet-to-WISC correlations vary with the age, intelligence level, and homogeneity of the samples; but generally they range between the coefficients of 0.60 and 0.90, which are good measures of the WISC's concurrent validity. Binet-to-WPPSI correlations range from 0.44 to 0.92 for the full-scale IQs, with median coefficients of 0.81, 0.67, and 0.82 for the verbal performances and full scales, respectively (see Sattler, 1974, p. 209).

**The Wechsler Intelligence Scale for Children (WISC).** On the children's version of the Wechsler-Bellevue scales (particularly Scale II), Wechsler added easier items to the low end of the subtests. Two WISC tests resulted, the original version of the WISC in 1949 and its revision, the WISC-R, in 1974. The WISC and its revision consists of twelve subtests, six forming the verbal scale (information, comprehension, arithmetic, similarities, vocabulary, and digit span), and six forming the performance scale (picture completion, picture arrangement, block design, object assembly, coding, and mazes).

The normative group for the WISC consisted of 2,200 white American boys and girls selected as representative of the 1940 United States census. However, according to Sattler, the normative group overrepresented the middle and upper socioeconomic levels, and "therefore, children from ethnic minority groups, or from lower socioeconomic groups, may be penalized because they were represented inadequately in developing the norms" (1974, p. 153).

To correct this imbalance, the WISC-R normative group was based on a stratified sampling of the 1970 census data, taking into account the children's geographic location, urban-rural residence, race, and socioeconomic level. Bilingual children were included in the normative sample if they both understood and spoke English fluently.

**The Wechsler Adult Intelligence Scale (WAIS).** The WAIS, as we indicated earlier, is a test for adults between the ages of sixteen and seventy-five. It contains eleven subtests, six covering predominantly verbal skills and five requiring the manipulation of objects and pictures. The verbal scales, as shown in Table 9–3, include tests of information, comprehension, arithmetic, similarities, digit span, and vocabulary; the performance scales include digit symbol, picture completion, block design, picture arrangement, and object assembly tasks. Together these

**Table 9-3** Description of the Verbal and Performance Scales of the WAIS.

**Verbal Scale**

1. *Information*: Questions covering a wide variety of general information that most persons can be expected to acquire in the course of everyday affairs.
2. *Comprehension*: The items covered on this scale measure common sense and practical judgment in a variety of situations. Also, the meaning of some common maxims must be explained by the examinee.
3. *Arithmetic*: About a dozen arithmetic problems, in ascending order of difficulty, are presented to the examinee. Each problem has a time limit for its solution.
4. *Similarities*: Pairs of words are presented, and the examinee is required to state the similarity of each pair, e.g., 'In what way are 'bird and leaf' alike?"
5. *Digit span*: The respondent must reproduce orally presented strings of digits (forward and backward).
6. *Vocabulary*: About forty words, in order of increasing difficulty, must be defined.

**Performance Scales**

1. *Digit symbol*: This is a timed test in which the respondent must place appropriate symbols in numbered squares.
2. *Picture completion*: Each of about two dozen picture cards is shown to the examinee, who must specify what is missing in each picture.
3. *Block design*: This is another timed test. The respondent reproduces, with four and nine blocks, designs of increasing difficulty.
4. *Picture arrangement*: Picture cards are laid out in front of the testee, who is required within specific time limits to rearrange these cards so that they make a story.
5. *Object assembly*: Several cut-up cardboard puzzle pieces are presented to the examinee, who is instructed to put them together to make objects. This is also a timed subtest.

Source: Based on Wechsler, D. *Manual for the Wechsler adult intelligence scale*. New York: Psychological Corporation, 1955, pp. 33-53.

make up the *full scale*. These scale scores, in turn, may be converted by "table-look-up" procedures to the *verbal IQ, performance IQ*, and *full scale IQ* scores. The scoring system, which incidentally is roughly comparable to those used to score the WISC and WPPSI tests, first adds up the correct raw-score responses to each item in each of the verbal and performance scales. Then these raw scores are converted to standard scores ($\bar{X} = 10$, standard deviation = 3) by using a conversion table. Subtest standard scores, in turn, are the totals of the verbal and performance scale's scores, which are then converted to verbal and performance IQs by using an age-relevant conversion table. Finally, the full scale IQ is obtained by adding together the verbal and the performance scale scores and once again consulting an age-relevant conversion table.

Interestingly, although the WAIS and the Stanford-Binet apply to entirely different age groups, their scores are closely related (see Sattler, 1974, p. 125). For normal college freshmen and adults, there is a median correlation of 0.77, with a range of coefficients from 0.40 to 0.83. Generally, the Stanford-Binet yields higher IQs than the WAIS does and correlates more closely with the WAIS's performance IQ. In samples of mentally retarded persons, the correlations are between 0.74 and 0.90 (the median correlation being 0.75), with Stanford-Binet IQs being lower than WAIS IQs.

The reliability and validity of the Wechsler tests, like those of the Stanford-Binet tests, are considered sufficiently high for most uses (see Anastasi, 1976; Matarazzo, 1972; Sattler, 1974; Wechsler, 1958). Split-half reliability subtests are in the 0.60s. For the digit span, which is a speeded test and therefore not suitable for split-half studies, equivalent forms reliabilities are also high. Validity studies tend to yield correlations in the 0.40s and 0.50s and run as high as the 0.70s and 0.80s in relation to other intelligence tests.

Some typical clinical interpretations of personality correlates of WAIS responding appeared in a recent survey on interpreting psychological test data (Gilbert, 1978, 1980) and included the following samples of performance: low arithmetic scores can be found among antisocial personalities, psychotic depressives, and simple schizophrenics; a decrement in block-design scores can be found among depressives; "I don't know" responses can reflect self-deprecating attitudes; the inability to say digits backwards may be an index of chronic undifferentiated schizophrenia; and evasiveness may be a sign of paranoid tendencies. These interpretations, as well as interpretations of the patterns of subtest scores as indices of personality disturbance, are based completely on clinical experience rather than on systematic studies, and therefore must await further documentation before they can be accepted.

Wechsler's tests made an important contribution to the concept and popular use of the deviation IQ, a contribution that, as we noted earlier, was adopted by Terman and Merrill in 1960.

There is some documented evidence, however, that many kinds of emotional factors interfere with children's intellectual functioning on the WISC (see Quay, 1972; Sattler, 1974). For example, one investigator (Woody, 1968) compared the WISC IQs of a group of children with problem behaviors (ages eight to thirteen) with those of a group of well-behaved children of the same age and found that the former's average IQ was 98, versus 110 for the well-behaved children. Although the WISC appears to be a reliable and consistent instrument, its validity for predicting emotional disturbance, like that of the Stanford-Binet, has not yet been documented (McHugh, 1963; Petrie, 1962; Schoonover & Hertel, 1970; Tigay & Kempler, 1971). In this regard, Sattler concluded, "The WISC, like the Stanford-Binet, does not provide any systematic patterns that can distinguish emotionally disturbed children from normal children or from children with other forms of psychopathology" (1974, p. 344).

## Group Tests of Intelligence

Because of the apparent success of tests administered to individuals, tests that could be administered to groups were developed. Not only could these tests be given to large numbers of people simultaneously, and hence save time and personnel, but they also could be given by teachers or others who had not been trained in the elaborate techniques required for the Binet and Wechsler testing. The major reason for developing group intelligence tests came about as a result of World War I. There was a need to select both military recruits with intelligence above a certain minimum level of functioning, and officer candidates with greater than average intelligence.

These group intelligence tests were patterned after existing group achievement examinations in that they were composed of large numbers of short items requiring multiple choice answers, the respondent having to underline or otherwise indicate the correct choice. Although these group tests were less varied than the Binet and Wechsler tests—mainly because of the more restricted paper-and-pencil format of group testing—they nonetheless covered many of the same intellectual processes, including vocabulary, analogies, classification, abstract reasoning, everyday information, and comprehension items, as well as pictorial materials and figures and shapes.

Around 1915, Arthur S. Otis (in the United States) and Cyril Burt (in England) were already experimenting with group intelligence testing so that, when the United States entered World War I in 1917, psychologists were able to use their experience in developing intelligence tests for recruits. In 1917, the American Psychological Association appointed a committee on tests, chaired by Robert M. Yerkes (1921), and this committee drew up two group intelligence tests: the Army Alpha Examination, which was administered to more than 1.5 million servicemen and consisted of eight parts, mostly involving verbal and number content; and the Army Beta Examination, which was designed for non-English speakers and illiterates and consisted of a set of performance or nonverbal tests. The Army Alpha covered such areas as following directions, arithmetic, practical judgment, synonyms-antonyms, disarranged sentences, number-series completion, analogies, and information. The Beta included mazes, cube analyses, digit symbols, picture completion, and geometrical construction.

Group intelligence tests have been said (Tyler & Walsh, 1979) to be more limited in their focus and more specific in their content than individual tests are. This is because such tests as the Binet or Wechsler are designed to measure some holistic concept like general intelligence, whereas group tests are geared to assess readiness for college admission, employment screening, or a job assignment in industry or the military. If the group tests are specific, they are better at predicting criterion measures, though not only group tests have this feature.

Other features of group intelligence tests worth noting are that they require less from the tester than individual tests do and permit objective scoring; and because of these features, group tests usually provide more and better-established normative data. But compared with individual tests, group tests' disadvantages are the inflexibility of the printed format and the limited relationship between examiner and examinee, which does not allow the examiner to sample how respondents cope with particular tasks.

The difference between the group intelligence test scores of emotionally disturbed children and the individual intelligence test scores of the same samples, according to Kessler (1966), was that the group test scores were higher because the disturbed children were less resistant in the group situation than in the individual test setting. This finding applied mainly to children with obsessional traits, and the studies on which it was based compared Stanford-Binet test scores, group intelligence test scores, and school grades.

Willis (1970), however, found just the opposite to be true in comparisons between the WISC and the Lorge-Thorndike Intelligence Test (see Thorndike & Hagen, 1969). Emotionally disturbed children between eight and fifteen years of age were found to obtain a mean IQ fifteen points higher (IQ = 108) on the WISC's verbal scale than on the Thorndike test's verbal section (IQ = 93). (The Thorndike test is a group intelligence test with three parts: nonreading tests for the primary grades, verbal tests for grades 4 through 13, and nonverbal tests for grades 4 through 13.) The emotionally disturbed children's relatively higher scores on the individual tests were attributed to the fact that the examiner was better able to hold the children's attention in this setting than he was in the group situation.

## Minority Group Testing

In the last decade, intelligence testing as it has been known for the past sixty years has come under severe criticism by psychologists who, in 1968 at the convention of the Black Psychological Association, called for a moratorium on the use of psychological and educational tests for disadvantaged students. Others have documented intelligence testing's history of systematic discrimination against blacks (Guthrie, 1976) and have asserted that it has been used as a political and social tool against most minorities who are out of the mainstream of American culture (Kamin, 1973, 1974).

The call for the moratorium on testing was articulated especially forcefully by Robert L. Williams of Washington University, who claimed that the current practices in intelligence testing were harmful to the mental well-being of black children (Williams, 1971). In response to the cultural discrimination inflicted by the existing, "made-for-whites-only" intelligence tests, Williams and Associates, Inc., of St. Louis, Missouri, devised an intelligence test specifically for American blacks. Williams (1972) called this test the Black Intelligence Test for Cultural Homogeneity (BITCH) and made no claims about its lack of cultural bias. Rather, he asserted that because test items of existing intelligence tests were in standard English, they penalized the black child; he therefore invented a test that was "culture specific" in that it reflected the life and cultural experiences of blacks living in this country.

Items from the BITCH are presented in Table 9–4, and it can be readily seen that they call for definitions of terms that are strange to people not familiar with black American life. Through the use of his "dialect fair" test, as he also calls it (1972), Williams demonstrated some interesting intelligence-testing differences between white and black children. Specifically, he showed that on the BITCH there were disparate mean differences between black and white students (high school and college), with blacks earning significantly higher scores than whites did. These differences, which were reliable and substantial, and his examination of the items seem to confirm Williams's belief that his test has the "advantage of dealing with content material which is familiar to the Black adolescent and adult. This means that he already has stored away mental images of the material so that he does not have to deal with the foreign or unfamiliar aspects of these materials. Thus a combination of dialect specific and culture specific tests would certainly enhance the possibility of measuring accurately what is inside the Black person's head" (1972, p. 5).

Unfortunately, however, although Williams intended the BITCH to be used as a measure of intelligence and although its items seem to be related to black American life, the BITCH has not yet been shown to predict academic success (see Humphreys's *Addendum*, 1975, pp. 95–96); nor has the BITCH yet been found to be valid as a selection device for any socially important purpose. This last conclusion is based on a study by Matarazzo and Wiens (1977), who reported that among black and white police-force applicants, there were low correlations between the BITCH and several WAIS subtest and full test IQ measures. These investigators also found that the BITCH test failed to discriminate

## BOX 9-3

## The Fallacies of Nature and Nurture in Testing

Interracial comparisons of intellectual ability have been the long-standing subject of national and international attention. In the United States, especially, there is ample documentation of the comparative performance of whites and blacks on intelligence tests and of the relatively poorer test standing of blacks. Theories espousing a racist or an egalitarian viewpoint on the question of racial differences have been advanced on the belief in the inherent intellectual superiority of whites, on the one hand, and in the cultural disadvantage of blacks, on the other. However, according to Ronald Samuda, "both the hereditarian and environmentalist position seem to rest on certain fallacies" (Samuda, 1975, pp. 50-62).

On the hereditarian side, Samuda contends that before any inference of racial differences in test performance can be made, one must first define "race" and then demonstrate that black Americans constitute a racial group distinct and separate from that of whites. Such a distinction is impossible because "in the gene pool of the 'Negro,' or 'colored man,' of the past and the black American of today are the genes of two of the major races, African and Caucasian. (Conversely, the white American must also claim some Negro ancestry, though quantitatively less.)" Thus, continues Samuda, "if the black American cannot be said to belong truly to the Negro race, it seems incongruous to call any black having the remotest trace of Negro ancestry black and to proceed to make 'racial' comparisons in test performances, as though white and black subjects belonged to scientifically determined, separate and distinct races" (Samuda, 1975, pp. 52-53).

It is equally fallacious, according to Samuda, to attempt to control adequately certain environmental, cultural, and sociopsychological variables that would clearly validate the relative intellectual superiority or inferiority of one group or the other. Procedures that attempt to equate the two racial groups in terms of nurture are doomed to failure because there is a scarcity of adequate instruments for measuring environments; in proportion to whites, blacks are grossly underrepresented in the professional and other white-collar occupations; blacks, especially in the South, have had a long history of limited educational opportunities; and although both blacks and whites have lived as compatriots for over 300 years, they do not, however, share in the same culture. Moreover, even in a hypothetical case in which all other variables could be controlled, writes Samuda, "the psychological effects of prolonged membership in a lower caste would still corrupt and hence nullify any comparisons between minority and majority groups" (Samuda, 1975, p. 58).

**Table 9-4** The BITCH Test (Black Intelligence Test of Cultural Homogeneity).

Name _____ Sex _____ Date _____

Age _____ Grade _____

DIRECTIONS: Below are some words, terms, and expressions taken from the Black experience. Select the correct answers and put a check (√) mark in the space provided on the right of the test sheet. Remember, we want the correct definition as Black People use the words and expressions. There is no time limit. Twenty to thirty minutes should be sufficient time to complete the test.
GO AHEAD.

|     |     |
| --- | --- |

1. *Alley Apple*                                      A   B   C   D
   (a) Brick                   (c) Dog
   (b) Piece of fruit       (d) Horse          1. ___ ___ ___ ___
2. *Black Draught*
   (a) Winter's cold wind  (c) Black soldier
   (b) Laxative           (d) Dark beer     2. ___ ___ ___ ___
3. *Blood*
   (a) A vampire         (c) An injured person
   (b) A dependent individual (d) A brother of color  3. ___ ___ ___ ___
4. *Boogie Jugie*
   (a) tired                (c) old
   (b) worthless         (d) well put together  4. ___ ___ ___ ___
5. *Boot* refers to a:
   (a) Cotton farmer     (c) Indian
   (b) Black              (d) Vietnamese citizen 5. ___ ___ ___ ___

SOURCE: *The Black intelligence test of cultural homogeneity* (B.I.T.C.H.) © 1972 by Robert L. Williams, Ph.D., 6372 Delmar Blvd., St. Louis, Missouri 63130. Reprinted by permission.

among black examinees because it did not yield a large enough range of scores. For example, among the blacks tested in the police selection program, the scores ranged from 79 to 91, a difference of only twelve points on a one hundred–item test. Clearly, if the BITCH is to be taken seriously as a useful and reliable measure of cognitive functioning, it must demonstrate that it can predict success in a variety of extratest situations.

Besides developing the BITCH, Williams helped draft six grievances regarding the testing of black children, and the Black Psychological Association charged that these tests

1. label black children as uneducable,
2. place black children in special classes,

# 330   Personality and Psychological Assessment

3. lead to inferior education,
4. assign black children to lower education tracks than whites are assigned to,
5. deny black children higher educational opportunities, and
6. destroy the positive intellectual growth and development of black children.

Leon Kamin, the author of *The Science and Politics of IQ* (1973, 1974), took a broader view than Williams did and argued that the intelligence-testing movement in the United States contributed to and supported the social climate and political legislation prevalent during World War I and thereafter. This view was not shared by Franz Samelson (1975), a philosopher and social science historian, who did not refute Kamin's facts but questioned the importance of psychological testing in shaping the social and political climates.

Leon Kamin traced this social history and the impact of testing on legislation to such notable early American testers as Lewis Terman (1916), who wrote the following about the performance of Indian and Mexican-American children: "Their dullness seems to be racial or at

---

**BOX 9-4**

### Items from R. B. Cattell's Culture Fair Intelligence Test

Most attempts to develop culture-free tests of intelligence have used group tests. Presumably, culture-free tests are designed to measure the intelligence of those not brought up in the average American milieu. Such tests achieve their aims by using items that tap elements common to, or shared by, many cultures. Examples of culture-free items are shown in the figure below, which was taken from the Culture Fair Intelligence Test (Cattell, 1950) developed at the Institute for Personality and Ability Testing (IPAT). On this particular test, which is available for three sample levels (Scale 1: ages four to eight and feebleminded adults, Scale 2: ages eight to twelve, Scale 3: high school to superior adults), some items must be administered individually (Scale 1), but most can be administered either individually or by the group-testing method. Generally, correlations between the IPAT-type and the Binet-type culture-free tests are in the 0.50s, and in the 0.60s and 0.70s with other group intelligence tests.

Below are examples of four types of tasks presented by the Cattell Culture Fair Intelligence Test (a measure of $g$): Series, classifications, matrices, directions.

**Source:** Copyright © 1950, 1959, 1963, Institute for Personality and Ability Testing, Inc., Champaign, Illinois. Reproduced by permission of the copyright owner

*(continued)*

# Maximum Performance Assessment

**BOX 9-4** *(Continued)*

### 1. Series

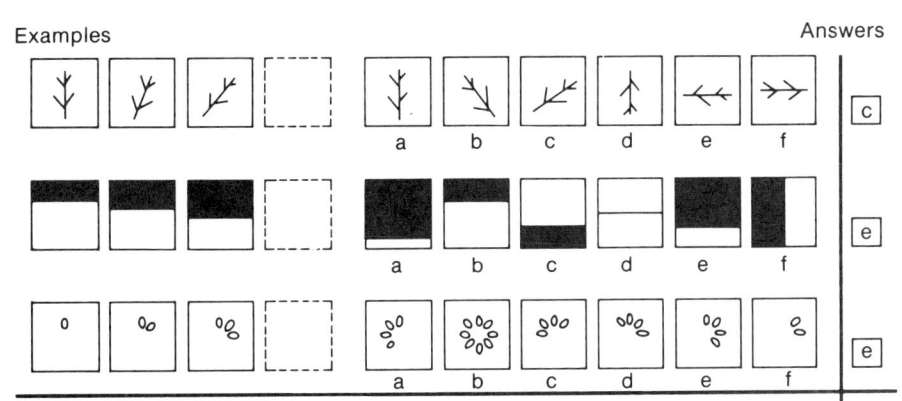

Examples                                                               Answers

Row 1 answer: c
Row 2 answer: e
Row 3 answer: e

Directions: On the left hand side of the page are 3 boxes with figures in them. Notice how the figure (1st row) leans to the right more and more as we go along the row of three boxes. Choose from the six boxes at the right which should go into the dotted space.

### 2. Classifications

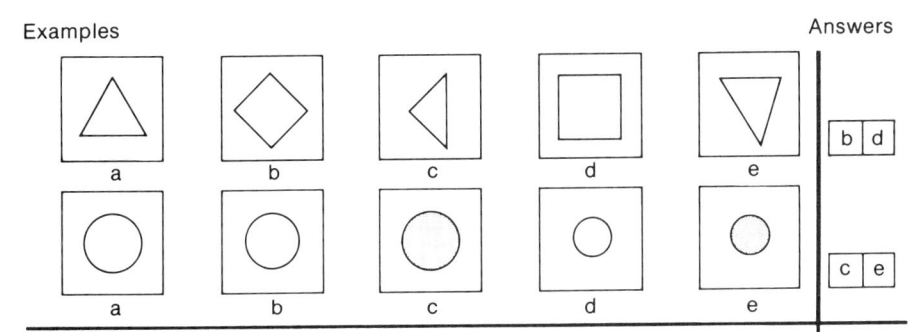

Examples                                                               Answers

Row 1 answers: b, d
Row 2 answers: c, e

Directions: There are 3 squares which are alike in some way, but the other two squares are different from these. Choose the *two* squares which are different in some way from the others.

*(continued)*

**332** Personality and Psychological Assessment

**BOX 9-4** *(Continued)*

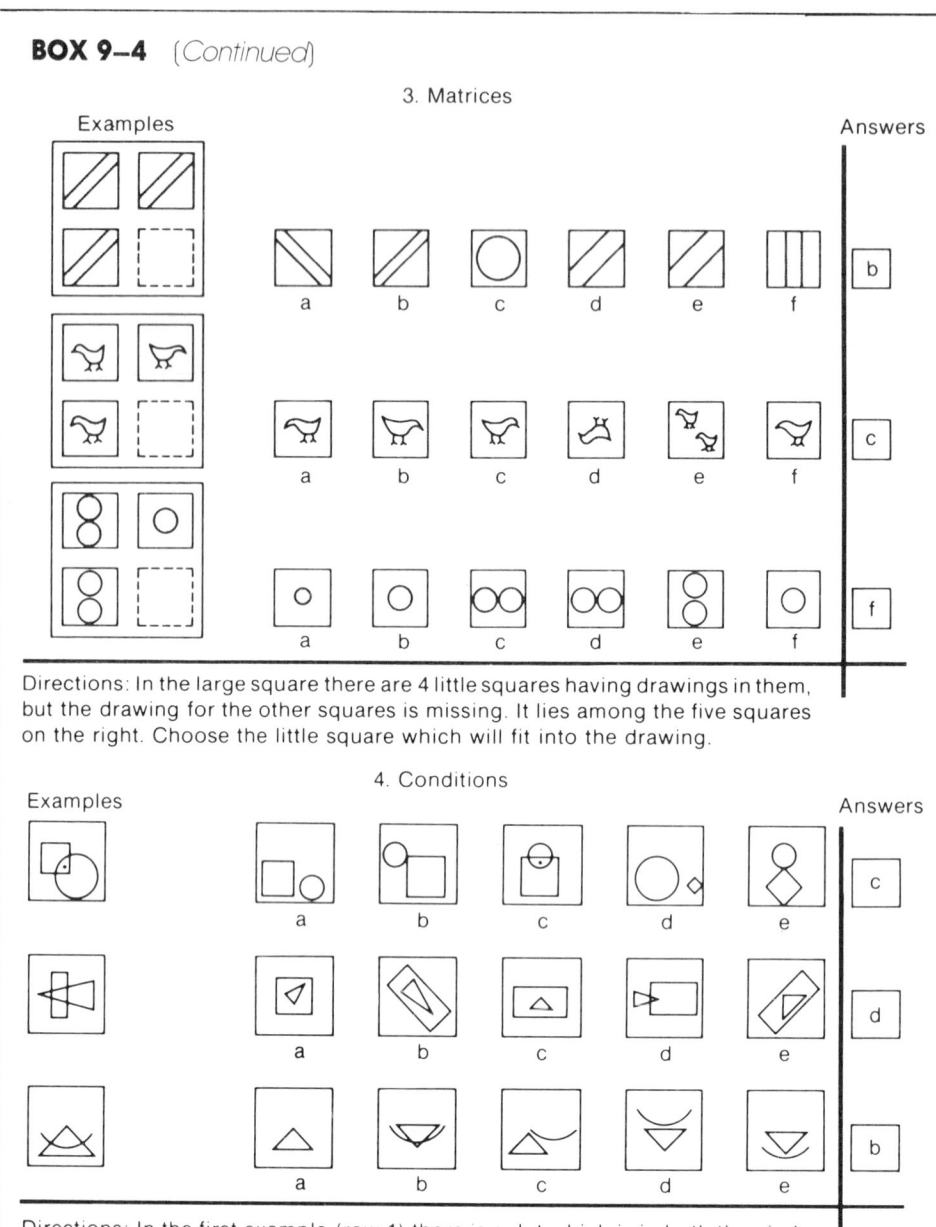

### 3. Matrices

Examples | | Answers

(matrix puzzle rows with answers: b, c, f)

Directions: In the large square there are 4 little squares having drawings in them, but the drawing for the other squares is missing. It lies among the five squares on the right. Choose the little square which will fit into the drawing.

### 4. Conditions

Examples | | Answers

(condition puzzle rows with answers: c, d, b)

Directions: In the first example (row 1) there is a dot which is in both the circle and the square. Now look over in the answer section and see if you can find a drawing there where you can put one dot which will be in both the circle and the square. Row 2: Here the dot is inside the triangle but outside the rectangle. In the answer section there is just one figure where you can place a dot in the triangle and not get it in the rectangle. Row 3: The dot is in the triangle and above the curved line, etc.

least inherent in the family stocks from which they come. The fact that one meets this type with such extraordinary frequency among Indians, Mexicans, and negroes suggests quite forcibly that the whole question of racial differences in mental traits will have to be taken up anew ... there will be discovered enormously significant racial differences ... which cannot be wiped out by any scheme of mental culture" (1973, pp. 1–2). Kamin then continued his social history by describing how in 1913, 1917, and 1920 Henry H. Goddard, another American testing pioneer, applied mental tests to shape the immigration policies of this country. Goddard (1913) reported that based upon his examination of the "great mass of average immigrants," 83 percent of the Jews, 80 percent of the Hungarians, 79 percent of the Italians, and 87 percent of the Russians were "feeble-minded." Goddard (1917) subsequently found that the use of mental tests for the detection of feebleminded aliens "had vastly increased the number of aliens deported" (Kamin, 1973, p. 3).

Kamin also implicated such other early testing notables as Robert M. Yerkes (1923) and Carl Brigham (1923) and argued that as a result of these and other similar reports, "the Congress passed in 1924 a law not only restricting the total *number* of immigrants, but also assigning 'national origin quotas'" (1973, p. 6). But Kamin used these sociopolitical facts only as background material. The theme of his argument was that there is little empirical evidence to substantiate the consensus view of many early as well as contemporary psychometricians that intelligence has a large hereditary component. To buttress his argument, the details of which are beyond the scope of this chapter, Kamin (1977, 1978) questioned the authenticity of Cyril Burt's identical twins studies (Burt, 1943, 1958, 1966) and adoption studies (Freeman et al., 1928; and also see Kamin, 1978; Munsinger, 1975, 1978). These studies were used extensively by Arthur Jensen in both his famous essay (1969) and his more recent book (1980), which set the stage for the heritability controversy. Kamin's suspicion of the authenticity of Cyril Burt's data was well founded. L. S. Hearnshaw, in a biography of *Cyril Burt, Psychologist*, (1979) provided compelling evidence that after 1950 Burt reported fraudulent twins studies and fabricated school surveys. The net effect of this fraud is that Burt's data on the heritability of intelligence are, to quote P. E. Vernon, "worthless apart from their contributions to genetical-statistical methodology" (1979, p. ix; also see Cronbach, 1979; Hawkes, 1979 for statements on Burt's scientific fraud).

But if the new tests fall short of the standards of psychometric excellence and if the existing tests discriminate unfairly, it is nevertheless important to ask what the alternatives to intelligence testing are. Proposals to eliminate intelligence testing do not usually consider

## BOX 9-5

### Jensenism

That there are measured IQ differences between black and white children of both sexes in America has, with some notable exceptions (Jones, 1972, p. 61), been repeatedly demonstrated by psychologists. But there is considerable controversy about whether these differences, which tend to be about ten to twenty points on the average in favor of white children, are due to environmental or hereditary determinants.

The central figure in this controversy is Arthur Jensen, a University of California (Berkeley) educational psychologist who, to support his heredity argument, invokes the concept of *heritability*. This is a technical term that he borrowed from quantitative genetics and that refers to the proportion of a trait that can be attributed to genetic factors. Using this concept, Jensen concludes that heredity accounts for up to 80 percent of the obtained IQ differences. His main thesis was contained in a lengthy article, "How Can We Boost IQ and Scholastic Achievement?" (Jensen, 1969), which appeared in the prestigious *Harvard Educational Review*. Its appearance, which stirred a considerable furor among psychologists and in the popular press, led one journalist (Edson, 1969, p. 10) to coin the term "jensenism," which he defined as a noun, describing "the theory that IQ is largely determined by genes."

Later, Jensen (1973) defended the heritability argument by placing the burden of the proof on the shoulders of the environmentalists. Thus he stated, "Of course, they [environmental causes] may be *possible* explanations of the IQ difference, but that does not necessarily make them the *most probable*. . . . I am not saying that they have been proven 100 percent wrong, only that they do not account for all of the black IQ deficit" (Jensen, 1973, p. 81).

Jensen's arguments for the genetic hypothesis consist mainly of counterproposals to the cultural and environmental explanations. Thus, in answer to the argument that blacks do less well than whites on culture-biased tests because blacks do not know this culture, he contends that studies indicate that Arctic Eskimos, Orientals and Mexican- and Native Americans do as well on IQ tests as white Anglos. He also discounts the effects of the tester's race as an influence lowering black children's scores, by pointing to a study of his own in which 9000 black and white children were administered a number of "standard mental tests" by both black and white examiners. No systematic differences could be attributed to the race of the examiner. All in all Jensen (1973, p. 80) believes that genetic factors have been ignored because of "fear and abhorrence of racism" and because research into the possible genetic influence has been considered "academically and socially taboo."

Jensen's critics are far more sophisticated than he cares to admit. For example, the noted geneticist Theodosius Dobzhansky (1973, p. 98) contends that Jensen's use of the term heritability is faulty in that its application to the individual case is spurious. Moreover he

*(continued)*

## BOX 9-5 (Continued)

notes that the "same gene constellation can result in a higher or lower score in different circumstances. Genes determine the intelligence (or stature or weight) of a person only in his particular environment. The trait that actually develops is conditioned by the interplay of the genes with the environment."

But perhaps even more convincing evidence of the fallacy of Jensen's heritability hypothesis can be found in a study by Sandra Scarr-Salapatek (1975), who demonstrated that different race and class IQ averages are less genetically determined than individual variations in IQ. Her study was conducted among 1521 pairs of twins attending public schools in Philadelphia. She compared test scores across races and socioeconomic levels and found that individual genetic differences show up more in persons who mature in favorable surroundings, but remain hidden or unused in individuals from adverse environments. Therefore, she concludes, both the percentage of genetic variance and the mean scores are very much influenced by the rearing condition of the population.

R. C. Lewontin (1976), a population geneticist, has criticized Jensen for equating "inherited" with "unchangeable," as well as incorrectly interpreting in several other respects the relationship among gene, environment, and organism. However, the most damaging objections to the biological determinist position grew out of an address to the American Psychological Association in 1973 in which psychologist Leon Kamin argued convincingly that Sir Cyril Burt, whose research supplied much of the "factual" basis for the genetic-determination-of-IQ hypothesis, had faked his data. In England Ann Clarke, a psychologist at Hull University, and her husband, Professor Alan Clarke, followed Kamin's lead and came up with additional evidence that Burt's data points had never existed outside his own mind. The crowning blow came when Oliver Gillie, the London *Sunday Times* medical correspondent, tried to locate two of Burt's collaborators, Margaret Howard and J. Conway, who should have been able to shed some light on the controversy. Gillie found that no one at University College (London) had any recollection of either of the two researchers, nor was there any official record that they had ever existed. Jensen himself first noted the difficulties with Burt's data, and has now conceded that Burt's data cannot be relied upon, but the controversy continues (see also Hearnshaw's 1979 biography of C. Burt).

**Source:** Kleinmuntz, B. *Essentials of abnormal psychology* (2nd ed.). New York: Harper & Row, 1980, pp. 60-61.

---

alternatives. The Committee on Educational Tests, established by the American Psychological Association in response to the call for a moratorium on testing, however, did suggest several other possibilities. Admittedly, most of these alternatives are not satisfactory. For example, it proposed using lotteries, which are random selections and assignments to categories. This alternative is unsatisfactory because "in addition to giving up any efficiencies, including remediation for which selection is usually exercised, it eliminates all 'feedback' from the selection process to prospective clients . . ." (Cleary et al., 1975, p. 32).

Another alternative listed by the committee was to use categorical selection, which is quotas or special treatment based on ethnic or socioeconomic grouping. This method does not eliminate the need for selection within categories and therefore does not necessarily eliminate testing if, as is usual, there are more applicants within categories than there are spaces in the programs or institutions in question.

There was also the proposal to eliminate formal tests from the prediction or selection process by basing decisions on unstructured interviews, written applications in the form of essays on various topics, letters of recommendation, or other subjective evaluations. But interviewing, and related methods of direct interaction between the examinee and the appraiser—as readers of this book should now be well aware—have been shown to be inadequate for most selection purposes (see Kelly & Fiske, 1951; Sines, L. K., 1959), and they have not fared well in comparison to more statistical approaches (Meehl, 1954, 1973). Thus they cannot be regarded as effective substitutes for tests. Cleary and her associates stated:

> Conceivably, future research may yield some improvement in interview effectiveness, but the present judgment must be that interviews are not effective alternatives to tests as predictors. Among other weaknesses of the interview is the fact that it is especially susceptible to biases of all sorts, including racial and religious bias. (1975, p. 34)

Eliminating intelligence and other ability tests has certain other hazards as well. For example, in situations other than screening, such as career and vocational counseling, tests can help discover abilities in children and adults that parents or others do not readily detect. Moreover, tests can indicate areas that need to be strengthened by further training or education. These are uses of tests that if stopped, according to black psychologist Kenneth B. Clark, would leave "black children . . . abandoned educationally even more than they are now" (1980, p. 104).

Therefore, rather than proposing to eliminate intelligence tests, some psychologists have turned to examining more closely the factors that go into intelligence tests. Other psychologists have elected to redefine the concept of intelligence. As an example of the first option, consider the work of John B. Carroll (1976), who observed that "traditional" intelligence testing can be divided into several cognitive and social tasks, especially cognitive tasks. He held that all of these cognitive tasks are related to what is contained in "intelligence tests" and that they have substantial correlations with measures of school success. Carroll theorized about some of the cognitive control factors probably used in arriving at responses on some standard intelligence tests. These factors include *spatial scanning*, or using different strategies to solve certain test problems; *memory span*, or retrieving information from short-term memory in order to solve task problems; *word fluency*, or drawing on long-term memory storage in order to respond to the meanings or concepts of words; *number facility*, or retrieving from long-term memory the appropriate numbers or operations associated with problem solution; and *general reasoning*, or retrieving from memory precise types of concepts in order to apply and relate these to the problems at hand. Admittedly, these are speculative concepts of cognitive controls currently under experimental investigation, but the hope is that the understanding gained by isolating these underlying factors will be paralleled by a comparable success in constructing better intelligence tests.

Attempts to redefine intelligence have consisted of a search for alternative concepts, preferably ones more broadly based than what is implied by the current concept. For example, Anderson and Messick (1974) and Mussen and his associates (1979) wrote about assessing competence rather than intelligence. They viewed competence as the broader concept of the two in that it includes cognitive functioning as well as realistic self-appraisal, social adeptness, self-reliance, and responsibility. Sundberg and his associates defined competence even more broadly as "personal characteristics (knowledge, skill, and attitudes) which lead to achievements having adaptive payoffs in significant environments" (Sundberg et al., 1978, p. 196). Competence is not a new concept. It has its roots in the earlier work of Robert White (1959), who described it as effectance motivation, or the motivation to explore and to master. But its recent rise is more closely related than its earlier use to the search for a concept to replace intelligence.

The attempt to redefine intelligence has led to the rediscovery of another time-honored term: *creativity*. Both Francis Galton (1869/1914, 1875) and William James (1890) were interested in creativity almost a century ago when they studied great men of science, and they distinguished between creative reasoning (Galton) and noncreative reasoning (James). In its newer form, the study of creativity has been sparked by the writings of J. P. Guilford (1950, 1959b, 1967), whose article on the *Structure of Intellect* (1967) distinguished between convergent and divergent thinking. Guilford considered only divergent thinking to be creative in that it requires novel, rather than just correct, responses to situations. One psychologist, Paul Torrance (1962, 1966), who was clearly influenced by Guilford's work, devised several tests of creativity. Still other investigators (Goldstein & Blackman, 1978; Shouksmith, 1973; Witkin & Goodenough, 1981) devised "cognitive style" intelligence tests, labeled according to their concepts of *field dependence* and *field independence*.

Finally, regardless of whether we label the new concepts intelligence, competence, creativity, cognitive style, or, as in the next sections, achievement, stability, and aptitude, it is probably true that as some writers have observed (Thorndike & Hagen, 1969, pp. 376–377), the tests measuring these concepts must have some significant correlation with the practical world. So far intelligence tests have had only modest success on this count. Paradoxically, when any of these tests do prove to be reliable and valid measures of their newly labeled constructs, they raise, as Bouchard pointed out, "all the same kinds of questions now raised about IQ testing" (1980).

## Achievement, Ability, and Aptitude Testing

Just as intelligence is a facet of personality in that performing well or poorly on an intelligence test influences one's self-concept and self-esteem, achievement, ability, and aptitude test performances also are important to a person's sense of self. To score high on an achievement test usually means that one can learn or master a subject matter; to score high on an abilities test means that one has the skills, either inherent or learned, to accomplish something; and to score high on an aptitude test, even after extensive practicing and coaching (e.g., as on the Scholastic Aptitude Test [SAT]), usually forecasts that one can learn certain subject matters or acquire certain skills.

To define these terms more specifically, *achievement* is learned information or skills following formal courses or training programs; *ability* is the available information or skill to answer certain questions or to solve certain problems; and *aptitude* is the natural talent and perhaps potential ability either to perform in a variety of situations or to grasp concepts. Aptitude seems to be a "readiness for learning" (Thorndike & Hagen, 1969, p. 644), which is precisely what intelligence tests should be measuring, but often do not. Instead, intelligence test items seem to tap a mix of all three of these constructs.

The fact that intelligence tests measure acquired skills rather than innate or potential abilities has been found objectionable by many prominent psychologists (see Vernon, 1979, pp. 21–23), who criticize this mix in intelligence tests because it means that those from deprived environments are unlikely to have been exposed to some of the information the test requires. The following is a list of items that require learned information and that are similar to those appearing on intelligence tests:

1. Name four poets who were famous in their time.
2. What is astronomy?
3. Who wrote *As You Like It*?
4. How are an aviary and sanctuary alike?
5. What is the color of a ripe banana?

Some of these items may not predict success in particular environments, or they may predict success but reflect natural talent or probably performance. But they may also depend on the acquisition of specific knowledge not available in many environments. Similar objections to the confusion among intelligence, achievement, abilities, and aptitude test items have been raised by others also (see Daniels, 1976; Fine, 1975; Kagan, 1974). The point is that intelligence tests should not measure past instruction but, rather, should indicate scholastic aptitude.

But although there is a lack of agreement on the distinctions among test items as they relate to intelligence testing, there is a consensus on what dimensions achievement, ability, and aptitude tests generally measure. We now examine some of these dimensions.

## Achievement Testing

Achievement testing, or the measurement of learning outcomes (see Hopkins & Stanley, 1981, and Payne, D. A., 1974, for extensive coverage of this topic), yields data on the level and breadth of a person's attainment. These tests usually contain items that represent the domain and subject matter taught in a course or program. They usually examine the knowledge or principles acquired, as well as the skill to apply these in new situations. Achievement tests may be individually or group administered, and they may be subjectively or objectively scored. The most common types of achievement tests are group-administered objective tests, often given in school settings.

The *Eighth Mental Measurements Yearbook* (Buros, 1978) listed 37 main types of general achievement batteries and about 350 specific fields of study and other miscellaneous achievement tests. Most achievement tests, however, are tailored to a specific subject and its coverage as taught by a particular teacher. Some of the more famous tests of achievement are the following, which measure general rather than specific course attainments: American School Achievement Tests, Iowa Tests of Basic Skills, Stanford Achievement Test, Tests of Adult Basic Education, Sequential Tests of Educational Progress, Wide Range Achievement Test, and Peabody Individual Achievement Test. These cover somewhat broader domains than the following, more specialized measures: Mathematics, Modern Geometry Tests, Bookkeeping Test, ACT Proficiency Examination in Health, and Sex Knowledge Test. And these, in turn, are somewhat broader than the classroom tests that measure the progress and outcome of specific courses.

An important distinction between achievement and other tests is that achievement tests, and to a somewhat lesser degree, ability tests directly sample the behavior in question; personality inventories, attitude and value questionnaires, interest tests, and many others indirectly sample their constructs. For example, in personality tests one samples verbal behavior presumed to characterize particular diagnostic groups. In achievement testing one samples the domain under investigation. Thus personality test items are farther removed than achievement test items are from the domain of interest. Of course the domain of interest must be sampled representatively in achievement testing, for to do otherwise would yield scores of questionable relevance, no matter how direct the sampling.

Achievement tests can be divided into three types, according to one source (Payne, D. A., 1974, p. 310): The *survey battery*, which contains various levels of individual subject matter tests; the *specific subject or area test*, which is self-explanatory; and the *diagnostic* test, which contains subareas of a subject matter and is designed to help determine someone's strengths and weaknesses in particular areas. The first is the staple of most schools' testing programs and provides important evaluative information about the effectiveness of training programs and courses. The content of a battery will vary according to the depth and breadth of coverage the tester needs to evaluate. Such batteries are the more general or broader-gauged measures mentioned earlier as the thirty-seven test areas listed in the *Eighth Mental Measurements Yearbook* (Buros, 1978, pp. 1–125). One advantage of the survey battery over a series of individual subject matter tests from different publishers is its simultaneous standardization and normatization of all subtests. Hence, standard administration and scoring procedures are ensured, and normative data for a large population are made available during the original test construction. Of course, the test user will still have to develop updated and local norms for his or her particular needs.

Specific subject tests on special topics differ mainly from the foregoing in that they cover individual topics in greater depth. This permits subdividing the general topics into subtopics, and then further subdividing these, and so on. Thus, a test on finite mathematics, for example, might contain subtests on connectives, logic, sets, probability theory, and so on; and these subtests might be broken down still further, according to what needs to be tested. Most of these tests are written by teachers and all too often do not meet minimal psychometric standards. Many teachers fail to collect norms, to obtain item analyses, or to conduct reliability and validity studies. Hence the measures they use are of questionable worth.

Diagnostic tests share many of the features and psychometric qualities of specific subject tests because they also are usually constructed by course instructors or committees assigned to evaluate instructional outcomes. Their main purpose, as we indicated above, is to detect strengths that can be built upon and weaknesses that can be remedied. D. A. Payne (1974, p. 334) listed four important features of these tests: (1) they should be tied to specific curricular objectives and stipulated learning outcomes; (2) they must include items that directly measure and analyze specific functions or operations of a subject matter; (3) they should yield information about errors and their possible correlation; and (4) they should cover reasonably detailed and integrated learning sequences.

**Criterion-Referenced Achievement Tests:** The criterion-referenced achievement tests, first popularized by Robert Glaser (1963), compare one's score with an established performance standard or criterion rather than with a reference or normative group. The idea of obtaining scores that measure one's performance according to criteria is not new; but a rekindled interest in it at the present time is due to the advent of *mastery learning*, a by-product of behavioral approaches, in which students learn at their own pace, sometimes with the help of intermediate incentives or reinforcements. This form of learning also received much attention in the 1960s and 1970s as a result of the revived interest in self-defined and student-tailored tests and the move away from competitiveness. Currently, the criterion-referenced test movement, according to one source (Hopkins & Stanley, 1981, p. 183), is in part a reaction to the misuse of classical test theory, especially reliability theory, which, as we indicated earlier in the book (chapter three), relies too heavily in its inferences about individuals on sample-based statistics. But it is interesting to note in this regard that often *prior* normative information is used in establishing the mastery level criterion (Popham, 1978), "a practice which blurs the distinction between normative and criterion-referenced testing but which helps avoid unrealistically high or low criteria" (Weiss & Davison, 1981, pp. 635–636).

The standards of performance on criterion-referenced tests, then, are often the same as those for norm-referenced tests except that their progress can be more closely monitored. Such monitoring is necessary because in criterion-referenced testing, initial performance measures depend on plotting from this starting point any changes and improvements in the expected direction. On the other hand, it is not possible to differentiate among the items on the two types of tests merely by inspecting them; the difference is only in the way their scores are obtained and interpreted. On criterion-referenced tests these scores are obtained by repeated testing and are interpreted by *progress made*; in norm-referenced testing the scores are obtained by one testing and are interpreted by comparison with a norm group. D. A. Payne referred to this difference as two ends of a continuum defined by "Interpretation Tied to Specific Objectives" at the mastery pole and by "Interpretation Tied to Relative Performance" at the other pole (1974, p. 290). Some other differences are listed in Table 9–5.

## Ability Testing

Since an ability is the available skill or power to perform at any given moment or in a given situation, it is a construct that lies somewhere between achievement and aptitude. A test score on an abilities test may represent a learned capability or an inherent talent; it is difficult to know which. Sometimes a factor analytic study helps define the specific abilities required in a particular activity, and this in turn may help differentiate between learned and inherent talents. In one such study, Berger, Guilford, and Christensen (1957) classified the abilities necessary in "planning." Among the twenty-five or so factors discovered, the following seem to have been a part: comprehension, numerical facility, visualization, general reasoning, judgment, psychomotor speed and coordination, visual memory, adaptive flexibility, and mathematical background. Clearly, the last of these is learned; the remainder may not have been. In an earlier factor analytic study, Thurstone (1944) isolated the three abilities most important to performing in a variety of perceptual tasks. They again were a mix of learned and natural abilities: reaction time, capacity to manipulate two configurations simultaneously or in succession, and speed of perception.

Most abilities tests are developed by means of factor analysis. There are four major types of abilities tests: (1) differential, (2) component, (3) analogous, and (4) work sample. The first of these is designed to assess a host of separate skills and usually consists of a battery of tests, each designed to measure a separate skill. These tests are accompanied by profile sheets on which the examiner can plot the examinee's score for his or her measured abilities in comparison with those of certain reference groups. The profile sheet thus permits both interindividual and intraindividual comparisons of competence in given tasks. The *component* ability test is a measure of only one ability rather than many, and it can easily become a part of a larger battery.

The formats of the *analogous* and *work sample* abilities tests are entirely different from those of the tests discussed above, in that they require performance on tasks similar to those demanded on a job. That is, they present the examinee with both a facsimile and a reproduction of a

**Table 9-5** Differences between Criterion-Referenced and Norm-Referenced Measures.

Several of the differences between criterion-referenced and norm-referenced measures are briefly summarized below. The differences are in most cases matters of degree rather than kind.

| Dimension | Criterion-Referenced Measures | Norm-Referenced Measures |
|---|---|---|
| 1. Intent | Information on degree to which absolute external performance standards have been met | Information for relative internal comparisons |
| | Description of maximum performance by individuals, groups, and treatment | Comparisons of individuals, particularly when high degree of selectivity is required |
| 2. Directness of measurement | Great emphasis | Lesser emphasis |
| 3. Variability among scores | Relatively low | Relatively high |
| 4. Difficulty of items | Items tend to be easy, but with some range | Item difficulty localized around 50 percent |
| 5. Item type | Great variety, but less reliance on selection-type items | Variety, but emphasis on selection-type items |
| 6. Discriminating ability of item | Not emphasized | Greatly emphasized |
| 7. Methods of establishing validity | Reliance on content validity | Emphasis on criterion-related validity |
| 8. Emphasis on reliability | Focus on reliability of domain sampling; therefore internal consistency of some interest | Greater concern with parallel form and test-retest estimates of performance stability |
| 9. Influence of guessing | Can be of consequence | Generally not a problem |
| 10. Importance of which items are missed | High | Emphasis on number of missed items |
| 11. Necessity for maintaining security of test items | Relatively low | Relatively high |
| 12. Area of education best served | Instruction | Guidance Selection Grading |

Source: Reprinted by permission of the Publisher, from *The assessment of learning: Cognitive and affective* by D.A. Payne pp. 293-294 (Lexington, Mass.: D.C. Heath and Company, 1974)

given job. The facsimile confronts the examinee with a mock-up or a simulation of the job or, more commonly, with tasks that use abilities similar to those that the job requires. The second presents the subject with the job itself and tests whether the person can perform all its tasks under the existing conditions. In aircraft piloting it would be the difference between testing a flyer in a mock-up airplane or in a real airplane, respectively.

All four of these formats are represented in the abilities tests currently available. Some of the test names (see Buros, 1978) and the abilities required for successful performance are General Clerical Test (clerical speed and accuracy, numerical ability, verbal facility), SRA Test of Mechanical Concepts (mechanical interrelationships, mechanical tools and devices, spatial relations), New Medical College Admission Test (biology, chemistry, physics, reading skills analysis, quantitative skills analysis), Entrance Level Firefighter (compatibility, map reading, spatial relations, visual pursuit), and National Occupational Competency Testing (abilities in twenty-six specific occupations including air conditioning, carpentry, plumbing, printing, and welding).

## Aptitude Testing

Having defined aptitude as a construct indicating natural talent, potential performance, and readiness to understand, we can now stipulate that the ideal aptitude test would be one that requires as little past learning or experience as possible. Thus, an intelligence test whose items do not draw on past instruction or cultural experience would be, as we indicated earlier, an ideal scholastic aptitude test. In other words, a scholastic aptitude test should measure "expected school achievement" (see Thorndike & Hagen, 1969, pp. 330–336) rather than past accomplishments.

Unfortunately, such ideal tests are rare, as we indicated throughout our preceding discussion. The problem seems to be that it is very difficult to differentiate between (and hence to construct) items that measure school learning and items that measure incidental learning. It might be helpful in constructing future aptitude test items to use a criterion of "susceptibility to coaching" (see Willerman, 1979, pp. 174–179). If an item is susceptible to coaching, then it is in all likelihood an achievement test item. If it is not, then it would be a proper aptitude test item. This criterion would ensure to some extent that aptitude tests include items that depend more on maturational development (e.g., the development of a biological and structural readiness to learn) than on formal learning. An example of a good aptitude test item to which this criterion can be applied was given by Willerman, who wrote that "it is very difficult to teach a five-year-old to copy a diamond, even though most five-year-olds can copy a square or a circle. Without explicit instruction, however, a seven-year-old can copy a diamond . . ." (1979, p. 176; also see Jensen, 1973). Furthermore, achievement test items call for more factual information than do aptitude test items. This also makes achievement tests more susceptible to coaching.

Of course, Jensen (1973) would have us believe that heritability, or genetic influences, is important to scholastic aptitude or intelligence testing. But this idea was fairly well discounted in a study by Willerman, Horn, and Loehlin (1977) who reported that genetically unrelated children reared together in adoptive homes scored no more alike on achievement tests than they did on intelligence tests, thus implying that "environmental variation has no greater influence on achievement tests than on IQ tests" (Willerman, 1979, p. 179).

Aptitude tests generally are divided into those that measure *restricted* or *special* aptitudes (clerical, spatial relations, observation, manipulation) or *general* or *multiaptitudes* (verbal reasoning, numerical ability, abstract reasoning, creativity, analytic thinking, judgment), and there also are *prognostic* tests which measure probable performance in some subject or segment of education. Thorndike and Hagen (1969) classified aptitude tests as vocational aptitude batteries, professional school aptitude batteries, musical aptitude tests, artistic aptitude tests, and prognostic tests.

The most widely known aptitude test battery is the Differential Aptitude Tests, which are an example of the multiaptitude format mentioned above. This group of tests was first published in 1947 by the Psychological Corporation, with the last edition appearing in 1975. These tests yield scores in such areas as verbal reasoning, numerical ability, abstract reasoning, clerical speed and accuracy, mechanical reasoning, space relations, spelling, and language usage. In many ways, this popular aptitude test battery is disappointing because some of its subtests clearly measure achievement rather than aptitude; many of its tests are not accompanied by norms or reliability data; and the whole battery "achieves very little differential validity and measures predominantly general intelligence" (Bouchard, 1978, p. 675). This criticism has been heard repeatedly (see Linn, 1978, p. 659) but does not seem to have affected the test's favorable receptions in counseling and employment settings.

## SUMMARY

This chapter included a discussion of intelligence and other maximum performance tests often omitted in other personality-testing texts. We defined intelligence as a mix of acquired and potential abilities to solve given problems or to adapt to certain environments. We also delineated several theories of intelligence, starting with the theoretical approach of Binet and Simon, who were charged with discovering why some children learn more slowly than others. Their Binet scales were the forerunners of the now well known Stanford-Binet IQ tests developed by Terman and Merrill at Stanford University.

Charles Spearman's theory of the general, or $g$, factor of intelligence, as well as his $s$ factor theory, set the stage for many subsequent factor analytic theories of and approaches to intelligence and its testing. The names of Cattell, Thurstone, and Guilford stand out in this tradition in the United States, and those of Spearman, Burt, and Eysenck, in England. Information-processing approaches to intelligence are becoming important in understanding cognitive functioning, and one theory by Sternberg is currently being developed.

Intelligence testing itself has been progressing, as evidenced by the numerous revisions of the Stanford-Binet scales and by the many tests for children and adults devised by David Wechsler over the past thirty years. Group tests of intelligence are also proliferating, and in many ways they are more economical to administer and score than the individual tests are.

A lively but sometimes acerbic debate is currently questioning the merits of ability and intelligence testing among disadvantaged and minority groups, with some critics recommending the cessation of such testing. This debate has intensified efforts to find alternatives to such testing, but the alternatives are in many ways as objectionable or as harmful as the tests they replace.

Achievement, ability, and aptitude tests also measure a part of the individual that relates to personality, revealing, respectively, what has been learned from instruction, the degree of available talent regardless of how acquired, and the potential ability to learn or understand. The last of these, when applied to probable school success, is an important component of intelligence testing. Unfortunately, however, the items on these tests are often a combination of information acquired from formal instruction and information and skills obtained from incidental learning and maturational development.

# FOR FURTHER READING

Cronbach, L.J. Five decades of public controversy over mental testing. *American Psychologist*, 1975, *30*, 1–14. In this important paper, Cronbach points out that the very success of intelligence and educational achievement testing has contributed to their downfall.

Guthrie, R.V. *Even the rat was white: A historical view of psychology.* New York: Harper & Row, 1976. In the chapter on psychometric scientism, Guthrie argues that "nativism, elitism, social class bias, and racism were as essential to the development of psychometric thought in America as the requirement of free enterprise was to capitalism" (p. 47).

Herrnstein, F.J. *IQ in the meritocracy.* Boston: Little Brown, 1973. In this polemic, Herrnstein argues for the social importance of IQ to real-life achievement.

Hunt, J.M. *Intelligence and experience.* New York: Ronald Press, 1961. Although written more than two decades ago, this book remains compulsory reading for students of intelligence testing and theory.

Jencks, C., Smith, M., Ackland, H., Bane, M.J., Cohen, D., Sintis, H., Heyns, B., Michelson, S. *Inequality.* New York: Basic Books, 1972. The authors' main concern is the extent to which social inequality, success, and failure in life depend on inequalities in family background, education, and personality factors that cannot readily be assessed.

Jensen, A.R. *Bias in mental tests.* New York: Macmillan, 1980. Confusing statistical with cultural bias, Jensen's latest contribution to the nature-nurture controversy of intellectual development is a lengthy recounting of much that he has already written.

Kamin, L. *The science and politics of IQ.* Potomac, MD: Lawrence Erlbaum, 1974. A recounting of the sorry history of the uses and abuses of intelligence testing throughout the twentieth century, this book should be must reading for most students of intelligence testing.

Loehlin, J.C., Lindzey, G., & Spuhler, J.N. *Race differences in intelligence.* San Francisco: W. H. Freeman & Company Publishers, 1975. These authors suggest that the intelligence measured by well-constructed tests comes close to intelligence as it would usually be defined by white culture.

Payne, D.A. *The assessment of learning: Cognitive and affective.* Lexington, MA: Heath, 1974. A comprehensive book on educational assessment with particular emphasis on planning, developing, and using a wide range of achievement and learning outcomes.

Vernon, P.E. *Intelligence: Heredity and environment.* San Francisco: W. H. Freeman & Company Publishers, 1979. Written by one of England's leading personality and assessment psychologists, this book is a superb review of the nature of intelligence and the effects on it of heredity and environment.

Willerman, L. *The psychology of individual and group differences.* San Francisco: W. H. Freeman & Company Publishers, 1979. Chapters four, five, and six of this book present the history, theory, and genetic and environmental contributors to the development of intelligence in humans.

Willerman, L., & Turner, R.G. (Eds.). *Readings about individual and group differences.* San Francisco: W. H. Freeman & Company Publishers, 1979. This book contains no less than eight papers on the topic of intelligence, beginning with Francis Galton's famous "Classification of Men according to Their Natural Gifts" and ending with Arthur Jensen's "Cumulative Deficit in IQ of Blacks in the Rural South."

# 10 Some Assessment Problems and Solutions

The study of personality has come a long way from psychology's common-sense notions of sizing up people, which existed until quite recently, and from Woodworth's pioneer adjustment inventory of World War I, which posed such questions as "Are you happy most of the time?" and naively expected truthful answers. Replacing these crude devices are many personality assessment tests and procedures available today, as well as extensive criticisms of these techniques (see Buros, 1978). In addition, there are even whole books written on the interpretation of a single test, as well as many large research-testing firms, such as the Psychological Corporation and the Educational Testing Service, which are devoted to developing personality and other tests. These developments have been accompanied by a greater understanding of, and concern about, the technical and ethical problems in studying people, as this book's evaluation of tests and procedures has emphasized.

In this chapter, we delineate some of these problems and suggest solutions, which are necessary if personality assessment is to surpass its prescientific origins. We also comment on the possible new directions in which the study of personality is moving.

## Technical Problems

Among the more persistent issues facing personologists, we list the following as important: the lack of consensus on personality definitions, the problem of continuous-versus-discrete personality variables, the many uses of personality tests, the nonutility of some assessment devices, the problem of reactivity in personality assessment, the inconsistency of observer and behavioral variables, and the poor quality of personality research.

## Lack of Consensus

The lack of consensus on personality definitions is most apparent in the paradigmatic differences (see Kuhn, 1970) among the *descriptive, dynamic*, and *behavioral* orientations. The descriptive orientation isolates dimensions of personality—types, traits, habits, response tendencies, or dispositions—and assigns them numbers. The dynamic, or depth, orientation is concerned with total or global personality patterns and their underlying psychodynamics. Dynamic theorists tend to be, in R.B. Cattell's and Kline's words, "innocent of measurement" (1977, p. 5). The behavioral orientation, with its origins in psychology's learning laboratories, focuses on the behavior unit as the most essential variable in the study of personality. In quantifying its observations, the behavioral approach falls somewhere in between the other two. But the important feature to note about these three approaches, other than their varying propensities toward quantification, is their separate views of personality. This disparity led Fiske to assert that the "discipline of personality as currently studied is and will remain prescientific" unless it achieves the kinds of consensus on definitions and theories that exist in the other sciences (1978, p. 20).

Why is this more true for personality than for other disciplines? Fiske stated that the "nature of the subject matter" is to blame, because it relies "on interpretive judgments that are determined by the observer as well as by the observed and that are produced for the special purposes of the research" (1978, p. 21). A major source of personality study problems is the different meanings of constructs and concepts.

Even within the three aforementioned approaches, there are disagreements about meanings. For example, in the descriptive, or trait, approach there is an almost arbitrary coining of trait names. Thus, there is Eysenck's *neuroticism* (see Eysenck & Rachman, 1965) and Bernreuter's *neurotic tendency*. Using factor analysis, Guilford (1959a), Eysenck (1956), and Cattell (1957) have independently isolated *extraversion* and *introversion* factors. These same dimensions also appear on the MMPI but seem there to have entirely different origins and meanings. To the personality researcher wanting to study these attributes and to the clinician needing to understand the individuals they describe, this state of affairs can be quite confusing. In an effort to clarify this confusion, Cattell and Kline seem to have added to it: "It was concluded that the factor analytic picture of personality drawn by Cattell . . . still remains the clearest, although there are genuine differences of interpretation between Cattell and Eysenck . . . " (1977, p. 109).

The principal disagreement in the dynamic approach, besides its variously defined concepts, is on its difficult-to-measure depth formulations. Such concepts as "authoritarianism," "ego," "anality," or "oedipal conflict" are based on depth interviews, and as such, they are difficult to separate from the observer's expectations. But even if they are identified by the consensus of other observers, their duration and intensity are difficult to measure, and they are almost impossible to validate against real-world criteria. What, for example, is a good criterion of "penis envy"? Or, how does one measure "self-actualization"?

At its inception the behavioral approach seemed to offer a more scientific alternative to interviewing or traditional psychometric methods. It has become apparent, however, that "as the nature of the behavioral problem being studied has changed . . . behavioral assessment looks more and more like traditional measurement (Fiske, 1978, p. 363). Fear of heights, for example, can be readily quantified in a laboratory by using latencies as dependent variables in approaching the ladder and the numbers of rungs climbed, but prosocial behavior and competency are less readily quantified. To assess these phenomena the behavioral observer has resorted to self-observations, self-reports, and rating scale procedures, which obviously are subject to all the problems and difficulties already mentioned in regard to these measures. Furthermore, the behavioral approach has several problems which are linked to its origin, several of which were listed by Liebert and Spiegler (1978). They include the behaviorist's overreliance on the concept of learning, which often fails to consider biogenic factors, and the overemphasis on situational tests, which have a poor record of reliability (as measured by interjudge agreement) and predictive validity (see Mischel, 1977, pp. 246–249, for a more positive view of behavioral assessment).

## Continuous-versus-Discrete Personality Variables

Besides the issue of whether descriptive, dynamic, or behavioral approaches best define personality, there is the problem that much of the clinical study of personality continues to be influenced by a diagnostic classification system (American Psychiatric Association, 1952, 1968, 1980) whose roots are in the medical or disease model of psychopathology (see Kleinmuntz, 1980, pp. 25–33, for a critique of classification). Most contemporary studies of personality seem to be concerned with continuous dimensions; yet the classification system of disordered personality is a typology composed of mutually exclusive and, in some instances, separate but overlapping categories. Any continuity among these categories, according to one source, "is somewhat grudgingly and unofficially provided by the expedient of various borderline states . . . "

(Draguns & Phillips, 1971, p. 5). In other words, the separate categories of psychiatric diagnosis have no continuity except that provided by clinical cases that do not fall easily into specific disease categories.

This problem had still not been resolved in the latest, or third, edition of the *Diagnostic and Statistical Manual of Mental Disorders* (American Psychiatric Association, 1980), and what is needed, according to another view, is a new personality taxonomy that enables psychologists "to organize the growing body of knowledge about human behavior, personality and psychopathology" (Dahlstrom, 1972, p. 24). This taxonomy should embody the diverse patterns of human behaviors over wide ranges of age, adjustment, and context. It may require us to consider a new set of qualitative and quantitative variations in the personality system and will in all likelihood require new conceptualizations and tools to measure personality behaviors.

## The Many Settings and Uses of Personality Assessment

Another problem in personality study is that personality assessment occurs in many settings and has many uses. We mentioned several settings and their uses in chapter one and throughout the book. These settings include clinical diagnosis, counseling and therapy, personnel selection, and research. Their uses include assessment of such varied and fragmented dimensions and constructs as mental health, adjustment, defenses, self-control, locus of control, aggression, self-esteem, androgyny, ascendance-submission, authoritarianism, extraversion-introversion, anxiety, phobia, frustration, as well as attitudes, intelligence, and achievement according to the broader definition of this book. This problem is complicated by the fact that many assessors use each other's techniques but score and interpret them differently, or they measure the same construct but attach different meanings to it. The resolution of this problem requires that the test user make several important prior decisions about the kinds of problems, kinds of phenomena, kinds of data, and kinds of settings he or she will study, plus the kinds of instruments to be used.

D.W. Fiske enumerated ten basic decisions that should be made regarding each of these considerations, which are presented in Table 10–1.

## The Nonutility of Assessment Devices

Another criticism of personality assessment strategies, according to James Butcher (1972, pp. 4–12), is that they are not useful for practical decision-making in clinical settings. Butcher traced this criticism to Carl

**Table 10–1** Basic Decisions Regarding Problems, Phenomena, Data, and Conditions for Personality Study.

| Topic | Decision | Choices |
|---|---|---|
| A. Problem | 1. Nature of problem to be solved. | 1a. Study problems of interest socially.<br>1b. Study problems of interest to me. |
| B. Phenomena | 2. Population of subjects of interest.<br>3. Type of behavior to be studied. | 3a. Study expressions.<br>3b. Study behavior more broadly defined (e.g., moving, speaking, gestures). |
| C. Observational Data | 4. Populations of persons to be studied. | 4a. Interest in observer's behavior.<br>4b. Interest in behavior of observer's subject's.<br>4c. Use a professional or lay observer? |
| D. Conditions | 5. Extent of observer participation in design.<br>6. Extent of subject awareness of research design and intent.<br>7. Natural or controlled setting. | 5a. Use knowledgeable and/or naive observers?<br>6a. Use knowledgeable or naive subjects?<br>7a. Natural and controlled stimuli. |

SOURCE: Fiske, D. W. *Strategies for personality research: The observation versus interpretation of behavior.* San Francisco: Jossey-Bass, 1978, pp. 204–205.

Rogers (1942, 1951), who cautioned against the biasing effects of personality testing on treatment because "when the locus of evaluation is seen as residing in the expert ... the long range social implications are in the direction of the social control of the many by the few ..." (Rogers, 1951, pp. 223–224).

As we indicated earlier, the nonutility criticism of traditional personality assessment is also supported by the behavioral therapists, who are often more interested in observable behavior and analyzing controlling, contingent, or reinforcing environmental stimuli than in global personality concepts or traits (see Peterson, 1968). But, again, behaviorists are currently moving more and more in the direction of traditional test procedures.

Quite aside from the above considerations, Robert Hogan and his associates at Johns Hopkins University (1977, pp. 259–260) countered the arguments of those test critics who suggest that tests have limited empirical utility because they account for only about 9 percent to 16 percent of the variance (e.g., a correlation between a test and a criterion of about 0.30 to 0.40) of the predicted extratest measure. Hogan pointed out that higher correlation coefficients could be achieved if certain important technical and conceptual considerations were not ignored: "When these considerations [e.g., base rates, the unreliability of criteria, and idiographic versus nomothetic ascription of traits] are taken into account, validity coefficients in competent research readily exceed 0.30 . . . " (Hogan, 1977, p. 260). He then cited several studies that support his argument and corroborate the utility of some existing self-report devices, although as we note later, even coefficients of 0.30 can have important predictive powers.

## The Problem of Reactivity

The problem of reactivity in studying persons has already been discussed in this book, and it is most thoroughly treated by Campbell (1957) and Webb and his associates (1966). According to them, personality tests affect or alter a behavior just by measuring it. One researcher recommended that "in order to achieve non-reactivity . . . it will be necessary to get beyond the standard 'test' kind of operation into the observation of behavior *in situ* and by means which conceal not only the nature of the measurement being conducted, but the fact that measurement is occurring at all" (Sechrest, 1968, p. 574). Specific examples of unobtrusive and nonreactive measures were presented in chapter five.

A form of nonreactivity different from that discussed in chapter five can be achieved by so-called archival studies of personality traces. There are several such studies (Barthell & Holmes, 1968; also see Meehl, 1973; Rabkin, 1980; Schofield & Balian, 1959), and we shall briefly describe that by Schofield and Balian as an example of what can be learned from a combined archival and interview comparison of a group of normal persons and a group of schizophrenic patients.

To test the popular view of many clinicians that severe life experience disruptions plant the seeds of mental illness, William Schofield and Lucy Balian compared the life histories of 150 psychiatrically normal subjects with those of 178 hospitalized schizophrenics. Their hypothesis was that the histories of the normals, when compared to those of the schizophrenics, would reveal markedly fewer of those events or experiences (traumas, deprivations, frustrations, conflicts, and the like) commonly associated with the origins and causes of schizophrenia.

Their findings were surprising and have held up over the years. Out of thirty-five early life events, thirteen (or 37 percent) did not reveal a reliable difference between the two samples. Of the five variables that did yield reliable differences, the normals had more undesirable or pathogenic factors (poverty, childhood invalidism, poor heterosexual adjustment, broken homes) than the schizophrenics did. Schizophrenics, however, had a reliably higher incidence of unfavorable relationships with their mothers and fathers, poorer attitudes toward achievement in school, less occupational success and satisfaction, higher rates of social withdrawal, and lack of initiative. Therefore, although there was not a complete reversal of expected early life events among normal and mentally ill persons, most of the expected early disruptions showed up more frequently in the lives of the normals than would have been predicted from clinical lore (also see Meehl, 1973, pp. 174–181; Schwarz, 1970).

A recent update by Rabkin (1980) on the influences of stressful life events on schizophrenia reported that in the number of events, there seemed to be no difference between the schizophrenics and the other patient groups, but that the findings in the research literature regarding event frequencies reported by schizophrenics and normals were inconsistent. Rabkin's general conclusion is worth quoting here because it casts the issue in a different, and somewhat more cautious, light: "Overall, the research evidence indicates a weaker relationship between life events and schizophrenia onset than the clinical literature suggests, although methodological limitations preclude firm conclusions at this time" (1980, p. 408).

## Problems of Observer and Behavioral Inconsistencies

As we indicated at the beginning of chapter five, the study of personality is difficult because the subjects of interest are people, and the units of observation are their moods, dispositions, and response tendencies. People are difficult to study because, more than any other subjects, they react to being observed, which itself alters their behavior. Moods, dispositions, and responses are equally as troublesome to study because they are probabilistic rather than all-or-none phenomena. Charitable people, for example, do not always display charitable traits; nor do honest people always act honestly; and in general, most individuals defined by personality descriptions (diagnostic class or other class membership) do not always possess or display the characteristics ascribed to them. Consequently, a "typical" antisocial, schizophrenic, or authoritarian personality is much harder to find than textbook descriptions of these and other designations suggest. Moreover, it is not unusual for two members of the same class or category of personality description to have few characteristics in common.

The situation is somewhat similar in medicine, as we also indicated in chapter five, which presumably deals with aspects of human behavior more stable than personality. Not all cases of the flu or other physical malfunctioning display the same cues, signs, or symptoms. The observed inconsistencies or irregularities may be due to a particularly unusual configuration of cues, the physician's skill in eliciting or discovering expected or existing cues, the circumstances prevailing at a given time, or some complex interaction of all of these.

Nevertheless, these apparent irregularities notwithstanding, personality psychologists search for regularities of behavior, a search that may be undermined by a failure to consider several aspects of the observational whole. Some psychologists (see Endler & Magnusson, 1976) have noted that expected behavioral consistencies cannot occur as a result of person-situation interactions and that unless these dynamic interactions are studied using appropriate techniques that take into account both the person and the environment, no science of personology can develop. Other psychologists (Block, 1976, pp. 91–92), who partially agree with this view, also have attributed these apparent "embarrassing inconsistencies" to the observer's search for behaviors that are not significant or salient for an individual and to poor personality research designs (see next section).

Worse yet, according to another psychologist, some personologists and clinicians tend to attribute consistencies of behavior where none exists because they need to "reconstrue and negate all sorts of discrepant behaviors" to their mold of what is expected (Mischel, 1976a, pp. 639–640). Any later behavior that is inconsistent with a given diagnosis or personality attribution is dismissed as irrelevant or extraneous. For example, after an observer has classified another person as "incompetent," but is subsequently confronted by new behavior inconsistent with this classification, he or she will then attribute the new behavior to factors other than the person's "real" or "true" self.

What is really needed, according to many of these personologists, are new methods and tools for studying dynamic person-by-situation interactions and perhaps even a taxonomy of situations (see Argyle & Little, 1972; Bem, 1976; Bem & Funder, 1978; Bowers, 1973; Endler, 1976; Magnusson & Endler, 1977; Mischel, 1977 for a complete discussion of the person-situation interaction controversy). Frederiksen (1976, pp. 487–502), for example, observed that although we have useful taxonomies to classify individual differences among persons (e.g., personality factors, cognitive factors, diagnostic classes, personality types, and so on), we have no satisfactory taxonomies to classify situations. He called for a "systematic way of conceptualizing the domain of situations and situational variables" (p. 489) and proposed some methods (factor and cluster analyses) for developing a taxonomy of situations, as well as some performance criteria (classification of situations based on elicited behavior) for doing so.

Bem and Funder (1978), who also address the problem of person-by-situation interactions, proposed the development of a common descriptive language and assessment strategy to study both persons and situations. They detail a template-matching technique that permits assessment of a person for similarity to a template or personality description of an idealized type of person expected to behave in specific ways in given situations. The probability of certain behaviors then depends on person-template similarity. For example, self-descriptive statements obtained from Q-sorts or other self-report devices can be matched with self-report templates derived from theory, or from the observations of judges familiar with the demands of particular situations, or from an algebraic weighting of the self-report items based on obtained item-response-criterion interrelations. Along the same lines, Siess and Jackson (1970) proposed that personality profiles of respondents be matched with those implied by certain situations (see Jackson & Paunonen, 1980).

But even if these new tools and methods for studying person-by-situation interactions were adopted, there would still be the problems of whether persons or situations control behavior, whether persons or situations are more important, and whether the relative importance of each can be quantified. And if these issues were resolved, there would be the new problem, according to Pervin, "about *what* in the person interacts *how* with *what* in the situation" (1980, p. 17).

In this regard, two psychologists (Kendrick & Stringfield, 1980) recently conducted studies in which they instructed subjects to select their own most consistent characteristics (on bipolar dimensions based on R.B. Cattell's Sixteen Personality Factors test). They found that these dimensions were highly and publicly visible, as judged by ratings of the subject's peers and parents. Having discovered such salient personality characteristics, Kendrick and Stringfield concluded that it should also "be possible to select a small but representative sample of salient classes of situations for each of the dimensions we have used herein.... [And] by allowing each subject to characterize his or her consistency in each of perhaps five such classes of situations, it should be possible to make very specific predictions for certain subsamples or persons and situations ... " (1980, p. 102).

In this regard also, Jackson and Paunonen (1980, pp. 511–512) dispute the argument used by Mischel (1968, pp. 23–25) and others that evidence from the classical study by Hartshorne and May (1928) indicating that situational tests of moral behavior show moderate to low intercorrelations is evidence for the specificity of behavior. This evidence is used to disparage the usefulness of general traits such as honesty. This argument, according to Jackson and Paunonen, together with Mischel's related observation that personality tests rarely predict specific behavior with correlations higher than 0.30, fails to take into account that "specific instances of honest behavior observed in different settings carry with them substantial systematic variance associated with the method of measurement and the influences attributable to the situation" (p. 511). But this is not good evidence that a general characteristic of honesty is not measurable, according to Jackson and Paunonen's disputation, and they demonstrate statistically that seven specific situational test measures reported in the Hartshorne and May study yield an estimate of internal consistency reliability of about 0.80. They then extrapolate beyond the seven-item test by using the Spearman-Brown formula (see chapter three) and demonstrate that the coefficient of 0.80 translates into a reliability of 0.97 if the test is lengthened to a fifty-item test. This implies that "honesty may be more reliable than, say, intelligence," and they speculate that this may "explain why even those who believe in the specificity of behavior would probably prefer that their pension funds not be administered by someone convicted of embezzlement" (p. 512).

## The Inadequacy of Personality Research

Concerning some of these person-situation issues, Block blamed the slow progress of personality study to several problems plaguing contemporary psychological research and stated that "perhaps 90 percent of the studies are methodologically inadequate, without conceptual implication, and even foolish" (1977, p. 41). To Block the reasons for this inadequacy are that many personality concepts are not well defined (an observation we made earlier in this chapter); that the implications of many personality constructs are not adequately conceptualized, or if properly conceptualized, are often not heeded in related research; and that the reliability of many assessment tools are poor, often as poor as the research designs of the studies that use them.

Block was therefore not surprised that personality seemed to be inconsistent. But "well-done ... studies," he argued, "demonstrate undeniable and impressive personality consistency and continuity ... in ... the individuals being studied" (1977, p. 62). As an example of such a study, he pointed to his own *Lives through Time* (1971), which reported on the well-known longitudinal studies at Berkeley that collected naturalistic data on a large number of people when they were young and again when they grew older. The information was collected at three points throughout these people's lives: in their junior high school, high school, and adult (mid-thirties) years. These data were then evaluated by three clinical psychologists who independently described the personalities of each subject at each of the three periods.

Block found that 59 percent (67/114) of the males' personality variables were highly consistent (0.001 significance level), and a corresponding 57 percent (65/114) of the females' variables were equally consistent. These consistencies were noted in junior and in senior high school but were somewhat less stable afterward until the subjects reached their mid-thirties, when the percentages of unchanged personality variables were 50 (25/50) and 30 (27/90) for males and females, respectively. The most stable personality variables were impulse control, inability to delay gratification, submissiveness, empathy, gregariousness, and nonconformance.

An interpretive comment by Pervin summarized the implications of Block's findings: "Block's arguments suggest that the evidence concerning consistency versus specificity of behavior is not clear-cut and that the issue is quite complex. At least part of the complexity . . . resides in the issue of [the question] . . . What does consistency mean and what type of data are necessary to justify a conclusion of consistency or one of situational specificity?" (1978, pp. 13–14).

Thus it could be argued that many of the personality inconsistencies were due to poor personality research rather than to the difficulties inherent in the complex person-by-situation interactions. To quote Pervin again: "The results found differ according to the type of study conducted. Studies using ratings by observers or self-observations . . . result in . . . consistency . . . [and] studies using . . . artificial tests or laboratory situations . . . result in evidence of situational specificity" (1978, p. 14).

## The Use of Traditional Measures

Most current personality assessments, with the already-noted exception of the behavioral approaches, use paper-and-pencil tests and responses to amorphous stimuli to measure people. The test scores obtained in this manner, as we indicated in chapters five and nine, are highly fallible indices of a person's present and future behavior. That is, these test scores, which stand as "signs"—and often questionable signs, at that—of a person's behavior and dispositions, are of only secondary interest to the investigator. The primary interest is the person's typical behavior in given situations.

One way to study a person more directly is to assess his or her tendency toward a personality-relevant behavior in situations designed to elicit that behavior (Fiske, 1963). Thus, if we want to study honesty, we can contrive situations maximally favorable for eliciting honest (or dishonest) responses. Likewise, if we want to study generosity, impulsiveness, aggression, or whatever, we can contrive correspondingly favorable situations for them also. Currently this practice is more in the experimental tradition than in the psychometric tradition, but there is no good reason why this cannot be changed (see Cronbach, 1957, 1975). In this regard, Jackson and Paunonen (1980) have noted that lately there has been an integration of measurement and experimental approaches to personality.

Several performance measures of personality can be studied, but most of these, except traditional self-report or projective approaches, are also somewhat removed from the behavior of interest. These measures are perceptual, conditioning phenomena, and physiological functioning.

**Perceptual Functioning.** One of the more interesting demonstrations relating perceptual phenomena to personality is H.J. Eysenck's (1947) early work on *dark vision*. He compared the dark vision ability of ninety-six neurotic patients with that of six thousand normal persons, on a scale of 0 to 32 objects perceived. The mean score for the latter was 19.3. Neurotics were able to perceive only 7.1 objects, indicating their marked inability to perceive objects in the dark. This perceptual measure has also been used to differentiate between seriously and less seriously symptomatic neurotics (also see Eysenck & Rachman, 1965).

Another possible perceptual phenomenon that may be related to personality is *vigilance*, namely, the ability of some people to attend to monotonous visual or auditory tasks. For example, two separate studies (Bakan, 1957; Claridge, 1960) reported that introverts have a significantly higher vigilance capacity than extraverts do. Two other experimenters (McGhie & Chapman, 1961) showed that also schizophrenics are unable to attend to incoming stimuli as well as normals can and that this deficit may be due to the schizophrenics' greater distractibility (Chapman & McGhie, 1962). This phenomenon seems to be related to both relatively complicated tasks and simple ones. For example, in a simple eye-tracking experiment, Philip Holzman and his associates (1973, 1977) reported that schizophrenics, when compared to normals, showed an erratic pattern of eye-tracking movements. Interestingly, this pattern of stops and starts was also displayed by a high proportion (44 percent) of first-degree relatives of schizophrenics (also see Shagass et al., 1974, 1976).

**Conditioning Experiments.** Conditioning experiments are a more subtle index of performance than dark vision or vigilance is. Eysenck's (1962) theory of personality, for instance, predicted that introverts would form conditioned responses more quickly, more strongly, and more persistently than extraverts would. Some studies using eyeblink conditioning to differentiate between introverts and extraverts yielded results favoring this theory (Brebner, 1957; Franks, 1956a; Symon, 1958), but others have been unfavorable (Farber et al., 1957; Spence & Spence, 1964; Sweetbaum, 1963).

In eyelid conditioning studies, a puff of air usually was the unconditioned stimulus (UCS) that elicited the conditioned or eyeblink response (CR). After several pairings between the UCS and a conditioned stimulus (CS), which was either a light or buzzer, the latter alone elicited the CR. It is beyond the scope of this book to detail the several methodological and theoretical issues concerning the differences between neurotics and normals, but it is important to emphasize that eyeblink conditioning may become a differentially diagnostic sign of some significance.

Another form of conditioning, in which the galvanic skin response (GSR) is the CR elicited by a buzzer or light (CS), has also been used as an index of personality (Franks, 1956b; Lykken, 1957; Vogel, 1960, 1961). An important study in this area was by David Lykken (1957) of the University of Minnesota, who showed that psychopaths were less likely than other prisoners and normals to display anxiety on a lie-detector test. An important feature of this study was Lykken's attempt to separate his antisocial study samples into *primary sociopaths* and the clinically similar appearing subtypes such as the *dyssocial* and *neurotic* sociopaths.

Specifically, he provided his psychologist judges with a fourteen-item criterion checklist to be used to identify primary sociopaths who fitted Cleckley's prototype descriptions of "pure psychopathy." In this way two experimental prisoner groups and one control group were selected. Group I (twelve males and seven females) consisted of primary sociopaths; group II (thirteen males and seven females) was made up of inmates who did not meet these criteria; and group III (ten males and five females) was selected from among normal high school and general college (junior college) students, matched with the other subjects for age, intelligence, and socioeconomic background.

The experimental hypothesis was that the group I subjects would not easily develop anxiety in the laboratory, that they would show abnormally little manifest anxiety in real-life situations, and that they would be relatively incapable of *avoidance learning* in the laboratory. To test the last part of this hypothesis, Lykken took a GSR measure of the blindfolded subjects, who were seated in the lab, while administering to them buzzer (CS)–shock (US) combinations. He found that group I showed significantly less GSR reactivity to the CS than the other two groups did. Of all the tests used, according to Lykken, this was the most important one because it showed that if a person "does *not* produce a GSR to a stimulus, one can be sure that he has not 'reacted emotionally' to that stimulus" (1957, p. 10).

In the avoidance-conditioning situation, primary psychopaths (group I subjects) showed the least avoidance, and hence the least anxiety;

neurotic and other types (group II) showed less avoidance; and normals (group III) showed the most avoidance. These results suggest that primary sociopaths are autonomically less reactive than normals or secondary antisocial types are.

To test the second part of this hypothesis—namely, that primary sociopaths have less real-life anxiety than others do—the subjects were given self-report questionnaires such as the Anxiety Index (AI) of the MMPI (Dahlstrom et al., 1972), the Taylor Manifest Anxiety Scale (Heineman, 1953; Taylor, J.A., 1953), and an "anxiety scale" especially constructed by Lykken for this study. The results on all tests except the last were that group II, as would be expected because of their neurotic anxiety, achieved the highest anxiety scores; and group I, unexpectedly, showed slightly higher scores than group III did. But on Lykken's special anxiety scale, the primary psychopaths showed the least anxiety, their scores being significantly lower than those of normals, with the scores of the neurotics and other sociopaths falling somewhere between those of the primaries and normals.

**Physiological Data.** The currently most promising physiological personality measures have been obtained from studies that relate behavior to autonomic nervous system functioning. The autonomic, or vegetative, nervous system regulates varying bodily states such as reaction to fear, alertness to danger, accommodation to heat, and most other reactions that require adjustment to an unusual set of internal or environmental circumstances. Some of the better-known physiological measures used as indices of behavioral states are electrical skin conductivity, or the galvanic skin response (GSR), blood pressure level, heart rate, basal metabolism rate, muscle tone, and respiration rate. All of these indices are included in the polygraph measurement, popularly mislabeled the "lie detector," which is routinely used to detect the presence of an emotional or aroused state but which may not detect deception at all (see Lykken, 1974, 1981; Szucko & Kleinmuntz, 1981). Unfortunately, psychologists rarely relate these indices to personality assessment.

That work in this area may also prove useful to the study of personality should be apparent from the studies that have reported positive relationships between physiological measures and the origins, or etiology, of schizophrenia. These studies, which focused on detailed biochemical agents, linked the various physiological components controlled by the autonomic nervous system to schizophrenia. Much of this work was based on the discovery that schizophrenics' blood chemistry differs from that of normal adults (see Rubin, 1959, 1962); that schizophrenics' rate of homeostatic adjustment differs from that of normals; and that psychotics' blood serum is toxic to both tadpoles

(Fischer, 1953) and human cell tissues (Federhoff & Hoffer, 1956). But the main point here is that these differences also could be used to study and to differentiate personality types.

It seems likely that the most efficient use of these physiological measures to predict personality would employ a multivariate approach (Sarason, 1972). For example, since the combined patterns of such physiological responses as heart rate, GSR, blood pressure, electrocardiogram (EKG), electroencephalogram (EEG), and several performance tasks seem to be more important to personality assessment than any one of these variables considered by itself is, the study of only one of these measures might complicate rather than clarify the empirical relationships discovered. Therefore, if there is to be progress in using physiological measures as personality predictors, it would be sensible to conduct multidimensional studies of physiological responses. This recommendation should come as no surprise to psychologists familiar with a similar movement in psychometrics, from univariate to multivariate measurement.

In the meantime, several aids in monitoring and computing physiological data on personality might be of interest in this regard and shall be mentioned briefly. The most promising future uses in assessment will probably come from biofeedback research, which uses electronic devices to inform subjects of their biological status in order to help them control their autonomic reactivity. For example, when one attempts to produce alpha EEG rhythms, and hence tranquility and relaxation (see Kamiya, 1969), by eliciting a desired tone or signal, that rhythm can be achieved by noting whether (or how many) these desired tones can be elicited within a given time. Similarly, since the single most important independent variable in biofeedback research is the display to the subject of the feedback under investigation, any of the types of feedback displays can be used as assessment devices. Many types of feedback displays have been used, according to a recent definitive source (Yates, 1980, pp. 36–44), including visual, auditory, and digital displays, and occasionally, tactual modality.

In the visual display, a scale like a speedometer or a radio-tuning grid is commonly used, as well as radarlike sweeps on an oscilloscope, flashing lights, moving horizontal or vertical lines, matched-needle displays like a camera's, and so forth. Digital displays, in which numbers represent the level of activity, are probably the wave of the future but are awaiting some essential technological advances not yet perfected. Auditory feedback usually is either a change in pitch or a change in click rate to indicate a different activity. It is probably more commonly used than visual displays are. For persons who cannot see or hear, other types of feedback are being devised.

Since these feedback displays are being used to implement the voluntary control of muscle and autonomic functions, as well as central nervous system reactivity, it follows that they also should be able to assess their functions. Or, more specifically, it might be feasible to assess some of the organism's conditions, such as alcoholism, anxiety, psychophysiological disorders, obsessive-compulsive behavior, phobias, and sexual disorders. Of course, in many of the behaviors to which biofeedback has been successfully applied (e.g., control of heart rate, blood pressure, and electrodermal responding), the direct assessment of these states is unimportant. But the personality dispositions that may underlie these states are not unimportant and might be able to be inferred or predicted from these indices.

To summarize these technical problems in the study of personality, we can state that although there has been considerable progress over the years, there is still little agreement on the definition of its subject matter. Its progress has been hampered, too, by the adherence to a medical model that may be inappropriate and by the fact that one of its main tools, personality assessment, must function in a variety of settings and uses for which it may not have been designed or intended. Furthermore, the research designs of many personality studies are inadequate and thus raise the question of whether discovered personality inconsistencies are due to poor observational techniques or to unstable characteristics and dispositions. There is also the problem that the subjects in the study of personality are people, which are inherently difficult to study. Finally, personality measurement has tended to stick rather closely to studying the person by means of traditional paper-and-pencil tests, a problem that can be solved by using performance and physiological measures.

## Ethical and Moral Considerations

Tests have also been criticized on ethical and moral grounds, as we noted in our chapter nine discussion of the problems of intelligence and aptitude testing among minority groups. But there are other, more specific criticisms.

### Invasion of Privacy

A recurring criticism of personality tests—particularly typical performance tests such as the MMPI and similar self-report inventories—is that they are an invasion of privacy. The argument here is that these tests probe into sexual practices and religious preferences, personal matters that are best confided only to psychologists, psychiatrists, physicians, or ministers.

Personality tests also have raised the larger issues of self-incrimination and due process, which were investigated in the 1960s by a special congressional committee chaired by Senator Sam J. Ervin, Jr., of later Watergate fame (see the American Psychological Association's 1965 special edition on testing). Specifically, this committee was concerned about the "procedural and due process issues involved in the administration of tests, including the employee's right to confront hs accusers when his emotional stability and mental competency are questioned" (p. 880).

Writing on the invasion of personal privacy, Congressman C. E. Gallagher stated, "Remember there is nothing voluntary about these tests ... What bothers me is that personnel often are interpreting these tests, and the answers are reposing in some Government file somewhere, all set to follow the person throughout his career or non-career" (American Psychological Association, 1965, pp. 881–882).

These are reasonable and understandable concerns, and they should motivate psychologists to consider carefully the gains and losses in using or not using tests. But surely there are occasions when personality tests can provide valuable information not otherwise available, and then they should be given under any circumstances. When one needs to determine, for example, whether certain persons might do serious harm to themselves or others in particular jobs or assignments, then psychiatric screening devices seem highly appropriate and useful. If testing were made voluntary in these circumstances, then the process of self-selection might eliminate the very candidates for whom it is most important to obtain test scores.

Examinees can be assured that psychologists are honor bound by the two principles contained in the *Ethical Standards of Psychologists* (American Psychological Association, 1977), which are intended to protect people's personal privacy. The violation of these or other ethical principles can mean expulsion from the American Psychological Association and forefeiture of one's state license or certificate to practice psychology.

Principle 5b

Information obtained in clinical or consulting relationships ... are discussed only for professional purposes and only with persons clearly concerned with the case. ...

Principle 8d

Psychologists accept responsibility for removing from clients' files test score information that has become obsolete, lest such information be misused or misconstrued to the disadvantage of the person tested.

The concern that personality tests pry into personal affairs is also understandable. They do pry. Items such as "I believe in the Resurrection," "My sex life has never been better," or "My bowel movements are irregular," are private matters. Critics have implied that "incorrect" responses to these items could cost someone a job. But this criticism must be judged within the context of the self-report tests' nature and aims. These and similar probing queries, which mainly pertain to fantasies, religiosity (e.g., excessive religiosity), sex practices, body functions, and other matters physically and psychologically relevant to a person, are not asked simply to probe; rather they are asked because they have been found to be pertinent to many psychological disorders. Starke R. Hathaway, cofounder of the MMPI, summed up the problem this way:

> If the psychologist cannot use these personal items to aid in the assessment of people, he suffers as did the Victorian physician who had to examine his female patients by feeling the pulse in the delicate hand thrust from behind a screen ... it is obvious that if we were making a new MMPI, we would again be faced either with being offensive to subgroupings of people by personal items they object to or, if we did not include personal items and were inoffensive, we would have lost the aim of the instrument.
>
> However, and we repeat, insofar as possible it is essential to safeguard the respondent's communications as confidential and to inform him or her of the purposes and uses of the testing. To do otherwise is unacceptable, regardless of the item contents. (1964, pp. 206–207)

But despite these safeguards and rationales there are still many opportunities for psychologists to misuse, and even to abuse, unintentionally or otherwise, the results of tests. A psychologist may be commercially motivated to misinterpret test findings or to extrapolate interpretations beyond reasonable bounds, or he or she may not know the proper interpretations of certain tests. In the first instance, of course, the psychologist runs the risk of sanctions; in the case of ignorance, he or she should be reminded of certain obligations to consumers, as spelled out in the *Standards for Educational and Psychological Tests*:

> *Paragraph G1.* A test user should have a general knowledge of measurement principles and of the limitations of test interpretations.
> *Paragraph G5.* Institutional test users should establish procedures for periodic internal review of test use.
> *Paragraph J7.* The test user should consider alternative considerations of a given score.
> *Paragraph J7.2.* A person tested should have more than one kind of opportunity to qualify for a favorable decision. (American Psychological Association, 1974)

Yet it may be argued that because psychological tests are the tools of those who will misuse or abuse them, these tools should be abolished.

Equally convincing arguments, however, could also be made for abolishing other artificial evils that might be destructive if not used properly. Gas, electricity, and nuclear energy come to mind. Regarding this issue, Hathaway observed:

> To attack tests is, to a certain extent, comparable to an attack upon knives. Both good and bad use of knives occurs because they are sharp instruments. To eliminate knives would, of course, have a limiting effect upon the occurrence of certain hostile acts, but it would also greatly limit the activities of surgeons. (1964, p. 204)

## Testing and Civil Rights

Closely related to the issues of privacy and the abuses of testing is the federal government's concern about minorities' civil rights in employment practices. In 1970, the Equal Employment Opportunity Commission issued the following statement regarding the use of tests for employee selection:

> The guidelines ... are based on the belief that properly validated and standardized employee selection procedures can significantly contribute to the implementation of nondiscriminatory personnel policies.... It is also recognized that professionally developed tests, when used in conjunction with other tools of personnel assessment and complemented by sound programs of job design, may significantly aid in the development and maintenance of an efficient work force and indeed, aid in the utilization and conservation of human resources generally.

Subsequently, in 1976 and again in 1978, the Equal Employment Opportunity Commission, together with the Civil Service Commission, the Department of Labor, and the Department of Justice, issued the *Testing and Selecting Employees Guidelines* (1978). The *Guidelines* were designed to "assist employers, labor organizations, employment agencies, and licensing and certification boards to comply with requirements of Federal law prohibiting employment practices which discriminate on grounds of race, color, religion, sex, and origin" (4010.01). The *Guidelines* also provide a framework for determining the proper use of tests and other selection procedures. This framework was largely based on, and was "intended to be consistent with generally accepted professional standards ... as ... described in the Standards for Educational and Psychological Tests (American Psychological Association, Washington, D.C., 1974)" (4010.05).

The *Guidelines* established what they called the "adverse impact and the four-fifths rule" for determining discriminatory uses (or discriminatory nonuses) of tests and procedures. Adverse impact, or a discriminatory selection practice, is established when the selection rate for any race, sex, or ethnic group is less than four-fifths (or 80 percent) of that group's representation in the labor market or, in the case of jobs filled from within, four-fifths of the applicable work force. The *Guidelines* also outlined in detail many of the essential attributes of psychometrically sound tests, as set down by the profession in its *Standards* (American Psychological Association, 1974).

An American Psychological Association publication, *Standards for Providers of Psychological Services* (1977b), specified minimally acceptable levels of quality for providers of psychological services. These *Standards*, which have been supplemented by another, more updated document (American Psychological Association, 1979b), cover both the psychologist's obligation to support the legal and civil rights of the user of psychological services and the establishment of a system to protect the confidentiality of psychological records. The users of such services include not only job applicants and employees but also the organization employing the service.

A recent review (London & Bray, 1980) of existing standards for psychologists listed various sources that prescribe ethical psychological practice. But these authors also noted that there are no standards for all situations and that research may be necessary to establish strategies for dealing with certain ethical issues; they also found that guarding against invasion of privacy, obtaining informed consent, guaranteeing confidentiality, and respecting the individual's right to know must be balanced against the need for high-quality evaluative information. This is a difficult balance to achieve in practice, and in some cases it may be necessary to sacrifice scientific rigor in favor of individual rights. In most cases, however, it is a matter of discovering and adjusting to new psychological practices that integrate the goals of the psychologists and the rights of those they serve. As Messick observed in "Test Validity and the Ethics of Assessment,"

> The primary concern . . . is the balancing of the instrumental value of the test in accomplishing its intended purpose with the instrumental value of any negative side effects and positive by-products of the testing. Most test makers acknowledge responsibility for providing general evidence of the instrumental value of the test. The terminal value of the test in terms of the social ends to be served goes beyond the test maker to include as well the decisionmaker, policymaker, and test user, who are responsible for specific evidence of instrumental value in their particular setting and for the specific interpretations and uses made of the test scores. (1980, p. 1025)

To sum up, then, we can say that tests do invade privacy but that they do so for a particular purpose. Whenever there have been misuses and abuses of tests and selection procedures, particularly in employment settings, they have not gone unnoticed by the profession or by the profession in cooperation with the federal government. Not only are these violations unethical according to the profession's guidelines, but they also are illegal according to the law of the land.

## Quasi-Ethical Objections

Several other objections to testing have been raised. These tend to be quasi-ethical because they fall midway between ethical and technical bounds. We list these objections in the order that they are usually listed by the critics.

**Tests Dehumanize.** Because of the recent large-scale testing programs and the ever-increasing use of computers to process persons and tests, more and more people (especially college students) have protested that humans have been reduced to numbers and computer data points. There is much truth in this because it is sometimes difficult to remember—perhaps because of the novelty of, and the enormous efficiency enjoyed by, automated data-processing hardware—that the processed numbers are really people. But if sometimes we do forget our responsibilities for our test and interview examinees, we need look no further than to the "Preamble" of the *Ethical Standards of Psychologists* (American Psychological Association, 1977a), which states that "psychologists respect the dignity and worth of the individual and honor the preservation and protection of fundamental human rights." And Principle 7a, regarding professional relationships, also expresses this concern:

> The absence of formal relationships with other professional workers does not relieve psychologists from the responsibility of securing for their clients the best possible professional service nor does it relieve them from the exercise of foresight, diligence, and tact in obtaining the complementary or alternative assistance needed by clients.

And for test users whose services may dehumanize because of their ignorance of good professional practices, there are these paragraphs from the *Standards for Educational and Psychological Tests* (American Psychological Association, 1974), which strongly urge them to remedy this situation:

> *Paragraph G1.* A test user should have a general knowledge of measurement principles and of the limitations of test interpretations. ESSENTIAL
> *Paragraph G3.* One who has the responsibility for decisions about individuals or policies that are based on test results should have an understanding of

psychological or educational measurement and of validation and other test research. ESSENTIAL

**Tests Can Be Faked and Therefore Encourage Dissembling.** Some years ago, William H. Whyte, Jr., wrote a book on *The Organization Man* (1956) in which he asserted that tests are inaccurate because they can be faked. Whyte's argument was that tests encourage lying and cheating because they create situations in which applicants for jobs or promotion are obligated to dissemble on tests because they must "look good."

In fact, it is not the tests but rather their critics who encourage cheating. For example, after cautioning about cheating on the MMPI, "which is not a test for the amateur to trifle with" (p. 452), Whyte gave this advice on how to cheat on personality tests (this is analogous to instructing patients to heat their thermometers or to raise their blood pressure): To settle on the most beneficial answer to any question, repeat to yourself . . .

a) I loved my father and my mother, but my father a little bit more.
b) I like things pretty well the way they are.
c) I never worry much about anything.
d) I don't care for books or music much.
e) I love my wife and children.
f) I don't let them get in the way of company work. (1956, p. 450)

Actually these rules do not work in practice. One psychologist (Shaw, 1962) tested them in a study in which he administered the Bernreuter Personality Inventory—a relatively easy test to distort—to fifty-one respondents, once under ordinary job applicant conditions and then again following Whyte's rules. He did not find any statistically significant differences in the two sets of test scores. However, *response set*—that is, the characteristics people consciously or unconsciously express in their answers to test items—and its possible effects on the accuracy of the test scores are real concerns to personality testers, and much has been done and written on this topic (see, for example, Berg, 1967; Block, 1965; Cronbach, 1950; Edwards, 1957; Jackson & Messick, 1958, 1961; and particularly, Wiggins, 1973, pp. 382–425).

The apparent vulnerability of some tests to faking is considered by some critics an open invitation to cheat. The net effect of such faking, according to one psychologist who testified against testing at the congressional hearings, is that it eliminates from jobs and assignments an honest segment of the population:

> A test like the MMPI probably most effectively picks out people who either know how to, or are willing to, carry on superficial lying in a situation when

## BOX 10-1

## Nader/Nairn Report on Tests as Poor Performance Predictors

Consumer advocate Ralph Nader issued his long-awaited, six-year study of the Educational Testing Service in mid-January charging that the giant test-maker's products—namely its array of standardized multiple-choice academic admissions tests—are of little value in predicting school performance and even less in forecasting later career achievement.

For the most part, Nader said, ETS' higher education admissions tests predict academic performance no better than a random toss of the dice. Nevertheless, he argued, it is on the basis of predictive utility that the nation's colleges and universities require such tests and that ETS has built what he characterized as an empire whose unchecked power routinely influences the lives of millions.

"ETS is the largest standardized testing corporation in America and one of the most powerful—though little known—corporations in the world," said Nader on releasing the report. "They have assumed a rare kind of corporate power, the power to change the way people think about their own potential, and through the passive acceptance of their test scores by admissions officers, to decide who will be granted and who will be denied access to education and career opportunities.

"What this report makes clear is that ETS' claims to measure aptitude and predict success are false and unsubstantiated, and can be described as a specialized kind of fraud," Nader charged, squaring off for the latest round in a years'-old battle with ETS over the unregulated power of standardized testing to allocate major life chances.

At a January 14 press conference, Nader and report author Allan Nairn focused on findings—later disputed by ETS chief William Turnbull as "inaccurate and misleading"—that the Scholastic Aptitude Test and other admission tests are poor predictors of first-year college grades.

According to the report, the ability to predict first-year academic grades in college, graduate school or professional school is "the empirical basis of ETS' claim to measure aptitude." However, it emphasizes, the predictive powers of ETS tests, whether the Scholastic Aptitude Test (SAT), the Law School Admission Test (LSAT), the Graduate Management Admission Test (GMAT) or the Graduate Record Examinations (GRE), are extremely weak.

For 90 percent of the time, the report argues, the tests predict first-year grades no better than a random selection process. Using figures compiled from ETS' own validity studies, the Nader/Nairn report calculates that the percentage of cases in which an ETS test predicts first-year grades better than chance is 12 percent for the SAT; 11 percent for the GRE; 13 percent for the LSAT and only 8 percent for the GMAT. Previous grades alone, it states, predict future grades twice as accurately as the tests. . . .

Turnbull challenged the report's statistical treatment, noting that the meth-

*(continued)*

**BOX 10-1** (*Continued*)

ods used by the authors would be likely to lead them to "minimize the apparent effect of using test scores in prediction" and, on the other hand, would invite "an overstatement of the difference between the predictive power of the grades and the test scores."

"I think from what I've seen, the data have been used in such a way that will immediately suggest very low value for test scores when, indeed, common experience indicates that the value is very much larger," he said. Turnbull also noted that while it is true that "colleges find a higher relationship between high school grades and college success than between test scores and college success," it's "not much" higher.

Arguing that test reform would bring about a major change in university admissions policies, Nader called for "application of a broader array of genuine standards which evaluate the diversity of human talents and experience excluded for too long by the ETS testing system." According to Nader, "the ETS-imposed definition of aptitude is undermining important standards demanding good writing, standards demanding active accomplishments, standards demanding, above all, actual performance and the ability to excel in more significant pursuits than multiple-choice test-taking."

In addition, Nader applauded the rising tide of truth-in-testing legislation. The National Public Interest Research Group noted that test laws will be considered in more than a dozen states in the next year. Such legislation, as recently passed in New York and currently being considered in Congress, would, according to Nader, encourage accountability in an industry too long veiled in secrecy.

**Source:** Excerpted from American Psychological Association. Nader releases ETS report, hits test as poor predictors of performance. *APA Monitor*, February 1980, p. 1.

---

it is more or less socially approved. The application of such a test to the Peace Corps means that you probably have in the Peace Corps a great number of people whose prime trait is the ability to lie in a minor way in situations where it is socially approved. These results are not our own results, but the results of some of the best studies which have ever been done on the MMPI. (Smith, 1965, p. 911)

Faking or lying on personality tests is a real problem, but for reasons other than those Smith suggested. Some of the "best studies" Smith referred to in his testimony were in fact motivated by the realization that particular test-taking attitudes have important influences on responses to test items and that these attitudes prevail even after great care has been taken to construct items that invite minimal misinterpretation. For example, faking "good" may occur because someone wants to be released from (or not admitted to) a psychiatric hospital or because someone wants to be hired or promoted. There are many possible reasons for faking in a "good," "bad," or other direction, but the important point here is that it is not as much the measuring instrument

## BOX 10-2

### Test Use and Validity: ETS Reply to the Nader/Nairn Report

A recent report on ETS, written by Allan Nairn and sponsored by Ralph Nader, has charged that the major admissions tests administered by ETS have undue influence on admissions to higher education, and that the tests have little value in predicting future academic performance. The Nairn report arrives at its remarkable conclusions by misrepresenting the purposes and uses of the tests, and by distorting or ignoring the results of research.

Nairn's claims that the SAT is a poor predictor of performance in college are based on faulty statistics. He uses an incorrect value for the characteristic validity of the SAT (.345) since he mistakenly averages the separate validities of the two parts of the SAT, rather than considering the validity of the whole test (.41). After squaring that coefficient and doing some further arithmetic, Nairn comes to the conclusion that "for 88% of the applicants . . . an SAT score will predict their grade rank no more accurately than a pair of dice."

Nairn's interpretation of this statistic is clearly wrong and would make no more sense to a layman than to a professional statistician. Even if the SAT had no predictive validity, it would be *no worse* than a random predictor. However, predictions based on valid information will be better than random predictions, and will certainly be more accurate more than 50 percent of the time. Yet Nairn claims that dice will be as good a predictor as the SAT for 88 percent of the applicants. Nairn's dice should be carefully inspected.

Admissions test scores are used with students' previous grades and other information in predicting later academic performance. The best predictor of college grades is the high school record, but the SAT is nearly as good, and the two together are better than either alone. At the graduate and professional school levels, admission test scores are most often the best available predictors of later grades.

Nairn charges that exaggerated and untrue claims are made for the tests. In support of this charge, Nairn quotes incorrectly from ETS publications. In one instance, he creates a quote, which he attributes to ETS, from parts of two separate and conflicting statements about aptitude testing from two different sources. They were used by ETS to illustrate the wide difference of opinion on that subject. Nairn also quotes from an SAT publication, deleting words and adding others in brackets to transform the meaning of the original passage. Nairn concludes that testers have assumed a right "to define the potential for thinking." The fact is that ETS claims only that the tests can be a useful measure of knowledge or academic ability. "No test," state College Board bulletins and manuals, "predicts with any certainty 'success in life' or is in any way a measure of an individual's total worth."

The tests administered by ETS are sponsored and controlled by associations of colleges and graduate and professional schools that use scores on

*(continued)*

> **BOX 10–2** (*Continued*)
>
> the tests as one factor in admissions decision-making. The tests that are described as aptitude tests were never meant to assess innate, unchanging abilities, but to measure learned skills. They are designed to provide a common basis for evaluation, to supplement students' academic records, and to permit students to satisfy admissions testing requirements of institutions across the country through taking a single examination at nearby testing centers, at relatively low cost.
>
> No doubt improvements in admissions can be made. But Nairn does not suggest alternatives that would perform the important functions now performed by admissions tests. Because of this and its misrepresentations, the report is unlikely to contribute to the improvement of admissions to higher education.
>
> **Source:** Educational Testing Service. *Test use and validity: A response to charges in the Nader/Nairn report on ETS.* Princeton, NJ: Educational Testing Service, February 1980, pp. 2–4.

that causes dissembling as it is the test taker and his or her needs and circumstances. But these reasons and the faking itself are not always conscious.

**Tests Assume Self-Knowledge.** Aside from the facts of conscious or unconscious test dissimulation, many critics have faulted self-report tests because they believe these tests are predicated on the notion that people understand their motivations for their behavior and have an accurate recall of the events and circumstances in their lives.

But self-report tests do not make such assumptions, for as Freud made us well aware, many of our motives, memories, and actions are inaccessible to us. Paradoxically, in many personality disorders, the degree of self-knowledge is inversely related to the severity of the disorder. Thus it is not uncommon to find schizophrenics who believe they are well, sometimes despite lengthy hospitalizations, and to find reasonably normal persons who believe they are going mad. The point is that test interpreters, particularly when dealing with responses made to self-report inventories, understand, and hence correct for, the fact that people have very little insight into their psychological functioning. Moreover, as we indicated in chapters three and seven, Paul Meehl (1945a) in his classic article on the dynamics of structured tests, has argued convincingly that although the stimulus situation—that is, the test items—seems to request a self-rating, the scoring does not assume that a valid self-rating has been given. In other words, what a person says about himself or herself may be a highly significant fact even though the interpreter of structured tests does not entertain with any confidence the proposition that this agrees with what complete knowledge of that person would lead others to say of him or her.

**BOX 10-3**

## Concerns about New York's Truth in Testing Law

Despite intense lobbying from major test producers, administrators and the New York State Psychological Association this summer, New York became the first state to enact sweeping new disclosure standards for major standardized admissions tests including the Scholastic Aptitude Test (SAT), the Law School Admission Test (LSAT) and the Graduate Record Exam (GRE), along with major dental and medical school admissions tests.

At the core of the controversial new law are provisions that require disclosure of actual test forms and individual answers at the request of those who take the exams. The measure spells trouble for major test producers such as the Education Testing Service, Inc. (ETS) in Princeton, New Jersey. ETS officials have said that such disclosure will certainly affect a test manufacturer's capacity to assure continued reliability and validity of various test instruments through processes based on years of reuse and screening. The new requirements are also expected to affect the reliability of various exams as predictors of academic success across varying geographical regions and from one year to another.

"I think you'll see it snowball in the future," commented ETS's Ernest Kimmel, director of test development for college board programs. Kimmel indicated that his view is shared by many in the Princeton headquarters, and that ETS is preparing to live with the trend. . . .

The issue has already been brought before legislatures in Ohio, Maryland and Colorado, and Rep. Ted Weiss (D-N.Y.) introduced a similar bill in Washington shortly after New York Governor Hugh Carey's approval of the measure last July.

California has already passed its own version of truth in testing law, but it stops short of requiring public access to actual tests and their corrected answers.

Most major test administrators, as of mid-summer, had yet to trim their policies and plans for changes in their testing programs in New York, but it was almost certain that the number of exam dates set for tests such as the SAT and the GRE would be cut back. Officials from the Dental Admissions Testing Program, administered by the American Dental Association, and the American College Testing Program, which administers the Medical College Admissions Test, have indicated that those exams would not be available in New York next year when the law takes effect.

Problems with the new law are not far off the horizon. There were 21 forms of the SAT used across the country last year, according to the College Board which oversees that program. ETS says that it has designed seven new forms of the test for the 1979–1980 academic year. "To publicly disclose and essentially exhaust those new instruments," said Kimmel, "would pretty much empty the bank." . . .

But the College Board, which admin-

*(continued)*

**BOX 10–3** (*Continued*)

istered 210,000 SATs in New York alone last year, has registered other objections to the new law in suggesting that it will be costly and complicated to comply with. New requirements for background data and statistical information, says the board, "would be costly, time consuming and, in some cases, improper or impossible" to produce.... Charles Marshall of the National Association of College Admissions Counselors, representing about 2,000 administrators in high school and college admissions, said the impact of the new law in New York is hard to predict at the moment, but he indicated it would be up to test developers like ETS and the American College Testing program to insure some kind of continued quality assurance for standardized tests. But he added that admissions policies he's familiar with have rendered standardized admissions tests as only one of many factors in college admissions and are seldom the pivotal factor, as some have charged.

Thus far, ETS has said it plans to comply with new requirements in New York, but as of yet, neither ETS nor the College Board knows what level of service New York students can expect next year. But ETS's Kimmel said the problem of constructing separate test forms for New York may solve itself if other states pick up the trend.

"Maybe it's paranoia," said Kimmel. "But ETS, ACT and the College Board are getting ready for the groundswell."

**Source:** Excerpted from Foltz, D. "Snowball effect" seen in truth in testing movement. *APA Monitor*, September/October 1979, p. 3.

**Tests Are Too Powerful.** A recent report sponsored by consumer advocate Ralph Nader and written by statistician Allan Nairn claimed that the Educational Testing Service (ETS) was exerting undue influence on the admissions policies of most major institutions of higher education. The so-called Nader/Nairn Report (see Box 10–1) charged also that large testing corporations, especially the ETS, use tests that have poor predictive efficiency. And the net effect of these two factors—power and poor tests—is that many qualified and creative young people are excluded from colleges, which is a waste of resources that this country can ill afford.

The Nader/Nairn report provoked a strong response from ETS president William Turnbull (see Box 10–2), who defended the Scholastic Aptitude Test's predictive usefulness and disputed the idea that the ETS was unduly influencing educational decision making. Turnbull's main arguments, however, were that all tests are fallible to some degree, that they certainly are aids to admission boards, and that the ETS never recommended using tests without also considering a student's previous high school performance.

Finally, as a sign of the consumers' current feelings about testing, there is now a "truth-in-testing" law effective in New York State (see Box 10-3). This law, which became effective on January 1, 1980, applies to all tests administered to more than five thousand persons, applying to colleges, professional schools, and graduate programs. Some of the tests affected by this law—almost all developed by the ETS—are the SATs, the MCATs (medical school), LSATs (law school), the GREs (Graduate Record Examinations), and the ACTs (American College Testing Program for undergraduate admissions, comparable to the SATs—not an ETS test).

The law contains three major provisions. First, the test takers must be told when they register how their scores will be computed; what the tester's contractual obligation to them is; and how test scores have been found to correlate with such background factors as socioeconomic class, education, race, and special coaching and preparations for the exam. Second, the companies (e.g., ETS, Psychological Corporation, American College Testing Program) must file information and studies on the validity of their exams with the office of the state education commissioner. And third, the testing companies must make available to the public the exams' questions and correct answers. Within thirty days of receiving the results, a student is entitled to see his or her graded answer sheet. Bills similar to this law are currently being considered in the legislatures of several states—clearly a sign that consumers are deeply displeased about what such tests have offered to the public.

## SUMMARY AND CONCLUSIONS

This final chapter dealt with the technical problems and ethical implications of psychological and personality testing. The technical problems are the disagreement on what personality is, an obsolete taxonomic system for classifying personality, testing's too numerous settings and aims, tests of sometimes questionable use, test subjects' reactivity, the inconsistency of observers and the behaviors they observe, and the generally inadequate methods used to study personality.

Several ethical issues were also raised, the two main ones being people's privacy and civil rights. Critics have also objected to testing's ethical implications, stating that tests dehumanize, encourage lying, and assume a self-awareness that does not exist. These critics also believe that tests exert an undue influence on educational policies and should be monitored more carefully or perhaps abolished.

These and similar problems and objections to testing have provoked rather strong, and sometimes emotional, public reactions. One of these reactions culminated in congressional hearings that investigated the tests' possible invasion of privacy. Another reaction resulted in a report sponsored by Ralph Nader, which charged that testing had become too powerful. These reactions are more than just a passing fad. They have been part of the testing scene since the mid-1960s and recently culminated in New York's adoption of a "truth-in-testing" law, which has seriously affected aptitude testing and which may be enacted by other states as well.

Taking a somewhat broader view than the summary of this chapter has, we conclude this book by noting that our journey through the various interdependent components of the information-processing system of Figure 1–1 of chapter one—with particular emphasis on the tools of assessment—has now come to a halt. En route, we encountered many important functions and uses of the system which served as the book's organizing scheme.

At the outset, we dwelt on properly preparing the input or data side of testing, which required formulating test goals relevant to the setting, purpose, and theory of the test user. We then selected the assessment tools and applied to them the criteria of objectivity, reliability, and validity before entering them into the information processor.

Once the test data had been entered, they were processed with the help of several interpretive aids which included norms and profiles, as well as systems to help formulate interpretations of and predictions about the person. After the test data were properly processed in this way, they entered the output side of the system, whose main purpose was the communication of findings and recommendations to the referral source.

Our information processor is, of course, not a real system installed and operating at a facility. We simply used it as a scheme to help illustrate some of the process's components and as a blueprint for a system that may become a reality in the future. In the meantime, we recognize that the prospect of using an information processor similar to the one we designed may, to some readers, seem to be a cold-hearted, even grim, method for giving, scoring, interpreting, and communicating tests and their scores. These readers might be willing to admit that machines may be all right for scoring tests—a function they have been routinely performing for about thirty-five years—but they are not ready to accept the idea that machines can make intelligent choices and inferences. We disagree with this view. We think that an information-processing system—much like the many automated systems currently used to interpret interviews and tests (see chapters four, six, seven, and eight)—can be useful to many testing and decision situations.

Is this desirable? The answer should rest on one decisive criterion: whether the automated system is superior to the human information processor. In other words, we should use the system that best administers, scores, interprets, and communicates tests and their findings.

The criteria of "superior" and "best" must be defined as the speed and efficiency of the system's processing capabilities, as well as the accuracy and comprehensiveness of its descriptive, interpretive, and communication skills. But before the image of the robot information processor arouses too much anxiety among our readers, we hasten to remind you that there still are many interpretive and inferential functions that humans perform better than machines do. And clearly, there are other, distinctly humanoid qualities that machines will never possess: namely, empathy, understanding, and warmth. The final decision about the balance between the cost effectiveness of machines and the warmth of humans also ultimately rests with humans, and making this decision, as Guion (1976) recently observed in another context, may still be an art.

# FOR FURTHER READING

American Psychological Association. *Ethical standards of psychologists.* Washington, DC: Directory of the American Psychological Association, 1978, pp. xxix–xxxiii. With its nine principles regarding, among other essentials, the responsibility, competence, and moral and legal standards of psychologists, the *Ethical Standards* are conveniently reprinted in every psychologist's favorite reference book: the *Directory.*

American Psychological Association. Special issue: Testing-concepts, policy, practice, and research. *American Psychologist,* 1981, *36,* 997–1189. This special edition of the psychologist's main professional journal deals exclusively with some of the technical and public policy issues discussed in this book.

American Psychological Association. *Standards for educational and psychological tests.* Washington, DC: American Psychological Association, 1974. The *Standards* are must reading for anyone who is a test user. Within its seventy-six pages (including index) it contains guidelines and principles pertaining to tests and their proper construction.

Bross, I.D.J. *Designs for decision. An introduction to decision-making.* New York: Free Press, 1953. An absolutely fascinating book on statistical decision theory. It has a light, humorous touch and has been an inspiration to us for the last twenty-five years.

Fiske, D.W. *Strategies for personality research: The observation versus interpretation of behavior.* San Francisco: Jossey-Bass, 1978. In one volume, Fiske tries to solve the problems of why the study of personality is not yet a science.

Holt, R.R. *Methods in clinical psychology: Projective assessment* (Vol. 1); *Prediction and research* (Vol. 2), 1978. The second of these volumes is particularly pertinent here for its coverage of experimental methods in clinical and personality research.

Magnusson, D. & Endler, N.S. (Eds.). *Personality at the crossroads: Current issues in interactional psychology.* Hillsdale, NJ: Lawrence Erlbaum, 1977. A compendium of contributions to the issues of the person-by-situations interactions for personality assessment.

Meehl, P.E. *Psychodiagnosis: Selected papers.* Minneapolis: University of Minnesota Press, 1973. The collection of papers by one of clinical psychology's most prolific contributors covers many important areas and issues of personality assessment.

Pervin, L.A. *Current controversies and issues in personality.* New York: John Wiley, 1978. Among the topics and issues covered in this ambitiously titled volume are "Am I me or am I the situation?" "The genetically determined person is the self-made person," "Why do and don't people help?" and "The tactics and ethics of personality research."

Weizenbaum, J. *Computer power and human reason: From judgment to calculation.* San Francisco: W. H. Freeman, 1976. As the title suggests, this book is a polemical, perhaps an even tongue-in-cheek, treatment of the limited powers of the computer. The author is one of the pioneers in computer interviewing and natural language processing.

# References

Abramson, P. R., & Mosher, D. L. Development of a measure of negative attitudes toward masturbation. *Journal of Clinical and Consulting Psychology*, 1975, *43*, 485–490.

Adair, F. L. Re MMPI computerized scoring and interpreting services. In O. K. Buros (Ed.), *Eighth mental measurements yearbook*. Highland Park, NJ: Gryphon Press, 1978.

Adcock, C. J. Review of the MMPI. In O. K. Buros (Ed.), *Sixth mental measurements yearbook*. Highland Park, NJ: Gryphon Press, 1965.

Adorno, T. W., Frenkel-Brunswik, E., Levinson, D. J., & Sanford, R. N. *The authoritarian personality*. New York: Harper & Row, 1950.

Aiken, L. R. *Psychological testing and assessment* (3rd ed.). Boston: Allyn & Bacon, 1979.

Alexander, M. J. *Information systems analysis: Theory and applications*. Palto Alto, CA: Science Research Associates, 1976.

Aiker, H. A. Review of the MMPI. In O. K. Buros (Ed.), *Eighth mental measurements yearbook*. Highland Park, NJ: Gryphon Press, 1978.

Allison, H. W., & Allison, S. G. Personality changes following transorbital lobotomy. *Journal of Abnormal and Social Psychology*, 1954, *49*, 219–223.

Allport, F. H., & Hartman, D. A. Measurement and motivation of a typical opinion in a certain group. *American Political Science Review*, 1925, *19*, 735–760.

Allport, G. W. *Personality: A psychological interpretation*. New York: Holt, Rinehart & Winston, 1937.

Allport, G. W. *The use of personal documents in psychological science*. New York: Social Science Research Council, Bulletin 49, 1942.

Allport, G. W., The trend in motivational theory. *American Journal of Orthopsychiatry*, 1953, *23*, 107–119.

Allport, G. W. *Pattern and growth in personality*. New York: Holt, Rinehart & Winston, 1961.

Allport, G. W., Traits revisited. *American Psychologist*, 1966, *21*, 1–10.

Allport, G. W., *Letters from Jenny*, New York: Harcourt, Brace & World, 1965.

Allport, G. W. & Odbert, H. S. Trait-names: A psycho-lexical study. *Psychological Monographs*, 1936, *47*, No. 211, 1–171.

Allport, G. W., & Vernon, P. E. A test for personal values. *Journal of Abnormal and Social Psychology*, 1931, *26*, 231–248.

Allport, G. W., Vernon, P. E., & Lindzey, G. *Study of values* (3rd ed.). Boston: Houghton Mifflin, 1960.

# References

Almy, T. P. The stress interview: Unfinished business. *Journal of Human Stress*, 1978, *4*, 3–8.

American Psychiatric Association, *Diagnostic and statistical manual of mental disorders* (DSM I). Washington, DC: American Psychiatric Association, 1952.

American Psychiatric Association. *Diagnostic and statistical manual of mental disorders* (DSM II). Washington, DC: American Psychiatric Association, 1968.

American Psychiatric Association. *Diagnostic and statistical manual of mental disorders* (DSM III). Washington, DC: American Psychiatric Association, 1980.

American Psychological Association. Special issue: Testing and public policy. *American Psychologist*, 1965, *20*, 857–993.

American Psychological Association. *Standards for educational and psychological tests and manuals*. Washington, DC: American Psychological Association, 1966.

American Psychological Association. *Standards for educational and psychological tests*. Washington, DC: American Psychological Association, 1974.

American Psychological Association. Ethical standards of psychologists. *APA Monitor*, March 1977 (also reprinted in the Directory of the American Psychological Association, 1978 edition). (a)

American Psychological Association. *Standards for providers of psychological services*. Washington, DC: American Psychological Association, 1977. (b)

American Psychological Association. *Standards for providers of industrial and organizational psychological services*. Washington, DC: American Psychological Association, 1979 (cited in London-Bray, 1979).

American Psychological Association. Nader releases ETS report, hits test as poor predictors of performance. *APA Monitor*, February 1980.

Anastasi, A. Review of the Personality Research Form. O. K. Buros (Ed.). *Seventh mental measurements yearbook*. Highland Park, NJ: Gryphon Press, 1972.

Anastasi, A. *Psychological testing* (4th ed.). New York: Macmillan, 1976.

Anderson, H. H., & Anderson, G. L. (Eds.). *An introduction to projective techniques*. Englewood Cliffs, NJ: Prentice-Hall, 1951.

Anderson, S., & Messick, S. Social competency in young children. *Developmental Psychology*, 1974, *10*, 282–293.

Angoff, W. H. Scales, norms, and equivalent scores. In R. L. Thorndike (Ed.), *Educational measurement* (2nd ed.). Washington, DC: American Council on Education, 1971.

Argyle, M., & Little, B. R. Do personality traits apply to social behavior? *Journal for Theory of Social Behavior*, 1972, *2*, 1–35.

Atkinson, J. W. *Studies in projective measurement of achievement motivation*. Unpublished doctoral dissertation, University of Michigan, 1950.

Atkinson, J. W. Thematic apperceptive measurement of motives within the context of a theory of motivation. In J. W. Atkinson (Ed.), *Motives in fantasy, action, and society*. Princeton, NJ: D. Van Nostrand, 1958.

Ayllon, T., & Azrin, N. H. *The token economy: A motivational system for therapy and rehabilitation*. New York: Appleton-Century-Crofts, 1968.

Azrin, N. H., & Powell, J. Behavioral engineering: The reduction of smoking behavior by a conditioning apparatus and procedure. *Journal of Applied Behavior Analysis,* 1968, *1,* 193–200.

Azrin, N. H., Rubin, H., O'Brien, F., Ayllon, T., & Roll, D. Behavioral engineering: Postural control by a portable operant apparatus. *Journal of Applied Behavior Analysis,* 1968, *1,* 99–108.

Babbie, E. R. *The practice of social research.* Belmont, CA: Wadsworth, 1975.

Bakan, P. Extraversion-introversion and improvement in an auditory vigilance task. *Medical Research Council,* 1957, A.P.U. 311/57.

Baldwin, A. L. Personal structure analysis. *Journal of Abnormal and Social Psychology,* 1942, *37,* 63–183.

Bandura, A. Psychotherapy as a learning process. *Psychological Bulletin,* 1961, *58,* 143–159.

Bandura, A. *Principles of behavior modification.* New York: Holt, Rinehart, & Winston, 1969.

Bandura, A. *Social learning theory.* Morristown, NJ: General Learning Press, 1971.

Bandura, A. Behavior theory and the models of man. *American Psychologist,* 1974, *29,* 859–869.

Bandura, A., Grusec, J. E., & Menlove, F. L. Vicarious extinction of avoidance behavior. *Journal of Personality and Social Psychology,* 1967, *5,* 16–23.

Bandura, A., & Menlove, F. L. Factors determining vicarious extinction of avoidance behavior through symbolic modeling. *Journal of Personality and Social Psychology,* 1968, *8,* 99–108.

Bannister, D., & Mair, J. M. *The evaluation of personal constructs.* New York: Academic Press, 1968.

Barker, H. R., Fowler, R. D., & Peterson, L. P. Factor analytic structure of the short form MMPI in a VA hospital population. *Journal of Clinical Psychology,* 1971, *27,* 228–233.

Barker, R. G. (Ed.). *The stream of behavior.* New York: Appleton-Century-Crofts, 1963.

Barker, R. G., & Wright, H. F. *Midwest and its children: The psychological economy of an American town.* New York: Harper & Row, 1955.

Barron, F. Some test correlates of responses to psychotherapy. *Journal of Consulting Psychology,* 1953, *17,* 234–241.

Barthell, C. N., & Holmes, D. S. High school yearbooks: A nonreactive measure of social isolation in graduates who later became schizophrenic. *Journal of Abnormal Psychology,* 1968, *73,* 313–316.

Baughman, E. E. Rorschach scores as a function of examiner difference. *Journal of Projective Techniques,* 1951, *15,* 243–249.

Baughman, E. E. *Personality: The psychological study of the individual.* Englewood Cliffs, NJ: Prentice-Hall, 1972.

Beck, S. J. *Rorschach's test: Basic processes* (Vol. 1). New York: Grune & Stratton, 1944.

Beck, S. J. *Rorschach's test: A variety of personality pictures* (Vol. 2). New York: Grune & Stratton, 1945.

Beck, S. J. How the Rorschach came to America. *Journal of Personality Assessment,* 1972, *36,* 105–108.

Bellak, A. S., & Hersen, M. *Introduction to clinical psychology.* New York: Oxford University Press, 1980.

Bellak, L. *The thematic apperception test and the children's apperception test in clinical use.* New York: Grune & Stratton, 1954.

Bellak, L., & Bellak, S. *The children's apperception test.* New York: CPS Company, 1952.

Bem, D. J. Constructing cross-situational consistencies: Some thoughts on Alker's critique of Mischel. In N. S. Endler & D. Magnusson (Eds.), *Interactional psychology and personality.* Washington, DC: Hemisphere Publishing, 1976.

Bem, D. J., & Bem, S. L. *Homogenizing the American woman: The power of an unconscious ideology.* Unpublished manuscript, Stanford University, 1972.

Bem, D. J., & Funder, D. C. Predicting more of the people more of the time: Assessing the personality of situation. *Psychological Review,* 1978, *85,* 485–501.

Bem, S. L. The measurement of psychological androgyny. *Journal of Consulting and Clinical Psychology,* 1974, *42,* 155–162.

Bem, S. L. Sex-role adaptability: One consequence of psychological androgyny. *Journal of Personality and Social Psychology,* 1975, *31,* 634–643.

Bem, S. L. On the utility of alternative procedures for assessing psychological androgyny. *Journal of Consulting and Clinical Psychology,* 1977, *45,* 196–205.

Bem, S. L. Theory and measurement of androgyny: A reply to the Pedhazur-Tetenbaum and Locksley-Colten critiques. *Journal of Personality and Social Psychology,* 1979, *37,* 1047–1054.

Bender, L. G. *Visual motor gestalt test.* Beverly Hills, CA: Western Psychological Services, 1938–1946.

Benjamin, A. *The helping interview.* Boston: Houghton Mifflin, 1969.

Berelson, B. Content analysis. In G. Lindzey (Ed.). *Handbook of social psychology.* Vol. 1. Cambridge, Mass.: Addison-Wesley, 1954.

Berg, I. A. The deviation hypothesis: A broad statement of its assumptions and postulates. In I. A. Berg (Ed.), *Response set in personality assessment.* Chicago: Aldine, 1967.

Berger, R. M., Guilford, J. P., & Christensen, P. R. A factor analytic study of planning abilities. *Psychological Monographs,* 1957, No. 435.

Bernstein, D. A., & Nietzel, M. T. *Introduction to clinical psychology.* New York: McGraw-Hill, 1980.

Bickman, L., Data collection: Observational methods (Vol. 1). In C. Selltiz, L. S. Wrightsman, & S. W. Cook (Eds.), *Research methods in social relations.* New York: Holt, Rinehart & Winston, 1976.

Bijou, S. W., & Peterson, R. F. Functional analysis in the assessment of children.

In P. McReynolds (Ed.), *Advances in psychological assessment* (Vol. 2). Palo Alto, CA: Science & Behavior Books, 1971.

Billingslea, F. Y. The Bender-Gestalt: A review and a perspective. *Psychological Bulletin*, 1963, *60*, 233–251.

Binet, A. & Henri, V. La psychologie individuelle. *Anné Psychologique*, 1895, *2*, 411–463.

Bingham, W. V. D., & Moore, B. V. *How to interview* (4th rev. ed.). New York: Harper & Brothers, 1959.

Bingham, W. V. D., Moore, B. V., & Gustad, J. W. *How to interview* (4th ed.). New York: Harper & Row, 1959.

Bjerstedt, A. Review of the Rosenzweig P-F study. In O. K. Buros (Ed.), *Sixth mental measurements yearbook*. Highland Park, NJ: Gryphon Press, 1965.

Black, J. D. *The interpretation of MMPI profiles of college women*. Unpublished doctoral dissertation, University of Minnesota, 1953 (reprinted in part in Welsh & Dahlstrom, 1956).

Blakemore, C. B. Review of Bender-Gestalt test. In O. K. Buros (Ed.), *Sixth mental measurements yearbook*. Highland Park, NJ: Gryphon Press, 1965.

Blanchard, E. B., & Young, L. D. Clinical applications of biofeedback training. *Archives of General Psychiatry*, 1974, *30*, 573–589.

Block, J. *The Q-sort method in personality assessment and psychiatric research*. Springfield, Ill., Thomas, 1960.

Block, J. *The challenge of response sets: Unconfounding meaning, acquiescence, and social desirability in the MMPI*. New York: Appleton-Century-Crofts, 1965.

Block, J. Personal communication, 1968.

Block, J. *Lives through time*. Berkeley, CA: Bancroft, 1971.

Block, J. Some reasons for the apparent inconsistencies of personality. In N. S. Endler & D. Magnusson (Eds.), *Interactional psychology and personality*. Washington, DC: Hemisphere Publishing, 1976.

Block, J. Advancing the psychology of personality: Paradigmatic shift or improving the quality of research. In D. Magnusson & N. S. Endler (Eds.), *Personality at the crossroads: Current issues in interactional psychology*. Hillsdale, NJ: Lawrence Erlbaum, 1977.

Block, J. H., & Block, J. The role of ego-control and ego-resiliency on the organization of behavior. In W. A. Collins (Ed.), *Minnesota symposia on child psychology* (Vol. 13). New York: Lawrence Erlbaum, 1979.

Block, J., Weiss, D. S., & Thorne, A. How relevant is a semantic similarity interpretation of personality ratings. *Journal of Personality and Social Psychology*, 1979, *37*, 1055–1074.

Block, N. J., & Dworkin, G. (Eds.). *The IQ controversy*. New York: Pantheon, 1976.

Blois, M. S. Clinical judgment and computers. *New England Journal of Medicine*, 1980, *303*, 192–197.

Blum, G. S. *The Blacky pictures: Manual of instructions*. New York: Psychological Corporation, 1950–1962.

Blumenthal, A. L. *The process of cognition.* Englewood Cliffs, NJ: Prentice-Hall, 1977.

Bootzin, R. R. *Abnormal psychology: Current perspectives.* New York: Random House, 1980.

Boring, E. G. Intelligence as the tests test it. *New Republic,* 1923, *35,* 35–37.

Bouchard, T. J. Review of the differential aptitude test. In O. K. Buros (Ed.), *Eighth mental measurements yearbook.* Highland Park, NJ: Gryphon Press, 1978.

Bouchard, T. J. Personal communication. April 16, 1980.

Borman, W. C., Exploring upper limits of reliability and validity in job performance ratings. *Journal of Applied Psychology,* 1978, *63,* 135–144.

Boulding, K. E. Role prejudice as an economic problem. *Monthly Labor Review,* 1974, *97,* 40. Cited in Diamond, E. E. Issues of sex bias and sex fairness in career interest measurement. In C. K. Tittle, & D. G. Zytowski (Eds.), *Sex-fair interest measurement.* Washington, DC: U.S. Government Printing Office, 1978.

Bowers, K. S. Situationism in psychology. *Psychological Review,* 1973, *80,* 307–336.

Bowers, K. S. Situationism in psychology. In N. S. Endler & D. Magnusson (Eds.), *Interactional psychology and personality.* Washington, DC: Hemisphere Publishing, 1976.

Boyd, V. S. Neutralizing sexist titles in Holland's self-directed search: What difference does it make? In C. K. Tittle & D. G. Zytowski (Eds.), *Sex-fair interest measurement: Research and implications.* Washington, DC: U.S. Government Printing Office, 1978.

Brady, J. *The craft of interviewing.* Cincinnati: Writer's Digest, 1976.

Brebner, J. M. T. *An experimental investigation of the relationship between conditioning and introversion-extraversion in normal subjects.* Unpublished master's thesis, University of Aberdeen, 1957.

Brigham, C. C. *A study of American intelligence.* Princeton, NJ: Princeton University Press, 1923.

Brody, E. B. & Brody, N. *Intelligence: Nature, determinants, and consequences.* New York: Academic Press, 1976.

Brody, N. *Personality: Research and theory.* New York: Academic Press, 1972.

Brooks, R., & Kleinmuntz, B. Design of an intelligent computer diagnostician. *Behavioral Science,* 1974, *19,* 16–20.

Bross, I. D. J. *Design for decision. An introduction to decision-making.* New York: Free Press, 1953.

Broverman, I. K., Vogel, S. R., Broverman, D. M., Clarkson, F. E., & Rosenkrantz, P. S. Sex-role stereotypes: A current appraisal. *Journal of Social Issues,* 1972, *28,* 59–78.

Brown, F. G. *Principles of educational and psychological testing.* New York: Holt, Rinehart & Winston, 1976.

Brown, W. R., & McGuire, J. M. Current psychological assessment practices. *Professional Psychology,* 1976, *7,* 475–484.

Buchwald, A. M. Verbal utterances as data. In H. Feigl & G. Maxwell (Eds.), *Current issues in the philosophy of science.* New York: Holt, 1961.

Buck, J. N., & Jolles, I. *H-T-P: House-tree-person projective technique.* Beverly Hills, CA: Western Psychological Services, 1946–1964.

Buck, R. W., Savin, V. J., Miller, R. E., & Caul, W. F. Communication of affect through facial expression in humans. *Journal of Personality and Social Psychology,* 1972, *23,* 362–371.

Buros, O. K. (Ed.). *The nineteen thirty-eight mental measurements yearbook of the school of education, Rutgers University.* New Brunswick, NJ: Rutgers University Press, 1938.

Buros, O. K. (Ed.). *The fifth mental measurements yearbook.* Highland Park, NJ: Gryphon Press, 1959.

Buros, O. K. (Ed.). *The sixth mental measurements yearbook.* Highland Park, NJ: Gryphon Press, 1965.

Buros, O. K. (Ed.). *Seventh mental measurements yearbook.* Highland Park, NJ: Gryphon Press, 1972.

Buros, O. K. (Ed.). *Eighth mental measurements yearbook.* Highland Park, NJ: Gryphon Press, 1978.

Burt, C. Ability and income. *British Journal of Educational Psychology,* 1943, *13,* 83–98.

Burt, C. The inheritance of mental ability. *American Psychologist,* 1958, *13,* 1–15.

Burt, C. The genetic determination of differences. *British Journal of Psychology,* 1966, *57,* 137–153.

Butcher, J. N. *Objective personality assessment.* Morristown, NJ: General Learning Press, 1971.

Butcher, J. N. Personality assessment: Problems and perspectives. In J. N. Butcher (Ed.), *Objective personality assessment: Changing perspective.* New York: Academic Press, 1972.

Butcher, J. N. Review of computerized scoring and interpreting services. In O. K. Buros (Ed.), *Eighth mental measurements yearbook.* Highland Park, NJ: Gryphon Press, 1978.

Butcher, J. N. *New developments in MMPI research.* Minneapolis: University of Minnesota Press, 1979.

Butcher, J. N., & Owen, P. L. Objective personality inventories: Recent research and some contemporary issues. In B. Wolman (Ed.), *Handbook of clinical diagnosis of mental disorders.* New York: Plenum, 1978.

Butcher, J. N., Pancheri, P., & Morgana, A. Computer interpretation of the MMPI in Europe. In J. N. Butcher & P. Pancheri (Eds.). *A handbook of cross-national MMPI research.* Minneapolis, University of Minnesota Press, 1976.

Cacioppo, J. T., & Petty, R. E. Electromyograms as measures of extent and affectivity of information processing. *American Psychologist,* 1981, *36,* 441–456.

Caldwell, A. B. *Caldwell report: An MMPI interpretation.* Santa Monica, CA: Caldwell Report, 1969.

Caldwell, A. B. Personal communication, July 1980.

Caldwell, A. B. Personal communication. May 29, 1981.

Campbell, D. P. The Strong vocational interest blank: 1927–1967. In P. McReynolds (Ed.), *Advances in psychological assessment* (Vol. 1). Palo Alto, CA: Science & Behavior Books, 1968.

Campbell, D. P. *Handbook for the Strong vocational interest blank.* Stanford, CA: Stanford University Press, 1971.

Campbell, D. P. The practical problems of revising an established psychological test. In J. N. Butcher (Ed.), *Objective personality assessment.* New York: Academic Press, 1972.

Campbell, D. P. *Manual for the Strong-Campbell interest inventory.* Stanford, CA: Stanford University Press, 1974.

Campbell, D. P. Review of the Strong-Campbell interest inventory. *Measurement and Evaluation Guidance,* 1976, *9,* 45–46.

Campbell, D. T. Factors relevant to the validity of experiments in social settings. *Psychological Bulletin,* 1957, *54,* 297–312.

Campbell, D. T., & Fiske, D. W. Convergent and discriminant validation by the multitrait-multimethod matrix. *Psychological Bulletin,* 1959, *56,* 81–105.

Campbell, D. T., & Stanley, J. C. *Experimental and quasi-experimental designs for research.* Chicago: Rand McNally, 1966.

Cannell, C. F., & Kahn, R. L. Interviewing. In G. Lindzey & E. Aronson (Eds.), *The handbook of social psychology* (Vol. 2). (2nd ed.). Reading, MA: Addison-Wesley, 1968.

Carey, G., & Gottesman, I. I. Reliability and validity in binary ratings: Areas of common misunderstanding in diagnosis and symptom ratings. *Archives of General Psychiatry,* 1978, *35,* 1454–1459.

Carroll, J. B. Psychometric tests as cognitive tasks: A new "structure of intellect." In L. Resnick (Ed.), *The nature of intelligence.* Hillsdale, NJ: Lawrence Erlbaum, 1976.

Cartwright, C. A., & Cartwright, G. P. *Developing observation skills.* New York: McGraw-Hill, 1974.

Cattell, R. B. *The culture fair intelligence test.* Champaign, IL: Institute for Personality and Ability Testing, 1950.

Cattell, R. B. *Personality and motivation structure and measurement.* New York: Harcourt, Brace & World, 1957.

Cattell, R. B. Theory of fluid and crystallized intelligence: A critical experiment. *Journal of Educational Psychology,* 1963, *54,* 1–22.

Cattell, R. B. (Ed.). *Handbook of modern personality theory.* Urbana: University of Illinois Press, 1971. (a)

Cattell, R. B. *Abilities: Their structure, growth, and action.* Boston: Houghton Mifflin, 1971. (b)

Cattell, R. B. *Manual for forms A, B, C, D, and E sixteen personality factor questionnaire.* Champaign, IL: IPAT, 1949–1976.

Cattell, R. B., & Kline, P. *The scientific analysis of personality and motivation.* New York: Academic Press, 1977.

Cautela, J. R. Covert sensitization. *Psychological Reports*, 1967, *20*, 459–468.

Cautela, J. R. Behavior therapy and the need for assessment. *Psychotherapy: Theory, Research, and Practice*, 1968, *5*, 175–179.

Cautela, J. R. Covert processes and behavior modification. *Journal of Nervous and Mental Disease*, 1973, *157*, 27–35.

Chapman, J., & McGhie, A. A comparative study of disordered attention in schizophrenia. *Journal of Mental Science*, 1962, *108*, 487–500.

Chapman, L. J., & Chapman, J. P. Genesis of popular but erroneous psychodiagnostic observations. *Journal of Abnormal Psychology*, 1967, *72*, 193–204.

Chapman, L. J., & Chapman, J. P. Illusory correlation as an obstacle to the use of valid psychodiagnostic signs. *Journal of Abnormal Psychology*, 1969, *74*, 271–280.

Chapple, E. D. "Personality" differences as described by invariant properties of individuals in interaction. *Proceedings of the National Academy of Sciences*, 1940, *26*, 10–16.

Chapple, E. D., Chamberlain, A. S., Egger, A. H., & Kline, N. S. Measurement of the activity patterns of schizophrenic patients. *Journal of Nervous and Mental Disease*, 1963, *137*, 258–267.

Ciminero, A. R. Behavioral assessment: An overview. In A. R. Ciminero, K. S. Calhoun, & H. E. Adams (Eds.), *Handbook of behavioral assessment*. New York: John Wiley, 1977.

Ciminero, A. R., Nelson, O. R., & Lipinski, D. P. Self-monitoring procedures. In A. R. Ciminero, K. S. Calhoun, & H. E. Adams (Eds.), *Handbook of behavior assessment*. New York: John Wiley, 1977.

Claridge, G. The excitation-inhibition balance in neurotics. In Eysenck, H. J. (Ed.), *Experiments in personality*. London: Routledge & Kegan Paul, 1960.

Clark, K. B. Quoted in *Newsweek*, February 18, 1980, p. 104.

Cleary, A. T., Humphreys, L. G., Kendrick, S. A., & Wesman, A. Educational uses of tests with disadvantaged students. *American Psychologist*, 1975, *30*, 15–41.

Cleckley, H. *The mask of sanity* (4th ed.). St. Louis: Mosby, 1964.

Cohen, J. Review of the Rokeach value survey. In O. K. Buros (Ed.), *Eighth mental measurements yearbook*. Highland Park, NJ: Gryphon Press, 1978.

Colby, K. M. Simulations of belief systems. In R. C. Schank & K. M. Colby (Eds.), *Computer models of thought and language*. San Francisco: W. H. Freeman & Company Publishers, 1973.

Colby, K. M., & Hilf, F. D. Multidimensional evaluation of a simulation of paranoid thought processes. In L. W. Gress (Ed.), *Knowledge and cognition*. Potomac, MD: Lawrence Erlbaum, 1974.

Colby, K. M., Hilf, F., & Weber, S. Artificial paranoia. *Artificial Intelligence*, 1971, *2*, 1–26.

Comrey, A. L. A factor analysis of items on the MMPI hypochondriasis scale. *Educational and Psychological Measurement*, 1957, *17*, 568–577.

Comrey, A. L. Factored homogeneous item dimensions: A strategy for personality research. In S. Messick & J. Ross (Eds.), *Measurement in personality and cognition.* New York: John Wiley, 1962.

Cook, T. D., & Campbell, D. T. *Quasi-experimentation: Design and analysis issues for field settings.* Chicago: Rand McNally, 1979.

Coombs, C. H., Dawes, R. M., & Tversky, A. *Mathematical psychology: An elementary introduction.* Englewood Cliffs, NJ: Prentice-Hall, 1970.

Cooper, P. Notes on psychological race differences. *Social Forces,* 1919, *8,* 426.

Corsini, R. J. (Ed.). *Current personality theories.* Itasca, IL: Peacock, 1977.

Cozby, P. C. *Methods in behavioral research.* Palo Alto, CA: Mayfield Publishing Company, 1977.

Craighead, W. E., Kazdin, A. E., & Mahoney, M. J. (2nd ed.). *Behavior modification: Principles, issues, and applications.* Boston: Houghton Mifflin, 1981.

Crandall, V. J., & Sinkeldam, C. Children's dependent and achievement behaviors in social situations and their perceptual field dependence. *Journal of Personality,* 1964, *32,* 1–22.

Crites, J. O. Critique of the Strong-Campbell interest inventory. In O. K. Buros (Ed.), *Eighth mental measurements yearbook.* Highland Park, NJ: Gryphon Press, 1978.

Cronbach, L. J. Statistical methods applied to Rorschach scores: A review. *Psychological Bulletin,* 1949, *46,* 393–429.

Cronbach, L. J. Further evidence on response sets and test design. *Educational and Psychological Measurement,* 1950, *10,* 3–31.

Cronbach, L. J. Coefficient alpha and the internal structure of tests. *Psychometrika,* 1951, *16,* 297–334.

Cronbach, L. J. The two disciplines of scientific psychology. *American Psychologist,* 1957, *12,* 671–684.

Cronbach, L. J. Review of the California psychological inventory. In O. K. Buros (Ed.), *Fifth mental measurements yearbook.* Highland Park, NJ: Gryphon Press, 1959.

Cronbach, L. J. *Essentials of psychological testing* (3rd ed.). New York: Harper & Row, 1970.

Cronbach, L. J. Test validation. In R. L. Thorndike (Ed.), *Educational measurement* (2nd ed.). Washington, DC: American Council on Education, 1971.

Cronbach, L. J. Five decades of public controversy over mental testing. *American Psychologist,* 1975, *30,* 1–14.

Cronbach, L. J. Hearnshaw on Burt. *Science,* 1979, *206,* 1392–1394.

Cronbach, L. J., & Gleser, G. C. *Psychological tests and personnel decisions* (2nd ed.). Urbana: University of Illinois Press, 1965.

Cronbach, L. J., Gleser, G., Nanda, H., & Rajaratnam, N. *The dependability of behavioral measurements.* New York: John Wiley, 1972.

Cronbach, L. J., & Meehl, P. E. Construct validity in psychological tests. *Psychological Bulletin,* 1955, *52,* 281–302.

Cronbach, L. J., Rajaratnam, N., & Gleser, G. C. Theory of generalizability: A liberalization of reliability theory. *British Journal of Statistical Psychology,* 1963, *16,* 137–163.

Cuadra, C. A., & Reed, C. F. *An introduction to the MMPI.* Downey, IL: Veterans Administration Hospital, 1954.

Curran, J. P., & Gilbert, F. S. A test of the relative effectiveness of a systematic desensitization program and an interpersonal skills training program with date anxious subjects. *Behavior Therapy,* 1975, *6,* 510–552.

Dahlstrom, W. G. *Personality systematics and the problem of types.* Morristown, NJ: General Learning Press, 1972.

Dahlstrom, W. G., & Dahlstrom, L. E. (Eds.), *Basic readings on the MMPI: A new selection on personality measurement.* Minneapolis: University of Minnesota Press, 1980.

Dahlstrom, W. G., & Welsh, G. S. *An MMPI handbook: A guide to use in clinical practice and research.* Minneapolis: University of Minnesota Press, 1960.

Dahlstrom, W. G., Welsh, G. S., & Dahlstrom, L. E. *An MMPI handbook: Clinical interpretation* (Vol. 1). (Rev. ed.). Minneapolis: University of Minnesota Press, 1972.

Dahlstrom, W. G., Welsh, G. S., & Dahlstrom, L. E. *An MMPI handbook: Research applications* (Vol. 2). (Rev. ed.). Minneapolis: University of Minnesota Press, 1975.

Dailey, C. A. The life history as a criterion of assessment. *Journal of Counseling Psychology,* 1960, *7,* 20–23.

Dailey, C. A. *Assessment of lives.* San Francisco: Jossey-Bass, 1971.

D'Andrade, R. G. Trait psychology and componential analysis. *American Anthropologist,* 1965, *67,* 215–228.

D'Andrade, R. G. Memory and the assessment of behavior. In H. Blalock (Ed.), *Measurement in the social sciences.* Chicago: Aldine, 1974.

Daniels, N. IQ, intelligence, and educability. *Philosophical Forum,* 1976, *6,* 56–69.

Darlington, R. B. A defense of "rational" personnel selection, and two new methods. *Journal of Educational Measurement,* 1976, *13,* 43–52.

Darlington, R. B. Cultural test bias: Comment on Hunter and Schmidt. *Psychological Bulletin,* 1978, *85,* 673–674.

De Risi, W. J., Alevizos, P., Ekman, T., Callahan, E. J., & Liberman, R. P. *The behavior observation instrument: Direct observation for program evaluation in applied settings* (Vol. 1). Unpublished manuscript, Camarillo State Hospital, Camarillo, CA, 1975.

Diamond, E. E. A case history of change: A review of responses to the challenge of sex bias in career interest inventories. In C. K. Tittle & D. G. Zytowski (Eds.), *Sex-fair interest measurement: Research and implications.* Washington, DC: U.S. Government Printing Office, 1978. (a)

Diamond, E. E. Issues of sex bias and sex-fairness in career interest measurement: Background and current status. In C. K. Tittle & D. G. Zytowski

(Eds.), *Sex-fair interest measurement: Research and implications.* Washington, DC: U.S. Government Printing Office, 1978. (b)

Dobzhansky, T. *Genetic diversity and human equality.* New York: Basic Books, 1973.

Doering, C. R., & Raymond, A. F. Additional note on reliability. In *Schizophrenia: Statistical studies from the Boston psychopathic hospital,* Reprint no. 6, 1935.

Dolliver, R. H. Review of Strong-Campbell interest inventory. In O. K. Buros (Ed.), *Eighth mental measurements yearbook.* Highland Park, NJ: Gryphon Press, 1978.

Dominowski, R. L. *Research methods.* Englewood Cliffs, NJ: Prentice-Hall, 1980.

Dougherty, F. E., Bartlett, E. S., & Izard, C. E. *A cross-cultural study of the responses of schizophrenics to facial expressions of the emotions.* Unpublished manuscript, Vanderbilt University, 1969.

Downey, J. E. *The Will-temperament and its testing.* New York: World Book Co., 1924.

Doyle, W. Recognition of sloppy, hand-printed characters. *Proceedings of the Western Joint Computer Conference,* 1960, *17,* 133–142.

Draguns, J. G., & Phillips, L. *Psychiatric classification and diagnosis: An overview and critique.* Morristown, NJ: General Learning Press, 1971.

Drake, L. E. A social I.E. scale for the MMPI. *Journal of Applied Psychology,* 1946, *30,* 51–54 (also reprinted in Welsh & Dahlstrom, 1956).

Drasgow, J., & Barnett, W. L. F-K in a motivated group. *Journal of Consulting Psychology,* 1957, *21,* 399–401.

Duncan, C. P. Cited as a 1963 personal communication in Webb et al., 1966.

Duncan, S., Jr., & Fiske, D. W. *Face-to-face interaction: Research, methods, and theory.* Hillsdale, NJ: Lawrence Erlbaum, 1977.

Dunlop, E. MMPI-ICA computer report. Glendale, CA: Institute of Clinical Analysis, 1963–1967.

Dunnette, M. D. Use of the sugar pill by industrial psychologists. *American Psychologist,* 1957, *12,* 223–225.

Dunphey, D. C., Stone, P. J., & Smith, M. S. The general inquirer. *Behavioral Science,* 1965, *10,* 468–480.

Dunsdon, M. I. A comparison of Terman-Merrill scale test responses among large samples of normal, maladjusted, and backward children. *Journal of Mental Science,* 1953, *99,* 720–731.

Ebbinghaus, H. Über eine neue Methode zur prüfung geister fähigkeiten und ihre Awendung bei Schulkindern. *Zeitschrift für Psychologie und Physiologie,* 1897, *13,* 401–459.

Eckhardt, W. K., & Ermann, M. D. *Social research methods: Perspective, theory, and analysis.* New York: Random House, 1977.

Edson, L. "Jensenism," n. The theory that IQ is largely determined by the genes. *The New York Times Magazine,* August 31, 1969.

Educational Testing Service. *Test use and validity: A response to charges in the Nader/Nairn report on ETS.* Princeton, NJ, February 1980.

Edwards, A. L. The relationship between the judged desirability of a trait and the probability that the trait will be endorsed. *Journal of Applied Psychology,* 1953, *37,* 90–93.

Edwards, A. L. *The social desirability variable in personality assessment and research.* New York: Dryden Press, 1957.

Edwards, A. L., Social desirability and performance on the MMPI. *Psychometrika,* 1964, *29,* 295–308.

Edwards, A. L. *The measurement of personality traits.* New York: Holt, Rinehart & Winston, 1970.

Efron, D., & Foley, J. P. A comparative investigation of gestural behavior patterns in Italian and Jewish groups living under different as well as similar environmental conditions. *Zeitschrift der Sozialforschung,* 1937, *6,* 151–159. Also reprinted in T. M. Newcomb & E. L. Hartley (Eds.). *Readings in social psychology.* New York: Holt, Rinehart & Winston, 1947, pp. 33–40.

Eichman, W. J. Review of computerized scoring and interpreting services. In O. K. Buros (Ed.). *Seventh mental measurements yearbook.* Highland Park, NJ: Gryphon Press, 1972.

Eichler, R. Experimental stress and alleged Rorschach indices of anxiety. *Journal of Abnormal and Social Psychology,* 1951, *46,* 344–355.

Einhorn, H. J., Kleinmuntz, D. N., & Kleinmuntz, B. Linear regression *and* process-tracing models of judgment. *Psychological Review,* 1979, *86,* 465–485.

Ekman, P. Body position, facial expression, and verbal behavior during interviews. *Journal of Abnormal and Social Psychology,* 1964, *68,* 295–301.

Ekman, P. Differential communication of affect by head and body cues. *Journal of Personality and Social Psychology,* 1965, *2,* 726–735.

Ekman, P. Universal and cultural differences in facial expression of emotions. *Nebraska Symposium on Motivation,* 1971, *19,* 207–283.

Ekman, P., & Friesen, W. V. The repertoire of nonverbal behavior: Categories, origins, usage, and coding. *Semiotica,* 1969, *1,* 49–98.

Ekman, P., & Friesen, W. V. *Unmasking the face.* Englewood Cliffs, NJ: Prentice-Hall, 1975.

Elliott, R. Interrelationships among measures of field dependence, ability, and personality traits. *Journal of Abnormal and Social Psychology,* 1961, *63,* 27–36.

Endler, N. S. The case for person-situation interactions. *Canadian Psychological Review,* 1975, *16,* 12–21.

Endler, N. S. The person versus the situation—A pseudo issue? A response to Alker. In N. S. Endler, & D. Magnusson (Eds.), *Interactional psychology and personality.* Washington, DC: Hemisphere Publishing, 1976.

Endler, N. S., & Magnusson, D. (Eds.), *Interactional psychology and personality.* Washington, DC: Hemisphere Publishing, 1976.

Epstein, L. H., Miller, P. M., & Webster, J. S. The effects of reinforcing concurrent behavior on self-monitoring. *Behavior Therapy,* 1976, *7,* 89–95.

Equal Employment Opportunity Commission (EEOC). Guidelines on employee selection procedures. *Federal Register,* 1970, *35,* 12333–12336.

## References

Equal Employment Opportunity Commission (EEOC). Testing and selecting employee guidelines. *Federal Register,* 1978, *51,* 2221–2225. (a)

Equal Employment Opportunity Commission (EEOC). *Testing and selecting employee guidelines.* Washington, DC: Commerce Clearing House, Inc., 1978, P4010.01–P4010.18. (b)

Erikson, E. H. *Young man Luther.* New York: W. W. Norton & Co., Inc., 1958.

Erikson, E. H. *Gandhi's truth: The origins of militant nonviolence.* New York: W. W. Norton & Co., Inc., 1969.

Ernst, F. Self-recording and counterconditioning of a self-mutilative compulsion. *Behavior Therapy,* 1973, *4,* 144–146.

Eron, L. D. Personal communication, 1980.

Eron, L. D., Terry, D., & Callahan, R. The use of rating scales for emotional tone of TAT stories. *Journal of Consulting Psychology,* 1950, *14,* 473–478.

Evans, C. C. Influence of "fake" personality evaluations on self-description. *Journal of Psychology,* 1962, *53,* 457–463.

Evans, C., & McConnell, T. R. *Minnesota T-S-E Inventory,* Princeton, NJ: Educational Testing Service, 1942–1957.

Exner, J. E. The self focus sentence completion: A study of egocentricity, *Journal of Personality Assessment,* 1973, *37,* 437–455.

Exner, J. E. Projective techniques. In I. B. Weiner (Ed.), *Clinical methods in psychology.* New York: Wiley Interscience, 1976.

Exner, J. E. *The Rorschach: A comprehensive system: Current research and advanced interpretation* (Vol. 2). New York: Wiley Interscience, 1978.

Eysenck, H. J. *Dimensions of personality.* London: Routledge & Kegan Paul, 1947.

Eysenck, H. J. The inheritance of extraversion-introversion. *Acta Psychologica,* 1956, *12,* 95–110.

Eysenck, H. J. Conditioning and personality. *British Journal of Psychology,* 1962, *53,* 299–305.

Eysenck, H. J. *The biological basis of perosonality.* Springfield, IL: Chas. C Thomas, 1967.

Eysenck, H. J. History and definition of the concept. In H. J. Eysenck (Ed.), *The measurement of intelligence.* Baltimore: Williams & Wilkins, 1973.

Eysenck, H. J., & Rachman, S. *The causes and cures of neurosis.* San Diego: Robert R. Knapp, 1965.

Faltz, D. "Snowball effect seen in truth in testing movement. *APA Monitor,* September/October.

Farber, I. E., Spence, K. W., & Bechtold, H. P. *Emotionality, introversion-extraversion, and conditioning.* Paper presented at Midwestern Psychological Association, Chicago, 1957.

Fast, J. *Body language.* New York: M. Evans, 1970.

Federhoff, S., & Hoffer, A. Toxicity of blood serum from schizophrenic and nonschizophrenic subjects. *Journal of Mental and Nervous Diseases.* 1956, *124,* 396–398.

Feldman, M. J. An evaluation scale for shock therapy. *Journal of Clinical Psychology*, 1958, *14*, 41–45.

Ferguson, E. D. The use of early recollections for assessing life style and diagnosing psychopathology. *Journal of Projective Techniques and Personality Assessment*, 1964, *28*, 403–442.

Festinger, L., & Katz, D. *Research methods in the behavioral sciences.* New York: Holt, Rinehart & Winston, 1953.

Festinger, L., Riecken, H. W., & Schacter, S. *When prophecy fails.* New York: Harper & Row, 1956.

Fine, B. *The stranglehold of the IQ.* New York: Doubleday, 1975.

Finney, J. C., Auvenshine, C. D., Smith, D. F., & Skeeters, D. E. *Behaviordyne psychodiagnostic laboratory service.* Stanford, CA: Behaviordyne, Inc., 1976.

Fischer, R. Stress and toxicity of schizophrenic serum. *Science*, 1953, *118*, 409–411.

Fiske, D. W. Variability of responses and the stability of scores and interpretations of projective protocols. *Journal of Projective Techniques*, 1959, *23*, 263–267.

Fiske, D. W. Problems in measuring personality. In J. M. Wepman & R. W. Heine (Eds.), *Concepts of personality.* Chicago: Aldine, 1963.

Fiske, D. W. *Strategies for personality research: The observation versus interpretation of behavior.* San Francisco: Jossey-Bass, 1978.

Fixsen, D. L., Phillips, E. L., & Wolf, M. M. Achievement place: Experiments in self government with pre-delinquents. *Journal of Applied Behavioral Analysis*, 1973, *6*, 31–47.

Flanagan, J. C. The critical incident technique. *Psychological Bulletin*, 1954, *51*, 327–358.

Forer, B. R. The fallacy of personal validations: A classroom demonstration of gullibility. *Journal of Abnormal and Social Psychology*, 1949, *44*, 118–123.

Forgus, R., & Shulman, B. *Personality: A cognitive view.* Englewood Cliffs, NJ: Prentice-Hall, 1979.

Forsyth, R. P., & Smith, S. F. MMPI related behavior in a student nurse group. *Journal of Clinical Psychology*, 1967, *23*, 224–229.

Fowler, R. D., Jr. *Roche MMPI computerized interpretation service.* Nutley, NJ: Roche Psychiatric Service Institute, 1966–1976.

Fowler, R. D., Jr. Automated interpretation of personality test data. In J. N. Butcher (Ed.), *MMPI research developments and clinical applications.* New York: McGraw-Hill, 1969.

Fowler, R. D., Jr. *Psychological assessment services.* Iowa City, Iowa: Psychological Assessment Service, Inc., 1973–1975.

Frank, G. Measures of intelligence and conceptual thinking, In I. B. Weiner (Ed.), *Clinical methods in psychology.* New York: John Wiley, 1976.

Frank, L. K. Projective methodology for the study of personality. *Journal of Psychology*, 1939, *8*, 349–413.

Franks, C. M. Conditioning and personality: A study of normal and neurotic subjects. *Journal of Abnormal and Social Psychology*, 1956, *52*, 143–150. (a)

Franks, C. M. L'échelle de Taylor et l'analyse dimensionelle de l'anxieté. *Revue de Psychologie Applique*, 1956, *6*, 35–44. (b)

Frederiksen, N. Toward a taxonomy of situations. In N. S. Endler & D. Magnusson (Eds.), *Interactional psychology and personality*. Washington, DC: Hemisphere Publishing, 1976.

Freeman, F. N., Holzinger, K. J., & Mitchell, B. C. The influence of the environment on the intelligence, school achievement, and conduct of foster children. *Yearbook of the National Society for the Study of Education* (Part 1). 1928, *27*, 103–205.

Freud, S. The psychopathology of everyday life. In S. Freud, *The basic writings of Sigmund Freud*. New York: Random House, 1938. (Originally published, 1904.)

Fruchter, B. *Introduction to factor analysis*. Princeton, NJ: D. Van Nostrand, 1954.

Fuller, P. R. Operant conditioning of a vegetative human organism. *American Journal of Psychology*, 1949, *62*, 587–590.

Galton, F. Statistical inquiries into the efficacy of prayer. *Fortnightly Review*, 1872, *12*, 125–135.

Galton, F. *English men of science*. New York: Appleton, 1875.

Galton, F. The measurement of character. *Fortnightly Review*, 1884, *42*, 179–185.

Galton, F. *Hereditary genius*. New York: Macmillan, 1914. (Originally published, 1869.)

Gamble, K. R. The Holtzman inkblot technique: A review. *Psychological Bulletin*, 1972, *77*, 172–194.

Gambrill, E. D., & Richey, C. A. An assertion inventory for use in assessment and research. *Behavior Therapy*, 1975, *6*, 550–561.

Garth, T. R. The will-temperament of Indians. *Journal of Applied Psychology*, 1927, *11*, 512–518.

Geer, J. H., & Turteltaub, A. Fear reduction following observation of a model. *Journal of Personality and Social Psychology*, 1967, *6*, 327–331.

Getzels, J. W., & Jackson, P. W. *Creativity and intelligence*. New York: John Wiley, 1962.

Ghiselli, E., Campbell, J. P., & Zedeck, S. *Measurement theory for the behavioral sciences*. San Francisco: Freeman, 1981.

Gilbert, J. *Interpreting psychological test data*. New York: Van Nostrand Reinhold, 1978.

Gilbert, J. *Interpreting psychological test data*. Vol. 2. New York: Van Nostrand Reinhold, 1980.

Gilliland, A. R., & Colgin, R. Norms, reliability, and forms of the MMPI. *Journal of Consulting Psychology*, 1951, *15*, 435–438.

Gilmore, S. K. *The counselor-in-training*. New York: Appleton-Century-Crofts, 1973.

Glaser, R. Instructural technology and the measurement of learning outcomes. *American Psychologist*, 1963, *18*, 519–522.

Goddard, H. H. The Binet tests in relation to immigration. *Journal of Psychoasthenics*, 1913, *18*, 105–107.

Goddard, H. H. Mental tests and the immigrant. *Journal of Delinquency*, 1917, *2*, 243–277.

Goddard, H. H. *Human efficiency and levels of ingelligence*. Princeton, NJ: Princeton University Press, 1920.

Goldberg, L. R. Diagnosticians vs. diagnostic signs: The diagnosis of psychosis vs. neurosis from the MMPI. *Psychological Monographs*, 1965, *79*, (9, Whole No. 602).

Goldberg, L. R. Seer over sign: The first good example? *Journal of Experimental Research in Personality*, 1968, *3*, 168–171. (a)

Goldberg, L. R. Simple models or simple processes? Some research on clinical judgments. *American Psychologist*, 1968, *23*, 483–496. (b)

Goldberg, L. R. Man vs. model of man: A rationale, plus some evidence for a method of improving on clinical inference. *Psychological Bulletin*, 1970, *73*, 422–432.

Goldberg, L. R. Review of the California psychological inventory. In O. K. Buros (Ed.). *Seventh mental measurements yearbook*. Highland Park, NJ: Gryphon Press, 1972.

Goldberg, L. R. Objective diagnostic tests and measures. *Annual Review of Psychology*, 1974, *25*, 343–366.

Goldberg, L. R. Review of the Jackson personality inventory. In O. K. Buros (Ed.). *Eighth mental measurements yearbook*. Highland Park, NJ: Gryphon Press, 1978.

Golden, M. Some effects of combining psychological tests on clinical inferences. *Journal of Consulting Psychology*, 1964, *28*, 440–446.

Goldfried, M. R. Behavioral assessment. In I. B. Weiner (Ed.), *Clinical methods in psychology*. New York: John Wiley, 1976.

Goldfried, M. R., & Kent, R. N. Traditional versus behavioral assessment. *Psychological Bulletin*, 1972, *77*, 409–420.

Goldfried, M. R., & Sprafkin, J. N. *Behavioral personality assessment*. Morristown, NJ: General Learning Press, 1974.

Goldfried, M. R., Stricker, G., & Weiner, I. B. *Rorschach handbook of clinical and research applications*. Englewood Cliffs, NJ: Prentice-Hall, 1971.

Goldman, L. *Using tests in counseling*. New York: Appleton-Century-Crofts, 1961.

Goldman, L. *Using tests in counseling* (2nd ed.). Englewood Cliffs, NJ: Prentice-Hall, 1971.

Goldstein, K. M., & Blackman, S. *Cognitive style: Five approaches and relevant research*. New York: John Wiley, 1978.

Gorden, R. L. *Interviewing: Strategy, techniques, and tactics* (3rd ed.). Homewood, IL: Dorsey Press, 1980.

Gottman, J. M., & Leiblum, S. R. *How to do psychotherapy and how to evaluate it.* New York: Holt, Rinehart & Winston, 1974.

Gough, H. G. Simulated patterns on the MMPI. *Journal of Abnormal and Social Psychology,* 1947, *42,* 215–225.

Gough, H. G. The F minus K dissimulation index for the MMPI. *Journal of Consulting Psychology,* 1950, *14,* 408–413 (also reprinted in Welsh & Dahlstrom, 1956).

Gough, H. G., McClosky, H., & Meehl, P. E. A personality scale for dominance. *Journal of Abnormal and Social Psychology,* 1951, *46,* 360–366 (also reprinted in Welsh & Dahlstrom, 1956).

Gough, H. G., McKee, M. G., & Yandell, R. J. *Adjective check list analyses of a number of selected psychometric and assessment variables.* Officer Education Research Laboratory, Technical Memorandum, OERL–TM–55–10, May 1955.

Gough, H. G. *California psychological inventory.* Palo Alto, CA: Consulting Psychologists Press, 1956–1975.

Graham, J. R., Schroeder, H. E., & Lilly, R. S. Factor analysis of items on the social introversion and masculinity-femininity scales of the MMPI. *Journal of Clinical Psychology,* 1971, *27,* 367–370.

Grand, S., Marcos, L. R., & Freedman, N. Relation of psychopathology and bilingualism to kinetic aspects of interview behavior in schizophrenia. *Journal of Abnormal Psychology,* 1977, *86,* 492–500.

Grimm, L. G. The maintenance of self- and drug-attributed behavior. *Journal of Abnormal Psychology,* 1980, *89,* 282–285.

Guertin, W. H. et al. Research with the Wechsler intelligence scales for adults: 1965–1970. *Psychological Record,* *21,* 289–339.

Guetzkow, H. S., & Bowman, P. H. *Men and hunger: A psychological manual for relief workers.* Elgin, Ill.: Brethren Publishing House, 1946.

Guilford, J. P. Creativity. *American Psychologist,* 1950, *5,* 444–454.

Guilford, J. P. *Personality.* New York: McGraw-Hill, 1959. (a)

Guilford, J. P. Three faces of intellect. *American Psychologist,* 1959, *14,* 469–479. (b)

Guilford, J. P. *The nature of human intelligence.* New York: McGraw-Hill, 1967.

Guilford, J. P., & Fruchter, B. *Fundamental statistics in psychology and education.* New York: McGraw-Hill, 1978.

Guilford, J. P., & Hoepfner, R. Sixteen divergent production abilities at the ninth-grade level. *Multivariate Behavioral Research,* 1966, *1,* 43–64.

Guilford, J. P., & Hoepfner, R. *The analysis of intelligence.* New York: McGraw-Hill, 1971.

Guion, R. M. *Personnel testing.* New York: McGraw-Hill, 1965.

Guion, R. M. The practice of industrial and organizational psychology. In M. D. Dunnette (Ed.). *Handbook of industrial and organizational psychology.* Chicago: Rand McNally, 1976.

Guion, R. M. Content validity—the source of my discontent. *Applied Psychological Measurement,* 1977, *1,* 1–10.

Guion, R. M. Scoring of content domain samples: The problem of fairness. *Journal of Applied Psychology,* 1978, *63,* 499–506.

Gullikson, H. *Theory of mental tests.* New York: John Wiley, 1950.

Gustafson, L. A., & Orne, M. T. Effects of heightened motivation on the detection of deception. *Journal of Applied Psychology,* 1963, *47,* 408–411.

Guthrie, G. M. Six MMPI diagnostic profile patterns. *Journal of Psychology,* 1950, *30,* 317–323 (also reprinted in Welsh & Dahlstrom, 1956).

Guthrie, R. V. *Even the rat was white: A historical view of psychology.* New York: Harper & Row, 1976.

Guttman, L. A basis for scaling quantitative data. *American Sociological Review,* 1944, *9,* 139–150.

Guttman, L. The Cornell technique for intensity analysis. *Educational and Psychological Measurement,* 1947, *7,* 247–279.

Gynther, M. D. White norms and black MMPIs: A prescription for discrimination? *Psychological Bulletin,* 1972, *78,* 386–402.

Gynther, M. D. Review of the California Personality Inventory. In O. K. Buros (Ed.). *Eighth mental measurements yearbook.* Highland Park, NJ: Gryphon, 1978.

Gynther, M. D., & Gynther, R. A. Personality inventories. In I. B. Weiner (Ed.), *Clinical methods in psychology.* New York: John Wiley, 1976.

Gynther, M. D., & Ullom, J. Objections to MMPI items as a function of interpersonal trust, race, and sex. *Journal of Consulting and Clinical Psychology,* 1976, *44,* 1020.

Hall, C. S., & Lindzey, G. *Theories of personality* (3rd ed.). New York: John Wiley, 1978.

Hall, E. T. *The silent language.* New York: Doubleday, 1959.

Hall, E. T. *The hidden dimension.* New York: Doubleday, 1966.

Hall, E. T. Learning the Arabs' silent language. *Psychology Today,* August 1979, pp. 45–54.

Hanson, G. R. *Assessing the career interests of college youth* (ACT Research Report No. 67). Iowa City, IA: American College Testing Program, 1974.

Hanson, G. R., & Rayman, J. Validity of sex-balanced interest inventory scales. In C. K. Tittle & D. G. Zytowski (Eds.), *Sex-fair interest measurement: Research and implications.* Washington, DC: U.S. Government Printing Office, 1978.

Hare, R. D. *Psychopathy: Theory and research.* New York: John Wiley, 1970.

Harmon, L. W. Review of Kuder Preference Record—Vocational. In O. K. Buros (Ed.), *Eighth mental measurements yearbook.* Highland Park, NJ: Gryphon Press, 1978.

Harris, B. Whatever happened to little Albert? *American Psychologist,* 1979, *34,* 151–160.

Harrison, G. The computer in the psychology of language. In M. J. Apter & G. Westby (Eds.), *The computer in psychology.* New York: John Wiley, 1973.

Harshbarger, T. *Introductory statistics: A decision map.* New York: Maxmillan, 1977.

Hartshorne, H., & May, M. A. *Studies in the nature of character. Vol. 1. Studies in deceit.* New York: Macmillan, 1928.

Hathaway, S. R. A coding system for MMPI profile classification. *Journal of Consulting Psychology*, 1947, *11*, 334–337.

Hathaway, S. R. Scales 5 (masculinity-femininity), 6 (paranoia), and 8 (schizophrenia). In G. S. Welsh & W. G. Dahlstrom (Eds.), *Basic readings on the MMPI.* Minneapolis: University of Minnesota Press, 1956.

Hathaway, S. R. MMPI: Professional use by professional people. *American Psychologist*, 1964, *19*, 204–210.

Hathaway, S. R. Where have we gone wrong? The mystery of the missing progress. In J. N. Butcher (Ed.), *Objective personality assessment: Changing perspectives.* New York: Academic Press, 1972.

Hathaway, S. R., & McKinley, J. C. *Minnesota multiphasic personality inventory.* Minneapolis: University of Minnesota Press, 1942.

Hathaway, S. R., & McKinley, J. C. *Manual for the Minnesota multiphasic personality inventory.* New York: Psychological Corporation, 1943.

Hathaway, S. R., & McKinley, J. C. *Minnesota multiphasic personality inventory* (Rev. ed.). New York: Psychological Corporation, 1951.

Hathaway, S. R., & Meehl, P. E. *An atlas for the clinical use of the MMPI.* Minneapolis: University of Minnesota Press, 1951. (a)

Hathaway, S. R., & Meehl, P. E. The Minnesota multiphasic personality inventory. *Military clinical psychology*, TM 8–242, AFM 160–45, U.S. Depts. of Army & Air Force, July 1951. (b)

Hathaway, S. R., & Meehl, P. E. *Adjective checklist correlates of MMPI scores.* Unpublished materials, 1952.

Hathaway, S. R., & Monachesi, E. D. The prediction of juvenile delinquency using the MMPI. *American Journal of Psychiatry*, 1951, *108*, 469–473.

Hathaway, S. R., & Monachesi, E. D. The MMPI in the study of juvenile delinquents. *American Sociological Review*, 1952, *17*, 704–710.

Hathaway, S. R., & Monachesi, E. D. *Analyzing and predicting juvenile delinquency with the MMPI.* Minneapolis: University of Minnesota Press, 1953.

Hathaway, S. R., & Monachesi, E. D. The personalities of predelinquent boys. *Journal of Criminal Law, Criminology, and Political Science*, 1957, *48*, 149–163.

Hathaway, S. R., & Monachesi, E. D. *An Atlas of juvenile MMPI profiles.* Minneapolis: University of Minnesota Press, 1961.

Hawkes, N. Tracing Burt's descent to scientific fraud. *Science*, 1979, *205*, 673–675.

Hawkins, R. P., & Dotson, V. A. Reliability scores that delude. In E. Ramp & G. Semb (Eds.), *Behavior analysis: Areas of research and application.* Englewood Cliffs, NJ: Prentice-Hall, 1975.

Hearnshaw, L. S. *Cyril Burt, psychologist.* Ithaca, NY: Cornell University Press, 1979.

Heineman, C. E. A forced choice form of the Taylor anxiety scale. *Journal of Consulting Psychology*, 1953, *17*, 447–454.

Heller, K. Interview structure and interview style in initial interviews. In A. N. Siegman, & B. Pope (Eds.). *Studies in dyadic communication.* New York: Pergamon, 1972.

Helman, Z. Rorschach et dessins dans un cas de lobotomie. *Bulletin Groups de Française Rorschach,* 1953, *3,* 9–15.

Helmstadter, G. C. *Research concepts in human behavior.* Englewood Cliffs, NJ: Prentice-Hall, 1970.

Helper, M. M., Wilcott, R. C., & Garfield, S. L. Effects of chlorpromazine on learning and related processes in emotionally disturbed children. *Journal of Consulting Psychology,* 1963, *27,* 1–9.

Helzer, J. E., Clayton, P. J., Pambakian, R., Reich, T., Woodruff, R. A., Jr., & Revole, M. A. Reliability of psychiatric diagnosis. II. The test retest reliability of diagnostic classification. *Archives of General Psychiatry,* 1977, *34,* 136–141. (a)

Helzer, J. E., Robins, L. N., Taibelson, M., Woodruff, R. A., Jr., Reich, T., & Wish, E. D. Reliability of psychiatric diagnosis. I. A methodological review. *Archives of General Psychiatry,* 1977, *34,* 129–133. (b)

Herrnstein, P. J. *IQ in the meritocracy.* Boston: Little, Brown, 1973.

Hersen, M. Fear scale norms for an inpatient population. *Journal of Clinical Psychology,* 1971, *27,* 375–378.

Hersen, M., & Bellak, A. S. (Eds.). *Behavioral assessment: A practical handbook.* New York: Pergamon, 1976.

Hersen, M., Eisler, R. M. Social skills training. In W. E. Craighead, A. E. Kazdin, & M. J. Mahoney (Eds.), *Behavior modification.* Boston: Houghton Mifflin, 1976.

Hertz, M. R. Reliability of Rorschach inkblot test. *Journal of Applied Psychology,* 1934, *18,* 461–477.

Hertz, M. R. *Frequency tables for scoring Rorschach responses.* Cleveland: Case Western Reserve University Press, 1970.

Hess, E. H. Attitude and pupil size. *Scientific American,* 1965, *212,* 46–54.

Hess, E. H. The role of pupil size in communication. *Scientific American,* 1975, *233,* 110–119.

Hilf, F. D. Non-nonverbal communication and psychiatric research. *Archives of General Psychiatry,* 1972, *27,* 631–635.

Hill, E. F. *The Holtzman inkblot technique.* San Francisco: Jossey-Bass, 1972.

Hogan, R. A dimension of moral judgment. *Journal of Consulting and Clinical Psychology,* 1970, *35,* 205–212.

Hogan, R. *Personality theory: The personological tradition.* Englewood Cliffs, NJ: Prentice-Hall, 1976.

Hogan, R. Review of personality research form. In O. K. Buros (Ed.). *Eighth mental measurements yearbook.* Highland Park, NJ: Gryphon Press, 1978.

Hogan, R., DeSoto, C. B., & Solano, C. Traits, tests, and personality research. *American Psychologist,* 1977, *32,* 255–264.

Hogarth, R. M. *Judgment and choice: The psychology of decision.* Chichester, England: Wiley, 1980.

Holden, C. Identical twins reared apart. *Science,* 1980, *207,* 1323–1326.

Holden, R. R., & Jackson, D. N. Item subtlety and face validity in personality assessment. *Journal of Consulting and Clinical Psychology,* 1979, *47,* 459–468.

Holland, J. L. *The self-directed search.* Palo Alto, CA: Consulting Psychologists Press, 1970.

Holmes, T. H., & Rahe, R. H. The social adjustment rating scale. *Journal of Psychosomatic Research,* 1967, *11,* 213–218.

Holmes, T. H., & Masuda, M. Psychosomatic syndrome: When mothers-in-law or other disasters visit, a person can develop a bad, bad cold, or worse. *Psychology Today,* 1972, p. 21.

Holmes, T. S., & Holmes, T. H. Short-term intrusions into the life style routine. *Journal of Psychosomatic Research,* 1970, *14,* 121–132.

Holsti, O. R. *Content analysis for the social sciences and humanities.* Reading, MA: Addison-Wesley, 1969.

Holt, R. R. Clinical and statistical prediction: A reformulation and some new data. *Journal of Abnormal and Social Psychology,* 1958, *56,* 1–12.

Holt, R. R. *Assessing personality.* New York: Harcourt Brace Jovanovich, 1971.

Holt, R. R. *Methods in clinical psychology: Projective assessment* (Vol. 1). New York: Plenum, 1978. (a)

Holt, R. R. *Methods in clinical psychology: Prediction and research* (Vol. 2). New York: Plenum, 1978. (b)

Holtzman, W. H. Objective scoring of projective techniques. In B. M. Bass & I. A. Bers (Eds.), *Objective approaches to personality assessment.* Princeton, NJ: D. Van Nostrand, 1959.

Holtzman, W. H. New developments in Holtzman inkblot technique. In P. McReynolds (Ed.), *Advances in psychological assessment* (Vol. 3). San Francisco: Jossey-Bass, 1974.

Holtzman, W. H. *Methods in psychology.* New York: Harper & Row, 1975.

Holtzman, W. H., Thorpe, J. S., Swartz, J. D., & Herron, E. W. *Inkblot perception and personality—Holtzman inkblot technique.* Austin: University of Texas Press, 1961.

Holtzman, W. H., Diaz-Guerrero, R., & Swartz, J. D. *Personality development in two cultures: A cross-cultural longitudinal study of school children in Mexico and the United States.* Austin: University of Texas Press, 1975.

Holzberg, J. D. Reliability re-examined. In M. A. Rickers-Osviankina (Ed.). *Rorschach psychology.* New York: John Wiley, 1960.

Holzberg, J. D. Projective techniques. In I. A. Bers & L. A. Pennington (Eds.), *An introduction to clinical psychology.* New York: Ronald Press, 1966.

Holzman, P., & Levy, D. L. Smooth pursuit eye movements and functional psychoses: A review. *Schizophrenia Bulletin,* 1977, *3,* 15–27.

Holzman, P., Proctor, L. R., & Hughes, D. W. Eyetracking patterns in schizophrenia. *Science,* 1973, *181,* 179–181.

Honig, W. K., & Staddon, J. E. R. (Eds.). *Handbook of operant behavior.* Englewood Cliffs, NJ: Prentice-Hall, 1977.

Hopkins, K. D., & Stanky, J. C. *Educational and psychological measurement and evaluation* (6th ed.). Englewood Cliffs, NJ: Prentice-Hall, 1981.

Horn, D. *An experimental study of the diagnostic process in the clinical investigation of personality.* Unpublished doctoral dissertation, Harvard University, 1943.

Horn, J. L. Intelligence—Why it grows, why it declines. In L. Willerman & R. G. Turner (Eds.), *Readings about individual and group differences.* San Francisco: W. H. Freeman & Company Publishers, 1979.

Horn, J. L., & Donaldson, G. On the myth of intellectual decline in adulthood. *American Psychologist*, 1976, *31*, 701–719.

Horn, J. L., & Knapp, J. R. On the subjective character of the empirical base of Guilford's structure-of-intellect model. *Psychological Bulletin*, 1973, *80*, 33–43.

Horrocks, J. E. *Assessment of behavior.* Columbus, Ohio: Charles E. Merrill Books, 1964.

Horst, P. Pattern analysis and configural scoring. *Journal of Clinical Psychology*, 1954, *10*, 3–11.

Hovey, H. B. MMPI profiles and personality characteristics. *Journal of Consulting Psychology*, 1953, *17*, 142–146 (also reprinted in Welsh & Dahlstrom, 1956).

Hovey, H. B. The questionable validity of some assumed antecedents of mental illness. *Journal of Clinical Psychology*, 1959, *15*, 270–272.

Howard, J. W. The Howard-inkblot test: A descriptive manual. *Journal of Clinical Psychology, Monograph Supplement*, 1953, *9*, 209–254.

Humphreys, L. G. Addendum to the report of the ad hoc Committee on Educational Uses of Tests with Disadvantaged Students. *American Psychologist*, 1975, *30*, 95–96.

Humphreys, L. G. To understand regression from parent to offspring, think statistically. *Psychological Bulletin*, 1978, *85*, 1317–1322.

Hunt, J. M. *Intelligence and experience.* New York: Ronald Press, 1961.

Hunter, J. E., & Schmidt, F. L. Bias in defining test bias: Reply to Darlington. *Psychological Bulletin*, 1978, *85*, 675–676.

Hurlock, E. B. The Will-temperament of white and negro children. *Pedagogical Seminary*, 1930, *38*, 91–99.

Hutt, M. L. *The Hutt adaptation of the Bender-Gestalt test* (2nd ed.). New York: Grune & Stratton, 1969.

Izard, C. E. *The face of emotion.* Englewood Cliffs, NJ: Prentice-Hall, 1971.

Izard, C. E. *Patterns of emotions.* New York: Academic Press, 1972.

Izard, C. E., & Tomkins, S. S. Affect and behavior: Anxiety as a negative affect. In C. D. Spielberger (Ed.), *Anxiety and behavior.* New York: Academic Press, 1966.

Jackson, D. N. The dynamics of structured personality tests: 1971. *Psychological Review*, 1971, *78*, 229–248.

Jackson, D. N. *Personality Research Form.* Port Huron, MI: Research Psychologists Press, 1967–1974.

Jackson, D. N. *Differential personality inventory.* London, Ontario: Author, 1972.

Jackson, D. N. *Jackson personality inventory.* Port Huron, MI: Research Psychologists Press, 1976.

Jackson, D. N., Hourany, L., & Vidmar, N. J. A four-dimensional interpretation of risk taking. *Journal of Personality,* 1972, *40,* 483–501.

Jackson, D. N., & Messick, S. J. Content and style in personality assessment. *Psychological Bulletin,* 1958, *55,* 243–252.

Jackson, D. N., & Messick, S. J. Acquiescence and desirability as response determinants on the MMPI. *Educational and Psychological Measurement,* 1961, *21,* 771–790.

Jackson, D. N., & Paunonen, S. V. Personality structure and assessment. *Annual Review of Psychology,* 1980, *31,* 503–551.

Jackson, G. D. On the report of the *ad hoc* committee on educational uses of tests with disadvantaged students. *American Psychologist,* 1975, *30,* 88–93.

Jacobs, A., & Baron, R. Falsification of the Guilford-Zimmerman temperament survey: II. Making a poor impression. *Psychological Reports,* 1968, *23,* 1271–1277.

James, W. *Principles of psychology.* Vol. 1. New York: Holt, 1890.

Jencks, C., Smith, M., Ackland, H., Bane, M. J., Cohen, D., Sintis, H., Heynes, B. & Michelson, S. *Inequality.* New York: Basic Books, 1972.

Jensen, A. R. How much can we boost IQ and scholastic achievement? *Harvard Educational Review,* 1969, *39,* 1–123.

Jensen, A. R. *Educability and group differences.* New York: Harper & Row, 1973.

Jensen, A. R. *Bias in mental tests.* New York: Macmillan, 1980.

Johnson, A. H. Teaching attitudes and skills in microcounseling. *Journal of Family Practice,* 1979, *9,* 255–263.

Johnson, J. A., & Hogan, R. Moral judgments and self-presentations. *Journal of Research in Personality,* 1981, *15,* 57–63.

Johnson, J. H., & Williams, T. A. The use of on-line computer technology in a mental health admitting system. *American Psychologist,* 1975, *30,* 380–390.

Johnson, R. W. Review of the Strong-Campbell interest inventory. *Measurement and Evaluation Guidance,* 1976, *9,* 40–45.

Jones, R. L. (Ed.). *Black psychology.* New York: Harper & Row, 1972.

Jung, C. G. *Contributions toward analytical psychology.* New York: Harcourt, Brace & World, 1928.

Kagan, J. What is intelligence? In A. Gartner, C. Greer, & F. Riesmann (Eds.), *The new assault on equality.* New York: Harper & Row, 1974.

Kagan, J., & Moss, H. A. Stability and validity of achievement fantasy. *Journal of Abnormal and Social Psychology,* 1959, *58,* 357–364.

Kamin, L. J. *Heredity, intelligence, politics, and psychology.* Unpublished paper, Princeton University, 1973.

Kamin, L. J. *The science and politics of IQ.* Potomac, MD: Lawrence Erlbaum, 1974.

Kamin, L. J. Comment on Munsinger's adoption study. *Behavior Genetics,* 1977, *7,* 403–406.

Kamin, L. J. Comment on Munsinger's review of adoption studies. *Psychological Bulletin*, 1978, *85*, 194–201.

Kamiya, J. Operant control of the EEG alpha rhythm and some of its reported effects on consciousness. In C. Tart (Ed.), *Altered states of consciousness: A book of readings*. New York: John Wiley, 1969.

Kanfer, F. H. Self-management techniques. In F. H. Kanfer & A. P. Goldstein (Eds.), *Helping people change*. New York: Pergamon, 1976.

Kanfer, F. H., & Grimm, L. G. Behavioral analysis: Selecting target behaviors in the interview. *Behavior Modification*, 1977, *1*, 7–28.

Kanfer, F. H., & Grimm, L. G. Managing clinical change: A process model of therapy. *Behavior Modification*, 1980, *4*, 419–444.

Kanfer, F. H., & Phillips, J. S. Behavior therapy: A panacea for all ills or a passing fancy? *Archives of General Psychiatry*, 1966, *15*, 114–128.

Kanfer, F. H., & Phillips, J. S. *Learning foundations of behavior therapy*. New York: John Wiley, 1970.

Kanfer, F. H., & Saslow, G. Behavioral diagnosis. In C. M. Franks (Ed.), *Behavior therapy: Appraisal and status*. New York: McGraw-Hill, 1969.

Kaplan, A. *The conduct of inquiry: Methodology for behavioral science*. San Francisco: Chandler, 1964.

Karson, S., & O'Dell, J. W. *Guide to the clinical use of the 16PE*. Champaign, IL: Institute for Personality and Ability Testing, 1976.

Kazdin, A. E., & Straw, M. K. Assessment of behavior of the mentally retarded. In M. Hersen & A. S. Bellack (Eds.), *Behavioral Assessment: A practical handbook*. New York: Pergamon Press, 1976.

Kelly, E. L. The Theory and techniques of assessment. *Annual Review of Psychology*, 1954, *5*, 281–310.

Kelly, E. L. *Assessment of human characteristics*. Belmont, CA: Brooks/Cole, 1967.

Kelly, E. L. Review of the personality research form. In O. K. Buros (Ed.), *Seventh mental measurements yearbook*. Highland Park, NJ: Gryphon Press, 1972.

Kelly, E. L., & Fiske, D. W. *The prediction of performance in clinical psychology*. Ann Arbor: University of Michigan Press, 1951.

Kelly, E. L., & Goldberg, L. R. Correlates of later performance and specialization in psychology. *Psychological Monographs*, 1959, *73* (12, Whole No. 482).

Kelly, G. A. *The psychology of personal constructs* (2 vols.). New York: W. W. Norton & Co., Inc., 1955.

Kendrick, D. T., & Stringfield, D. O. Personality traits and the eye of the beholder: Crossing some traditional philosophical boundaries in the search for consistency in all of the people. *Psychological Review*, 1980, *87*, 88–104.

Kennedy, W. A. *Intelligence and economics: A confounded relationship*. Morristown, NJ: General Learning Press, 1973.

Kent, R. N., & Foster, S. L. Direct observational procedures: Methodological issues in naturalistic settings. In A. R. Ciminero, K. S. Calhoun, & H. E. Adams (Eds.), *Handbook of behavioral assessment*. New York: John Wiley, 1977.

Kerlinger, F. N. *Foundations of behavioral research* (2nd ed.). New York: Holt, Rinehart & Winston, 1973.

Kessler, J. W. *Psychopathology of childhood.* Englewood Cliffs, NJ: Prentice-Hall, 1966.

King, G. D. Review of the MMPI. In O. K. Buros (Ed.), *Eighth mental measurements yearbook.* Highland Park, NJ: Gryphon Press, 1978.

Kitwood, T. Review of the Rokeach value survey. In O. K. Buros (Ed.), *Eighth mental measurements yearbook.* Highland Park, NJ: Gryphon Press, 1978.

Kleinmuntz, B. *An investigation of the verbal behavior of paranoid psychotic patients and normals.* Unpublished doctoral dissertation, University of Minnesota, 1958.

Kleinmuntz, B. An extension of the construct validity of the ego-strength scale. *Journal of Consulting Psychology,* 1960, *24,* 463–464. (a)

Kleinmuntz, B. Identification of maladjusted college students. *Journal of Counseling Psychology,* 1960, *7,* 209–211. (b)

Kleinmuntz, B. Two types of paranoid schizophrenia. *Journal of Clinical Psychology,* 1960, *16,* 310–312. (c)

Kleinmuntz, B. The college maladjustment scale (Mt): Norms and predictive validity. *Educational and Psychological Measurement,* 1961, *21,* 1029–1033.

Kleinmuntz, B. MMPI decision rules for the identification of college maladjustment: A digital computer approach. *Psychological Monographs,* 1963, *77* (14, Whole No. 577). (a)

Kleinmuntz, B. Personality test interpretation by digital computer. *Science,* 1963, *139,* 416–418. (b)

Kleinmuntz, B. A portrait of the computer as a young clinician. *Behavioral Science,* 1963, *8,* 154–156. (c)

Kleinmuntz, B. *Personality measurement: An introduction.* Homewood, IL: Dorsey Press, 1967 (Reprinted by R. E. Krieger, 1975). (a)

Kleinmuntz, B. Sign and seer: Another example. *Journal of Abnormal Psychology,* 1967, *72,* 163–165. (b)

Kleinmuntz, B. (Ed.). *Formal representation of human judgment.* New York: John Wiley, 1968.

Kleinmuntz, B. Personality test interpretation by computer and clinician. In J. N. Butcher (Ed.). *MMPI: Research developments and clinical applications.* New York: McGraw-Hill, 1969, pp. 97–104.

Kleinmuntz, B. The computer as clinician. *American Psychologist,* 1975, *30,* 379–387.

Kleinmuntz, B. Psychological assessment. In W. H. Holtzman (Ed.). *Introductory psychology in depth: Developmental topics.* New York: Harper & Row, 1978.

Kleinmuntz, B. *Essentials of abnormal psychology* (2nd ed.). New York: Harper & Row, 1980.

Kleinmuntz, B., & Alexander, L. B. Computer program for the Meehl-Dahlstrom MMPI profile rules. *Educational and Psychological Measurement,* 1962, *22,* 193–199.

Kleinmuntz, B., & McLean, R. S. Diagnostic interviewing by digital computer. *Behavioral Science,* 1968, *13,* 75–80.

Kline, P. (Ed.). *New approaches in psychological measurement.* New York: John Wiley, 1973.

Klopfer, B., Ainsworth, M. D., Klopfer, W. G., & Holt, R. R. *Developments in the Rorschach technique.* Vol. 1. New York: Harcourt, Brace & World, 1954.

Klopfer, B., & Davidson, H. H. *The Rorschach technique: An introductory manual.* New York: Harcourt, Brace & World. 1962.

Klopfer, B., & Kelley, D. M. *The Rorschach technique.* New York: Harcourt, Brace & World, 1942.

Klopfer, B., Meyer, M. M., & Brawer, F. *Developments in the Rorschach technique.* New York: Harcourt Brace Jovanovich, 1970.

Korchin, S. J. *Modern clinical psychology: Principles of intervention in the clinic and community.* New York: Basic Books, 1976.

Korchin, S. J., & Heath, H. A. Somatic experience in the anxiety state: Some sex and personality correlates of "autonomic feedback." *Journal of Consulting Psychology,* 1961, *25,* 398–404.

Kostlan, S. A method for the empirical study of psychodiagnosis. *Journal of Consulting Psychology,* 1954, *18,* 83–88.

Kraepelin, E. *Lehrbuch* (9th ed.). Berlin: 1926.

Krasner, L. The operant approach in behavior modification. In J. T. Spence, R. C. Carson, & J. W. Thibaut (Eds.), *Behavioral approaches to therapy.* Morristown, NJ: General Learning Press, 1976.

Kuder, G. F. *Kuder preference record—personal.* Chicago: Science Research Associates, 1934–1976. (a)

Kuder, G. F. *Kuder preference record—vocational.* Chicago: Science Research Associates, 1934–1976. (b)

Kuder, G. F. *Kuder occupational interest survey.* Chicago: Science Research Associates, 1956–1976.

Kuhn, T. S. *The structure of scientific revolutions* (2nd ed.). Chicago: University of Chicago Press, 1970.

Lachar, D. *Automated psychological assessment.* Pontiac, MI: Automated Psychological Assessment, Inc., 1976.

Lans, P. J., & Lazovik, A. D. Experimental desensitization of a phobia. *Journal of Abnormal and Social Psychology,* 1963, *66,* 519–525.

Lanyon, R. I., & Goodstein, L. D. *Personality assessment.* New York: John Wiley, 1971.

Lazarsfeld, P. F. The controversy over detailed interviews. An offer for negotiation. *Public Opinion Quarterly,* 1944, *8,* 38–60.

Lazarus, A. A. Has behavior therapy outlived its usefulness? *American Psychologist,* 1977, *32,* 550–554. (a)

Lazarus, A. A. *Multimodal life history questionnaire.* Kingston, NJ: Multimodal Therapy Institute, 1977. (b)

Lazarus, R. S. *Adjustment and personality.* New York: McGraw-Hill, 1961.

Lemke, E., & Wiersma, W. *Principles of psychological measurement.* Chicago: Rand McNally, 1976.

Lentz, R. J., Paul, G. L., & Calhoun, J. F. Reliability and validity of three measures of functioning with "hard core" chronic patients. *Journal of Abnormal Psychology*, 1971, *78*, 69–76.

Levine, K. M., Grassi, J. R., & Gerson, M. J. Hypnotically induced mood changes in the verbal and graphic Rorschach, a case study. *Rorschach Research Exchange*, 1943, *7*, 130–144.

Levy, L. H. *Conceptions of personality.* New York: Random House, 1970.

Lewontin, R. C. The fallacy of biological determinism. *The Sciences*, 1976, *16*, 6–10.

Liebert, R. M., & Spiegler, M. D. *Personality: Strategies for the study of man.* (3rd ed.). Homewood, IL: Dorsey Press, 1978.

Likert, R. A technique for the measurement of attitudes. *Archives of Psychology*, 1932, No. 140.

Lindsley, O. R. A reliable wrist counter for recording behavior rates. *Journal of Applied Behavior Analysis*, 1968, *1*, 77–78.

Lindzey, G. Seer versus sign. *Journal of Experimental Research in Personality*, 1965, *1*, 17–26.

Lindzey, G., & Herman, P. S. Thematic apperception test: A note on reliability and situational validity. *Journal of Projective Techniques*, 1955, *19*, 36–42.

Lingoes, J. C. Review of the MMPI. In O. K. Buros (Ed.), *Sixth mental measurements yearbook.* Highland Park, NJ: Gryphon Press, 1965.

Linn, R. L. Review of differential aptitude tests. In O. K. Buros (Ed.), *Eighth mental measurements yearbook.* Highland Park, NJ: Gryphon Press, 1978.

Locksley, A., & Colten, M. E. Psychological androgyny: A case of mistaken identity? *Journal of Personality and Social Psychology*, 1979, *37*, 1017–1031.

Loehlin, J. C., Lindzey, G., & Spuhler, J. N. *Race differences in intelligence.* San Francisco: W. H. Freeman & Company, Publishers, 1975.

Loevinger, J. Objective tests as instruments of psychological theory. *Psychological Reports*, 1957, *3*, 635–694. (Monograph)

Loevinger, J. Objective tests as instruments of psychological theory. In D. N. Jackson & S. Messick (Eds.), *Problems in human assessment.* New York: McGraw-Hill, 1967.

Loevinger, J. Some limitations of objective personality tests. In J. N. Butcher (Ed.), *Objective personality assessment: Changing perspectives.* New York: Academic Press, 1972.

Loevinger, J., & Wessler, R. *Measuring ego development: Construction and use of a sentence completion test* (Vol. 1). San Francisco: Jossey-Bass, 1970.

Loevinger, J., Wessler, R., & Redmore, C. *Measuring ego development: Scoring manual for women and girls* (Vol. 2). San Francisco: Jossey-Bass, 1970.

Lofland, J. *Doomsday cult: A study of conversion, proselytization, and maintenance of faith.* Englewood Cliffs, NJ: Prentice-Hall, 1966.

London, M., & Bray, D. W. Ethical issues in testing and evaluation for personnel decisions. *American Psychologist*, 1980, *35*, 890–901.

Lopez, F. M., Jr. *Personnel interviewing: Theory and practice.* New York: McGraw-Hill, 1965.

Lord, F. M., & Novick, M. R. *Statistical theories of mental test scores.* Reading, MA: Addison-Wesley, 1968.

Lorr, M. Assessing psychotic behavior by the IMPS. In P. Pichot, & R. Oliver-Martin (Eds.), *Psychological measurements in psychopharmacology.* Basel, Switzerland: S. Karger, 1974.

Lorr, M. Measurement of the major psychotic syndromes. *Annals of the New York Academy of Science,* 1962, *93,* 851–856.

Lorr, M., Klett, C. J., McNair, D. M., & Lasky, J. J. *Inpatient Multidimensional Psychiatric Rating Scale, 1966 rev.* Palo Alto, CA: Consulting Psychologists Press, 1966.

Lorr, M., McNair, D. M., Klett, C. J., & Lasky, J. J. Evidence of ten psychotic syndromes. *Journal of Consulting Psychology,* 1962, *26,* 185–189.

Lorr, M., & Vestie, N. D. *Psychotic inpatient profile.* Los Angeles, CA: Western Psychological Services, 1961.

Lorr, M., McNair, D. M., Klett, C. J., & Lasky, J. J. Canonical variates and second-order variates: a reply. *Journal of Consulting Psychology,* 1963, *27,* 180–181.

Lubin, A. *A methodological study of configural scoring.* USA Personnel Research Branch Note No. 42, 1954.

Luborsky, L., & Spence, D. P. Quantitative research on psychoanalytic therapy. In A. E. Bergin, & S. L. Garfield (Eds.), *Handbook of psychotherapy and behavior change: An empirical analysis.* New York: John Wiley, 1971.

Lucas, R. W., Mullin, P. J., Luna, C. B., & McInroy, D. C. Psychiatrists and a computer as interrogators of patients with alcohol-related illness: A comparison. *British Journal of Psychiatry,* 1977, *131,* 160–167.

Lumsden, J. Test theory. *Annual Review of Psychology,* 1976, *27,* 251–280.

Lunneborg, P. W. Review of Strong-Campbell interest inventory. In O. K. Buros (Ed.), *Eighth mental measurements yearbook.* Highland Park, NJ: Gryphon Press, 1978.

Lushene, R. E. *Factor structure of the MMPI item pool.* Unpublished master's thesis, Florida State University, 1967.

Lykken, D. T. A study of anxiety in the sociopathic personality. *Journal of Abnormal and Social Psychology,* 1957, *55,* 6–10.

Lykken, D. T. Psychology and the lie detector industry. *American Psychologist,* 1974, *29,* 725–739.

Lykken, D. T. Review of the Jackson personality inventory. In O. K. Buros (Ed.), *Eighth mental measurements yearbook.* Highland Park, NJ: Gryphon Press, 1978.

Lykken, D. T. *A tremor in the blood: Uses and abuses of the lie detector.* New York: McGraw-Hill, 1981.

Lyman, H. B. *Test scores and what they mean* (2nd ed.). Englewood Cliffs, NJ: Prentice-Hall, 1971.

McBee, G. W., & Justice, B. The effect of interviewer bias on mental illness questionnaire responses. *Journal of Psychology*, 1977, *95*, 67–75.

Mahoney, M. J., & Thoresen, C. E. *Self-control: Power to the person.* Monterey, CA: Brooks/Cole, 1974.

McCall, R. B. *Fundamental statistics for psychology* (3rd ed.). New York: Harcourt Brace Jovanovich, 1980.

McClelland, D. C. Measuring motivation in fantasy: The achievement motive. In D. C. McClelland (Ed.), *Studies in motivation.* New York: Appleton-Century-Crofts, 1955.

McClelland, D. C. Methods of measuring human motivation. In J. W. Atkinson (Ed.), *Motives in fantasy, action, and society.* Princeton, NJ: D. Van Nostrand, 1958. (a)

McClelland, D. C. Risk taking in children into high and low need for achievement. In J. W. Atkinson (Ed.), *Motives in fantasy, action, and society.* Princeton, NJ: D. Van Nostrand, 1958. (b)

McClelland, D. C. *The achieving society.* Princeton, NJ: D. Van Nostrand, 1961.

McClelland, D. C. Love and power: The psychological signals of war. *Psychology Today*, 1975, *8*, 44–48.

McClelland, D. C., Atkinson, J. W., Clark, R. A., & Lowell, E. L. *The achievement motive.* New York: Appleton-Century-Crofts, 1953.

McDonald, R. L., & Gynther, M. D. Relationship of self and ideal-self descriptions with sex, race, and class in southern adolescents. *Journal of Personality and Social Psychology*, 1965, *1*, 85–88.

McFadden, J. H., & Dashiell, J. F. Racial differences as measured by the Downey-Will temperament test. *Journal of Applied Psychology*, 1923, *7*, 30–53.

McGhie, A., & Chapman, J. Disorders of attention and perception in early schizophrenia. *British Journal of Medical Psychology*, 1961, *34*, 103–116.

McGown, N. A. (Ed.). *The natural history of an interview.* Microfilm collection of manuscripts on cultural anthropology. (Fifteenth Series.) Chicago: University of Chicago Joseph Regenstein Library Department of Photo Duplication, 1971.

MacDonough, T. S. A critique of the first Feldman and MacCulloch avoidance conditioning treatment of homosexuals. *Behavior Therapy*, 1972, *3*, 104–111.

Machover, K. *Personality projection in the drawing of the human figure.* Springfield, IL: Chas. C Thomas, 1948.

Machover, K. Drawing of the human figure: A method of personality investigation. In H. H. Anderson & G. L. Anderson (Eds.), *An introduction to projective techniques.* Englewood Cliffs, NJ: Prentice-Hall, 1951.

MacKinnon, D. W. An assessment study of air force officers: Part V. Summary and applications. *WADC technical report 58–91*, Wright Air Development Center, 1958.

McHugh, A. F. WISC performance in neurotic and conduct disturbances. *Journal of Clinical Psychology*, 1963, *19*, 423–424.

McKinley, J. C., & Hathaway, S. R. A multiphasic personality schedule (Minnesota): II. A differentiated study of hypochondriasis. *Journal of Psychology,* 1940, *10,* 255–268 (also reprinted in Welsh & Dahlstrom, 1956).

McKinley, J. C., & Hathaway, S. R. The MMPI: V. Hysteria, hypomania, and psychopathic deviate. *Journal of Applied Psychology,* 1944, *28,* 153–174 (also reprinted in Welsh & Dahlstrom, 1956).

McNemar, Q. *Psychological statistics* (4th ed.). New York: John Wiley, 1969.

Magnusson, D. *Test theory.* Reading, MA: Addison-Wesley, 1966.

Magnusson, D., & Endler, N. S. (Eds.). *Personality at the crossroads: Current issues in interactional psychology.* Hillsdale, NJ: Lawrence Erlbaum, 1977.

Maguire, P., Roe, P., Goldberg, D., Jones, S., Hyde, C., & O'Dowd, T. The value of feedback in teaching interviewing skills to medical students. *Psychological Medicine,* 1978, *8,* 695–704.

Mahoney, M. J. Self-reward and self-monitoring techniques for weight control. *Behavior Therapy,* 1974, *5,* 48–57.

Mahoney, M. J. Reflections on the cognitive-learning trend in psychotherapy. *American Psychologist,* 1977, *32,* 5–13.

Mahoney, M. J., & Thoresen, C. E. *Self-control: Power to the person.* Monterey, CA: Brooks/Cole, 1974.

Manaster, G. J., & King, M. Early recollections of male homosexuals. *Journal of Individual Psychology,* 1973, *29,* 26–33.

Mandler, G., Mandler, J. M., Kremen, I., & Sholiton, R. D. The response to threat: Relations among verbal and physiological indices. *Psychological Monographs,* 1961, *75* (9, Whole No. 511).

Marcos, L. R. Nonverbal behavior and thought processing. *Archives of General Psychiatry,* 1979, *36,* 940–943.

Marks, P. A., & Seeman, W. *Actuarial descriptions of abnormal personality: An atlas for use with the MMPI.* Baltimore: Williams & Wilkins, 1963.

Marks, P. A., Seeman, W., & Haller, D. L. *The actuarial use of the MMPI with adolescents and adults.* Baltimore: Williams & Wilkins, 1974.

Marlatt, G. A., Demming, B., & Reid, J. B. Loss of control drinking of alcoholics: An experimental analogue. *Journal of Abnormal Psychology,* 1973, *81,* 233–241.

Mash, E. J. & Terdal, L. Modification of mother-child interaction: Playing with children. *Mental Retardation,* 1973, *11,* 44–49.

Maslow, A. H. *Towards a psychology of being.* Princeton, NJ: D. Van Nostrand, 1962.

Maslow, A. H. *Toward a psychology of being* (2nd ed.). New York: D. Van Nostrand, 1968.

Maslow, A. H. Self-actualizing and beyond. In A. H. Maslow (Ed.), *The farther reaches of human nature.* New York: Viking, 1972.

Matarazzo, J. D. The interview. In B. B. Wolman (Ed.), *Handbook of clinical psychology.* New York: McGraw-Hill, 1965.

Matarazzo, J. D. *Wechsler's measurement and appraisal of adult intelligence* (5th ed.). Baltimore: Williams & Wilkins, 1972.

Matarazzo, J. D., & Wiens, A. N. Black intelligence test of cultural homogeneity and Wechsler adult intelligence scale scores of black and white police applicants. *Journal of Applied Psychology*, 1977, *62*, 57–63.

Matarazzo, J. D., Wiens, A. N., Matarazzo, R. G., & Soslow, G. Speech and silence behavior in clinical psychotherapy and its laboratory correlates. In J. Shlien, H. Hunt, J. D. Matarazzo, & C. Savage (Eds.), *Research in Psychotherapy*. Vol. 3. Washington, D.C. American Psychological Association, 1968.

Meehan, K. A., Woll, S. B., & Abbot, R. D. The role of dissimulation and social desirability in the measurement of moral reasoning. *Journal of Research in Personality*, 1979, *13*, 25–38.

Meehl, P. E. The dynamics of "structured" personality tests. *Journal of Clinical Psychology*, 1945, *1*, 296–303.

Meehl, P. E. Profile analysis of the MMPI in differential diagnosis. *Journal of Applied Psychology*, 1946, *30*, 517–524 (also reprinted in Welsh & Dahlstrom, 1956).

Meehl, P. E. Configural scoring. *Journal of Consulting Psychology*, 1950, *14*, 165–171.

Meehl, P. E. *Clinical versus statistical prediction*. Minneapolis: University of Minnesota Press, 1954.

Meehl, P. E. When shall we use our heads instead of the formula? *Journal of Counseling Psychology*, 1957, *4*, 268–273.

Meehl, P. E. A comparison of clinicians with five statistical methods of identifying psychotic MMPI profiles. *Journal of Counseling Psychology*, 1959, *2*, 102–109. (a)

Meehl, P. E. Some ruminations on the validation of clinical procedures. *Canadian Journal of Psychology*, 1959, *13*, 102–108. (b)

Meehl, P. E. The cognitive activity of the clinician. *American Psychologist*, 1960, *15*, 19–27.

Meehl, P. E. Seer over sign: The first good example. *Journal of Experimental Research in Personality*, 1965, *1*, 27–32.

Meehl, P. E. Nuisance variables and *ex post facto* design. In M. Radno & S. Winokur (Eds.), *Minnesota studies in the philosophy of science* (Vol. 4). Minneapolis: University of Minnesota Press, 1970.

Meehl, P. E. High school yearbooks: A reply to Schwarz. *Journal of Abnormal Psychology*, 1971, *77*, 143–148.

Meehl, P. E. Reactions, reflections, projections. In J. N. Butcher (Ed.), *Objective personality assessment: Changing perspectives*. New York: Academic Press, 1972.

Meehl, P. E. (Ed.). *Psychodiagnosis: Selected papers*. Minneapolis: University of Minnesota Press, 1973.

Meehl, P. E. Theoretical risks and tabular asterisks: Sir Karl, Sir Ronald, and the slow progress of soft psychology. *Journal of Consulting and Clinical Psychology*, 1978, *46*, 806–834.

Meehl, P. E., & Dahlstrom, W. G. Objective configural rules for discriminating psychotic from neurotic MMPI profiles. *Journal of Consulting Psychology*, 1960, *24*, 375–387.

Meehl, P. E., & Hathaway, S. R. The K factor as a suppressor variable in the MMPI. *Journal of Applied Psychology*, 1946, *30*, 525–564 (also reprinted in Welsh & Dahlstrom, 1956).

Meehl, P. E., & Rosen, A. Antecedent probability and the efficiency of psychometric signs, patterns, or cutting scores. *Psychological Bulletin*, 1955, *52*, 194–216.

Megargee, E. I. The California *psychological inventory handbook*. San Francisco: Jossey-Bass, 1972.

Mehrabian, A. *Silent messages*. Belmont, CA: Wadsworth, 1971.

Meichenbaum, D. Cognitive factors in behavior modification: Modifying what clients say to themselves. In C. Franks & T. Wilson (Eds.), *Annual Review of Behavior Therapy: Theory and Practice*. New York: Bruner/Mazel, 1973.

Meichenbaum, D. *Cognitive behavior modification*. Morristown, NJ: General Learning Press, 1974.

Meichenbaum, D. *Cognitive behavior modification: An integrative approach*. New York: Plenum, 1977.

Meichenbaum, D. H., Bilmore, J. B., & Fedoravicius, A. Group insight versus group desensitization in treating speech anxiety. *Journal of Consulting and Clinical Psychology*, 1971, *36*, 410–421.

Menninger, K. A. *A manual for psychiatric case study*. New York: Grune & Stratton, 1952.

Merton, R. K. *The focused interview*. New York: Free Press, 1956.

Messick, S. The standard problem: Meaning and values in measurement and evaluation. *American Psychologist*, 1975, *30*, 955–966.

Messick, S. Test validity and the ethics of assessment. *American Psychologist*, 1980, *35*, 1012–1027.

*Methods of expressing test scores* (Test Service Bulletin, No. 48). New York: The Psychological Corporation, January, 1955.

Mettler, F. A. (Ed.). *Columbia Greystone associates: Selective partial ablations of the frontal cortex*. New York: Harper & Row, 1949.

Miklich, D. R. Radio telemetry in clinical psychology. *American Psychologist*, 1975, *30*, 419–425.

Mikulas, W. L. *Behavior modification: An overview*. New York: Harper & Row, 1970.

Miller, N. E., & Dollard, J. *Social learning and imitation*. New Haven, CT: Yale University Press, 1941.

Millon, T. *Modern psychopathology*. Philadelphia: Saunders, 1969.

Millon, T. *Millon multiracial clinical inventory manual*. Minneapolis: Interpretive Scoring Systems (NCS), 1977.

Millon, T. Millon clinical multiaxial inventory (MCMI). Interpretive Scoring Systems (NCS), 1979.

Mills, C., & Hogan, R. A role theoretical interpretation of personality scale item responses. *Journal of Personality*, 1978, *46*, 778–785.

Mischel, W. *Personality and assessment*. New York: John Wiley, 1968.

Mischel, W. On the empirical dilemmas of psychodynamic approaches. *Journal of Abnormal Psychology*, 1973, *82*, 335–344.

Mischel, W. On the empirical dilemmas of psychodynamic approaches: Issues and alternatives. In N. S. Endler & D. Magnusson (Eds.), *Interactional psychology and personality*. Washington, DC: Hemisphere Publishing, 1976. (a)

Mischel, W. *Introduction to personality*. New York: Holt, Rinehart & Winston, 1976. (b)

Mischel, W. On the future of personality measurement. *American Psychologist*, 1977, *32*, 246–254.

Mischel, W. *Introduction to personality* (3rd ed.). New York: Holt, Rinehart & Winston, 1981.

Mischel, W., & Metzner, R. Preference for delayed reward as a function of age, intelligence, and length of delay interval. *Journal of Abnormal and Social Psychology*, 1962, *64*, 425–431.

Morris, B. S. Officer selection in the British army, 1942–1945. *Occupational Psychology*, 1949, *23*, 219–234.

Morris, D. *Intimate behavior*. New York: Random House, 1971.

Morris, D. *Manwatching: A field guide to human behavior*. New York: Harry N. Abrams, 1977.

Mosier, C. I. Problems and designs of cross-validation. *Educational and Psychological Measurement*, 1951, *11*, 5–11.

Munroe, R. L. *Schools of psychoanalytic thought*. New York: Dryden Press, 1955.

Munsinger, H. The adopted child's IQ: A critical review of adoption studies. *Psychological Bulletin*, 1975, *82*, 623–659.

Munsinger, H. Reply to Kamin. *Psychological Bulletin*, 1978, *85*, 202–206.

Murray, H. A. (and collaborators). *Explorations in personality*. New York: Oxford University Press, 1938.

Murray, H. A. Thematic apperception test. Cambridge, MA: Harvard University Press, 1943.

Murray, H. A. *Explorations in personality*. New York: Science Editions, 1962.

Mussen, P. H., Conger, J. J., & Kagan, J. *Child development and personality* (5th ed.). New York: Harper & Row, 1979.

Myers, C. R., & Gifford, E. V. Measuring abnormal patterns on the revised Stanford-Binet scale (form L). *Journal of Mental Science*, 1943, *89*, 92–101.

Nathan, P. E., & O'Brien, J. S. An experimental analysis of the behavior of alcoholics and nonalcoholics during prolonged experimental drinking. *Behavior Therapy*, 1971, *2*, 455–476.

Nay, W. R. *Multimethod clinical assessments*. New York: Gardner Press, 1979.

Newell, A., & Simon, H. A. *Human problem solving*. Englewood Cliffs, NJ: Prentice-Hall, 1972.

Norman, A. Response contingency and human gastric acidity. *Psychophysiology*, 1969, *5*, 673–682.

Norman, A., & Melville, C. H. Potential applications of telemetered heart rate data to developmental psychology. *Developmental Psychology*, 1971, *5*, 190–194.

Norman, W. T. Toward an adequate taxonomy of personality attributes: Replicated factor structure in peer nomination personality ratings. *Journal of Abnormal and Social Psychology*, 1963, *66*, 574–583.

Norman, W. T. *2800 personality trait descriptors: Normative operating characteristics for a university population.* Department of Psychology, University of Michigan, Ann Arbor, 1967.

Norman, W. T. Psychometric considerations for a revision of the MMPI. In J. N. Butcher (Ed.), *Objective personality assessment: Changing perspectives.* New York: Academic Press, 1972.

Nunnally, J. C. *Introduction to psychological measurement.* New York: McGraw-Hill, 1970. (a)

Nunnally, J. C. *Introduction to statistics for psychology and education.* New York: McGraw-Hill, 1970. (b)

Nunnally, J. C. *Psychometric theory* (2nd ed.). New York: McGraw-Hill, 1978.

Office of Strategic Services Assessment Staff (OSS). *Assessment of men.* New York: Rinehart, 1948.

O'Leary, K. D., Kent, R. N., & Kanowitz, J. Shaping data collection congruent with experimental hypotheses. *Journal of Applied Behavioral Analysis*, 1975, *8*, 43–51.

O'Leary, K. D., & Wilson, G. T. *Behavior therapy: Applications and outcome.* Englewood Cliffs, NJ: Prentice-Hall, 1975.

Orne, M. T. On the social psychology of the psychological experiment: With particular reference to demand characteristics and their implications. *American Psychologist*, 1962, *17*, 776–783.

Osgood, C. E. The nature and measurement of meaning. *Psychological Bulletin*. 1952, *49*, 197–237.

Osgood, C. E., Suci, G. J., & Tannenbaum, P. H. *The measurement of meaning.* Urbana: University of Illinois Press, 1957.

Office of Strategic Services. *Assessment of men.* New York: Rinehart, 1948.

Owens, W. A. A quasi-actuarial basis for individual assessment. *American Psychologist*, 1971, *26*, 992–999.

Owens, W. A. Background data. In M. D. Dunnette (Ed.), *Handbook of industrial psychology.* New York: Rand-McNally, 1975.

Paige, J. M. Summary of "Automated content analysis of 'Letters from Jenny'." In P. J. Stone, D. C. Dunphey, M. S. Smith, & D. M. Ogilvie (Eds.), *General Inquirer.* Cambridge, Mass.: MIT Press, 1966.

Parlee, M. B. Conversational politics. *Psychology Today*, May 1979, pp. 48–56.

Pascal, G. R., & Suttell, B. J. *The Bender-Gestalt test.* New York: Grune & Stratton, 1951.

Patterson, G. R. *Families: Applications of social learning to family life.* Champaign, IL: Research Press, 1971.

Paul, G. L. Outcome of systematic desensitization. I: Background procedures, and uncontrolled reports of individual treatment. In C. M. Franks (Ed.), *Behavior therapy: Appraisal and status.* New York: McGraw-Hill, 1969.

Pavlov, I. *Conditioned reflexes.* New York: Oxford University Press, 1927.

Payne, A. F. *Sentence completions.* New York: New York Guidance Clinic, 1928.

Payne, D. A. *The assessment of learning: Cognitive and affective.* Lexington, MA: Heath, 1974.

Pearson, J. S., & Swenson, W. M. The psychological corporation MMPI reporting service. New York: The Psychological Corporation, 1967.

Pedhazur, E. J., & Tetenbaum, T. J. Bem sex role inventory: A theoretical and methodological critique. *Journal of Personality and Social Psychology,* 1979, *37,* 996–1016.

Pervin, L. A. *Current controversies and issues in personality.* New York: John Wiley, 1978.

Pervin, L. A. *Personality; Theory, assessment, and research.* New York: John Wiley, 1980.

Peterson, D. R. *The clinical study of social behavior.* New York: Appleton-Century-Crofts, 1968.

Peterson, R. A. Review of the Holtzman inkblot test. In O. K. Buros (Ed.), *Eighth mental measurements yearbook.* Highland Park, NJ: Gryphon Press, 1978. (a)

Peterson, R. A. Review of the Rorschach. In O. K. Buros (Ed.), *Eighth mental measurements yearbook.* Highland Park, NJ: Gryphon Press, 1978. (b)

Petrie, I. R. J. Residential treatment of maladjusted children: A study of some factors related to progress in adjustment. *British Journal of Educational Psychology,* 1962, *32,* 29–37.

Phares, E. J. *Locus of control.* Morristown, NJ: General Learning Press, 1972.

Phares, E. J. *Locus of control in personality.* Morristown, NJ: General Learning Press, 1976.

Phares, E. J. *Clinical psychology: Concepts, methods, and profession.* Homewood, IL: Dorsey, 1979.

Phillips, J. L., Jr. *Statistical thinking: A structural approach.* San Francisco: W. H. Freeman & Company Publishers, 1973.

Phillips, J. P. N. A note on the scoring of the sexual orientation method. *Behavior Research and Therapy,* 1968, *6,* 121–123.

Pignatelli, M. L. A comparative study of mental functioning patterns of problem and non-problem children seven, eight, and nine years of age. *Genetic Psychology Monographs,* 1943, *27,* 69–162.

Piotrowski, Z. A. *Perceptanalysis.* New York: Macmillan, 1957.

Piotrowski, Z. A. Digital computer interpretation of ink-blot test data. *Psychiatric Quarterly,* 1964, *38,* 1–24.

Piotrowski, Z. A. The Rorschach inkblot method. In B. B. Wolman (Ed.), *Handbook of clinical psychology.* New York: McGraw-Hill, 1965.

Piotrowski, Z. A. CPR: The psychological x-ray in mental disorders. In J. Sidowski, J. H. Johnson, & T. A. Williams (Eds.), *Technology in mental health care delivery systems.* Norwood, NJ: Ablex Publishers, 1980. (a)

Piotrowski, Z. A. Personal communication. August 1980. (b)

Popham, W. J. *Criterion-referenced measurement.* Englewood Cliffs, NJ: Prentice-Hall, 1978.

Potkay, C. R. The role of personal history data in clinical judgment: A selective focus. *Journal of Personality Assessment,* 1973, *37,* 203–213.

Quay, H. C. Patterns of aggression, withdrawal, and immaturity. In H. C. Quay & J. S. Werry (Eds.), *Psychopathological disorders of childhood.* New York: John Wiley, 1972.

Rabkin, J. G. Stressful Life Events and Schizophrenia: A review of the research literature. *Psychological Bulletin,* 1980, *87,* 408–425.

Radcliffe, J. A. A note on questionnaire faking with 16PFQ and MMPI. *Australian Journal of Psychology,* 1966, *18,* 154–157.

Rahe, R. H., & Holmes, T. H. Social, psychologic, and psychophysiologic aspects of inguinal hernia. *Journal of Psychosomatic Research,* 1965, *8,* 487.

Ramzy, I., & Pickard, P. M. A study in the reliability of scoring the Rorschach inkblot test. *Journal of General Psychology,* 1949, *40,* 3–10.

Rapaport, D., Gill, M. M., & Schafer, R. *Diagnostic psychological testing* (Rev. ed. by R. R. Holt). New York: International Universities Press, 1968.

Raush, H. L., Dittman, A. T., & Taylor, T. J. The interpersonal behavior of children in residential treatment. *Journal of Abnormal and Social Psychology,* 1959, *58,* 9–27.

Rayman, J. *Sex and the simple interest inventory: The empirical validation of sex-balanced vocational interest inventory items.* Unpublished doctoral dissertation, University of Iowa, 1974.

Remmers, H. H., & Silance, E. F. Generalized attitude scales. *Journal of Social Psychology,* 1934, *5,* 298–312.

Renaud, H. R. *Clinical correlates of the masculinity-femininity scale of the MMPI.* Unpublished doctoral dissertation, University of California, Berkeley, 1950.

Richardson, S. A., Dohrenwend, B. S., & Klein, D. *Interviewing: Its forms and functions.* New York: Basic Books, 1965.

Rioch, M. J. The use of the Rorschach test in the assessment of change in patients under psychotherapy. *Psychiatry,* 1949, *12,* 427–434.

Robinson, A. L. Tournament competition fuels computer chess. *Science,* 1979, *204,* 1396–1398.

Rogers, C. R. *Counseling and psychotherapy.* Boston: Houghton Mifflin, 1942.

Rogers, C. R. *Client-centered therapy.* Boston: Houghton Mifflin, 1951.

Rogers, C. R. *On becoming a person.* Boston: Houghton Mifflin, 1961.

Rogers, C. R., & Stevens, B. *Person to person: The problem of being human.* New York: Pocket Books, 1971.

Rohde, A. R. *Sentence completion method: Its diagnostic and clinical application to mental disorders.* New York: Ronald Press, 1951–1957.

Rokeach, M. *Rokeach value survey.* New York: Free Press, 1967–1973.

Rorschach, H. *Psychodiagnostik.* Leipzig: Ernst Bircher Verlag, 1921.

Rosen, A. Detection of suicidal patients: An example of some limitations in the prediction of infrequent events. *Journal of Consulting Psychology*, 1954, *18*, 397–403.

Rosen, G. M. Effects of source prestige on subjects' acceptance of the Barnum effect: Psychologist versus astrologer. *Journal of Consulting and Clinical Psychology*, 1975, *43*, 95.

Rosenhan, D. L. On being sane in insane places. *Science*, 1973, *179*, 250–258.

Rosenthal, R. The effect of the experimenter in the results of psychological research. In B. A. Maher (Ed.), *Progress in experimental personality research* (Vol. 1). New York: Academic Press, 1964.

Rosenthal, R. Interpersonal expectations: Effects of the experimenter's hypothesis. In R. Rosenthal & R. L. Rosnow (Eds.), *Artifact in behavioral research*. New York: Academic Press, 1969.

Rosenthal, R. *Experimenter effects in behavioral research* (Enlarged ed.). New York: Halsted Press, 1976.

Rosenthal, R., Friedman, C. J., Johnson, C. A., Fode, K. L., Shill, T. R., White, C. R., & Vikom-Kline, L. L. Variables affecting experimenter bias in a group situation. *Genetic Psychological Monographs*, 1964, *70*, 271–296.

Rosenzweig, S. *Rosenzweig picture frustration study*. Rosenzweig, Inc., 1944–1964.

Rosenzweig, S. The Rosenzweig picture frustration study, children's form. In A. I. Rubin & M. R. Haworth (Eds.), *Projective techniques with children*. New York: Grune & Stratton, 1960.

Rosnow, R. L., & Rosenthal, R. Volunteer effects in behavioral research. In T. M. Newcomb (Ed.), *New directions in psychology* (Vol. 4). New York: Holt, Rinehart & Winston, 1970.

Rotter, J. B. *Social learning and clinical psychology*. Englewood Cliffs, NJ: Prentice-Hall, 1954.

Rotter, J. B. Generalized expectancies for internal vs. external control of reinforcement. *Psychological Monographs*, 1966, *80* (1, Whole No. 609).

Rotter, J. B. A new scale for the measurement of interpersonal trust. *Journal of Personality*, 1967, *35*, 651–665.

Rotter, J. B., Chance, J. E., & Phares, E. J. (Eds.), *Applications of a social learning theory of personality*. New York: Holt, Rinehart & Winston, 1972.

Rotter, J. B., & Rafferty, J. E. *Manual for the Rotter incomplete sentences Blank, College Form*. New York: Psychological Corporation, 1950.

Rubin, L. S. Recent advances in the chemistry of psychotic disorders. *Psychological Bulletin*, 1959, *56*, 375–383.

Rubin, L. S. Patterns of adrenergic-cholinergic imbalance in the functional psychoses. *Psychological Review*, 1962, *69*, 501–519.

Samelson, F. On the science and the politics of the IQ. *Social Research: An International Quarterly of the Social Sciences*, 1975, *42*, 466–488.

Samuda, R. J. *Psychological testing of American minorities: Issues and consequences*. New York: Harper & Row, 1975.

Sarason, I. G. The effects of anxiety and threat on the solution of a difficult task. *Journal of Abnormal and Social Psychology*, 1961, *62*, 165–168.

Sarason, I. G. *Personality: An objective approach.* New York: John Wiley, 1972.

Sarbin, T. R. The relative accuracy of clinical and statistical predictions of academic achievement. *Psychological Bulletin*, 1941, *38*, 714. (Abstract)

Sarbin, T. R. A contribution to the study of actuarial and individual methods of prediction. *American Journal of Sociology*, 1943, *48*, 593–602.

Sattler, J. M. *Assessment of children's intelligence.* Philadelphia: Saunders, 1974.

Sawyer, J. Measurement and prediction, clinical and statistical. *Psychological Bulletin*, 1966, *66*, 178–200.

Scarr, S., & Weinberg, R. A. IQ test performance of black children adopted by white families. *American Psychologist*, 1976, *31*, 726–739.

Scarr, S., & Weinberg, R. A. Intellectual similarities in adoptive and biologically related families of adolescents. In Z. Willerman & R. G. Turner (Eds.), *Readings about individual and group differences.* San Francisco: W. H. Freeman & Company Publishers, 1979.

Scarr-Salapatek, S. Race, social class, and IQ. *Science*, 1971, *174*, 1285–1295. (a)

Scarr-Salapatek, S. Unknowns in the IQ equation. *Science*, 1971, *174*, 1223–1228. (b)

Scarr-Salapatek, S. Review in *American Scientist*, September-October, 1975, *63*, 588.

Schafer, R. *Psychoanalytic interpretation in Rorschach testing: Theory and application.* New York: Grune & Stratton, 1954.

Schank, R. C. Identification of conceptualizations underlying natural language. In R. C. Schank & K. M. Colby (Eds.), *Computer models of thought and language.* San Francisco: W. H. Freeman & Company Publishers, 1973.

Schank, R. C., & Colby, K. M. (Eds.). *Computer models of thought and language.* San Francisco: W. H. Freeman & Company Publishers, 1973.

Schmidt, H. O. Notes on the MMPI: The K factor. *Journal of Consulting Psychology*, 1948, *12*, 337–342.

Schofield, W., & Balian, L. A comparative study of the personal histories of schizophrenic and nonpsychiatric patients. *Journal of Abnormal and Social Psychology*, 1959, *59*, 216–225.

Schoonover, S. M., & Hertel, R. K. Diagnostic implications of WISC scores. *Psychological Reports*, 1970, *26*, 967–973.

Schwartz, G. E., Shapiro, B., & Tursky, B. Learned control of cardiovascular integration in man through operant conditioning. *Psychosomatic Medicine*, 1971, *33*, 57–62.

Schwarz, J. C. Comment on "High school yearbooks: A nonreactive measure of social isolation in graduates who later became schizophrenic." *Journal of Abnormal Psychology*, 1970, *75*, 317–318.

Schwitzgebel, R. K., & Kolb, D. A. *Changing human behavior: Principles of planned intervention.* New York: McGraw-Hill, 1974.

Sechrest, L. B. Incremental validity: A recommendation. *Educational and Psychological Measurement*, 1963, *23*, 153–158. (a)

Sechrest, L. B. The psychology of personal constructs: George Kelly. In J. M.

Wepman & R. W. Heine (Eds.), *Concepts of personality*. Chicago: Aldine, 1963, 206–233. (b)

Sechrest, L. B. Testing, measuring, and assessing people. In E. F. Borsatta & W. W. Lambert (Eds.), *Handbook of personality theory and research*. Chicago: Rand McNally, 1968.

Selfridge, O. G. Pandemonium: A paradigm for learning. *Proceedings of the Symposium on Mechanisation of Thought Processes*. London: H. M. Stationery Office, 1959.

Selltiz, C., Wrightsman, L. S., & Cook, S. W. *Research methods in social relations* (3rd ed.). New York: Holt, Rinehart & Winston, 1976.

Shagass, C., Amadeo, M., & Overton, D. A. Eye-tracking performance in psychiatric patients. *Biological Psychiatry*, 1974, *9*, 245–260.

Shagass, C., Roemer, R. A., & Amadeo, M. Eye-tracking performance and engagement of attention. *Archives of General Psychiatry*, 1976, *33*, 121–125.

Shannon, C., & Weaver, W. *The mathematical theory of communication*. Urbana: University of Illinois Press, 1949.

Shaw, M. E. The effectiveness of Whyte's rules: "How to cheat on personality tests." *Journal of Applied Psychology*, 1962, *46*, 21–25.

Shneidman, E. S. *The Make-A-Picture Story Test*. New York: Psychological Corporation, 1952.

Shneidman, E. S. Projective techniques. In B. B. Wolman (Ed.), *Handbook of Clinical Psychology*. New York: McGraw-Hill, 1965.

Shoben, E. J., Jr. Toward a concept of the normal personality. *American Psychologist*, 1957, *12*, 183–189.

Shouksmith, G. *Intelligence, creativity, and cognitive style*. London: Angus Robertson, 1973.

Shweder, R. A. How relevant is an individual theory of personality? *Journal of Personality*, 1975, *43*, 455–484.

Shweder, R. A. Illusory correlations and the MMPI controversy. *Journal of Consulting and Clinical Psychology*, 1977, *45*, 917–924. (a)

Shweder, R. A. Illusory correlation and the MMPI controversy. Reply to some of the allusions and elusions in Block's and Edwards' commentaries. *Journal of Consulting and Clinical Psychology*, 1977, *45*, 936–940. (b)

Shweder, R. A., & D'Andrade, R. G. Accurate reflection or systematic distortion? A reply to Block, Weiss, and Thorne. *Journal of Personality and Social Psychology*, 1979, *37*, 1075–1084.

Siesman, A. W. The meaning of silent pauses in the initial interview. *Journal of Nervous and Mental Diseases*, 1978, *166*, 642–654.

Siess, T. F., & Jackson, D. N. Vocational interests and personality: An empirical integration. *Journal of Counseling Psychology*, 1970, *17*, 27–35.

Simmons, R. F. Semantic networks: Their computation and use for understanding English sentences. In R. C. Schank & K. M. Colby (Eds.), *Computer models of thought and language*. San Francisco: W. H. Freeman & Company Publishers, 1973.

Sines, J. O. Actuarial methods as appropriate strategy for the validation of diagnostic tests. *Psychological Review*, 1964, *71*, 517–523.

Sines, J. O. Actuarial methods in personality assessment. In B. A. Maher (Ed.), *Progress in experimental personality research* Vol. 3). New York: Academic Press, 1966.

Sines, L. K. The relative contribution of four kinds of data to accuracy in personality assessment. *Journal of Consulting Psychology*, 1959, *23*, 483–492.

Skinner, B. F. *The behavior of organisms.* New York: Appleton, 1938.

Skinner, B. F. *Science and human behavior.* New York: Macmillan, 1953.

Sloan, I. J., & Pierce-Jones, J. The Bordin-Pepinsky diagnostic categories. Counselor agreement and MMPI comparisons. *Journal of Counseling Psychology*, 1958, *5*, 189–193.

Slovic, P., & Lichtenstein, S. Comparison of Bayesian and regression approaches to the study of information processing in judgment. *Organizational Behavior and Human Performance*, 1971, *6*, 649–744.

Smith, K. U. Testimony before the senate subcommittee on constitutional rights. *American Psychologist*, 1965, *20*, 907–915.

Snyder, C. R. Acceptance of personality interpretations as a function of assessment procedures. *Journal of Consulting and Clinical Psychology*, 1974, *42*, 150.

Sobell, L. C., & Sobell, M. B. A self-feedback technique to monitor drinking behavior in alcoholics. *Behavior Research and Therapy*, 1973, *11*, 237–238.

Sobell, M. B., & Sobell, L. C. Alcoholics treated by individualized behavior therapy: One year treatment outcome. *Behavior Research and Therapy*, 1973, *11*, 599–618.

Sobell, M. B., & Sobell, L. C. Assessment of addictive behavior. In M. Hersen & A. S. Bellak (Eds.), *Behavioral assessment.* New York: Pergamon Press, 1976.

Soskin, W. F. Influence of four types of data on diagnostic conceptualization in psychological testing. *Journal of Abnormal and Social Psychology*, 1959, *58*, 69–78.

Spearman, C. *The nature of "intelligence" and the principle of cognition.* London: Macmillan, 1923.

Spearman, C. *The abilities of man.* New York: Macmillan, 1927.

Spence, J. T., Helmreich, R., & Stepp, J. The personal attributes questionnaire: A measure of sex-role stereotypes and masculinity-femininity. JSAS *Catalog of Selected Documents in Psychology*, 1974, *4*, 43 (Ms. No. 617).

Spence, J. T., Helmreich, R. & Stapp, J. Ratings of self and peers on sex-role attributes and their relation to self-esteem and conceptions of masculinity-femininity. *Journal of Personality and Social Psychology*, 1975, *32*, 29–39.

Spence, J. T., & Helmreich, R. L. The many faces of androgyny: A reply to Locksley and Colten. *Journal of Personality and Social Psychology*, 1979, *37*, 1032–1046.

Spence, K. W., & Spence, J. T. Relation of eyelid conditioning to manifest anxiety, extraversion, and rigidity. *Journal of Abnormal and Social Psychology*, 1964, *68*, 144–149.

Spielberger, C. D. Theory and research on anxiety. In C. D. Spielberger (Ed.), *Anxiety and behavior*. New York: Academic Press, 1966.

Spitzer, R. L., & Endicott, J. The value of the interview for the evaluation of psychopathology. In M. Hammer, K. Salzinger, & S. Sutton (Eds.), *Psychopathology: Contributions from the social, behavioral, and biological sciences*. New York: John Wiley, 1973.

Spranger, G. *Types of men*. New York: Hafner, 1928.

Stagner, R. The gullibility of personnel managers. *Personnel Psychology*, 1958, *11*, 347–352.

Stanley, J. C. Reliability. In R. L. Thorndike (Ed.), *Educational measurement* (2nd ed.). Washington, DC: American Council on Education, 1971.

Stanley, J. C., & Hopkins, K. D. *Educational and psychological measurement and evaluation*. Englewood Cliffs, NJ: Prentice-Hall, 1972.

Steinhauer, J. C. Review of the Strong-Campbell interest inventory. *Measurement and Evaluation Guidance*, 1976, *9*, 47–48.

Stephenson, W. *The study of behavior: Q-Technique and its methodology*. Chicago: University of Chicago Press, 1953.

Stephenson, W. Newton's fifth rule and Q methodology: Application to educational psychology. *American Psychologist*, 1980, *35*, 882–889.

Sternberg, R. J. *Intelligence, information processing, and analogical reasoning: The componential analysis of human abilities*. Hillsdale, NJ: Erlbaum, 1977.

Sternberg, R. J. The nature of mental abilities. *American Psychologist*, 1979, *34*, 214–230. (a)

Sternberg, R. J. Stalking the IQ quark. *Psychology Today*, September 1979, pp. 42–54. (b)

Sternberg, R., & Detterman, D. K. (eds.). *Human intelligence: Perspectives on its theory and measurement*. Norwood, NJ: Ablex, 1979.

Stevens, S. S. Mathematics, measurement and psychophysics. In S. S. Stevens (Ed.). *Handbook of experimental psychology*. New York: John Wiley, 1951.

Stricker, L. J. "Test-wiseness" on personality scales. *Journal of Applied Psychology Monographs*, 1969, *53*(3, Pt. 2).

Strong, E. K., Jr. A vocational interest test. *Educational Record*, 1927, *8*, 107–121.

Strong, E. K., Jr. Vocational interests of men and women. Stanford, CA: Stanford University Press, 1943.

Strong, E. K., Jr. Permanence of interest scores after 22 years. *Journal of Applied Psychology*, 1951, *35*, 89–92.

Strong, E. K., Jr. Vocational interests eighteen years after college. Minneapolis: University of Minnesota Press, 1955.

Strong, E. K., Jr. Reworded versus new interest items. *Journal of Applied Psychology*, 1963, *47*, 111–116.

Stuart, R. B. *Trip or treatment: How and when psychotherapy fails*. Champaign, IL: Research Press, 1970.

Sullivan, H. S. *The interpersonal theory of psychiatry*. New York: W. W. Norton & Co., Inc., 1953.

Sullivan, H. S. *The psychiatric interview*. New York: W. W. Norton & Co., Inc., 1954.

Sundberg, N. D. The acceptability of "fake" versus "bona fide" personality test interpretations. *Journal of Abnormal and Social Psychology*, 1955, *50*, 145–147.

Sundberg, N. D. *Assessment of persons*. Englewood Cliffs, NJ: Prentice-Hall, 1977.

Sundberg, N. D., Snowden, L. P., & Reynolds, W. M. Toward assessment of personal competence and incompetence. *Annual Review of Psychology*, 1978, *29*, 179–221.

Sundberg, N. D., Tyler, L. E., & Taplin, J. R. *Clinical psychology: Expanding horizons* (2nd ed.). Englewood Cliffs, NJ: Prentice-Hall, 1973.

Sutherland, J. D., & Gill, H. S. *Language and psychodynamic appraisal*. London: Research Publications Services, 1970.

Swartz, J. D. Review of TAT. In O. K. Buros (Ed.), *Eighth mental measurements yearbook*. Highland Park, NJ: Gryphon Press, 1978.

Sweetbaum, H. A. Comparison of the effects of introversion-extraversion and anxiety on conditioning. *Journal of Abnormal and Social Psychology*, 1963, *66*, 249–254.

Swensen, C. H. Empirical evaluations of human figure drawings. *Psychological Bulletin*, 1957, *54*, 431–466.

Swensen, C. H. Empirical evaluations of human figure drawings: 1957–1966. *Psychological Bulletin*, 1968, *70*, 20–44.

Symon, S. M. *An investigation of the relationship between conditioning and introversion-extraversion in normal students*. Unpublished master's thesis, University of Aberdeen, 1958.

Szasz, T. S. *The manufacture of madness*. New York: Dell Pub. Co., Inc., 1971.

Szucko, J. J., & Kleinmuntz, B. Statistical versus clinical lie detection. *American Psychologist*, 1981, *36*, 488–496.

Taft, J. The function of a mental hygienist in a children's agency. *Proceedings of the National Conference of Social Work, 1927*. Chicago: University of Chicago Press, 1927.

Taulbee, E. S., & Sisson, B. D. Configurational analysis of MMPI profiles of psychiatric groups. *Journal of Consulting Psychology*, 1957, *21*, 413–417.

Taylor, E. M. *Psychological appraisal of children with cerebral defects*. Cambridge, MA: Harvard University Press, 1961.

Taylor, H. C., & Russell, J. T. The relationship of validity coefficients to the practical effectiveness of tests in selection. *Journal of Applied Psychology*, 1939, *23*, 565–578.

Taylor, J. A. The relationship of anxiety to the conditioned eyelid response. *Journal of Experimental Psychology*, 1951, *41*, 81–92.

Taylor, J. A. A personality scale of manifest anxiety. *Journal of Abnormal and Social Psychology*, 1953, *48*, 285–290.

Tendler, A. D. A preliminary report on a test for emotional insight. *Journal of Applied Psychology*, 1930, *14*, 123–136.

Tenopyr, M. L. Personnel selection and placement. *Annual Review of psychology*, 1982, *33*, in press.

# References

Terman, L. M. *The measurement of intelligence.* Boston: Houghton Mifflin, 1916.

Terman, L. M., & Merrill, M. A. *Measuring intelligence.* Boston: Houghton Mifflin, 1937.

Terman, L. M. &. Merrill, M. A. *Stanford-Binet intelligence scale: Manual for the third revision, form L-M.* Boston: Houghton Mifflin, 1960.

Terman, L. M., & Merrill, M. A. *Stanford-Binet intelligence scale: 1972 norms edition.* Boston: Houghton Mifflin, 1973.

Thompson, C. E. The Thompson modification of the thematic apperception test. *Rorschach Research Exchange,* 1949, *13,* 469–478.

Thoreson, C. E., & Mahoney, M. J. *Behavioral self-control.* New York: Holt, Rinehart & Winston, 1974.

Thorndike, R. L. *The fundamentals of learning.* New York: Teachers College Press, 1932.

Thorndike, R. L. Review of the California psychological inventory. In O. K. Buros (Ed.), *Fifth mental measurements yearbook.* Highland Park, NJ: Gryphon Press, 1959.

Thorndike, R. L. (Ed.). *Educational measurement* (2nd ed.). Washington, DC: American Council on Education, 1971.

Thorndike, R. L. *Stanford-Binet intelligence scale, form L-M, 1972 norms tables.* Boston: Houghton Mifflin, 1973.

Thorndike, R. L., & Hagen, E. *Measurement and evaluation in psychology and education* (3rd ed.). New York: John Wiley, 1969.

Thurstone, L. L. The nature of intelligence. *Psychological Bulletin,* 1923, *20,* 78–79.

Thurstone, L. L. The mental age concept. *Psychological Review,* 1926, *33,* 268–278.

Thurstone, L. L. A factorial study of perception. *Psychometric Monographs,* Chicago: University of Chicago Press, 1944.

Thurstone, L. L., & Chase, E. J. *Measurement of attitude toward the church.* Chicago: University of Chicago Press, 1929.

Tigay, B., & Kempler, H. L. Stability of WISC scores of children hospitalized for emotional disturbance. *Perceptual and Motor Skills,* 1971, *32,* 487–490.

Tolor, A., & Schulberg, H. *Evaluation of the Bender-Gestalt test.* Springfield, IL: Chas. C Thomas, 1963.

Tomkins, S. S. *The positive affects: Affect, imagery, consciousness.* Vol. 1. New York: Springer Verlag, 1962.

Tomkins, S. S. Simulation of personality: The interrelationships between affect, memory, thinking, perception, and action. In S. S. Tomkins & S. J. Messick (Eds.), *Computer simulation of personality.* New York: John Wiley, 1963.

Tomkins, S. S., & McCarter, R. What and where are the primary affects? some evidence for a theory. *Perceptual and Motor Skills,* 1964, *18,* 119–158.

Torrance, E. P. *Guiding creative talent.* Englewood Cliffs, NJ: Prentice-Hall, 1962.

Torrance, E. P. *Torrance tests of creative thinking.* Princeton, NJ: Personnel Press, 1966.

Turner, R. K., James S. R. N., & Orwin, A. A note on the internal consistency of the sexual orientation method. *Behavior Research and Therapy*, 1974, *12*, 273-278.

Tyler, L. E., & Walsh, W. B. (3rd ed.). *Tests and measurements*. Englewood Cliffs, NJ: Prentice-Hall, 1979.

Ullmann, L. P., & Krasner, L. *A psychological approach to abnormal behavior* (2nd ed.). Englewood Cliffs, NJ: Prentice-Hall, 1975.

Urban, W. H. *The draw-a-person*. Beverly Hills, CA: Western Psychological Services, 1963.

Vernon, P. E. The Rorschach inkblot test. II. *British Journal of Medical Psychology*, 1933, *13*, 179-205.

Vernon, P. E. *Intelligence: Heredity and environment*. San Francisco: W. H. Freeman & Company Publishers, 1979.

Vogel, M. D. The relation of personality factors to GSR conditioning of alcoholics: an exploratory study. *Canadian Journal of Psychology*, 1960, *14*, 275-280.

Vogel, M. D. GSR conditioning and personality factors in alcoholics and normals. *Journal of Abnormal and Social Psychology*, 1961, *63*, 417-421.

Wagner, M. E., & Schubert, H. J. P. Figure drawing norms: Reliability and validity indices for normal adolescents. II. Development of a pictorial scale of draw-a-person quality. *American Psychologist*, 1955, *30*, 321.

Wallace, C. J. Assessment of psychotic behavior. In M. Hersen & A. S. Bellak (Eds.), *Behavioral assessment: A practical handbook*. New York: Pergamon Press, 1976.

Walsh, J. A. Review of the California psychological inventory. In O. K. Buros (Ed.), *Seventh mental measurements yearbook*. Highland Park, NJ: Gryphon Press, 1972.

Wanderer, Z. W. Validity of clinical judgments based on human figure drawings. *Journal of Consulting and Clinical Psychology*, 1969, *33*, 143-150.

Watson, J. B., & Raynor, R. Conditioned emotional reactions. *Journal of Experimental Psychology*, 1920, *3*, 1-14.

Webb, E. J., Campbell, D. T., Schwartz, R. D., & Sechrest, L. *Unobtrusive measures: Nonreactive research in the social sciences*. Chicago: Rand McNally, 1966.

Wechsler, D. *The measurement of adult intelligence*. Baltimore: Williams & Wilkins, 1939.

Wechlser, D. *Manual for the Wechsler intelligence test for children*. New York: Psychological Corporation, 1949.

Wechsler, D. *Manual for the Wechsler adult intelligence scale*. New York: Psychological Corporation, 1955.

Wechsler, D. *The measurement and appraisal of adult intelligence* (4th ed.). Baltimore: Williams & Wilkins, 1958.

Wechsler, D. *Manual for the Wechsler intelligence scale for children—Revised*. New York: Psychological Corporation, 1974.

Wechsler, D. Intelligence defined and undefined. *American Psychologist*, 1975, *30*, 135–139.

Weick, K. E. Systematic observational methods. In G. Lindzey & E. Aronsen (Eds.), *The handbook of social psychology* (Vol. 2). (2nd ed.). Reading, MA: Addison-Wesley, 1968.

Weinberg, G. H., & Schumaker, J. A. *Statistics: An intuitive approach* (3rd ed.). Monterey, CA: Brooks/Cole, 1974.

Weiner, B. *Theories of motivation*. Chicago: Markham, 1972.

Weiner, B., Runquist, W., Runquist, P. A., Raven, B. H., Meyer, W. J., Leiman, A., Kutscher, G. L., Kleinmuntz, B., & Haber, R. N. *Discovering psychology*, New York: St. Martin's, 1977.

Weiner, I. B. Approaches to Rorschach validation. In M. A. Rickers-Ovsiankina (Ed.), *Rorschach psychology* (Rev. ed.). New York: Krieger, 1977.

Weiss, D. J., & Davison, M. L. Test theory and methods. In *Annual Review of Psychology, 1981, 32,* 629–658.

Weitz, S. Attitude, voice, and behavior: A repressed affect model of interracial interaction. *Journal of Personality and Social Psychology*, 1972, *24*, 14–21.

Weizenbaum, J. Eliza—A computer program for the study of natural language communication between man and machine. *Communications of the ACM*, 1966, *9*, 36–45.

Weizenbaum, J. *Computer power and human reason: From judgment to calculation*. San Francisco: W. H. Freeman, 1976.

Wells, F. L., & Reusch, J. *Mental examiner's handbook* (2nd ed.). New York: Psychological Corporation, 1945.

Welsh, G. S. An extension of Hathaway's MMPI profile coding system. *Journal of Consulting Psychology*, 1948, *12*, 343–344 (also reprinted in Welsh & Dahlstrom, 1956).

Welsh, G. S. An anxiety index and an internationalization ratio for the MMPI. *Journal of Consulting Psychology*, 1952, *16*, 65–72 (also reprinted in Welsh & Dahlstrom, 1956).

Welsh, G. S., & Dahlstrom, W. G. (Eds.). *Basic readings on the MMPI in psychology and medicine*. Minneapolis: University of Minnesota Press, 1956.

Wesman, A. G. Intelligent testing. *American Psychologist*, 1968, *23*, 267–274.

White, R. W. Motivation reconsidered: The concept of competence. *Psychological Review*, 1959, *66*, 297–333.

White, R. W. *Lives in progress*. New York: Holt, Rinehart & Winston, 1966.

Whyte, W. H., Jr. *The organization man*. New York: Simon & Schuster, 1956.

Wiens, A. N. The assessment interview. In I. B. Weiner (Ed.), *Clinical methods in psychology*. New York: John Wiley, 1976.

Wiggins, J. S. Interrelationships among MMPI measures of dissimulation under standard and social desirability instructions. *Journal of Consulting Psychology*, 1959, 419–427.

Wiggins, J. S. Social desirability estimation and "faking good" well. *Educational and Psychological Measurement*, 1966, *26*, 329–341.

Wiggins, J. S. Personality structure. *Annual Review of Psychology*, 1968, *19*, 293–350.

Wiggins, J. S. *Personality and prediction: Principles of personality assessment.* Reading, MA: Addison-Wesley, 1973.

Wiggins, J. S. Personality research form. In O. K. Buros (Ed.), *Seventh mental measurements Yearbook*, Vol. 1. Highland Park, NJ: Gryphon Press, 1972.

Wiggins, J. S., Renner, K. E., Clore, G. L., & Rose, R. J. *Principles of personality.* Reading, MA: Addison-Wesley, 1976.

Wile, I. S., & Davis, R. M. A study of failures on the Stanford-Binet in relation to behavior and school problems. *Journal of Educational Psychology*, 1941, *32*, 275–284.

Willerman, L. *The psychology of individual and group differences.* San Francisco: W. H. Freeman & Company, 1979.

Willerman, L., Horn, J. M., & Loehlin, J. C. The aptitude-achievement test of distinction: A study of unrelated children reared together. *Behavior Genetics*, 1977, *7*, 465–470.

Willerman, L., & Turner, R. G. (Eds.). *Readings about individual and group differences.* San Francisco: W. H. Freeman & Company, 1979.

Williams, J. G., & Kleinmuntz, B. A process for detecting correlations between dichotomous variables. In B. Kleinmuntz (Ed.), *Clinical information processing by computer.* New York: Holt, Rinehart & Winston, 1969.

Williams, R. L. Abuses and misuses in testing black children. *The Counseling Psychologist*, 1971, *3*, 62–73.

Williams, R. L. *Manual of directions: Black intelligence test of cultural homogeneity.* St. Louis: Author, 1972.

Willis, J. Group vs. individual intelligence tests in one sample of emotionally disturbed children. *Psychological Reports*, 1970, *27*, 819–822.

Winch, R. F., & More, D. M. Does TAT add information to interviews? Statistical analysis of the increment. *Journal of Clinical Psychology*, 1956, *12*, 316–321.

Windle, C. Psychological tests in psychopath's logical prognosis. *Psychological Bulletin*, 1952, *49*, 451–482.

Winfield, D. L. An investigation of the relationship between intelligence and the statistical reliability of the MMPI. *Journal of Clinical Psychology*, 1952, *8*, 146–148.

Winkler, R. C. Management of chronic psychiatric patients by a token reinforcement system. *Journal of Applied Behavior Analysis*, 1970, *3*, 47–55.

Winkler, R. L., & Hays, W. L. *Statistics: probability and decision.* New York: Holt, Rinehart & Winston, 1975.

Winograd, T. A program for understanding natural language. *Cognitive Psychology*, 1972, *3*, 1–192.

Winograd, T. A procedural model of language understanding. In R. C. Schank & K. M. Colby (Eds.), *Computer models of thought and language.* San Francisco: W. H. Freeman & Company Publishers, 1973.

Witkin, H. A., & Goodenough, D. R. *Cognitive styles: Essence and origins.* New York: International Universities Press, 1981.

# References

Wittenborn, J. R. *Wittenborn Psychiatric Rating Scales.* New York: The Psychological Corporation, 1955 (revised, 1964).

Wittson, C. L., & Hunt, W. A. The predictive value of the brief psychiatric interview. *American Journal of Psychiatry,* 1951, *107,* 582–585.

Wolfe, J. *Psychotherapy by reciprocal inhibition.* Stanford, CA: Stanford University Press, 1958.

Wolfe, J. *The practice of behavior therapy.* New York: Pergamon Press, 1969.

Wolfe, J. *The practice of behavior therapy* (2nd ed.). New York: Pergamon Press, 1973.

Wolfe, J., & Lang, P. J. *Fear survey schedule.* San Diego: Educational & Industrial Testing Service, 1969.

Wolfe, J., & Lazarus, A. A. *Behavior therapy techniques.* Oxford, England: Pergamon Press, 1966.

Woodworth, R. S. *Personal Data Sheet.* Chicago: Stoelting, 1917.

Woody, R. H. Diagnosis of behavioral problem children: Mental abilities and achievement. *Journal of School Psychology,* 1968, *6,* 111–116.

Wrightsman, L. S. Wallace supporters and adherence to "law and order." *Journal of Personality and Social Psychology,* 1969, *13,* 17–22.

Yates, A. J. The validity of some psychological tests of brain damage. *Psychological Bulletin,* 1954, *51,* 359–379.

Yates, A. J. *Theory and practice in behavior therapy.* New York: John Wiley, 1975.

Yates, A. J. *Biofeedback and the modification of behavior.* New York: Plenum, 1980.

Yerkes, R. M. (Ed.). Psychological examining in the United States Army. *Memorandum of the National Academy of Sciences,* 1921, 15.

Yerkes, R. M., & Foster, J. C. *A point scale for measuring mental ability.* Baltimore: Warwick & York, 1923.

Sax, M., & Specter, G. A. *An introduction to community psychology.* New York: John Wiley, 1974.

Zubin, J. Rorschach test. In F. A. Mettler (Ed.). Columbia Greystone Associates. New York: Harper & Row, 1949.

Zubin, J., Eron, L. D., & Schumer, F. *An experimental approach to projective techniques.* New York: John Wiley, 1965.

Zulliser, H. *Einführuns in den Behn-Rorschach test.* Berne: Verlag Hans Huber, 1941.

Zulliser, H. *Der Behn-Rorschach test.* Band: Text (Vol. 1). Berne: Verlag Hans Huber, 1952.

Zulliser, H. *The Behn-Rorschach test.* Berne: Verlag Hans Huber, 1956.

# Indexes

# Subject Index

Ability Testing, 13–14, 338, 342, 344
  analogous, 342, 344
  component, 342
  defined, 338
  differential, 342, 344
  rationale for inclusion of, 13–14
Achievement Testing, 338, 339–342
  defined, 338
  diagnostic, 340, 341
  specific, 340
  survey battery, 340
  varieties of, 339–342
Actuarial Prediction, *See* Clinical Versus Statistical Prediction
Adler's Interview Technique, 192–193
Aptitude Testing, 338, 344–345
  defined, 338
  multiaptitudes, 345
  special aptitudes, 345
Archival Records, 148–150
Assertion Inventory, 155
Assessment, 5–7, 55–56
  defined, 6
  logic of, 55–56
  measurement and, 5
  need for in personality, 1
  testing and, 6
Assessment Logic, 55–56
Assessment Problems, 348–376
  ethical and moral, 363
  quasi-ethical, 368–376
  technical, 348–363
Attitude Scaling, 253–259
  Guttman scaling, 255–256
  Likert scaling, 254
  Semantic differential, 256–259
  Thurstone scaling, 254

Bandwidth-Fidelity Dilemma, 105–107
Base Rates, 104–105

Behavior, 52–55, 162
  importance of defining, 162
  sampling of, 54–55
Behavior Assessment Form, 160
Behavioral Assessment, 151–163
  evaluation of, 161–163
  methods of, 153–161
  origins of, 152–153
  versus traditional methods, 151–161
Bem Sex Role Inventory (BSRI), 219–220
Bender Visual-Motor Gestalt Test, 293–294
Binet-type Tests, 314–321
B.I.T.C.H., 327, 329
  evaluation of, 327
  example of, 329
  items on, 329
  rationale of, 327

California Psychological Inventory (CPI) 98, 244–247
  profile sheet of, 245
Case History Interview, 186–187, 189–191
  evaluation of, 190–191
Cattell's Culture Fair Test, 330–332
Civil Rights, 366–368
Class Interval, 28
Classical Test Theory, 50–51
  alternatives to, 51
Classification, 15–16
Clinical Versus Statistical Prediction, 109–113
  defined, 109–110
  empirical evidence for, 110, 112–113
  guidelines for, 111–112
  sophisticated clinical prediction, 110–111

# Subject Index

Cognitive Behavioral Assessment, 159–161
Combining Test Information, 108–113
   clinical versus statistical, 109–113
Communicating Test Findings, 113–115
Computer, 23–24, 199–207, 230–237, 375–376
   functional components of, 23–24
   interviewing by, 199–207
   modeling with, 231–232
   test scoring and interpreting by, 230–237, 377–378
Computer Interviewing, 199–207, 377–378
   ELIZA, 199–200
   evaluation of, 206–207, 375–376
   mental status, 201–206
   PARRY, 200–201
Computer Modeling, 231–232
Computer Test Scoring and Interpretation, 230–237, 375–376
   Caldwell Report, 233–237
   consequences of, 377–378
Conditioning, 152–153
   classical or respondent, 152
   operant or instrumental, 152–153
Configural Scoring, 99
Consensual Problems, 349–350
Construct Validity, 80–82
   convergent, 81
   discriminant, 81
   factor analysis, 81–82
   multitrait-multimethod, 81
   nomological network and, 80
Content Analysis, 145–146
   defined, 145
   example of, 145–146
Content Validity, 71–72
Continuous-Versus-Discrete Variables, 350–351
Correlation Coefficients, 35–41
   computation of, 37–39
   Pearson product moment, 37, 41
   reliability indices and, 65
   validity indices and, 73, 102

Counseling and Psychotherapy, 16
Criterion Keying, 53–54, 85
Criterion-referenced Testing, 51, 341–342, 343
   achievement, 341–342
   compared to norm-referenced tests, 343
   defined, 341
Criterion Reliability, 73–77
Criterion Validity, 73–78
   reliability and, 77–78
   standard error of estimate and, values of, 75–77
Criterion Variables, 56
Crossvalidation, 78–80
   and shrinkage, 78
   as validity generalization, 79

Dehumanization, 368
Derived Scores, 92–97
   normalization, 95
   percentiles, 93–94
   raw scores and, 92–95
   relationships among, 94
   standard scores, 92
   stanines, 95, 96
   $T$-scores, 95–96
   $z$-scores, 92–93
Descriptive Statistics, 27–43
Differential Personality Inventory (DPI), 241–242
Direct Observation, 120–144
   controlled, 139
   naturalistic, 121–139
Draw-A-Person Test (DAP), 292–293
DSM III, 8, 202, 243, 348

Early Recollections, 188–189
*Eighth Mental Measurements Yearbook*, 88–89, 230, 239, 242, 262, 283, 386, 339, 340, 344, 348
Empirical Keying, 53–54, 214, 247–248
Employment or Personnel Interview, 182–183
Error Variance, 45, 58–61
   random, 45, 58–61
   systematic, 45, 58

## Subject Index

Expectancy Tables, 100–104
Experimental MMPI Scales, 223–224
   Do(dominance), 224
   Es(ego strength), 224
   MAS(manifest anxiety scale), 224
   Mt(college maladjustment), 224
   SD(social desirability), 224
Expressive Behavior, 125–131
   body language, 127
   facial expressions, 127
   gestures, 126–130
   handwriting, 131
   pupil size and, 130–131
Extraversion, 349
   lack of consensus and, 349

Face Validity, 72–73
Factor Analysis, 81–82, 86
   method of, 81–82
   test construction by, 86
False Negatives, 101–102
False Positives, 101–102
Fear Survey Schedule III, 155
Forced-choice Keying, 85–86
Free Association, 175, 192
Frequency Distribution, 28–30
Frequency Polygon, 29–30
Freud's Interview Technique, 175, 192

Group Tests, 87
Guttman Scaling, 255–256

Hardware Aids for Observation, 132–133
Histogram, 29
Hogan's Survey of Ethical Attitudes (SEA), 88
Holtzman Inkblot Test (HIT), 285–287

Incident Sampling, 123–124
   critical incidents, 124
   self-monitoring, 124
Inconsistencies, 354–357
   behavioral, 354–357
   observer, 354–357
   person-by-situation, 355–357

Incremental Validity, 107–108
Indirect Observation, 144–151
Individual Tests, 87
Inferential Statistics, 43–48
   and degree of confidence, 45
   and hypothesis testing, 47
   and null hypothesis, 47–48
Initial Interview Outline, 158–183
Inpatient Multidimensional Psychiatric Scale, 133
Intake Interview, 183
Intelligence, 303–313, 314
   Binet-Simon theory of, 305–306
   Cattell theory of, 307–309
   definitions of, 303–313
   Guilford's theory of, 309–310
   Sternberg's theory of, 310–313
Intelligence Quotient (IQ), 5, 304, 313–325, 335
   as example of interval scale, 5
   varieties of, 313–325
Intelligence Testing, 313–338
   evaluation of, 333–338
   group tests of, 325
   individual tests of, 313–325
   minority groups and, 326–338
   nature and nurture in, 328
Interview, 167–207
   analysis of, 169–170
   as conversational politics, 171
   as data collection, 168–169
   computers and, 199–207
   evaluation of, 175, 195–199
   history of, 170
   initial, 158
   psychotherapy and, 170, 173
   structured, 176–181
   theoretical orientation of, 192–195
   types of, 181–192
   unstructured, 173–176
Interview Errors, 195–199
   due to interview process, 195–196
   due to interviewee, 196–197
   due to interviewer, 197–198
   validity and, 198–199
Interview Schedule, 176
Introversion, 349
   lack of consensus and, 349

## Subject Index

Invasion of Privacy, 363–366
Item Response Theory, 51

Jackson Personality Inventory, 242
Jensenism, 334–335

Kuder Preference Records, 251–253

Latent Test Theory, 51
Legal Testing, 16–18
Levels of Measurement, 3–5
  absolute scale, 4
  compared, 3
  interval scale, 4
  nominal scale, 4
  ordinal scale, 4
  ratio scale, 5
Life History Assessment, 190–191
Likert Scaling, 254

Maximum Performance Test, 85–87, 303–345
McClelland's Achievement Needs, 290–291
Measurement, 3–6
  assessment and, 5–6
  defined, 3–4
  levels of, 4–5
  testing and, 6
Measurement Error, 45, 58–61
  sources of, 59–61
Measures of Central Tendency, 30–33
  compared, 32–33
  mean, 31
  median, 31
  mode, 31–32
Measures of Correlation, 35–41
  computation of, 37–39
  correlation coefficient, 37–39
  linear regression line, 40
  scatter diagrams, 36
Measures of Variability, 33–35
  computation of, 34–35
  range, 33
  standard deviation, 33–34
  variance, 34–35
Mental Status Interview, 183–186

Millon Clinical Multiaxial Inventory (MCMI), 242–244
Minnesota Multiphasic Personality Inventory (MMPI), 9, 18, 79, 85, 87, 91, 212–240
  clinical scales of, 215–222
  construction of, 214
  decision rules, 79
  evaluation of, 237–240
  interpretation of, 227–237
  replacement of, 240–244
  validity scales of, 222–223
MMPI Profile, 213, 225, 226, 228
MMPI Scales, 215–224
  coding of, 224–227
  correction scale (K), 223
  F scale, 223
  interpretation of, 227–237
  items on, 216
  Lie scale (L), 223
  new scales of, 223–224
  Question scale (?), 222
  Scale 1 (Hs), 215, 217
  Scale 2 (D), 217
  Scale 3 (Hy), 217–218
  Scale 4 (Pd), 218
  Scale 5 (Mf), 218
  Scale 6 (Pa), 218, 220–221
  Scale 7 (Pt), 221
  Scale 8 (Sc), 221
  Scale 9 (Ma), 222
  Scale 0 (Si), 222, 223
Motivation and Personality, 10–11
Multimodal Life History Questionnaire, 155
Murray's Needs, 11, 287–291
  $n$ Achievement, 11, 290–291
  $n$ Affiliation, 11
  $n$ Dominance, 11
  $n$ Order, 287

Naturalistic Personality, Data, 124–131
  expressive behavior as, 125–131
  signs and cues of, 125
Neuroticism, 349
  lack of consensus and, 345

## Subject Index

Nondirective Interviews, 175
Normal Curve of Probability, 41–43
  defined, 41–42
  properties of, 43
Normality, 9–10
Norms, 90–92
Null Hypothesis, 47–48
  confidence intervals, 48
  levels of confidence, 48

Objectivity, 52
Observation, 117–163
  behavioral, 151–163
  defined, 117–118
  direct, 120–144
  indirect, 144–151
  kinds of, 119–120
  naturalistic and controlled compared, 139–144
  observer participation in, 118–119
  reliability and validity of, 140–141
Observation Learning, 159
Observational Error, 131
  aids for limiting, 131–136
Observer Error, 162–163
Operant Assessment, 155–157
  rating scales used in, 157
  self-reporting in, 159
Order Models, 51

Paper-and-Pencil Tests, 86
Paralanguage, 170
  in interviewing, 170
Pearson $r$, 37–41
Percentile Score, 93–94
Performance Tests, 86–87
  maximum versus typical, 86–87
Person-by-Situation Interaction, 355–357
Personal Documents, 145–148
  evaluation of, 147–148
Personality Assessment Methods, 20–21, 88, 90–99
  interpretive aids for, 88, 90–99
  sources of information about, 20–21
Personality Assessment Purposes, 14–20, 351

Personality Assessment Settings, 14–20, 351
Personality Definitions, 7–14
Personality Research Form (PRF), 241–242
Personality Research, 348–376
  ethical problems and, 363–368
  quasi-ethical problems and, 368–376
  technical problems and, 368–376
Personality Research Settings, 19–20
Personality Traits and Types, 11–13, 349–350
  consensual problems and, 349–350
Personnel Selection, 17–19
Physical Traces, 150–151
Plan of the Book, 22–25
Polygraph "Lie Detection," 113
Posttest Interview, 191–192
Predictor Variables, 56, 368–371
  Nader/Nairn report, 370–371
  reply to Nader/Nairn report, 372–373
  tests as poor, 370–371, 372–373
Press, 11, 287
  $p$ Achievement, 11
  $p$ Affiliation, 11
  $p$ Dominance, 11
Pretest Interview, 191
Profiles, 97–99, 213, 225, 226, 228, 245
  analysis of, 97
  California Psychological Inventory as example of, 245
  MMPI as example of, 213, 225, 226, 228
Projection, 265–266
  projective techniques and, 265–266
  psychoanalytic concept of, 265
Projective Techniques, 264–299
  definition of, 265–266
  projection and, 265
  psychometric standards of, 298–299
  self-reports and, 264
Psychoanalysis, 192
Psychodiagnosis, 14–16

# Subject Index

Psychological Reporting, 113–115
Psychopathology, 8–9

Quantification, 2–3
  measurement and, 3
  need for, 2–3
Q-sort, 133–136, 256

Rating Scale Errors, 136–138
  ambiguity, 137
  central tendency, 137
  halo effect, 137
  leniency, 136
  logical, 137
  proximity, 137
Rating Scales, 133–139
  defined, 133
  evaluation of, 139
  as rater fictions, 138
  improvement of, 138–139
Raw Scores, 92–95
  derived scores and, 92–95
Reactivity, 144, 353, 354
  as a problem, 353–354
Reliability, 56–70, 77–78
  equivalent forms, 63, 66
  generalizability, 56–57
  importance of, 57
  internal consistency, 68–69
  measurement error and, 58
  random error and, 58
  scorer, 69–70
  sources of error and, 59–61
  split-half, 63, 67
  standard error of measurement, 61–64
  systematic error and, 58
  test-retest, 64–66
  true score and, 58, 59
  validity and, 77–78
Respondent Assessment, 154–155
  questionnaires used in, 155
Rogers' Nondirective Interview, 194–195
Rokeach Value Survey, 260–261
Role Construct Repertory Test, 295–298
  administration of, 296
  interpretation of, 298
  scoring of, 297–298
  theory of, 296–297
Rorschach inkblots, 9, 85, 266–285
  administration of, 267–269
  applications of, 276
  computer interpretation of, 276–279
  evaluation of, 279–285
  interpretation of, 272–279
  reliability of, 280–282
  scoring of, 269–272
  validity of, 282–285
Rosenzweig Picture-Frustration Study, 294–295

Scholastic Aptitude Test, 28–29, 94, 95
Selection Ratio, 103–104
Self-knowledge, 373
  assumption of, 373
Self-Report Inventories, 87–88, 210–253
  California Psychological Inventory, 244–247
  Differential Personality Inventory, 241–242
  dissimulation on, 87–88
  interest testing, 248–253
  Jackson Personality Inventory, 242
  Millon's MCMI, 242–244
  Personality Research for, 241–242
Semantic Differential, 256–259
Sentence Completions, 291–292
Sexual Orientation Questionnaire, 155
Skewed Distributions, 44
Social Learning Theory, 159–161
  locus of control, 159, 161
  modeling, 159
  observation learning, 159
Standard Deviation, 33–35
  computation of, 33–35
Standard Error of Estimate, 75–77
  computation of, 76
  meaning of, 75, 76, 77
Standard Error of Measurement, 61–64

## Subject Index

computation of, 62
definition of, 61–62, 63
Standard Error of Sample Means, 45–48
Standard Score, 47–48, 92–95
  computation of, 47
  meaning of, 47–48
  z-score and, 47–48, 92–95
*Standards for Educational and Psychological Tests*, 57, 90, 91, 96
Standardization, 51–52
Stanford-Binet IQ, 94, 95
Stanines, 95–96
Statistical Prediction, *See* Clinical Versus Statistical Prediction
Statistical Reasoning, 28
Statistical Symbols, 32
Stress Interview, 181
Strong-Campbell Interest Inventory (SCII), 248–251
  description of, 249–251
  evaluation of, 249
  items on, 250–251
Strong Vocational Interest Blank (SVIB), 248–249
Structured Interviews, 174, 176–181
  evaluation of, 179–181
  fixed alternatives in, 176–177, 178
  open-ended, 176–177
Structured Tests, 84–85
Sullivan's Interpersonal Interview, 193–194
Systems Analysis, 22–25
  decision maker and, 24
  information processor and, 22, 23, 24, 25
  inputs and, 22–23, 24
  outputs and, 22, 23, 24

*T*-score, 95–96, 97
Taylor-Russell Tables, 103–104
Test Construction, 53–54, 85–86
  criterion keying and, 53–54, 85
  domain sampling and, 85
  factor analysis and, 86
  forced-choice keying, 85–86
Test Decision Making, 100–108
Test Faking, 369, 371, 373

Test, 5, 6, 84–88
  assessment and, 6
  classification of, 84–88
  construction of, 84–86
  measurement and, 6
  structuredness of, 84–88
Thematic Apperception Test (TAT), 11, 85, 287–291
  adaptations, 290–291
  administration of, 287
  evaluation of, 289–291
  hero, 287
  interpretation of, 288
  scoring of, 287
  themes, 287
  uses of, 287–288
Thompson TAT (T-TAT), 290
Thurstone Scaling, 254
Time Sampling, 121–123
Traditional Personality Measures, 359–363
  aids to monitor, 362–363
  conditioning, 359–360
  perceptual functioning, 359
  physiological data, 361
Traits, 11–13, 349–350
  consensual problems and, 349–350
Truth-in-Testing Law, 374, 376
Typical Performance Tests, 86–87, 303

Unobtrusive Measures, 144–151
  archival records as, 148–150
  nonreactivity and, 144
  personal documents as, 145–148
  physical traces as, 150–151
Unstructured Interviews, 173–176, 179–181
  evaluation of, 179–181
Unstructured Tests, 85

Valid Negatives, 101–102
Valid Positives, 101–102
Validity, 70–82, 102–103
  compared, 71, 74–77
  content, 71–72
  construct, 80–82
  criterion, 73

crossvalidation, 78–80
effects of reliability on, 77–78
face, 72–73
importance of, 57
reliability of criterion and, 73–77
Validity Generalization, 79–80
Value Measurement, 259–261
   Allport-Vernon Study of Values, 259
   Allport-Vernon-Lindzey Study of Values, 259–260
Variance, 33–35, 45, 58–61
   computation of, 33–35
   random error as, 45, 58–61
   system error as, 45, 58–61

Wechsler Tests, 94–95, 321–325
   IQ, 94, 95
   WAIS, 322–324
   WAIS-R, 323
   WISC, 322–324
   WISC-R, 322
   WPPSI, 321
*Wittenborn Psychiatric Rating Scales*, 133, 134
Woodworth Personal Data Sheet, 53, 211–212
$z$ Score, 47–48, 92–95
   computation of, 47
   meaning of, 47–48
   standard score and, 92

# Name Index

Abramson, P. R., 155
Adair, F., 237
Adcock, C. I., 239
Adler, A., 7, 8, 146, 192–194, 208
Adorno, T., 175
Aiken, L. R., 285
Alexander, M. J., 22
Alker, H. A., 239
Allison, H. W., 284
Allison, S. G., 284
Allport, G., 7, 9, 10, 12, 145–147, 259
Almy, T. P., 191
Anastasi, A., 51, 56, 78, 238, 242, 265, 292, 295, 313, 319, 324
Anderson, G. L., 293
Anderson, H. H., 293
Anderson, S., 337
Angoff, W. H., 101
Argyle, M., 355
Ashear, J. B., 131
Atkinson, J. W., 287, 289
Ayllon, T., 162
Azrin, N. H., 151, 162

Babbie, E. R., 147
Bakan, P., 359
Baldwin, A. L., 146
Balian, L. A., 189, 353
Bandura, A., 151, 159
Bannister, D., 298
Barker, R. G., 121
Barnett, W. L., 238
Barron, F., 224, 238
Barthell, C. N., 149, 353
Baughman, E. E., 6, 12, 280
Beck, S., 267
Bellak, A. S., 151
Bellak, L., 290
Bellak, S., 290
Bem, D. J., 219, 355–356
Bem, S. L., 219, 220

Bender, L., 293
Benjamin, A., 174
Berelson, B., 145
Berg, I. A., 369
Berger, R. M., 342
Bernreuter, P., 349
Bickman, L., 124, 142
Bijou, S. W., 151
Billingslea, F. Y., 293
Bingham, W. V. D., 170–173, 180–182
Binet, A., 305–306, 309, 314–315, 346
Bjerstedt, A., 295
Black, J. G., 227–228
Blackman, S., 337–338
Blakemore, C. B., 293
Block, J., 135, 138, 224, 355, 357–358, 369
Block, J. H., 138
Blois, M. S., 113
Blum, G. S., 290
Bootzin, R. R., 190
Boring, E. G., 304
Borman, W. C., 73
Bouchard, T. J., 338, 345
Bowers, K. S., 355
Bowman, P. H., 19
Brady, J., 170
Bray, D. W., 367
Brebner, J. M. T., 359
Brigham, C., 333
Brody, E. B., 310, 313
Brody, N., 13, 310, 313
Brooks, R., 204, 206
Broverman, I. K., 219
Brown, F. G., 65, 68, 74–75, 79, 282–283, 298–299
Buck, J. N., 293
Buck, R. W., 127
Buros, O. K., 84, 88–89, 212, 230, 247, 285, 286, 289, 290, 293, 295,

## Name Index

339, 340, 344, 348
Burt, C., 325, 333, 335, 346
Butcher, J. N., 20, 230, 236, 238, 240–241, 351–352

Cacioppo, J., 129
Caldwell, A. B., 230, 233–234, 236
Campbell, D. P., 248, 249
Campbell, D. T., 71, 81, 353
Cannell, C. F., 198
Carey, G., 198–199
Carey, H., 374
Carroll, J. B., 310, 336–337
Cartwright, C. A., 121
Cartwright, G. P., 121
Cattell, R. B., 12, 82, 307, 309, 330, 346, 349, 356
Cautela, J. R., 151
Chapman, J. P., 21, 292, 359
Chapman, L. J., 21, 292
Chapple, E. D., 133
Chase, E. J., 254
Christensen, P. R., 342
Ciminero, A. R., 124, 151, 159
Claridge, G., 359
Clark, K. B., 336
Clarke, Alan, 335
Clarke, Ann, 335
Cleary, A. T., 336
Cleckley, H., 9, 360
Cohen, J., 261
Colby, K. M., 200–201
Colgin, R., 238
Colten, M. E., 220
Conway, J., 335
Cook, T. D., 71
Coombs, C. H., 4
Corsini, R. J., 192
Craighead, W. E., 157
Crites, J. O., 249
Cronbach, L. J., 12, 54, 56–59, 67, 69, 77, 79, 80, 86, 99, 103–107, 135, 137, 162, 265, 282, 333, 358, 369
Cuadra, C. A., 217
Curran, J. P., 155

Dahlstrom, L. E., 227, 236–237
Dahlstrom, W. G., 218, 224, 227–230, 236–239, 351, 361

Dailey, C. A., 187, 197
D'Andrade, R. G., 138
Daniels, N., 339
Darwin, C., 129–130
Davidson, H. H., 267, 275, 341
Davis, R. M., 320
Davison, M. L., 50, 51, 255
De Risi, W. J., 163
Dittman, A. T., 121–122
Dobzhansky, T., 334–335
Doering, C. R., 189
Dollard, J., 159
Dolliver, R., 249
Donaldson, G., 307
Dotson, V. A., 163
Dougherty, F. E., 127–129
Doyle, W., 131
Draguns, J. G., 350–351
Drake, L. E. A., 222
Drasgow, J., 238
Duncan, C. P., 150
Duncan, S. J., 169
Dunette, M. D., 278
Dunlop, E., 230
Dunphy, D. C., 146
Dunsdon, M. I., 320

Ebbinghaus, H., 291
Eckhardt, W. K., 255–256
Edwards, A. L., 85–86, 224, 369
Eichler, R., 284
Eichman, W. J., 230
Einhorn, H. J., 111
Ekman, P., 127
Endler, N. S., 355
Epstein, L. H., 159
Erikson, E. H., 7, 8
Ermann, M. D., 255–256
Ernst, F., 159
Eron, L. D., 276, 287, 290
Ervin, S., Jr., 364
Esquirol, 315
Evans, C. C., 222, 278
Exner, J. E., 267, 276, 278, 281–283, 287, 289, 291, 292
Eysenck, H. J., 12, 13, 305, 313, 346, 349, 359

Farber, I. E., 359
Fast, J., 127

## Name Index

Feldman, M. J., 238
Festinger, L., 124, 256
Fine, B., 339
Finney, J. C., 230
Fischer, R., 362
Fiske, D. W., 81, 169, 198, 281, 336, 349–351, 358
Fixsen, D. L., 159
Flanigan, J. C., 124
Forer, B. R., 278
Forsyth, R. P., 229
Foster, S. L., 142
Fowler, R. D., Jr., 230
Frank, G., 305, 313
Franks, C. M., 221, 359, 360
Frederiksen, N., 355
Freeman, F. N., 333
Freud, S., 7, 8, 10, 125, 146, 175, 192–194, 208, 265, 373
Friesen, W. V., 127
Fromm, E., 7
Fruchter, B., 12, 61, 77, 81
Funder, D. C., 355–356

Gallagher, C. E., 364
Galton, Sir F., 2, 149, 337
Gamble, K. R., 286
Gambrill, E. D., 155
Geer, J. H., 159
Gifford, E. V., 320
Gilbert, F. S., 155
Gilbert, J., 274, 293, 324
Gill, H. S., 292
Gillie, O., 335
Gilliland, A. R., 238
Gilmore, S. K., 197
Glaser, R., 341
Gleser, G. C., 99, 103, 106
Goddard, H. H., 333
Goldberg, L. R., 110, 198, 241, 242, 246
Golden, M., 107, 108, 189
Goldfield, M. R., 151, 162, 283
Goldman, L., 16, 99, 111–112
Goldstein, K. M., 237–238
Goodenough, D. R., 337–338
Goodshin, L. D., 108–110
Gorden, R. L., 172, 174

Gottesman, I. I., 198–199
Gottman, J. M., 151, 154
Gough, H. G., 87, 97, 244, 246
Grand, S., 130
Grimm, L. G., 151, 155, 159
Guetzkow, H. S., 19
Guilford, J. P., 12, 61, 65, 77, 81, 309, 310, 337, 342, 346, 349
Guion, R. M., 72, 378
Gulliksen, H., 59
Gustafson, L. A., 138
Guthrie, G. M., 217, 221, 229
Guthrie, R. V., 327
Guttman, L., 254–256
Gynther, M. D., 246, 247

Hagen, E., 135, 326, 338, 344, 345
Hall, C. S., 7, 192
Hall, E. T., 127
Hare, R. D., 9
Harmon, L. W., 253
Harshbarger, T., 48
Hartshorne, H., 357
Hathaway, S. R., 97, 212, 214, 215, 217, 223, 227, 228, 237–238, 246, 365, 366
Hawkes, N., 333
Hawkins, R. P., 163
Hays, W. L., 48
Hearnshaw, L. S., 333, 335
Heath, H. A., 221
Heineman, C. E., 361
Heller, K., 195
Heller, R., 197–198
Helman, Z., 284
Helmreich, R. L., 220
Helmstadter, G. C., 12, 28, 61, 137, 138
Helzer, J. E., 180
Henri, V., 315
Herman, P. S., 289
Hersen, M., 151, 155
Hertel, R. K., 324
Hess, E., 130–131
Hertz, M. R., 282
Hilf, F. D., 200–201
Hill, E. F., 286
Hoepfner, R., 310
Hogan, R., 9, 54, 87–88, 352–353

# 442  Name Index

Holden, R. R., 73
Holmes, D. S., 149, 353
Holmes, T. H., 190
Holsh, O. R., 147
Holt, R. R., 17, 110–111, 113, 175, 267, 276, 287, 289
Holtzman, W. H., 87, 276, 279, 281, 285, 286
Holzberg, J. D., 276, 279, 281
Holzman, P., 359
Honig, W. K., 151
Hopkins, K. D., 339, 341
Horn, D., 187
Horn, J. L., 307
Horn, J. M., 345
Horney, K., 7
Horrocks, J. E., 253
Horst, P., 99
Howard, J. W., 281
Howard, M., 335
Humphreys, L. G., 327
Hutt, M. L., 293

Izard, C., 127

Jackson, D. N., 54, 69, 73, 74, 241, 242, 261, 356–359, 369
James, W., 337
Jensen, A. R., 313, 333–335, 345
Johnson, A. H., 170
Johnson, J. A., 54, 87, 88
Johnson, J. H., 202
Johnson, R., 249
Jones, R. L., 334
Jung, C., 7, 8, 13, 146

Kagan, J., 289, 339
Kahn, R. I., 198
Kamin, L. J., 327, 330, 333, 335
Kamiya, J., 362
Kanfer, F. H., 151, 155, 159, 198
Kaplan, A., 132
Katz, D., 256
Kelley, D. M., 267
Kelly, E. L., 6, 198, 242, 336
Kelly, G., 295–297, 300
Kempler, H. L., 324
Kendrick, D. T., 356

Kent, R. N., 142
Kerlinger, F. N., 56, 135, 143, 146–147, 178
Kessler, J. W., 320, 326
Kimmel, E., 374–375
King, G. D., 239
Kitwood, T., 261
Kleinmuntz, B., 9, 79, 99, 110, 111, 113, 202, 204, 206, 221, 224, 231, 238, 259, 350, 361
Kleinmuntz, D. N., 111
Kline, P., 82, 349
Klopfer, B., 267, 275
Knapp, J. R., 307
Korchin, S. J., 16, 114–115, 221
Kostlan, S. A., 107, 187
Kraepelin, E., 8
Krasner, L., 15, 151, 157
Kuder, G. F., 69, 249–251, 253
Kuhn, T. S., 349

Labor, W., 171
Lachar, D., 230
Lang, P. J., 155
Lanyon, R. I., 108–110
Lazarsfeld, P. F., 177–178
Lazarus, A. A., 154, 155
Lazarus, R. S., 189
Lazovik, A. D., 155
Leiblum, S. R., 151, 154
Lemke, E., 77, 78
Lewontin, R. C., 335
Lichtenstein, S., 110
Liebert, R. M., 7, 350
Likert, R. A., 254, 256
Lindzey, G., 7, 110, 192, 259, 289
Lingoes, J. C., 239
Linn, R. L., 345
Little, B. R., 355
Locksley, A., 220
Loehlin, J. C., 345
Loewinger, J., 54, 80
London, M., 367
Lopez, F. M., 182
Lord, F. M., 59, 67
Lorr, M., 133, 157
Lubin, A., 99
Luborsky, L., 113

# Name Index

Lucas, R. W., 207
Lumsden, J., 50, 299
Lunnenberg, P., 249
Lykken, D. T., 77, 242, 360, 361
Lyman, H. B., 99

McCarter, R., 127
McClelland, D. C., 287, 290, 300
McConnell, T. R., 222
MacDonough, T. S., 155
McGhie, A., 359
Machover, K., 292
McHugh, A. F., 324
McKinley, J. C., 212, 214, 215, 217, 238, 246
McLean, R. S., 202
McNemar, Q., 37
Magnusson, D., 59, 65, 66, 70, 74, 355
Mahoney, M. J., 124, 159
Mair, J. M., 298
Mandler, G., 221
Marcos, L. R., 130
Marshall, C., 375
Mash, E. J., 151
Maslow, A., 8–10
Masuda, M., 190
Matarazzo, J. D., 196, 321, 327–329
May, M. A., 357
Meehan, K. A., 87–88
Meehl, P. E., 16, 53, 54, 60, 80, 88, 99, 104, 107, 109–113, 149, 150, 192, 205–206, 217, 223, 227, 228, 239, 336, 353, 354, 373
Megargee, E. I., 246, 247
Mehrabian, A., 125, 127
Menlove, F. L., 159
Menninger, K. A., 183
Merrill, M. A., 315, 318, 319, 324, 346
Messick, S. J., 80, 337, 367, 369
Mettler, F. A., 284
Miklich, D. R., 124
Mikulas, W. L., 151
Miller, N. E., 159
Millon, T., 242–243, 261
Mills, C., 54, 88

Mischel, W., 7, 12–13, 151, 305, 350, 351, 356
Monachesi, E. D., 237–238
Moore, B. V., 170–173, 181–182
More, D. M., 107, 108
Morgan, 290
Morgana, A., 230
Morris, D., 127
Mosher, D. L., 155
Mosier, C. I., 78
Moss, H. A., 289
Munroe, R. L., 192
Munsinger, H., 333
Murray, H. A., 11, 241, 265, 287, 290
Mussen, P. H., 337
Myers, C. R., 320

Nader, R., 370–372, 375, 377
Nairn, A., 370, 372–373, 375
Nathan, P. E., 162
Newell, A., 310
Norman, W. T., 12
Novick, M. R., 59, 67
Nunnally, J. C., 59, 74, 81, 99, 135

O'Brien, J. S., 162
Odbert, H. S., 12
O'Leary, K. D., 142
Orne, M. T., 138
Osgood, C. E., 256
Otis, A. S., 325
Owen, P. L., 240–241
Owens, W. A., 189

Paige, J. M., 146
Panchari, P., 230, 238
Parlee, M. B., 171
Pascal, G. R., 293
Paterson, D. G., 278
Patterson, G. R., 133
Paunonen, S. V., 69, 74, 356–359
Pavlov, I., 152
Payne, A. F., 291
Payne, D. A., 339–342
Pearson, J. S., 230
Pearson, K., 37
Pedhazur, E. J., 220

## Name Index

Pervin, L. A., 356, 358
Peterson, D. R., 352
Peterson, R. A., 283, 286
Peterson, R. F., 151
Petrie, I. R. J., 324
Petty, R., 129
Phares, E. J., 16, 159, 160
Phillips, J. L., Jr., 48
Phillips, J. P. N., 155
Phillips, J. S., 151, 155, 159, 198
Phillips, L., 350–351
Pickard, P. M., 279
Pierce-Jones, J., 238
Pignatelli, M. L., 320
Piotrowski, Z. A., 267, 276–279
Plato, 170
Popham, W. J., 341
Powell, J., 151

Quay, H. C., 324

Rabkin, J. G., 353, 354
Rachman, S., 349, 359
Rafferty, J. E., 291–292
Rahe, R. H., 190
Ramzy, I., 280
Rank, O., 7
Rappaport, D., 267
Rausch, H. L., 121–122
Raymond, A. F., 189
Reed, C. F., 217
Reik, T., 7
Renaud, H. R., 218
Reusch, J., 183
Richardson, S. A., 69, 178
Richey, C. A., 155
Rioch, M. J., 285
Robinson, A. L., 113
Rogers, C. R., 8, 9, 175, 194, 208, 351–352
Rohde, A. R., 292
Rokeach, M., 260
Rorschach, H., 266, 299
Rosen, A., 104, 111, 205–206
Rosen, G. M., 278
Rosenhan, D. L., 15
Rosenthal, R., 142
Rosenzweig, S., 294, 295

Rotter, J. B., 159–161, 291–292
Rubin, L. S., 361
Russell, J. T., 103

Samelson, T., 330
Samuda, R., 328
Sarason, I. G., 239, 240, 362
Sarbin, T. R., 198
Saslow, G., 151
Sattler, J. M., 315, 320, 322, 324–325
Sawyer, J., 111
Scarr-Salapatek, S., 335
Schafer, R., 197
Schank, R. C., 146
Schmidt, H. O., 87
Schofield, W., 189, 353
Schoonover, S. M., 324
Schubert, H. J. P., 293
Schulberg, H., 293
Schumer, F., 276
Schwarz, J. C., 150, 354
Sechrest, L., 107, 353
Selfridge, O. G., 131
Selltiz, C., 176, 255
Shagass, C., 359
Shannon, C., 106
Shaw, M. E., 369
Shneidman, E. S., 290
Shoben, E. J., 197
Shouksmith, G., 337–338
Shweder, R. A., 138
Siegman, A. W., 198
Siess, T. F., 356
Simmons, R. F., 146
Simon, H. A., 310
Simon, T., 305–306, 309, 314–315, 346
Sines, J. O., 111
Sines, L. K., 107, 108, 189, 336
Sisson, B. D., 238
Skinner, B. F., 152–153
Sloan, I. J., 238
Slovic, P., 110
Smith, K. U., 369–371
Smith, S. F., 229
Snyder, C. R., 278
Sobell, L. C., 156

Sobell, M. B., 156
Socrates, 170
Soskin, W. F., 187–189
Spearman, C., 50, 304–307, 309, 310, 346
Spence, D. P., 113
Spence, J. T., 220
Spence, K. W., 359
Spiegler, M. D., 7, 350
Sprafkin, J. N., 151, 162
Spranger, G., 259
Stagner, R., 278
Stanley, J. C., 59, 71, 77, 339, 341
Stephenson, W., 133
Sternberg, R. J., 310, 313, 346
Steinhaurer, J., 249
Stevens, B., 194
Stevens, S. S., 4
Stringfield, D. O., 356
Strong, E. K., Jr., 85, 248–249
Stuart, R. B., 151
Sullivan, H. S., 8, 192–194, 208
Sundberg, N. D., 16, 149, 187, 265, 278, 290, 299, 305, 337
Sutherland, J. D., 292
Suttell, B. J., 293
Swartz, J. D., 287, 290
Sweetbaum, H. A., 359
Swenson, C. H., 292
Swenson, W. M., 230
Symon, S. M., 359
Szasz, T. S., 15
Szucko, J. J., 110, 113, 361

Taft, J., 186
Taulbee, E. S., 238
Taylor, E. M., 320
Taylor, H. C., 103
Taylor, J. A., 221, 224, 238, 361
Taylor, T. J., 121–122
Tendler, A. D., 291
Tenopyr, M. L., 17
Terdal, L., 151
Tetenbaum, T. J., 220
Terman, L., 315, 318, 319, 324, 330, 346
Thompson, C. E., 290
Thoresen, C. E., 124, 159

Thorndike, R. L., 138, 152, 246–247, 321, 326, 338, 344, 345
Thurstone, L. L., 254–256, 303, 342, 346
Tigay, B., 324
Tolor, A., 293
Tomkins, S. S., 127, 207
Torrance, E. P., 337
Turnbull, W., 275, 370–371
Turner, R. K., 155
Turtletaub, A., 139
Tyler, L. E., 265, 325–326

Ullmann, L. P., 15, 151, 157
Urban, W. H., 292

Vernon, P. E., 259, 282, 306, 307, 313, 333, 338
Vogel, M. D., 360

Wagner, M. E., 293
Wallace, C. J., 163
Walsh, J. A., 246–247
Walsh, W. B., 265, 325–326
Wanderer, Z. W., 21
Weaver, W., 106
Webb, E. J., 125, 144, 149, 353
Wechsler, D., 304, 321–322, 324, 325, 346
Weick, K. E., 117, 143
Weiner, B., 298
Weiner, I. B., 276
Weiss, D. J., 50, 51, 255, 341
Weiss, T., 374
Weitz, S., 124–125
Weizenbaum, J., 113, 119–200
Wells, F. L., 183
Welsch, G. S., 97, 227, 228, 236–239
Wesman, A. G., 314
White, R., 337
Whyte, H., Jr., 369
Wiens, A. N., 124–125, 170, 196, 198, 327–329
Wiersma, W., 77, 78
Wiggins, J. S., 7, 12, 53, 59, 61, 104, 117, 161, 224, 241, 298, 369
Wile, I. S., 320
Willerman, L., 303, 306–307, 310,

313, 344–345
Williams, R. L., 99, 202, 327, 330
Willis, J., 326
Winch, R. F., 107, 108
Windle, C., 285
Winfield, D. L., 238
Winkler, R. C., 163
Winkler, R. L., 48
Winograd, T. A., 146
Witkin, H. A., 337–338
Wittenborn, J. R., 133

Wolfe, J., 154, 155
Woodworth, R. S., 53, 211–212, 348
Woody, R. H., 324
Wright, H. F., 121
Wrightsman, L. S., 150

Yates, A. J., 293, 362
Yerkes, R. M., 325, 333

Zubin, J., 276, 282, 284
Zulliger, H., 281